The Inner World of
Abraham Lincoln

The Inner World of
Abraham Lincoln

Michael Burlingame

University of Illinois Press
Urbana and Chicago

Illini Books edition, 1997
© 1994 by the Board of Trustees of the University of Illinois
Manufactured in the United States of America
3   4   5   C   P   6   5   4   3

This book is printed on acid-free paper.

Library of Congress Cataloging-in-Publication Data

Burlingame, Michael, 1941–
    The inner world of Abraham Lincoln / Michael Burlingame.
       p.   cm.
    Includes bibliographical references (p.) and index.
    ISBN 0-252-02086-3 (cloth : alk. paper). —
    ISBN 0-252-06667-7 (pbk. : alk. paper)
    ISBN 978-0-252-02086-5 (cloth : alk. paper). —
    ISBN 978-0-252-06667-2 (pbk. : alk. paper)
    1. Lincoln, Abraham, 1809–1865—Psychology. I. Title.
E457.2.B97   1994
973.7'092—dc20   93-34650
                                              CIP

*This book is lovingly dedicated
to Susie, for putting me up;
to Lois, for putting up with me;
and to Lloyd, for both.*

Contents

Acknowledgments	ix
Introduction	xi
A Note on Sources	xxiii
1. Lincoln's Midlife Crisis: From Party Hack to Statesman	1
2. "I Used to Be a Slave": The Origins of Lincoln's Hatred of Slavery	20
3. "Unrestrained by Parental Tyranny": Lincoln and His Sons	57
4. Surrogate Father Abraham	73
5. Lincoln's Depressions: "Melancholy Dript from Him as He Walked"	92
6. Lincoln's Attitude toward Women: The Most Striking Contradiction of a Complex Character	123
7. Lincoln's Anger and Cruelty	147
8. "The Most Ambitious Man in the World"	236
9. The Lincolns' Marriage: "A Fountain of Misery, of a Quality Absolutely Infernal"	268
Epilogue	357
Appendix: Stephen A. Douglas as a Target of Lincoln's Lyceum Address	365
Index	369

Acknowledgments

I am grateful to the many people have read and commented on this work. A special debt of gratitude is owed to two of them: Gabor S. Boritt and John Y. Simon. Neither accepts all of my interpretations; in fact, they object vigorously to some. But despite our differences, they have encouraged me unstintingly. Robert V. Bruce and Richard N. Current were also supportive early on, which meant a great deal to me. Douglas L. Wilson not only read the manuscript but has also shared with me valuable information about Lincoln that he has unearthed as he edits the William H. Herndon interviews and works on his study of Lincoln's early adulthood. In addition, I would also like to thank Robert Bray, Maura Casey, Rodney O. Davis, Carl N. Degler, Don E. Fehrenbacher, Eric Foner, John H. B. Knowlton, James M. McPherson, John McGuigan, Peter Shaw, Thomas F. Schwartz, William Styron, Hans L. Trefousse, Thomas R. Turner, Paul H. Verduin, Major L. Wilson, and Frank J. Williams, all of whom scrutinized the manuscript in whole or part. For their comments and suggestions I am grateful; for my mistakes they are blameless.

I have benefited from knowledgable, kind librarians, especially Jennifer Lee and her colleagues at Brown University's John Hay Library, Margaret Moser of the Pelletier Library at Allegheny College, Meadville, Pennsylvania, and the cordial, efficient staff of the Manuscripts Division at the Library of Congress. I also wish to express hearty thanks to their counterparts at the Illinois State Historical Library in Springfield, the Sterling and Beinecke Libraries at Yale University, the Chicago Historical Society, the National Archives, the University of Chicago Library, the Butler Library at Columbia University, the Henry E. Huntington Library in San Marino, California, the Massachusetts Historical Society, the Houghton Library at Harvard University, the Connecticut State Library, the Connecticut Historical Society, the Watkinson Library at Trinity College, Hartford, and the Lincoln Room at the University of Illinois Library at Urbana-Champaign. Helen Aitner, interlibrary loan officer at Connecticut College, helped me immeasurably.

At Princeton and Johns Hopkins universities, I had the good fortune to be trained as a historian by David Herbert Donald, to whom I owe much, both personally and professionally. For this book, I am particularly grateful for his permission to examine the James G. Randall Papers at the Library of Congress.

I would also like to acknowledge Connecticut College's R. Francis Johnson Faculty Development Fund and History Department Gift Fund, both of which defrayed some research expenses, and the staff of the college's computer center, who have patiently nursed me through many a crisis. Dorothy B. James, formerly dean of the faculty at Connecticut College, kindly authorized the purchase of a portable computer, which has done yeoman service and upon which I write these words. I am also grateful to my copy editor, Mary Giles, at the University of Illinois Press.

Finally, I want to thank my daughter Rebecca, who helped check the accuracy of quotations in this volume.

Introduction

Many questions go unasked, or at least unanswered, in standard accounts of Lincoln's life. Fawn Brodie was not entirely accurate when she maintained that "thanks to the industry of an unending parade of Lincoln scholars, there are almost no important mysteries left."[1] As she herself pointed out, we lack satisfactory accounts of Lincoln's depressions and his marriage.[2] In addition, historians and biographers have yet to analyze fully the psychological origins of Lincoln's hatred of slavery, his aversion to women, his anger and cruelty, his role as a father figure, his relationship with his children, his intense ambition, and his transformation from the party hack of the 1830s and 1840s to the statesman of the 1850s and 1860s. To answer these questions, I, like Brodie, use the tools of psychobiography.

A prominent Lincoln scholar has justly deemed psychobiographical studies of the sixteenth president "unmitigated disasters."[3] Recent essays in the genre have been so far-fetched as to discredit the psychohistorical enterprise.[4] Thus it is not surprising that some Lincoln authorities scorn the idea of psychobiography.[5] However, as Gabor S. Boritt, a substantial contributor to the Lincoln literature, has counseled other historians, "We must not fear psychoanalytic concepts."[6] I share the belief of another Lincoln scholar, John W. Starr, Jr., that "we can never arrive at an approximately full understanding [of Lincoln's character] until an extended and intensive study of it is made from a psychological standpoint."[7]

In the 1920s, when Albert J. Beveridge was preparing his biography of Lincoln, Samuel Eliot Morison wrote to him concerning Lincoln's bouts of depression: "I do not know whether it has occurred to you to call the psychologists and psychiatrists into consultation," Morison noted, "but it seems to me they would be more useful advisers than historians."[8] The findings of psychologists can indeed help illuminate aspects of Lincoln, including his melancholia, that traditional approaches leave dark. Lincoln's law partner William H. Herndon once wrote that the "world will never rest till it knows all about Lincoln, inside & outside."[9] But his contemporary Schuyler Colfax told a biographer in 1875 that the "special feature" of his Lincoln book "should be the Inner Life of Lincoln," because the "outer life is pretty well known."[10]

I have taken Colfax's advice and do not go over the well-plowed ground of Lincoln's outer life yet again. Because my approach is topical, a brief chronology of the important events of Lincoln's life might be useful. His age at each event is given in parentheses:

1809 February 12: born in Kentucky
ca. 1811 (two): Lincoln's infant brother dies
1816 December (seven): Lincoln's family moves to Indiana
1818 October 5 (nine): Lincoln's mother dies
1819 December 2 (ten): Lincoln's father remarries
1828 January 20 (eighteen): Lincoln's sister dies
1828 (nineteen): first trip to New Orleans
1830 March 1 (twenty-one): Lincoln family moves to Illinois
1831 April–July 8 (twenty-two): second trip to New Orleans
1831 July (twenty-two): leaves home, settles in New Salem
1832 May–August (twenty-three): runs unsuccessfully for state legislature
1834 August 4 (twenty-five): wins election to state legislature
1835 August 25 (twenty-six): Ann Rutledge dies
1837 (twenty-eight): moves to Springfield, admitted to the bar, issues protest against slavery
1838 January 27 (twenty-eight): delivers Lyceum Address in Springfield
1841 January 1 (thirty-one): breaks engagement to Mary Todd
1842 November 4 (thirty-three): weds Mary Todd, retires from legislature
1843 August 1 (thirty-four): first son, Robert Todd, is born
1846 March 10 (thirty-seven): second son, Edward Baker, is born
1846 August (thirty-seven): elected to Congress
1847–49 (thirty-eight to forty): serves in Congress
1849–54 (forty to forty-five): semiretirement from politics
1850 February 1 (forty): son Eddie dies
1850 December 21 (forty-one): third son, William Wallace, is born
1851 January 15 (forty-one): father dies
1853 April 4 (forty-four): fourth son, Thomas, is born
1854 fall (forty-five): reenters politics, gives Peoria Speech

1855 February 8 (forty-five): defeated for U.S. Senate
1858 summer–fall (forty-nine): runs for Senate against Douglas
1859 January (forty-nine): defeated for Senate
1860 November (fifty-one): elected president
1861 March (fifty-two): inaugurated as president
1862 February (fifty-three): son Willie dies
1865 April 15 (fifty-six): dies

This book supplements the standard biographies, which pay scant attention to Lincoln's emotional life.[11] Because, as one psychiatrist lamented, "we have no data of his inner life, essential for . . . diagnosing his case," historians must speculate, an activity frowned upon by many scholars.[12] I have taken the advice of an authority on Lincoln, Nathaniel Wright Stephenson, who argued that "the biographer is a person who has by long and arduous concentration upon the particular subject put himself in a unique relation to it. His views ought to be more valuable than the views of other people. Of course, I don't want him to dogmatize ever about anything that he can't prove; at the same time I do want him wherever the subject becomes obscure to give me tentatively his own views."[13] For nearly a decade I have steeped myself in Lincoln sources and offer in this book what I hope are informed guesses about my subject's inner life.

Eminent historians have maintained that Lincoln's personality was the North's secret weapon in the Civil War, the key variable that spelled the difference between victory and defeat. James G. Randall thought it "doubtful whether any other leader of the North could have matched him in dramatizing the war to the popular mind, in shaping language to his purpose, in smoothing personal difficulties by a magnanimous touch or a tactful gesture, in avoiding domestic and international complications, in courageously persisting in the face of almost unendurable discouragements, in maintaining war morale while refusing to harbor personal malice against the South." David M. Potter contended that "it hardly seems unrealistic to suppose that if the Union and the Confederacy had exchanged presidents with one another, the Confederacy might have won its independence." James Ford Rhodes concluded that "the preponderating asset of the North proved to be Lincoln."[14]

Because Lincoln's leadership played such a vital role in preserving the Union and abolishing slavery, his personality deserves the fullest analysis. Perhaps the greatest strength of his character was his lack of egotism. In his twenties and thirties, Lincoln was, according to several historians whose view I share, something of a party hack, known best for his talents as a skilled wheeler-dealer in legislative halls and as a clever belittler of Democrats on the stump. In his forties and fifties, however, he became a statesman as he dealt with the issues of slavery and union. During those same years he shed his cruel habit of humiliating and ridiculing opponents (a habit that I document at length), overcame his egotism, abandoned cheap partisanship, and in other ways showed that he had grown dramatically. Chapter 1 is devoted to illustrating the truth of Herman Belz's observation that Lincoln "negotiated a mid-life crisis in a highly constructive and positive manner."[15] The work of psychologist Daniel J. Levinson has influenced my understanding of Lincoln in his early forties.[16]

To help put Lincoln's transformation between 1849 and 1854 in perspective, I devote chapter 7 to his cruelty and anger, which were most conspicuous in his younger years. Historians have said little about Lincoln's negativity, but it must be acknowledged if his capacity for growth and his essential humanity are to be appreciated fully. Clearly, he did forgo in his later life the ugly tendency to belittle and wound others, but he never lost his capacity for anger. I have gathered all the evidence I could find about his temper, and the information in chapter 7 does modify the popular image of the man of infinite forbearance. What is most impressive about the mature Lincoln is not how often he expressed his anger, but how seldom he did so, considering the provocations he endured. My findings complement those of Richard N. Current, whose essay "The Tenderhearted" shows Lincoln to be not as "hopelessly sentimental and soft" as is often thought.[17]

Lincoln's treatment of the slavery issue generates heated debate, especially about whether he was liberal, moderate, or conservative. Several recent historians assert that he demonstrated in word and deed far more passionate opposition to slavery than the customary portrayal of Lincoln as a "Reluctant Emancipator" suggests.[18] Acknowledgment of Lincoln's essential radicalism suggests another question: Why did he hate slavery so fiercely? If Lincoln had been born in New England, had imbibed antislavery views from the atmosphere around him, and had sought political office there, his aversion to the peculiar institution would hardly be surprising. But he was a native of Kentucky, raised in Negrophobic southern Indiana, and a practical politician, eagerly seeking honor and fame in central Illinois, where strong antislavery views were not calculated to bring much of either. In addition, he had married into a prominent slave-holding family in Kentucky. Rational self-interest would not have impelled Lincoln into the antislavery camp.

To understand Lincoln's hatred of slavery, one must penetrate beneath the surface of the conscious ego and explore the personal meanings that slavery had for him. I believe that Lincoln's well-documented estrangement from his father helps explain his later aversion to slavery, which lay at the core of his ideology. Because his father treated him like a slave, Lincoln empathized with the bondsmen and felt a special urgency about freeing them.

A full understanding of Lincoln's marriage helps clarify aspects of his presidential leadership as well as his inner life. If, as I believe, the Lincolns' domestic life was miserable, several questions arise. Why did he marry someone so utterly different from himself? What did she see in him? Why were they so unhappy? I suggest in chapter 9 that the marriage was a kind of psychodrama in which Mary Todd displaced buried anger at her father on Lincoln, and that both Abraham and Mary had been so wounded by the early deaths of their mothers that they were bound to have serious matrimonial troubles. I further suggest that the Lincolns were polar opposites in psychological typology and in their archetypal identity.

Much as one may deplore Mary Lincoln's behavior, she is more to be pitied than censured. She did not, after all, ask that her mother die when Mary was only six, or that her father abandon her emotionally and marry a woman unsympathetic to the children of his first marriage. Nor did she ask to have her husband slain by her side and to have three of her four sons die in childhood. It is hard not to sympathize with the widow who lamented in 1867, "Without my All in this life, my dearly beloved husband, why should I seek to find a house, the ever vacant chair is always there and I cannot have a settled feeling, where none exists in my heart. Alas!"[19] Nor did she ask to be born into a sexist society that thwarted her ambition and gave insufficient scope to her talents. Considering the hardships that befell her, the amazing thing about Mary Todd Lincoln is not that she behaved so badly, but that she behaved as well as she did.[20]

I agree with William Herndon, who acknowledged that even though Mary Lincoln "was a terrible woman," she "would have led society anywhere" if *"hell* [had] not got into her neck," for "she was a highly cultured woman—witty—dashing—pleasant and a lady." Herndon added that "I have always sympathized with Mrs. Lincoln.

Remember that every effect must have its cause. Mrs. Lincoln was not a she wolf—wildcat without a cause."[21] I share that view; the moody, introspective, emotionally withdrawn Lincoln was far from an ideal husband.

I also share Mrs. John A. Logan's admiration for Mary Lincoln's education and her "intellectual ability," while simultaneously deploring, along with Mrs. Logan, the First Lady's "personal vanity" and her "temper that was really a species of madness." Mrs. Logan sadly and accurately concluded, "Loftiness of soul, consecrated purpose, broad and profound sympathy, self-sacrificing endeavor—all these, unhappily, were wanting in the character of the Mistress of the White House." Another woman who observed Mary Lincoln during the war concurred: "She was incapable of lofty, impersonal impulse. She was self-centered, and never in any experience rose above herself."[22] A Springfield matron put it more bluntly: Mary Lincoln, she said, was "a perfect termagant."[23] I also share William Howard Russell's amazement at Mary Lincoln's behavior: "Mrs. L's meanness is beyond belief," he confided to his private diary.[24]

Ultimately, my feelings about the Lincolns are irrelevant. Rather than judging their subjects, biographers should describe and analyze them, making them understandable; that is what I try to do in the chapter on their marriage, and indeed throughout this book. The aim of historians is to relate the past, as Leopold von Ranke put it, "wie es eigentlich gewesen ist [as it really happened]," or, as contemporary scholars—more aware than Ranke was of the problems of subjectivity—might put it, "wie es wahrscheinlich gewesen ist [as it probably happened]." In telling that story, I marshall facts in abundance because their cumulative weight discredits the notion that there "is no reliable evidence that their marriage was especially stormy." During the Civil War, Victorian delicacy about women protected Mary Lincoln. As Thurlow Weed explained in 1867, "but for a generous forbearance on the part of political opponents, there would have been discreditable revelations [about the First Lady] in Congress."[25] In our era, historians are freer to tell the objective truth without fear of seeming ungallant.

Intentionally and unintentionally, Mary Lincoln shaped her husband's character and career. Had Lincoln found her a more sympathetic soul, he might not have devoted so much time and energy to politics and thus would probably not have attained the presidency. As Captain Shotover says in George Bernard Shaw's *Heartbreak House,* "Who are the men that do things? The husbands of the shrew and the drunkard, the men with the thorn in the flesh." From his long years of marital unhappiness, Lincoln developed a knack for handling difficult people, a knack that stood him in good stead during the Civil War. He might never have occupied the Executive Mansion had it not been for Mary Todd's constant stoking of his political ambition, for she yearned to be First Lady.

Her goading, however, did not create Lincoln's ambition. From his youth, Lincoln had shown a keen desire to rise above his crude frontier background, of which he seemed ashamed. What was the source of that ambition? Why did he strive so hard for political honor and recognition? Following the lead of Harold D. Lasswell, who argued that political ambition is rooted in a damaged sense of self-esteem, I have tried in chapter 8 to identify the inner wounds that required the balm that political success offered.

Lincoln's troubles with Mary Todd reflected a larger problem that he had with women in general. Why was he so awkward and uncomfortable around females? Why did he dislike them? The answers to these questions can be found, I think, in his relationship with his own mother, whose death when he was nine profoundly affected his attitude toward women, making him mistrustful of the whole sex. I agree with Charles B. Strozier's contention that the death of Lincoln's mother was "the critical point in Lincoln's childhood," but I disagree with his argument that Lincoln felt guilty because he believed that "his own earlier forbidden sexual wishes" caused her death. That conclusion—which Strozier himself acknowledges "seems fanciful"—has been discredited by Don E. Fehrenbacher.[26]

The most obvious feature of Lincoln's psyche that cries out for explanation is his well-known tendency to suffer from depression (chapter 5). Many clinical studies support the hypothesis that depression can result from inadequate mourning for an early loss, especially the loss of a parent. Lincoln is a case in point. The lonely nine-year-old, who helped build his mother's coffin in an isolated frontier cabin, never fully recovered from her death. In later years, other losses would trigger subconscious memories of that grievous event and cause Lincoln untold agony, which could take the form of near-suicidal depressions.

Among those losses were the deaths of two of Lincoln's four sons: Eddie died in 1850 at the age of three; Willie died in 1862 at the age of eleven. In dealing with his boys, Lincoln scandalized proper Victorians with his notorious indulgence. Why did he so conspicuously flout the childrearing conventions of his era? I believe it was Lincoln's way of reacting to the harsh treatment he had suffered at the hands of his father. As the victim of what he later called "parental tyranny," Lincoln evidently promised himself that he would not repeat his father's mistakes. The famous engraving of Lincoln and Tad with a book has fixed an image of the loving, gentle father in the popular mind. Although that image is for the most part accurate, it can be overdrawn. Lincoln was devoted to Willie and Tad, but he was curiously distant with his first-born, Robert Todd. Why should there be such a discrepancy between his relations with Robert on the one hand and with Willie and Tad on the other? Strozier has offered a Freudian explanation, but I believe that the answer is simpler. Willie was a clone of his father, sharing his temperament, values, attitudes, personality, and character. After Willie died, Lincoln transferred to Tad, a very different but nonetheless lovable boy, the intense devotion he had felt for Willie. But Lincoln shared almost nothing in common with the stuffy, humorless, conventional Robert, who took after his mother's family. Thus, Lincoln's problems with Robert, in my view (chapter 3), had less to do with Oedipal tensions than with the intractable, inborn differences between the two. For Lincoln it was understandably easier to love a child like Willie, who was a clone, than it was to love a child like Robert, who was, in effect, a stranger.

Lincoln's paternal feelings extended to many men, women, and children beyond his household. He felt most comfortable in dealing with others on a father-child basis. Something deep in his psyche radiated a fatherlike quality that drew others to him and inclined them to trust him as a child trusts a loving father. This mysterious power was an invaluable component of his successful leadership during the Civil War. When Northerners sang, "We are coming Father Abraham, 300,000 more," they expressed an abiding confidence in their president's integrity, judgment, and wisdom that helped inspire Northern morale even in the darkest periods of the war.

The source of Lincoln's power can be found, I believe, in what Carl Jung called an archetype. Throughout this volume, I rely on the insights of Jungian psychology, which maintains that in addition to the personal unconscious, upon which Freud concentrated—the product of the individual's own experiences, especially in childhood—all people have a transpersonal unconscious that powerfully shapes them and that has nothing to do with childhood events.

This book does not, however, attempt to vindicate Jungian, Freudian, Levinsonian, or Lasswellian theory. As Gabor Boritt has observed, the "meager work" done on Lincoln's inner life "suffers from a not infrequent disease of psychohistory: too much psychodogmatism on the one hand and too little knowledge of the historical subject, in our case Lincoln, on the other."[27] I approach this subject as a historian rather than as a psychologist and have been militantly eclectic in using theory to shed light in dark corners of Lincoln's life.

Beveridge bemoaned the existence of a "conspiracy to make Lincoln an impossible and unhuman angel who could not possibly make a mistake and who was without any human weakness whatever." Some authors do, in fact, maintain that anyone trying to show that Lincoln was unhappily married or loved Ann Rutledge or was estranged from his father is guilty of perpetrating "legends that libel Lincoln."[28] Such naive hero worship has no place in serious historical writing. What I present here is not intended to libel Lincoln, but to make him more human and understandable.

I hope that the interpretations in this volume achieve that end. For readers unconvinced by those interpretations, perhaps at least the new information here adduced will serve as compensation. While conducting research for this book, I was repeatedly amazed at the number of new data about Lincoln I kept stumbling across, especially in manuscript collections (most notably those of biographers and historians like Allan Nevins, Ward Hill Lamon, John Hay, John G. Nicolay, William H. Herndon, Jesse W. Weik, Josiah G. Holland, Ida M. Tarbell, William E. Barton, Harry E. Pratt, Albert J. Beveridge, James G. Randall, and Ruth Painter Randall); in newspapers (especially among the clipping collections at the Lincoln Museum in Fort Wayne, Indiana, and the Illinois State Historical Library in Springfield); and in the National Archives. A half century ago, James G. Randall published an influential article entitled "Has the Lincoln Theme Been Exhausted?" Based on what I and other scholars, for example, G. Cullom Davis, Douglas L. Wilson, Mark E. Neely, Jr., John Y. Simon, and Paul Verduin, are finding, another version of Randall's article might carry the title "The Lincoln Theme in American Historiography: Has the Surface Really Been Scratched?"[29]

NOTES

1. Fawn M. Brodie, *Thomas Jefferson: An Intimate History* (New York: W. W. Norton, 1974), 23.

2. Brodie, *Thomas Jefferson*, 25.

3. Mark E. Neely, Jr., *The Abraham Lincoln Encyclopedia* (New York: McGraw-Hill, 1982), 248n.

4. This is particularly true of Dwight G. Anderson, *Abraham Lincoln: The Quest for Immortality* (New York: Alfred A. Knopf, 1982). Charles B. Strozier, *Lincoln's Quest for Union: Public and Private Meanings* (New York: Basic Books, 1982) is a conspicuous exception. I have tried to build on Strozier's insights. I disagree with many conclusions in George B. Forgie, *Patricide in the House Divided: A Psychological Interpretation of Lincoln and His Age* (New York: W. W. Norton, 1979), but his work raises important questions. See Don E. Fehrenbacher, "The Deep Reading of Lincoln," in *Lincoln in Text and Context: Collected Essays* (Stanford: Stanford University Press, 1987), 214-27; Richard O. Curry, "Conscious or Unconscious Caesarism? A Critique of Recent Scholarly Attempts to Put Abraham Lincoln on the Analyst's Couch," *Journal of the Illinois State Historical Society* 77 (Spring 1984): 67–71; Gabor S. Boritt and Norman O. Forness, eds., *The Historian's Lincoln: Pseudohistory, Psychohistory, and History* (Urbana: University of Illinois Press, 1988), 242–51, 275–83, 302–12; and Richard N. Current, "Lincoln after 175 Years: The Myth of the Jealous Son," *Papers of the Abraham Lincoln Association* 6 (1984): 15–24.

5. Gabor S. Boritt, "The Voyage to the Colony of Linconia: The Sixteenth President, Black Colonization, and the Defense Mechanism of Avoidance," *The Historian* 37 (Aug. 1975): 630–31.

6. Quoted in Mark E. Neely, Jr., "The Lincoln Theme since Randall's Call: The Promise and Perils of Professionalism," *Papers of the Abraham Lincoln Association* 1 (1979): 64.

7. John W. Starr, *"The Dual Personality of Abraham Lincoln": A Brief Psychological Study* (Privately printed, 1928), 5.

8. Morison to Beveridge, Oxford [England], 15 June 1925, Beveridge MSS, DLC.

9. Herndon to Jesse W. Weik, Springfield, 9 Feb. 1889, H-W MSS, DLC.

10. Colfax to John Hay, Baltimore, 22 Oct. 1875, Hay MSS, RPB.

11. The best one-volume biography remains Benjamin P. Thomas, *Abraham Lincoln: A Biography* (New York: Alfred A. Knopf, 1952). David Donald and William Gienapp are both writing single-volume biographies of Lincoln. There is a crying need for a new multivolume biography to replace the detailed but inadequate works by Carl Sandburg and James G. Randall.

12. Morton Prince to Albert J. Beveridge, Nahant, Mass., 13 Oct. 1925, Beveridge MSS, DLC.

13. Stephenson to Albert J. Beveridge, New Haven, Conn., 23 June 1926, Beveridge MSS, DLC.

14. James G. Randall, "Abraham Lincoln," in *Dictionary of American Biography*, 20 vols., ed. Dumas Malone (New York: Charles Scribner's Sons, 1933), 11:258; David M. Potter, "Jefferson Davis and the Political Factors in Confederate Defeat," in *Why the North Won the Civil War*, ed. David Donald (Baton Rouge: Louisiana State University Press, 1960), 112; Rhodes quoted by David Donald in *Why the North Won*, x. For a brief summary of the argument, see James M. McPherson, "American Victory, American Defeat," in *Why the Confederacy Lost*, ed. Gabor S. Boritt (New York: Oxford University Press, 1992), 37.

15. Herman Belz, "Commentary on 'Lincoln's Quest for Union,'" in *The Historian's Lincoln*, ed. Boritt and Forness, 250. Cf. Joel H. Silbey, "'Always a Whig in Politics': The Partisan Life of Abraham Lincoln," *Papers of the Abraham Lincoln Association* 8 (1986): 21–42; Thomas, *Lincoln*, 143, 130; Helen Nicolay, *Personal Traits of Abraham Lincoln* (New York: Century, 1912), 57–62; Benjamin P. Thomas, *Portrait for Posterity: Lincoln and His Biographers* (New Brunswick: Rutgers University Press, 1947), 256; Albert J. Beveridge, *Abraham Lincoln, 1809–1858*, 2 vols. (Boston: Houghton, Mifflin, 1928), 1:493, 2:244. Don E. Fehrenbacher contends that Lincoln's growth was not most dramatic after 1860, but after 1854: "If greatness is the response of inner strength to an extraordinary challenge, Lincoln had first met such a challenge and begun to show such strength in 1854, after the repeal of the Missouri Compromise." Fehrenbacher, *Prelude to Greatness: Lincoln in the 1850s* (Stanford: Stanford University Press, 1962), 161.

16. Daniel J. Levinson et al., *The Seasons of a Man's Life* (New York: Alfred A. Knopf, 1978).

17. Richard N. Current, *The Lincoln Nobody Knows* (New York: Hill and Wang, 1958), 164–86.

18. Robert W. Johannsen's *Lincoln, the South, and Slavery: The Political Dimension* (Baton Rouge: Louisiana State University Press, 1991) is a conspicuous exception. In that slender volume, the author maintains that Lincoln's expression of antislavery convictions "was shaped and directed by political exigencies and motivations" (xii). Although he explicitly states that he does not "mean that one must question the sincerity of Lincoln's antislavery convictions," his book suggests that indeed one should do so. Johannsen focuses on the years from 1854 to 1861, playing down abundant evidence that Lincoln expressed moral repugnance for the peculiar institution on many occasions before 1854, when it was hardly politically expedient to do so. In this book, I gather that evidence which, as far as I know, has never before been assembled in one place.

19. Mary Lincoln to Elizabeth Emerson Atwater, Racine, 30 June [1867], in *Mary Todd Lincoln: Her Life and Letters*, ed. Justin G. Turner and Linda Levitt Turner (New York: Alfred A. Knopf, 1972), 425.

20. Cf. Jean Baker, *Mary Todd Lincoln: A Biography* (New York: W. W. Norton, 1987), xiv–xv, 331.

21. Herndon to Weik, Springfield, 16 Jan. 1886, H-W MSS, DLC. She did lead society as First Lady and deserves the journalistic tribute she received in 1863: "Since the time that Mrs. Madison presided at the White House, it has not been graced by a lady as well fitted by nature and by education to dispense its hospitalities as is Mrs. Lincoln." Washington correspondence, 30 Nov. 1863 Boston *Journal*, 1 Dec. 1863, signed "Perley" [Ben: Perley Poore], in Ruth Painter Randall, *Mary Todd Lincoln: Biography of a Marriage* (Boston: Little, Brown, 1953), 243.

22. Mrs. John A. Logan, *Thirty Years in Washington; or, Life and Scenes in Our National Capital* (Hartford: A. D. Worthington, 1901), 646, 648; Mary Clemmer [Ames], *Ten Years in Washington; or, Inside Life and Scenes in Our National Capital as a Woman Sees Them* (Hartford: Hartford Publishing Company, 1882), 242.

23. Remarks of a Mrs. Forrest, in conversation with Ida Tarbell, memo marked "Lincoln—Items," in folder "Mary Todd Lincoln," Tarbell MSS, Allegheny College.

24. Russell's remark was not included in the version of his diary that appeared in print in 1863. Martin Crawford, ed., *William Howard Russell's Civil War: Private Diary and Letters, 1861–1862* (Athens: University of Georgia Press, 1992), 162 [entry for 3 Nov. 1861].

25. Neely, *Lincoln Encyclopedia,* 181; New York *Commercial Advertiser,* 7 Oct. 1867, 2.

26. Strozier, *Lincoln's Quest for Union,* 28, 25–26; Fehrenbacher, *Lincoln in Text and Context,* 21–22.

27. Boritt, "The Voyage to the Colony of Linconia," 630–31.

28. Beveridge to Nathaniel Wright Stephenson, Beverly Farms, Mass., 18 Dec. 1925, copy, Beveridge MSS, DLC; Montgomery S. Lewis, *Legends That Libel Lincoln* (New York: Rinehart, 1946).

29. Neely, "The Lincoln Theme since Randall's Call."

A Note on Sources

In old age, Mark Twain said, "When I was younger I could remember anything, whether it had happened or not; but my faculties are decaying now, and soon I shall be so [old] I cannot remember any but the things that never happened."[1] This witticism illustrates a serious problem for scholars: How much credence should be given to the reminiscences of people who knew Lincoln, especially to those recalling events from the distant past?

One Lincoln scholar, James G. Randall, cautioned that "the vagueness of reminiscence given after many years is familiar to all careful historical students; if, in the haste of general reading, this matter is disregarded, the essence of the subject is overlooked. Huge tomes could be written to show the doubtfulness of long-delayed memories." Randall sensibly noted that "the historian must use reminiscence, but he must do so critically. Even close-up evidence is fallible. When it comes through the mists of many years some of it may be true, but a careful writer will check it with known facts. Contradictory reminiscences leave doubt as to what is to be believed; unsupported memories are in themselves insufficient as proof; statements induced under suggestion, or psychological stimulus . . . call especially for careful appraisal."[2]

Randall urged particular caution in using the reminiscences gathered by William H. Herndon, Lincoln's law partner, shortly after the Civil War. Following Randall's lead, subsequent scholars have tended to shy away from the Herndon materials, regarding them as unreliable.[3]

But the most thorough student of the Herndon collection, Douglas L. Wilson, has cogently argued that Randall's skepticism was exaggerated.[4] In dealing with the Ann Rutledge story, for example, Randall scrutinized Herndon's informants as if they were witnesses at a criminal trial. Like a defense attorney, Randall sought to discredit every informant who told Herndon that Lincoln and Ann Rutledge loved each other. "Historical scholarship," Wilson argues, "for whatever similarities it might bear to trying a case in a court of law, is a very different kind of enterprise and employs different methods. Observing the evidentiary safeguards of a criminal trial would, after all, bring a substantial portion of historical inquiry to a halt, for much of what we want to know about the past simply cannot be established on these terms. Abraham Lincoln's early life is a perfect example. Virtually everything we know about Lincoln as a child and as a young man—his incessant reading and self-education, his storytelling, his honesty, his interest in politics, and so forth—comes exclusively from the recollections of the people who knew him. Non-contemporary, subjective, often unable to be confirmed even by the recollections of others, to say nothing of contemporary documents, this evidence is sheer reminiscence." Wilson acknowledges that "Randall's caveats about such evidence and the admixture of error and bias it may contain are certainly justified," but adds that "the historian or biographer has no alternative but to find a way to work with it and, indeed, with anything that may be indicative of the truth."[5]

I have made extensive use of the Herndon materials, which Wilson rightly calls "the richest source of information on Lincoln's life extant, which even at the present day is far from exhausted."[6] He points out that "Herndon spent a prodigious amount of time and effort pursuing and procuring information about Abraham Lincoln." The documents he collected "show that he examined and cross-examined his informants with care, that he sought information both open-endedly and on a wide variety of specific topics, that he checked up on doubtful or conflicting stories, and that he acted in accordance with his stated purpose, which was to learn and publish the truth about his great law partner."[7]

The people Herndon interviewed have also been underestimated, Wilson argues: "It is sometimes maintained by an appeal to common experience that Herndon's informants could not have been expected to summon up obscure events from the distant past with anything like accuracy, much less historical reliability, and that Herndon was naive to have believed them." Such objections, Wilson contends, "make it appear that Herndon asked his informants to recall . . . things they had not thought about or discussed with anyone for twenty-five or thirty years." In fact, the people whom Herndon consulted had, during the years when Lincoln's fame grew, "frequent occasion to recall their own personal contacts with him and keep alive their memories of his early days."[8]

Having immersed myself in the Herndon archive, I agree with Wilson as well as Albert J. Beveridge, who, after examining Herndon's papers closely, wrote that "everywhere it is obvious that Herndon is intent on telling the truth himself and getting the truth from those who could give personal, first-hand information."[9] Beveridge told a Lincoln biographer, "I have examined the credibility of Herndon very much as if he were a hostile witness in a murder trial; and there is absolutely no doubt that the old man (he was not very old when he collected this data) was well-nigh fanatically devoted to truth. It is only when he assumes to analyze the 'souls' of other people that he is untrustworthy. . . . But I repeat, that when he states a fact as a fact, you can depend upon it that it is a fact."[10] The Herndon-Weik collection is not without it faults and must be used carefully, but it is time that historians stop treating it as if it were high-level nuclear waste.[11]

I have also made extensive use of other reminiscent material, including memoirs and diaries. Next to the Herndon-Weik Papers, the most valuable has been the newspaper clipping collections at the Lincoln Museum in Fort Wayne, Indiana and at the Illinois State Historical Library.[12] These sources, too, must be treated with caution, especially when Lincoln's exact words are cited. Purists might argue that, given the vagaries of memory, all such quotations should be dismissed out of hand. Yet as Don E. Fehrenbacher says in a thoughtful examination of the issue, there is "a great accumulation of spoken words attributed to Lincoln that cannot be ignored." By being too "fastidious," he warns, historians might produce works "impoverished as a consequence."[13]

Although acknowledging that there "is no simple formula for judging the authenticity of recollected utterances," Fehrenbacher offers Lincoln scholars reasonable guidelines, which I have tried to follow in this volume.[14] "First," he says, "it should be recognized that many a quotation has a provenance too weak and/or a substance too dubious to be incorporated in serious historical writing." In order to judge whether a quote is marred by a "substance too dubious," I have examined Lincoln's own writings closely, as well as the vast literature about him, developing in the process a nose for what "smells" authentically Lincolnian. This procedure is hardly scientific, and there is room for disagreement among historians of good will. I have also tried to learn as much as possible about those reporting Lincoln's words so that I may judge their veracity.

Fehrenbacher also advises that "insofar as the pace of narrative or argument will allow it, the reader should be given some measure of a quotation's authenticity." It would be tedious to clutter the text with such qualifiers as "if we can believe the recollective memory of X,"[15] and the reader should supply such a disclaimer before all recollected quotes, which are identified in the notes. While seeking to avoid such clumsiness, I have tried to distinguish canonical utterances of Lincoln from "recollective testimony." I have not heeded Fehrenbacher's advice to treat such testimony as indirect rather than direct discourse. To be sure, such language may not be strictly accurate, but paraphrasing Lincoln's alleged words robs them of much of their impact.

Fehrenbacher also suggests that "the interpretive weight placed on a quotation should be compatible with the quality of its authentication." Whenever possible, I rest my arguments on Roy P. Basler's edition of Lincoln's *Collected Works*. Often, however, no canonical evidence sheds light on an aspect of Lincoln's inner life; then I try to alert readers to the quality of the reminiscent material used. I have used the following abbreviations for the books, manuscript collections, and repositories that I cite most frequently:

Angle, *HL*	Paul M. Angle, ed., *Herndon's Life of Lincoln: The History and Personal Recollections of Abraham Lincoln as Originally Written by William H. Herndon and Jesse W. Weik* (Cleveland: World, 1942)
Baker, *MTL*	Jean Baker, *Mary Todd Lincoln: A Biography* (New York: W. W. Norton, 1987)
Basler, *CWL*	Roy P. Basler, ed., with Lloyd A. Dunlap and Marion Dolores Pratt, asst. eds., *The Collected Works of Abraham Lincoln*, 8 vols. plus index (New Brunswick: Rutgers University Press, 1953–55)
CSmH	Henry E. Huntington Library, San Marino, California
DLC	Library of Congress, Washington, D.C.
Hertz, *HL*	Emanuel Hertz, ed., *The Hidden Lincoln: From the Letters and Papers of William H. Herndon* (New York: Viking, 1938)
H-W MSS	Herndon-Weik Papers
ICHi	Chicago Historical Society
IHi	Illinois State Historical Library, Springfield
JGR MSS	James G. Randall Papers
LMFW	Lincoln Museum, Fort Wayne, Indiana
Randall, *MTL*	Ruth Painter Randall, *Mary Todd Lincoln: Biography of a Marriage* (Boston: Little, Brown, 1953)

Rice, *RL*   Allen Thorndike Rice, ed., *Reminiscences of Abraham Lincoln by Distinguished Men of His Time* (New York: North American Review, 1888)

RPB   Brown University, Providence, Rhode Island

Turner and
Turner, *MTL* Justin G. Turner and Linda Levitt Turner, eds., *Mary Todd Lincoln: Her Life and Letters* (New York: Alfred A. Knopf, 1972)

Weik, *RL*   Jesse W. Weik, *The Real Lincoln: A Portrait* (Boston: Houghton Mifflin, 1922)

NOTES

1. Albert Bigelow Paine, ed., *Mark Twain's Autobiography,* 2 vols. (New York: Harper and Brothers, 1924), 1:96.

2. J. G. Randall, *Lincoln the President: Springfield to Gettysburg,* 2 vols. (New York: Dodd, Mead, 1945), 2:324–25.

3. Douglas L. Wilson, "William H. Herndon and His Lincoln Informants," *Journal of the Abraham Lincoln Association* 14 (Winter 1993): 15–34.

4. Douglas L. Wilson, "Abraham Lincoln, Ann Rutledge, and the Evidence of Herndon's Informants," *Civil War History* 36 (December 1990): 301–23. Wilson, with Rodney O. Davis, is preparing a new edition of the Herndon collection, a welcome supplement to the Lincoln literature. It will replace Emanuel Hertz's woefully edited volume *The Hidden Lincoln: From the Letters and Papers of William H. Herndon* (New York: Viking, 1938).

5. Wilson, "Lincoln, Ann Rutledge, and Herndon's Informants," 321.

6. Ibid., 306.

7. Wilson, "Herndon and His Lincoln Informants," 26.

8. Ibid., 31.

9. Albert J. Beveridge, "Lincoln as His Partner Knew Him," *Literary Digest International Book Review* 1 (Sept. 1923): 33.

10. Beveridge to Nathaniel Wright Stephenson, Beverly Farms, Mass., 18 Dec. 1925, copy, Beveridge MSS, DLC.

11. On the shortcomings of the Herndon archive, see David Donald, *Herndon's Lincoln* (New York: Alfred A. Knopf, 1948), 195–96. On Donald's shortcomings as a biographer of Herndon and analyst of the Herndon materials, see Wilson, "Herndon and His Lincoln Informants," 20–21.

12. The Lincoln Museum recently photocopied its collection and sent the originals to the John Hay Library at Brown University, where I read them. Lincoln scholars in New England are indebted to Frank J. Williams, president of the Abraham Lincoln Association, for obtaining this treasure trove, and to Jennifer Lee and her colleages at Brown University for making them available to researchers.

13. Don E. Fehrenbacher, *Lincoln in Text and Context: Collected Essays* (Stanford: Stanford University Press, 1987), 277–78.

14. Fehrenbacher, *Lincoln in Text and Context*, 281, 278.

15. Fehrenbacher uses this construction when discussing a quote from Horace White. Ibid., 277.

The Inner World of
Abraham Lincoln

1

Lincoln's Midlife Crisis:
From Party Hack to Statesman

Lincoln underwent a profound change between 1849, when at the age of forty he retired temporarily from public life, and 1854, when he returned to the political fray, emerging like a butterfly from a caterpillar's chrysalis. At the time he withdrew from politics, Lincoln was, in Benjamin P. Thomas's words, "an honest, capable, but essentially self-centered small-town politician of self-developed but largely unsuspected talents" and "a lucid thinker and a clever man before a crowd." After five years on the political sidelines, he came back a "political analyst and debater of surpassing power," speaking "with a new seriousness, a new explicitness, a new authority," and thus he grew into "a statesman." The years from 1849 to 1854 were "among the most fruitful of his life," for "as he put aside all thought of political advancement and devoted himself to personal improvement, he grew tremendously in mind and character."[1]

Albert J. Beveridge described the period from 1849 to 1854 as one "of waiting, thought, and growth" during which Lincoln shed "narrow partisanship and small purposes" and laid "the foundations of greatness" that were clearly "visible even to hostile eyes." Beveridge had been rather critical as he scrutinized Lincoln's record in the Illinois legislature. "I wish to the Lord he could have gone straight-forward about something or other," he lamented to a friend. "Of all [the] uncertain, halting and hesitating conduct, his takes the prize." In Lincoln's 1854 Peoria speech, which marked the end of his political retirement, Beveridge detected a new man speaking, for it was "wholly unlike any before made by him. Indeed, if it and his public utterances thereafter were placed side by side with his previous [pre-1854] speeches, and the authorship of them all were unknown, it would appear impossible that they had been written by the same man."[2]

Others noted that in his early political career Lincoln was little more than "a clever speaker, talking for political ends," whose early oratorical efforts were merely "rattling good stump speeches," whereas his

public utterances from 1854 on showed that "he had received his Pen-
tecostal touch of flame and become a teacher—a leader of men."[3] The
historian Joel H. Silbey argues that Lincoln in the 1830s and 1840s
"was a total political operator," "a virulent political point man," and
"a nineteenth century political partisan to his boots," possessed of "a
very partisan outlook"; in short, Silbey concludes, Lincoln was a "party
hack."[4]

Lord Charnwood observed that "Lincoln left political life in 1849,
a praiseworthy self-made man with good sound views but with nothing much to distinguish him above many others, and at a sudden call
returned to political life in 1854 with a touch of something quite uncommon added to those good sound views." As a result of "long and
deep and anxious thought," Lincoln succeeded in "making himself a
bigger man."[5] Don E. Fehrenbacher's monograph on Lincoln in the
1850s concludes that the key turning point in his subject's life was not
his elevation to the presidency in 1861 but his return from self-imposed
political exile seven years earlier.[6] In a study of Lincoln's law career,
John J. Duff called the 1849–54 period "in some respects, the most
important preparatory stage of the pre-presidential years."[7] An Illinois
contemporary of Lincoln's thought the period from 1849 to 1854, although "apparently . . . uneventful and even unimportant" for Lincoln,
"was really the period in which by thought and much study he prepared
himself for his great life work."[8]

While noting the central importance of Lincoln's early forties, historians do not analyze how he became a deeper, bigger, more profound
man. Given the dearth of autobiographical material that Lincoln left
behind, especially dealing with his inner life, scholarly agnosticism is
understandable. The findings of psychology, however, help shed light
onto those years and make an understanding of Lincoln's early forties,
and indeed his whole life, less shadowy. Psychologists such as Daniel
J. Levinson have studied closely the changes that men undergo in their
late thirties and early forties, a period that Levinson calls "the mid-life
transition."[9]

The chief task of that transition is *individuation*, a term coined by
Carl Jung, one of the first major psychologists to explore the significant changes men make as they pass from the first to the second half
of life. "Individuation," he said, "means becoming a single, homoge-
neous being, and, in so far as 'individuality' embraces our innermost,
last, and most incomparable uniqueness, it also implies becoming one's
own self. We could therefore translate individuation as 'coming to self-

hood.'" It is "a process of psychological development . . . by which a man becomes the definite, unique being he in fact is."[10]

Specifically, individuation at midlife requires several things of a man: to reappraise his past; to ask fundamental questions about what is truly important; to develop atrophied areas of his psyche; to abandon inappropriate qualities of youthfulness and accept appropriate aspects of aging; to acknowledge and integrate the dark, destructive qualities of his self as well as the feminine components of his total personality; to pay more attention to his inner voice and less attention to the outer voice of the collective; to let go of some of his attachment to the external world; to become a mentor to younger men; to come to terms with his mortality; and to find his true calling and fully engage his creative gifts. This is a tall order indeed, and most men experience either a moderate or severe crisis as they try to fill it. If successful, a man emerges from this crisis less egocentric and more conscious, rooted, centered in himself, creative, and self-accepting. In short, he becomes individuated.[11]

Lincoln clearly underwent such a crisis between 1849 and 1854, a period that Beveridge called "five desolate years"—and so they were.[12] Outwardly his life appeared uneventful; as Lincoln himself put it in autobiographical sketches, "he went to the practice of the law with greater earnestness than ever before" and "was losing interest in politics."[13] In 1860 he reportedly said that early in the previous decade, "I was clean out of politics and contented to stay so; I had a good business, and my children were coming up, and were interesting to me."[14] Three years later he told White House callers that "in Congress I was then [1849] so disgusted" with politics that "I made up my mind to retire to private life and practice my profession."[15] Although he continued to participate in Whig party affairs in Illinois, he sought no office and seldom campaigned for the party's standard-bearers. When in 1850 a Whig newspaper suggested that Lincoln run for Congress, he firmly declined.[16] That same month he did not take part in a large public meeting to endorse the Compromise of 1850.[17] Two years later, he turned down the Whig nomination for a seat in the state legislature, citing "business arrangements."[18] He spent several months every year on the legal circuit, traveling throughout central Illinois, and devoted the rest of the year to clients in Springfield.[19]

Inwardly, however, Lincoln used this time to find his true identity, for, like most men, he had not by the age of forty yet developed a deep sense of self, of his own uniqueness. It was a period of intense, painful yet creative depression. Many friends noted that Lincoln was afflicted in his early forties with "a sadness so profound that the depths of it cannot be sounded or estimated by normal minds."[20] He would sit silent for hours, preoccupied with his inner thoughts. His colleagues on the legal circuit recalled many occasions when Lincoln rose early and stared into the fire, mumbling with great sadness (chapter 5). Lincoln's sister-in-law observed similar behavior in his home, where he "would lean back, his head against the tip of a rocking chair, sit abstracted that way for . . . 20 or 30 minutes, and all at once burst out in a joke, though his thoughts were not on a joke."[21]

Although it is impossible to know precisely what those thoughts were, it seems clear that he brooded on his lack of success. As John G. Nicolay noted, Lincoln had failures aplenty to brood about: "He went into the Black Hawk war as a captain, and . . . came out a private. He rode to the hostile frontier on horseback, and trudged home on foot. His store 'winked out.' His surveyor's compass and chain, with which he was earning a scanty living, were sold for debt. He was defeated in his first campaign for the legislature—defeated in his first attempt to be nominated for Congress—Four times he was defeated as a candidate for Presidential Elector, because the Whigs of Illinois were yet in a hopeless minority—He was defeated in his application to be appointed Commissioner of the General Land Office."[22] Reflecting on these setbacks was painful, for Lincoln was "keenly sensitive to his failures," and any mention of them made him "miserable," according to Herndon.[23]

Returning to Illinois in 1849 after his one term in the U.S. House of Representatives, the forty-year-old Lincoln considered himself a failure as a lawyer and a politician. "I am not an accomplished lawyer," he wrote in 1850. "I find quite as much material for a lecture, in those points wherein I have failed, as in those wherein I have been moderately successful."[24] With some justification, Lincoln was disappointed in the results of his term in Congress and, according to Herndon, "he despaired of ever rising again in the political world."[25] In 1855 Lincoln said "with much feeling" that "men are greedy to publish the successes of [their] efforts, but meanly shy as to publishing the failures of men. Men are ruined by this one sided practice of concealment of blunders and failures."[26] The following year he lamented that "with *me*, the race of ambition has been a failure—a flat failure."[27]

All this suggests that Lincoln struggled to come to terms with his own failure and realized that such an effort might be fruitful. As Jung wrote, *"The experience of the self is always a defeat for the ego."* Only through such experiences, however, can true psychological growth occur: "The widening of consciousness is at first upheaval and darkness, then a broadening out of man to the whole man."[28]

While brooding on his failures, Lincoln also contemplated the meaning of his life. One day in 1851 he "gloomily—despairing—sadly" observed to Herndon: "How hard—Oh how hard it is to die and leave one's Country no better than if one had never lived for it."[29] Lincoln's closest friend, Joshua Speed, recalled a similar conversation: "He said to me that he had done nothing to make any human being remember that he had lived—and that to connect his name with the events transpiring in his day & generation and so impress himself upon them, as to link his name with something that would redound to the interest of his fellow man was what he desired to live for."[30]

Lincoln was obviously grappling with one of the dominant issues of the midlife transition: shaping a legacy. According to Levinson,

> In the midlife transition a man comes to the depressing realization that his previous successes are not so grand as he had imagined. At best, they form a prelude to the main work, a basis on which a more substantial project can be constructed. But the important achievements remain for the future. His initial success is like a promissory note: an assurance but by no means a guarantee of better work to come. It is still more deflating to realize that, even if he is very effective in his new work, the result will not be as monumental as the omnipotent young man might have wished. . . . To the extent that he heals the wounds produced by this ego deflation, he can get on with the serious work and form a "good enough" legacy.[31]

Between 1849 and 1854, Lincoln seems to have worked hard on this task of healing the wounds of ego deflation and thus prepared himself well for leaving behind a legacy that, as it turned out, was monumental indeed.

Lincoln in his early forties mastered Euclid, whose works he carried with him on business trips. This suggests a desire to strip away all superfluous mental baggage and get at the heart of matter, psychologically as well as logically. Herndon reports that Lincoln also "read much in the political world," presumably about the slavery issue. When he emerged from his political semiretirement in 1854, he had formulated a basic critique of the proslavery and popular sovereignty cases, arguing with Euclidian coherence.[32]

In these years Lincoln also indulged his taste for somber verse. His favorite poems, for example, "Mortality," "The Last Leaf," and "The Burial of Sir John Moore," reflected his long-standing preoccupation with death.[33] This issue assumed even greater salience when Lincoln reached his early forties and grew more aware of mortality. His three-year-old son Eddie died in 1850, and his father a year later. But even without these grim reminders, Lincoln probably would have become more concerned with death between 1849 and 1854, for, as Levinson observed, "At 40 a man knows more deeply than ever before that he is going to die. He feels it in his bones, in his dreams, in the marrow of his being." Such awareness can cause deep pain and even depression because "at mid-life, the growing recognition of mortality collides with the powerful wish for immortality and the many illusions that help to maintain it."[34] Lincoln did yearn for immortality, and hence his despair was all the more acute as he came to terms with his eventual death.[35]

Another major task confronting a man in his early forties is to come "to grasp more clearly the flow of generations and the continuity of the human species. . . . He feels more responsible for the generations that will follow his own."[36] One manifestation of that heightened sense of responsibility is the willingness to become a mentor to younger men. This Lincoln did gladly in the two realms where he had gained some mastery: law and politics. Several attorneys fondly remembered how, when they were young, Lincoln advised them, helped them solve problems, and guided them in their careers (chapter 4).

He also offered guidance to aspiring politicos. Lincoln told his partner in 1848 how to get ahead in politics: "The way for a young man to rise, is to improve himself every way he can, never suspecting that any body wishes to hinder him. Allow me to assure you, that suspicion and jealousy never did help any man in any situation. There may sometimes be ungenerous attempts to keep a young man down; and they will succeed too, if he allows his mind to be diverted from its true channel to brood over the attempted injury."[37] In another letter of the same period, he advised Herndon, "Now as to the young men. You must not wait to be brought forward by the older men. . . . You young men get together and form a . . . club, and have regular meetings and speeches. . . . Let every one play the part he can play best—some speak, some sing, all hollow [holler]."[38]

That Lincoln became a mentor to young lawyers and politicians indicates that he was successfully achieving another goal of the midlife transition: integrating the feminine side of his nature. As a mentor, a man nurtures the careers of others and concerns himself with connecting the generations.[39] Such tasks require making greater use of eros than logos.

A significant challenge in midlife is developing the weakest part of the psyche. According to Jung, everyone has four psychological functions: thinking, feeling, intuition, and sensation. One is dominant, one is inferior, and the other two are auxiliary.[40] Clearly, Lincoln's strongest function was thinking, as his fondness for Euclid suggests. At the age of twenty-eight he enunciated a thinker's credo: "Reason, cold, calculating, unimpassioned reason, must furnish all the materials for our future support and defence."[41] Lawyers marveled at his powerful, analytical mind. One recalled that "the quality in which he excelled all other men was that of analysis. In the crucible of his mind every question was resolved into its pristine elements."[42] Herndon thought that "Lincoln was entirely logical, had no intuition at all."[43]

According to Jung, "When thinking is the dominant or superior function, feeling is necessarily an inferior function." In Jung's typology, feeling is a rational enterprise that assigns value: "Feeling informs you through its feeling-tone whether a thing is agreeable or not. It tells you what a thing is *worth* to you."[44] James Hillman has noted that "the feeling function on a more primitive level is mainly a reaction of yes and no, like and dislike, acceptance and rejection. As it develops, there forms in us a subtle appreciation of values, and even of value systems, and our judgments of feeling then rest more and more on a rational hierarchy, whether it be in the realm of aesthetic taste, ethical goods, or social forms and human relationships. . . . The developed feeling function is the reason of the heart which the reason of the mind does not quite understand."[45]

Between 1849 and 1854, Lincoln apparently struggled to develop his feeling function, especially in the realm of political values. Before 1849, he was something of a hack politician, stressing partisanship above all else. To be sure, he had expressed aversion to slavery, but he had not worked out a thorough or deep analysis of the peculiar institution. By 1854 he had done so, and his Peoria speech that year examined the issue with more than "cold, calculating, unimpassioned reason." Heatedly he denounced as well as analyzed the proslavery and popular sovereignty arguments, and for the rest of his life continued with passion to attack slavery as "a vast moral evil" and "the sum of all villa[i]nies" (chapter 2). That he did so immediately after his return to politics suggests that he used the five years of his semiretirement not only to study the issue, but also to assimilate his feeling function as he addressed it.

Another major task of the midlife transition is to acknowledge one's shadow—that dark, destructive underside of the personality that is repressed and then projected onto others. In midlife, Levinson found, "It is necessary that a man recognize and take responsibility for his own destructive capabilities."[46] In the first half of his life, Lincoln cruelly belittled and satirized his political opponents, often wounding them deeply (chapter 7). After his midlife transition, he abandoned that practice. In 1864 he said, with much justice, "So long as I have been here [in Washington] I have not willingly planted a thorn in any man's bosom."[47] Clearly, Lincoln came to terms with his destructiveness between 1849 and 1854.

The psychological growth described here is not an act of will. The learning that takes place in a man's early forties is, according to Levinson, "not purely conscious or intellectual. It cannot be acquired simply by reading a few books, taking a few courses, or even having some psychotherapy. . . . we often learn by going through intense periods of suffering, confusion, rage against others and ourselves, grief over lost opportunities and lost parts of the self."[48]

After five years of such suffering, confusion, rage, and grief, Lincoln emerged with what his law partner William Herndon called "that peculiar nature . . . which distinguishes one person from another, as much to say 'I am myself and not you.'"[49] In 1859 an admirer noted that "what he [Lincoln] does & says is all his own. What Seward and others do you feel that you have read in books or speeches, or that it is a sort of deduction from what the world is full of. But what Lincoln does you feel to be something newly mined out—something above the ordinary."[50] Although he remained ambitious, he no longer desperately needed collective approval. On September 30, 1863, he explained "with considerable feeling" to a group of Missourians, "It is my ambition and desire to so administer the affairs of the government while I remain president that if at the end I shall have lost every other friend on earth I shall at least have one friend remaining and that one shall be down inside of me."[51] Nor did he lose his desire to be accommodating, but it was now tempered. In 1864 he told one of his secretaries that in dealing with congressional Radicals who opposed him on Reconstruction, "I must keep some consciousness of being somewhere near right: I must keep some standard of principle fixed within myself."[52]

His firmly rooted sense of self, his marked individuality and integrity, had a numinous quality that impressed many contemporaries and historians. Beveridge said that it "is impossible for us to realize the spell he exercised by sheer personal presence, for cold print cannot recreate the magic with which he imbued his utterances, but when vitalized and lighted by his presence and personality, all he said had [a] compelling effect upon his companions, a sort of wizardry, not to be understood nor even apprehended by those who never saw nor heard him."[53] An Illinois congressman remembered that Lincoln "personally won men to him, and those who came in contact with him felt the spell and submitted to its thraldom, led by the invisible chords of his marvelous power. . . . As well might the hasheesh-eater attempt to analyze its seductive influence as for those who felt the spell of Lincoln's voice and presence, to say where and what it was."[54] Francis Grierson, who heard Lincoln debate Stephen A. Douglas at Alton in 1858, noted the same phenomenon:

> From every feature of Lincoln's face there radiated the calm, inherent strength that always accompanies power. . . . Here, then, was one man out of all the millions who believed in himself, who did not consult with others about what to say, who never for a moment respected the opinion of men who preached a lie. . . . What thrilled the people who stood before Abraham Lincoln on that day was the sight of a being who, in all his actions and habits, resembled themselves, gentle as he was strong, fearless as he was honest, who towered above them all in that psychic radiance that penetrates in some mysterious way every fibre of the hearer's consciousness. . . . Lincoln's presence infused into the mixed and uncertain throng something spiritual and supernormal. His looks, his words, his voice, his attitude, were like a magical essence dropped into the seething cauldron of politics, reacting against the foam, calming the surface and letting the people see to the bottom.[55]

The following year Lincoln gave a speech in Wisconsin that similarly impressed at least one listener, who later wrote, "His voice had something peculiarly winning about it, some quality which I can't describe, but which seemed to thrill every fiber of one's body."[56]

Lincoln's "psychic radiance" should not be confused with flashy charisma. As Lord Charnwood put it, Lincoln "is remembered as a personality with a 'something' about him—the vague phrase is John Bright's—which widely endeared him, but his was by no means that 'magnetic' personality which we might be led to believe was indispensable in America."[57]

That "something" was frequently referred to as "honesty" or "integrity," but more was involved than is usually connoted by those terms. Beveridge concluded that

> Lincoln's honesty was so striking that those who came in contact with him were impressed by it in an unaccountable fashion—unaccountable because many other men were as honest as he. But the manifestation of that quality in Lincoln was so unlike the same characteristic in others, that everybody who knew him felt called upon to assert it particularly and with emphasis. And it should be said . . . that the esteem in which he was held for truthfulness and integrity was a priceless possession in that political career. . . without precedent or parallel in our history.[58]

Many observers used words other than "truthfulness," "honesty," and "integrity" to describe Lincoln's special quality. His cousin Dennis Hanks noted that even when a boy, Lincoln had "suthin' peculiarsome about him."[59] His closest friend, Joshua Speed, wrote that "if I was asked what it was that threw such charm around him, I would say it was his perfect naturalness. He could act no part but his own. He copied no one either in manner or style."[60] Lincoln "had no affectation in any thing," Speed noted. "True to nature[,] true to himself, he was true to every body and every thing about and around him—When he was ignorant on any subject no matter how simple it might make him appear he was always willing to acknowledge it—His whole aim in life was to be true to himself & being true to himself he could be false to no one."[61] Henry C. Whitney observed that although Lincoln was "awkward and ungainly . . . there nevertheless was in his *tout ensemble* an indefinable *something* that commanded respect."[62]

Young lawyers in particular manifested such respect (chapter 4). A student of the relations between Herndon and his partner concluded that "there was something exquisite in Lincoln, a native majesty and refinement of soul, which impressed young men deeply."[63] In court, witnesses and judges also felt the power of Lincoln's personality. A scholar who analyzed Lincoln's career at the bar was impressed by his "psychic qualities of extraordinary power" which "exerted a remarkable personal influence upon every one with whom he came into contact. . . . [T]here was something mysterious in Lincoln's personality which played an important part in his success as a cross-examiner."[64]

In little towns on the Illinois circuit where Lincoln peripatetically practiced law, his visits were eagerly awaited. A resident of one of the judicial circuits where Lincoln practiced recalled that "everyone in his presence felt lighter in heart and more joyous. He brought light with him."[65] In the town of Highland, he enjoyed special favor. When he stopped there one day during the 1858 senatorial campaign, the largely German-born population flocked to the house where he was staying. Joseph Gillespie, who accompanied him, recalled that the "people were perfectly enraptured; the bare sight of the man threw them into ecstacies. I, here got the first inkling of the amazing popularity of Mr. Lincoln among the Germans. I could perceive that there was some magnetic influence at work, that was perfectly inexplicable, which brought him and the masses into a mysterious correspondence with each other."[66]

David Davis noted in his eulogy of Lincoln that "his presence on the circuit was watched for with interest, and never failed to produce joy and hilarity. When casually absent, the spirits of both bar and people were depressed."[67] Another observer recalled that, on the circuit, people would keenly await his arrival: "Sometimes he might happen to be a day or two late, and then, as the Bloomington stage came in at sundown, the Bench and the Bar, jurors, and the general citizens would gather in crowds at the hotel where he always put up, to give him a welcome."[68]

A young man who heard Lincoln speak in Ohio in 1861 wrote that "to see Lincoln was to feel closely drawn to him. His personal appearance and his manner, so perfectly natural, absolutely free from anything like ostentation, and yet so manly, made every one feel instinctively that he was preeminently a man of the people. There was an air of freedom and good humor in all that was said and done."[69] A few days later, Lincoln cast a spell over an audience in Trenton, New Jersey. A journalist reported in the New York *World* on February 22, 1861 that when "he asked them to stand by him so long as he did right" there "was a peculiar naivette in his manner and voice, which produced a strange effect upon his audience. It was hushed for a moment to a silence which was like that of the dead. I have never seen an assemblage more thoroughly captivated and entranced by a speaker than were his listeners . . . by the grim and stalwart Illinoisan."

Four years later another young man, Ervin Chapman, observed that as Lincoln was about to deliver his second inaugural address, "currents of mystic power that were resistless in their influence upon the convictions and purposes of those about him" flowed from "his tremendous personality." Chapman was at a loss to explain this mysterious power: "My sensitive nature responded to those waves of magnetic force while in rapturous bewilderment I sought to discover the secret of his greatness, and I was unconsciously lifted to a higher level of purpose by a silent influence which I felt but could not understand." John G. Nicolay marveled at Lincoln's "subtle and indefinable magnetism" that enabled him to control "dangerously disturbed and perverted forces" that might have defeated the North.[70] The youthful John Russell Young similarly detected in Lincoln "a deep, unfathomable sense of power."[71]

Horace White, a leading Illinois Republican, described how "Lincoln quickly gained the confidence of strangers, and . . . their affection as well. I found myself strongly drawn to him from the first. . . . This personal quality, whose influence I saw growing and widening among the people of Illinois from day to day, eventually penetrated to all the Northern States. . . . It was this magical personality that commanded all loyal hearts. It was this leadership that upheld confidence in the dark hours of the war and sent back to the White House the sublime refrain: 'We are coming, Father Abraham, three hundred thousand more.'"[72]

Henry B. Rankin, who knew Lincoln in Springfield, thought that photographs and paintings of him failed to capture "the inner Abraham Lincoln." Rankin said that occasionally "he arose from *within himself,* and through his seamed and battle-scarred visage something from his inner life, . . . lit up the outer visage of the man, startling the beholder as prophetic in its intensity, when his inner power and grandeur revealed itself."[73]

Jane Grey Swisshelm also was struck by Lincoln's "grandeur." When she visited the president early in 1863, she found his personality disarming. She "went into his presence with a feeling of scorn for the man who had tried to save the Union and slavery" but was "startled to find a chill of awe pass over me as my eyes rested upon him. It was as if I had suddenly passed a turn in a road and come into full view of the Matterhorn. . . . I have always been sensitive to the atmosphere of those I met, but have never found that of any one impress me as did that of Mr. Lincoln, and I know no word save 'grandeur' which expresses the quality of that atmosphere."[74]

Although he may have radiated grandeur, Lincoln had not the slightest trace of megalomania. An Illinois railroad conductor, who often had eminent politicians on his run, deemed Lincoln "the most folksy of them. He put on no airs. He did not hold himself distant from any man." Nevertheless, "there was something about him which we plain people couldn't explain that made us stand a little in awe of him.

. . . You could get near him in a sort of neighborly way, as though you had always known him, but there was something tremendous between you and him all the time."[75]

Like anyone who has come to grips with his own shadow, Lincoln cherished no exalted self-image. "I am very sure," he told Noah Brooks one day in the White House, "that if I do not go away from here a wiser man, I shall go away a better man, for having learned here what a very poor sort of a man I am."[76] To a delegation of clergy, he declared, "I may not be a great man—(straightening up to his full height) I know I am not a great man."[77] John Hay was impressed by the difference between the president and the petty egomaniacs surrounding him. To his diary Hay confided on July 31, 1863, "While the rest are grinding their little private organs for their own glorification[,] the old man is working with the strength of a giant and the purity of an angel to do this great work."

Lincoln had so little egotism that even when he used the first-person singular pronoun it hardly seemed egocentric. James Russell Lowell, commenting on Lincoln's "unconsciousness of self," noted that "he forgets himself so entirely in his object as to give his *I* the sympathetic and persuasive effect of *We* with the great body of his countrymen." This lack of egotism enabled Lincoln to relate to the people of the North easily, so that, in Lowell's words, "When he speaks, it seems as if the people were listening to their own thinking aloud."[78] The rapport he enjoyed with the people allowed him to infuse his "unconquerable spirit" into them "in some mysterious manner," as Douglas Southall Freeman put it.[79]

Leo Tolstoy detected a God-like quality in Lincoln. Admiring his "peculiar moral power" and "the greatness of his character," Tolstoy said, "He was what Beethoven was in music, Dante in poetry, Raphael in painting, and Christ in the philosophy of life. He aspired to be divine—and he was."[80] Some of his constituents believed that if Lincoln were not divine, at least he had been placed in office to do the work of the Almighty. John Hay told his fellow White House secretary John G. Nicolay in the summer of 1863 that their boss "is in fine whack. I have rarely seen him more serene & busy. He is managing this war, the draft, foreign relations, and planning a reconstruction of the Union, all at once. . . . There is no man in the country, so wise, so gentle and so firm. I believe the hand of God placed him where he is."[81]

In 1864 a White House caller who had expected to find the president a mere joker reached a conclusion like Hay's. Lincoln, he recorded in his diary, appeared "a man of deep convictions," the "great guiding intellect of the age," whose "Atlantian shoulders were fit to bear the weight of mightiest monarchies." This visitor was so impressed by Lincoln's "transparent honesty, his republican simplicity, his gushing sympathy for those who offered their lives for their country, his utter forgetfulness of self in his concern for his country," that he concluded, "He was Heaven[']s instrument to conduct his people thro[ugh] this red sea of blood to a Canaan of peace & freedom."[82]

Lincoln inspired such confidence and esteem because he had followed the path of individuation so uncompromisingly and, as Herman Belz has suggested, he had "negotiated a midlife crisis in a highly constructive and positive manner."[83] Had he not become so conscious, he could not have been a successful president. His remarkable individuation endowed him with that "wizardry," "magical personality," "subtle and indefinable magnetism," "indefinable something," "psychological honesty," "mystic power," "perfect naturalness," "grandeur," "native majesty and refinement of soul," "psychic radiance," "suthin' peculiarsome"—call it what you will—that formed the cornerstone of his personality and commanded so much respect.

Lincoln's high degree of consciousness enabled him to suppress his own egotism while steadily focussing on the main goal: victory in the Civil War. As a friend observed, "He managed his politics upon a plan entirely different from any other man the country has ever produced. . . . In his conduct of the war he acted upon the theory that but one thing was necessary, and that was a united North. He had all shades of sentiments and opinions to deal with, and the consideration was always presented to his mind: How can I hold these discordant elements together?"[84] In a less conscious man, envy, jealousy, self-righteousness, false pride, vanity, and the other foibles of ordinary humanity would have undermined his ability to maintain Northern unity and resolve. That task required "utter forgetfulness of self," and such forgetfulness of self, the ability to overcome the petty tyranny of the ego, developed only after he had wrestled long and hard—and successfully—with the challenges of midlife.

NOTES

1. Benjamin P. Thomas, *Abraham Lincoln: A Biography* (New York: Alfred A. Knopf, 1952), 143, 130.

2. Claude G. Bowers, *Beveridge and the Progressive Era* (Boston: Hough-

ton Mifflin, 1932), 569; Albert J. Beveridge, *Abraham Lincoln, 1809–1858,* 2 vols. (Boston: Houghton, Mifflin, 1928), 1:493, 2:244. Beveridge told Edward Channing that "the Lincoln of youth, early and middle adulthood showed few signs of the Lincoln of the second inaugural." As he was conducting research, Beveridge concluded that "not one faint glimmer appears in his whole life, at least before his Cooper Union speech, which so much as suggests the radiance of the last two years." Bowers, *Beveridge,* 565–66. Obviously, Beveridge had changed his mind by the time he wrote his biography.

    3. Helen Nicolay, *Personal Traits of Abraham Lincoln* (New York: Century, 1912), 57–62.

    4. Joel H. Silbey, "'Always a Whig in Politics': The Partisan Life of Abraham Lincoln," *Journal of the Abraham Lincoln Association* 8 (1986): 21–42.

    5. Lord Charnwood, *Abraham Lincoln* (New York: Henry Holt, 1916), 108, 101, 103.

    6. Don E. Fehrenbacher, *Prelude to Greatness: Lincoln in the 1850s* (Stanford: Stanford University Press, 1962), 160–61.

    7. John J. Duff, *A. Lincoln: Prairie Lawyer* (New York: Holt, Rinehart and Winston, 1960), 163.

    8. [John M. Scott], "Lincoln on the Stump and at the Bar," typescript, 4, Ida Tarbell MSS, Allegheny College.

    9. Daniel J. Levinson et al., *The Seasons of a Man's Life* (New York: Alfred A. Knopf, 1978), 191–313. Other studies tend to confirm Levinson's findings, especially Roger L. Gould, *Transformations: Growth and Change in Adult Life* (New York: Simon and Schuster, 1978), 217–307. See also George E. Vaillant, *Adaptation to Life* (Boston: Little, Brown, 1977), 219–30. Vaillant does, however, conclude that "there is nothing magical about a given year," for example, forty (223). Cf. Lois M. Tamir, *Men in Their Forties: The Transition to Middle Life* (New York: Springer, 1982), who reviews the then-available literature and concludes, "Clearly, something unique seems to occur to a man as he becomes middle aged, for, time and again, studies that range over the entire life span of the individual uncover an atypical statistic, a slump in a curve, or a qualitative shift among their middle-aged subjects, although more often than not this group originally was not meant to be the focus of attention" (5).

    Levinson's conclusions have been challenged by some psychologists. The critics, foremost among them Paul T. Costa, rely heavily on questionnaires rather than the in-depth, long-term interviews that Levinson used. This methodological weakness renders their objections suspect, as does their tendency to oversimplify the subtle, complex analysis that Levinson offers. See Susan Krauss Whitbourne and Comilda S. Weinstock, *Adult Development,* 2d ed. (New York: Praeger, 1986), 229–48. For further literature on the subject, see Lois Tamir's bibliography in Ski Hunter and Martin Sundel, *Midlife Myths: Issues, Findings, and Practice Implications* (Newbury Park: Sage Publications, 1989), 177–79.

    10. Carl Jung, *Two Essays on Analytical Psychology,* vol. 7 of *The Collected Works of C. G. Jung* (New York: Pantheon Books, 1953), 171–72. Cf. Edward F. Edinger, *Ego and Archetype: Individuation and the Religious Function of the Psyche* (New York: G. P. Putnam's Sons, 1972).

11. Levinson et al., *Seasons of a Man's Life*, passim.

12. Beveridge, *Lincoln*, 1:493.

13. Basler, *CWL*, 4:67, 3:512.

14. Henry C. Whitney's recollections, quoted in John W. Starr, Jr., *Lincoln and the Railroads: A Biographical Study* (New York: Dodd, Mead, 1927), 167.

15. Charles H. Hart to [William H. Herndon], Philadelphia, 3 March 1866, Jesse W. Weik MSS, IHi. Hart's parents and sister heard Lincoln utter these words, or words like them, in February 1863; Hart himself was not present.

16. Lincoln to the editors of the *Illinois Journal*, 5 June 1850, in Basler, *CWL*, 2:79.

17. Paul M. Angle, *"Here I Have Lived": A History of Lincoln's Springfield, 1821–1865* (New Brunswick: Rutgers University Press, 1935), 205–6.

18. Herndon, speaking for Lincoln at the Whig county convention, *Illinois State Journal* [Springfield], 11 Aug. 1852, in *Lincoln Day by Day: A Chronology, 1809–1865*, ed. Earl Schenck Miers et al., 3 vols. (Washington, D.C.: Lincoln Sesquicentennial Commission, 1960), 2:80 [entry for 9 Aug.].

19. Despite all this, Don E. Fehrenbacher argues that Lincoln did not really retire between 1849 and 1854. He has a point, for Lincoln did not completely absent himself from political life, but he certainly reduced his commitment to it drastically. Fehrenbacher, *Prelude to Greatness*, 20–21.

20. Beveridge, *Lincoln*, 1:525.

21. Frances Todd Wallace, in Beveridge, *Lincoln*, 1:507.

22. John G. Nicolay, "Abraham Lincoln," speech of 14 April 1894, Nicolay MSS, DLC.

23. Herndon to Weik, Springfield, 7, 10 Jan. 1886, H-W MSS, DLC.

24. "Fragment: Notes for a Law Lecture" [1 July 1850?], in *The Collected Works of Abraham Lincoln, Supplement, 1832–1865*, ed. Roy P. Basler (Westport: Greenwood Press, 1974), 18.

25. Herndon to Weik, Springfield, 28 Oct. 1885, H-W MSS, DLC. Cf. Dwight G. Anderson, *Abraham Lincoln: The Quest for Immortality* (New York: Alfred A. Knopf, 1982), 7, 110–14.

26. Herndon to Weik, [Springfield], 15 Dec. 1886, in Beveridge, *Lincoln*, 1:520. Cf. a similar statement Lincoln made to Herndon in 1857, quoted in Herndon to Weik, Springfield, 27 Feb. 1891, H-W MSS, DLC.

27. "Fragment on Stephen A. Douglas" [Dec. 1856?], in Basler, *CWL*, 2:383.

28. Carl Jung, *Mysterium Coniunctionis: An Inquiry into the Separation and Synthesis of Psychic Opposites in Alchemy*, in *The Collected Works of C. G. Jung*, ed. Herbert Read, Michael Fordham, and Gerhard Adler, 21 vols. (New York: Pantheon Books, 1953–79), 14:546 [paragraph 778], 171 [paragraph 209].

29. Herndon to Ward Hill Lamon, Springfield, 6 March 1870, Lamon MSS, CSmH; William Henry Herndon, "Facts Illustrative of Mr. Lincoln's Patriotism and Statesmanship" [lecture delivered 24 Jan. 1866], *Abraham Lincoln Quarterly* 3 (Dec. 1944): 188–89.

30. Speed to Herndon, Louisville, 9 Feb. 1866, H-W MSS, DLC. Here Speed offers no date for this conversation, but in another place he dates a similar conversation 1851. Joshua F. Speed, *Reminiscences of Abraham Lincoln and Notes of a Visit to California: Two Lectures* (Louisville: John P. Morton, 1884), 39.

31. Levinson et al., *Seasons of a Man's Life*, 226.

32. Herndon to Weik, Springfield, 28 Oct. 1885, 11 Feb. 1887, H-W MSS, DLC.

33. See Douglas L. Wilson, "Abraham Lincoln's Indiana and the Spirit of Mortal," *Indiana Magazine of History* 87 (June 1991): 155–70; Robert V. Bruce, *Lincoln and the Riddle of Death* (Fort Wayne: Louis A. Warren Lincoln Library and Museum, 1981); and chapter 5 in this volume.

34. Levinson et al., *Seasons of a Man's Life*, 215.

35. See Anderson, *Lincoln: The Quest for Immortality*, passim.

36. Levinson et al., *Seasons of a Man's Life*, 217.

37. Lincoln to Herndon, Washington, 10 July 1848, in Basler, *CWL*, 1:497.

38. Lincoln to Herndon, Washington, 22 June 1848, in Basler, *CWL*, 1:491.

39. Levinson et al., *Seasons of a Man's Life*, 237–38.

40. C. G. Jung, *Psychological Types; or, The Psychology of Individuation*, trans. H. Godwin Baynes (New York: Harcourt, Brace, 1926).

41. "Address Before the Young Men's Lyceum of Springfield, Illinois," 27 Jan. 1838, in Basler, *CWL*, 1:115.

42. Joseph Gillespie to James Fairman, Edwardsville, 21 Dec. 1874, Miscellaneous Manuscripts no. 97, Sterling Library, Yale University. Cf. Gillespie to Herndon, Edwardsville, 8 Dec. 1866, in Hertz *HL*, 323.

43. Herndon to Weik, Springfield, 12 Dec. 1889, in Hertz, *HL*, 243.

44. C. G. Jung, *Analytical Psychology, Its Theory and Practice: The Tavistock Lectures* (New York: Pantheon, 1968), 16, 12.

45. James Hillman, "The Feeling Function," in Marie Louise von Franz and James Hillman, *Lectures on Jung's Typology* (Irving: Spring, 1979), 91.

46. Levinson et al., *Seasons of a Man's Life*, 222–28 [quote on 224].

47. "Response to a Serenade," 10 Nov. 1864, in Basler, *CWL*, 8:101.

48. Levinson et al., *Seasons of a Man's Life*, 225.

49. William Henry Herndon, "Lincoln Individually," H-W MSS, DLC.

50. N. M. Knapp to Ozias M. Hatch, N.p., 12 May 1859, Hatch MSS, IHi.

51. Enos Clarke, a member of the delegation, in "Lincoln and the Radical Union Men of Missouri," unidentified clipping, LMFW. Cf. Ida M. Tarbell, *The Life of Abraham Lincoln*, 4 vols. (New York: Lincoln History Society, 1903), 3:175. According to John Hay's notes taken during the meeting, Lincoln said, "I am well aware that by many . . . I have been . . . charged with tyranny and wilfulness, with a disposition to make my own personal will supreme. I do not intend to be a tyrant. At all events I shall take care that in my own eyes I do not become one. I shall always try and preserve one friend within me, whoever else fails me, to tell me that I have not been a tyrant, and that I have acted right." Nicolay-Hay MSS, IHi.

52. John Hay, diary, 4 July 1864, Hay MSS, RPB.

53. Beveridge, *Lincoln,* 1:536–37.

54. Reminiscences of James A. Connolly, Peoria [Ill.] *Journal,* 11 Feb. 1910.

55. Francis Grierson, *The Valley of Shadows* (New York: History Book Club, 1948; originally published in 1909 by Houghton, Mifflin, with the subtitle *Recollections of the Lincoln Country, 1858–1863*), 198–99. Cf. Harold P. Simonson, "Francis Grierson: A Biographical Sketch and Bibliography," *Journal of the Illinois State Historical Society* 54 (Summer 1961): 198–203. Grierson was a boy of ten when he heard this speech, and he wrote about it some fifty years later in a book that contains many fictionalized passages. See Robert Bray's introduction to an abridged version of *The Valley of the Shadows: Sangamon Sketches* (Urbana: University of Illinois Press, 1990), xi–xxvii. Still, because Grierson's account coincides with so many other impressions of Lincoln, it rings true.

56. Reminiscences of Peter van Dechten, Milwaukee *Free Press,* 3 Feb. 1909.

57. Charnwood, *Lincoln,* 235.

58. Beveridge, *Lincoln,* 1:543–45.

59. Robert McIntyre, "Lincoln's Friend," Charleston [Ill.] *Courier,* N.d., Paris [Ill.] *Gazette,* N.d., Chicago *Tribune,* 30 May 1885.

60. Speed, *Reminiscences of Lincoln,* 34.

61. Speed to Herndon, Louisville, 6 Dec. 1866, photostatic copy, Beveridge MSS, DLC. I am grateful to Douglas L. Wilson for calling my attention to this important document, the original of which is not in the Herndon-Weik Papers.

62. Henry C. Whitney, "Abraham Lincoln: A Study from Life," *Arena* 19 (April 1898): 466.

63. Joseph Fort Newton, *Lincoln and Herndon* (Cedar Rapids: Torch Press, 1910), 254. Cf. chapter 4 of this volume.

64. Frederick Trevor Hill, *Lincoln the Lawyer* (New York: Century, 1906), 227–28.

65. Francis Fisher Browne, *The Every-Day Life of Abraham Lincoln,* 2d ed. (New York: G. P. Putnam's Sons, 1913), 75.

66. A document in Gillespie's papers, quoted in Josephine G. Prickett, "Joseph Gillespie," *Transactions of the Illinois State Historical Society for the Year 1912* (Publication no. 17 of the Illinois State Historical Library), 108. Gillespie added: "This relation increased and was intensified to such an extent that afterwards at Springfield I witnessed a manifestation of regard for Mr. Lincoln, such as I did not suppose was possible."

67. Davis's address to the U.S. District and Circuit Courts, 17 June 1865, [Springfield] *Daily State Journal,* 19 June 1865, 3. On the circuit Herndon observed Lincoln "keep . . . crowds of people in full laugh till near daylight. In villages the whole male population would assemble about early candle-light of an evening at the tavern at which Mr. Lincoln put up." Herndon to "Mr. N.," Chinkapin Hill, Ill., 4 Feb. 1874, in Grandview [Ind.] *Monitor,* 15 March 1934.

68. "Personal Reminiscences of the Late Abraham Lincoln," by "a contributor to the Bulletin," San Francisco *Steamer Bulletin,* 22 April 1865, 4.

69. Smith Stimmel, *Personal Reminiscences of Abraham Lincoln* (Minneapolis: William H. M. Adams, 1928), 10–11.

70. Ervin S. Chapman, *Latest Light on Abraham Lincoln and War-Time Memories,* 2 vols. (New York: Fleming H. Revell, 1917), 2:283; John G. Nicolay, *Abraham Lincoln* (Boston: Little Brown, 1882), 21.

71. John Russell Young, *Men and Memories: Personal Reminiscences,* ed. May D. Russell Young, 2 vols. (New York: F. Tennyson Neely, 1901), 1:68.

72. Horace White, *Abraham Lincoln in 1854* (Springfield: Illinois State Historical Society, 1908), 21.

73. Henry B. Rankin, *Intimate Character Sketches of Abraham Lincoln* (Philadelphia: J. B. Lippincott, 1924), 249.

74. Swisshelm in Rice, *RL,* 413.

75. E. J. Edwards, quoting the conductor Gilbert Finch, then retired and living in Connecticut, New York *Times,* 24 Jan. 1909.

76. Noah Brooks, "Personal Recollections of Abraham Lincoln," *Harper's New Monthly Magazine* 31 (July 1865): 226.

77. Undated statement by one Dr. Parker, in Nicolay's hand, Nicolay-Hay MSS, IHi.

78. James Russell Lowell, "Abraham Lincoln," in *Political Essays,* vol. 5 in *The Writings of James Russell Lowell,* 10 vols. (Cambridge: Riverside Press, 1890), 207–8.

79. Douglas Southall Freeman, *R. E. Lee: A Biography,* 4 vols. (New York: Charles Scribner's Sons, 1935), 3:264.

80. Count S. Stakelberg, "Tolstoi Holds Lincoln World's Greatest Hero," New York *World,* 7 Feb. 1909.

81. Hay to Nicolay, Washington, 7 Aug. 1863, Hay MSS, RPB.

82. Diary of Joseph T. Mills, 19 Aug. 1864, in Basler, *CWL,* 7:507.

83. Herman Belz, "Commentary on 'Lincoln's Quest for Union,'" in *The Historian's Lincoln: Pseudohistory, Psychohistory, and History,* ed. Gabor S. Boritt and Norman O. Forness (Urbana: University of Illinois Press, 1988), 250.

84. Leonard Swett to Herndon, Chicago, 17 July 1866, in Hertz, *HL,* 298.

2

"I Used to Be a Slave": The Origins of Lincoln's Hatred of Slavery

More than a decade after Appomattox, the celebrated abolitionist and former slave Frederick Douglass called Abraham Lincoln's opposition to slavery "swift, zealous, radical, and determined," especially when compared to "the sentiment of his country, a sentiment he was bound as a statesman to consult."[1] Another Radical Republican, George S. Boutwell, asserted that "in the steps taken for the emancipation of the slaves, Mr. Lincoln *appeared* to follow rather than to lead the Republican party. But his own views were more advanced usually than those of his party, and he waited patiently and confidently for the healthy movements of public sentiment which he well knew were in the right direction."[2] Lincoln was hardly a reluctant emancipator. As his friend the Marquis de Chambrun put it, the Emancipation Proclamation cannot be viewed merely as "a concession made to the aroused feelings of the moment, or a measure that was destined to stab the enemy in the heart; no, it corresponded to the generous tendencies of his mind and realized the yearnings of his soul."[3]

Historians long ignored such conclusions, arguing instead that Lincoln dealt with the peculiar institution conservatively.[4] Recently, however, scholars have begun to acknowledge the validity of judgments like those by Douglass, Boutwell, and Chambrun.[5] LaWanda Cox, for example, portrays Lincoln during his presidency as "a determined, though circumspect, emancipator and friend of black civil and political rights, consistently striving to obtain what was possible in the face of constitutional restraints, political realities, and white prejudice."[6] Similarly, David Lightner argues that in treating slavery, Lincoln "was guided by egalitarian idealism. Political circumstances sometimes compelled Lincoln to say things that were inconsistent with his commitment to the egalitarian ideal, but in his actions he displayed an overall consistency of purpose."[7]

Scholars also point out that before entering the White House, Lincoln had taken risks in attacking slavery. To be sure, his white supremacist assertions during the 1858 debates with Stephen A. Douglas grate on modern ears, but as Charles B. Strozier has aptly observed, "In the 1850s white supremacy was taken for granted; what was remarkable was that Lincoln had the courage to brand slavery wrong, oppose its extension into the territories on moral and political grounds, and risk association with abolitionism."[8]

These important points cry out for explanation. Lincoln was, after all, born in the slave state of Kentucky, was raised in Negrophobic southern Indiana, was an ambitious practical politician hungry for honors and distinction, and was the son-in-law of a prominent Kentucky slaveholding family. Where did such a man, as one historian asked, "get his *strong and early* convictions against Slavery?"[9] And why did he act so decisively against the institution once he had the power to do so? Why was slavery, as one of Lincoln's Illinois friends put it, "about the only public question on which he would become excited"?[10] Walt Whitman's contention that "the only thing like passion or infatuation in the man was the passion for the Union" is belied by Lincoln's words and deeds, which show how deeply he "abhorred" slavery.[11] An analysis of the 175 speeches he delivered between 1854 and 1860 shows that Lincoln was a "one-issue man" who was "almost a monomaniac on the question of slavery in politics from 1854 forward."[12]

. . .

It is not clear exactly when Lincoln's aversion to slavery emerged. He told a Kentucky editor in 1864 that "I am naturally anti-slavery. If slavery is not wrong, nothing is wrong. I can not remember when I did not so think, and feel."[13] It is possible that Lincoln imbibed antislavery views from his parents; he said in an 1860 autobiographical sketch that his family had moved from Kentucky to Indiana in 1816 "partly on account of slavery."[14] Christopher Columbus Graham, who knew Thomas and Nancy Hanks Lincoln well and attended their wedding, recalled that "Tom and Nancy and Sally Bush were just steeped full of [the Reverend] Jesse Head's notions about the wrong of slavery and the rights of man as explained by Thomas Jefferson and Thomas Paine." Head, pastor of the church where the Lincolns worshipped, had married Thomas and Nancy.[15]

Lincoln spent his first seven years in Hardin County, Kentucky, where, in 1811, 1,007 slaves lived together with 1,627 whites and where debates over slavery had begun at the time of the Revolution and continued throughout his youth, especially among the Baptists. Lincoln's parents belonged to the Little Mount Baptist Church, whose ministers opposed slavery, and Lincoln as a lad may have heard sermons denouncing human bondage. Because his cabin faced the Cumberland Road from Louisville to Nashville, he may have seen slave coffles pass by his front door.[16] In Indiana from 1816 to 1830, Lincoln might also have listened to antislavery preachers, have read newspaper debates about the peculiar institution, have been angered by the slavecatchers who infested his neighborhood, and have heard abolitionist remarks made by his neighbor, who opposed slavery and ran for lieutenant governor in 1819.[17]

In 1828 and 1831, Lincoln, as a hired hand on a flatboat, traveled to New Orleans, where he doubtless saw slavery and slave traders. His cousin John Hanks accompanied him on the second trip and later claimed that in the Crescent City Lincoln saw "negroes chained—maltreated—whipt—& scourged," and that "his heart bled," that he "said nothing much—was silent from feeling—was sad—looked bad—felt bad—was thoughtful & abstracted." Hanks contended that "it was on this trip that he formed his opinions of slavery: it ran its iron in him then & there—May 1831." Hanks added, "I have heard him say [so]— often and often."[18] The interviewer who jotted down this story as it was told, William Herndon, corroborated it: "I have also heard Mr. Lincoln refer to it himself."[19] Historians are skeptical about Hanks's account, for Lincoln himself wrote that Hanks had left the boat well before it reached New Orleans.[20]

Others have left evidence supporting Paul Angle's contention that "it is likely that Lincoln witnessed some such scene as Hanks described."[21] E. Grant Gentry told a historian that his relative Allen Gentry and Lincoln had, during their trip to New Orleans in 1828– 29, observed slaves being bought and sold. The sight prompted Lincoln to exclaim, "Allen, that's a disgrace!"[22] Around 1851, a young man who worked in David Davis's law office told Lincoln how, after observing slave auctions and pens in St. Louis, he had become an abolitionist. Alluding to his own experience in New Orleans, Lincoln replied: "I saw it all myself when I was only a little older than you are now, and the horrid pictures are in my mind yet."[23] In April 1852, at the Metamora court house, Lincoln allegedly told his fellow attorneys that he became "disgusted" when he "saw young women, as white as any that walk these streets to-day, sold on the auction-block simply because they had some Negro blood in their veins."[24]

If these accounts are accurate, they may help explain Lincoln's intense aversion to slave traders, whom he reviled as "enemies of the human race."[25] During the Civil War, a Massachusetts congressman appealed to the president on behalf of a slave trader who had served the full term of his sentence but had been unable to pay his fine. After perusing the relevant documents, Lincoln said, "I believe I am kindly enough in nature and can be moved to pity and to pardon the perpetrator of almost the worst crime that the mind of man can conceive or the arm of man can execute; but any man, who, for paltry gain and stimulated only by avarice, can rob Africa of her children to sell into interminable bondage, I never will pardon, and he may stay and rot in jail before he will ever get relief from me."[26]

Two years earlier he had similarly "put his foot down," rebuffing numerous pleas to spare the life of Nathaniel Gordon, the only American ever hanged for slave trading.[27] Lincoln told the district attorney prosecuting the case, "You do not know how hard it is to have a human being die when you know that a stroke of your pen may save him."[28] But he resisted the impulse to commute the death sentence, telling Gordon's intercessors that the "slave-trade will never be put down till our laws are executed, and the penalty of death has once been enforced upon the offenders."[29] Three years later he told Judge H. P. H. Brownell, "That was a case where there must be an example, and you don't know how they followed and pressed to get him pardoned, or his sentence commuted; but there was no use of talking. It had to be done."[30]

Lincoln was evidently influenced by his attorney general, who argued that the chief executive "has no right to stop the course of law, except on grounds of excuse or mitigation found in the case itself—and not to arrest the execution of the statute merely because he thinks the law wrong or too severe."[31] Lincoln may also have been swayed by Charles Sumner, with whom he discussed the case at length.[32] Sumner argued that Gordon must be executed in order to "deter slave traders," to "give notice to the world of a change of policy," and to show "that the Govt. can hang a man."[33] In any event, the president counseled Gordon to relinquish "all expectation of pardon by Human Authority" and "refer himself alone to the mercy of the common God and Father of all men."[34]

When the Confederate cavalry leader and slave trader John Hunt Morgan was killed in 1864, Lincoln expressed his satisfaction to a Union chaplain. "Well, I wouldn't crow over anybody's death," the president remarked, "but I can take this as *resignedly* as any dispensation of Providence. Morgan was a coward, nigger-driver; a low creature, such as you Northern men know nothing about." He added, "Southern slaveholders despise them. But such a wretch has been used to carry on their rebellion."[35]

In 1854, he spoke with similar vehemence while urging Southerners to admit that slavery was wrong: "You have amongst you, a sneaking individual, of the class of native tyrants, known as the 'SLAVE DEALER.' . . . You despise him utterly. You do not recognize him as a friend, or even as an honest man. Your children must not play with his; they may rollick freely with the little negroes, but not with the 'slave-dealers' children. If you are obliged to deal with him, you try to get through the job without so much as touching him." Ostensibly Lincoln was describing the hostility of Southerners toward slave traders, but it seems clear that the remarks also reflect Lincoln's own antipathy.[36]

In any event it is easy to imagine Lincoln recoiling from slavery on his trips to New Orleans. Cruelty to humans would doubtless have offended him, for as a boy he had protested vigorously against cruelty to animals.[37] In Illinois, Lincoln could not observe slavery firsthand, but he did on trips to Kentucky to visit his wife's family and his friend Joshua Speed.[38] He told Speed how in 1841 he had witnessed in Kentucky a coffle of "ten or a dozen slaves, shackled together with irons," a sight that "was a continual torment" to him. He claimed that he saw such things "every time I touch the Ohio, or any other slave-border," and that those sights had "the power of making me miserable."[39]

• • •

Whatever episodes may have prompted his revulsion, Lincoln first gave public expression to it in 1837. During his second term in the Illinois state legislature, he and a colleague issued a formal protest against an antiabolitionist resolution that had passed the Illinois legislature by the lopsided vote of 77–6. The dissenters asserted that slavery was "founded on both injustice and bad policy."[40] Later that year the people of Springfield joined the legislature in condemning the abolitionists.[41] As a young man, Lincoln seldom flouted public opinion so dramatically.[42] While running for president many years later, he described his 1837 protest as one that "briefly defined his position on the slavery question; and so far as it goes, it was then the same that it is now."[43] That document lends credence to Lincoln's assertion, made in 1858, that "I have always hated slavery, I think as much as any Abolitionist." He explained that he had not been active in antislavery politics before 1854 because until that fateful year he had assumed that the institution was on the road to ultimate extinction.[44]

The following year, in his Lyceum Address, Lincoln protested against mob violence, including the killing of Elijah Lovejoy and the burning of a black man in St. Louis. He risked offending his antiabolitionist audience by alluding sympathetically to Lovejoy and speaking with compassion about the "horror-striking scene at St. Louis," which he termed "highly tragic." Paraphrasing Lovejoy's account of the St. Louis crime, Lincoln said, "A mulatto man, by the name of McIntosh, was seized in the street, dragged to the suburbs of the city, chained to a tree, and actually burned to death; and all within a single hour from the time he had been a freeman, attending to his own business, and at peace with the world."[45]

Other pre-1854 evidence supports Lincoln's statement to Robert H. Browne that "the slavery question often bothered me as far back as 1836–1840. I was troubled and grieved over it."[46] A close friend observed that while riding a train to Alton in 1837, "Lincoln was talking and men were standing up around him listening to the conversation. . . . One of them asked him if he was an abolitionist. Mr. Lincoln in reply, reached over and laid his hand on the shoulder of Mr. Alsopp who was a strong abolitionist and said, 'I am mighty near one.'"[47] When a Springfield businessman, Benjamin Fox, complained that the postmaster would not deliver an abolitionist journal, Lincoln persuaded that reluctant official to do his duty. The gesture was not entirely altruistic, for Lincoln often visited Fox's store to read what the abolitionist editors had to say.[48]

Lincoln told a Canadian abolitionist during the Civil War that "I have always been an anti-slavery man. Away back in 1839, when I was a member of the Legislature of Illinois, I presented a resolution asking for the emancipation of slavery in the District of Columbia, when, with but few exceptions, the popular mind of my State was opposed to it."[49] It was actually 1837 when Lincoln offered an amendment to an Illinois legislative resolution concerning slavery in Washington. The main motion affirmed that Congress had no right to abolish slavery in the nation's capital. Lincoln's unsuccessful amendment would have paved the way for emancipation there; it called for the insertion of the following language: "unless the people of said District petition for the same."[50]

Twelve years later, in 1849, as a member of the U.S. House of Representatives, Lincoln proposed abolishing slavery in Washington with the consent of the owners.[51] While the Southern press criticized him as an abolitionist, his measure enjoyed the support of the radical antislavery congressman Joshua R. Giddings.[52] When as president he signed a law ending human bondage in Washington, he said privately: "Little did I dream in 1849, when . . . I proposed to abolish slavery at this capital, and could scarcely get a hearing for the proposition, that it would be so soon accomplished."[53]

In 1838, Lincoln alluded to slavery in a somewhat delphic fashion while warning against the dangers of Caesarism: "Towering genius disdains a beaten path. . . . It thirsts and burns for distinction; and, if possible, it will have it, whether at the expense of emancipating slaves, or enslaving freemen."[54] It is hard to know what to make of this curious remark. Isaac N. Arnold speculated that it may have been a "mysterious presentiment that in some unknown way he was to be the deliverer of the slaves."[55]

Another strange reference to slavery occurs in Lincoln's 1842 temperance address. Because he had not mentioned slavery at all in the main body of this speech, an allusion to it in the peroration seems like a non-sequitur: "When the victory shall be complete—when there shall be neither a slave nor a drunkard on the earth—how proud the title of that *Land,* which may truly claim to be the birth-place and cradle of both those revolutions, that shall have ended in that victory."[56] Arnold believed that this language indicated that Lincoln "was always dreaming, it would seem, of the time when there should be *no slave* in the republic."[57] That may be farfetched speculation, but Lincoln did tell Joshua Speed shortly after issuing the Emancipation Proclamation that it represented "the fulfillment of his long cherished hope."[58]

In 1839, Lincoln helped defeat a resolution in the Illinois legislature declaring that slavery should be preserved in Washington, D.C., that more slave states should be allowed to enter the Union, and that any move to grant Illinois blacks equal rights was "unconstitutional."[59]

Two years later, he was forced to pay close attention to the slavery issue as he prepared to argue a case before the Illinois supreme court. In *Bailey vs. Cromwell,* Lincoln and his partner John T. Stuart successfully contended that slavery had been outlawed in Illinois both by the Northwest Ordinance of 1787 and by the state Constitution of 1818, and that therefore that no person could be bought or sold in Illinois.[60] In 1847, however, Lincoln agreed to serve as co-counsel for a slave-holder, Robert Matson, who sued to force Illinois blacks to return to slavery in Kentucky.[61] Why he would help compel blacks to return to slavery is "one of the greatest enigmas of his career," because, as he told Speed in discussing captured runaway slaves, "I hate to see the poor creatures hunted down, and caught, and carried back to their stripes, and unrewarded toils."[62]

In the 1850s, a conductor on the Underground Railroad told a fellow abolitionist that Lincoln "was often a contributor to the funds needed for the protection of the fugitives."[63] After the passage of the Fugitive Slave Act of 1850, Lincoln avoided cases dealing with run-aways because, according to his friend and colleague Leonard Swett, he was unwilling "to be a party to a violation of the Fugitive Slave Law, arguing that the way to overcome the difficulty was to repeal the law."[64] In private, however, he denounced the statute as "very obnoxious" and exclaimed that it was "ungodly! no doubt it is ungodly!"[65]

Even though he avoided fugitive slave cases, sometime in late 1856 or early 1857 Lincoln responded positively to the appeal of a free black woman whose son faced enslavement in New Orleans. The incautious young man had worked on a steamboat and was seized in the Crescent City because he lacked "free papers." Lincoln asked an attorney in New Orleans to represent the young man, a native of Springfield, and offered to pay all costs. With William Herndon, he also called on Illinois Governor William Bissell, who claimed he had no power to help rescue the unfortunate fellow. According to Herndon, his partner "exclaimed with some emphasis: 'By God, Governor, I'll make the ground in this country too hot for the foot of a slave, whether you have the legal power to secure the release of this boy or not.'" Thwarted at first by technical complications, Lincoln eventually raised money to procure the young man's freedom.[66] As president, he similarly tried to cut through red tape to save a young slave boy by offering to pay the owner up to $500 for his freedom.[67]

In May 1845, Lincoln heard Anson S. Miller arraign slavery and Illinois's discriminatory black laws in the most scorching terms. While delivering his philippic, Miller noticed that Lincoln was paying close attention. Afterward, Lincoln greeted him warmly and "was particularly emphatic in his commendation of the passage which denounced slavery."[68] That October he told a fervent abolitionist that "we should never knowingly lend ourselves directly or indirectly" to any measure that would "prevent ... slavery from dying a natural death."[69] The following year, when Lincoln ran for Congress, Free-Soilers in his district questioned him about the slavery issue. As one of the delegation later wrote, "We called on him and were so well pleased with what he said on the subject that we advised our anti-slavery friend[s] throughout the district [that they should] should cast their vote for Mr. Lincoln; which was generally done."[70]

In 1855 Lincoln passed a similar test when radical abolitionists investigated him.[71] One antislavery militant, Charles H. Ray, told a friend in December 1854, "I must confess I am afraid of 'Abe.' He is Southern by birth, Southern in his associations and Southern, if I mistake not, in his sympathies. I have thought that he would not come squarely up to the mark in a hand to hand fight with Southern influence and dictation. His wife, you know, is a Todd, of a proslavery family, and so are all his kin." Ray thought that abolitionists were especially upset because a Democrat captured the legislative seat that Lincoln had won and then turned down. But within a few weeks Ray decided to back Lincoln for the U.S. Senate.[72] At the time of that election, Zebina Eastman and Cassius M. Clay visited Springfield to learn about the depth and sincerity of Lincoln's antislavery views. They talked with Herndon, who convinced them that his partner was sound. Later Eastman wrote Herndon, "You satisfied me. ... After that visit [to Springfield] I told all my Liberty Party friends to stand by Abraham Lincoln."[73] Some abolitionists demanded that he pledge to vote for the repeal of the 1850 Fugitive Slave Act. Lincoln refused, saying that the statute was rooted in the Constitution; if elected to the Senate, however, he would vote to strip the law "of its obnoxious features."[74]

After he won the 1846 race for Congress, Lincoln took his seat in the House and followed the slavery debates closely. One day in the Senate Chamber he listened intently as Hannibal Hamlin denounced the peculiar institution. Lincoln nodded enthusiastically whenever the senator from Maine "made a good point against slavery."[75] Many years later, when they first met as president-elect and vice-president-elect, Lincoln said, "I have just been recalling the time when, in '48, I went to the Senate to hear you speak. Your subject was not new, but the ideas were sound. You were talking about slavery, and I now take occasion to thank you for so well expressing what were my own sentiments at that time."[76]

While in Congress in 1848 and 1849 he supported antislavery measures such as the Wilmot Proviso, which excluded slavery from the territory acquired from Mexico, as well as framing legislation to abolish slavery in the District of Columbia. A fellow representative from Illinois, Orlando B. Ficklin, believed that Joshua Giddings, the leading antislavery champion in Congress, helped convert Lincoln to the cause. "I had not known him to favor the abolition of slavery" before he entered Congress, Ficklin wrote. "But he was thrown in a mess [rooming house] with Joshua R. Giddings. In this company his views crystallized, and when he came out from such association he was fixed in his views on emancipation."[77] But he did not accord the slavery issue high priority. In September 1848, after hearing William Henry Seward attack the peculiar institution, he told the New York senator: "I have been thinking about what you said. . . . I reckon you are right. We have got to deal with this slavery question, and got to give much more attention to it hereafter than we have been doing."[78]

In 1850 Lincoln expressed firm antislavery sentiments to colleagues at the bar. While returning with Lincoln from a swing around the legal circuit, John T. Stuart predicted that soon all men would have to choose between abolitionism and the Democratic party. Lincoln replied "in an Emphatic tone" that "when that time comes my mind is made up. The Slavery question can[']t be compromised[."][79] In Shelbyville soon after the Kentucky constitutional convention of 1849, Lincoln warned Joseph Gillespie that slavery might well spread across the entire country. Alluding to the convention, he noted incredulously that whites who did not hold slaves outnumbered those who did by a margin of nearly twenty to one, yet all the delegates to the convention favored slavery. Indignantly he repeated what a Kentuckian had told him about the popularity of slavery: A slave was the most glittering status symbol in the south. To have a slave in tow indicated not only wealth but also a disdain for work. As Gillespie remembered it, "These things Mr. Lincoln regarded as highly seductive to the thoughtless and giddy headed young men who looked upon work as vulgar and ungentlemanly. Mr. Lincoln was really excited and said with great earnestness that this spirit ought to be met and if possible checked[,] That slavery was a great crying injustice[,] an enormous national crime and that we could not expect to escape punishment for it." Lincoln conceded that he had no practical solution for the problem, but Gillespie inferred that "he made up his mind from that time that he would oppose slavery actively."[80] Lincoln's second law partner, Stephen T. Logan, said that he knew Lincoln's "early opinions" on the peculiar institution and that "no man felt more repugnance to slavery than Mr. Lincoln."[81]

While visiting Cincinnati in 1855, Lincoln again deplored the baleful effects of slavery on white Kentuckians. Walking with a friend along the banks of the Ohio, he

> suddenly turned and pointed across the river to Kentucky, and said: "Here is this fine city of Cincinnati, and over there is the little town of Covington. Covington has just as good a location as Cincinnati, and a fine country back of it. It was settled before Cincinnati. Why is it not a bigger city? Just because of slavery, and nothing else. My people used to live over there, and I know. Why the other day I went to ship my family on a little railroad they have got down there from Covington back into the country. I went to the ticket office and found a lank fellow sprawling over the counter, who had to count up quite a while on his fingers how much two and one-half fares would come to. While over here in Cincinnati, when I shove my money through the window, the three tickets and the change would come flying back at me quick. And it is just the same way in all things through Kentucky. That is what slavery does for the white man."[82]

In 1852 Lincoln said that he imagined he might become "something of a leader against slavery encroachments."[83] In fact, he became a manager of the Illinois State Colonization Society, addressed their annual meetings in 1853 and 1855, contributed money to the society, and enjoyed speaking with its agents.[84] During the Civil War, he continued to promote colonization (a pet scheme of his "beau ideal of a statesman" Henry Clay) despite criticism from some Radical Republicans.[85]

In 1854, the passage of the Kansas-Nebraska Act gave Lincoln the occasion to follow through more forcefully on his resolve. In the Springfield courthouse that summer, he attended a meeting to discuss the slavery issue and nominate candidates for office. Most of the thirty attendees, although angry about "the encroachments of slavery," hesitated to take action to combat them. Lincoln, however, purportedly "said if we hold these opinions in regard to the outrages upon the black man why should we fear to avow them and say what we think and do what we can in behalf of right and justice."[86] In the fall he made his first extensive analysis and denunciation of slavery, which he regarded as "a moral, social and political evil," "the sum of all villa[i]nies," "a vast moral evil," and a "monster."[87] He told an Illinois audience why he opposed Douglas's indifference to whether slavery "was voted up or down." Speaking "with unusual warmth and energy" and quivering "with emotion," Lincoln said "I hate it because of the monstrous injustice of slavery itself. I hate it because it deprives our republican example of its just influence in the world—enables the enemies of free institutions, with plausibility, to taunt us as hypocrites—causes the real friends of freedom to doubt our sincerity, and especially because it forces so many really good men amongst ourselves into an open war with the very fundamental principles of civil liberty—criticising the Declaration of Independence, and insisting that there is no right principle of action but *self-interest.*"[88]

What did Lincoln mean by "the monstrous injustice of slavery itself"? A close reading of his speeches and letters suggests that Lincoln found slavery monstrous because it represented the systematic theft of the fruits of hard labor, a kind of institutionalized robbery.[89] He made this point heatedly and often. At the start of the 1858 campaign for Douglas's Senate seat, Lincoln characterized the proslavery argument as "the same old serpent that says you work and I eat, you toil and I will enjoy the fruits of it." He declared that "each individual is naturally entitled to do as he pleases with himself and the fruit of his labor."[90] At the end of the campaign he summarized the difference between his stand on slavery and Douglas's:

> It is the eternal struggle between . . . two principles—right and wrong—throughout the world. They are the two principles that have stood face to face from the beginning of time; and will ever continue to struggle. The one is the common right of humanity and the other the divine right of kings. . . . It is the same spirit that says, "You work and toil and earn bread, and I'll eat it." No matter in what shape it comes, whether from the mouth of a king who seeks to bestride the people of his own nation and live by the fruit of their labor, or from one race of men as an apology for enslaving another race, it is the same tyrannical principle.[91]

When Douglas charged that the Republicans favored racial equality, Lincoln conceded that "certainly the negro is not our equal in color—perhaps not in many other respects" but insisted that "in the right to put into his mouth the bread that his own hands have earned, he is the equal of every other man, white or black."[92] According to one observer, Lincoln delivered that last sentence with special fervor, lifting himself "to his full height" and reaching "his hands towards the stars of that still night."[93]

At the same time, Lincoln scouted the argument that slaves were content with their bondage. "The ant," he wrote, "who has toiled and dragged a crumb to his nest, will furiously defend the fruit of his la-

bor, against whatever robber assails him." By the same token, he added, "the most dumb and stupid slave that ever toiled for a master, does
constantly *know* that he is wronged."[94]

Lincoln also mocked the Union-saving and democratic pretensions
of slavery's defenders. In 1857 he told a Springfield audience that "the
Republicans inculcate . . . that the negro is a man; that his bondage is
cruelly wrong, and that the field of his oppression ought not to be enlarged. The Democrats deny his manhood; deny . . . the wrong of his
bondage; . . . crush all sympathy for him, and cultivate and excite hatred and disgust against him; compliment themselves as Union-savers
for doing so; and call the indefinite outspreading of his bondage 'a
sacred right of self-government.'"[95]

Theological justifications for slavery aroused Lincoln's indignation.
He told the American Baptist Home Mission Society in 1864 that "to
read in the Bible, as the word of God himself, that 'In the sweat of *thy*
face shalt thou eat bread,['] and to preach therefrom that, 'In the sweat
of *other mans* faces shalt thou eat bread,' to my mind can scarcely be
reconciled with honest sincerity."[96] After a Tennessee woman had successfully pleaded with Lincoln to release her spouse from a prison camp,
the president thus bade her farewell: "You say your husband is a religious man; tell him when you meet him, that I say I am not much of a
judge of religion, but that, in my opinion, the religion that sets men to
rebel and fight against their government, because, as they think, that
government does not sufficiently help *some* men to eat their bread on
the sweat of *other* men's faces, is not the sort of religion upon which
people can get to heaven!"[97]

To the Southern contention "that the institution [of slavery] is a 'necessity' imposed on us by the negro race," Lincoln scoffingly replied:
"That the going many thousand miles, seizing a set of savages, bringing
them here, and making slaves of them is a necessity imposed on us by
them involves a species of logic to which my mind will scarcely assent."[98]

Dr. Frederick A. Ross, a leading proslavery member of the clergy,
infuriated Lincoln. He imagined that Ross owned a slave named Sambo and that the question of whether God intended Sambo to be free
arose:

> The Almighty gives no audable answer to the question. . . . No one
> thinks of asking Sambo's opinion on it. So, at last, it comes to this,
> that *Dr. Ross* is to decide the question. And while he consider[s] it,
> he sits in the shade, with gloves on his hands, and subsists on the bread

that Sambo is earning in the burning sun. If he decides that God Wills Sambo to continue a slave, he thereby retains his own comfortable position; but if he decides that God will's Sambo to be free, he thereby has to walk out of the shade, throw off his gloves, and delve for his own bread.

Lincoln scorned the argument that slaveholders were motivated by benevolence toward their bondsmen: "Nonsense! Wolves devouring lambs, not because it is good for their own greedy maws, but because is [is] good for the lambs!!!"[99]

A spectator who heard this denunciation of Ross also recalled Lincoln describing his emotions as he beheld slaves at work: "When I see strong hands sowing, reaping, and threshing wheat and those same hands grinding and making that wheat into bread, I cannot refrain from wishing, and believing, that those hands some way, in God's good time, shall own the mouth they feed!"[100] He told an audience in Charleston, Illinois, in 1856 that he would continue to work against slavery "until everywhere on this wide land, the sun shall shine and the rain shall fall and the wind shall blow upon no man who goes forth to unrequited toil."[101] In his second inaugural address he said that it "may seem strange that any men should dare to ask a just God's assistance in wringing their bread from the sweat of other men's faces; but let us judge not that we be not judged."[102]

Lincoln's rejoinder to those who denounced emancipation as a violation of the liberty of the slaveholder was scathing. As he told a crowd in Baltimore in 1864, "The world has never had a good definition of the word liberty, and the American people, just now, are much in want of one. We all declare for liberty; but in using the same *word* we do not all mean the same *thing*. With some the word liberty may mean for each man to do as he pleases with himself, and the product of his labor; while with others the same word may mean for some men to do as they please with other men, and the product of other men's labor." Lincoln's gloss on the latter definition was contemptuous; alluding to the Emancipation Proclamation and its Southern critics, he said, "The shepherd drives the wolf from the sheep's throat, for which the sheep thanks the shepherd as a *liberator,* while the wolf denounces him for the same act as the destroyer of liberty."[103]

In the second inaugural, he argued that the Civil War might be God's punishment on both North and South for the evil of slavery and that the bloodshed might not end "until all the wealth piled by the bond-man's two hundred and fifty years of unrequited toil shall be sunk."[104]

On occasion, Lincoln treated the theme with humor. Anatomy, he told an audience in Cincinnati in 1859, proved that "whatever any one man earns with his hands and by the sweat of his brow, he shall enjoy in peace." He contended:

> Whereas God Almighty has given every man one mouth to be fed, and one pair of hands adapted to furnish food for that mouth, if anything can be proved to be the will of Heaven, it is proved by this fact, that that mouth is to be fed by those hands, without being interfered with by any other man who has also his mouth to feed and his hands to labor with. I hold if the Almighty had ever made a set of men that should do all the eating and none of the work, he would have made them with mouths only and no hands, and if he had ever made another class that he had intended should do all the work and none of the eating, he would have made them without mouths and with all hands.[105]

In reminiscences by people who knew Lincoln, this same theme recurs. In 1860 he remarked to Cassius M. Clay, "I always thought that the man who made the corn should eat the corn."[106] When first introduced to Ward Hill Lamon in 1847, Lincoln teased the younger man, a native of Virginia, about white Southerners' aversion to hard work. When Lamon protested, Lincoln sarcastically replied, "Oh, yes; you Virginians shed barrels of perspiration while standing off at a distance and superintending the work your slaves do for you. It is different with us. Here it is every fellow for himself, or he doesn't get there."[107]

When Lincoln felt himself cheated of the fruits of his labor, he grew indignant. In 1849, after Justin Butterfield of Chicago beat him out for the commissionership for the General Land Office, Lincoln complained to a fellow Whig that he had, by dint of hard work for the Whig party, earned the office, whereas Butterfield had not:

> In 1840 we fought a fierce and laborious battle in Illinois, many of us spending almost the entire year in the contest. The general victory came, and with it, the appointment of a set of drones, including this same Butterfield, who had never spent a dollar or lifted a finger in the fight. . . . Again, winter and spring before the last, when you and I were almost sweating blood to have Genl. Taylor nominated, this same man was ridiculing the idea, and going for Mr. Clay; and when Gen: T. was nominated, if he [Butterfield] went out of the city of Chicago to aid in his election, it is more that I ever heard, or believe.

Yet, when the election is secured, by other men's labor, and even against his effort, why, he is the first man on hand for the best office that our state lays any claim to. Shall this thing be? Our whigs will throw down their arms, and fight no more, if the fruit of their labor is thus disposed of.[108]

Slavery was not the only issue that galvanized Lincoln into a passionate defense of workers' rights to keep what they had earned by the sweat of their brow. His pre-1854 economic views are for the most part consonant with his later antislavery positions.[109] In an 1847 analysis of the tariff controversy, he said that "it has so happened in all ages of the world, that *some* have laboured, and *others* have, without labour, enjoyed a large proportion of the fruits. This is wrong, and should not continue. To [secure] to each labourer the whole product of his labour . . . is a most worthy object of any good government."[110] In a discussion of the rights of workers, he said in 1859 that "as Labor is the common *burthen* of our race, so the effort of *some* to shift their share of the burthen on to the shoulders of *others,* is the great, durable, curse of the race."[111] A few months later he defended New England workers who were on strike to win a fair share of the fruits of their labor: "I am glad to know that there is a system of labor where the laborer can strike if he wants to!"[112] This pro-labor stand was, according to a close student of Lincoln's economic thought, "the product of his own mind, not that of his party."[113]

Such emphasis on the rights of workers, white or black, to enjoy what they had earned was hardly unique to Lincoln, but it is noteworthy that he stressed it so heavily. Other opponents of slavery focused on the physical cruelty of the peculiar institution, on its baleful effects on the economy of the South and on the poor whites, on its destruction of family ties among slaves, on the way it corrupted the personality of the slaveholder, and on its tendency to promote an aristocratic social order in the South.[114] Such arguments, however, had little appeal for Lincoln.

He so emphatically deplored the way that owners robbed slaves of their rightful earnings because, as Gabor Boritt suggests, Lincoln "sympathized and, to a degree, identified with the downtrodden black man."[115] At the age of twenty-nine, he stated that the experience of bondage was not unfamiliar to him. Describing how he had managed to free himself from an engagement to be married, he said, "Through life I have been in no bondage, either real or immaginary from the thral-

dom of which I so much desired to be free."[116] An Illinois friend, John
E. Roll, recalled that Lincoln made a speech in which he asserted that
"we were all slaves one time or another," but noted "that white men
could make themselves free and the [N]egroes could not." To illustrate
his point, Lincoln said, "There is my old friend John Roll. He used to
be a slave, but he has made himself free, and I used to be a slave, and
now I am so free that they let me practice law."[117]

Frederick Douglass thought that Lincoln's cordiality toward him
stemmed in part from their common status as poor boys who had made
good. Douglass recalled that in all his dealings with the president, "I
was impressed with his entire freedom from popular prejudice against
the colored race. He was the first great man that I talked with in the
United States freely, who in no single instance reminded me of the difference between himself and myself, of the difference of color, and I
thought that all the more remarkable because he came from a State
where there were black laws [forbidding blacks to migrate into the
state]. I account partially for his kindness to me because of the simi-
larity with which I had fought my way up, we both starting at the lowest
round of the ladder."[118] This may well be true, for Lincoln felt some
pride in overcoming the poverty of his youth. In his first annual message to Congress, he declared that "no men living are more worthy to
be trusted than those who toil up from poverty—none less inclined to
take, or touch, aught which they have not honestly earned."[119] In his
eulogy on Henry Clay, Lincoln described that Kentucky statesman's
ideology in terms that apply equally well, if not better, to himself: "Mr.
Clay's predominant sentiment, from first to last, was a deep devotion
to the cause of human liberty—a strong sympathy with the oppressed
every where, and an ardent wish for their elevation."[120]

A month before his death, Lincoln told a regiment of Union soldiers that he had "always thought that all men should be free; but if
any should be slaves it should be first those who desire it for *themselves,*
and secondly those who *desire* it for *others.*" Then, in terms that suggest he knew firsthand what it meant to be a slave, he added that
"whenever [I] hear any one, arguing for slavery I feel a strong impulse
to see it tried on him personally."[121]

Lincoln seldom accepted favors because he believed that "those
who receive favors owe a debt of gratitude to the giver and to that
extent are obedient and abject slaves."[122] Herndon thought him "wholly self-reliant, asking no man anything."[123] Henry C. Whitney wrote

that Lincoln "kept his own counsels, and asked the fewest favors of all kinds of any man of his station." His "absolute desire to be wholly independent," according to Whitney, led him to milk his own cow, groom his own horse, clean his own stable, chop his own wood, and perform other such chores unaided.[124] Egbert L. Viele recalled that Lincoln "never liked to be waited upon, or to ask any one to do anything for him that he could possibly do himself."[125]

Herndon remembered that Lincoln in court "was altogether commonplace, except when fired by the thought of injustice or oppression. Then he became transformed. To speak well he must think that someone, black or white, had been 'abused.'"[126] Because Lincoln with reason felt that he had been abused as a child, he could identify best with clients, black or white, in the same position. During his political career after 1854, he became, in effect, an attorney for all slaves.

• • •

As a youth, Lincoln was like a slave to his father, who insisted that his son not only labor on the family farm but also that he work for neighbors and then turn over every penny that he had earned.[127] Soon after Lincoln started school in Indiana, Thomas Lincoln removed him and set him to work for neighbors in order to help solve Thomas's financial problems and perhaps to thwart the boy's interest in reading.[128] No direct evidence illuminates Lincoln's feelings about being forced to work hard and then turn over all the earnings to his father, but an anecdote from his presidential years is suggestive. One day during the Civil War he described the joy he felt at earning his first money, a whole dollar given him for rowing two men from a riverbank to a steamboat. "I could scarcely credit that I, the poor boy, had earned a dollar in less than a day; that by honest work I had earned a dollar. The world seemed wider and fairer before me; I was a more hopeful and thoughtful boy from that time."[129] It was, perhaps, the first money that he had earned without being leased out by his father and thus could keep; his obvious delight indicates that it may have been.[130]

Lincoln harshly satirized one of the employers to whom he was rented and who, he felt, had taken unfair advantage of him. Josiah Crawford made him work three full days pulling fodder as compensation for damage done to a borrowed book. This seemed excessive to young Lincoln, who also disliked the way that Crawford docked his meager wages (twenty-five cents a day) if he should be a few minutes

late. In retaliation, Lincoln wrote poems, songs, and chronicles ridiculing Crawford's large nose.[131] Some of the anger Lincoln aimed at
Crawford was probably displaced animosity felt for Thomas Lincoln.

Lincoln's relationship with his father was chilly. Much evidence
supports Richard N. Current's conclusion that "there must have been
a real estrangement" between the two.[132] Lincoln's cousin, Dennis
Hanks, who lived with the Lincoln family from the time Abraham was
seven, doubted whether "Abe Loved his father very well or Not," and
concluded "I Don[']t think he Did."[133] Although a relatively placid,
easy-going man, Thomas Lincoln could treat his son with "great barbarity," according to Hanks's son-in-law.[134] Hanks testified that Thomas Lincoln would sometimes "slash" his boy for reading instead of
doing chores. Hanks also recalled other episodes of physical abuse:
"When strangers would ride along and up to his father's fence, Abe
always, through pride and to tease his father, would be sure to ask the
stranger the first question, for which his father would sometimes knock
him a rod. . . . Abe, when whipped by his father, never balked, but
dropped a kind of silent unwelcome tear."[135]

Sophie Hanks, who lived with the Lincolns in Indiana, recalled that
rather than whipping Abraham in front of guests, Tom Lincoln would
wait until they had gone and then deal with the boy.[136] She told her
children that one morning a poor, usually barefoot neighbor named
Jenkins called on Tom Lincoln. When young Abe saw him, he said,
"Hello, Mr. Jenkins. You are doing better than you used to. You have
a new pair of boots." Tom Lincoln took his boy inside a "gave Abe a
little drilling" because his remarks might have offended Jenkins. "'Well,'
said Abe, 'he's got the boots.'"[137] According to her son, Sophie Hanks
"always said that the worst trouble with Abe was when people was
talking—if they said something that wasn't right Abe would up and tell
them so. Uncle Tom had a hard time to break him of this."[138] She also
recalled how Lincoln "very often would correct his father in talking
when his father was telling how anything happened and if he didn[']t
get it jest right or left out any thing, Abe would but[t] in right there
and correct it."[139] This recollection was borne out by Lincoln's stepmother, who related how he once challenged his father's version of story,
saying "Paw, that was not jest the way it was." For this act of lèse-
majesté, Tom slapped Abe in the face.[140] As the Lincolns prepared to
leave Indiana for Illinois, Jimmy Grigsby observed Thomas Lincoln
impatiently awaiting his tardy son. When Abraham finally arrived, his
father, carrying an ox whip, approached him. Grigsby then whispered

to a friend, "Watch old Tom flail him." But instead the elder Lincoln handed his son the whip and told him to lead the procession.[141]

What Lincoln thought of his father's disciplinary methods is unknown, but a beating is inordinately severe punishment for initiating a conversation with passers-by. As a parent, Lincoln rejected the pattern of his own father and indulged his sons so much that he scandalized polite society (chapter 3).

Young Abraham may have resented even more than physical abuse the favoritism that his father displayed toward his stepbrother. According to Dennis Hanks's son-in-law, "Tho[ma]s Lincoln never showed by his actions that he thought much of his son Abraham when a boy. [He] treated him rather unkindly than otherwise, [and] always appeared to think much more of his stepson John D. Johnston than he did of his own son Abraham." John Y. Simon speculates plausibly that his father's preference for Johnston hurt Lincoln deeply.[142]

The source of Tom Lincoln's attitude may in part have been Abraham's distaste for farm work. "Farming, grubbing, hoeing, [and] making fences" held no charm for the boy, according to his cousin John Hanks. His stepmother told Herndon that "Abe was a good boy," but "he didn't like physical labor."[143] Abraham often worked for a neighbor, who recalled that the boy "was always reading and thinking, [so] I used to get mad at him. . . . I say Abe was awful lazy. [H]e would laugh and talk and crack jokes and tell stories all the time. . . . Lincoln said to me one day that his father taught him to work but never learned him to love it."[144]

Thomas Lincoln scarcely tolerated his boy's obsession with learning. John B. Helm stated that the father of the future president "looked upon bone and muscel [as] sufficient to make the man and that time spent in school as doubly wasted."[145] To discourage the reading habit, Thomas used to conceal Abraham's books and sometimes even threw them away.[146] According to Sarah Bush Johnston Lincoln, her husband "was not easily reconciled" to the suggestion that young Abraham be allowed to attend school and to read at home, but in time he relented.[147] Five years after Abraham had struck out on his own at the age of twenty-two, Thomas Lincoln told William G. Greene, "I suppose that Abe is still fooling hisself with eddication. I tried to stop it, but he has got that fool idea in his head, and it can't be got out. Now I hain't got no eddication, but I get along far better than ef I had." At that point Thomas Lincoln demonstrated how he kept accounts by marking a rafter with a piece of coal and then proudly remarked, "That thar's a heap better 'n yer eddication."[148] He added that "if Abe don't fool away all his time on his books, he may make something yet."[149]

When Thomas tried to instruct Abraham in his own trade of carpentry, the boy demonstrated so little interest that the effort was soon abandoned.[150] He was equally unenthusiastic about his father's favorite leisure pursuits, hunting and fishing, partly because of his tender feelings for animals.[151] Those feelings were not strong enough, however, to keep him from deliberately killing one of his father's dogs.[152] That may have been an act of unconscious revenge for Thomas's slaughter of young Abraham's pet pig, to which the boy had been devoted.[153]

By the time he was nineteen, Abraham had grown so alienated that he seriously considered running away from home, even though the law required him to stay there and obey his father's command until he reached his majority. After returning from his first trip to New Orleans and handing over all the money he had earned to his father, Lincoln visited William Wood and said, "I want you to go to the river and give me a recommendation to some boat. I want a start." Wood refused, saying, "Abe, your age is against you. You're not twenty-one. I won't do it for your own good."[154]

Some who knew Tom Lincoln thought him shiftless. Nathaniel Grigsby, an Indiana neighbor of the Lincolns, called Thomas "a piddler" who "was happy, lived easy and contented." Grigsby noted that he "wanted few things and supplied them easily."[155] Other Hoosiers shared this poor opinion of Thomas Lincoln. "Many people of the Indiana hills," wrote Grace Jeannette Bullock Maas, "did not like Thomas Lincoln" because he "was satisfied to live in the good *old* fashioned way; his shack kept out the rain; there was plenty of wood to burn . . . the old ways were good enough for him." This author claimed that "Abe had to bear the brunt of the older man's unpopularity."[156] Elizabeth Crawford "said they [the Lincolns] were very poor people. They had little of even the comforts of that time in their home. Life in the Lincoln home was so hard that she invited Sarah, Lincoln's sister, to come and live in the Crawford home and pay for her board by helping with the house work." It seemed "very funny" to Mrs. Crawford that the Lincolns "didn't have anything to offer their guests, as was customary among those very hospitable pioneer people."[157] An Illinois neighbor, George B. Balch, had similar recollections: "It is generally supposed that he [Thomas] was a farmer; and such he was, if one who tilled so little land by such primitive modes could be so called. He never planted more than a few acres, and instead of gathering and hauling his crop in a wagon he usually carried it in baskets or large trays. He was uneducated, illiterate, content with living from hand to mouth."[158] Balch called Lincoln a "rough man" who "never drank" but was "lazy & worthless." He owned "few sheep," he "talked and walked slow," and was, in sum, "an excellent spec[imen] of poor white trash."[159] William G. Greene spent a few days at the Lincolns' farm in Goosenest Prairie and observed that Thomas was barely able to eke out a living.[160] Sophie Hanks's son ascribed Thomas Lincoln's lack of ambition to the economic conditions of the Midwest frontier: "Well, you see, he was like the other people in that country. None of them worked to get ahead. There was n't no market for nothing unless you took it across two or three states. The people raised just what they needed."[161]

Three years after he had asked William Wood to help him escape from home, Lincoln fled the quasi-slavery he endured at the hands of his father and drifted off to New Salem; thereafter he had little to do with Thomas Lincoln. When his law practice took him to Coles County, as it occasionally did in the 1840s, Lincoln as a rule stayed at the home of his cousin Dennis Hanks or at the Union Hotel rather than at his father's house.[162] Although he helped his father financially now and then, he did so seldom and grudgingly.[163] Also surprising is Lincoln's reluctance to name a son after his father until after Thomas's death. Mary and Abraham Lincoln named their first boy after her father, Robert Todd; their second after Lincoln's friend, Edward D. Baker; and their third after Mrs. Lincoln's brother-in-law, William Wallace. Only the fourth and final son, born two years after Thomas Lincoln died, was given his name. Even so, Lincoln never called this boy Thomas or Tom, but rather Tad.

When notified in 1851 that his father lay dying, Lincoln refused to make the relatively short journey to honor his father's request that they say farewell. Coldly he instructed his stepbrother to tell Thomas "that if we could meet now, it is doubtful whether it would not be more painful than pleasant."[164] When the old man died shortly afterward, Lincoln did not attend the funeral, nor did he have the gravesite marked with a stone.[165]

Whenever he referred to his father, Lincoln emphasized Thomas's lack of education and seemed to be embarrassed to have had such a parent. In 1848 he said, "Owing to my father being left an orphan at the age of six years, in poverty, and in a new country, he became a wholly uneducated man."[166] Twelve years later he stated in an autobiography that Thomas, "by the early death of his father, and the very narrow circumstances of his mother, even in childhood was a wandering laboring boy, and grew up litterally without education. He never did more in the way of writing than to bunglingly sign his own name."[167] The word *bunglingly* suggests contempt for his father's ignorance.

Lincoln ascribed his own positive traits—his "power of analysis, his logic, his mental activity, [and] his ambition"—to his maternal grandfather rather than to his father.[168] This grandfather was, as Lincoln told Herndon, "a nobleman so called of Virginia," who had sired Lincoln's mother out of wedlock. "My mother inherited his qualities and I hers. All that I am or hope ever to be I get from my mother, God bless her."[169] This remark is as much a rejection of his father as it is a paean to his mother. Lincoln also belittled his father when, in referring to Thomas's brother Mordecai, he told a fellow lawyer, "I have often said that Uncle Mord had run off with all the talents of the family."[170]

Lincoln's deep aversion to the way his father treated him made him sensitive to the injustice suffered by slaves, with whom he probably felt a bond of identity. Just as slaveowners robbed their bondsmen of the fruits of their labor, thwarted their attempts to gain an education, and abused them physically, so too did Thomas Lincoln rob Abraham of the fruits of his labor, hinder his efforts to educate himself, and occasionally beat him for no good reason.

Lincoln's hatred of formal slavery was matched by his hostility toward quasi-slavery and led him once to challenge his wife on a matter of household management, something he rarely did (chapter 9). In 1844, Dennis Hanks's daughter Harriet came to stay with the Lincolns in Springfield while she attended school there.[171] According to Herndon, "Mrs. Lincoln tried to make a servant—a slave of her," and "this created a fight[,] a fuss[,] between Lincoln and his wife."[172] Lincoln could easily identify with the girl, striving to get an education while being treated like a slave at home. That was the story of his youth. Painful memories of his childhood struggles to make something of himself despite his father's opposition must have provoked him to cross his notoriously difficult wife, just as they prompted him to speak out strongly against slavery and ultimately to take decisive action to abolish it.

NOTES

1. Frederick Douglass, "Freedmen's Monument to Abraham Lincoln: An Adddress Delivered in Washington, D.C., on April 14, 1876," in *The Freder-*

ick Douglass Papers: Series 1, *Speeches, Debates, and Interviews,* ed. John W. Blassingame and John R. McKivigan, 5 vols. (New Haven: Yale University Press, 1991), 4:436.

2. Rice, *RL,* 136; emphasis added.

3. Marquis de Chambrun, "Personal Recollections of Mr. Lincoln," *Scribner's Magazine,* Jan. 1893, 33. Cf. Thomas Wentworth Higginson to an unidentified correspondent, N.p., N.d., Boston *Evening Transcript,* 31 May 1865, 4.

4. This tendency is most obvious in the writings of the school known as "revisionists." Cf. James G. Randall, who termed Lincoln "a moderate liberal," in *Lincoln the President: From Springfield to Gettysburg,* 2 vols. (New York: Dodd, Mead, 1945), 1:91, 2:151–204. A modern variant on this theme is Robert W. Johannsen's sugggestion that Lincoln's antislavery views were rooted in political expediency rather than in moral principle. See *Lincoln, the South, and Slavery: The Political Dimension* (Baton Rouge: Louisiana State University Press, 1991).

5. See Arthur Zilversmit, "Lincoln and the Problem of Race: A Decade of Interpretations," *Papers of the Abraham Lincoln Association* 2 (1980): 22–45; Kenneth M. Stampp, *The Imperiled Union: Essays on the Background of the Civil War* (New York: Oxford University Press, 1980), 123–35; Richard H. Sewell, *Ballots for Freedom: Antislavery Politics in the United States, 1837–1860* (New York: Oxford University Press, 1976), 321–42; Don E. Fehrenbacher, *Lincoln in Text and Context: Collected Essays* (Stanford: Stanford University Press, 1987), 95–112; John Hope Franklin, "Lincoln's Evolving View of Freedom," in *Lincoln and Lincolniana at Brown,* ed. John Hope Franklin (Providence: Friends of the Library of Brown University, 1985), 37–48; Eugene H. Berwanger, "Lincoln's Constitutional Dilemma: Emancipation and Black Suffrage," *Papers of the Abraham Lincoln Association* 5 (1983): 25–38. One of the few historians of the revisionist era to appreciate Lincoln's essential radicalism on the slavery issue was Dwight Lowell Dumond; see *Antislavery Origins of the Civil War in the United States* (Ann Arbor: University of Michigan Press, 1939), 106–14.

6. LaWanda Cox, "From Emancipation to Segregation: National Policy and Southern Blacks," in *Interpreting Southern History: Historiographical Essays in Honor of Sanford W. Higginbotham,* ed. John B. Boles and Evelyn Thomas Nolen (Baton Rouge: Louisiana State University Press, 1987), 223. This statement summarizes the conclusions of Cox's *Lincoln and Black Freedom: A Study in Presidential Leadership* (Columbia: University of South Carolina Press, 1981). There she maintains that Lincoln "was well in advance of northern opinion generally and at times in advance of a consensus within his own party [on slavery]. Viewed against his deference to the processes of persuasion and the limitations set by the Constitution, the persistence and boldness of his actions are striking" (7).

7. David Lightner, "Abraham Lincoln and the Ideal of Equality," *Journal of the Illinois State Historical Society* 75 (Winter 1982): 308.

8. Charles B. Strozier, *Lincoln's Quest for Union: Public and Private Meanings* (New York: Basic Books, 1982), 175.

9. J. Edward Murr to Albert J. Beveridge, New Albany, Ind., 21 Nov. 1924, Beveridge MSS, DLC.

10. Joseph Gillespie to William Herndon, Edwardsville, 31 Jan. 1866, H-W MSS, DLC. An Illinois lawyer recalled that Lincoln's 1840 speeches showed that economic issues "were not such questions as enlisted and engaged his best thoughts—they did not take hold of his great nature and had no tendency to develope it." "Lincoln on the Stump and at the Bar," John M. Scott typescript, 1, Ida M. Tarbell MSS, Allegheny College.

11. Gillespie to Herndon, Edwardsville, 31 Jan. 1866, H-W MSS, DLC; Walter Lowenfels, ed., *Walt Whitman's Civil War* (New York: Alfred A. Knopf, 1960), 264. Strozier's *Lincoln's Quest for Union* rests on Whitman's erroneous assumption. For a thoughtful critique of Strozier's work, see Herman Belz, "Commentary on 'Lincoln's Quest for Union,'" in *The Historian's Lincoln: Pseudohistory, Psychohistory, and History,* ed. Gabor S. Boritt and Norman O. Forness (Urbana: University of Illinois Press, 1988), 247–52.

12. Waldo W. Braden, *Abraham Lincoln: Public Speaker* (Baton Rouge: Louisiana State University Press, 1988), 35–36; John S. Wright, *Lincoln and the Politics of Slavery* (Reno: University of Nevada Press, 1970), 132.

13. Lincoln to A. G. Hodges, Washington, 4 April 1864, in Basler, *CWL,* 7:281.

14. "Autobiography Written for John L. Scripps" [ca. June 1860], in Basler, *CWL,* 4:61.

15. Ida M. Tarbell, *The Life of Abraham Lincoln,* 4 vols. (New York: Lincoln History Society, 1903), 1:35. J. Edward Murr speculated that Lincoln's aversion to slavery came "to some extent by way of his forbears—The Elder ABRAHAM—his grand Father [—] as well as his more immediate forbe[a]rs who perhaps in no single instance ever owned slaves? It must have been easily possible at least for his rather well-to-do Grandfather to have owned slaves. I wonder if we do not find here at least some *family* or tribal opposition to this regime?" Murr to Albert J. Beveridge, New Albany, Ind., 21 Nov. 1924, Beveridge MSS, DLC.

16. Louis A. Warren, *The Slavery Atmosphere of Lincoln's Youth* (Fort Wayne: Lincolniana Publishers, 1933), passim. The tax lists for 1810, according to one source, indicate that there were 739 blacks in Hardin County that year and 1,736 whites the following year. Bayless E. Hardin, secretary-treasurer of the Kentucky Historical Society, to Harry E. Pratt, Frankfort, Ky., 3 Aug. 1953, Harry E. Pratt Papers, University of Illinois Library, Urbana-Champaign. William Herndon thought that Lincoln as a boy in Kentucky saw slavery "and shrank from it" because of "his tender & sensitive nature." "Lincoln in Ky.," undated manuscript, H-W MSS, DLC.

17. Francis Marion Van Natter, *Lincoln's Boyhood: A Chronicle of His Indiana Years* (Washington: Public Affairs Press, 1963), 131–48.

18. Hanks's undated statement to Herndon, H-W MSS, DLC.

19. Angle, *HL,* 64.

20. "Autobiography Written for John L. Scripps," in Basler, *CWL,* 4:64. Hanks, however, insisted that he accompanied Lincoln to New Orleans. Hanks to Herndon, Chicago, 13 June 1865, copy, H-W MSS, DLC. It is pos-

sible that Lincoln's memory was faulty when he said that Hanks left the boat at St. Louis.

21. Angle, *HL,* 64.

22. Van Natter, *Lincoln's Boyhood,* 145, citing an affidavit by E. Grant Gentry in Van Natter's possession.

23. Robert H. Browne, *Abraham Lincoln and the Men of His Time,* 2 vols. (Cincinnati: Jennings and Pye; New York: Eaton and Mains, 1901), 1:506. In July 1860 Lincoln's friend James H. Matheny of Springfield described to an audience how the sight of a slave trader separating a mother and child enraged him and led him to become a Republican. The next day, when Lincoln was told about this speech, he "seemed greatly interested . . . and showed not a little emotion when told of the deep sympathy the people manifested in the poor slave mother and her child." John W. Harman, Brooklyn, N.Y., March 1891, "Why He Became a Republican," *Magazine of Western History Illustrated* 14 (May 1891): 55–56.

24. G. A. Owen, "The Lincoln Country," clipping identified as "C. E. World, 14 Feb. 1924," LMFW.

25. "Annual Message to Congress," 6 Dec. 1864, in Basler, *CWL,* 8:140.

26. John B. Alley, in Rice, *RL,* 582–83.

27. James A. Rawley, "Captain Nathaniel Gordon, the Only American Executed for Violating the Slave Trade Laws," *Civil War History* 39 (Sept. 1993): 216–24; Warren S. Howard, *American Slavers and the Federal Law, 1837–1862* (Berkeley: University of California Press, 1963), 199–202; Edward Dicey, *Spectator of America,* ed. Herbert Mitgang (Chicago: Quadrangle Books, 1971; originally published in 1863 as *Six Months in the Federal States*), 56–60 [quote on 58].

28. Ethan Allen, "Lincoln and the Slave Trader Gordon," in *Abraham Lincoln, Tributes of His Associates: Reminiscences of Soldiers, Statesmen and Citizens,* ed. William Ward Hayes (New York: Thomas Y. Crowell, 1895), 168.

29. Edward Dicey, "Lincolniana," *Macmillan's Magazine* 12 (June 1865): 191.

30. Denver *Tribune,* 18 May 1879.

31. Howard K. Beale, ed., *The Diary of Edward Bates, 1859–1866,* vol. 4 of the Annual Report of the American Historical Association for 1930 (Washington, D.C.: Government Printing Office, 1933), 229, 233–34 [entries for 5, 18, 19 Feb. 1862, quote from 233].

32. On January 31, 1862, Ralph Waldo Emerson recorded in his journal that Lincoln "argued to Sumner the whole case of Gordon, the slave-trader, point by point, and added that he was not quite satisfied yet, & meant to refresh his memory by looking again at the evidence." In *The Journals and Miscellaneous Notebooks of Ralph Waldo Emerson,* ed. Linda Allardt et al., 15 vols. (Cambridge: Harvard University Press, 1982), 15:187.

33. Charles Sumner to Orestes A. Brownson, Washington, 2 Feb. 1862, in *The Selected Letters of Charles Sumner,* ed. Beverly Wilson Palmer, 2 vols. (Boston: Northeastern University Press, 1990), 2:100.

34. "Stay of Execution for Nathaniel Gordon," 4 Feb. 1862, in Basler, *CWL,* 5:128. Three years later Lincoln pardoned the slave trader Zeno Kelley,

mistakenly thinking he had merely fitted out a slave ship rather than engaged in the trade. Lincoln to Thomas D. Eliot, 28 Feb., 2 March 1865, in Basler, *CWL,* 8:323–24; David Rankin Barbee, "A Lost Incident in Lincoln's Life," *Tyler's Quarterly Historical and Genealogical Magazine* 27 (July 1945): 27–35.

35. Joseph P. Thompson [pastor, Broadway Tabernacle Church, New York], *Abraham Lincoln; His Life and Its Lessons: A Sermon Preached on Sabbath, April 30, 1865* (Loyal Publication Society, no. 85), 2; J. P. Thompson, "A Talk with President Lincoln," *The Congregationalist,* 30 March 1866.

36. Speech of 16 Oct. 1854, in Basler, *CWL,* 2:264.

37. Statement by Lincoln's stepsister, Matilda Johnston Hall Moore, [Goosenest Prairie, Ill.], 8 Sept. 1865, H-W MSS, DLC; Ruth Painter Randall, *Lincoln's Animal Friends* (Boston: Little, Brown, 1958), 46–49; Nat Grigsby in Francis F. Browne, *The Every-Day Life of Abraham Lincoln* (Boston: Mason and Fowler, 1886), 65.

38. Cf. William H. Townsend, *Lincoln and His Wife's Home Town* (Indianapolis: Bobbs-Merrill, 1929), v, 223, and *Lincoln and the Bluegrass: Slavery and the Civil War in Kentucky* (Lexington: University Press of Kentucky, 1955), vii–viii, 126–32, 190–91.

39. Lincoln to Speed, Springfield, 24 Aug. 1855, in Basler, *CWL,* 2:320.

40. "Protest in Illinois Legislature on Slavery," 3 March 1837, in Basler, *CWL,* 1:75. That colleague, Dan Stone, was not a candidate for reelection, see *Lincoln Day by Day: A Chronology, 1809–1865,* ed. Earl Schenck Miers et al., 3 vols. (Washington, D.C.: Lincoln Sesquicentennial Commission, 1960), 1:74 [entry for July 1]. Johannsen contends that this protest "carefully skirted the moral question." But surely Lincoln's denunciation of the "injustice" of slavery expresses moral repugnance; had he and Stone wished to skirt the moral question, they could simply have omitted the words "both injustice and." Johannsen further argues that it "seems clear that Lincoln was protesting against the new militancy of the abolitionists more than he was objecting to slavery." That does not seem clear at all, especially because a short time earlier he was one of the six members of the Illinois legislature who voted against a resolution denouncing the abolitionists. In addition, Johannsen points out that the Lincoln-Stone protest called for the abolition of slavery in the District of Columbia only with the consent of its inhabitants, a provision that was not "acceptable to the abolition movement." But when Lincoln in 1849 introduced a bill in Congress with such a stipulation, it won the approval of the abolitionist Congressman Joshua Giddings. See Johannsen, *Lincoln, the South, and Slavery,* 14. Johannsen's statement is valid only if one adopts a narrow definition of abolitionist, a definition that Johannsen himself rejects later in his book (66–68).

41. Paul M. Angle, *"Here I Have Lived:" A History of Lincoln's Springfield, 1821–1865* (Springfield: Abraham Lincoln Association, 1935), 79–80; *Sangamo Journal* [Springfield], 28 Oct. 1837, 2.

42. Aryeh Maidenbaum, "Sounds of Silence: An Aspect of Lincoln's Whig Years," *Illinois Historical Journal* 82 (Autumn 1989): 167–76, argues that political expediency kept Lincoln, unlike some other Whigs, silent on such controversial issues as the murder of Elijah Lovejoy and attacks against the

Mormons. But he took a bold stand on the slavery issue in 1837, suggesting that it stirred him deeply.

43. "Autobiography Written for John L. Scripps," in Basler, *CWL*, 4:65.

44. "Speech at Chicago, Illinois," 10 July 1858, in Basler, *CWL*, 2:492.

45. "Address Before the Young Men's Lyceum of Springfield, Illinois," 27 Jan. 1838, in Basler, *CWL*, 1:108–15. In this much-analyzed speech, Lincoln indirectly condemned slavery while sympathizing with persecuted abolitionists and blacks. Although Lincoln did not mention Lovejoy by name, he alluded to mobs who "throw printing presses into rivers, [and] shoot editors," clear references to Lovejoy's killing on November 7, 1837, in Alton. See Basler, *CWL*, 1:111n; and Neil Schmitz, "Murdered McIntosh, Murdered Lovejoy: Abraham Lincoln and the Problem of Jacksonian Address," *Arizona Quarterly* 44 (Autumn 1988): 15–39.

46. Lincoln said this in 1854; Browne, *Lincoln and the Men of His Time*, 1:285. A friend allegedly heard him in 1830 spontaneously reply to a proslavery speaker, asserting that "he was opposed to slavery and ever expected to be so long as the whip cracked over the yellow girl's back." Statement of A. H. Goodpasture (who heard the story from George Close), Petersburg, Ill., 31 March 1869, Herndon-Weik Papers, Record Group 4, reel 9, frames 1518–19. While working in the neighborhood, Close and Lincoln took time off to listen to an orator named John F. Posey.

Goodpasture's account seems improbable, for other descriptions of the speech contain no reference to slavery, suggesting that Lincoln dealt exclusively with internal improvements. Cf. W. D. Howells, *Life of Abraham Lincoln* (Bloomington: Indiana University Press, 1960), 28; Otto R. Kyle, *Abraham Lincoln in Decatur* (New York: Vantage Press, 1957), 23–26; and "Lincoln's First Political or 'Lincoln Square' Speech," in Macon County Historical Society, *The Lincolns, the Hanks, and Macon County* (Decatur: Privately published, 1971); and John Hanks's undated statement to Herndon, H-W MSS, DLC.

47. Reminiscences of John E. Roll, in John Linden Roll, "Sangamo Town," *Journal of the Illinois State Historical Society* 19 (1926–27): 159. According to the author, this conversation took place "during the abolitionist excitement" in Alton, where antislavery editor Elijah P. Lovejoy was murdered in 1837.

48. Reminiscences of Mrs. Benjamin Fox, "Greeting Lincoln Gave to Bride," unidentified clipping, LMFW.

49. Alexander Milton Ross, *Recollections and Experiences of an Abolitionist; From 1855 to 1865* (Toronto: Rowsell and Hutchinson, 1875), 137.

50. Paul Simon, *Lincoln's Preparation for Greatness: The Illinois Legislative Years* (Norman: University of Oklahoma Press, 1965), 132; Miers, ed., *Lincoln Day by Day*, 1:65 [entry for Jan. 20]. In 1839 he voted to table a resolution declaring that Congress should not abolish slavery in the District of Columbia or the territories, or prohibit the interstate slave trade. Ibid., 1:104 [entry for February 2].

51. "Remarks and Resolution, Introduced in the United States House of Representatives Concerning Abolition of Slavery in the District of Columbia," 10 Jan. 1849, in Basler, *CWL*, 2:20–22.

52. "Another Abolition Appointment by Taylor," *Sentinel* [no city indicated], reprinted in the *Yazoo Democrat* [Yazoo City, Miss.], 10 Oct. 1849; Giddings wrote in his diary, "This evening (January 11), our whole mess remained in the dining-room after tea, and conversed upon the subject of Mr. Lincoln's bill to abolish slavery. It was approved by all; I believe it as good a bill as we could get at this time, and am willing to pay for slaves in order to save them from the Southern market." Cleveland *Post*, 31 March 1878, quoted in John G. Nicolay and John Hay, *Abraham Lincoln: A History,* 10 vols. (New York: Century, 1890) 1:286–87. This casts doubt on Robert W. Johannsen's contention that Lincoln's proviso calling for a referendum on slavery by the white male inhabitants of the District "was angrily rejected by the abolitionists." See *Lincoln, the South, and Slavery,* 17. Again, Johannsen's statement assumes a narrow definition of the term *abolitionist,* a definition that he himself rejects (66–68). During that session, the other members of the mess were all from Pennsylvania: John Blanchard, John Dickey, A. R. McIlvaine, James Pollock, and John Strohm. See Elihu B. Washburne, "Abraham Lincoln in Illinois," *North American Review,* Oct. 1885, 314. Cf. James Pollock, *Douglas the Loyal,* ed. Esther Cowles Cushman [Providence: 1930], 5.

53. This statement dates from April 1862. Francis Fisher Browne, *The Every-Day Life of Abraham Lincoln,* 2d ed. (New York: G. P. Putnam's Sons, 1913), 421. In May 1860, Lincoln told an interviewer: "My mind has been in process of education since that time, do not know that I would now approve of the Bill, but in the main *think* that I would." James Quay Howard's notes, [May 1860], Lincoln MSS, DLC.

54. "Address Before the Young Men's Lyceum of Springfield, Illinois," 27 Jan. 1838, in Basler, *CWL,* 1:114.

55. Isaac N. Arnold, *The Life of Abraham Lincoln* (Chicago: Jansen, McClurg, 1885), 65. Cf. 253, 342. For a discussion of scholarly interpretations of this speech, see chapter 8 and the Appendix, "Stephen A. Douglas as a Target of Lincoln's Lyceum Address," in this book.

56. "Temperance Address," Springfield, 22 Feb. 1842, in Basler, *CWL,* 1:279.

57. Arnold, *Life of Lincoln,* 66. Cf. Isaac N. Arnold, *The History of Abraham Lincoln, and the Overthrow of Slavery* (Chicago: Clarke, 1866), 685–86.

58. Speed to Herndon, Louisville, 14 Feb. 1866, H-W MSS, DLC.

59. Simon, *Lincoln's Preparation for Greatness,* 135.

60. John J. Duff, *A. Lincoln: Prairie Lawyer* (New York: Holt, Rinehart and Winston, 1960), 86–87; Isaac N. Arnold, *Reminiscences of the Illinois Bar Forty Years Ago: Lincoln and Douglas as Orators and Lawyers* (Chicago: Fergus, 1881), 23–24.

61. Orlando B. Ficklin in the Tuscola [Ill.] *Review,* 7 Sept. 1922, originally published in the Charleston [Ill.] *Courier,* 15 Jan. 1885, copy, Beveridge MSS, DLC; D. W. McIntyre, "History of the Matson Slave Trial in 1847," copy, Beveridge MSS, DLC; Duff, *Prairie Lawyer,* 130–47; Jesse W. Weik, "Lincoln and the Matson Negroes: A Vista into the Fugitive-Slave Days," *Arena* 17 (April 1897): 752–58; Charles H. Coleman, *Abraham Lincoln and Coles*

County, *Illinois* (New Brunswick: Scarecrow Press, 1955), 104–11; Albert A. Woldman, *Lawyer Lincoln* (Boston: Houghton, Mifflin, 1937), 56–66.

62. Woldman, *Lawyer Lincoln,* 56; Lincoln to Speed, Springfield, 24 Aug. 1855, in Basler, *CWL,* 2:320. In 1839 he expressed ambivalence about legislative resolutions condemning those who aided fugitive slaves. "Remarks in Illinois Legislature in Relation to Fugitive Slaves," 5 Jan. 1839, in Basler, *CWL,* 1:126.

63. Letter by Zebina Eastman, unidentified clipping, Eastman Scrapbook, ICHi. Cf. Eastman, "History of the Anti-Slavery Agitation, and the Growth of the Liberty and Republican Parties in the State of Illinois," in Rufus Blanchard, *Discovery and Conquests of the North-west, with the History of Chicago* (Wheaton: R. Blanchard, 1879), 671. Eastman states that he and Cassius Clay visited Erastus Wright, a wealthy client of Lincoln's who served as an agent of the Underground Railroad. On Wright, see *Bulletin of the Abraham Lincoln Association,* no. 50 (Dec. 1937). No mention of this event appears in Cassius M. Clay, *The Life of Cassius Marcellus Clay: Memoirs, Writings, and Speeches* (Cincinnati: J. Fletcher Brennan, 1886).

64. Statement made to Jesse W. Weik, in Weik, *RL,* 198. Cf. Lincoln to Salmon P. Chase, Springfield, 20 June 1859, in Basler, *CWL,* 3:386.

65. Browne, *Lincoln and the Men of His Time,* 1:517; Alonzo J. Grover's reminiscences in Browne, *Every-Day Life of Lincoln,* 2d ed., 248–49; cf. Lincoln to Grover, Springfield, 15 Jan. 1860, in Basler, *CWL,* 3:514.

66. Annie E. Jonas to Herndon, Quincy, Ill., 28 Oct. 1866, Jesse W. Weik Papers, IHi; Angle, *HL,* 308–9; J. G. Holland, *The Life of Abraham Lincoln* (Springfield, Mass.: Gurdon Bill, 1866), 127–28; Charles M. Segal, "Lincoln, Benjamin Jonas and the Black Code," and "Postscript to 'Black Code' Article," *Journal of the Illinois State Historical Society* 46 (1953): 277–82, 428–30.

67. Lincoln to George Robertson, Washington, 20, 26 Nov. 1862, in Basler, *CWL,* 5:502–3, 512–14. Cf. Townsend, *Lincoln and the Bluegrass,* 299–304; Roy P. Basler, "'Beef! Beef! Beef! Lincoln and Judge Robertson," *Abraham Lincoln Quarterly* 6 (Sept. 1951): 400–407; and J. Winston Coleman, Jr., "Lincoln and 'Old Buster,'" *Lincoln Herald* 46 (Feb. 1944): 3–9.

68. Summary of an interview with Miller in Moses Coit Tyler, "One of Mr. Lincoln's Old Friends," in the New York *Independent,* 12, 19 March 1868, reprinted in the *Journal of the Illinois State Historical Society* 29 (Jan. 1936): 251.

69. Lincoln to Williamson Durley, Springfield, 3 Oct. 1845, in Basler, *CWL,* 1:348.

70. Franklin T. King to William Herndon, Kempton, Ill., 12 Sept. 1890; cf. Herndon to Weik, Springfield, 24 Sept. 1890, both in H-W MSS, DLC.

71. Edward Magdol, *Owen Lovejoy: Abolitionist in Congress* (New Brunswick: Rutgers University Press, 1967), 132–33.

72. Charles H. Ray to Elihu B. Washburne, North Norwich, N.Y., 16, 24 Dec. 1854; Chicago, 29 Dec. 1854; Springfield, 2, 12 Jan. 1855, copies, Ray MSS, CSmH.

73. Eastman to Herndon, Bristol [England], 2 Jan. 1866, photocopy,

Beveridge MSS, DLC. Cf. Herndon to Eastman, Springfield, 6 Feb. 1866, copy, Beveridge MSS, DLC.

74. Reminiscences of Thomas J. Henderson, a member of the legislature, typescript, 10, Ida M. Tarbell MSS, Allegheny College.

75. Charles Eugene Hamlin, *The Life and Times of Hannibal Hamlin* (Cambridge: Riverside Press, 1899), 194, 367.

76. Hamlin told this to C. J. Prescott. Reminiscences of C. J. Prescott, "Hamlin" folder, Ida M. Tarbell MSS, Allegheny College.

77. Interview with Ficklin, *The Classmate: A Paper for Young People* [Cincinnati], 6 Feb. 1926.

78. Beveridge, *Lincoln*, 1:476.

79. Statement of John T. Stuart, N.d. [21 July 1865?], H-W MSS, DLC. Cf. a similar statement by Stuart, H-W MSS, DLC. In Browne, *Every-Day Life of Lincoln*, this conversation is dated 1850 (242).

80. Joseph Gillespie to Herndon, Edwardsville, [Ill.], 31 Jan. 1866, H-W MSS, DLC. On the Kentucky constitutional convention and Lincoln's response to it, see Townsend, *Lincoln and the Bluegrass*, 157–75, and Lincoln to George Robertson, Springfield, 15 Aug. 1855, in Basler, *CWL*, 2:317–18.

81. Paraphrase of Logan's remarks at the meeting of the U.S. district and circuit courts, 17 June 1865, Springfield [Ill.] *Daily State Journal*, 19 June 1865.

82. Ralph Emerson, *Mr. & Mrs. Ralph Emerson's Personal Recollections of Abraham Lincoln* (Rockford: [Wilson Bros.], 1909), 9.

83. Browne, *Lincoln and the Men of His Time*, 2:517.

84. The Rev. Dr. James Miller to the editor, *McClure's Magazine*, Atlanta, 20 Nov. 1895, Ida M. Tarbell MSS, Allegheny College; interview with Dr. Miller, St. Louis *Globe Democrat*, 26 Aug. 1894. Lincoln had been scheduled to speak at the 1854 meeting, but illness in the family prevented him from doing so. Gary R. Planck, "Abraham Lincoln and Black Colonization: Theory and Practice," *Lincoln Herald* 72 (Summer 1970): 61–62. Cf. Jason H. Silverman, "'In Isles Beyond the Main'; Abraham Lincoln's Philosophy on Black Colonization," *Lincoln Herald* 80 (Fall 1978): 115–22; Michael Vorenberg, "Abraham Lincoln and the Politics of Black Colonization," *Journal of the Abraham Lincoln Association* 14 (Summer 1993): 23–45.

85. Benjamin Quarles, *Lincoln and the Negro* (New York: Oxford University Press, 1962), 108–23; G. S. Boritt, "The Voyage to the Colony of Linconia: The Sixteenth President, Black Colonization, and the Defense Mechanism of Avoidance," *The Historian* 37 (Aug. 1975): 619–32. Many vigorous opponents of slavery, including Benjamin F. Wade, Salmon P. Chase, Horace Greeley, Thaddeus Stevens, Samuel C. Pomeroy, Harriet Beecher Stowe, Henry Ward Beecher, James G. Birney, Martin R. Delany, Lyman Trumbull, Henry Wilson, and Gerrit Smith, favored colonization. See Hans L. Trefousse, *The Radical Republicans: Lincoln's Vanguard for Racial Justice* (New York: Alfred A. Knopf, 1969), 29–30, and Sewell, *Ballots for Freedom*, 323–26.

86. Reminiscences of A. W. French, N.d., Ida M. Tarbell MSS, Allegheny College.

87. Basler, *CWL*, 2:454, 444, 3:226; F. B. Carpenter, *Six Months at the*

White House with Abraham Lincoln: The Story of a Picture (New York: Hurd and Houghton, 1867), 75.

88. Angle, *HL*, 296; "Speech at Peoria, Illinois," 16 Oct. 1854, in Basler, *CWL*, 2:255.

89. Cf. Henry C. Whitney, *Lincoln the Citizen*, vol. 1 of *A Life of Lincoln*, ed. Marion Mills Miller, 2 vols. (New York: Baker and Taylor, 1908), 1:174.

90. "Speech at Chicago," 10 July 1858, in Basler, *CWL*, 2:500, 493.

91. "Seventh and Last Debate with Stephen A. Douglas at Alton," 15 Oct. 1858, in Basler, *CWL*, 3:315.

92. "Speech at Springfield, Illinois," 17 July 1858, in Basler, *CWL*, 2:520. Cf. "Speech at Springfield, Illinois," 26 June 1857, 2:405.

93. Lawrence Weldon, "Reminiscences of Lincoln as a Lawyer," in Hayes, ed., *Lincoln, Tributes from His Associates*, 249.

94. "Fragment on Slavery," [1 July 1854?], in Basler, *CWL*, 2:222.

95. "Speech at Springfield, Illinois," 26 June 1857, in Basler, *CWL*, 2:409.

96. Lincoln to George B. Ide et al., Washington, 30 May 1864, in Basler, *CWL*, 7:368.

97. "Story Written for Noah Brooks," [6 Dec. 1864], in Basler, *CWL*, 8:155.

98. Lincoln to C. H. Fisher, Springfield, 27 Aug. 1860, draft of a letter probably not sent, in Basler, *CWL*, 4:101.

99. "Fragment on Pro-slavery Theology," [1 Oct. 1858?], in Basler, *CWL*, 3:204–5.

100. Henry B. Rankin, *Personal Recollections of Abraham Lincoln* (New York: G. P. Putnam's Sons, 1916), 215. Cf. Noah Brooks, *Abraham Lincoln and the Downfall of American Slavery* (New York: G. P. Putnam's Sons, 1894), 157–58. Brooks had observed Lincoln campaigning in 1856. Brooks and Rankin date this speech 1856; Basler puts it two years later.

101. Holland, *Lincoln*, 149–50.

102. Basler, *CWL*, 8:333.

103. "Address at Sanitary Fair, Baltimore, Maryland" 18 April 1864, in Basler, *CWL*, 7:301–2.

104. "Second Inagural Address," in Basler, *CWL*, 8:333.

105. "Speech at Cincinnati, Ohio—Omitted Portion," 17 Sept. 1859, in *The Collected Works of Abraham Lincoln: Supplement, 1832–1865*, ed. Roy P. Basler (Westport: Greenwood Press, 1974), 44.

106. Clay in Rice, *RL*, 297.

107. Ward Hill Lamon, *Recollections of Abraham Lincoln, 1847–1865*, 2d ed., ed. Dorothy Lamon Teillard (Washington: Published by the editor, 1911), 14–15.

108. Lincoln to William B. Preston, Springfield, 16 May 1849, in Basler, *CWL*, 2:49. Cf. Thomas F. Schwartz, "'An Egregious Political Blunder': Justin Butterfield, Lincoln and Illinois Whiggery," *Papers of the Abraham Lincoln Association* 8 (1986): 9–19.

109. Gabor S. Boritt, *Lincoln and the Economics of the American Dream* (Memphis: Memphis State University Press, 1978), passim.

110. "Fragments of a Tariff Discussion," [1 Dec. 1847?], in Basler, *CWL,* 1:412.

111. "Fragment on Free Labor," [17 Sept. 1859?], in Basler, *CWL,* 3:462.

112. "Speech at Hartford, Connecticut," 5 March 1860, in *CWL,* 4:7.

113. Boritt, *Lincoln and the Economics of the American Dream,* 182. See 182–85 and 217–21 for a thoughtful discussion of Lincoln's attitude toward labor unions. See also James A. Stevenson, "Abraham Lincoln on Labor and Capital," *Civil War History* 38 (Sept. 1992): 197–209.

114. See William H. Pease and Jane H. Pease, eds., *The Antislavery Argument* (Indianapolis: Bobbs-Merrill, 1965).

115. Boritt, *Lincoln and the Economics of the American Dream,* 173.

116. Lincoln to Mrs. O. H. Browning, Springfield, 1 April 1838, in Basler, *CWL,* 1:118.

117. Reminiscences of John Roll, Chicago *Sunday Times-Herald,* 25 Aug. 1895, reprinted in Garda Ann Turner, "John E. Roll Recalls Lincoln," *Lincoln Herald* 62 (Fall 1960): 105. Cf. Roll, "Sangamo Town," 153–60, and an interview with Roll, Springfield correspondence, 7 May 1892, St. Louis *Globe-Democrat,* N.d., clipping, LMFW.

118. Douglass in Rice, *RL,* 193. Cf. Cox, *Lincoln and Black Freedom,* 35–36. Unlike Douglass, Lincoln never grew snobbish about those at the bottom of the social heap. On Douglass's "contempt" for "working men," see William S. McFeely, *Frederick Douglass* (New York: W. W. Norton, 1991), 80, 140, 242, 256, 330, 315–16. Nor did Lincoln share Douglass's arrogant touchiness (121–22, 145).

119. "Annual Message to Congress," 3 Dec. 1861, in Basler, *CWL,* 5:52–53.

120. "Eulogy on Henry Clay," 6 July 1852, in Basler, *CWL,* 2:126.

121. "Speech to One Hundred Fortieth Indiana Regiment," 17 March 1865, in Basler, *CWL,* 8:361.

122. William Herndon to C. O. Poole, Springfield, 5 Jan. 1886; cf. Herndon to Weik, Springfield, 18 Feb. 1887, both in H-W MSS, DLC.

123. Herndon to Jesse W. Weik, 8 Oct. 1881, in Hertz, *HL,* 84.

124. Herndon to Isaac N. Arnold, Springfield, 24 Oct. [18]83, Lincoln Collection, ICHi; Whitney, *Lincoln,* 1:231. Cf. Henry C. Whitney, "Abraham Lincoln: A Study from Life," *Arena* 19 (April 1898): 468.

125. Egbert L. Viele, "A Trip with Lincoln, Chase, and Stanton," *Scribner's Monthly* 16 (Oct. 1878): 816.

126. Emanuel Hertz, ed., *Lincoln Talks: A Biography in Anecdote* (New York: Viking, 1939), 26.

127. Beveridge, *Lincoln,* 1:65; Browne, *Every-Day Life of Lincoln,* 89.

128. Ezra M. Prince, recalling a conversation with Lincoln in October 1856, "A Day and a Night with Abraham Lincoln," typescript, H-W MSS, DLC; Leonard Swett to J. H. Drummond, Bloomington, Ill., 27 May 1860, copy, H-W MSS, DLC; Swett in Rice, *RL,* 458–59; Nathaniel Grigsby, in Angle, *HL,* 32; John F. Cady, "Why Abraham Lincoln Never Joined the Baptist Church," *Missions,* N.d., reprinted in the Grandview [Ind.] *Monitor,* undated clipping, LMFW.

129. William D. Kelley in Rice, *RL,* 279–80. Cf. Leonard Swett, ibid., 457–58; Anna L. Boyden, *Echoes from Hospital and White House: A Record of Mrs. Rebecca R. Pomroy's Experience in War-Times* (Boston: D. Lothrop, 1884), 83–84; Viele, "A Trip with Lincoln," 816–17; Alban Jasper Conant, "A Portrait Painter's Reminiscences of Lincoln," *McClure's Magazine* 32 (March 1909): 514; and George W. Shaw, *Personal Reminiscences of Abraham Lincoln* (Moline: Carlson, 1924), 15–16.

130. At the time, Lincoln was living with James Taylor at Troy, Indiana, sixteen miles from home. According to one source, the "money he often sent to his father." From this statement it could be inferred that he sometimes kept his earnings for himself. Sallie Logan Bergonroth, "Some Early Troy History," typescript, Papers of the Southwest Indiana Historical Society, Evansville Central Library; cf. Warren, *Lincoln's Youth,* 144–46.

131. Statement of A. H. Chapman, Charleston, Ill., 8 Sept. 1865, H-W MSS, DLC; Dennis Hanks to Herndon, Chicago, 13 June 1865, in Hertz, *HL,* 281; extracts from an address by William Fortune, who in 1884 interviewed Mrs. Josiah Crawford, in Bess V. Ehrmann, *The Missing Chapter in the Life of Abraham Lincoln: A Number of Articles, Episodes, Photographs, Pen and Ink Sketches Concerning the Life of Abraham Lincoln in Spencer County, Indiana, between 1816–1830 and 1844* (Chicago: Walter M. Hill, 1938), 73–74. Lincoln often worked for Crawford. Will Adams, "Biographical Sketch of Josiah and Elizabeth (Anderson) Crawford," typescript, Papers of the Southwest Indiana Historical Society, Evansville Central Library.

132. Current, *Lincoln Nobody Knows,* 30. The most thoughtful analysis of the relations between Abraham and Thomas Lincoln is John Y. Simon, *House Divided: Lincoln and His Father* (Fort Wayne: Louis A. Warren Lincoln Library and Musem, 1987). Cf. Charles B. Strozier and Stanley H. Cath, "Lincoln and the Fathers: Reflections on Idealization," in *Fathers and Their Families,* ed. Stanley H. Cath, Alan Gurwitt, and Linda Gunsberg (Hillsdale: Analytic Press, 1989), 285–99. For a defense of Thomas Lincoln, see Louis Austin Warren, *Lincoln's Parentage and Childhood: A History of the Kentucky Lincolns Supported by Documentary Evidence* (New York: Century, 1926), 72, 133–35, 157ff, and C. T. Baker, "The Disposal of the Lincoln Farm," Grandview [Ind.] *Monitor,* 11 Jan. 1934. In their biography of Lincoln, Nicolay and Hay presented Thomas Lincoln in a favorable light in order to please Robert Todd Lincoln. Hay told Richard Watson Gilder, "The only weak link in the chain is Tom Lincoln—but I can't dwell on that. His grandson is extremely sensitive about it. It is not an ignoble feeling in R. T. L. He says 'he feels sorry for the old man, and does not think it right to jump on him, in the the broad light of his son's fame.'" Hay to Gilder, N.p., 29 Dec. [1886], Lincoln File, CSmH.

133. Hanks to Herndon, N.p., 26 Jan. 1866, H-W MSS, DLC.

134. Augustus H. Chapman, in Ward H. Lamon, *The Life of Abraham Lincoln from His Birth to His Inauguration as President* (Boston: James R. Osgood, 1872), 40n.

135. Hanks to Herndon, Chicago, 13 June 1865, in Hertz, *HL,* 278, 280. Cf. Hanks to Herndon, N.p., 26 Jan. 1866, H-W MSS, DLC; Robert

McIntyre, "Lincoln's Friend," Charleston [Ill.] *Courier,* N.d., Paris [Ill.] *Gazette,* N.d., Chicago *Tribune,* 30 May 1885; Hanks in Browne, *Every-Day Life of Lincoln,* 53.

136. Arthur E. Morgan, "New Light on Lincoln's Boyhood," *Atlantic Monthly* 125 (Feb. 1920): 214. This article is based primarily on interviews with Sophie Hanks's son, Dr. James LeGrande, who noted that "people in them days believed that whipping was good for children."

137. Notes of Arthur E. Morgan's interview with Nancy Davison, Feb. 1909, Morgan MSS, DLC. Davison was the half-sister of Sophie Hanks's son, James LeGrande.

138. "Notes on Arthur E. Morgan's first trip—Jasper [Ark., Feb. 1909]," Morgan MSS, DLC.

139. Undated questionnaire filled out by James LeGrande, Morgan MSS, DLC.

140. Reminiscences of Lincoln's stepnephew, John J. Hall, in Eleanor Gridley, *The Story of Abraham Lincoln; or, The Journey from the Log Cabin to the White House* (Chicago: Monarch, 1902), 96.

141. Van Natter, *Lincoln's Boyhood,* 152. Cf. Andrew W. Sweeney's reminiscences, Indianapolis *Star,* 16 April 1933.

142. Augustus H. Chapman to Herndon, Charleston, 28 Sept. 1865, H-W MSS, DLC. Cf. Carl Sandburg, *Lincoln Collector: The Story of Oliver R. Barrett's Great Private Collection* (New York: Harcourt, Brace, 1950), 88; Simon, *House Divided,* 18.

143. Hanks to Herndon, N.p., 13 June 1865, in Beveridge, *Lincoln,* 1:67; Mrs. Lincoln's statement, [Goosenest Prairie, Ill.], 8 Sept. 1865, in Hertz, *HL,* 350.

144. John Romaine's statement, in Beveridge, *Lincoln,* 1:68, as well as similar statements by Dennis Hanks, Matilda Johnston Moore, A. H. Chapman, and Mrs. Josiah Crawford. Ibid.

145. Helm to Herndon, Hannibal, Mo., 20 June 1865, H-W MSS, DLC.

146. Mrs. Mary J. Scott, a great-niece of Lincoln's friend Joseph C. Richardson, in C. T. Baker, "How Abe Saved the Farm," Grandview [Ind.] *Monitor,* 26 Aug. 1920, reprinted on 14 Oct. 1926. Cf. C. T. Baker, "The Lincoln Family in Spencer County," typescript dated 1928, Papers of the Southwest Indiana Historical Society, Evansville Central Library.

147. Angle, *HL,* 33.

148. Whitney, *Lincoln,* 1:75.

149. Browne, *Every-Day Life of Lincoln,* 88.

150. Angle, *HL,* 33.

151. Randall, *Lincoln's Animal Friends,* passim; Albert R. Beatty, "Dogs Ever Were a Joy to Lincoln," *American Kennel Gazette,* 1 Feb. 1933, 9–13, 77, 80; A. Y. Ellis in Browne, *Every-Day Life of Lincoln,* 124. Benjamin P. Thomas thought it "strange that Abraham never developed any liking" for hunting or fishing, but it can be understood as a sign of his aversion toward his father and all that he represented. Thomas, *Lincoln,* 10.

152. J. R. Herndon to William Herndon, Quincy, 21 June 1865, H-W MSS, DLC.

153. Charles T. White, "Lincoln's First Pet: An Experience of Lincoln When He Was Six Years Old, Told by Lincoln Himself to Captain Gilbert J. Greene," *McClure's Magazine*, Feb. 1923. Cf. a similar article in *Success*, Sept. 1901. Greene was a compositor on the *Illinois State Journal* in Springfield in the late 1850s, when Lincoln told him this story. During the Civil War, Lincoln named him marshal of Winchester, Illinois, and subsequently a dispatch carrier for General Grant. See also Randall, *Lincoln's Animal Friends*, 12–20, 96–97. There is some evidence that Thomas killed a dog of Abraham's, which may also have prompted the boy to take revenge on his father's cur. Lincoln's stepnephew, John J. Hall, in Gridley, *Story of Lincoln*, 68. Cf. A. H. Chapman to Herndon, Charleston, Ill., 8 Oct. 1865, H-W MSS, DLC.

154. Statement by Wood, 14 Sept. 1865, H-W MSS, DLC, quoted in Van Natter, *Lincoln's Boyhood*, 58.

155. Statement by Grigsby, Gentryville, Ind., 12 Sept. 1865, in Hertz, *HL*, 355.

156. Mass, "Jonesboro," transcript, Papers of the Southwest Indiana Historical Society, Evansville Central Library.

157. William Fortune's interview with Mrs. Crawford, 1881, summarized in Fortune's 1925 address to the Southwest Indiana Historical Society, typescript, Ida M. Tarbell MSS, Allegheny College.

158. Balch's reminiscences in Browne, *Every-Day Life of Lincoln*, 2d ed., 22.

159. Balch's undated interview with Jesse W. Weik, Weik MSS, IHi.

160. Greene to Herndon, Tallulah, Ill., 29 May 1865, H-W MSS, DLC.

161. Morgan, "New Light on Lincoln's Boyhood," 213.

162. Amanda Hanks Poorman, daughter of Dennis Hanks, in St. Louis *Post-Dispatch*, 26 May 1901, in Coleman, *Lincoln and Coles County*, 67, 80–81; Duff, *Prairie Lawyer*, 135. Strozier concludes that "Lincoln generally avoided" his father. *Lincoln's Quest for Union*, 50–51. Thomas's home in Goosenest Prairie was about eight miles outside of Charleston.

163. Coleman, *Lincoln and Coles County*, 65–66; Strozier, *Lincoln's Quest for Union*, 52–53.

164. Lincoln to John D. Johnston, Springfield, 12 Jan. 1851, in Basler, *CWL*, 2:97.

165. According to Mary Todd Lincoln, "My husband a few weeks before his death mentioned to me, that he intended *that* summer, paying proper respect to *his* father's grave, by a head & foot stone, with his name, age && and I propose very soon carrying out his intentions." Mary Lincoln to Sarah Bush Johnston, Chicago, 19 Dec. [18]67, in Turner and Turner, *MTL*, 465. Not until 1880 did Thomas Lincoln's grave have a monument, erected at the behest of Robert Todd Lincoln.

166. Lincoln to Solomon Lincoln, Washington, 6 March 1848, in Basler, *CWL*, 1:456.

167. "Autobiography Written for John L. Scripps," in Basler, *CWL*, 4:61. Cf. "Autobiography" enclosed in Lincoln to Jesse W. Fell, Springfield, 20 Dec. 1859, in Basler, *CWL*, 3:511. It might be argued that Lincoln was, in this document, simply being politically astute and portraying himself as a

humble man of the people. But he would have had no such incentive to make the same point about his father in the private letter of 1848 cited in the previous note.

168. Lincoln's speculation represents a twist on what Freud called the "Family Romance," the "fantasy of being the child of other parents, usually those of higher standing, such as royalty or celebrities." In childhood, most people have such fantasies and outgrow them. Some adults, notably the "exceptional individual" or men "whose father was far removed from a palpable relationship with them," will "persist in an intense family romance." Linda Joan Kaplan, "The Concept of the Family Romance," *Psychoanalytic Review* 61 (Summer 1974): 169–202 (quotations from 183). Cf. Sigmund Freud, "Family Romances," *Collected Papers,* vol. 5 of *Miscellaneous Papers, 1888–1938* (London: Hogarth Press, 1950), 74–78; and Otto Rank, *The Myth of the Birth of the Hero* (1909, repr. New York: Vintage, 1959).

169. Herndon to Ward Hill Lamon, Springfield, 6 March 1870, Lamon MSS, CSmH. Cf. Paul H. Verduin, "New Evidence Suggests Lincoln's Mother Born in Richmond County, Virginia, Giving Credibility to Planter-Grandfather Legend," *Northern Neck of Virginia Historical Magazine* 38, no. 1 (1988): 4354–89, and "Plantation Overseers, Patriots, Pioneers: New Light on Lincoln and His Hanks Forbears," unpublished paper delivered at the Lincoln home, Springfield, Ill., 12 Feb. 1992. Lincoln allegedly told his stepnephew John J. Hall that "I can't bear to think that I don't know who my grandfather was." Gridley, *Story of Lincoln,* 172–73. Cf. chapter 8 of this volume.

170. Usher F. Linder, *Reminiscences of the Early Bench and Bar of Illinois* (Chicago: Chicago Legal News, 1879), 38. Cf. Augustus H. Chapman to Herndon, Charleston, Ill., 8 Oct. 1865, H–W MSS, DLC.

171. Harriet Hanks Chapman's interview with Jesse W. Weik, Weik MSS, IHi.

172. Herndon to Weik, Springfield, 1 Dec. 1885, H-W MSS, DLC.

3

"Unrestrained by Parental Tyranny": Lincoln and His Sons

William Herndon complained that Lincoln was "so blinded to his children's faults" that if "they s[hi]t in Lincoln's hat and rubbed it on his boots, he would have laughed and thought it smart. . . . He worshipped his children and *what* they worshipped; . . . *disliked* what the[y] hated, which was everything that did not bend to their . . . whims." Herndon was exasperated by the way the boys came to the office with their father and "would take down the books—empty ash buckets—coal ashes—inkstands—papers—gold pens—letters etc., etc. in a pile and then dance on the pile."[1]

Many contemporaries agreed with Herndon that Lincoln "was too kind, too tender & too gentle to his children: he had no domestic government—administration or order." Herndon added that Lincoln "was liberal—generous—affectionate to his children, loving them with his whole heart, . . . as loving & tender as a nursing mother."[2] According to Mary Lincoln, her husband summed up his views on child-rearing thus: "It is my pleasure that my children are free and happy, and unrestrained by parental tyranny. Love is the chain whereby to bind a child to its parents."[3] When the youngest of their four sons, Tad, showed signs of learning difficulties, Lincoln expressed no alarm.[4] A Springfield neighbor recalled dining with several others at the Lincoln home one day: "Mr. Lincoln was carving the chicken, and the first thing he did was to cut off the drumstick and gave it to Tad . . . , and then he said, smiling at the rest of the company, 'Children have first place here, you know.'"[5]

He was indulgent to children in general, not just his own. In New Salem, Lincoln became "a kind of elder brother to the children," who "clustered about" him "whenever he appeared, fairly worshipping him."[6] When he moved to Springfield, Lincoln quickly acquired the reputation of a man "exceedingly fond of children."[7] One of the youngsters he befriended, Joseph P. Kent, remembered that "Mr. Lincoln was well liked by the boys of our neighborhood. . . . He seemed to understand as well as enjoy boy nature perfectly."[8] J. L. Kain noted the same quality: "He had a rare insight into boy nature, and . . . took uncommon pains to remember the faces and names of children." In addition, Lincoln "made use of every chance for pleasant, mostly whimsical conversation with the young, and he entered, as few men have the knack of doing, into their small concerns, easily winning their confidence." Lincoln treated Kain like a son, reading to him, coaching him in declamation, and suggesting ways to study.[9] William B. Thompson, who grew up in a house near Eighth and Jackson, encountered Lincoln many times on the street. As he later recalled, "He walked along with his hands behind him, gazing upward and noticing nobody. But it was usual for all of the boys in the neighborhood to speak to him as we met him. He had endeared himself to all of us by reason of the interest he took in us. When one of us spoke to him as he was walking along in his absorbed manner he would stop and acknowledge the greeting pleasantly. If the boy was small Mr. Lincoln would often take him up in his arms and talk to him. If the boy was larger Mr. Lincoln would shake hands and talk with him."[10]

Fred Dubois, son of Jesse K. Dubois, remembered that he and his playmates would rig a string to knock the hat from Lincoln's head as he walked the street. When he looked around for the boys who had tricked him, they would "set up a great shout, and instead of running away from him, . . . would run up to him and cling to his hands and legs and make a mighty noise." Lincoln, smiling at them "in a fatherly sort of way," then bought them cakes and nuts.[11]

As a twelve-year-old, Robert H. Browne met Lincoln in Springfield and took an instant liking to him, as did the other boys in town. Browne later wrote that Lincoln found "pleasure in making us his friends and in telling us delightful little stories . . . [and] tales so well suited to our tastes and boyish ways that we always wanted to hear him tell another little story."[12] A minister who lived across the street from the Lincolns' home in Springfield called Lincoln "a great lover of children" and noted that "he loved his neighbors['] children too. Many a time we have seen troops of children, living on the same street, run out to meet him, when he was coming to his meals, and would gambol by his side, and as many as could get hold on him, would swing from his hands."[13]

Lewis H. Waters told a friend that on the streets of Springfield when Lincoln was talking to people, "little children (not his own) would run up to him and catch hold of his long legs and hang on to his pants and perhaps tug at them." Even though he paid them little heed, the youngsters would "stand close beside him or sit down at his feet." When he finished his conversation, "he would perhaps pick up one and place it on his shoulder, the others trotting along after him."[14]

Lincoln was particularly devoted to the infant son of his next-door neighbor Stephen Smith, a relative of Mary Lincoln's. Mrs. Smith recalled that Lincoln loved to play with her baby, and a friend of the Smiths' wrote that "this tiny boy was Lincoln's constant companion and solace." Lincoln "was utterly devoted to him." Often in late 1859 and early 1860, he "would hoist the youngster over his shoulder and carry him there so gently that he slept almost continually, with his head against Lincoln's neck." This baby "satisfied something which he was always shy about explaining." When Lincoln learned that Mrs. Smith planned to travel east in early 1860, he asked her to delay her departure so that she and her infant might join him on his trip to New York to speak at Cooper Union. En route, Lincoln delighted in walking about with the baby on the platform whenever the train stopped at a station.[15]

Girls also received kind, paternal treatment. The daughter of near neighbors, Emanuel and Justina De Crastos, visited the house at Eighth and Jackson streets, where she was, to her delight, given "hossy" rides on Lincoln's leg.[16] He was also solicitous of the health of children. While visiting the family of John Albert Jones, he noticed that Jones's two-year-old son was limping. Lincoln inspected the boy's foot and discovered a stone bruise, which he promptly treated with his penknife.[17]

During the Civil War, Lincoln continued to show marked solicitude for children. A member of his cavalry guard recalled that the president "never passed by a child without a smile, and some way, in spite of sad eyes and heavy brows, the children always took to him." One morning, this observer watched the president talk to some schoolchildren playing on the White House steps. "He stopped and had a word of pleasantry with them, took one or two of their books and glanced through them, and while he did so, the children crowded around him as if he had been their father."[18] Lincoln often played with the grandchildren of Francis P. Blair, Sr. One of them recalled how the president would "join ardently" in the children's games: "He entered into the spirit of the play as completely as any of us, and we invariably hailed his coming with delight."[19]

Inside the White House, Lincoln was exposed to few youngsters other than his own sons, but those he did see aroused his paternal interest. The children of Mr. and Mrs. Horatio Nelson Taft regularly played at the Executive Mansion with Willie and Tad. Lincoln treated the Tafts' daughter Julia with avuncular warmth. As she recalled, "He was to me a good, uncle-like person, sometimes quizzical, but always smiling and kind to 'little Julie.'"[20] The president "seemed to take a great liking" to her brother Bud and used him occasionally as a messenger boy for personal and state business.[21] But the Taft children were hardly unique; a White House secretary observed that "all children are favorites of his."[22]

In Illinois, Lincoln was an absent parent as well as an indulgent one.[23] In order to avoid conflict with his difficult wife, he spent an inordinate amount of time away from home. Such a tactic may have made his unfortunate marriage tolerable, but it deprived the children of much contact with their father.

Ironically, the child who saw Lincoln most often, the first-born Robert, was the one who felt least close to him. Anecdotes about Lincoln's permissive and loving treatment of his children mostly concern the third and fourth sons, Willie and Tad; the second, Eddie, died at the age of three and little is known about his relationship with his father. In one of the saddest documents of the Lincoln story, Robert told a biographer of his father shortly after the assassination that

> my Father's life was of a kind which gave me but little opportunity to learn the details of his early career. During my childhood and early youth he was almost constantly away from home, attending courts or making political speeches. In 1859 when I was sixteen and when he was beginning to devote himself more to practice in his own neighborhood, and when I would have had both the inclination and the means of gratifying my desire to become better acquainted with the history of his struggles, I went to New Hampshire to school and afterward to Harvard College, and he became President. Henceforth any great intimacy between us became impossible. I scarcely even had ten minutes quiet talk with him during his Presidency, on account of his constant devotion to business.[24]

Robert also complained that his father seldom wrote to him at college.[25]

Another grievance Robert had against his parents was their reluctance to let him join the army during the Civil War. Lincoln favored the idea, but his wife objected. A White House guest once heard them discuss the matter:

"Of course, Mr. Lincoln, I know that Robert's plea to go into the Army is manly and noble and I want him to go, but oh! I am so frightened he may never come back to us!"

"Mr. Lincoln said sadly, 'Many a poor mother, Mary, has had to make this sacrifice and has given up every son she had—and lost them all.'

"'Don't I know that only too well?' cried Mary; 'before this war is ended I may be like that poor mother, like my poor mother in Kentucky, with not a prop left in her old age.'"[26]

Finally, as the war drew to a close, Mary Lincoln relented, and Robert, with the help of his father, joined the staff of General Grant.[27]

Robert remembered with some bitterness one of the few occasions when the president carved time from a busy schedule to see him: "I returned [after graduating] from college in 1864 and one day I saw my father for a few minutes. He said: 'Son, what are you going to do now?' I said: 'As long as you object to my joining the army, I am going back to Harvard to study law.'" Lincoln coolly replied, "If you do, you should learn more than I ever did, but you will never have so good a time." Robert added resentfully, "That is the only advice I had from my father as to my career."[28] The distance between them obviously pained Robert, who confided twelve days after his father's death that "in all my plans for the future, the chief object I had in view was the approbation of my Father, and now that he is gone . . . , I feel utterly without spirit or courage."[29]

Robert failed to win his father's approval even as a young boy. When Lincoln informed Joshua Speed of the birth of Eddie, his second child, he included some unflattering remarks about his first-born: "Bob is 'short and low,' and, I expect, always will be. . . . He is quite smart enough. I some times fear he is one of the little rare-ripe sort, that are smarter at about five than ever after. He has a great deal of that sort of mischief, that is the offspring of much animal spirits." As Lincoln was writing, Bob ran off and had to be fetched. In a statement that indicates that the boy was more strictly treated than his brothers would be, Lincoln told Speed that "by the time I reached the house, his mother had found him, and had him whip[p]ed—and by now, very likely he is run away again."[30]

Robert seems to have baited his mother. According to a childhood friend and schoolmate, "Bob Lincoln was an awful tease. He never made trouble at school but at home he delighted in tormenting his mother. I've seen her fly into a rage at his pranks."[31]

Lincoln used botanical imagery to describe all the boys. Mary Lincoln was "very proud of her sons"[32] and, according to Herndon, liked to show them off to important visitors. She would "get them to monkey around—talk—dance—speak—quote poetry, etc." and grow "enthusiastic & eloquent over the children much to the annoyance of the visitor and to the mortification of Lincoln. . . . After Mrs. Lincoln had exhausted the English language and broken herself down in her rhapsodies on her children, Lincoln would smooth things over by saying— 'These children may be something sometimes, if they are not merely rareripes—rotten ripes—hothouse plants. I have always noticed that a rare-ripe child quickly matures, but rots as quickly.'"[33] Robert's waywardness may have stemmed in part from the emotional dislocation he suffered when Eddie's birth provided unwanted competition for the love and attention of his parents.[34]

Robert may also have been upset by his mother's general ineptitude in her maternal role. As her cousin Elizabeth Todd Grimsley recalled, Mary Lincoln, "always over-anxious and worried about the boys and withal not a skillful nurse, was totally unfitted for caring for them" when they took sick.[35] She tended to fly into hysterics when anything untoward happened to her children. A Springfield neighbor, Elizabeth A. Capps, recalled that Mrs. Lincoln "was a very nervous, hysterical woman who was incessantly alarming the neighborhood with her outcries. It was a common thing to see her standing out on their terrace in front of the house, waving her arms and screaming, 'Bobbie's lost! Bobbie's lost!' when perhaps he was just over in our house. This was almost an every day occurrence." Mrs. Capps remembered how one day "when Robert could just barely walk Mrs. Lincoln came out in front as usual, screaming, 'Bobbie will die! Bobbie will die!' My father ran over to see what had happened. Bobbie was found sitting out near the back door by a lime box and had a little lime in his mouth. Father took him, washed his mouth out and that's all there was to it." On another occasion, Mary Lincoln overreacted to the illness of one of her babies and dispatched their black maid to summon the doctor. Evidently thinking that "there wasn't much wrong with the child," the servant stopped to chat with a friend. Observing this, Mrs. Lincoln burst out, "Charity! Charity! run for your life and I'll give you fifty dollars when you get back." According to Mrs. Capps, Mary Lincoln's "many outcries frightened us children and we were afraid of her so we stayed at home and let Bob do the visiting."[36]

Perhaps Robert also resented his mother's resort to corporal punishment and his father's failure to prevent her from having him whipped. A next-door neighbor in Springfield said that, in disciplining her children, Mary Lincoln "was prone to excitability and rather impulsive, saying many things that were sharp and caustic, and which she afterward usually regretted."[37] Margaret Ryan, a servant in the Lincolns' home in Springfield, recalled that "Mrs. L would whip Bob a good deal."[38] Frank Edwards, a playmate of Tad's, recalled that Mary Lincoln "held a private-strapping party" with her son after he had fallen into a mud puddle.[39]

Lincoln sometimes intervened to protect his younger sons from his wife's wrath. A playmate of Tad's remembered one summer afternoon when Mary Lincoln accused the boy of stealing a dime, flew into a rage when he denied it, and beat his legs with a switch. The punishment ceased as Lincoln entered the room, where the boy cringed in fright as his mother stood over him. When asked what had happened, she replied incoherently. Lincoln solved the crisis by having the boy empty his pockets, then turned to his wife and said tenderly, "Mary! Mary!"[40]

Later evidence suggests that Mary Lincoln continued to be a harsh disciplinarian during her husband's presidency. A young girl named Mary Pinkerton, who frequently visited the White House to play with the Lincoln children, later recalled how Tad would sometimes tease her and pull her hair. When she complained to the president, he "would dry my tears and tell Tad he should be ashamed for teasing such a little girl—and then maybe for a whole hour Tad and I would be good friends again." But, she noted, "It was different when Mrs. Lincoln was the judge. She had a terrible temper—and when I would go to her with my stories about Tad, she would punish him severely." Although the president "was always so kind and gentle," his wife "was often short-tempered and bitter-tongued."[41]

One reason why Lincoln, if not his wife, tended to indulge Willie and Tad more than he did Robert was the grief he felt at the death in 1850 of his second son, Eddie. A more basic reason for Lincoln's closer relationship with his younger sons is that he felt a stronger bond with Willie and Tad than with Robert, who in some ways was as much a stranger to his father as Thomas Lincoln had been to Abraham. Robert and his father shared little in common; the son did not inherit Lincoln's temperament or values. In vain one seeks to find in Robert the sense of humor, idealism, personal warmth and humanity, egalitarianism, wisdom, relative indifference to money, and generosity that distinguished his father's character.[42] As Herndon put it, Robert was "a

Todd and not a Lincoln."⁴³ Ida Tarbell, who interviewed Robert Todd Lincoln on several occasions, described him as "all Todd."⁴⁴ According to Ruth Painter Randall, "Robert seems to have been born with the Todd tastes, abilities, and inclinations. . . . The Todd kin whom Robert knew had the things he liked, high standards of social correctness, prosperity and the comfortable type of living that goes with it."⁴⁵

Robert, in fact, was something of a prig and a snob. When Tom Thumb visited the White House during the war, Mary Lincoln suggested that her eldest son attend the party honoring their diminutive guest. Haughtily, Robert said, "No, mother, I do not propose to assist in entertaining Tom Thumb. My notions of duty, perhaps, are somewhat different from yours."⁴⁶ When Tad played a harmless prank, Robert indignantly complained, with more than a tinge of sibling jealousy and resentment. "I have just had a great row with the President of the United States!" he told the painter Francis B. Carpenter:

> "Tad" went over to the War Department to-day, and Stanton, for the fun of the thing, . . . commissioned him "lieutenant." On the strength of this, what does "Tad" do but go off and order a quantity of muskets sent to the house! Tonight he had the audacity to discharge the guard, and he then mustered all the gardeners and servants, gave them the guns, drilled them, and put them on duty in their place. I found it out an hour ago, and thinking it a great shame, as the men had been hard at work all day, I went to father with it; but instead of punishing "Tad," as I think he ought, he evidently looks upon it as a good joke, and won't do anything about it!⁴⁷

Lincoln occasionally erupted in anger at Robert. In Springfield one day, the boy and his friends put on a dog show in the family barn. To get the canines to rise up, the children slung ropes over a rafter then tied them around the dogs' necks, practically hanging them. Lincoln heard the howls and, after rescuing the poor animals, expressed his indignation to Robert.⁴⁸ On the way from Springfield to Washington in 1861, the president-elect entrusted to Robert's safekeeping a satchel containing the only copies of his inaugural address. When the seventeen-year-old boy misplaced it, his father, with the help of Ward Hill Lamon, frantically searched for the highly sensitive document. Lamon recalled that "I had never seen Mr. Lincoln so much annoyed, so much perplexed, and for the time so angry." Lincoln, he added, "seldom manifested a spirit of anger toward his children—this was the nearest approach to it I had ever witnessed."⁴⁹ Part of that anger may be at-

tributed to the tone of "bored and injured virtue" that Robert affected when replying to his father's anxious query about the satchel.[50] When
it was finally retrieved, Lincoln returned it to his son's custody, saying,
"There, Bob, see if you can't take better care of it next time."[51] Lincoln later showed irritation when Robert, at the request of friends at
Harvard, indiscreetly appealed on behalf of a candidate for the postmastership of Cambridge. The president, who loathed patronage squabbles, reportedly said, "If you do not attend to your studies and let
matters such as you write about alone I will take you away from college."[52] Earlier, when Robert was enrolled at Illinois State University,
his father was also alarmed by reports that the boy frequently skipped
classes. Lincoln visited the campus and spoke at length with a professor "to see what could be done to get Bob to attend classes regularly
again."[53]

Little evidence survives of Lincoln's anger at his other boys. Once
he did scold Tad for stealing a piece of stove pipe. As he marched his
son back to the store, Tad was heard "complaining bitterly at the heat
of the way on his bare feet." His father replied "that heat was as nothing
to what he would suffer if he went on taking what did not belong to
him."[54]

Charles B. Strozier speculates that the bad blood between Lincoln
and his eldest son may be ascribed in part to Oedipal tensions. Arguing that "in many respects Robert was much like his father," Strozier
suggests that Lincoln harbored "an inability to tolerate the competi-
tive thrust of Robert's intelligence" and that "Robert obstructed in some
way Lincoln's largely unconscious grandiosity, holding back by his
presence the father's tendency to fill the male space within the family."[55] Some Oedipal rivalry may have existed between father and son,
but there seems to have been no such problems with the other boys.
Strozier suggests that Lincoln was a very different man in 1850, the
year of Willie's birth, from the man he had been in 1843, when Robert was born. "With seven years and one child [Eddie] spanning the
distance between the birth of these two sons, and Lincoln's greater
emotional distance from the family itself, he could relate warmly and
easily to Willie."[56]

Although that may be true, a more fundamental explanation is that
Robert from birth had a temperament and character profoundly different from those of his father; such differences transcended in importance the events of Robert's childhood. Willie, on the other hand, was
born a near-clone of his father. Ruth Randall sensibly concluded that

Lincoln and his first-born son "seem to have been too different in make-up for either to feel essential kinship with the other. There are cases of incompatibility where the chemistries of two personalities simply will not mix."[57] Contemplating Robert and Willie, Lincoln, who knew his Shakespeare well, might have recalled Kent's observation on the dissimilarity between King Lear's daughter Cordelia and her sisters, Goneril and Regan: "It is the stars, / The stars above us govern our conditions; / Else one self mate and make could not beget / Such different issues."

Willie, described by a playmate as "the most lovable boy I ever knew, bright, sensible, sweet-tempered and gentle mannered," was so close to his father that Lincoln could almost read the boy's mind.[58] One day at the White House breakfast table, the volatile Tad burst into tears because soldiers to whom he had given religious tracts had laughed at him. When presidential hugs and kisses failed to console the lad, Willie set his mind to discover some balm for the wounded feelings of his younger brother. One of the diners recalled that Willie "lapsed into a profound, absorbed silence, which Mr. Lincoln would not allow to be disturbed. This lasted ten or fifteen minutes, then he clasped both hands together, shut his teeth firmly over the under lip, and looked up smilingly into his father's face, who exclaimed, 'There! you have it now, my boy, have you not?'" Turning to his wife's cousin, Lincoln said, "I know every step of the process by which that boy arrived at his satisfactory solution of the question before him, as it is by just such slow methods I attain results."[59]

The poet and editor Nathaniel P. Willis, a friend of the Lincolns' in Washington, thought Willie "faithfully resembled his father" in all important ways.[60] A Springfield neighbor recalled that "Will was the true picture of Mr. Lincoln, in every way, even to carrying his head slightly inclined toward his left shoulder."[61] Ruth Painter Randall concluded that Willie "was his father over again both in magnetic personality and in his gifts and tastes" and that "with Willie his father could get that special joy that comes to a parent when he recognizes that his child is mentally like him."[62]

Of the many sorrows Lincoln endured in his fifty-six years, Willie's death in February 1862 was among the most crushing. To lose any child is hard enough, but to lose such a remarkably gifted and lovable child as Willie was especially devastating (chapter 5). In the household, Willie had been a great consolation to Lincoln, who derived little emotional satisfaction from his spouse or eldest child. On the last day of his life, Lincoln told Mary, "We must both be more cheerful in the future; between the war and the loss of our darling Willie, we have been very miserable."[63]

Lincoln had always loved Tad, but with the death of Willie that love was intensified as he displaced his powerful feeling for Willie onto his youngest son. He told a friend that he wanted to give Tad "everything he could no longer give Willie."[64] John Hay said that after Willie's death, Lincoln's "bereaved heart seemed . . . to pour out its fullness on his youngest child."[65] The daughter of Hay's fellow-secretary John G. Nicolay wrote that after Willie's death, "The President was even more tender and indulgent toward [Tad] than before, if such a thing were possible. . . . The bond that had always been uncommonly close between them grew stronger after the older boy's death."[66] Julia Taft Bayne described at length how Lincoln indulged Tad's whims.[67]

Tad was not the clone that Willie had been. A Springfield observer noted that Bob and Tad "were *Mama* boys. They neither one had the slightest personal appearance or deliberate easy manner of Mr. Lincoln. They both resembled their mother in looks and actions."[68] Unlike Willie, Tad had his mother's ungovernable temper and, like her, was "implacable in his dislikes."[69] He also suffered from learning disabilities, including a speech impediment that rendered him almost unintelligible, and he was markedly slow in learning to read.[70]

Nevertheless, some detected resemblances between Tad and his father. A presidential bodyguard thought that "the boy was like his father" and added, "I believe he was the best companion Mr. Lincoln ever had—one who always understood him, and whom he always understood."[71] Thus Tad became, in some ways, another Willie for his father.

Now and then Lincoln sought to tame his youngest son, but he acknowledged the futility of the effort. Late one night during the Civil War, when the White House servants complained that they could not get Tad into bed, the president told his guests, "I must go and suppress Tad." Upon returning, he observed, "I don't know but I may succeed in governing the nation, but I do believe I shall fail in ruling my own household."[72]

During the Civil War, Lincoln "took infinite comfort in the child's rude health, fresh fun, and uncontrollable boisterousness," according to John Hay. "He was pleased to see him growing up in ignorance of books, but with singularly accurate ideas of practical matters. . . . 'Let him run,' the easy-going President would say; 'he has time enough left to learn his letters and get pokey. Bob was just such a little rascal, and now he is a very decent boy.'"[73]

Lincoln's unorthodox approach to child-rearing probably had its roots in his own unhappy childhood. From Thomas Lincoln he had learned first-hand the meaning of "parental tyranny" and was determined not to subject his offspring to it. Just as he hoped to see all slaves free, he evidently wanted his sons, and indeed all youngsters, to have the emotional indulgence and kindness so conspicuously absent in his boyhood home.

NOTES

1. Herndon to Jesse Weik, Springfield, 18 Feb. 1887, H-W MSS, DLC.

2. William Henry Herndon, "Analysis of the Character of Abraham Lincoln" [lecture of 26 Dec. 1865], *Abraham Lincoln Quarterly* 1 (Dec. 1941): 417–18; Ruth Painter Randall, *Lincoln's Sons* (Boston: Little, Brown, 1955), 36–48.

3. Mary Lincoln's statement to Herndon in Angle, *HL*, 413.

4. Noah Brooks, *Washington, D.C. in Lincoln's Time*, ed. Herbert Mitgang (Chicago: Quadrangle Books, 1971), 249.

5. Reminiscences of Annie Lanphier Walters, daughter of the state printer, Captain William Walters of Springfield, Chicago *Examiner,* 13 Feb. 1909.

6. Albert J. Beveridge, *Abraham Lincoln, 1809–1858,* 2 vols. (Boston: Houghton, Mifflin, 1928), 1:142.

7. Reminiscences of Mrs. Stephen Smith, Bloomington [Ill.] *Pantagraph,* 19 Feb. 1895, reprinted in "When Lincoln Left Town with Another Woman," ed. Wayne C. Temple, *Lincoln Herald* 68 (Winter 1966): 183.

8. Weik, *RL,* 124.

9. J. L. Kain, "A Boy's Recollections of Lincoln," *Youth's Companion,* 30 May 1907, 259.

10. St. Louis *Globe Democrat,* 7 Feb. 1909.

11. Fred Dubois, "I Knew Lincoln When I Was a Boy," *National Republic,* Oct. 1926, 20. Cf. Lincoln Dubois, "Personal Reminiscences of Lincoln," IHi, copy, JGR MSS, DLC.

12. Robert H. Browne, *Abraham Lincoln and the Men of His Time,* 2 vols. (Cincinnati: Jennings and Pye; New York: Eaton and Mains, 1901), 1:173.

13. Noyes W. Miner, "Personal Reminiscences of Abraham Lincoln," 11, manuscript dated 10 July 1881, SC 1052, folder 2, IHi.

14. French Quinn to Albert J. Beveridge, Decatur, Ind., 15 June 1925, Beveridge MSS, DLC.

15. Temple, ed., "When Lincoln Left Town," 183; Elizabeth Irons Folsom, "New Stories of Abraham Lincoln," *American Magazine* 96 (July 1923): 47, 120, 129–30.

16. New York *Times,* 6 Feb. 1938, sec. 2, 6.

17. Eugenia Jones Hunt, "My Personal Recollections of Abraham and Mary Todd Lincoln," *Abraham Lincoln Quarterly* 3 (March 1945): 241–42.

18. Smith Stimmel, *Personal Reminiscences of Abraham Lincoln* (Minneapolis: William H. M. Adams, 1928), 96. Cf. Robert W. McBride, *Personal Recollections of Abraham Lincoln by a Member of His Bodyguard* (Indianapolis: Bobbs Merrill, 1926), 59.

19. Statement by Frank P. Blair of Chicago to J. McCan Davis, 9 Dec. 1898, Ida M. Tarbell MSS, Allegheny College.

20. Julia Taft Bayne, *Tad Lincoln's Father* (Boston: Little, Brown, 1931), 14.

21. Bayne, *Tad Lincoln's Father,* 88–92.

22. William O. Stoddard, *Inside the White House in War Times* (New York: Charles L. Webster, 1890), 91.

23. Charles B. Strozier, *Lincoln's Quest for Union: Public and Private Meanings* (New York: Basic Books, 1982), 126–27.

24. Robert T. Lincoln to J. G. Holland, Chicago, 6 June 1865, in *Intimate Memories of Lincoln,* ed. Rufus Rockwell Wilson (Elmira: Primavera Press, 1945), 499.

25. Robert Lincoln to Herndon, Chicago, 1 Oct. 1866, H-W MSS, DLC.

26. Diary of Emilie Todd Helm, in Katherine Helm, *The True Story of Mary, Wife of Lincoln* (New York: Harper and Brothers, 1928), 227–28. This statement belies Baker's assertion that Mary Lincoln did not "affirm what other mothers recognized as the choke on their maternal power: their future dependence as widows on their children. Only years later, with three sons and a husband dead, did she explain that in old age she had hoped that her sons would take care of her." Baker, *MTL,* 122.

27. John S. Goff, *Robert Todd Lincoln: A Man in His Own Right* (Norman: University of Oklahoma Press, 1969), 64–68.

28. Randall, *Lincoln's Sons,* 177.

29. Robert Todd Lincoln to Professor Francis J. Child, [27 April 1865], ibid., 219. There is nothing unusual about a child wanting to succeed in order to please its parents, but this letter suggests that Robert had failed to win his father's approval.

30. Lincoln to Speed, Springfield, 22 Oct. 1846, in Basler, *CWL,* 1:391. This letter does not square with Ruth Painter Randall's claim that "the Lincolns did not spank their children." *Lincoln's Animal Friends* (Boston: Little, Brown, 1958), 89. If Mary Lincoln did not do so herself, she obviously instructed someone else to whip Robert.

31. Reminiscences of W. C. Atkinson, Davenport [Iowa] *Democrat and Leader,* 3 July 1927.

32. Olivia Leidig Whiteman, in the Vandalia, Ill., correspondence, 4 Feb. 1929, New York *Herald,* 10 Feb. 1929.

33. Herndon to Jesse Weik, Springfield, 8 Jan. 1886, H-W MSS, DLC. Lincoln's comments about his children may have stemmed from his essential humility rather than a distant attitude toward his offspring. For an example of Mary Lincoln's tendency to brag about her children, see Frances A. Seward,

diary, 11 April 1862, William Henry Seward MSS, University of Rochester Library.

34. Randall, *Lincoln's Sons*, 16. Sibling rivalry is, of course, common, but it can be seriously dislocating, as it may have been for Robert.

35. Elizabeth Todd Grimsley, "Six Months in the White House," *Journal of the Illinois State Historical Society* 19 (Oct. 1926–Jan. 1927): 54.

36. Elizabeth A. Capps, "My Early Recollections of Abraham Lincoln . . . ," Vertical File, "Reminiscences," Lincoln Collection, IHi.

37. Olivia Leidig Whiteman, in the Vandalia, Illinois, correspondence, 4 Feb. 1929, New York *Herald*, 10 Feb. 1929.

38. Margaret Ryan's interview with Jesse W. Weik, 27 Oct. 1886, Weik MSS, IHi. I am indebted to Douglas L. Wilson for calling this to my attention.

39. Frank Edwards, "A Few Facts along the Lincoln Way," typescript enclosed in Mrs. Jacob H. Stoner to William E. Barton, Waynesboro, Penn., 21 July 1930, uncatalogued material, Box 10, folder 180, Barton MSS, University of Chicago.

40. Anna Eastman Jackson, quoted in A. Longfellow Fiske, "A Neighbor of Lincoln," *Commonweal*, 2 March 1932, 494. This story and Mrs. Grimsley's remarks cast doubt on Baker's curious claim and that "some women berated their children in unseen outbursts of temper inside their homes, but Mary Lincoln's fury appeared in unladylike public displays against hired girls and greengrocers." *MTL*, 122. Baker cites Anna Eastman Jackson's recollection in her notes but ignores it in the text of her book. It does not strain credulity to imagine Mary Lincoln lashing out at her children, given her general lack of self-control. It is also clear that she had nothing against corporal punishment, for in a letter quoted above (and also by Baker) it is clear that Mary Lincoln had Robert beaten when he misbehaved. Margaret Ryan's reminiscences further confirm that Mary Lincoln used corporal punishment.

41. Reminiscences of Mrs. Mary Virginia Pinkerton Thompson, in Frazier Hunt, "The Little Girl Who Sat on Lincoln's Lap," *Good Housekeeping*, Feb. 1931, 17.

42. Randall, *Lincoln's Sons*, 10, 27, 126, 143–53.

43. Quoted in Benjamin P. Thomas, *Portrait for Posterity; Lincoln and His Biographers* (New Brunswick: Rutgers University Press, 1947), 154.

44. Ida M. Tarbell, *All in the Day's Work: An Autobiography* (New York: Macmillan, 1939), 166.

45. Randall, *Lincoln's Sons*, 26. Robert and his mother, according to Randall, shared common "tastes and traits" but "never understood each other." Ibid., 124, 251. Cf. Strozier, *Lincoln's Quest for Union*, 136–37.

46. Elizabeth Keckley, *Behind the Scenes: Thirty Years a Slave and Four Years in the White House* (New York: G. W. Carleton, 1868), 123.

47. Francis B. Carpenter, *Six Months at the White House with Abraham Lincoln: The Story of a Picture* (New York: Hurd and Houghton, 1867), 300.

48. Obituary of Chauncey H. Graves, *Holt County Independent* [Mound City, Mo.], 13 Dec. 1928, 1; Walter Graves to Ida Tarbell, Salina, Kansas, 18 Aug. 1929, Ida M. Tarbell MSS, Allegheny College; Chauncey H. Graves's reminiscences, "An Abraham Lincoln Anecdote," *Catskill* [N.Y.] *Recorder*, 23

Aug. 1929; C. H. Graves to Amelia De Motte, [Mound City, Mo.], 3 Oct. 1926, copy, enclosure in Amelia De Motte to Roy P. Basler, Jacksonville, Ill., N.d., Lincoln Collection, Vertical File, "Reminiscences," folder 5, IHi; Randall, *Lincoln's Animal Friends*, 89. Graves recalled that Lincoln spanked Robert and the other boys.

49. Ward Hill Lamon, *Recollections of Abraham Lincoln, 1847–1865*, 2d ed., ed. Dorothy Lamon Teillard (Washington: Published by the editor, 1911), 35–36.

50. Helen Nicolay, *Lincoln's Secretary: A Biography of John G. Nicolay* (New York: Longmans, Green, 1949), 64.

51. Recollections of an unidentified friend of Robert Lincoln's, who heard this story from him. Wayne Whipple, "Lincoln's Love for Billy Herndon and How It Was Requited," *Illinois State Journal* [Springfield], 11 Feb. 1912.

52. H. S. Huidekoper, *Personal Notes and Reminiscences of Lincoln* (Philadelphia: Bicking Print, 1896), 6.

53. Mrs. K. T. Anderson, Rock Island, Ill., "Some Reminiscences of Pioneer Rock Island Women," *Transactions of the Illinois State Historical Society* (1912): 75. Anderson's husband was the professor with whom Lincoln spoke.

54. Horace R. Boynton, Jr., to Milton H. Shutes, Santa Barbara, Calif., 20 Feb. 1948, copy, Lincoln Collection, Vertical File, "Reminiscences," IHi. Boynton was the grandson of the victimized merchant who overheard this exchange between father and son.

55. Strozier, *Lincoln's Quest for Union*, 131, 128–29. As evidence of the similarities between father and son, Strozier unpersuasively cites Robert's sense of humor, which in fact was almost nonexistent. Randall suggests that the only interest Robert and his father shared in common was mathematics. She might have added astronomy. See *Lincoln's Sons*, 20–21.

56. Strozier, *Lincoln's Quest for Union*, 138.

57. Randall, *Lincoln's Sons*, 153.

58. Bayne, *Tad Lincoln's Father*, 8.

59. Grimsley, "Six Months in the White House," 53–54.

60. Randall, *Lincoln's Sons*, 117–18.

61. Joseph P. Kent, in the *Illinois State Journal*, 9 Jan. 1909, in *Intimate Memories of Lincoln*, ed. Wilson, 136–37.

62. Randall, *Lincoln's Sons*, 8, 51–53.

63. Carpenter, *Six Months at the White House*, 293.

64. Nicolay, *Lincoln's Secretary*, 133. When he bought gifts for Tad, he said, "I want to give him all the toys . . . that I would have given the boy who went away." Randall, *Lincoln's Sons*, 181.

65. "Life in the White House in the Time of Lincoln," *Century Magazine* 41 (Nov. 1890): 35. Cf. Noah Brooks, *Abraham Lincoln and the Downfall of American Slavery* (New York: G. P. Putnam's Sons, 1894), 420.

66. Nicolay, *Lincoln's Secretary*, 133.

67. Bayne, *Tad Lincoln's Father*, especially 108–10, 128–38. See also Thomas Hicks's recollections, in Rice, *RL*, 597–98.

68. Joseph Kent, in *Intimate Memories of Lincoln*, ed. Wilson, 136.

69. Bayne, *Tad Lincoln's Father,* 8.

70. Randall, *Lincoln's Sons,* 159–60, 197–98.

71. William H. Crook, quoted in Randall, *Lincoln's Sons,* 202.

72. "Death of 'Tad' Lincoln,' unidentified clipping, John Hay scrapbook, Hay MSS, RPB.

73. John Hay, "Tad Lincoln," New York *Tribune,* 19 July 1871, 4.

4

Surrogate Father Abraham

In 1844, the thirty-five-year-old Lincoln chose an inexperienced, erratic, impulsive attorney nearly ten years his junior, William H. Herndon, to be his law partner. The reasons for this curious selection puzzled Lincoln's friends and biographers, as well as Herndon himself. John J. Duff, a close student of Lincoln's career at the bar, argued that although Lincoln's partnerships first with John T. Stuart, lasting from 1837 to 1841, and then with Stephen T. Logan, from 1841 to 1844, made sense because they were "valuable apprenticeships," his "reason for joining forces with Herndon defies analysis."

After examining various explanations—among them that Lincoln wanted a steady partner without distracting political ambitions and that he felt it was time to be the senior rather than the junior partner—Duff concluded that "it is not clear on any rational ground why Lincoln, in the secret soul of him, should have made the choice he did, especially considering how radically their personalities differed."[1] Herndon himself was surprised at his selection, and later, when asked why Lincoln chose him, replied, "I don't know and no one else does."[2]

If no "rational ground" can be found, an irrational one may provide the answer. Carl Jung maintained that everyone is dominated by an archetypal figure, a condition that has nothing to do with the experiences of childhood.[3] Lincoln's archetype seems to have been the Old Man, who combines the qualities of the Wise Elder and the Great Father.[4] People in Illinois regarded him with a kind of filial reverence. In early 1861, when Lincoln visited his stepmother in Charleston, the townspeople received him warmly. One recalled that "[o]ld men and women talked to Mr. Lincoln with the confidence and assurance of loving children in a great family reunion."[5] An Illinois train conductor recalled of Lincoln that "I have eaten with him many times at the railroad eating houses, and you get very neighborly if you eat together in a railroad restaurant. . . . Everybody tried to get as near Lincoln as possible when he was eating, because he was such good company, but we always looked at him with a kind of wonder. We couldn't exactly

make him out. . . . [T]here was something about him that made plain
folks feel toward him a good deal as a child feels toward his father."[6]
That mysterious "something" was Lincoln's Old Man archetype.

As one dominated by the Old Man archetype, Lincoln seemed old
even while he was young. An Indiana friend of Lincoln's recalled that
"Abe was always a man though a boy."[7] Gibson W. Harris, who worked
in the Lincoln-Herndon office in the mid-1840s, recalled that "'Honest
Old Abe' was a colloquialism familiar to all Springfield before he was
thirty-seven" and that Lincoln deemed himself old "when in his late
thirties."[8] E. B. Washburne first heard the sobriquet "Old Abe" applied
to Lincoln when he was but thirty-eight.[9] Lincoln himself at that age
referred to his "old, withered, dry eyes" and at thirty-nine told Herndon, "I suppose I am now one of the old men."[10] Allegedly he once said
that "I . . . have been kept so crowded with the work of living that I felt
myself comparatively an old man before I was forty."[11]

These are puzzling remarks, for he did not look elderly. When he
was fifty, a journalist in Cincinnati remarked that he was "so exceedingly 'well preserved' that he would not be taken for more than thirty
eight," and the following year a New York paper observed that "he
certainly has no appearance of being so old" as his actual age.[12] Yet,
as Lincoln himself told a friend in 1854, people began calling him "old"
before he had turned thirty.[13] The answer to this paradox seems to be
that Lincoln, dominated as he was by the Old Man archetype, radiated the quality of being old despite his physical appearance.

Lincoln needed to have surrogate sons in addition to his own offspring. Gibson W. Harris recalled that Lincoln "took undisguised pleasure in fathering many of us younger persons, including some already
in their thirties."[14] As a young man, R. R. Hitt, the noted shorthand
reporter who became a congressman, worked for Lincoln and wrote
in his journal that "he treated me with the utmost kindness, almost like
a father."[15] Herndon, like many other young men in Lincoln's life, was
well suited for the role. He described Lincoln as "truly paternal in every sense of the word" and as "the best friend I ever had or expect ever
to have except my wife & mother."[16] A mutual friend of the partners
recalled that "it was a quaint, peculiar power that Lincoln exerted" over
Herndon: "silent, steady, masterful. No father or brother I ever knew
exerted a more complete control over his own kin than did this senior
partner over his junior. It was not a changeful influence only occasionally exercised, but one constantly maintained throughout the period
of their close personal relations," which lasted from 1837 to 1861.[17]

As Herndon himself put it, Lincoln "moved me by a shrug of the shoulder—by a nod of the head—by a flash of the eye and by the quiver of the whole man."[18] Herndon's biographer argues that "Lincoln had an unexplainable fascination for the younger man" and that it was not Lincoln's appearance or his mind but rather "the character of the senior partner" that "inspired respect; Lincoln's heart was in the right place. . . . Herndon had no stupid, dog-like devotion and he thought there were greater men than his partner, yet there was no one else he would ever trust so fully. Lincoln was his friend."[19]

Lincoln in fact was more than a friend; he was a surrogate father to Herndon, who had grown estranged from his bibulous, proslavery sire. While in college, Herndon became an antislavery Whig, whereupon his father evidently withdrew all financial support. The son then quit school, left home, and went to live at the Springfield store of Joshua Speed, where Lincoln also roomed. Herndon soon became a temperance zealot, perhaps as a gesture of rebellion against his father, and later spoke of Lincoln as though he were a father, calling him "the great big man of our firm" and himself "the little one" and remarking that the "little one looked *naturally* up to the big one."[20] Lincoln defended Herndon as if he were his own son. Once, when the junior partner lay sick for three months, some of Lincoln's friends urged him to end the partnership. In reply Lincoln "exclaimed vehemently: 'Desert Billy! No, never! If he is sick all the rest of his days, I will stand by him.'"[21]

Herndon acknowledged that he was scarcely unique: "Mr. Lincoln was kind and tender to all members of the bar, especially the younger ones whom he always assisted." He recalled that when "Mr. Lincoln was on one side of a case and . . . a young practitioner was on the other side; and in the trial of the case [the young man] had failed or certainly would fail—Mr. Lincoln kindly—cautiously—not with offensive pomp, took witnesses and examined both sides—trying all the while to conceal from the crowd the cause of his action. All young lawyers cry—'Heaven bless Mr. Lincoln.'"[22] Gibson W. Harris also noted how Lincoln "was ever kind and courteous to . . . young beginners when he was the opposing counsel. He had a happy knack of setting them at their ease and encouraging them. In consequence he was the favorite of all who came in contact with him."[23]

Among them was Joe Blackburn, who received assistance from Lincoln in a case before the U.S. Circuit Court in Chicago. As Blackburn later recalled, he was only nineteen, "inexperienced, and naturally felt diffident and nervous. . . . I said but little, and that in a very bewildered manner, and was about ready to sit down, and let the case go by default, as it were, when a tall, homely, loose-jointed man sitting in the bar, whom I had noticed as giving close attention to the case, arose and addressed the court in behalf of the position I had assumed in my feeble argument, making the points so clear that when he closed the Court at once sustained my demurrer." This act of kindness prompted the opposing counsel, Isaac N. Arnold, to rebuke his friend for meddling. Lincoln replied "that he claimed the privilege of giving a young lawyer a boost when struggling with his first case, especially if he was pitted against an experienced practitioner."[24]

Another beneficiary of such kindness was James H. Hosmer, who when handling his first important case "found himself hopelessly enmeshed in a mass of intricate details." While the poor novice was floundering, Lincoln told him, "Young man, I have handled cases like this in the past. Let us see if I can't help you out." With coaching by the veteran attorney, Hosmer won the case.[25] Early in his legal career, Lewis H. Waters advised a client to hire Lincoln to help him argue a case. Although much the senior of the two attorneys, Lincoln "insisted" that Waters serve as chief counsel and wrote the instructions, which he suggested that Waters copy and present to the bench as his own work.[26]

E. B. Washburne recalled that "Mr. Lincoln was always a great favorite with young men, particularly with the younger members of the bar. It was a popularity not run after, but which followed."[27] Unlike Washburne, Henry C. Whitney felt that Lincoln was more active than passive in establishing ties with younger attorneys. "It seemed," he wrote, "as if he wooed me to close intimacy and familiarity." Whitney added that "Lincoln was so good natured, and so willing to give advice, that young lawyers went to him a great deal."[28] A county court clerk, William H. Somers, recalled that no other attorney "was so ready and willing to aid, and give encouragement, to younger members of the bar. He was always helping them along the rugged road that led to success in the profession of the law. . . . Few men were so loved as Abraham Lincoln by the young men of those times." In 1857, when he was first elected clerk, Lincoln congratulated Somers warmly; Somers later said that gesture "was so in contrast with that of the other members of the bar that it touched me deeply and made me, ever afterwards, his steadfast friend."[29] Jonathan Birch, who as a young man applying for admission to the bar had received kind treatment from Lincoln, wrote that "somehow—probably because of the recollection of his own early struggles—his heart seemed especially filled with sympathy and concern for the young man whose footsteps took him in the direction of the law."[30] Attorney John M. Scott, who made the rounds with Lincoln, said he "was remarkably gentle with young lawyers," even the cocky ones, and termed him "the much beloved senior member of the bar." "No young lawyer," Scott added, "ever practiced in the courts with Mr. Lincoln who did not in all his after life have a regard for him akin to personal affection."[31]

Lincoln often visited the students pursuing legal studies with his close friend and political ally Edward D. Baker. One of them, William Walker, recalled fondly "his great kindness and generous sympathy for the young men, who were struggling night and day, to reach a place at the bar." Lincoln would greet them cheerfully, examine the books they perused, quiz them genially, tell anecdotes, and even play ball with them in a nearby yard.[32] According to Whitney, Lincoln did not confide in these young men, yet he "took a deep interest in them, studying their natures and loving them for their personal loyalty to him, and for their enthusiasm in his cause which they had made their own."[33]

Other young men from Illinois developed quasi-filial ties with Lincoln during his presidency, most notably his secretaries, John G. Nicolay, John Hay, and William O. Stoddard. The relations between the president and Hay "came closely to resemble those of father and son," according to a biographer of Hay.[34] Helen Nicolay wrote that Lincoln regarded Hay "almost as a son."[35] Hay's friend Charles H. Halpine also thought that Lincoln "loved him as a son."[36] Other biographers noted that "for Hay, Lincoln proved to be a father figure who combined the values and personalities of both John's father and uncle."[37] Living in the White House as assistant secretary to the president, Hay enjoyed easy access to Lincoln. In fact, he seems to have been a more congenial soulmate to the president than his eldest child Robert, five years Hay's junior.

The speaker of the House, Galusha Grow, recalled that "Lincoln was very much attached" to Hay and "often spoke to me in high terms of his ability and trustworthiness." Grow could think "of no person in whom the great President reposed more confidence and to whom he confided secrets of State as well as his own personal affairs with such great freedom."[38] Hay's diary supports Grow's claim.

In some ways the relationship between Hay and Lincoln resembled that of an earlier wartime surrogate-father-surrogate-son pair, Alexander Hamilton and George Washington. As John Russell Young noted, Hay "knew the social graces and amenities, and did much to make the atmosphere of the war[-]environed White House grateful, tempering unreasonable aspirations, giving to disappointed ambitions the soft answer which turneth away wrath, showing, as Hamilton did in similar offices, the tact and common sense which were to serve him as they served Hamilton in wider spheres of public duty."[39] A fellow boarder with Hay from 1862 through the end of the war recalled that he was "a hard practical worker . . . , as his twelve or fourteen hours a day of hard work at the White House . . . sufficiently attested. He was a trusted and intimate friend of Lincoln's and probably lived nearer to that good man's heart during the years of the civil war, than any other man."[40]

Among his other chores, Hay composed letters for the president's signature. Lincoln "wrote very few letters," Hay told William Herndon in 1866. "He did not read one in fifty that he received. At first we tried to bring them to his notice, but at last he gave the whole thing over to me, and signed without reading them the letters I wrote in his name."[41] One of those was, in all probability, the letter of condolence to the Widow Bixby.[42]

Lincoln also "took a fatherly interest" in John G. Nicolay, according to Nicolay's daughter.[43] Nicolay's father had died when John was only fourteen. As the principal White House secretary, Nicolay saw Lincoln often and developed close ties with him. Nicolay later recalled that "the five years during which he gave me his confidence and intimacy, I learned to know him perhaps better than any other person, except the members of his own family."[44]

At the White House Nicolay became known as "the bulldog in the ante-room" with a disposition "sour and crusty."[45] A New Yorker complained to the president early in his first term: "If the stories I hear about Nicolay . . . are true, you ought to dismiss him. If he is sick, he has a right to be cross and ungentlemanly in his deportment, but not otherwise. People say he is very disagreeable and uncivil."[46] Thurlow Weed called Nicolay's temperament "bilious."[47] A journalist described Nicolay as the "grim Cerberus of Teutonic descent who guards the last door which opens into the awful presence."[48]

William O. Stoddard described his colleague more generously: "A fair French and German scholar, with some ability as a writer and much natural acuteness, he nevertheless—thanks to a dyspeptic tendency—had developed an artificial manner the reverse of 'popular,' and could say 'no' about as disagreeably as any man I ever knew." But, Stoddard added, Nicolay served Lincoln well: "That . . . for which we all respected him, which was his chief qualification for the very important post he occupied, was his devotion to the president and his incorruptible honesty Lincoln-ward. He measured all things and all men by their relations to the president, and was of incalculable service in fending off much that would have been unnecessary labor and exhaustion to his over-worked patron. For this, and more, he deserves the thanks of all who loved Mr. Lincoln."[49] Stoddard recalled that Lincoln "put entire confidence" in all three of his secretaries; in return, "there was in the feeling with which they all regarded him something quite as strong as any tie of blood could possibly have been."[50]

A young man slated to become Lincoln's secretary in his second administration, Noah Brooks, also grew close to the president. "I knew and loved Abraham Lincoln well," he wrote shortly after the assassination. "It was my good fortune to make his acquaintance years ago, during the early days of Republicanism, in Illinois, and since my sojourn in Washington [starting in the fall of 1862] that early acquaintance has ripened into intimacy near and confiding."[51] During his final two and a half years, Lincoln saw Brooks, a correspondent for a California newspaper, "almost daily."[52]

Another young man in Illinois, Elmer Ellsworth, also became a surrogate son. Ellsworth, a student in the Lincoln and Herndon office, accompanied the president-elect to Washington, where he become part of the White Household. Whitney noted that a "relation like that of knight and squire of the age of chivalry existed between the two" and that Lincoln had an "almost fatherly affection" for Ellsworth.[53] A biographer of Ellsworth concluded that Lincoln regarded him "with a father's love."[54]

Lincoln may well have identified with young Ellsworth, a self-educated poor boy, ambitious for honors and distinction, too proud to accept favors, alienated from his father (who expected his son to earn money for him), with a paternal streak, a sensitive conscience, and a heart full of compassion and generosity.[55] For years Ellsworth had been seeking an "aged . . . gentleman . . . who only awaits a convenient opportunity to pat me on the head and adopt me as his own."[56]

That gentleman turned out to be Abraham Lincoln, who met Ellsworth in 1860 and was strongly attracted to the energetic young militia enthusiast. A friend in Springfield reported to Ellsworth that Lincoln had expressed "an earnest desire that you should make this place your home & his office your head quarters. He has taken a greater interest in you than I ever knew him to manifest in any one before."[57]

Eventually Lincoln appealed directly to Ellsworth, who accepted his offer in October 1860. Ostensibly an apprentice lawyer, he spent most of his time working in his new surrogate father's presidential campaign.[58] Lincoln, who according to Hay "loved him like a younger brother," called his diminutive new surrogate son "the greatest little man I ever met."[59]

When Ellsworth was killed early in the war while hauling down a Confederate flag in Alexandria, Lincoln was devastated and "mourned him as a son."[60] Upon receipt of the news, he burst into tears, telling his official callers, "Excuse me, but I cannot talk." After he had collected himself, he explained, "I will take [make] no apology, gentlemen, for my weakness; but I knew poor Ellsworth well, and held him in great regard."[61] When a congressman expressed satisfaction that the Stars and Stripes now flew in Alexandria, Lincoln replied, "'Yes, but it was at a terrible cost!' and the tears rushed into his eyes as he said it."[62] At the funeral conducted in the White House, the president cried out as he viewed the corpse, "My boy! my boy! was it necessary this sacrifice should be made!"[63]

The president reacted similarly when he learned of the fearsome battle wounds sustained by William P. Black and his brother John C. Black, whom he knew well and whose parents he had often visited in Danville, Illinois. He exclaimed, "My God, my God! It is too bad! They worked hard to earn money enough to educate themselves, and this is the end! I loved them as if they were my own."[64]

Other young Union officers whose relations with Lincoln had a filial quality included commanders of the Army of the Potomac. In his dealings with George B. McClellan, "the problem child of the Civil War," Lincoln repeatedly had to exercise his legendary patience to the utmost.[65] One observer accurately noted that the president "indulge[d] him in his whims and complaints and shortcomings as a mother would indulge her baby."[66]

No Union general brought out Lincoln's paternal qualities so strikingly as Joseph Hooker. In January 1863, the president wrote one of his most fatherly letters to "Fighting Joe":

> I have placed you at the head of the Army of the Potomac. Of course I have done this upon what appear to me to be sufficient reasons. And yet I think it best for you to know that there are some things in regard to which, I am not quite satisfied with you. I believe you to be a brave and skilful soldier, which, of course, I like. I also believe you do not mix politics with your profession, in which you are right. You

have confidence in yourself, which is a valuable, if not an indispensable quality. You are ambitious, which, within reasonable bounds, does good rather than harm.

After this preliminary praise, Lincoln then turned to a delicate matter: Hooker's indiscreet belittling of General Ambrose E. Burnside, his predecessor as commander of the Army of the Potomac:

> I think that during Gen. Burnside's command of the Army, you have taken counsel of your ambition, and thwarted him as much as you could, in which you did a great wrong to the country, and to a most meritorious and honorable brother officer. I have heard . . . of your recently saying that both the Army and the Government needed a Dictator. Of course it was not *for* this, but in spite of it, that I have given you the command. Only those generals who gain successes, can set up dictators. What I now ask of you is military success, and I will risk the dictatorship. The government will support you to the utmost of it's ability, which is neither more nor less than it has done and will do for all commanders. I much fear that the spirit which you have aided to infuse into the Army, of criticizing their Commander, and withholding confidence from him, will now turn upon you. I shall assist you as far as I can, to put it down. Neither you, nor Napoleon, if he were alive again, could get any good out of an army, while such a spirit prevails in it.

Lincoln concluded with a rousing injunction: "And now, beware of rashness. Beware of rashness, but with energy, and sleepless vigilance, go forward, and give us victories."[67]

Upon receiving this remarkable document, Hooker said of its author: "He talks to me like a father. I shall not answer the letter until I have won him a great victory."[68] He also planned to have it published after he captured Richmond. "It will be amusing," he remarked. When told of this, Lincoln sighed, "Poor Hooker! I am afraid he is incorrigible."[69] Three months later at the battle of Chancellorsville, Hooker failed conspicuously to achieve that victory and was soon removed from command. He then asked Noah Brooks what the president thought of him. As Brooks recalled the scene, "I . . . said that Lincoln had told me that he regarded Hooker very much as a father might regard a son who was lame, or who had some other incurable physical infirmity. His love for his son would be even intensified by the reflection that the lad could never be a strong and successful man." Moved to tears, Hooker told Brooks, "Well, the President may regard me as a cripple; but if he will give me a chance, I will yet show him that I know how to fight." Hooker did in fact achieve distinction later as a corps commander.[70] A general who bore some of the opprobrium for Hooker's Chancellorsville debacle was the leading German-American public figure of the nineteenth century, Carl Schurz, who also regarded the president with almost filial reverence.[71]

The enlisted men's fond sobriquet for Lincoln was "Father Abraham." A Union chaplain reported that after the president had visited the troops on the Virginia Peninsula in 1862, "The boys liked him. In fact, his popularity in the army is and has been universal. Many of our rulers and leaders fall into odium, but all have faith in Lincoln. 'When he finds out (they say of this or that matter of complaint) it will be stopped.'"[72]

The following year, when Lincoln and several other dignitaries paid a visit to the Army of the Potomac, one solider recalled that he and his comrades "had no eyes save for our revered President, the Commander-in-Chief of the army, the brother of every soldier." The men were especially impressed by the president's sad countenance. Later they said to one another, "Did you ever see such a look on any man's face?" "He is bearing the burdens of the nation." "It is an awful load; it is killing him."[73] A senator noted that Lincoln's "tender sympathy" for young men who joined the army unaware of what they were undertaking "rendered him . . . popular with the private soldiers in the army. They all felt they had a friend in the President."[74] A scholar who examined the common Union solider extensively concluded that the troops esteemed Lincoln because of his mercy, kindness, solicitousness, integrity, and lack of pretense. But above all, his fatherly concern for their welfare was the most important factor "contributing to Lincoln's popularity among the rank and file."[75] In conversation he would refer to the Union soldiers as "my boys."[76]

In September 1862 a young Union cavalryman who served as a White House dispatch-bearer rode with Lincoln to General Halleck's home. En route, the president asked the young man about his family and urged him to be good to his mother. The soldier was "astonished" that "this great man, even under all his strain and anxiety, could turn his thoughts to a nineteen-year-old cavalryman and talk to the lad like a kind, wise father."[77]

Lincoln regarded even the Confederates paternally. A telegraph operator heard Lincoln call Robert E. Lee "Bobby Lee" and Jefferson Davis "Jeffy D." and concluded that he "seemed to be thinking of the leaders of the Rebellion as wayward sons rather than as traitorous brethren."[78] This was especially true of General Benjamin Hardin Helm, husband of Mary Lincoln's half-sister Emilie.[79] Lincoln got to know Helm as a lawyer in 1857 and developed a high regard for him. Thus began a relationship that the Helms' daughter thought "was more like the affection of brothers than the ordinary liking of men." She added that "Mary and Mr. Lincoln treated their young brother-in-law with so much kindness and affection and consideration that he felt they had indeed accepted him as a brother."[80]

But Emilie Todd Helm viewed the Lincolns more as parents than siblings. To her diary, she confided gratefully that her sister and brother-in-law "pet me as if I were a child."[81] At the outset of the war, Lincoln vainly offered Helm, a West Point graduate, the post of paymaster with the rank of major in the Union army. Helm later said, "The most painful moment of my life was when I declined the generous offer of my brother-in-law."[82] When that life was cut short in September 1863 at the battle of Chickamauga, Lincoln's paternal feeling for Helm caused him to lament that "I feel as David of old did when he heard of the death of Absalom. 'Would God I had died for thee, O Absalom, my son, my son!'"[83]

In the eyes of slaves freed by his Emancipation Proclamation, the president was a father as well as a deliverer. Blacks "beheld in Lincoln a father image," according to the historian Benjamin Quarles.[84] A correspondent for the New York *Independent* described how blacks reacted to the president in 1864: "I had noticed, at sundry times during the summer, the wild fervor and strange enthusiasm which our colored friends always manifest over the name of Abraham Lincoln. His name with them seems to be associated with that of his namesake, the Father of the Faithful." On New Year's Day 1865, when the president warmly greeted black callers at a White House reception, they were even more demonstrative than usual. "They laughed and wept, and wept and laughed,—exclaiming, through their blinding tears: 'God bless you! God bless Abraham Lincoln!'"[85] When Lincoln visited the black troops of the Eighteenth Corps in 1864, they cheered him, saying among other things, "De Lord save Fader Abraham!"[86]

News of the president's assassination saddened no group more than the blacks. As Quarles put it, Lincoln's death "burdened every black with a personal sense of loss."[87] A correspondent of the New York *Tribune* noted that when word of the president's death reached Charleston, the black population there seemed stricken: "I never saw such sad faces, or heard such heavy hearts beatings, as here in Charleston the day the dreadful news came! The colored people—the native loyalists—were like children bereaved of an only and loved parent." One woman, "so absorbed in her grief that she noticed no one," cried loud and long. The journalist concluded that "her heart told her that he whom Heaven had sent in answer to her prayers was lying in a bloody grave, and she and her race were left—*fatherless.* "[88] Gideon Welles noted that on the day of the president's funeral, there "were no truer mourners . . . than the poor colored people . . . bewailing the loss of him whom they regarded as a benefactor and father."[89] Another observer noted that the blacks of Washington sorrowfully declared that they "had lost their best friend."[90]

The foremost black leader of the era, Frederick Douglass, shared this filial regard. He remembered that when with Lincoln he "was in the presence of a very great man, as great as the greatest," and felt "as though I could go and put my hand on him if I wanted to, to put my hand on his shoulder. . . . I felt as though I was in the presence of a big brother, and that there was safety in his atmosphere."[91]

Many who came into contact with the president felt the same way. One of his bodyguards, William Crook, said, "I followed him as a child would follow his father."[92] A White House secretary noted that members of Congress "became bound to him by near ties of mutual understanding and respect. A sort of family feeling grew in the hearts of many, unconsciously regarding themselves as watching the control of the common household by a man who oddly combined the functions of a father and an elder brother."[93]

One of the most important elements in Lincoln's success as president was his ability to inspire in Congress and its constituents filial trust and devotion. In part, it stemmed from the eloquence of his public utterances, which Harriet Beecher Stowe said "more resembled a father's talks to his children than a State paper."[94] In the first inaugural address, his words to the South, in the view of a Republican congressman, contained "conciliatory promises" and "such winning arguments and admonitions only, as a tender father might employ with a wayward offspring."[95] An early biographer, J. G. Holland, said that Lincoln "more than any of his predecessors was . . . regarded as the father of his people. . . . Every man seemed to think that Mr. Lincoln could settle his little difficulty, or provide for his little want. . . . It was the story of his younger life re-enacted. He had always been a reconciler of difficulties between men; and he remarked, while in the presidential chair, that it seemed as if he was regarded as a police justice, before whom all the petty troubles of men were brought for adjustment."[96]

A good example of this phenomenon occurred in March 1865, when a New Orleans real estate holder complained to Lincoln that he was unable to collect his rents. A journalist who observed the interview later described it: "Your case, my friend," said the president, "may be a hard one, but it might have been worse. If, with your musket, you had taken your chance with our boys before Richmond, you might have found your bed before now. But the point is, what would you have me do for you? I have much to do, and the courts have been opened to relieve me in this regard." The applicant, still embarrassed, said, "I am not in the habit of appearing before big men." "And for that matter," it was quickly responded, "you have no need to change your habit, for you are not before very big men now." Lincoln added playfully, "I can't go into the collection business." The New Orleans man was finally satisfied that a president cannot do everything necessary to redress individual grievances.[97]

Lincoln reacted similarly when a delegation asked him to help the Washington fire department obtain new equipment. He interrupted them, "gravely" observing, "It is a mistake to suppose that I am at the head of the fire department of Washington. I am simply the President of the United States."[98]

In the fall of 1862 Charles G. Halpine heard Lincoln tell an old woman, "I am really very sorry, madam, very sorry. But your own good sense must tell you that I am not here to collect small debts. You must appeal to the courts in regular order." After she departed, the president mused to Halpine, "What odd kinds of people come in to see me, and what odd ideas they must have about my office! Would you believe, Major, that the old lady who has just left, came in here to get from me an order for stopping the pay of a Treasury clerk, who owes her a board bill of about $70. . . . She may have come here a loyal woman, but I'll be bound she has gone away believing that the worst pictures of me in the Richmond press only lack truth in not being half black and bad enough."[99]

• • •

Thus Lincoln radiated the positive Old Man archetype, embodying the Wise Father. Many Northerners sensed this intuitively and trusted him. Without that trust, Northern morale might well have flagged, crippling the administration and the war effort. Few things contributed more to Lincoln's success as president than his ability to inspire the kind of confidence that children accord a benevolent father.

NOTES

1. John J. Duff, *A. Lincoln: Prairie Lawyer* (New York: Holt, Rinehart and Winston, 1960), 97–103 [quotes on 97, 100]. Joseph Fort Newton observed that "no two men were ever more unlike in temper of mind and habits of thought." *Lincoln and Herndon* (Cedar Rapids: Torch Press, 1910), 21.

2. Herndon to Jesse Weik, Springfield, 24 Feb. 1887, H-W MSS, DLC. Cf. Angle, *HL,* 211

3. For an elaboration on this fundamental point, see M. Esther Harding, *The "I" and the "Not-I": A Study in the Development of Consciousness,* Bollingen Series 79 (New York: Pantheon Books, 1965), 130–76.

4. Jung uses the term *Senex* to describe the archetype. I use the English translation *Old Man.* For a brief outline of the qualities of the Senex, both positive and negative, see James Hillman, "Senex and Puer: An Aspect of the Historical and Psychological Present," in James Hillman et al., *Puer Papers* (Irving: Spring, 1979), 15–23.

5. Reminiscences of R. H. Osborne, "Lincoln with His People," Lerna [Ill.] *Weekly Eagle,* Lincoln anniversary issue, Feb. 1928, broadside, Barton MSS, uncatalogued addendum, Box 7, folder 129, University of Chicago.

6. E. J. Edwards, quoting the conductor, Gilbert Finch, then retired and living in Connecticut, New York *Times,* 24 Jan. 1909.

7. Statement of William Wood, 15 Sept. 1865, in Hertz, *HL,* 364.

8. Gibson William Harris, "My Recollections of Abraham Lincoln," *Woman's Home Companion* (Dec. 1903): 15.

9. Washburne in Rice, *RL,* 16.

10. Lincoln to Herndon, Washington, 2 Feb., 10 July 1848, in Basler, *CWL,* 1:448, 497. George Harris Monroe said that in 1848, when Lincoln was "verging upon middle life, . . . he had the aspect of one considerably older than his real age." "Lincoln in Massachusetts," unidentified clipping, LMFW.

11. Robert H. Browne, *Abraham Lincoln and the Men of His Time,* 2 vols. (Cincinnati: Jennings and Pye; New York: Eads and Mains, 1901), 1:86.

12. Cincinnati *Commercial,* 17 Sept. 1859; Springfield correspondence, 6 Nov. 1860, New York *Tribune,* 10 Nov. 1860, both in *Abraham Lincoln: A Press Portrait,* ed. Herbert Mitgang (Chicago: Quadrangle Books, 1971), 137, 202–3.

13. Janet Jennings, in *Abraham Lincoln, Tributes from His Associates: Reminiscences of Soldiers, Statesmen and Citizens,* ed. William Hayes Ward (New York: Thomas Y. Crowell, 1895), 237–38.

14. Harris, "My Recollections of Abraham Lincoln," 15.

15. R. R. Hitt, Journal, 274, Hitt MSS, DLC. The date for this entry is unclear, but probably sometime between Nov. 1860 and Feb. 1861.

16. William Henry Herndon, "Analysis of the Character of Abraham Lincoln" [lecture of 26 Dec. 1865], *Abraham Lincoln Quarterly* 1 (Dec. 1941): 417; Herndon to Francis B. Carpenter, Springfield, 11 Dec. 1866, H-W MSS, DLC. Significantly, Herndon did not mention his father in addition to his wife and mother.

17. Henry B. Rankin, *Personal Recollections of Abraham Lincoln* (New York: G. P. Putnam's Sons, 1916), 141.

18. Herndon, "Analysis of the Character of Lincoln," 411–12.

19. David Donald, *Lincoln's Herndon* (New York: Alfred A. Knopf, 1948), 129.

20. Donald, *Lincoln's Herndon*, 13–14, 65–71, 129. Cf. Charles B. Strozier, *Lincoln's Quest for Union: Public and Private Meanings* (New York: Basic Books, 1982), 81.

21. Reminiscences of John H. Littlefield, in "Abe Lincoln's Wisdom," unidentified clipping, LMFW.

22. Herndon "Analysis of the Character of Lincoln," 431–34.

23. Gibson W. Harris in Francis Fisher Browne, *The Every-Day Life of Abraham Lincoln*, 2d ed. (New York: G. P. Putnam's Sons, 1913), 130.

24. Reminiscences of Blackburn, in "Joe Blackburn and Mr. Lincoln," Chicago *News*, N.d., clipping, LMFW.

25. "A Helping Hand," unidentified clipping, LMFW.

26. Unidentified newspaper article, quoted in Nelle S. Mills to French Quinn, Kansas City, Mo., 8 July 1925, enclosed in French Quinn to Albert J. Beveridge, Decatur, Ind., 20 July 1925, Beveridge MSS, DLC.

27. Washburne in Rice, *RL*, 16–17.

28. Whitney to Herndon, N.p., 27 Aug. 1887, in Albert J. Beveridge, *Abraham Lincoln, 1809–1858*, 2 vols. (Boston: Houghton, Mifflin, 1928), 1:527.

29. Somers to James R. B. Van Cleave, N.p., 7 Dec. 1908, in *Intimate Memories of Lincoln*, ed. Rufus Rockwell Wilson (Elmira: Primavera Press, 1945), 100; Somers to S. S. McClure, El Cajon, Calif., 1 Nov. 1895, Ida M. Tarbell MSS, Allegheny College.

30. Jesse W. Weik, ed., "A Law Student's Recollection of Abraham Lincoln," *Outlook*, 11 Feb. 1911, 312.

31. [John M. Scott], "Lincoln on the Stump and at the Bar," typescript, 10–11, Ida M. Tarbell MSS, Allegheny College.

32. Walker in *The Lincoln Memorial: Album-Immortelles*, ed. Osborn H. Oldroyd (New York: G. W. Carleton, 1883), 213.

33. Henry C. Whitney, *Lincoln the President*, vol. 2 of *A Life of Lincoln*, 2 vols., ed. Marion Mills Miller (New York: Baker and Taylor, 1908), 2:87.

34. Tyler Dennett, *John Hay: From Poetry to Politics* (New York: Dodd, Mead, 1934), 39.

35. Helen Nicolay, *Lincoln's Secretary: A Biography of John G. Nicolay* (New York: Longmans, Green, 1949), 85.

36. Halpine's headnote to Hay's poem "God's Vengeance," undated clipping from the New York *Citizen*, Hay scrapbook, Hay MSS, RPB.

37. Howard I. Kushner and Anne Hummel Sherrill, *John Milton Hay: The Union of Poetry and Politics* (Boston: Twayne, 1970), 27.

38. James T. DuBois and Gertrude S. Mathews, *Galusha Grow: Father of the Homestead Law* (Boston: Houghton Mifflin, 1917), 266–67.

39. John Russell Young, "John Hay, Secretary of State," *Munsey's Magazine*, 8 Jan. 1929, 247. Cf. John Russell Young, "Lincoln as He Was," Pitts-

burgh *Dispatch,* 23 Aug. 1891. On the relationship between Hamilton and Washington, see Fawn M. Brodie, *Thomas Jefferson: An Intimate History* (New York: W. W. Norton, 1974), 257–75.

40. Sedalia [Mo.] *Times,* 11 May 1871.

41. Hay to Herndon, Paris, 5 Sept. 1866, Hay MSS, RPB.

42. The debate over the authorship of the Bixby letter has created a scholarly furor, based largely on stylistic considerations and on the secondhand and thirdhand testimony by people who recall Hay claiming that he wrote the letter. Hitherto overlooked pieces of documentary evidence seem to clinch the argument in favor of Hay. Among the Hay Papers at Brown University and at the Library of Congress are scrapbooks of newspaper clippings, including copies of the Bixby letter. The overwhelming bulk of the items in the books are Hay's own writings. It is hard to imagine why Hay would have pasted the Bixby letter in these scrapbooks, full of his own literary creations, unless he had composed it himself. Combined with Hay's 1866 statement to Herndon and the reminiscences of John Morley, Walter Hines Page, Louis Coolidge, W. C. Brownell, and Spencer Eddy (Hay's personal secretary), Hay's scrapbooks suggest that it is highly likely that Hay, not Lincoln, is the true author of what has been called "the most beautiful letter ever written." For Spencer Eddy's testimony, see Catherine Beveridge's memo of 22 July 1949, Albert J. Beveridge MSS, DLC. For the other testimony, see F. Lauriston Bullard, *Abraham Lincoln and the Widow Bixby* (New Brunswick: Rutgers University Press, 1946); and William E. Barton, *A Beautiful Blunder: The True Story of Lincoln's Letter to Mrs. Lydia A. Bixby* (Indianapolis: Bobbs-Merrill, 1926).

43. Nicolay, *Lincoln's Secretary,* 214.

44. Nicolay quoted by David McWilliams, *Northwestern Christian Advocate,* N.d., reprinted in the St. Louis *Globe Democrat,* 12 Feb. 1901.

45. William O. Stoddard, "White House Sketches," New York *Citizen,* 25 Aug. 1866, and *Inside the White House in War Times* (New York: Charles L. Webster, 1890), 104.

46. Robert Colby to Lincoln, New York, 18 May 1861, Lincoln MSS, DLC.

47. Weed to John Bigelow, N.d., in William Roscoe Thayer, *The Life and Letters of John Hay,* 2 vols. (Boston: Houghton Mifflin, 1915), 1:222.

48. Noah Brooks, Washington correspondence, 7 Nov. 1863, in Sacramento *Daily Union,* 4 Dec. 1863, 1. Brooks added, "The President is affable and kind, but his immediate subordinates are snobby and unpopular." Another discontented observer lamented that "Mr. Lincoln has no private secretary that fills the bill and the loss is a national one." Henry Smith to Charles H. Ray and Joseph Medill, [Washington], 4 Nov. 1861, Ray MSS, CSmH.

49. Stoddard, "White House Sketches," New York *Citizen,* 25 Aug. 1866. Cf. John Russell Young, "Lincoln as He Was," Pittsburgh *Dispatch,* 23 Aug. 1891.

50. William O. Stoddard, *Abraham Lincoln: The True Story of a Great Life* (New York: Fords, Howard, and Hulbert, 1884), 243. He added: "Towards his immediate subordinates, private secretaries, messengers, and other officials or servants, it may almost be said that he had no manner at all, he took their presence and the performance of their duties so utterly for granted.

Not one of them was ever made to feel, unpleasantly, the fact of his inferior position by reason of any look or word of the President. All were well assured that they could not get a word from him unless the business which brought them to his elbow justified them in coming" (403).

51. Washington correspondence, 16 April 1865, Sacramento *Daily Union,* 17 May 1865, 3.

52. Noah Brooks, *Abraham Lincoln and the Downfall of American Slavery* (New York: G. P. Putnam's Sons, 1894), vi.

53. Whitney, *Lincoln,* 2:87–88.

54. Ruth Painter Randall, *Colonel Elmer Ellsworth: A Biography of Lincoln's Friend and First Hero of the Civil War* (Boston: Little, Brown, 1960), 261. This is the standard biography of Ellsworth. See also John R. Turner Ettlinger, "A Young Hero—Elmer Ellsworth, 1837–1861," *Books at Brown* 19 (May 1963): 23–68, and Charles A. Ingraham, *Elmer E. Ellsworth and the Zouaves of '61* (Chicago: University of Chicago Press, 1925).

55. Randall, *Ellsworth,* passim.

56. Ibid., 134–35.

57. John Crook to Ellsworth, Springfield, March 1860, ibid., 4.

58. John Hay, "A Young Hero: Personal Reminiscences of Colonel E. E. Ellsworth," *McClure's Magazine* 6 (March 1896): 358.

59. [John Hay], "Ellsworth," *Atlantic Monthly* 8 (July 1861): 124; Randall, *Ellsworth,* 7.

60. John Hay, "A Young Hero," New York *World,* 16 Feb. 1890, 26.

61. Washington correspondence, 24 May 1861, New York *Herald,* 25 May 1861, 1.

62. Recollections of John A. Kasson, in Rice, *RL,* 36.

63. Randall, *Ellsworth,* 263.

64. Ward Hill Lamon, *Recollections of Abraham Lincoln, 1847–1865,* 2d ed., ed. Dorothy Lamon Teillard (Washington: Published by the editor, 1911), 104–5.

65. T. Harry Williams, *Lincoln and His Generals* (New York: Alfred A. Knopf, 1952), 25.

66. John G. Nicolay to Therena Bates, Washington, 9 Nov. 1862, Nicolay MSS, DLC. Cf. Williams, *Lincoln and His Generals,* 25–178, and Stephen W. Sears, *George B. McClellan: The Young Napoleon* (New York: Ticknor and Fields, 1988), 133–34, and chapter 7 of this volume.

67. Lincoln to Hooker, Washington, 26 Jan. 1863, in Basler, *CWL,* 6:78–79.

68. Whitney, *Lincoln,* 2:171. According to John Nicolay, Hooker thought Lincoln's letter "a compliment," although Nicolay believed "it would be difficult to find a severer piece of friendly criticism." Nicolay to Robert T. Lincoln, 1878 [no day or month given], in Nicolay, *Lincoln's Secretary,* 278.

69. Brooks, *Lincoln and the Downfall of American Slavery,* 356–57.

70. Noah Brooks, *Washington, D.C. in Lincoln's Time,* ed. Herbert Mitgang (Chicago: University of Chicago Press, 1971), 62–63.

71. Michael Burlingame, "The Early Life and Career of Carl Schurz," Ph.D. diss., Johns Hopkins University, 1971, 357–58.

72. Joseph H. Twichell to his father, N.p., 9 July 1862, in Twichell, "Army Memories of Lincoln: A Chaplain's Reminiscences," *Congregationalist and Christian World*, 30 Jan. 1913, 154.

73. Ira Seymour Dodd, in Tarbell, *The Life of Abraham Lincoln*, 3:137–38.

74. [Morton] S. Wilkinson, "A Statesman's Tact," New York *Tribune*, 12 July 1885, 3. The author is identified as "W. S. Wilkinson," but it seems clear that Minnesota Senator M. S. Wilkinson wrote the article.

75. Bell Irvin Wiley, "Billy Yank and Abraham Lincoln," *Abraham Lincoln Quarterly* 6 (June 1950): 103–20 [quote on 104]. Cf. Tarbell, *The Life of Abraham Lincoln*, 3:146–69, and William H. Seward, "Reminiscences of Lincoln," *Magazine of History* 9 (Feb. 1909): 104–5.

76. Reminiscences of a Union nurse, Helen B. Cole, Chicago *Tribune*, 5 Feb. 1931.

77. William H. Tisdale's recollections in the Washington *Star*, 10 Feb. 1924.

78. David Homer Bates, "Lincoln and Charles A. Dana," in *Lincoln, Tributes from His Associates*, ed. Ward, 229. According to Captain D. V. Derickson, of Company D of the 150th Pennsylvania Volunteers, which served as a presidential bodyguard, Lincoln always referred to the Confederate leadership as "those Southern gentlemen." Pittsburgh *Gazette Times*, 29 Nov. 1908. In early 1865 Lincoln praised Davis highly: "Our adversaries have been more fortunate than we; for it has been their good luck to have for their chief one of the ablest of men,—very capable of conducting at the same time both civil and military affairs. As minister of war, Mr. Davis had known all the officers of the regular army. I had never seen but three of them before I came to Washington as President." [Antoine] Auguste Laugel, *The United States during the War* (New York: Bailliere Brothers, 1866), 264.

79. On Helm, see R. Gerald McMurtry, *Ben Hardin Helm: "Rebel" Brother-in-Law of Abraham Lincoln—with a Biographical Sketch of His Wife and an Account of the Todd Family of Kentucky* (Chicago: Privately printed for the Civil War Roundtable, 1943).

80. Katherine Helm, *The True Story of Mary, Wife of Lincoln* (New York: Harper and Brothers, 1928), 127, 130.

81. Helm, *The True Story of Mary*, 224.

82. Ibid., 188.

83. Washington City *Herald*, N.d., quoting a statement made by David Davis in 1877, reprinted in *Lincoln Talks: A Biography in Anecdote*, ed. Emanuel Hertz (New York: Viking, 1939), 660.

84. Benjamin Quarles, *The Negro in the Civil War* (New York: Russell and Russell, 1953), 345.

85. F. B. Carpenter, *Six Months at the White House with Abraham Lincoln: The Story of a Picture* (New York: Hurd and Houghton, 1867), 206.

86. Horace Porter, *Campaigning with Grant* (New York: Century, 1906), 219.

87. Quarels, *The Negro in the Civil War*, 345.

88. Carpenter, *Six Months at the White House*, 207–8.

89. Howard K. Beale, ed., *Diary of Gideon Welles, Secretary of the Navy under Lincoln and Johnson,* 3 vols. (New York: W. W. Norton, 1960), 2:293 [entry for 19 April 1865].

90. B. F. Winslow to his grandfather, Washington, 18 April 1865, S. Griswold Flagg Collection, Box 2, Sterling Library, Yale University.

91. Rice, *RL,* 195.

92. Margarita Spalding Gerry, ed., *Through Five Administrations: Reminiscences of Colonel William H. Crook, Body-Guard to President Lincoln* (New York: Harper and Brothers, 1910), 25.

93. Stoddard, *Abraham Lincoln,* 359.

94. *Christian Watchman and Reflector* [Boston], 7 July 1864, 1.

95. Henry C. Deming, *Eulogy of Abraham Lincoln* (Hartford: A. N. Clark, 1865), 25.

96. J. G. Holland, *The Life of Abraham Lincoln* (Springfield: Gurdon Bill, 1866), 429.

97. "Reminiscences of President Lincoln," by the editor of the Lowell *Citizen,* in *Anecdotes, Poetry and Incidents of the War: North and South, 1861–1865,* ed. Frank Moore (New York: Printed for the subscribers, 1866), 482–83.

98. William Bender Wilson, *A Few Facts and Actors in the Tragedy of the Civil War* (Philadelphia: Published by the author, 1892), 109–10.

99. Charles G. Halpine, "Personal Recollections of Mr. Lincoln," New York *Citizen,* N.d., reprinted in the *Illinois State Journal* [Springfield], 10 June 1865, 1.

5

Lincoln's Depressions:
"Melancholy Dript from Him as He Walked"

Intense melancholy was among the most striking features of Lincoln's personality. Henry C. Whitney, recalling travels on the Illinois legal circuit with Lincoln in the 1850s, thought that "no element of Mr. Lincoln's character was so marked, obvious and ingrained as his mysterious and profound melancholy." Whitney remembered one morning in Danville, where he and Lincoln were bunkmates: "I was awakened early . . . by my companion sitting up in bed, his figure dimly visible by the ghostly firelight, and talking the wildest and most incoherent nonsense all to himself." A stranger observing this behavior, Whitney speculated, "would have supposed he had suddenly gone insane." But Whitney knew better, for he was familiar with Lincoln's "idiosyncracies." After at least five minutes of weird gabbling, Lincoln jumped up, hurriedly washed and dressed, then stoked the fire, before which he sat "moodily, dejectedly, in a most somber and gloomy spell" for two full hours.

Such episodes, according to Whitney, were not uncommon. He first observed this characteristic in court during the spring of 1855 in Bloomington. John T. Stuart, Lincoln's former law partner, told him that Lincoln was "a hopeless victim of melancholy" and pointed to where Lincoln sat alone in a corner, far from anyone else, "wrapped in abstraction and gloom." Whitney imagined that Lincoln was pursuing some "sad subject, regularly and systematically through various sinuosities, and his sad face would assume, at times, deeper phases of grief: but no relief came from dark and despairing melancholy, till he was roused by the breaking up of the court, when he emerged from his cave of gloom and came back, like one awakened from sleep, to the world in which he lived, again."[1]

Whitney was not alone in noting Lincoln's intense melancholy. Jesse W. Weik interviewed many of Lincoln's friends and acquaintances and reported that "almost every man in Illinois I met, including not only Herndon, but John T. Stuart, Samuel H. Treat, James C. Conkling, James H. Matheny, David Davis, [and] Leonard Swett . . . reminded me" of his "predisposition to melancholy."[2] Albert J. Beveridge concluded that the last decade and a half of Lincoln's life were dominated by "a sadness so profound that the depths of it cannot be sounded or estimated by normal minds."[3] Herndon noted that Lincoln "was a sad looking man: his melancholy dript from him as he walked" and recounted innumerable instances of Lincoln's gloomy abstraction.[4] During the 1850s, Joseph Wilson Fifer saw Lincoln in Bloomington often and recalled that "his face was about the saddest I ever looked upon. The melancholy seemed to roll from his shoulders and drip from the ends of his fingers."[5]

Like Whitney, attorney Lawrence Weldon observed Lincoln rise early and sit before the fire, musing, pondering, and sometimes reciting lugubrious verses "with the saddest expression I have ever seen in a human being's eyes." Weldon noted that Lincoln, in addition to being an early riser, "would frequently lapse into reverie and remain lost in thought long after the rest of us had retired for the night."[6] Jonathan Birch remembered Lincoln sitting by himself for hours, "the very picture of dejection and gloom. . . . defying the interruption of even his closest friends."[7]

Lincoln's bouts of depression began early. Beveridge incorrectly stated that "no evidence exists of gloom or despondency in his talk or conduct until December, 1840," when Lincoln was thirty-one.[8] As a boy in Indiana, Lincoln would, according to his friend and fellow student James Grigsby, "get fits of blues, then he wouldn't study for two or three days at a time."[9]

A close friend of Lincoln's once asked William Herndon, "What gave him that peculiar melancholy? What cancer had he inside?"[10] For more than a century, biographers and historians have put forth many answers to those questions, but as Fawn Brodie lamented in 1974, the "essential nature of Lincoln's melancholy still resists analysis."[11] Brodie herself offered a tentative solution: "It can, I believe, be demonstrated that his mother's death was related to Lincoln's life-long tendency to melancholy."[12] She did not, however, marshall the evidence to test her hypothesis. Charles B. Strozier emphasizes the importance of Nancy Hanks's death in molding her son's inner life, but his analysis of how it created an abiding sense of guilt in Lincoln is implausible.[13]

Lincoln's depressions probably stemmed from a series of childhood losses, which included the death of his newborn younger brother when Lincoln was about three years old; the death of his mother, along with her aunt and uncle, when he was nine; and the death of his sister when he was eighteen. Psychologists have found that "bereavement in childhood is one of the most significant factors in the development of depressive illness in later life," and that "a depressive illness in later years is often a reaction to a present loss or bereavement which is associated with a more serious loss or bereavement in childhood."[14] Specialists have not determined why this should be the case, but some studies indicate that if a parent dies, the quality of the child's relationship with the surviving parent is of critical importance.[15] The central cause of later depressions seems to be "lack of adequate care" for the child.[16]

The historical record says nothing about Lincoln's reaction to the death of his brother, but he seems to have been profoundly distraught when his mother succumbed to a then-mysterious disease known as "the milk sick" in 1818. Two years earlier, Thomas Lincoln had moved his wife and children from Kentucky to Indiana, where the family eked out a precarious existence along Pigeon Creek. They had been joined later by Nancy Hanks Lincoln's aunt and uncle, Thomas and Betsy Sparrow, and her cousin, Dennis Hanks, ten years Abraham's senior.[17]

In September 1818, the milk sick killed the Sparrows. While tending them, Nancy Lincoln contracted the disease and within a week was dead. Typically, victims of tremetol poisoning, brought on by drinking the milk of cows that had eaten white snakeroot, lie on their backs with their legs up and spread apart. Their breath grows ever shorter, their skin turns clammy and cold, their pulse becomes irregular, finally they slip into a coma.[18] To observe his mother endure such agony must have horrified young Abraham. No minister was available at the time in the remote Pigeon Creek area, but the following June an itinerant preacher from Kentucky, David Elkin (or Elkins), led a service for Nancy Lincoln and the other victims of the milk sick.[19]

Twenty-eight years later, Lincoln sadly told a friend about how lonely life was during the months following his mother's death, and how he cherished hearing the Bible stories she had once told him, for they brought her voice back to his mind's ear.[20] Augustus H. Chapman recalled a conversation with Lincoln as he drove the president-elect to visit his stepmother in January 1861: "He alluded to the sad, if not pitiful condition of his father's family at the time of the marriage to his stepmother."[21]

The loneliness that Lincoln felt may well have been compounded by his father's decision to leave the two children with Sophie Hanks to fend for themselves while he made an expedition down the Ohio River to sell pork.[22] He later left the children alone when he traveled to Kentucky to woo Sarah Bush Johnston. According to family tradition, he had planned to be gone only three months but actually spent half a year in Kentucky. One source claims that "the children had given him up as having been killed by some wild animal. They had become almost nude for the want of clothes and their stomachs became leathery from the want of food."[23] The newcomer provided more than "adequate care" for Abraham and his sister, but the year and a quarter that separated her arrival from Nancy Hanks Lincoln's death must have been miserable indeed for the children (chapter 2).

Lincoln doubtless had his mother's death in mind when he wrote from the White House to a young girl whose father had been killed in the war: "It is with deep grief that I learn of the death of your kind and brave Father; and, especially, that it is affecting your young heart beyond what is common in such cases. In this sad world of ours, sorrow comes to all; and, to the young, it comes with bitterest agony, because it takes them unawares." He may well have identified with the girl, for he too seems to have suffered the "bitterest agony" at the sudden death of his mother and to have been affected "beyond what is common in such cases." He urged the youngster not to despair: "You are sure to be happy again. To know this, which is certainly true, will make you some less miserable now." Significantly, he added, "I have had experience enough to know what I say."[24]

In the fifteen months following Nancy Lincoln's death, her daughter Sarah became the woman of the house, cooking, cleaning, and acting as a surrogate mother. She relinquished these roles to Sarah Bush Johnston, whom Thomas Lincoln wed in late 1819. Little is known about Lincoln's feelings for his sister, but he was affected deeply when she died in childbirth in 1828. Her brother-in-law, Redmond Grigsby, recalled that Lincoln, who "dearly loved his sister, she having been his only companion after the death of his mother," upon hearing the news "sat down on a log and hid his face in his hands while the tears rolled down through his long bony fingers. Those present turned away in pity and left him to his grief."[25] According to a neighbor, "Abe was in a little smoke-house when the news came to him that she had died. He came to the door and sat down, burying his face in his hands. The tears trickled through his large fingers, and sobs shook his frame. From then on he was alone in the world you might say." This neighbor added that the blow was a "great grief, which affected Abe through his life."[26] Henry C. Whitney plausibly speculated that Sarah's death reawakened painful memories of his mother's a decade earlier.[27] Lincoln blamed his sister's death on the neglect shown her by her husband, Aaron Grigsby.[28] He also resented the elder Grigsbys, who, some thought, had let his sister "lay too long" during the difficult childbirth.[29]

In 1835, Lincoln was deeply affected when Ann Rutledge died, and there is good reason to believe Robert V. Bruce's suggestion that "long-repressed grief at the death of his mother may have broken out again to swell Lincoln's grief at the similar death of Ann."[30] It is clear that "Lincoln took her death unusually hard."[31] Mrs. Elizabeth Abell, at whose home Lincoln was staying when Ann Rutledge died, recalled that "it was a great shock to him and I never seen a man mourn for a companion more than he did for her." Lincoln told her one rainy day that "he could not bare the idea of its raining on her Grave." Mrs. Abell noted that "he was very disponding a long time."[32] W. G. Greene told Herndon that after Ann Rutledge's death, he and other friends of Lincoln's felt "compelled to keep watch" over him because "from the sudden shock" he had become "somewhat temporarily deranged." They paid especially close attention during "storms—fogs—damp gloomy weather," for Lincoln said, "I can never be reconciled to have the snow—rains & storms . . . beat on her grave."[33]

Henry McHenry remembered that Lincoln "seemed quite *changed*" and *"Retired"* and that he "loved *Solitude*" and "seemed wrapped in *profound thought, indifferent* to transpiring events." He had "little to say but would take his gun and wander off in the woods by himself." This "gloom seemed to deepen for some time, so as to give anxiety to his friends in regard to his mind."[34] Lincoln allegedly told the schoolteacher Mentor Graham that "death took my mother, and my sister, Sarah, unnecessarily. It took Ann. And now—it is my evil luck—I shall always lose the women I love." Graham remembered that "Lincoln told me he felt like committing suicide after her death."[35] Ann's brother averred that the effect of his sister's death on Lincoln's mind "was terrible; he became plunged in despair, and many of his friends feared that reason would desert her throne. His extraordinary emotions were regarded as strong evidence of the existence of the tenderest relations between himself and the deceased."[36] For three weeks after Ann Rutledge's death, Lincoln stayed with Bowling Greene and his wife, mourning his loss and neglecting his duties as postmaster of New Salem.[37]

Within a year he managed to recover sufficiently from his depression to begin courting another woman, Mary Owens (chapter 6). To her Lincoln complained during his melancholy moods. In December 1836, while attending a meeting of the state legislature in Vandalia, he told her that he had been sick and that the illness had conspired "with other things I can not account for" to get "my spirits so low, that I feel that I would rather be any place in the world than here. I really can not endure the thought of staying here ten weeks." Lincoln evidently felt embarrassed by his moaning, for he closed by saying, "This letter is so dry and [stupid] that I am ashamed to send it, but with my pre[sent feel]ings I can not do any better."[38] Six months later, after having moved to Springfield, which he called a "busy wilderness," he lamented that "this thing of living in Springfield is rather a dull business after all, at least it is so to me." He was, he said, "quite as lonesome here as [I] ever was anywhere in my life."[39]

That same year, Lincoln told Robert L. Wilson "that although he appeared to enjoy life rapturously, Still he was the victim of ter[r]ible melancholly." Although he liked company, Lincoln added that, when alone, "he was so overcome with mental depression, that he never dare[d] carry a knife in his pocket."[40] Herndon remembered Lincoln talking often about suicide, and Joshua Speed alleged that he published a poem on the subject in 1840 or 1841.[41]

In March 1837 depression afflicted Lincoln as he returned from the capitol in Vandalia with three other legislators, including William Butler. According Butler, that night as the four of them bedded down, Lincoln "was uneasy, turning over and thinking and studying, so much so that he kept me awake." When asked what was wrong, Lincoln replied, "All the rest of you have something to look forward to, and all are glad to get home, and will have something to do when you get there. But it isn't so with me. I am going home, Butler, without a thing in the world. I have drawn all my pay I got at Vandalia, and have spent it all. I am in debt—I am owing Van Bergen, and he has levied on my horse and my compass, and I have nothing to pay the debt with, and no way to make any money. I don't know what to do." To Butler's suggestion that he become an attorney, Lincoln responded, "How can I study law when I have nothing to pay my board with?" Butler then offered to feed him in his own home and pay off his debts.[42]

That same month Lincoln moved from New Salem to Springfield and spoke to Joshua Speed as despairingly as he had to Butler. With the same remarkable generosity that Butler showed, Speed volunteered to share the sleeping quarters above his store with the newcomer. Speed later recalled, "I never saw so gloomy and melancholy a face in my life." This depression may have been partly a result of Lincoln's poverty and bleak prospects, for he told Speed in a "melancholy" voice that he had no money: "If you will credit me until Christmas, and my experiment here as a lawyer is a success, I will pay you then. If I fail in that I will probably never pay you at all."[43]

As he launched his "experiment" as a lawyer, Lincoln encountered depressing setbacks. Psychologists have found among people who suffer the early loss of a parent that "any frustration of ambition" as well as the "loss of subsequent love objects" can "lead to re-experience of the depression surrounding the original loss."[44] One day Lincoln unburdened himself to Stephen T. Logan, his law partner from 1841 to 1844. Logan recalled that "he had got very much discouraged" because at Danville court Edward D. Baker had bested him in some cases. Lincoln complained to Logan that "Baker had got so much the start of him that he despaired of getting even with him in acquirements and skill." Logan replied, "It does not depend on the start a man gets, it depends on how he keeps up his labors and efforts until middle life." Those words evidently consoled Lincoln.[45] Around 1840 Lincoln had a similar conversation with Mentor Graham.[46] Fifteen years later he told Ralph Emerson that he feared the competition of "college-trained men, who have devoted their whole lives to study."[47]

During the 1855 McCormick reaper patent infringement case tried in Cincinnati, Lincoln grew morose after being replaced by Edwin M. Stanton, a high-powered attorney from Pittsburgh who referred to Lincoln a "giraffe" and a "long-armed baboon."[48] George Harding, Stanton's principal partner in the case, recalled that "in all his experience he had never seen one man insult another more grossly, and that too without reason, than Stanton insulted Lincoln on that occasion." Stanton "conducted himself toward Lincoln in such a way that it was evident that he, Stanton, thought Lincoln was of no importance, and deserved no consideration whatever from himself, and he refused to talk with him, and told Harding that it was shameful that such a low-down country lawyer should be sent to associate with them." Stanton "refused to walk with Lincoln or to be seen on the street with him." In court, Stanton "refused to talk with, or say anything to Lincoln, but utterly ignored him, even refusing to take from Lincoln's hands one of the models used in the case."[49]

Stanton once rudely jerked Lincoln by the coattails and told him to step aside as the lawyers examined the reapers on display, Harding remembered.[50] Thereafter, Lincoln "did not attempt to conceal his unkind feelings" toward Stanton until he appointed him secretary of war in 1862.[51] According to William Martin Dickson, at whose home Lincoln stayed, his guest "was deeply grieved and mortified." All during the trial, as he sat on the sidelines while Stanton argued the case, Lincoln "seemed to be greatly depressed, and gave evidence of that tendency to melancholy which so marked his character." As he left town, Lincoln told his hostess, "You have made my stay here most agreeable, and I am a thousand times obliged to you; but in reply to your request for me to come again I must say to you I never expect to be in Cincinnati again. I have nothing against the city, but things have so happened here as to make it undesirable for me ever to return here."[52] Failure at the ballot box had the same depressing effect as failure at the bar.[53]

But personal rather than professional woes cast Lincoln into his blackest depression. It struck in early 1841, when he broke his engagement to Mary Todd and was spurned by Matilda Edwards (chapter 9). Orville H. Browning, who recalled that Lincoln "was so much affected as to talk incoherently, and to be delirious to the extent of not knowing what he was doing," believed that "Mr. Lincoln's aberration of mind resulted entirely from the situation he . . . got himself into—he was engaged to Miss Todd, and in love with Miss Edwards, and his conscience troubled him dreadfully for the supposed injustice he had done, and the supposed violation of his word which he had committed."[54]

As his closest confidant, Joshua Speed, recalled, "a gloom came over him till his friends were alarmed for his life."[55] "It was terrible," Speed said, for "Lincoln went crazy"; his friends "had to remove razors from his room" and "take away all knives and other such dangerous things."[56] Martinette Hardin McKee told her brother John Hardin that "we have been very much distressed, on Mr. Lincoln's account; hearing that he had two Cat fits and a Duck fit since we left."[57] Two days later, James Conkling told his fiancée that Lincoln "was confined about a week, but though he now appears again he is reduced and emaciated in appearance and seems scarcely to possess strength enough to speak above a whisper." Conkling thought Lincoln's case "truly deplorable."[58] A Springfield woman reported that "Lincoln is in rather a bad way . . . the doctors say he came within an inch of being a perfect lunatic for life."[59] James H. Matheny recalled that Lincoln went "crazy for a week or so, not knowing what to do." In fact, for many months thereafter Matheny "thought L[incoln] would commit suicide."[60] Ninian Edwards and his wife Elizabeth both used the word "crazy" to describe Lincoln's condition in January 1841.[61]

To his law partner John T. Stuart, Lincoln acknowledged on January 20 that "I have, within the last few days, been making a most discreditable exhibition of myself in the way of hypochondriaism [i.e., depression]." Three days later he elaborated, "I am now the most miserable man living. If what I feel were equally distributed to the whole human family, there would not be one cheerful face on the earth. Whether I shall ever be better I can not tell; I awfully forebode I shall not. To remain as I am is impossible; I must die or be better, it appears to me."[62] In his despondency, Lincoln evidently wrote to Dr. Charles Drake in Cincinnati, describing his symptoms and asking advice. The doctor sensibly replied that he could make no recommendations without a personal interview.[63] In early January, the morose Lincoln neglected his duties as Whig floorleader in the legislature, but, like his depression after Ann Rutledge's death, this one lifted after three weeks.[64]

Compounding Lincoln's depression was the imminent departure of Joshua Speed, his bunkmate for nearly four years. Speed dissolved his business partnership, sold his store on January 1, and in the spring returned to his native Kentucky. To lose such a close friend was doubtless painful.[65] In fact, when Speed married the following year, Lincoln wrote to him, "I feel som[e]what jealous of both of you now; you will be so exclusively concerned for one another, that I shall be forgotten entirely."[66] On other occasions he also expressed a fear of abandonment (chapter 9).

Another unsettling event took place in January 1841: Lincoln ended his law partnership with John T. Stuart, the attorney who had encouraged him to aspire for a place at the bar. When Lincoln moved in with Speed in the spring of 1837, he also formally joined forces with Stuart; now both ties were being severed.[67] Stuart seems to have played an important psychological as well as professional role in Lincoln's life. Young men in their twenties need a mentor, an older man who acts as a teacher, sponsor, guide, exemplar, and source of counsel and support as they strive to form a profession. According to Daniel J. Levinson, a mentor "fosters the young adult's development by believing in him, sharing the youthful Dream and giving it his blessing, helping to define the newly emerging self in its newly discovered world, and creating a space in which the young man can work on a reasonably satisfactory life structure that contains the Dream."[68] Stuart served this function well, although he was but a year older than Lincoln. William

Dean Howells's 1860 campaign biography, which Lincoln read and corrected, says "Stuart advised Lincoln to study law" during the legislative campaign of 1834, "and after the election he borrowed some of Stuart's books, and began to read."[69] Stuart had served with Lincoln in the Black Hawk War two years earlier and had come to respect and admire him.[70] Lincoln received his law license in September 1836 and began to practice informally with Stuart; the following spring they announced their partnership.[71]

In politics as well as law, Stuart had acted as a guide and mentor. When Lincoln entered the Illinois legislature in 1834, Stuart, a two-year veteran of the house, "introduced him to his colleagues" and "showed him the ropes."[72] As Stuart's "protégé," Lincoln "drafted legislation which Stuart introduced and frequently . . . voted on the same side" with him.[73]

Levinson found that mentorships usually last two to three years, rarely more than eight to ten, and that mentor-protégé relationships often end painfully.[74] Lincoln and Stuart were partners from 1837 to 1841; there seems to have been no ill will between the two attorneys, whose political aspirations evidently dictated that each needed a partner more devoted to the law.[75] It is not known how Lincoln felt about severing his tie with Stuart but, coming when it did, the ending of their partnership must have been dislocating. Stuart was no ordinary figure; Lincoln had unbosomed himself to him during this psychological crisis as he did to no one else, at least in writing. And he had gotten much from the association. A close student of Lincoln's career at the bar argued that the years with Stuart constituted "a brief, though valuable apprenticeship, during which Lincoln compressed into a few years experiences which would have ordinarily occupied a decade or more" and that "from Lincoln's standpoint the association had been fruitful of knowledge and experience beyond measure."[76]

To recuperate from the emotional earthquake that had shaken him so badly, Lincoln took a vacation in the summer of 1841, spending four weeks at Joshua Speed's family home in Kentucky. There he benefited, as Herndon put it, from the "congenial associations at the Speed farm, the freedom from unpleasant reminders, the company of his staunch friend, and above all the motherly care and delicate attention of Mrs. Speed."[77] According to Speed, his mother solicitously looked after Lincoln, and one day, when she observed him "very melancholy," she "with a woman[']s instinct being much pained at his deep depression" presented him with a Bible, "advising him to read it, [and] to adopt its precepts." This gesture "made a deep impression," Speed noted.[78] Lincoln thanked her in a letter to her step-daughter: "Tell your mother that I have not got her 'present' with me; but that I intend to read it regularly when I return home. I doubt not that it is really, as she says, the best cure for the 'Blues' could one but take it according to the truth."[79] In October 1861, Lincoln gratefully inscribed a photograph: "For Mrs. Lucy G. Speed, from whose pious hand I accepted the present of an Oxford Bible twenty years ago."[80] Thus, in the midst of unconscious mourning for his own mother, Lincoln seemed to derive solace from his friend's mother, just as he had found comfort from Mrs. Bowling Greene, a surrogate mother, after the death of Ann Rutledge.[81]

When Mrs. Greene's husband died in February 1842, Lincoln was prostrated by grief. Like Stuart, Squire Greene, a justice of the peace and the most influential citizen in New Salem, had been a mentor figure, helping Lincoln get started in the law. In Greene's court, Lincoln argued minor cases even before he had obtained a license. The rotund judge loved jokes, and Lincoln's sense of humor amused him vastly; he also respected the young man's intellectual ability and allowed him to peruse the law books in his small personal library.[82] Although he was the leading Democrat in New Salem, Greene urged Lincoln, a Whig, to make his second run for the state legislature.[83] A temperance advocate, Greene was a cultivated man of refined manners, and his authority as an arbiter of disputes was widely respected.[84]

When apoplexy killed Greene, Lincoln immediately left Springfield to see his widow. He had consented to make a few remarks at the funeral, but when he looked upon the face of his old friend in the casket, he broke down. According to two observers, Lincoln's "whole frame began trembling with suppressed emotion." To the assembled mourners he "spoke a few words—broken sentences only,—tremulous vibrations of the thoughts he found it impossible to coherently articulate." With tears in his eyes, Lincoln "vainly struggled to regain that self-control under which he had always held his feelings before these friends on so many occasions. He had no words that could express adequately the thoughts that thronged him as he stood beside the body of his friend whose life had been so near his, and had meant so much to him." Finally he seized his hat, "buried his face a moment in his handkerchief," then escorted Mrs. Greene to the gravesite.[85]

He demonstrated no such grief when his father died in 1851. Deeply estranged from him for many years, Lincoln refused to visit Thomas Lincoln on his deathbed, to attend his funeral, or to provide a stone for his grave (chapter 2). It seems likely that he had realized as a youth that his father was, in effect, dead to him emotionally, for the two shared little in common. The bond between them was exceptionally weak, and Lincoln tried to distance himself from his father physically, socially, culturally, and politically. It has even been argued that his depressions "may have been related to his ambition and guilt over the radical revolt against his father's world to which it had led him."[86]

This hypothesis is suggestive, and doubtless a connection exists between Lincoln's melancholy and his poor relationship with his father. But it seems more plausible to argue that Lincoln in effect lost his father, as he had his mother, early in life. Tom Lincoln did not die physically, but the young Lincoln was forced to recognize that his father was hardly a sympathetic, loving, supportive force, and that knowledge may have hurt as much as the sudden shock of his mother's death. When Thomas Lincoln did die, his son was already depressed and coping with a painful midlife crisis (chapter 1).

Other losses, especially the death of two children and several child surrogates, plunged Lincoln into despair. In 1850, his three-year-old son Eddie died, an event that Lincoln called to mind as he bade farewell to Springfield eleven years later: "No one, not in my situation, can appreciate my feeling of sadness at this parting. . . . Here my children have been born, and one is buried."[87] He wrote to his step-brother about Eddie's death, saying that "we miss him very much."[88] A minister in Springfield who spoke with Lincoln at the time found him "much depressed and downcast at the death of his son," and Herndon stated that Lincoln read him a tender, sad threnody that he composed in Eddie's honor.[89]

In 1862, eleven-year-old Willie, who was like a clone of Lincoln, died. When he learned that Willie had finally succumbed to the fever that had prostrated him for weeks, Lincoln told his secretary, "Well, Nicolay, my boy is gone—he is actually gone" and then burst into tears.[90] Tears also stood in his eyes as he told Elizabeth Keckley that Willie "was too good for this earth . . . but then we loved him so. It is hard, hard to have him die!"[91] Repeatedly he exclaimed, "This is the hardest trial of my life. Why is it? Oh, why is it?"[92] Keckley observed this outpouring of sorrow and later said, "I never saw a man so bowed down with grief."[93] Three months later he "broke down in most convulsive weeping" after reciting from Shakespeare's *King John* the lament of Constance for her dead son: "And, Father Cardinal, I have heard you say / That we shall see and know our friends in heaven. / If that be true, I shall see my boy again." He explained that he had dreamed of Willie and felt that he engaged in "sweet communion" with the boy although he realized that "it was not a reality."[94]

Once again, he was probably reminded of the death of his mother, who evidently was much on his mind as he grieved for Willie.[95] At the war's end, Lincoln told his wife, "We must both be more cheerful in the future; between the war and the loss of our darling Willie, we have been very miserable."[96] The wartime deaths of surrogate sons like Elmer Ellsworth and Ben Hardin Helm also deeply saddened the president (chapter 4).

The news that his old friend Edward D. Baker had been killed at the battle of Ball's Bluff "smote upon him like a whirlwind from a desert." Lincoln deemed it the "keenest blow" he suffered in "all the war."[97] When he learned of Baker's fate, an "expression of awe and grief solemnized the massive features of Lincoln."[98] He emerged from the telegraph office "with bowed head, and tears rolling down his furrowed cheeks, his face pale and wan, his heart heaving with emotion" and "almost fell as he stepped into the street. . . . With both hands pressed upon his heart he walked down the street, not returning the salute of the sentinel pacing his beat before the door."[99] At the funeral, the president "wept like a child."[100]

When General James S. Wadsworth died in the Battle of the Wilderness three years later, John Hay wrote: "I have not known the President so affected by a personal loss since the death of Baker." Lincoln said, "No man has given himself up to the war with such self-sacrificing patriotism as Genl. Wadsworth. He went into the service not wishing or expecting great success or distinction in his military career & profoundly indifferent to popular applause, actuated only by a sense of duty which he neither evaded nor sought to evade."[101]

Throughout the war Lincoln suffered emotional agony, especially in the wake of Union defeats. The day after the first battle of Bull Run, he confided to John D. Defrees, "If hell is [not] any worse than this, it has no terror for me."[102] Similarly, he exclaimed to General Robert Schenck after bad news arrived from the front, "If to be at the head of Hell is as hard as what I have to undergo here, I could find it in my heart to pity Satan himself."[103] In the summer of 1864 he told another caller, "When the Peninsular campaign terminated suddenly at Harrison's Landing [in July 1862], I was as nearly inconsolable as I could be and live."[104] A few weeks after that disappointment, when word reached the White House that Lee had thrashed John Pope at Second Bull Run, Lincoln "said he felt almost ready to hang himself."[105]

On December 16, 1862, shortly after the debacle at Fredericksburg, he exclaimed, "If there is a worse place than hell[,] I am in it"; on the eighteenth he lamented that "if there was any worse Hell than he had been in for two days, he would like to know it."[106] When the governor of Pennsylvania described to him the "terrible slaughter" at Fredericksburg, Lincoln "groaned, wrung his hands and showed great agony of spirit. He . . . moaned and groaned in anguish. He walked the floor, wringing his hands and uttering exclamations of grief, . . . saying over and over again: 'What has God put me in this place for.'"[107] Lincoln's face "was darkened with particular pain after the Fredericksburg fight," according to a White House secretary.[108] A War Department telegraph operator, to whom Lincoln dictated several messages while the battle raged, later wrote, "When it was learned that over 13,000 men were killed, the calamity seemed to crush Lincoln. He looked pale, wan and haggard. He did not get over it for a long time and, all that winter of 1863, he was downcast and depressed. He felt that the loss was his fault."[109]

Things improved little the following spring, when Joseph Hooker marched the Army of the Potomac toward Richmond. To the secretary of war, who brought news of Hooker's defeat at Chancellorsville, Lincoln cried out: "My God! Stanton, our cause is lost! We are ruined—we are ruined; and such a fearful loss of life! My God! this is more than I can endure! . . . Defeated again, and so many of our noble countrymen killed! What *will* the people say?" The secretary feared that the despondent president might commit suicide.[110] "I am the loneliest man in America," he lamented at that time to Bishop Charles Gordon Ames.[111]

A year later the Army of the Potomac, now under Grant, suffered heavy losses at the Battle of the Wilderness. The next day Lincoln exclaimed to a congressman, "Why do we suffer reverses after reverses! Could we have avoided this terrible, bloody war! Was it not forced upon us? Is it never to end!"[112] The speaker of the house recalled that Lincoln suffered even when the Union won a victory: "I was with him often when he was receiving news of some great battle, and whether our side won or lost his great heart seemed to shudder at the slaughter of soldiers."[113] In the midst of such carnage, he told a visitor, "I shall never be glad any more."[114] Dispiriting as military setbacks were, one sensitive observer remarked, "The deep careworn lines about his rugged face told of trouble or melancholy of far older standing than any late misfortune could have occasioned."[115]

To relieve the gloom, Lincoln resorted to humor; his legendary storytelling and joking were essential to his mental balance. He told Herndon, "If it were not for these stories—jokes—jests I should die: they give vent—are the vents of my moods & gloom."[116] Similarly, he explained to an Iowa congressman why he needed to read humorists like Orpheus C. Kerr: "I have hours of depression, and I must be unbent." He added, "You flaxen men with broad faces are born with cheer, and don't know a cloud from a star. I am of another temperament."[117] He told a Springfield neighbor, "You know I am not a man of a very hopeful temperament."[118]

Lincoln prescribed a different set of techniques for dealing with depression to a gloomy Joshua Speed: "Let me urge you, as I have ever done, to remember in the dep[t]h and even the agony of despondency, that verry shortly you are to feel well again." He also counseled Speed to "avoid being *idle;* I would immediately engage in some business, or go to making preparations for it."[119] When depressed, Lincoln would sometimes seek the company of a congenial friend. According to an associate of Admiral John Dahlgren, Lincoln said, evidently early in the Civil War, "When I am depressed, I like to talk with Dahlgren. I learn something of the preparations for defence, and I get from him consolation and courage."[120]

Some attribute Lincoln's depressions to heredity. His cousins seem to have suffered from depression.[121] Herndon speculated that possibly "Lincoln inherited this sadness and sensitiveness from his mother."[122] Whitney was less tentative in making the same point: "His melancholy was stamped on him while in the period of gestation. It was part of his nature."[123] A neighbor of the Lincolns in Kentucky recalled that Thomas Lincoln "often got the 'blues,' and had some strange sort of spells, and wanted to be alone all he could when he had them. He would walk away out on the barrens alone, and stay out sometimes half a day." Once he was overheard "talkin' all alone to hisself about God and his providence and sacrifices, and how thar war a better, more promised land." Some neighbors feared that Thomas "was losin' his mind."[124] Bipolar depression can be hereditary, but Lincoln himself seems to have suffered from "unipolar depression" without accompanying bouts of inordinate high spirits.[125]

Charles B. Strozier contends that Lincoln felt guilty and suffered depressions because he believed that "his own earlier forbidden sexual wishes" had caused his mother's death. That hypothesis, which Strozier himself acknowledges "seems fanciful," has been challenged by Don E. Fehrenbacher.[126]

A psychiatrist discussing Lincoln's "marked depression" told Albert J. Beveridge that "the data are inadequate to form much of an opinion," but went on to state that Lincoln "suffered from mental conflicts from which many 'tender-minded' people (to use W[illia]m James's expression) suffer, with just such symptoms as Lincoln manifested. . . . The 'tough-minded' have no conflicts or if they have are not torn by them."[127]

Other historians have pointed to the loneliness of Lincoln's youth as a source of his depression. Lord Charnwood noted that, early on, young Lincoln "must have been intensely ambitious, and discovered in himself intellectual power; but from his twelfth year to his twenty-first there was hardly a soul to comprehend that side of him. This chill upon his memory unmistakably influenced the particular complexion of his melancholy."[128]

Herndon speculated that "his father's cold and inhuman treatment of him" may have predisposed Lincoln to depression.[129] Modern psychologists have found that "punishment in childhood always has been one of the most powerful generators of depression in adulthood."[130] As already noted, Thomas Lincoln showed "great barbarity" in punishing his son.[131] Lincoln may have also resented the way his mother resorted to corporal punishment. Austin Gollaher, a playmate of Lincoln's in Kentucky, recalled how he rescued Abraham from drowning one day. After this exciting adventure, the boys' relief was tempered by the knowledge that, as Gollaher said, "If our mothers discovered our wet clothes they would whip us. This we dreaded from experience, and determined to avoid." They did so by shedding their soaked garments and drying them in the sun.[132]

But the most important cause of Lincoln's depression was his mother's death, not her spankings. The debilitating effects of that trauma were exacerbated by the deaths of siblings, his great-aunt and great-uncle, and the emotional coldness of his father. The subsequent events in Lincoln's life that plunged him into stygian gloom had such power because they reawakened memories of the painful losses he suffered as a youth.

. . .

Lincoln's taste in literature bears out this hypothesis. He preferred such lugubrious works as the poem "Mortality" by William Knox.[133] "I would give all I am worth, and go into debt, to be able to write so fine a piece as I think that is," he said in 1846.[134] Lawrence Weldon observed him, at day's end on the circuit, sit "by the decaying embers of an old-fashioned fire-place" and "quote at length" from "Mortality."[135] He told friends that Knox's verses "sounded to him as much like true poetry as anything that he had ever heard."[136] Evidently he first made its acquaintance in New Salem but came to love it intensely after visiting southwestern Indiana during the 1844 presidential campaign.[137] He described that trip as a visit to "the neighborhood in that State where I was raised, where my mother and only sister were buried, and from which I have been absent about fifteen years."[138] The memories thus conjured up rendered him susceptible to the appeal of Knox's dirgelike quatrains:

> Oh why should the spirit of mortal be proud!
> Like a swift flying meteor—a fast flying cloud—
> A flash of lightning—a break of the wave,
> He passeth from life to his rest in the grave.

> The leaves of the Oak, and the Willow shall fade,
> Be scattered around, and together be laid.
> And the young and the old, and the low and the high,
> Shall moulder to dust, and together shall lie.

The third stanza may have been particularly meaningful:

> The infant a mother attended and loved—
> The mother that infant's affection who proved
> The husband that mother and infant who blest,
> Each—all are away to their dwellings of rest.

This might well have brought back images of his mother, his mother's aunt and uncle, and his infant brother, all of whom died in Lincoln's youth. The fourth stanza perhaps summoned up memories of Ann Rutledge, or his sister, or both:

> The maid on whose brow, on whose cheek, on whose eye
> Shone beauty and pleasure—her triumphs are by;

And alike from the memory of the living erased
And the memory of mortals, who loved her and praised—

The remaining ten stanzas continue in a similar vein but without such obvious reference to Lincoln's life.

In a poetry anthology Lincoln found Cowper's "On Receipt of My Mother's Picture" and marked one stanza that may well have called to mind his own mother:

> Oh that those lips had language! Life has pass'd
> With me but roughly since I heard thee last.
> Those lips are thine—thy own sweet smile I see,
> The same that oft in childhood solaced me.[139]

His own 1846 poem, "My Childhood Home I See Again," is similarly obsessed with "loved ones lost." The first canto clearly deals with Lincoln's own family and friends.

> My childhood-home I see again,
>   And gladden with the view;
> And still as mem'ries crowd my brain,
>   There's sadness in it too.
>
> O memory! thou mid-way world
>   'Twixt Earth and Paradise,
> Where things decayed, and loved ones lost
>   In dreamy shadows rise.
>
> And freed from all that's gross or vile
>   Seem hallowed, pure, and bright,
> Like scenes in some enchanted isle,
>   All bathed in liquid light.
>
> As distant mountains please the eye,
>   When twilight chases day—
> As bugle-tones, that, passing by,
>   In distance die away—
>
> As leaving some grand water-fall
>   We ling'ring, list it's roar,
> So memory will hallow all
>   We've known, but know no more.
>
> Now twenty years have passed away,
>   Since here I bid farewell

> To woods, and fields, and scenes of play
>   And school-mates loved so well.
>
> Where many were, how few remain
>   Of old familiar things!
> But seeing these to mind again
>   The lost and absent brings.
>
> The friends I left that parting day—
>   How changed, as time has sped!
> Young childhood grown, strong manhood grey,
>   And half of all are dead.
>
> I hear the lone survivors tell
>   How nought from death could save,
> Till every sound appears a knell,
>   And every spot a grave.
>
> I range the fields with pensive tread,
>   And pace the hollow rooms;
> And feel (companions of the dead)
>   I'm living in the tombs.[140]

This resembles poetry found in Lincoln's commonplace book of 1824–26, into which the adolescent copied (or created himself) the following verses:

> Time what an em[p]ty vaper [']tis and days how swift they are
> swift as an indian arr[ow] fly on like a shooting star
> the presant moment Just [is here] then slides away in h[as]te
> that we can never say they['re ours] but [only say] th[ey]'re past.[141]

Lincoln was also fond of "The Inquiry" by Charles Mackay, which is about death and the afterlife:

> Tell me, ye winged winds
> That round my pathway roar,
> Do ye not know some spot
> Where mortals weep no more?
> Some lone and pleasant vale
> Some valley in the West,
> Where, free from toil and pain,
> The weary soul may rest?
> The loud wind dwindled to a whisper low,
> And sighed for pity as it answered, No.

Tell me, thou mighty deep,
Whose billows round me play,
Knows't thou some favored spot,
Some island far away,
Where weary man may find
The bliss for which he sighs;
Where sorrow never lives
And friendship never dies?
The loud waves rolling in perpetual flow
Stopped for awhile and sighed to answer, No.

And thou, serenest moon,
That with such holy face
Dost look upon the earth
Asleep in Night's embrace—
Tell me, in all thy round
Hast thou not seen some spot
Where miserable man
Might find a happier lot?
Behind a cloud the moon withdrew in woe,
And a voice sweet but sad responded, No.

Tell me, my secret soul,
Oh, tell me, Hope and Faith,
Is there no resting-place
From sorrow, sin, and death?
Is there no happy spot
Where mortals may be blessed,
Where grief may find a balm
And weariness a rest?
Faith, Hope, and Love, best boon to mortals given,
Waved their bright wings and whispered, Yes, in Heaven.[142]

One of Lincoln's favorite speeches from Shakespeare was Richard
II's lament, which John Hay heard him read in Springfield and Washington:

For heaven's sake, let us sit upon the ground,
And tell sad stories of the death of kings:—
How some have been deposed, some slain in war,
Some haunted by the ghosts they have deposed;
Some poisoned by their wives, some sleeping killed;
All murdered:—For within the hollow crown
That rounds the mortal temples of a king

> Keeps Death his court; and there the antic sits,
> Scoffing his state, and grinning at his pomp,—
> Allowing him a breath, a little scene
> To monarchize, be feared, and kill with looks;
> Infusing him with self and vain conceit,—
> As if this flesh, which walls about our life,
> Were brass impregnable,—and humored thus,
> Comes at the last, and with a little pin
> Bores through his castle walls and—farewell, King!

The speech had, Hay recalled, "a peculiar fascination for him."[143]

Lincoln also liked a prose version of such sentiments that appeared in Gibbon's *Philosophical Refections:*

> A being of the nature of man, endowed with the same faculties, but with a larger measure of existence, would cast down a smile of pity and contempt on the crimes and follies of human ambition, so eager in a narrow space to grasp at a precarious and short-lived enjoyment. It is thus that the experience of history exalts and enlarges the horizon of our intellectual view. In a composition of some days, in a perusal of some hours, six hundred years have rolled away, and the duration of a life or reign is contracted to a fleeting moment. *The grave is ever beside the throne;* the success of a criminal is almost instantly followed by the loss of his prize, and our immortal reason survives and disdains the sixty phantoms of kings who have passed before our eyes and faintly dwell upon our remembrance.[144]

Lincoln had a fondness for sad songs. As a boy in Indiana, he used to sing "John Anderson's Lamentation," which contained the line "In yonder cold graveyard, her body doth lie."[145] Milton Hay recalled hearing Lincoln in 1839 and 1840, singing in his office "pathetic pieces" like "Mary's Dream," "Lord Ullin's Daughter," and "The Soldier's Dream."[146] His favorite song, according to Ward Hill Lamon, was a "simple ballad" entitled "Twenty Years Ago," which Lamon heard him sing often in Illinois and later in the White House. The verses that most affected him were these:

> I've wandered to the village, Tom; I've sat beneath the tree
> Upon the schoolhouse play-ground, that sheltered you and me:
> But none were left to greet me, Tom, and few were left to know
> Who played with us upon the Green, some twenty years ago.
>
> Near by the spring, upon the elm you know I cut your name,—
> Your sweetheart's just beneath it Tom; and you did mine the same.

Some heartless wretch has peeled the bark,—t'was dying sure but slow,
Just as *she* died whose name you cut, some twenty years ago.

My lids have long been dry, Tom, but tears came to my eyes;
I thought of her I loved so well, those early broken ties:
I visited the old churchyard, and took some flowers to strew
Upon the graves of those we loved, some twenty years ago.[147]

Lincoln especially admired Oliver Wendell Holmes's "The Last Leaf," which also treated the death of loved ones.[148] He was fondest of the following stanza:

The mossy marbles rest
On lips that he has pressed
In their bloom;
And the names he loved to hear
Have been carved for many a year
On the tomb.

Of these verses he said, "For pure pathos, in my judgment, there is nothing finer than those six lines in the English language!"[149] To Herndon, Lincoln would "recite it, praise it, laud it, and swear by it." Herndon told Henry C. Whitney that "it took him in all moods and fastened itself upon him as never poem on man."[150] Whitney himself remembered frequent occasions when Lincoln recited the stanza and "tears would come unbidden to his eyes." Whitney was doubtless right in speculating that those tears were shed because the poetry called to Lincoln's mind the "grave [of his mother and sister] at Gentryville, or that [of Ann Rutledge] in the bend of the Sangamo."[151]

NOTES

1. Henry C. Whitney, *Life on the Circuit with Lincoln* (Boston: Estes and Lauriat, 1892), 47–48, 139, and "Abraham Lincoln: A Study from Life," *Arena* 19 (April 1898): 479.

2. Weik, *RL*, 111–12. Cf. Albert J. Beveridge, *Abraham Lincoln, 1809–1858*, 2 vols. (New York: Houghton, Mifflin, 1928), 1:521–26.

3. Beveridge, *Lincoln*, 1:525.

4. William Henry Herndon, "Analysis of the Character of Abraham Lincoln" [lecture delivered in Springfield, 12 Dec. 1865], *Abraham Lincoln Quarterly* 1 (Sept. 1941): 359. Cf. Herndon to Weik, Springfield, 12 Nov. 1885, H-W MSS, DLC.

5. Fifer's speech to the Bar Association of Illinois, 1880, in *Intimate*

Memories of Lincoln, ed. Rufus Rockwell Wilson (Elmira: Primavera Press, 1945), 155.

6. Statement of Weldon, 1 Aug. 1865, H-W MSS, DLC; statement to Frederick Trevor Hill, in Hill, Lincoln the Lawyer (New York: Century, 1906), 190–91.

7. Jesse W. Weik, ed., "A Law Student's Recollection of Abraham Lincoln," Outlook, 11 Feb. 1911, 312.

8. Beveridge, Lincoln, 1:305.

9. Grigsby's statement to Andrew M. Sweeney, who had boarded with Grigsby in 1870, in Francis Marion Van Natter, Lincoln's Boyhood: A Chronicle of His Indiana Years (Washington: Public Affairs Press, 1963), 187.

10. Leonard Swett to Herndon, Chicago, 14 Feb. 1866, H-W MSS, DLC.

11. Fawn M. Brodie, Thomas Jefferson: An Intimate History (New York: W. W. Norton, 1974), 25. Among the more implausible explanations are intense eyestrain caused by the tendency of his left eye to turn upward; or the poor functioning of his liver; or "intestinal toxemia" brought on by "putrification of food residues in the colon"; or "chronic constipation." Thomas Hall Shastid in Lincoln among His Friends: A Sheaf of Intimate Memoirs, ed. Rufus Rockwell Wilson (Caldwell: Caxton, 1942), 67; Henry C. Whitney to Herndon, [Chicago], 23 Aug. 1887, H-W MSS, DLC; Good Health [Battle Creek], N.d., quoted in The Literary Digest, 24 May 1924, 24; Chicago Tribune, 3 Sept. 1929.

12. Fawn M. Brodie, "Hidden Presidents," Harpers 254 (April 1977): 71.

13. Charles B. Strozier, Lincoln's Quest for Union: Public and Private Meanings (New York: Basic Books, 1982), 25–27; Don E. Fehrenbacher, Lincoln in Text and Context: Collected Essays (Stanford: Stanford University Press, 1987), 224–26. Strozier's response to Fehrenbacher's criticism is unpersuasive. Gabor S. Boritt, ed., The Historian's Lincoln: Rebuttals (Gettysburg: Gettysburg College, 1988), 21–22.

14. Felix Brown, "Depression and Childhood Bereavement," Journal of Mental Science 107 (1962): 770. The results of all the many studies, while not conclusive, do show an association between early bereavement and depression among adults. E. S. Paykel, "Life Events and Early Environment," in Handbook of Affective Disorders, ed. E. S. Paykel (New York: Guilford Press, 1982), 146–61.

15. Alan Breier et al., "Early Parental Loss and Development of Adult Psychopathology," Archives of General Psychiatry 45 (Nov. 1988): 987–93; Louis A. Warren, "The Mystery of Lincoln's Melancholy," typescript, Papers of the Southwest Indiana Historical Society, Evansville Central Library.

16. Tirrill Harris, George W. Brown, and Antonia Bifulco, "Loss of Parent in Childhood and Adult Psychiatric Disorder: The Role of Lack of Adequate Parental Care," Psychological Medicine 16 (Aug. 1986): 657.

17. The childless aunt and uncle had raised Nancy Hanks and Dennis Hanks as if they were their own offspring, and young Abraham evidently thought of the Sparrows as his grandparents. William E. Barton, The Women Lincoln Loved (Indianapolis: Bobbs-Merrill, 1927), 47–50.

18. Philip D. Jordan, "The Death of Nancy Hanks Lincoln," Indiana Magazine of History 40 (June 1944): 103–10.

19. Van Natter, *Lincoln's Boyhood*, 65–67.

20. Lincoln told this to Henry B. Rankin's mother in 1846. Rankin, *Personal Recollections of Abraham Lincoln* (New York: G. P. Putnam's Sons, 1916), 320–21.

21. Weik, *RL*, 293.

22. Statement by Dr. James LeGrande, son of Sophie Hanks, Jasper, Ark., 15 Feb. 1909, Arthur E. Morgan MSS, DLC.

23. Address by Clarence W. Bell in Mattoon, Ill., 11 Feb. 1931, in *Shelby County* [Ill.] *Leader*, 19 March 1931. Bell was the grandson of Elisha Linder, a friend of Lincoln's and a neighbor of Thomas Lincoln in Illinois. This story comes from his family tradition. Bell claims that he was "closely related to Sarah Bush Lincoln." Cf. Bell's address delivered 18 Sept. 1930, in Lerna [Ill.] *Weekly Eagle*, 7 Nov. 1930.

24. Lincoln to Fanny McCullough, Washington, 23 Dec. 1862, in Basler, *CWL*, 6:16–17.

25. Lincoln City, Ind., correspondence, 1 Oct. [1902], Evansville *Journal News*, N.d., clipping, LMFW; Rockport [Ind.] correspondence, 21 Dec. 1895, Chicago *Times Herald*, 22 Dec. 1895.

26. John W. Lamar in Indianapolis *News*, 12 April 1902, in J. T. Hobson, *Footprints of Abraham Lincoln* (Dayton: Otterbein Press, 1909), 24.

27. Henry C. Whitney, *Lincoln the Citizen*, vol. 1 of *A Life of Lincoln*, ed. Marion Mills Miller, 2 vols. (New York: Baker and Taylor, 1908), 1:56.

28. John W. Lamar's statement in Hobson, *Footprints of Lincoln*, 24.

29. Van Natter, *Lincoln's Boyhood*, 53; Beveridge, *Lincoln*, 1:92–94.

30. Robert V. Bruce, *Lincoln and the Riddle of Death* (Fort Wayne: Louis A. Warren Lincoln Library and Museum, 1981), 7. Brodie incorrectly stated that Lincoln "did not give way" to the melancholy produced by his mother's death "save when he broke off his first engagement to Mary Todd." See "Hidden Presidents," 71. Clearly he succumbed to it at the time of Ann Rutledge's death. Cf. John Y. Simon, "Abraham Lincoln and Ann Rutledge," *Journal of the Abraham Lincoln Association* 11 (1990): 33, and Douglas L. Wilson, "Abraham Lincoln, Ann Rutledge, and the Evidence of Herndon's Informants," *Civil War History* 36 (Dec. 1990): 301–23, esp. 310; John Evangelist Walsh, *The Shadows Rise: Abraham Lincoln and the Ann Rutledge Legend* (Urbana: University of Illinois Press, 1993).

31. Benjamin P. Thomas, *Abraham Lincoln: A Biography* (New York: Alfred A. Knopf, 1952), 49.

32. E[lizabeth] Abell to Herndon, N.p., 15 Feb. 1868, H-W MSS, DLC. Henry Rankin thought Lincoln's grief was compounded by the deaths of several friends and acquaintances shortly before Ann's demise. See *Personal Recollections*, 72–75.

33. Statement of Greene, Elm Wood, 30 May 1865, H-W MSS, DLC.

34. McHenry to Herndon, 8 Jan. 1866, H-W MSS.

35. Kunigunde Duncan and D. F. Nickols, *Mentor Graham: The Man Who Taught Lincoln* (Chicago: University of Chicago Press, 1944), 175; Graham's answer to Herndon's questionnaire about Ann Rutledge is on page 253. John J. Hall remembered his uncle Lincoln saying, "I am almost inclined

to believe that the curse of God rests upon my family." Eleanor Gridley, *The Story of Abraham Lincoln; or, The Journey from the Log Cabin to the White House* (Chicago: Monarch, 1902), 49.

36. R. B. Rutledge to Herndon, N.p., N.d., H-W MSS, DLC.

37. Mathew S. Marsh to George Marsh, New Salem, 17 Sept. 1835, in Illinois State Historical Society Library, *Transactions* (1926): 122. James G. Randall misconstrued Marsh's letter to show that "Lincoln was attending to his postmaster duties as usual." See *Lincoln the President: Springfield to Gettysburg*, 2 vols. (New York: Dodd, Mead, 1945), 2:335. In fact, Marsh complains that Lincoln carelessly left the post office unlocked and was not there when Marsh called to pick up his mail. This small distortion is part of a larger pattern. Randall minimizes the evidence of Lincoln's profound grief and thus avoids the obvious inference, that he loved Ann Rutledge. Cf. Wilson, "Abraham Lincoln, Ann Rutledge, and the Evidence of Herndon's Informants," 301–23, esp. 320.

38. Lincoln to Mary Owens, Vandalia, 13 Dec. 1836, in Basler, *CWL*, 1:54–55.

39. Lincoln to Mary Owens, Springfield, 7 May 1837, in Basler, *CWL*, 1:78–79.

40. Robert L. Wilson to Herndon, Sterling, 10 Feb. 1866, H-W MSS, DLC. Wilson told this same story to Henry Whitney, dating Lincoln's remarks 1837. Whitney, *Life on the Circuit*, 140.

41. Speed to Herndon, Louisville, 13 Sept. 1866, H-W MSS, DLC; Herndon to Lamon, Springfield, 25 Feb. 1870, in Hertz, *HL*, 67; Herndon's memo on Nancy Hanks, Greencastle, Ind., 20 Aug. 1887, ibid., 412. When Herndon went to the files of the *Sangamo Journal* in search of this poem, he found that the spot where the piece was to have appeared had been clipped out of the paper. In his biography of Lincoln, Herndon dated the poem at 1841 and suggested that Lincoln himself clipped it from the newspaper. In his letter to Lamon, he dated it 1838. Angle, *HL*, 172. I have examined the surviving files of the *Sangamo Journal* and found no issue with a portion clipped out. It is possible that a single page or the entire issue is missing that contained the poem, if in fact it was published.

42. John G. Nicolay's interview with William Butler, June 1875, Hay MSS, RPB. Cf. William J. Butler, grandson of William Butler, in the *Illinois State Journal*, 28 Feb. 1937, 11; John G. Nicolay, "Lincoln's Personal Appearance," *Century Magazine* 42 (Oct. 1891): 936; Francis Fisher Browne, *The Every-Day Life of Abraham Lincoln* (New York: N. D. Thompson, 1886), 150–51. Butler's grandson stated that Lincoln actually moved into the Butler home after a few months and remained there until he was married in 1842. Herndon maintained that Lincoln boarded with Butler for free from 1837 to 1842. Herndon to Weik, N.p., 16 Jan. 1886, H-W MSS, DLC.

43. Speed to Herndon, N.d., in Angle, *HL*, 148.

44. Constance M. Dennehy, "Childhood Bereavement and Psychiatric Illness," *British Journal of Psychiatry* 112 (1966): 1063.

45. Logan's interview with John G. Nicolay, 6 July 1875, Hay MSS, DLC.

46. Duncan and Nickols, *Mentor Graham*, 175.

47. Emerson's reminiscences, in Ida M. Tarbell, *The Life of Abraham Lincoln*, 4 vols. (New York: Lincoln History Society, 1903), 2:60.

48. John J. Duff, *A. Lincoln: Prairie Lawyer* (New York: Holt, Rinehart and Winston, 1960), 323; Donn Piatt, in Benjamin P. Thomas and Harold M. Hyman, *Stanton: The Life and Times of Lincoln's Secretary of War* (New York: Alfred A. Knopf, 1962), 66.

49. William B. H. Dowse to Albert J. Beveridge, Boston, 16 Oct. 1925, Beveridge MSS, DLC.

50. Harding told this story to Benjamin Rush Cowen. Cowen, *Abraham Lincoln: An Appreciation by One Who Knew Him* (Cincinnati: Robert Clarke, 1909), 10–12. Cf. George Alfred Townsend's interview with Harding, clipping marked "Globe 11-9-1909," LMFW.

51. Report of a statement by Harding, N.d., typescript, Ida M. Tarbell MSS, Allegheny College. Later Stanton allegedly said, "What a mistake I made about that man when I met him in Cincinnati." Ibid.

52. W. M. Dickson, "Abraham Lincoln at Cincinnati," *Harper's New Monthly Magazine* 69 (June 1884): 62.

53. See chapter 8 in this volume. These setbacks may also have reinforced Lincoln's determination to succeed.

54. Nicolay's interview with Browning, Springfield, 17 June 1875. In January 1841, legal business took Browning to Springfield; he stayed at the home of William Butler, where Lincoln then boarded. Browning said "L[incoln]'s insanity was but an exaggerated attack of the fits of despondency or melancholy to which he was subject. . . . his greater trials and embarrassments pressed him down to a lower point than at other times."

55. Joshua F. Speed, *Reminiscences of Abraham Lincoln and Notes of a Visit to California: Two Lectures* (Louisville: John P. Morton, 1884), 39.

56. Statement by Speed, N.p., N.d., H-W MSS, DLC.

57. Letter from Jacksonville, 22 Jan. 1841, quoted in Basler, *CWL*, 1, 229n. Basler mistakenly identifies the author as "Martin McKee" instead of Martinette Hardin McKee.

58. Conkling to Mercy Levering, [Springfield], 24 Jan. 1841, in Carl Sandburg and Paul M. Angle, *Mary Lincoln, Wife and Widow* (New York: Harcourt, Brace, 1932), 179.

59. Jane D. Bell to Anne Bell, Springfield, 27 Jan. 1841, copy, JGR MSS, DLC.

60. Statement to Herndon, 3 May 1866, in Beveridge, *Lincoln*, 1:315, 316n.

61. Statement of Ninian Edwards, 22 Sept. 1865, and Mrs. Elizabeth Edwards's first statement, N.d., both in Beveridge, *Lincoln*, 1:314–15.

62. Lincoln to Stuart, Springfield, 20, 23 Jan. 1841, in Basler, *CWL*, 1:228–29.

63. Lincoln read parts of this letter to Speed. Speed to Herndon, N.p., 30 Nov. 1866, H-W MSS, DLC.

64. Beveridge, *Lincoln*, 1:289–90.

65. Strozier, *Lincoln's Quest for Union*, 42–45.

66. Lincoln to Speed, Springfield, 25 Feb. 1842, in Basler, *CWL*, 1:281.

67. Duff, *Prairie Lawyer,* 23–24, 35–36, 73.

68. Daniel J. Levinson et al., *The Seasons of a Man's Life* (New York: Alfred A. Knopf, 1978), 97–101 [quote on 99]. Mentors are usually eight to fifteen years older than protégés.

69. W. D. Howells, *Life of Abraham Lincoln* (Bloomington: Indiana University Press, 1960), 48.

70. Beveridge, *Lincoln,* 1:133.

71. Thomas, *Lincoln,* 54–55; Duff, *Prairie Lawyer,* 35–36.

72. William E. Baringer, "Lincoln Enters Politics," in *Lincoln for the Ages,* ed. Ralph G. Newman (Garden City: Doubleday, 1960), 71. Cf. Baringer, *Lincoln's Vandalia: A Pioneer Portrait* (New Brunswick: Rutgers University Press, 1949), 60–62; Paul Stroble, *High on the Okaw's Western Bank: Vandalia, Illinois, 1819–39* (Urbana: University of Illinois Press, 1992).

73. Mark E. Neely, Jr., *The Abraham Lincoln Encyclopedia* (New York: McGraw-Hill, 1982), 292. Cf. Rankin, *Personal Recollections,* 102–7.

74. Levinson et al., *The Seasons of a Man's Life,* 100–101.

75. Thomas, *Lincoln,* 95.

76. Duff, *Prairie Lawyer,* 73.

77. Angle, *HL,* 172–73. Cf. Beveridge, *Lincoln,* 1:318–21.

78. Speed to Herndon, Louisville, 17 Sept. 1866, H-W MSS, DLC.

79. Lincoln to Mary Speed, Bloomington, Ill., 27 Sept. 1841, in Basler, *CWL,* 1:261.

80. Basler, *CWL,* 4:546.

81. Rankin, *Personal Recollections,* 81–83, stresses how maternal Mrs. Greene was toward Lincoln.

82. Beveridge, *Lincoln,* 1:141; Benjamin P. Thomas, *Lincoln's New Salem,* 2d ed. (New York: Alfred A. Knopf, 1954), 115–16.

83. Thomas, *Lincoln's New Salem,* 112–13.

84. Duncan and Nickols, *Mentor Graham,* 104.

85. Rankin, *Personal Recollections,* 53–56, based on the recollections of W. G. Greene and Mentor Graham.

86. James Hurt, "All the Living and the Dead: Lincoln's Imagery," *American Literature* 52 (Nov. 1980): 357–60 [quote on 360].

87. "Farewell Address at Springfield, Illinois" version A, 11 Feb. 1861, in Basler, *CWL,* 4:190. Cf. Ruth Painter Randall, *Lincoln's Sons* (Boston: Little, Brown, 1955), 28–30.

88. Lincoln to John D. Johnston, Springfield, 23 Feb. 1850, in Basler, *CWL,* 2:77.

89. The Rev. James Smith, in Milton H. Shutes, *Lincoln and the Doctors: A Medical Narrative of the Life of Abraham Lincoln* (New York: Pioneer Press, 1933), 55; memo by Herndon, N.d., H-W MSS, DLC; "Little Eddie," *Sangamo Journal,* 7 Feb. 1850. Cf. Ida M. Tarbell, *In the Footsteps of the Lincolns* (New York: Harper and Brothers, 1924), 296–97.

90. John G. Nicolay notebook, Feb. 1862, quoted in *Lincoln Day by Day: A Chronology, 1809–1865,* ed. Earl Schenck Miers et al., 3 vols. (Washington, D.C.: Lincoln Sesquicentennial Commission, 1960), 3:96 [entry for 20 Feb. 1862].

91. Elizabeth Keckley, *Behind the Scenes: Thirty Years a Slave, and Four Years in the White House* (New York: G. W. Carleton, 1868), 103.

92. Anna L. Boyden, *Echoes from Hospital and White House: A Record of Mrs. Rebecca R. Pomroy's Experience in War-Times* (Boston: D. Lothrop, 1884), 56.

93. Keckley, *Behind the Scenes,* 103.

94. LeGrand B. Cannon, *Personal Reminiscences of the Rebellion, 1861–1866* (New York: Burr, 1895), 173–74.

95. Holland, *Lincoln,* 436.

96. Carpenter, *Six Months at the White House with Abraham Lincoln: The Story of a Picture* (New York: Hurd and Houghton, 1867), 293.

97. Noah Brooks, "Personal Recollections of Abraham Lincoln," *Harper's New Monthly Magazine* 31 (July 1865): 228.

98. John Hay's anonymous Washington dispatch, 22 Oct. 1861, *Missouri Republican* [St. Louis], 27 Oct. 1861, 2.

99. Charles Carlton Coffin in Rice, *RL,* 172.

100. J. Wainwright Ray to John G. Nicolay, Washington, 18 Oct. 1886, Nicolay MSS, DLC. Ray cites his wife as the authority for this description. At Baker's funeral, Charles Carlton Coffin observed Lincoln as "the tears rolled down his cheeks." In Rice, *RL,* 174.

101. John Hay diary, 14 May 1864, Hay MSS, RPB.

102. Statement by George P. Goff, enclosed in Goff to John G. Nicolay, Washington, 9 Feb. 1899, Nicolay MSS, DLC.

103. Introduction to Rice, *RL,* xxvii–xxix.

104. Henry C. Deming, *Eulogy of Abraham Lincoln* (Hartford: A. N. Clark, 1865), 40. Lincoln thought that had McClellan seized the initiative after the battle of Malvern Hill, he might have taken Richmond. Ibid. Cf. Lew Wallace's reminicences, clipping dated 1898, Indianapolis *Journal,* LMFW.

105. Annotation by Edward Bates on a letter of 2 Sept. 1862, in Basler, *CWL,* 5:486n.

106. William Henry Wadsworth to S. L. M. Barlow, Washington, 16 Dec. 1862, Barlow MSS, CSmH, copy of an excerpt, Allan Nevins MSS, Columbia University; Samuel Wilkeson to Sidney Howard Gay, [Washington, 19 Dec. 1862], Gay MSS, Columbia University. Another version of this statement appeared in the Chicago *Tribune,* 7 Feb. 1909: "If there is a man out of hell that suffers more than I do, I pity him."

107. Curtin's reminiscences, in William A. Mowry, "Some Incidents in the Life of Abraham Lincoln," *Uxbridge and Whitinsville* [Mass.] *Transcript,* 1913 (no day or month indicated), clipping, Harry E. Pratt MSS, University of Illinois Library, Urbana-Champaign.

108. William O. Stoddard, "White House Sketches, No. VII," New York *Citizen,* 29 Sept. 1866.

109. Reminiscences of Edward Rosewater, in Victor Rosewater, "Lincoln in Emancipation Days," *St. Nicholas* 65 (Feb. 1937): 13. Cf. interviews with Rosewater, 21 March 1898, Ida M. Tarbell MSS, Allegheny College and in Frank G. Carpenter, "President Lincoln's Telegraph Operators," unidentified clipping dated Omaha, 27 June (probably 1896), LMFW.

110. Noah Brooks, *Abraham Lincoln and the Downfall of American Slavery* (New York: G. P. Putnam's Sons, 1894), 358; Edwin Stanton, quoted by John Russell Young, Philadelphia *Times,* 1895, clipping, LMFW. The Lincoln believed that had Hooker reinforced Sedgwick when he heard his artillery on the far right of the Union line, he might have won a great victory. Deming, *Eulogy of Abraham Lincoln,* 40–41.

111. W. H. Smith claims he heard Ames tell this story in Washington in 1863. "Lincoln as the Loneliest Man," clipping from the *Drayter* [?] *Gleaner,* 2 Nov. 1937, LMFW.

112. Schuyler Colfax, quoted in "Ellsworth's Death Was Lincoln's Personal Sorrow," unidentified clipping, LMFW. Cf. Robert C. Ogden's recollections of a story Colfax told him, unidentified clipping, Judd Stewart Collection, Lincoln Scrapbooks, 3:6–7, CSmH.

113. James T. DuBois and Gertrude Mathews, *Galusha A. Grow: Father of the Homestead Law* (Boston: Houghton Mifflin, 1917), 267.

114. Delia A. P. Harvey to Col. J. H. Howe, Washington, 13 Sept. 1863, photcopy of typed manuscript, Civil War Miscellaneous Manuscripts Collection, series 2, Box 29, Sterling Library, Yale University.

115. Edward Dicey, "Lincolniana," *Macmillan's Magazine* 12 (June 1865): 191.

116. Herndon to Weik, Springfield, 17 Nov. 1885, H-W MSS, DLC. Cf. Herndon, "Double Consciousness of Lincoln," H-W MSS, DLC, and J. M. Ashley, *Reminiscences of the Great Rebellion: Calhoun, Seward and Lincoln; Address of Hon. J. M. Ashley at Memorial Hall, Toledo, June 2, 1890* (New York: Evening Post, 1890), 39.

117. Josiah Bushnell Grinnell, *Men and Events of Forty Years: Autobiographical Reminiscences of an Active Career from 1850 to 1890* (Boston: D. Lothrop, 1891), 171.

118. The Rev. Dr. Noyes W. Miner, "Personal Reminiscences of Abraham Lincoln," 46, manuscript dated 10 July 1881, SC 1052, folder 2, IHi. In April 1862 Lincoln said this to Miner, who shortly thereafter wrote "full notes" of the conversation.

119. Lincoln to Speed, Springfield, 13 Feb. 1842, in Basler, *CWL,* 1:269–70.

120. Charles Cowley, *Leaves from a Lawyer's Life Afloat and Ashore* (Boston: Lee and Shepard, 1879), 192.

121. William E. Barton, "Why Lincoln Was Sad," *Dearborn Independent,* 28 Aug. 1923, 6, 22. Barton claims that the correspondence of Mordecai Lincoln's children show that "they were all subject to the same depression and melancholy which was so characteristic of Abraham Lincoln." The correspondence about Cousin Mordecai is contained in two scrapbooks, both marked "The Illinois Lincolns," Barton MSS, University of Chicago. In Hancock County, people described Bernice V. Lovely's grandmother, Mary Rowena Lincoln (whose father, James Lincoln, was a cousin of Lincoln's) as a victim of the "Lincoln hippo." Another cousin, the second Mordecai, and Benjamin Mudd, son of Elizabeth Lincoln Mudd, suffered from what was called "the Lincoln horrors" (gloomy spells). Lovely to W. A. Evans, Colchester, Ill., 21 April 1921,

and Lovely to Barton, Colchester, Ill., 14 May 1922, vol. 1, "The Illinois Lincolns" scrapbook, Barton MSS, University of Chicago. A. R. Simmons, son of a neighbor of Lincoln's, heard his father talk about "moody spells" as one of the Lincoln family characteristics. Simmons to Barton, Colchester, Ill., 7 March 1923, Barton MSS, University of Chicago. Lincoln physically resembled Robert and his brother Hezekiah (Lincoln's cousins), as well as Mordecai, according to A. R. Simmons of Colchester. Interview with Barton, 12 Oct. 1923, Barton MSS, University of Chicago.

122. Herndon to C. O. Poole, Springfield, 5 Jan. 1886, H-W MSS, DLC.

123. Whitney to Herndon, [Chicago], 23 June 1887, H-W MSS, DLC.

124. Robert H. Browne, *Abraham Lincoln and the Men of His Time*, 2 vols. (Cincinnati: Jennings and Pye; New York: Eaton and Mains, 1901), 1:82–83.

125. Carlo Perris, "The Distinction between Bipolar and Unipolar Affective Disorders," in *Handbook of Affective Disorders*, ed. Paykel, 45–58.

126. Strozier, *Lincoln's Quest for Union*, 26, 28; Fehrenbacher, *Lincoln in Text and Context*, 224–26. Cf. Strozier's response in *The Historian's Lincoln*, ed. Boritt, 21–22. Lincoln as a youth may well have felt common Oedipal urges. In a careful analysis of Lincoln's satirical poem "The Chronicles of Reuben," Howard M. Feinstein argues that its author harbored illicit sexual wishes for his sister or his mother. Feinstein, "'The Chronicles of Reuben': A Psychological Test of Authenticity," *American Quarterly* 18 (Winter 1966): 637–54.

127. Morton Prince to Beveridge, Nahant, Mass., 1, 26 Sept., 13 Oct. 1925, Beveridge MSS, DLC.

128. Lord Charnwood, *Abraham Lincoln* (London: Constable, 1916), 7. Cf. John G. Nicolay and John Hay, *Abraham Lincoln: A History*, 10 vols. (New York: Century, 1890), 1:187–90.

129. Herndon to C. O. Poole, Springfield, 5 Jan. 1886, H-W MSS, DLC; and Herndon to Lamon, Springfield, 25 Feb. 1870, in Lamon MSS, CSmH.

130. Philip Greven, *Spare the Child: The Religious Roots of Punishment and the Psychological Impact of Physical Abuse* (New York: Alfred A. Knopf, 1991), 130–35 [quote from 130].

131. Augustus H. Chapman, in Ward H. Lamon, *The Life of Abraham Lincoln from His Birth to His Inauguration as President* (Boston: James R. Osgood, 1872), 40n. Also see chapter 2 in this volume.

132. Interview with Gollaher by D. J. Thomas, in Ida M. Tarbell with J. McCan Davis, *The Early Life of Abraham Lincoln* (New York: McClure, 1896), 44, 46. Gollaher told the same story to Howard Burba. See Burba, "A Story of Lincoln's Boyhood," *American Boy* [Detroit], Feb. 1905.

133. Maurice Boyd, *William Knox and Abraham Lincoln: The Story of a Poetic Legacy* (Denver: Sage Books, 1966); William D. Kelley in Rice, *RL*, 268–70; James Grant Wilson in *Intimate Memories of Lincoln*, ed. Wilson, 423–24; Lawrence Weldon's speech before the Springfield bar, June 1865, in Angle, *HL*, 496–97; Carpenter, *Six Months at the White House*, 58–61.

134. Lincoln to Andrew Johnston, Tremont, 18 April 1846, in Basler, *CWL*, 1:378.

135. Weldon in Rice, *RL*, 213.

136. Lamon, *Recollections of Lincoln*, 155; cf. Lamon to S. J. Perkins, Washington, 30 Sept. 1864, Lamon MSS, CSmH.

137. Douglas L. Wilson, "Abraham Lincoln's Indiana and the Spirit of Mortal," *Indiana Magazine of History* 87 (June 1991): 155–70.

138. Lincoln to Andrew Johnston, Tremont, 18 April 1846, in Basler, *CWL*, 1:378.

139. According to William H. Townsend, Lincoln "was particularly impressed with Cowper's poem . . . and drew a hand with the index finger pointing to the stanza" that he found in *Elegant Extracts; Or, Useful and Entertaining Passages from the Best English Authors and Translations*. Lincoln "marked or underscored heavily with a lead pencil" certain passages when he visited his in-laws in Kentucky in 1847 and 1849. Townsend, *Lincoln and the Bluegrass: Slavery and Civil War in Kentucky* ([Lexington]: University Press of Kentucky, 1955), 136.

140. Basler, *CWL*, 1:378–79.

141. Basler, *CWL*, 1:1.

142. Angle, *HL*, 259–60.

143. John Hay, "Life in the White House in the Time of Lincoln," in Hay, *Addresses of John Hay* (New York: Century, 1906), 334–35.

144. James M. Scovel, in *Intimate Memories of Lincoln*, ed. Wilson, 525.

145. Reminiscences of Elizabeth Crawford, in Hertz, *HL*, 293.

146. Milton Hay to John Hay, Springfield, 8 Feb. 1887, Hay MSS, RPB.

147. Lamon, *Reminiscences of Lincoln*, 150–51.

148. See Whitney, *Life on the Circuit*, 482–83.

149. Carpenter, *Six Months in the White House*, 59. Cf. James Grant Wilson's reminiscences in *Intimate Memories of Lincoln*, ed. Wilson, 423–24; Hay, "Life in the White House in the Time of Lincoln," 336; Angle, *HL*, 258.

150. Angle, *HL*, 258.

151. Whitney, *Lincoln*, 1:238.

6

Lincoln's Attitude toward Women: The Most Striking Contradiction of a Complex Character

Abraham Lincoln did not like women.[1] His stepmother, with whom he lived from his eleventh to his twenty-third year, recalled that he "was not very fond of girls," a conclusion supported by his stepbrother, who said that he "didn't take much truck with the girls" because "he was too busy studying."[2] One schoolmate with whom he studied during his Indiana years, Anna C. Roby, testified from firsthand experience that Lincoln "didn't like girls much" and "did not go much with the girls" because he thought them "too frivolous."[3] Lincoln's cousin Sophie Hanks, who lived with the Lincolns for several years during his youth, told her son that young Abraham "didn[']t like the girls['] company."[4] Another of Lincoln's cousins, John Hanks, who also stayed with the Lincoln family for many years, recalled that "I never could get him in company with women; he was not a timid man in this particular, but he did not seek such company."[5]

Some accounts suggest that once he reached the age of seventeen, Lincoln began to take a romantic interest in Indiana girls, but little evidence documents these adolescent affairs of the heart.[6] They were unknown to such friends and neighbors as Joseph C. Richardson, who said that Lincoln "never seemed to care for the girls," or to David Turnham, who averred that Lincoln "did not seem to seek the company of the girls and when [with] them was rather backward."[7] Another companion of Lincoln's youth, Jason Duncan, maintained that Lincoln "was very reserved toward the opposite sex" and never "paid address" to them.[8] His cousin, Dennis Hanks, also recalled that Lincoln "didn[']t love the company of girls" and was the "bashfullest boy that ever lived."[9]

The feeling was reciprocated by females Lincoln knew in Indiana. One later recalled, "I never found any fault with him excepting he was so tall and awkward. All the young girls my age made fun of Abe.

They'd laugh at him right before his face, but Abe never 'peared to care. He was so good and he'd just laugh with them. Abe tried to go with some of them, but no sir-ee, they'd give him the mitten every time, just because he was . . . so tall and gawky, and it was mighty awkward I can tell you trying to keep company with a fellow as tall as Abe was."[10] Another was repelled by "his awkwardness and large feet."[11] Yet another remembered that Lincoln "wus so quiet and awkward and so awful homely" that "girls didn't much care" about him, and he in turn "never made up to the girls."[12] When Elizabeth Tuley was courted by Lincoln, her friends teased her "unmercifully" about "his coatsleeves and pantlegs always being too short."[13]

When he moved to Illinois at the age of twenty-one, Lincoln continued to show little interest in the opposite sex, according to N. W. Brandon, a New Salem acquaintance. Echoing John Hanks, Brandon said Lincoln "didn't go to see the girls much. He didn't appear bashful, but it seemed as if he cared but little for them." Although he "always liked lively, jovial company," Lincoln "would just as lieve the company were all men as to have it a mixture of the sexes."[14] William Greene observed that in New Salem "Lincoln was fearfully awkward and timid when girls were around." A friend of Greene's, J. Q. Spears, recalled that Lincoln in New Salem was "very bashful and about the gawkiest young man you ever saw."[15]

A young New Salem woman, Susan Reid, stated that when Lincoln courted her in 1836, he seemed to be "a very queer fellow": "very bashful," "very awkward," and "very homely."[16] Later in Springfield he did not grow more sophisticated, according to Martinette Hardin, whom he also courted. He was "so awkward that I was always sorry for him," she told a visitor. "He did not seem to know what to say in the company of women. . . . While he was never at ease with women, with men he was a favorite companion."[17]

At work as well as social gatherings, Lincoln would rather deal with males. Abner Y. Ellis, owner of a New Salem store where he clerked, remembered that Lincoln "always disliked to wait on the Ladies," preferring, he said, "trading with the Men & Boys." Even when eating, Lincoln avoided women. Ellis told Herndon that "on one occasion while we boarded at this Tavern there came a family containing an old Lady[,] her Son and Three stilish Daughters from the State of Virginia and stopped there for 2 or 3 weeks and during their stay I do not remember of Mr. Lincoln ever eating at the same table when they did."[18] As a young legislator, he was, a colleague recalled, "very awkward, and very much

Self &
confidence

embarrassed in the presence of ladies."[19] A New Salem woman remembered that "Lincoln was not much of a beau and seemed to prefer the company of the elderly ladies to the young ones."[20] Those more mature women included Hannah Armstrong, Nancy Greene, and Mrs. Bennett Abell, who were in effect surrogate mothers.[21]

Lincoln once humiliated a New Salem girl with his barbed wit, which he normally unleashed only on political opponents. He was serving food at a party when, as one of the guests recalled, "a girl there who thought herself pretty smart" protested when he filled her plate with an exceptionally generous portion. She said "quite pert and sharp, 'Well, Mr. Lincoln, I didn't want a cart-load.'" Later, when she said she would like some more food, he announced in a voice loud enough for everyone in the room to hear, "All right, Miss Liddy, back up your cart and I'll fill it again." The party-goers all laughed save for Miss Liddy, who "went off by herself and cried the whole evening."[22]

Once married, Lincoln still felt uncomfortable around women. William Herndon stated flatly that "after his marriage it cannot be said that he liked the society of ladies; in fact, it was just what he did not like."[23] Henry C. Whitney often observed Lincoln's painful embarrassment and concluded that "he had very little courage to confront the fair sex; on the contrary, he was very shy, bashful, and awkward in [the] presence of ladies: unless, and sometimes even if, he knew them very well." One day Lincoln and Whitney attended a tea at the home of the mayor of Urbana. Joining them were the mayor's wife and Whitney's mother. Lincoln "got along so-so" until Whitney had to leave briefly; upon returning, he found Lincoln "as demoralized and ill at ease as a bashful country boy. He would put his arms behind him, and bring them to the front again, as if trying to hide them, and he tried apparently but in vain to get his long legs out of sight." In 1858, Whitney and Lincoln were introduced to a group of women as they awaited a train. Lincoln "bowed as awkwardly and under as much embarrassment as could be imagined—and then with extreme awkwardness put down his carpet bag, and shifting his umbrella to his other hand, and putting out his disengaged hand, said, 'Howdo! Howdo!! I don't know how to talk to ladies; Whitney can tell you that.'"[24] Two years later he penned a brief note to one Mrs. M. J. Green in which he confessed, "I have never corresponded much with ladies; and hence I postpone writing letters to them, as a business which I do not understand."[25] Toward the end of the Civil War, the president told a crowd at a Sanitary Fair that he had "never studied the art of paying compliments to women."[26]

In light of such evidence, it is hard to quarrel with Albert J. Beveridge's conclusion that "Lincoln never got on well with women" and "did not understand" them.[27]

· · ·

According to Helen Nicolay, "Nothing showed his patience and kindliness more than his manner with the women who came to the Executive Office—and many were the militant females he encountered."[28] Shortly after her October 29, 1864, interview with the chief executive, Sojourner Truth wrote that "I never was treated by any one with more kindness and cordiality than were shown to me by that great and good man, Abraham Lincoln."[29] White House secretary William O. Stoddard recalled that Lincoln's "manner with the softer sex was kindly and courteous," and that he was especially solicitous of "the ministering angels who went to and fro among our camps and hospitals" and the "sorrowing and broken hearted mothers, wives, or sisters, of suffering or erring men in the army." And yet, Stoddard noted, Lincoln's "chivalrous deference for women" seldom led him to "yield special privileges." In fact, "it seemed an unpleasant and irksome thing to him to have a lady present a petition for any favor when the same duty could as well have been performed by a man; and if there was anything contrary to propriety or policy in the matter presented, or if the petitioner presumed upon her feminine prerogative to press too far upon his good-nature, she was very likely to receive an answer in which there was far more of truth and justice than flattery."[30]

Among the "militant females" who provoked Lincoln to respond with little flattery were two strong-willed women who, in the opinion of Roy P. Basler, received shabby treatment from the president.[31] The first was Anna E. Dickinson, a Quaker abolitionist known as the American Joan of Arc.[32] In 1862 she publicly criticized Lincoln for being "not so far from . . . a slave-catcher after all" and privately denounced him as "an Ass . . . for the Slave Power to ride."[33] Two years later she called him "the wisest scoundrel in the country" and declared that "I would rather lose all the reputation I possess & sell apples & peanuts on the street, then say aught, that would gain a vote for him."[34] That same year Dickinson visited the president and urged a more vigorous enforcement of the Emancipation Proclamation. As she later explained to an audience in Boston, the president tried to divert her by telling a story. She interrupted, saying "I didn't come to hear stories. I can read better ones in the papers any day than you can tell me."

The president then showed Dickinson some letters regarding the progress of reconstruction in Louisiana. When he asked her opinion of his reconstruction policy, she called it "all wrong; as radically bad as can be." In response, Lincoln paid her some compliments and closed by saying, "If the radicals want me to lead, let them get out of the way and let me lead." The indignant Dickinson told a friend, "I have spoken my last word to President Lincoln." As she related this tale in Boston, she ridiculed Lincoln's appearance, especially "his old coat, out at the elbows[,] which look[ed] as if he had worn it three years and used it as a pen wiper" and his "stocking limp and soiled."[35]

One of Anna Dickinson's mentors, J. M. McKim, heard the interview described in much different terms: "A. E. D. said but very few words. She was more a witness than a party. What she did say was 'fool'ish according to her own acknowledgment at the time. She burst into tears—struck an attitude and begged Mr. L. to excuse her for coming there to make a fool of herself. The President was paternally kind and considerate in what he said to her."[36] If Dickinson's version of the interview is accurate, her abrasive, not to say rude, manner makes Lincoln's conduct seem restrained. Had she been a male, he might well have responded as he did to an insolent man whom he threw out of the office with the explanation, "I can bear censure, but not insult!"[37]

The other woman who, in Basler's judgment, fared poorly at the hands of Lincoln was Anna Ella Carroll, a gifted writer, political activist, and member of a distinguished Maryland family. She also possessed a streak of vanity, an "imperious nature," and an "obsession for power and recognition."[38] In the 1850s the militantly anti-Catholic Carroll toiled for nativist candidates on the state and national levels, and during the secession crisis she helped keep Maryland in the Union. Early in the war she wrote two eloquent pamphlets: a reply to Kentucky Senator John C. Breckinridge, who had urged the border states to secede, and a defense of the Lincoln administration's sweeping assertions of executive power. In 1862 she again vindicated the administration in "The Relation of the National Government to the Revolted Citizens Defined."[39] In May 1862, Lincoln allegedly told several congressmen that Carroll, "the head of the Carroll race," will "stand a good deal taller than ever old Charles Carroll did" when "the history of this war is written."[40]

When three months later Carroll presented a bill of $50,000 for writing, printing, and distributing these three documents, Lincoln was not so laudatory. He called her demand "the most outrageous one, ever made to any government, upon earth." In an angry reply, she said, "The difference between us, was in our views, upon the value of intellectual laber."[41] Basler considered Lincoln's reaction "understandable, but scarcely justifiable."[42] Yet it seems reasonable considering that her bill was twice the amount of Lincoln's annual salary. Historians have, for the most part, found her claims insupportable.[43] Carroll's biographer presents evidence that she was a "swindler, guilty of forgery, lying, and fraudulent misrepresentation."[44]

Basler incorrectly stated that Lincoln "did not treat any man who interviewed him or wrote to him . . . with so little apparent respect for his intelligence for holding views at odds with those of the president of the United States."[45] In fact, he did address equally sharp words to male callers who, in his opinion, made excessive demands on the government (chapter 7). Basler's suggestion that Lincoln exploded solely because Carroll disagreed with him on a general policy matter is also misleading. The president simply thought that she was vastly overcharging a beleaguered government for her modest if helpful services, a conclusion that seems unexceptionable. Later she would make the dubious claim that she alone was responsible for the strategy of General Grant's 1862 Tennessee River campaign; for this contribution to the cause she demanded a quarter of a million dollars.[46]

Basler did not fault Lincoln for losing patience with Jessie Benton Frémont, wife of General John C. Frémont. In September 1861 she delivered to the president a letter from her husband, whom Lincoln had chastised for unilaterally freeing the slaves in Missouri. She reported that Lincoln treated her rudely and failed to offer her a seat. As she later wrote, the president accepted the letter "with an expression that was not agreeable." After she defended her husband's actions, Lincoln said in "a sneering tone" that she was "quite a female politician."[47]

Lincoln's version of the interview differs from Jessie Benton Frémont's. He told friends that she "taxed me so violently with many things that I had to exercise all the awkward tact I have to avoid quarreling with her. . . . She more than once intimated that if Gen. Fremont should conclude to try conclusions with me he could set up for himself."[48] To an Iowa congressman, Lincoln recalled that Mrs. Frémont, after "opening her case with mild expostulation . . . left in anger flaunting her handkerchief before my face, and saying, 'Sir, the general will try titles with you. He is a man and I am his wife.'"[49] After she left, Lincoln wrote to her, denying that he doubted her husband's "honor or integrity" and protesting "against being understood as acting in any hostility towards him."[50] If Lincoln did "lose his cool" with her, as Basler put it, one can scarcely wonder.

Basler suggested that Lincoln managed to retain his equanimity when dealing with "forceful women such as Jane Swisshelm, Dorothea Dix, and Clara Barton" because "their work did not take them out of the male-approved female role of nurse and comforter of the sick and wounded."[51] This statement is misleading. In fact, Jane Swisshelm was not much interested in care for the sick and wounded; rather, she lobbied primarily for a more vigorous antislavery policy and then for harsh punishment of the Sioux in Minnesota, who had risen up in 1862. "Exterminate the wild beasts and make peace with the devil and all his host sooner than with these red-jawed tigers whose fangs are dripping with the blood of the innocents," she counseled. But she, like Barton and Dix, did not resort to rudeness in dealing with the president.[52]

Furthermore, Lincoln did respond sharply to Cordelia A. P. Harvey, who in the summer of 1863 lobbied him on six occasions to establish military hospitals in the North as well as near the Southern battlefields. Unlike the Frémont episode, only one version of this story has survived—Harvey's. If she is to be believed, she was treated sharply by the president. While explaining how wounded soldiers perished in the unhealthy climate of the lower South, she noted, "There are thousands of graves all along the Mississippi and the Yazoo, for which the government is responsible, ignorantly, undoubtedly, but this ignorance must not continue." Bristling at this criticism, Lincoln challenged her almost contemptuously, calling the plan "a fine way to decimate the army," for the troops would desert from hospitals in the North.

In later interviews, the president displayed more pique. When Cordelia Harvey pressed him for a decision, he "impatiently" snapped, "I believe this idea of Northern hospitals is all a great humbug, and I am tired of hearing about them." As she continued her pleas, he sharply interjected, "You assume to know more than I do!" and, later, "You assume to know more than surgeons do!" Exasperated by her manner, Lincoln finally asked her how many Wisconsin men were in the army and said, "I have a good mind to dismiss them all from the service and have no more trouble with them."

In the end, Lincoln approved Cordelia Harvey's plan, informing her that a military hospital would be named after her late husband, Wisconsin Governor Lewis Harvey. As they discussed the matter, the president asked, "Don't you ever get angry? I know a little woman not very unlike you that gets mad sometimes." She replied that she did not and thanked him effusively for his action.[53]

Lincoln may have had Harvey in mind when, in 1864, he paid tribute to the women who had aided sick and wounded troops. At a Sanitary Fair he told the crowd that "if all that has been said by orators and poets since the creation of the world in praise of woman were applied to the women of America, it would not do them justice for their conduct during this war. . . . God bless the women of America!"[54]

The story of Lincoln's clash with Harvey illustrates why he told a female petitioner, "I never could argue with women, they always get the best of me."[55] Similarly, he described Mrs. Gabriel R. Paul, who lobbied to have her husband awarded a general's stars, as "a saucy woman" and concluded that "I am afraid she will keep tormenting me till I may have to do it."[56]

A female "Quaker Preacher" once taxed Lincoln's patience as she self-righteously pleaded for the end of slavery. He listened "with an air of ill-subdued impatience" as she told him that the Almighty has chosen him to end human bondage. "I have neither time nor disposition to enter into discussion with the Friend," Lincoln responded curtly, "and end this occasion by suggesting for her consideration the question whether, if it be true that the Lord has appointed me to do the work she has indicated, it is not probable that He would have communicated knowledge of the fact to me as well as to her."[57]

Women from the opposite end of the political spectrum also could arouse presidential anger. When a Mississippi widow whose slaves had been confiscated appealed to Lincoln to lend her some freedmen to run her farm, he "became very excited." He "said with great vehemence that he had rather take a rope and hang himself" or *"throw up"* than to do what was asked. He pointed out that "there were a great many poor women who had never had any property at all who were suffering as much" as the petitioner, and "that her condition was a necessary consequence of the rebellion, and that the government could not make good the losses occasioned by rebels."[58]

In November 1864 Lincoln refused a woman's plea for the release of her spouse from prison. After reading her petition he said, "This will not do. I can do nothing for your husband."

"Why not?"

"Because he is not loyal."

"But he intends to be; he wants to take the oath of allegiance."

"That is the way with all who get into prison. I can do nothing for you."

"But you would if you knew my circumstances."

"No, I would not. I am under no obligation to provide for the wives of disloyal husbands." Sarcastically he asked, "Hasn't your husband the consumption?"

"No."

"Well, it is the only case. Nearly all have the consumption."[59]

Lincoln lost his composure when dealing with another Confederate matron, Martha Todd White, his wife's half-sister. In the spring of 1864 she called at the White House, where the Lincolns would not see her. The president did, however, send her a pass for travel back to the South. She returned it, asking for special permission to have her luggage exempt from inspection. When Lincoln refused, White dispatched emissaries to plead her case. To one of those gentlemen, Lincoln said that "if Mrs. W[hite] did not leave forthwith she might expect to find herself within twenty-four hours in the Old Capitol Prison."[60] Thomas F. Pendel, a White House servant, remembered that the president once refused two beautiful Southern women a pass to Richmond: "No, I won't give it to you. You will go down there and tell them what our army is doing." The women stayed on while Lincoln transacted other business. Finally he said, "If I don't give you the pass, you will only stay here and smuggle information to Richmond, so you might as well take it in person."[61]

These stories tend to confirm Ward Hill Lamon's assertion that Lincoln granted passes to pro-Confederate women after rebuking them: "He would scold them—saying—'You would kill me if you could—and still you are asking favors of me—.'" As the weeping suppliant started to leave, the president would say, "Now if you go back South, you will do some mischief—You would overturn the Government if you could," but he would issue a pass nonetheless.[62]

Lincoln was abrupt with such a woman from Baltimore who wanted to visit a sick relative in Richmond. With a few questions, he learned that his caller was "intensely rebel." He offered her a deal: "I'll compromise with you. I don't know but I would be willing to give you a pass to Richmond if you will promise to not come back again." Indignantly the offended matron bustled from the office without further words.[63]

Shortly after this interview, another woman appealed to the president to release her son, who had been caught smuggling vital supplies to the Confederates. To bolster her case, she presented a letter from a prominent Marylander who, it developed, was dead. Lincoln then dismissed her, saying, "Now, Madam, I do not think you are treating me fairly. Your son has been tried by a sworn court, and convicted. . . . and now you ask me to pardon him and set the verdict aside just as a matter of humanity and kindness to you. I do not think that fair to me, and while I would like to gratify you, I suspect if I should do so, it would not be two weeks before he would be doing the same thing again: and I am not at all sure but that is just what you would like to have him do."[64] Lot M. Morrill recalled a similar event:

> At one time when I went into the room to President Lincoln, there were two women from Baltimore there who had come to try to obtain the release and parole of a prisoner of war who had been captured, and was then confined at Point Lookout. One of them was the mother of the young rebel, and after detailing his alleged sufferings wound up her sympathetic appeals with the usual finale of such interviews, a copious shower of tears. At this point the president, who had patiently listened to the recital, asked casually when and how the boy had gone into the confederate service? The mother with evident pride, quickly responded with the whole history: he had gone south early in the war, served in such and such campaigns, made such and such marches, and survived such and such battles.
> "And now that he is taken prisoner it is the first time, probably, that you have ever shed tears over what your boy has done?["] asked the President with emphasis.
> The question was so direct, and so completely described the true situation of affairs that the woman could frame no equivocation[.] She sat dumb, and visibly convicted of her secession sympathies, by the very simple inquiry.
> "Good morning Madam," said the President[,] "I can do nothing for your boy today."[65]

Early in 1864 Lincoln rejected a wife's appeal on behalf of her husband, who had, in the president's words, "knowingly and willfully helped a rebel to get out of our lines to the enemy to join in fighting and killing our people." He was blunt in his dismissal of the woman's protestations of devotion to the Union cause: "You pretend . . . that you and he are loyal, and you may really think so, but this is a view of loyalty which it is difficult to conceive that any sane person could take, and one which the government may not tolerate and hope to live—And even now, what is the great anxiety of you and your husband to get to

Washington but to get into a better position to repeat this species of loyalty? There is certainly room enough North of the Susquehanna for a great variety of honest occupations."[66]

Inspired by a vision of how to win the war, a female congregant of Henry Ward Beecher's church in Brooklyn called at the White House and insisted that she see the president immediately. Obligingly, Lincoln left a meeting to learn what the woman wanted. After she recounted her strategy for subduing the rebellion, he said "with abruptness and impatience" before taking his leave, "Madam, all this has been thought of a hundred times before!"[67]

· · ·

Lincoln's romantic dealings with women were marked by a strange passivity.[68] Nowhere is that more clearly illustrated than in his peculiar courtship of Mary Owens, which sheds much light on his attitude toward women. Kentucky-born, well educated, attractive, wealthy, and socially poised, Owens was, as her son described her, "a good conversationalist and a splendid reader" and "light-hearted and cheery."[69] Lincoln met her in 1833, while she was visiting her sister, Mrs. Bennett Abell, in New Salem. He thought her "intel[l]igent and agreeable." After a month in Illinois, she returned to Kentucky.

Three years later, Mrs. Abell made a strange proposal to Lincoln: She was going to visit relatives in Kentucky and would bring back her sister if he would agree to wed her "with all convenient dispatch." Incredibly, Lincoln accepted the offer, for, as he later wrote, he "was most confoundedly well pleased with the project," seeing "no good objection to plodding life through hand in hand with her."

When Mrs. Abell returned with Mary Owens, however, Lincoln regretted his rash promise. She was so fat that, he said, she "appeared a match for Falstaff" and had such a "weather-beaten appearance" that she seemed to be in her late thirties, although in fact she was but a few months senior to the twenty-seven-year-old Lincoln. But he felt honor-bound to carry out his pledge. As he explained to the wife of his friend Orville Browning, "What could I do? I had told her sister that I would take her for better or for worse; and I made a point of honor and conscience in all things, to stick to my word, especially if others had been induced to act on it." Still, he "dreaded as much—perhaps more, than an irishman does the halter" the thought of marriage.[70]

Rather than renege on his promise to Mrs. Abell, Lincoln courted Mary Owens for several months before screwing up the courage to propose. When he finally did so, it was in a most self-deprecating, passive manner. Acutely self-conscious because of his social awkwardness and poverty, he told the young woman that she should reject his offer of marriage.[71]

> I want in all cases to do right, and most particularly so, in all cases with women. I want . . . more than any thing else, to do right with you, and if I *knew* it would be doing right, as I rather suspect it would, to let you alone, I would do it. And for the purpose of making the matter as plain as possible, I now say, that you can now drop the subject, dismiss your thought (if you ever had any) from me forever, and leave this letter unanswered, without calling forth one accusing murmur from me. And I will even go further, and say, that if it will add any thing to your comfort, or peace of mind, to do so, it is my sincere wish that you should. Do not understand by this, that I wish to cut your acquaintance. I mean no such thing. What I do wish is, that our further acquaintance shall depend upon yourself. If such further acquaintance would contribute nothing to your happiness, I am sure it would not to mine. If you feel yourself in any degree bound to me, I am now willing to release you, provided you wish it; while, on the other hand, I am willing, and even anxious to bind you faster, if I can be convinced that it will, in any considerable degree, add to your happiness.[72]

Not surprisingly, Mary Owens rejected this diffident proposal. As she later explained, "Mr. Lincoln was deficient in those little links which make up the chain of woman's happiness. . . . Not that I believed it proceeded from a lack of goodness of heart; but his training had been different from mine; hence there was not that congeniality which would otherwise have existed."[73]

Lincoln had behaved in ways that she understandably considered thoughtless and insensitive to her feelings. One day, for example, while riding with other New Salem young women and their swains, they came to a creek. All the men save Lincoln gallantly helped their companions cross. Owens chided her escort, "You are a nice fellow! I suppose you did not care whether my neck was broken or not." Lincoln replied laughingly that he reckoned she was plenty smart enough to care for herself.[74]

In Springfield, another woman, Rosanna Schmink, also found Lincoln gauche, for when he called to take her to a "wool picking" he failed to provide her with a horse. According to her granddaughter, Schmink "had to ride behind him, and being a southern girl and very proud, she did not like that and said she would never go any place with him again."[75] To Mary Owens Lincoln frankly acknowledged his awkwardness around women. Shortly after moving to Springfield, he told her, "I have been spoken to by but one woman since I've been here, and should not have been by her, if she could have avoided it."[76]

When Mary Owens spurned his proposal, Lincoln found himself "mortified beyond endurance." As he told Mrs. Browning,

> I was mortified . . . in a hundred different ways. My vanity was deeply wounded by the reflection, that I had so long been too stupid to discover her intentions, and at the same time never doubting that I understood them perfectly; and also, that she whom I had taught myself to believe no body else would have, had actually rejected me with all my fancied greatness; and to cap the whole, I then, for the first time, began to suspect that I was really a little in love with her. But let it all go. I'll try and out live it. Others have been made fools of by the girls; but this can never be with truth said of me. I most emphatically, in this instance, made a fool of myself. I have now come to the conclusion never again to think of marrying; and for this reason; I can never be satisfied with any one who would be block-head enough to have me.[77]

The bizarre courtship illustrates several important aspects of Lincoln's attitude toward women: his passivity, his feelings of inadequacy, his deep ambivalence about marriage and intimacy, and his scrupulous determination to carry out promises, even bad ones.

Lincoln was also turned down by Sarah Rickard, the sister of another one of his surrogate mothers, Mrs. William Butler. From 1837 to 1842, Lincoln boarded at the Butlers' house, where Rickard was living. When they first met, she was twelve, and Lincoln, considerably her senior, took her to a play. Four years later he paid her serious court and eventually proposed marriage, suggesting that, because her name was Sarah, she was destined to marry Abraham. She declined because of their age difference and because, as she put it, "his peculiar manner and his general deportment would not be likely to fascinate a young girl just entering the society world."[78]

The importance of Lincoln's relationship with Ann Rutledge, the pretty daughter of the owner of the New Salem tavern where Lincoln boarded for a time, has been skeptically dismissed by some scholars. As John Y. Simon concluded, however, "Available evidence overwhelmingly indicates that Lincoln so loved Ann that her death plunged him into severe depression." Lincoln wooed Ann, and she probably accepted his proposal before she died in 1835.[79]

Sometimes Lincoln joked about his inability to attract the opposite sex. He once told his colleagues in the Illinois legislature that "if any woman, old or young, ever thought there was any peculiar charm in this distinguished specimen . . . I have, as yet, been so unfortunate as not to have discovered it."[80] In the mid-1850s he was strongly attracted to Lois E. Hillis, a singer performing with a traveling concert troupe. When his colleagues at the bar chaffed him about her, he replied, "Don't trouble yourselves, boys; there's no danger. She's actually the only woman in the world, outside of my wife, who ever dared to pay me a compliment, and if the poor thing is attracted to my handsome face and graceful figure it seems to me you homely fellows are the last people on earth who ought to complain."[81] One day, at her request, Lincoln recited to Hillis his favorite poem, the lugubrious "O Why Should the Spirit of Mortal Be Proud" by William Knox. Later he wrote it out for her and, as he gave it to her, called her "my dear."[82]

Although Lincoln felt uneasy around women and did not much like them, little evidence suggests that he regarded them as inherently inferior to men.[83] In fact, he endorsed women's suffrage during his campaign for reelection to the Illinois legislature in 1836: "I go for admitting all whites to the right of suffrage, who pay taxes or bear arms, (by no means excluding females)."[84] In the late 1850s he told a young woman who expressed a desire to vote, "I believe you will vote, my young friend, before you are much older than I."[85] Lincoln also deplored the sexual double standard. According to Herndon, Lincoln's "idea was that a woman had the same right to play with her tail that a man had and no more nor less and that he had no moral or other right to violate the sacred marriage vow."[86]

During the Civil War, Lincoln eagerly sought excuses to spare soldiers condemned to death by courts martial. According to the judge advocate general, the president made an exception to this rule for rape cases: ["]He shrank with evident pain from even the idea of shedding human blood. . . . In every case he always leaned to the side of mercy. His constant desire was to save life. There was only one class of crimes I always found him prompt to punish—a crime which occurs more or less frequently about all armies—namely, outrages upon women. He never hesitated to approve the sentence in these cases."[87]

Wife-beaters also provoked Lincoln's anger. In 1839 he and some friends warned a shoemaker to stop whipping his spouse or else they would whip him. One of those friends later recalled that when the shoemaker ignored the threat and hit his wife, Lincoln and his accomplices "tied him to a post near a well back of [the] Court House[,] stripped his shirt—sent for his wife—who whaled him tremendously." Lincoln had "wanted to do it himself a few days before."[88]

. . .

The origins of Lincoln's feelings about women are unclear. As Albert J. Beveridge put it, "Of the many contradictions in his complex character, no one is more striking than his attitude toward women."[89] Evidently Lincoln feared that he might be abandoned by a woman, just as his mother had abandoned him by dying when he was a boy of nine. The bitter agony that he experienced as a youth in Indiana probably crippled his capacity for trusting and loving women lest they, like Nancy Hanks, desert him.

Lincoln's relationship with his mother is often portrayed sentimentally, with heavy emphasis laid on his purported declaration that "all that I am, or hope to be, I owe to my angel mother."[90] That celebrated statement has been widely misinterpreted. In his biography of Lincoln, Herndon recounts how his partner said one spring day about 1851 as they rode to court in Petersburg, "God bless my mother; all that I am or ever hope to be I owe to her."[91] But in an 1870 letter, Herndon remembered the words differently: "All that I am or hope ever to be I get from my mother, God bless her."[92] When Lincoln made this remark, he was "dwelling on her characteristics, and mentioning and enumerating what qualities he inherited from her."[93] Most notable was Lincoln's speculation about his maternal grandfather, supposedly a Virginia aristocrat who had sired Nancy Hanks out of wedlock.[94] Thus, as Gabor and Adam Boritt point out, he was essentially saying, "All I am or ever hope to be I owe to her *noble bloodline.*"[95] These remarks tell us more about Lincoln's estrangement from his father than they do about his devotion to his mother.

Other evidence suggests that he might have felt deeply ambivalent about Nancy Hanks. Herndon speculated that Lincoln may not have really known "the benign influence of a mother's love" until his stepmother, Sarah Bush Johnston, entered his life when he was ten.[96] W. Helm believed that Sarah Bush Johnston "was doubtless the first person that ever treated him [Lincoln] like a human being."[97] Lincoln referred to Nancy Hanks rather harshly in one of the surprisingly few surviving references he made to her. Writing to Mrs. Orville H. Browning about how Mary Owens had changed between the first time he saw her in 1836 and her return to Illinois after two years, Lincoln said, "I could not for my life avoid thinking of my mother; and this, not from withered features, for her skin was too full of fat, to permit its contracting to wrinkles; but from her want of teeth, [and] weather-beaten appearance in general."[98] The tone of this document suggests little filial devotion to the memory of a mother. In his autobiographical sketches, Lincoln says much about his father's family but almost nothing about Nancy Hanks and hers. He seldom if ever visited his mother's grave, nor did he have it marked with a stone.[99] Herndon thought Lincoln was ashamed of his mother's family.[100]

Aside from his mother's early demise, Lincoln may have held other things against her. Like her husband, Nancy Hanks seems to have beaten young Abraham (chapter 5). Some evidence supports Herndon's statement that "she had a bad reputation."[101] Laurinda Mason Lanman of Indiana, who was roughly Lincoln's age, told an interviewer: "My Mother was neighbor to the Lincolns and she liked them but she always said that not only was Nancy Hanks an illegitimate child herself but that *Nancy was not what she ought to have been herself. Loose.*"[102] It is possible that Lincoln knew of that sullied reputation.[103] He told Herndon that "his relations were *lascivious—lecherous* not to be trusted."[104]

In any event, Nancy Hanks's death profoundly affected her nine-year-old son. As an adult, he harbored irrational fears of abandonment. After his best friend, Joshua Speed, married Fanny Henning, Lincoln told them, as noted earlier, "I feel som[e]what jealous of both of you now; you will be so exclusively concerned for one another, that I shall be forgotten entirely."[105] When defeated for the Senate by Stephen A. Douglas in 1858, he remarked to a friend that "I expect everybody to desert me."[106] At the age of thirty, he concluded a speech with a strange peroration, envisioning himself abandoned by all in his defense of the right: "If ever I feel the soul within me elevate and expand to those dimensions not wholly unworthy of its Almighty Architect, it is when I contemplate the cause of my country, deserted by all the world beside, and I standing up boldly and alone and hurling defiance at her victorious oppressors."[107] In his political career, he expressed his greatest anger at former allies who abandoned the party and principles he supported (chapter 7).

Thus Lincoln seems to have learned from his relationship with his mother, and especially from her death, that women are untrustworthy and unreliable. He could overcome this mistrust enough to court a few women and to wed one, but that marriage turned out badly. Emotionally scarred as he was in childhood, Lincoln lacked the capacity to trust women and relate easily to them.

NOTES

1. For an overview of Lincoln's fondness for male company and aversion to women, see Robert H. Wiebe, "Lincoln's Fraternal Democracy," in *Abraham Lincoln and the American Political Tradition*, ed. John L. Thomas (Amherst: University of Massachusetts Press, 1986), 19–28.

2. Statements by Sara Bush Johnston Lincoln, 8 Sept. 1865, in Hertz, *HL*, 352, and Dennis Franklin Johnston, son of John D. Johnston, Lincoln's stepbrother, in Los Angeles *Times*, 12 Feb. 1929. According to George W. Balch, "Lincoln[']s stepmother said when her own boy was away at dances Abraham was at home with [his] head at the fire place reading or studying." Balch, undated interview with Jesse W. Weik, Weik MSS, IHi.

3. Statement of Mrs. Allen Gentry (née Anna Roby), Rockport, Ind., 17 Sept. 1865, H-W MSS, DLC.

4. Dr. James LeGrande's answers to a questionnaire, [ca. 1909], Arthur E. Morgan MSS, DLC.

5. Hanks's undated statement, H-W MSS, DLC.

6. Louis A. Warren, *Lincoln's Youth: Indiana Years, 1816–1830* (Indianapolis: Indiana Historical Society, 1959), 155–58; Francis Marion Van Natter, *Lincoln's Boyhood: A Chronicle of His Indiana Years* (Washington, D.C.: Public Affairs Press, 1963), 125–30; William E. Barton, *The Women Lincoln Loved* (Indianapolis: Bobbs-Merrill, 1927), 123–66.

7. Richardson quoted in Albert J. Beveridge, *Abraham Lincoln, 1809–1858*, 2 vols. (Boston: Houghton, Mifflin, 1928), 1:80; statements by Turnham, 15 Sept. 1865, 17 Dec. 1866, H-W MSS, DLC.

8. Undated statement by Duncan, H-W MSS, DLC.

9. Undated statement by Hanks, H-W MSS, DLC; Hanks quoted in the Charleston, Ill., correspondence, 24 July [1891], in the Chicago *Republic*, N.d., clipping collection, LMFW.

10. Polly Richardson Agnew, in J. Edward Murr, "Lincoln in Indiana," *Indiana Magazine of History* 14 (March 1918): 57. Cf. Murr to Albert J. Beveridge, New Albany, Ind., 21 Nov. 1924, Beveridge MSS, DLC.

11. Elizabeth Wood, quoted in Warren, *Lincoln's Youth*, 157.

12. Mrs. Samuel Chowning, in Eleanor Gridley, *The Story of Abraham Lincoln; or, The Journey from the Log Cabin to the White House* (Chicago: Monarch, 1902), 136. Cf. statement of Lincoln's stepnephew, John J. Hall, 75–76.

13. Nora Bender, granddaughter of Elizabeth Tuley, to an unidentified correspondent, N.p., N.d., typescript, Papers of the Southwest Indiana Historical Society, Evansville Central Library. Cf. interviews with Elizabeth Tu-

ley, Evansville *Courier and Journal,* 12 Feb. 1928, and Chicago *Times-Herald,* 22 Dec. 1895.

14. Brandon to Herndon, Petersburg, Ill., 3 Aug. 1865, H-W MSS, DLC.

15. Dispatches by G. A. P[ierce], Chicago *Inter-Ocean,* 13, 23 April 1883.

16. Interview with Susan Reid Boyce, Calistoga, Calif., correspondence, 22 May 1897, San Franciso *Call,* N.d., *Iowa State Register,* 6 June 1897.

17. Interview with Mrs. Alexander R. McKee (née Martinette Hardin), Marietta Holdstock Brown, "A Romance of Lincoln," clipping identified as "Indianapolis 1896," LMFW.

18. Undated statement of A. Y. Ellis, H-W MSS, DLC.

19. O. H. Browning, interview with John G. Nicolay, Springfield, 17 June 1875, Hay MSS, RPB.

20. A "Mrs. Rule" of Talulah, Ill., quoted in G. A. P[ierce]'s dispatch in the Chicago *Inter-Ocean,* 13 April 1883.

21. Benjamin P. Thomas, *Lincoln's New Salem,* 2d ed. (New York: Alfred A. Knopf, 1954), 121. Cf. T. G. Onstot, *Pioneers of Menard and Mason Counties* (Peoria: J. W. Frank, 1902), 69. In Indiana, Mrs. Josiah Crawford played a similar role. J. W. Wartman to Jesse Weik, N.p., 20 July [1888], H-W MSS, DLC.

22. Reminiscences of Riley Potter, Petersburg, Ill., correspondence [by Walter B. Stevens, 18 Sept. 1877?], St. Louis *Globe Democrat,* N.d., clipping, LMFW; Walter B. Stevens, *A Reporter's Lincoln* (St. Louis: Missouri Historical Society, 1916), 8.

23. Angle, *HL,* 342. Cf. Herndon's undated "Lincoln's Domestic Life," H-W MSS, DLC.

24. Henry C. Whitney, *Life on the Circuit with Lincoln* (Boston: Estes and Lauriat, 1892), 36-37.

25. Lincoln to Mrs. Green, Springfield, 22 Sept. 1860, in Basler, *CWL,* 4:118.

26. "Remarks at Closing of Sanitary Fair, Washington, D.C.," 18 March 1864, in Basler, *CWL,* 7:254.

27. Beveridge, *Lincoln,* 1:306. Richard N. Current has suggested that "Lincoln's fear of women and his gaucherie with them have been overemphasized," but the document he cites to bolster his point is not persuasive. It is a joint appeal written by Lincoln and signed by several young men urging Mrs. Orville H. Browning to attend a cotillion with her sisters and friends. This merely suggests that Lincoln could in Springfield, as well as in New Salem, be at ease with wives of his friends. Current, *The Lincoln Nobody Knows* (New York: Hill and Wang, 1958), 34. In 1836, Mrs. Browning had gone out of her way to cultivate Lincoln and "treated him with a certain frank cordiality—which put Lincoln entirely at his ease." He grew "very much attached to her." O. H. Browning, interview with John G. Nicolay, Springfield, 17 June 1875, Hay MSS, RPB.

28. Helen Nicolay, *Personal Traits of Abraham Lincoln* (New York: Century, 1912), 271–72.

29. Letter to a New Jersey Quaker, 17 Nov. 1864, in *The National Anti-Slavery Standard,* 17 Dec. 1864, quoted in Carleton Mabee, "Sojourner Truth

and President Lincoln," *New England Quarterly* 61 (Dec. 1988): 521. The woman who introduced Sojourner Truth to Lincoln reported that Lincoln received his two female guests "with real politeness and pleasing cordiality." Washington correspondence, N.d., Rochester *Express,* N.d., clipping, John Hay scrapbook, vol. 55, Hay MSS, DLC.

30. William O. Stoddard, "White House Sketches, no. X," New York *Citizen,* 20 Oct. 1866.

31. Roy P. Basler, "Lincoln, Blacks, and Women," in *The Public and the Private Lincoln: Contemporary Perspectives,* ed. Cullom Davis et al. (Carbondale: Southern Illinois University Press, 1979), 44–48. Cf. Robert H. Wiebe's contention that "Lincoln made the demeaning of women his stock in trade—not a casual or occasional happening but the heart of his social style." "Lincoln's Fraternal Democracy," 27.

32. See Giraud Chester, *Embattled Maiden: The Life of Anna Dickinson* (New York: G. P. Putnam's Sons, 1951), and Wendy Hamand Venet, *Neither Ballots nor Bullets: Women Abolitionists and the Civil War* (Charlottesville: University Press of Virginia, 1991).

33. James M. McPherson, *The Struggle for Equality: Abolitionists and the Negro in the Civil War and Reconstruction* (Princeton: Princeton University Press, 1964), 108.

34. Anna E. Dickinson to [Elizabeth Cady Stanton?], Philadelphia, 12 July 1864, Harper Collection, CSmH.

35. Boston *Daily Courier,* 28 April 1864, in James Harvey Young, "Anna Elizabeth Dickinson and the Civil War: For and Against Lincoln," *Mississippi Valley Historical Review* 31 (June 1944): 72. Cf. John Hay diary, 14 May 1864, Hay MSS, RPB.

36. McKim to William Lloyd Garrison, 5 May 1864, quoted in Young, "Dickinson and the Civil War," 73. McKim described this version as "testimony not to be questioned." His source may have been Pennsylvania Congressman William D. Kelley, who was with Dickinson at the time of her meeting with Lincoln. Kelley told McKim, "That interview helped me to the conclusion in which I abide, that 'Abraham Lincoln is the wisest radical of us all.' . . . [T]he impression made on my mind by the interview was much to Mr. Lincoln's advantage." Kelley to McKim, 1 May 1864, ibid.

37. Francis Fisher Browne, *The Every-Day Life of Abraham Lincoln,* 2d ed. (New York: G. P. Putnam's Sons, 1913), 478. Cf. chapter 7 in this volume.

38. Janet L. Coryell, *Neither Heroine nor Fool: Anna Ella Carroll of Maryland* (Kent: Kent State University Press, 1990), and "Anna Ella Carroll and the Historians," *Civil War History* 35 (June 1989): 120–37; Sydney Greenbie, *Anna Ella Carroll and Abraham Lincoln* (Manchester: University of Tampa Press, 1952). Carroll once wrote, "I . . . mean to be a power yet in this land, which it will be well to propitiate." Coryell, *Carroll,* 31.

39. Ibid., 13–89.

40. William Mitchell to an unidentified correspondent, Washington, 13 May 1862, in Lucinda B. Chandler, "Woman in Lincoln's Cabinet," Chicago *Times Herald,* clipping dated only 1895, LMFW. Lincoln's remarks were reportedly made the previous evening.

41. Carroll to Lincoln, N.p., 14 Aug. 1862, in Basler, *CWL*, 5:382.

42. Basler, "Lincoln, Blacks, and Women," 46.

43. Kenneth P. Williams, "The Tennessee River Campaign and Anna Ella Carroll," *Indiana Magazine of History* 46 (Sept. 1950): 221–48, a review of Sydney Greenbie, *Anna Ella Carroll and Abraham Lincoln* in *Lincoln Herald* 54 (Summer 1952): 54–56, and "A Reply to Sydney Greenbie," *Lincoln Herald* 55 (Fall 1953): 40–42; E. B. Long, "Anna Ella Carroll: Exaggerated Heroine?" *Civil War Times Illustrated* 14 (July 1975): 29, 33, 35; F. Lauriston Bullard, "Anna Ella Carroll and her 'Modest' Claim," *Lincoln Herald* 50 (Oct. 1948): 2–10.

44. Coryell, *Carroll,* 31–36, 85, 96.

45. Basler, "Lincoln, Blacks, and Women," 48.

46. Coryell, *Carroll,* 83–89, 95–109.

47. Jessie Benton Frémont's memoirs, "Great Events," (1891), in *The Letters of Jessie Benton Frémont,* ed. Pamela Herr and Mary Lee Spence (Urbana: University of Illinois Press, 1993), 266. In 1888 and 1890 she wrote two other versions of this interview, which are not reproduced in the volume edited by Herr and Spence but can be found in the Frémont Papers, Bancroft Library, University of California, Berkeley. Herr and Spence note that the earlier accounts were "provoked by publication of a distorted version of the meeting in John G. Nicolay and John Hay's *Abraham Lincoln: A History*" (267n). Because Nicolay and Hay's version is based on an account given by Lincoln in 1863 and recorded at that time, and Mrs. Frémont's is based on her memory in 1888, it may well be that Nicolay and Hay provided a less distorted version than the one given here.

48. John Hay, diary, 9 Dec. 1863, Hay MSS, RPB.

49. Josiah Bushnell Grinnell, *Men and Events of Forty Years: Autobiographical Reminiscences of an Active Career from 1850 to 1890* (Boston: D. Lothrop, 1891), 174.

50. Lincoln to Mrs. John C. Frémont, Washington, 12 Sept. 1861, in Basler, *CWL,* 4:519.

51. Basler, "Lincoln, Blacks, and Women," 45.

52. Frank Klement, "Jane Grey Swisshelm and Lincoln: A Feminist Fusses and Frets," *Abraham Lincoln Quarterly* 6 (Dec. 1950): 227–38 [quote on 233].

53. Delia A. P. Harvey to Col. J. H. Howe, Washington, 13 Sept. 1863, photcopy of typed manuscript, and "Recollections of Hospital Life and Personal Interviews with President Lincoln," photocopy of typed manuscript, both in Civil War Miscellaneous Manuscripts Collection, series 2, Box 29, Sterling Library, Yale University; J. G. Holland, *The Life of Abraham Lincoln* (Springfield, Mass.: Gurdon Bill, 1866), 443–53.

54. "Remarks at Closing of Sanitary Fair, Washington, D.C.," 18 March 1864, in Basler, *CWL,* 7:254.

55. Enclosure in Alice Eve McCardell to Ida Tarbell, Cumberland, 3 Oct. [1895?], Ida M. Tarbell MSS, Allegheny College; cf. Edward D. Neill, in *Lincoln Talks: A Biography in Anecdote,* ed. Emanuel Hertz (New York: Viking Press, 1939), 428.

56. "Memorandum: Appointment of Gabriel R. Paul," 23 Aug. 1862, in Basler, *CWL,* 5:390–91.

57. William D. Kelley, in Rice, *RL*, 284–85.

58. Theodore Calvin Pease and James G. Randall, eds., *The Diary of Orville Hickman Browning*, 2 vols. Collections of the Illinois State Historical Library, vols. 20 and 22 (Springfield: Illinois State Historical Library, 1925, 1933), 1:659 [entry for 6 Feb. 1864].

59. Diary of the Reverend G. H. Blakeslee [entry for 2 Nov. 1864], in Francis Durbin Blakeslee, *Personal Recollections and Impressions of Abraham Lincoln* (Gardena: Spanish American Institute Press, 1927), 11–12.

60. Howard K. Beale, ed., *Diary of Gideon Welles, Secretary of the Navy under Lincoln and Johnson*, 3 vols. (New York: W. W. Norton, 1960), 2:21 [entry for 29 April 1864]. Cf. Mrs. H. C. Ingersol to the editor, 1 June 1875, Springfield *Republican*, 7 June 1875, 4; Elizabeth Todd Grimsley, "Six Months in the White House," *Journal of the Illinois State Historical Society* 19 (Oct. 1926): 56–57; Baker, *MTL*, 226; Margaret Leech, *Reveille in Washington, 1860–1865* (New York: Harpers, 1941), 307–8; William H. Townsend, *Lincoln and the Bluegrass: Slavery and Civil War in Kentucky* ([Lexington]: University Press of Kentucky, 1955), 314–17; Helen Nicolay, *Lincoln's Secretary: A Biography of John G. Nicolay* (New York: Longmans, Green, 1949), 202–4.

61. Lida Rose McCabe, "Lincoln's Body-Guard: Reminiscences of Lincoln's Last Days in the White House," clipping from an unidentified Chicago newspaper, 16 April 1893, LMFW.

62. William Herndon's interview with Lamon, no date, copy in the Lincoln Records, 2:76–77, Lamon MSS, CSmH.

63. John Jay Janney, "Talking with the President: Four Interviews with Abraham Lincoln," *Civil War Times Illustrated* 26 (Sept. 1987): 35.

64. Janney, "Talking with the President, 35."

65. John G. Nicolay's interview with Lot M. Morrill, [probably 20 Sept. 1878], Nicolay MSS, DLC.

66. Lincoln to Mrs. J. J. Neagle, [13 Feb. 1864], in *The Collected Works of Abraham Lincoln: Second Supplement, 1848–1865*, ed. Roy P. Basler and Christian O. Basler (New Brunswick: Rutgers University Press, 1990), 89. Cf. "The Case of J. J. Neagle: Two Unpublished Lincoln Documents," *Lincoln Lore*, no. 1781 (July 1987): 4.

67. Frazer Kirkland, ed., *Reminiscences of the Blue and Gray, '61–'65* (Chicago: Preston, 1895), 55.

68. Lord Charnwood, *Abraham Lincoln* (New York: Henry Holt, 1916), 87–88.

69. Angle, *HL*, 117–18.

70. Lincoln to Mrs. Orville Browning, Springfield, 1 April 1838, in Basler, *CWL*, 1:117–19. During the Civil War, Mrs. Browning, who thought the letter was a joke, asked the president about it. "He then, very much to her surprise told her that there was much more truth in that letter than she supposed." O. H. Browning, interview with John G. Nicolay, Springfield, 17 June 1875, Hay MSS, RPB. Cf. Browning to Isaac N. Arnold, Quincy, Ill., 25 Nov. 1872, Arnold MSS, ICHi.

71. Statement of Johnson Green, N.d., H-W MSS, DLC. Cf. Lincoln to Mary Owens, Springfield, 7 May 1837, in Basler, *CWL*, 1:78.

72. Lincoln to Mary Owens, Springfield, 16 Aug. 1837, in Basler, *CWL,* 1:94.

73. Mary S. Vineyard to Herndon, Weston, Mo., 22 May 1866, in Angle, *HL,* 119–20.

74. Mary S. Vineyard to Herndon, Weston, Mo., 22 July 1866, in Angle, *HL,* 121. Mentor Graham's granddaughter recounted how Mary Owens complained about Lincoln's "lack of knowledge of etiquette" and lamented that "our whole outlook on life is so different, and our training." Kunigunde Duncan and D. F. Nickols, *Mentor Graham: The Man Who Taught Lincoln* (Chicago: University of Chicago Press, 1944), 164–65. Cf. William Greene's description of Mary Owens's reaction to Lincoln's uncouth behavior. G. A. P[ierce]'s dispatch, Chicago *Inter-Ocean,* 23 April 1881.

75. Edna Bell Howell to "My dear friend," Los Angeles, 20 March [19]38, copy enclosed in Charles Gunther to the Lincoln National Life Foundation, Lexington, Mo., 27 Sept. 1943, clipping collection, LMFW.

76. Lincoln to Mary Owens, Springfield, 7 May 1837, in Basler, *CWL,* 1:78.

77. Lincoln to Mrs. Browning, Springfield, 1 April 1838, in Basler, *CWL,* 1:119.

78. Sarah A. Basset (née Rickard) to Herndon, Connors, Kan., 3, 12 Aug. 1888, H-W MSS, DLC. Cf. Herndon to Weik, Springfield, 8 Aug. 1888, H-W MSS, DLC, and an interview with Sarah Rickard Barrett by Nellie Crandall Sanford, Kansas City *Star,* 10 Feb. 1907. Herndon's wife, whose mother was Sarah Rickard's sister, heard the story of Lincoln's courtship and proposal from her sister. Jesse W. Weik interviewed Sarah Rickard about the courtship and was told that her elder sister had opposed the match because of the girl's youth. Weik, *RL,* 66–68.

Despite this evidence, some biographers doubt the whole story. See Carl Sandburg and Paul M. Angle, *Mary Lincoln: Wife and Widow* (New York: Harcourt, Brace, 1932), 54–55, 344–50. After the spring of 1841, when Speed returned to Kentucky, Lincoln may have roomed as well as boarded with the Butlers. Sandburg and Angle, *Mary Lincoln,* 54; William J. Butler, grandson of William Butler, in the *Illinois State Journal* [Springfield], 28 Feb. 1937, 11. Cf. Nicolay's interview with William Butler, Springfield, June, 1875, Hay MSS, RPB.

According to one Springfield resident, Ninian Edwards "had been sufficiently interested in the young lawyer [Lincoln] to go to his friend William Butler, the owner of one of the largest homes, and persuade him to take Lincoln to board, representing him as a fine, industrious young man, pitifully poor, who, if he were helped a little for a few years, was sure to succeed. Mr. Butler, therefore, took him into his family, and after boarding him for a short time also gave him a large and comfortable room, which Speed shared with him, abandoning the room at the store." Octavia Roberts, "Our Townsman: Pictures of Lincoln as a Friend and Neighbor," *Collier's,* 12 Feb. 1909, 17.

79. John Y. Simon, "Abraham Lincoln and Ann Rutledge," *Journal of the Abraham Lincoln Association* 11 (1990): 33. Cf. Douglas L. Wilson, "Abraham Lincoln, Ann Rutledge, and the Evidence of Herndon's Informants," *Civil War History* 36 (Dec. 1990): 301–23, which, like Simon's article, effectively

rebuts James G. Randall's argument in "Sifting the Ann Rutledge Evidence," in Randall, *Lincoln the President: From Springfield to Gettysburg*, 2 vols. (New York: Dodd, Mead, 1945), 2:321–42; John Evangelist Walsh, *The Shadows Rise: Abraham Lincoln and the Ann Rutledge Legend* (Urbana: University of Illinois Press, 1993).

80. "Speech in the Illinois Legislature Concerning Apportionment," [9 Jan. 1841?], in Basler, *CWL*, 1:227–28.

81. Henry Whitney's recollections, in Weik, *RL*, 76–77. Cf. Whitney, *Life on the Circuit*, 51, and "Reminiscences of Abraham Lincoln by Col. W. J. Anderson," in Henry B. Rankin, *Intimate Character Sketches of Abraham Lincoln* (Philadelphia: Lippincott, 1924), 72–82.

82. Memoirs of Mrs. Hillis, in Weik, *RL*, 77–80.

83. In discussing Lincoln's treatment of Anna E. Dickinson and Anna Ella Carroll, Basler suggests that Lincoln betrayed signs of sexism. See "Lincoln, Blacks, and Women," 47–48.

84. Letter to the editor of the *Sangamo Journal* [New Salem], 13 June 1836, in Basler, *CWL*, 1:48.

85. The young woman was Lillian Conlee, who told this story to her granddaughter, Helen Ruth Reed. See Reed, "A Prophecy Lincoln Made," Boston *Herald*, 9 Feb. 1930.

86. Herndon to Weik, Springfield, 23 Jan. 1890, H-W MSS, DLC. Cf. Herndon to Gen. James H. Wilson, N.p., 23 Sept. 1889, copy of excerpt, and Herndon to Weik, Springfield, 23 July 1890, H-W MSS, DLC.

87. Joseph Holt, interview with John G. Nicolay, 29 Oct. 1879, Nicolay MSS, DLC. Of the 276 Union soldiers executed during the Civil War, twenty-two were found guilty of rape. Once convicted, they were speedily dispatched, usually within seventy-two hours. Robert I. Alotta, *Civil War Justice: Union Army Executions under Lincoln* (Shippensburg: White Mane, 1989), 30. Alotta notes (31) that Lincoln "provided clemency for all types of military offenders, except rapists." On July 18, 1863, after spending six hours with the president and with Holt on courts martial decisions, John Hay noted in his diary: "I was amused at the eagerness with which the President caught at any fact which would justify him in saving the life of a condemned soldier. He was only merciless in cases where meanness or cruelty were shown." Hay diary, Hay MSS, RPB.

88. James Matheny interview with Jesse W. Weik, 12 Sept. 1888, Weik MSS, IHi. Lincoln's friends in this affair were Evan Butler, Noah Rickard, and James Matheny.

89. Beveridge, *Lincoln*, 1:306.

90. Noah Brooks, *Abraham Lincoln and the Downfall of American Slavery* (New York: G. P. Putnam's Sons, 1894), 21.

91. Angle, *HL*, 3. A memo by Weik states that "H[erndon] says when L[incoln] told of his mother's illegitimate birth that L[incoln] requested him to say nothing about it while he L[incoln] lived. There followed a long spell of sadness[.]" Weik MSS, IHi.

92. Herndon to Ward Hill Lamon, Springfield, 6 March 1870, Lamon MSS, CSmH. Cf. Herndon to Lamon, Springfield, 26 Feb. 1870, Herndon to Jesse Weik, Springfield, 19 Jan. 1886, and Herndon's memoir on Nancy Hanks,

dated Greencastle, Ind., 20 Aug. 1887, in Hertz, *HL*, 63, 139, 411–12. Cf. Herndon to Charles Hart, Springfield, 2 March 1867, Lamon MSS, CSmH.

93. Angle, *HL*, 2; Herndon to Lamon, Springfield, 6 March 1870, Lamon MSS, CSmH.

94. Herndon to Charles H. Hart, Springfield, 2 March 1867, and to Ward Hill Lamon, Springfield, 25 Feb., 6 March 1870, Lamon MSS, CSmH. On the identity of this grandfather, see Paul H. Verduin, "New Evidence Suggests Lincoln's Mother Born in Richmond County, Virginia," *Northern Neck of Virginia Historical Magazine* 38 (Dec. 1988): 4354–89.

95. Gabor S. Boritt and Adam Boritt, "Lincoln and the Marfan Syndrome: The Medical Diagnosis of a Historical Figure," *Civil War History* 29 (Sept. 1983): 228. The Boritts have some doubt about the authenticity of this quote.

96. Angle, *HL*, 29.

97. Helm to Herndon, N.p., [1 Aug. 1865], H-W MSS, DLC.

98. Lincoln to Mrs. Browning, Springfield, 1 April 1838, in Basler, *CWL*, 1:118.

99. Herndon to James H. Wilson, N.p., 15 Oct. 1889, copy, H-W MSS DLC. In 1860 Lincoln allegedly told Nathaniel Grigsby of "his intention to return to Spencer county and . . . to erect a suitable monument at his mother's grave, feeling it was his sacred duty." But he did not, and it was left to Joseph Davis Armstrong to mark Nancy Hanks's grave. Ida D. Armstrong, unidentified article [1923], paraphrased in Thomas James de la Hunt, "The Pocket Periscope," N.d., clipping collection, LMFW. According to an Indiana tradition, Lincoln in the 1850s arranged with Nat and Jim Grigsby to fence in his mother's gravesite to keep livestock from grazing on it. C. T. Baker, "Spencer County Lincolniana," Grandview [Ind.] *Monitor*, 22 Feb. 1934.

100. Herndon to James H. Wilson, N.p., 1 Oct. 1889, copy of an excerpt, H-W MSS, DLC.

101. Herndon to Truman Bartlett, Springfield, 25 Sept. 1887, Bartlett Scrapbook, Massachusetts Historical Society, Boston. Cf. Herndon to Charles Hart, Springfield, 28 Dec. 1866, Lamon MSS, CSmH.

102. J. Edward Murr to Albert J. Beveridge, New Albany, Ind., 21 Nov. 1924, Beveridge MSS, DLC. Murr omits the remarks about Nancy Hanks's reputation as a loose woman in the published version of Mrs. Lanman's remarks. See Murr, "Lincoln in Indiana," 333–34. In his letter, Murr refers to Mrs. Lanman as "Mrs. Laymon." Her full name, correctly spelled, was provided me by Paul H. Verduin, to whom I am grateful.

103. William Herndon to Charles H. Hart, Springfield, 28 Dec. 1866, Lamon MSS, CSmH.

104. Herndon to Ward Hill Lamon, Springfield, 25 Feb. 1870, Lamon MSS, CSmH.

105. Lincoln to Speed, Springfield, 25 Feb. 1842, in Basler, *CWL*, 1:281.

106. Whitney, *Life on the Circuit*, 467. Cf. Whitney to Herndon, N.p., 18 July 1887, in David Donald, *Lincoln's Herndon* (New York: Alfred A. Knopf, 1948), 126.

107. "Speech on the Sub-Treasury," [26] Dec. 1839, in Basler, *CWL*, 1:178.

7

Lincoln's Anger and Cruelty

Like the crew of H.M.S. *Pinafore,* readers of William Herndon's Lincoln biography, when informed that its subject "never lost his temper," might well wonder "what, *never?!*"[1] In Herndon's defense, it must be noted that many other observers echoed his statement. John G. Nicolay maintained that Lincoln's "self control was simply wonderful." Day in and out for more than four years, Nicolay was able "to witness his bearing under most trying conditions and circumstances, and during the whole time never saw him manifest any extraordinary excitement . . . , or indulge in any violence of speech or action beyond that of impressive emphasis."[2] Nicolay told a journalist that Lincoln "listened patiently to all, seldom protecting himself even from bores. I never saw him angry but twice, and then only momentarily. He turned one man out of the room and laid his hands on his shoulder to hasten his departure."[3]

Lincoln's bodyguard William Crook maintained that "no employee of the White House ever saw the president moved beyond his usual controlled calm."[4] In his early life Lincoln "never got angry," according to N. W. Brandon.[5] Charles A. Dana informed an audience that "I never heard him say a harsh word to anybody" or "an unkind thing about anybody." Dana "never heard him speak a word of complaint even."[6] Jackson Grimshaw, who knew Lincoln for two decades, doubted that he "ever exchanged an angry word with any person in his life."[7] He "was always of even temperament, never showing anger," said Thomas Dowling, who frequently saw Lincoln on his visits to Charleston, Illinois.[8]

In fact, like the captain of the *Pinafore,* Lincoln "hardly ever" lost his celebrated equanimity. Abundant evidence supports the contention of Paul M. Angle that Lincoln "would not always turn the other cheek." Angle rightly observed that such an assertion "is, of course, at variance with the common concept of a man of infinite patience" and "infinite endurance of imposition."[9]

Other historians have noted a similar phenomenon: Lincoln's tendency toward cruelty, at least in his early years, when he "could be cutting and scornful" as he inflicted "pain and humiliation" on opponents, both political and personal.[10] But scholars have generally shied away from a close examination of Lincoln's anger and cruelty.

· · ·

Long before his biography of Lincoln appeared, Herndon conceded that his law partner would occasionally erupt in anger: "As he was grand in his good nature, so he was grand in his rage," he told an interviewer.[11] Other Illinois lawyers concurred, including Lincoln's second partner Stephen T. Logan, who said that he "had at times, when he was roused, a very high temper" that he controlled "in a general way, though it would break out sometimes—and at those times it didn't take much to make him whip a man."[12] Henry C. Whitney, who observed Lincoln closely on the circuit, found him usually imperturbable: "The only excitement he ever betrayed in court was when he got righteously indignant at the actions of some one in a case—then he was terrible in his wrath; he has been known (though rarely) to transcend the bounds of decorum on such occasions."[13] Now and then Whitney recalled seeing Lincoln's face "lurid with majestic and terrifying wrath."[14] Isaac N. Arnold wrote that "personal abuse, injustice, and indignity offered to himself did not disturb him, but gross injustice and bad faith towards others" so enraged him that "his eyes would blaze with indignation, and his denunciation few could endure."[15] David Davis noted that "many a man, whose fraudulent conduct was undergoing review in a court of justice, has writhed under his terrific indignation and rebukes."[16] A former student in Lincoln's law office recalled that he "had within him . . . all of the scorn of scorn and hate of hate if his moral sensibilities and indignation had been fully aroused. He seldom considered it necessary to use this quality of his manhood in political debate, or at the bar, but when he did he was transformed."[17]

Lincoln allegedly said that he grew angry only when frustrated intellectually: "When a mere child, I used to get irritated when anybody talked to me in a way that I could not understand. I do not think I ever got angry at anything else in my life; but that always disturbed my temper, and has ever since."[18] Near the end of the Civil War, he acknowledged that he could become deeply infuriated at people as well. He told Virginia Governor Francis H. Pierpont that, amid all the trials he had endured, "I have been angry but once since I came to the White

House. Then, if I had encountered the man who caused my anger, I certainly would have hurt him."[19]

Years before he became president, Lincoln had, in fact, hurt several men, wounding them with ridicule and insults rather than with fists or weapons.[20] If, as president, he could with some justice state that "I have not willingly planted a thorn in any man's bosom," during his youth he had in fact delighted in planting thorns.[21] He was especially adept at cruel mimicry of accents, mannerisms, gestures, and physical defects.[22] Herndon recalled seeing "whole crowds lifted off their seats by his unequaled powers of mimicry. . . . It was only on rare occasions that he resorted to this method of killing off . . . an enemy."[23] Sometimes he goaded his victims to retaliation. At a corn husking bee where two teams raced to finish their assigned quotas, the young Lincoln taunted a member of the opposition so badly that the aggrieved man hurled a rocklike corn nub that created an ugly gash above Lincoln's eye.[24]

Among the earliest recorded victims of Lincoln's harsh, belittling humor were the brothers of Aaron Grigsby, who had married Lincoln's sister Sarah. Lincoln thought her death in childbirth less than two years after her wedding "was due to neglect" and thereafter bore a grudge against the Grigsby family.[25] In 1829, he humiliated Aaron's brothers Reuben and Charles when they were married in a joint ceremony to two sisters. Lincoln contrived to have the grooms and brides switched on the wedding night; later he lampooned the men in a satire entitled "The Chronicles of Reuben." Soon thereafter, Lincoln mocked yet another of Aaron's brothers for his baldness, ungainly figure, and lack of popularity with the opposite sex.[26] These early exercises in what Herndon called "merciless satire" enraged the Grigsbys and evidently touched off a row.[27]

Another target of Lincoln's acid-dipped pen was Josiah Crawford, an Indiana neighbor who had compelled him to labor three days to compensate for damage done to a book that Crawford had lent the young man. Angry at this arrangement and also at the way that Crawford docked his meager wages when he was the slightest bit late for chores at Crawford's farm, Lincoln retaliated by satirizing his employer's large nose.[28]

Lincoln's ripostes could be clever as well as crude. In New Salem, a Major Hill "abused" him "a great deal," speaking "very roughly & insultingly" in the mistaken belief that Lincoln had disparaged his wife.

Lincoln "kept his temper—denied having said anything against her—
[and] told the Major that he had a very high opinion of her, and that if
he knew anything in the world against her it was the fact of her being
his wife."[29]

• • •

Early in his political career, Lincoln would scorn his opponents,
sometimes insulting them roundly. In the 1834 election campaign, he
attacked Democrat Peter Cartwright as "a most abondoned hypocrite"
who was "continually exposing" the people of his community "to ridicule by making a public boast of his power to hoodwink them." He
contended that "none has a greater thirst for political distinction than
Cartwright," that he had been "long dealing in duplicity," and that an
"intelligent" observer "will be much puzzled to decide" whether Cartwright "is [a] greater fool or knave; although he may readily see that
he has but few rivals in either capacity."[30]

During his 1836 campaign for reelection to the Illinois legislature,
he was attacked by one George Forquer, a noted orator who had recently converted from the Whig to the Democratic party and had been
rewarded for this switch with a government job. He also owned a
Springfield house that had a lightning rod, a new invention that fascinated Lincoln. Forquer delivered a "slasher-gaff" speech, full of ridicule and sarcasm, to which Lincoln replied in kind. "I would rather
die now," he mocked, "than, like the gentleman, change my politics,
and simultaneous with the change receive an office worth $3,000 per
year, and then have to erect a lightning-rod over my house to protect a
guilty conscience from an offended God."[31]

In that same year, Lincoln unleashed his "crushing power of sarcasm and ridicule" on other Democratic leaders. Residents of Sangamon County remembered for decades how he replied to Dr. Jacob M.
Early. As Isaac N. Arnold summarized their recollections, at first Lincoln "was embarrassed, spoke slowly, and with some hesitation and
difficulty, but soon becoming warm, and excited by his subject, he for-
got himself entirely, and went on with argument and wit, anecdote and
ridicule, until his opponent was completely crushed."[32]

Another victim of the campaign was Colonel Dick Taylor, whose
assaults on the Whigs as elitists nettled Lincoln. In the midst of one
harangue, Taylor, "a talkative, noisy fellow, with a fatal fondness for
fine clothes,"[33] was surprised when his vest popped open, revealing a
ruffled shirt and gold watch chain. Lincoln denounced Taylor's hypoc-

risy: "Behold the hard-fisted democrat," he taunted while pointing at his opponent. "Look, gentlemen, at this specimen of the bone and sinew." Pointing to his own jeans and coarse shirt, he added, "And here, gentlemen, here at your service, here is your aristocrat!" The crowd laughed at Taylor's discomfiture.[34] In that same canvass Lincoln called an anonymous critic "a *liar* and a *scoundrel*" and threatened "to give his proboscis a good wringing."[35]

The following year Lincoln engaged in what Paul M. Angle called "one of the bitterest personal and political fights that Springfield has ever witnessed."[36] Amid the horsewhippings and stabbings that attended the electioneering, Lincoln contemptuously and angrily attacked James Adams, the Democratic candidate for probate justice of the peace, a post that Lincoln's friend Anson G. Henry also sought. Lincoln excoriated Adams as a forger, a whiner, a fool, and a liar.[37] It is not clear whether he wrote the series of anonymous letters in the Sangamo *Journal* that skewered Adams, but it seems likely, given the intensity of the rancor of his public assaults and the way he had used anonymous writings to scourge the Grigsbys and later to ridicule James Shields.[38] Lincoln's war against Adams amounted to a vendetta that one biographer aptly described as "squalid political campaigning."[39]

That summer Lincoln nearly came to blows with a Democratic legislator, William L. D. Ewing, who lambasted the Whigs in a cutting, sarcastic speech. Leaders of that maligned party chose Lincoln to reply, and he did so "with great severity." Ewing then asked the Whigs, "Have you no other champion than this coarse and vulgar fellow to bring into the lists against me? Do you suppose that I will condescend to break a lance with your low and obscure colleague?" A spectator recalled that "we were all very much alarmed for fear there would be a personal conflict between Ewing and Lincoln. It was confidently believed that a challenge must pass between them, but the friends on both sides took it in hand, and it was settled without anything serious growing out of it."[40] Later, when Ewing defeated Lincoln for the speakership of the Illinois house of representatives, Lincoln, in a rare outburst of profanity, told his law partner that Ewing "is not worth a damn."[41]

During the "hard cider and log cabin" presidential campaign of 1840, Lincoln continued his partisan assaults on Democrats. In preliminary skirmishing for that contest, he denounced Stephen A. Douglas as "stupid" and "deserving of the world's contempt" and derided the editors of the state's foremost Democratic newspaper as "liars."[42] He was also quick to label opponents in court "liars."[43]

But he reserved his sharpest barbs for Judge Jesse B. Thomas, who had been accused of writing anonymous letters in the press. It turned out that Lincoln and his fellow Whigs had been the authors, and Thomas attacked them in a speech. Arriving just in time to hear the end of Thomas's remarks, Lincoln rose to answer as the judge took his seat. One witness reported that Lincoln was "terrific in his denunciation" and "had no mercy" as he mimicked Thomas's gestures and accent. Another observer wrote that "Lincoln's effort was absolutely overwhelming and withering. He had not proceeded far, indeed, before Judge Thomas began to blubber like a baby, and left the assembly." The Democratic press chided Lincoln for his "rude assault upon the private character of . . . Thomas." The next day Lincoln apologized. In the annals of Illinois politics, the episode became celebrated as "the skinning of Thomas."[44]

Lincoln often ridiculed Democrats as "locofocos," a term widely used to designate the most radical wing of the party, which, in the eyes of some, had abandoned the principles of Jefferson and Jackson. When his opponents protested against such name-calling, Lincoln replied with a joke about the farmer who caught a skunk in his hen house. The animal averred that he was no polecat but a friend to the farmer, who responded, "You look like a polecat, . . . act like one, smell like one and you are one, by God, and I'll kill you, innocent & friendly to me as you say you are." The locofocos, Lincoln continued, "'claim to be true democrats, but they are only locofocos—they look like locofocos, . . . act like locofocos,' and turning up his nose and backing away a little . . . as if the smell was about to smother him, 'are locofocos by God.'" His listeners "nearly bursted their sides laughing."[45]

At the end of the 1840 campaign, a leading Democrat, William G. Anderson, repeatedly interrupted Lincoln's speech at Lawrenceville, Indiana, charging that the speaker was "falsifying the acts and record of the Democratic party."[46] Lincoln evidently replied heatedly, for Anderson charged that Lincoln's attack on him "imported insult" and ominously demanded an explanation. A duel seemed likely, but Lincoln obviated the threat with a conciliatory reply: "I entertain no unkind feeling to you, and none of any sort upon the subject, except a sincere regret that I permitted myself to get into such an altercation."[47]

Two years later, however, he was unable to avoid a challenge to a duel after ridiculing the Democratic state comptroller James Shields in an anonymous newspaper satire. Writing under the pen name "Rebecca," Lincoln contemned Shields as "a fool as well as a liar" with whom "truth is out of the question, and as for getting a good bright passable lie out of him, you might as well try to strike fire from a cake of tallow."[48] As Mark E. Neely, Jr., rightly observed, "It must be said that the 'Rebecca' letter was abusive enough to provoke Shields' challenge."[49] When the enraged Shields demanded satisfaction, Lincoln picked up the gage; the duel, however, was called off at the last minute through the intervention of mutual friends.[50]

Albert J. Beveridge called this "the most lurid personal incident in Lincoln's entire life" and concluded that Lincoln had "needlessly and heedlessly assailed" Shields. In Beveridge's view, the episode marked a key turning point in Lincoln's life: "At last his habit, formed in boyhood, of ridiculing other persons through offensive, anonymous writing, had been sternly checked. . . . Never did Lincoln forget that experience. Never again did he write an anonymous letter, never again say any insulting word about any human being. From the time of the Shields duel Lincoln was infinitely circumspect and considerate in his dealings with others."[51]

Beveridge was only partially correct. To be sure, Lincoln allegedly felt that his acceptance of Shields's challenge was "the meanest thing he ever did in his life" and sought to put it out of mind.[52] After a participant in the duel later attempted to get him to discuss the event, Lincoln remarked, "That man is trying to revive his memory of a matter that I am trying to forget."[53] A few weeks before his death, he replied abruptly to a question about the Shields duel: "If you desire my friendship you will never mention the circumstance again!"[54]

Although the chastened Lincoln did stop writing anonymous letters, he nevertheless continued to pour sarcasm and ridicule over opponents. In 1844, for example, he humiliated W. L. May during a debate in Peoria. May, who, like Forquer had switched from the Whigs to the Democrats, joked about a pole raised by the Whigs, saying that at its base it was hollow and heartless, just like the Whig party. Lincoln's reply was that the pole was hollow at the butt end in order to allow May to crawl out of the party and that his former friends intended to close off the hole to prevent May's return. The audience howled, and May later criticized Lincoln for introducing personalities into the debate. Lincoln jocularly confessed, "Colonel, I was like the little boy who kissed the girl at school. When the teacher asked him why he had acted so rudely, [he] replied, 'She stood so fair I couldn't help it!'"[55]

Another fugitive from the Whig ranks, Charles H. Constable, so aroused Lincoln's ire that fisticuffs nearly resulted.[56] In October 1851,

Constable complained to Lincoln that the Whigs had neglected him and that the party was dominated by old fogies indifferent to younger men. David Davis recalled how Lincoln, who in 1849 and again in 1851 had vainly tried to secure a government job for Constable, "turned fiercely upon him, and said, 'Mr. Constable, I understand you perfectly, and have noticed for some time back that you have been slowly and cautiously picking your way over to the democratic party.'" Only Davis's intervention prevented a fight.[57] Anthony Thornton, speaking of the encounter, said, "I shall never forget the aspect of Lincoln's face. The glare of his eye and the working of his countenance were terrific."[58] He denounced James W. Singleton, an old Whig who joined the Democrats in the mid-1850s, "with emphasis" as "a miracle of meanness."[59]

In the presidential canvass of 1848 Lincoln attacked Democratic nominee Lewis Cass for abandoning his antislavery principles. Scornfully he summarized Cass's waffling course on the Wilmot Proviso, which banned slavery from the territory acquired from Mexico: "When the question was raised in 1846, he was in a blustering hurry to take ground for it. He sought to be in advance, and to avoid the uninteresting position of a mere follower; but soon he began to see glimpses of the great democratic ox-gad waving in his face, and to hear, indistinctly, a voice saying 'Back' 'Back sir' 'Back a little'. He shakes his head, and bats his eyes, and blunders back." Lincoln also ridiculed Cass's military record, saying that if the Democrats should ever nominate him for the presidency, "I protest they shall not make fun of me, as they have of Gen: Cass, by attempting to write me into a military hero."[60]

In the presidential campaign eight years later, Lincoln denounced former Whigs who refused to support the new Republican party and instead backed the Know-Nothing candidate, Millard Fillmore, because he was a "good man." With "scornful emphasis" he suggested that "they vote for God—the best Being—who had as good a chance for being elected President as Fillmore had."[61]

Attorney Henry C. Whitney, who saw Lincoln lose his temper only thrice in the many years they worked together on the circuit, recalled him exploding at the action of T. Lyle Dickey, an influential lawyer who had been a friend and political ally. In 1858, however, Dickey supported Stephen A. Douglas. This desertion pained Lincoln, who, shortly after hearing of Dickey's act, erupted in anger. In order to prepare a case to be argued in federal court, Lincoln and Whitney visited Chicago. The opposing counsel, Dickey, sent Lincoln a note saying that he could not appear in court and asking Lincoln to go ahead and make his argument first. As Whitney remembered it, Lincoln "exclaimed . . . with the utmost impatience and anger: 'I hain't got any argument to make!'" Whitney tried vainly to discover the reason for Lincoln's anger. In fact, Lincoln was probably furious that Dickey, like Forquer, May, Constable, and the pro-Fillmore Whigs, had deserted the party.[62]

Benjamin P. Thomas suggested Lincoln's failure "to appreciate the pain and humiliation his scathing satire inflicted on its victims" was simply "another of those crudities originating in his rough-and-tumble background and the tough school in which he learned his politics."[63] Although that is doubtless true, Thomas's explanation does not account for the special venom that Lincoln had for those who abandoned party or principle. Lincoln feared abandonment,[64] probably because in childhood he felt abandoned by his mother, who died when he was nine, and his father, who was emotionally distant.[65] Lincoln seems to have displaced the repressed anger he felt for his parents onto political "abandoners."

• • •

Turncoats may have been the victims of Lincoln's most heated and cruel outbursts, but they were not alone. As Herndon asserted, Lincoln sometimes "got angry at the bar and when he did get mad he was then ugly." In 1859, Herndon witnessed "a terrible spectacle" when his partner denounced a judge's decision in a murder case, becoming "so angry that he looked like Lucifer in an uncontrollable rage." Carefully keeping "within the bounds of propriety just far enough to avoid a reprimand for contempt of court," Lincoln "was fired with indignation and spoke fiercely [and] strongly" of the decision of the judge, whom "he pealed . . . from head to foot."[66] Lincoln "roared like a lion suddenly aroused from his lair," the court crier remembered.[67]

Lincoln also skinned a pension agent, Erastus Wright, who had flagrantly overcharged his client, the poor widow of a Revolutionary War veteran. Speaking of that case, David Davis said that if Lincoln "believed his client was oppressed . . . he was hurtful in denunciation. When he attacked meanness, fraud, or vice, he was powerful, merciless in his castigation."[68] Herndon recalled that as Lincoln explained how Wright had fleeced the widow, he "rose up to about 9 f[ee]t high—grew warm—then eloquent," assailing "as with a thunderbolt the miscreant who had robbed one that helped the world to liberty." Herndon never saw his partner "so wrought up."[69] Another example of Lincoln's wrath in attacking meanness was observed by Samuel C.

Parks, who termed "his denunciation of a defendant (before a jury in Petersburg) who had slandered an almost friendless schoolmistress" perhaps "as bitter a Philippic as was ever uttered."[70]

In a courtroom Lincoln would occasionally explode at witnesses, especially those he thought untruthful. As one lawyer put it, "Woe betide the unlucky and dishonest individual who suppressed the truth, or colored it against Mr. Lincoln's side."[71] Herndon once observed such a witness "turn pale—& tremble, great big drops of sweat—drops of agony stood out all over the man's face."[72] While defending an orphan girl who "had been betrayed to her ruin," Lincoln grew indignant at "disgusting testimony" against his client and "turned upon the offending witness a torrent of invective and denunciation of such severity as rarely ever falls from the lips of an advocate at the bar."[73]

If opposing counsel tried to browbeat his witness, Lincoln "was terrific in denunciation" and "had no mercy," according to David Davis.[74] In the spring of 1851 Davis observed him as he "bore down savagely" during his closing remarks in a bastardy case in which the married defendant "has been using extraordinary exertions to procure testimony, to prove that the woman had permitted the embraces of other men."[75] Whitney remembered that such conduct made Lincoln "get pugnacious." When attorney Amzi McWilliams shouted "No! No!! No!!!" at one of Lincoln's witnesses, Lincoln yelled, "Oh! Yes! Yes!! Yes!!!" while "looking daggers at McWilliams, who quailed under Lincoln's determined look."[76] A famous surgeon, testifying as an expert witness, aroused Lincoln's scorn when he made "some very extreme statements." During cross-examination, Lincoln asked him how much his fee was for testifying. The large sum stunned the jurors and court observers. Lincoln then "rose, turned, and, stretching out his long right arm and forefinger, . . . cried in a shrill voice, overflowing with the hottest indignation: 'Gentlemen of the jury, big fee, big swear.'"[77]

During a trial at Jimtown on the Sangamon River, Lincoln attacked another lawyer, a young man with "an exceedingly glib tongue" that he used "quite briskly in referring to Mr. Lincoln." Finally Lincoln "told the jury that the young man reminded him of an old mud scow that used to run on the Sangamon river. Its engine was a rather weak affair and when they blew the whistle the wheels would stop, and Mr. Lincoln thought that the young man was in a somewhat similar condition, that when he was using his tongue so vigorously, his brain failed to work."[78]

Although hardly a model of sartorial fastidiousness, Lincoln once ridiculed "a very eminent lawyer, of Springfield, who was extremely careless, almost slatternly, in his dress and manners." Arguing a minor case against this gentleman, Lincoln found himself in danger of losing. To avert defeat, he addressed the jury:

> My learned friend has made an able speech to you. He has analyzed the testimony with his accustomed acuteness and skill, and laid down to you the law with his usual ability and confidence. And I am not going to assert, positively, that he is mistaken, either as to the law or the evidence. It would not become me to do so, for he is an older and better lawyer than I am. Nevertheless I may properly make a suggestion to you, gentlemen of the jury. And I now ask you, and each of you, to look, closely and attentively, at my friend, the counsel on the other side, as he sits there before you,—look at him all over, but especially at the upper part of him, and then tell me if it may not be possible that a lawyer who is so unmindful of the proprieties of this place as to come into the presence of his Honor and into your presence, gentlemen of the jury, with his standing collar on wrong-end-to, may not possibly be mistaken in his opinion of the law?

This provoked uproarious laughter as observers noted that, indeed, the attorney had buttoned his collar on improperly, with its two points "sticking out behind, like horns."[79]

Boasters sometimes felt the sting of Lincoln's ridicule in court. During a seduction trial at Urbana, a witness hostile to Lincoln's client intimated that he was a lady's man. Lincoln belittled him in graphic terms: "Ther[e] is Busey—he pretends to be a great heart smasher—does wonderful things with the girls—but I'll venture that he never entered his flesh but once & that is when he fell down & stuck his finger in his —— [anus]."[80]

Less crudely, Lincoln ridiculed a hostile witness who called himself J. Parker Green. During cross-examination, Lincoln made fun of his name to discredit Green: "*Why J. Parker Green? . . . What did the J. stand for? . . . John? . . . Well, why did n't the witness call himself John P. Green? . . . That was his name, was n't it? . . . Well, what was the reason he did not wish to be known by his right name? . . . Did J. Parker Green have anything to conceal; and if not, why did J. Parker Green part his name in that way?*" Green quickly became a laughing stock, and Lincoln won his case.[81]

Opposing counsel was not immune from Lincoln's ridicule. He once took offense when a lawyer challenged some potential jurors on the grounds that they knew Lincoln, who then asked members of the jury pool whether they were acquainted with the other lawyer. Judge David Davis reprimanded him, saying, "Now, Mr. Lincoln, you are wasting time. The mere fact that a juror knows your opponent does not disqualify him."

"'No, your Honor,' responded Lincoln, dryly. 'But I am afraid some of the gentlemen may *not* know him, which would place me at a disadvantage.'"[82]

Clients could also anger Lincoln. One rejected his advice, saying, "I will be d[amne]d if I do." Lincoln replied "in the same spirit," saying, "I will be d[amne]d if I attend to your suit if you don't."[83] In 1853 he snapped at a party in a fraud suit when that gentleman complained "sulkily" about the verdict, which awarded him some money. At that point Lincoln "became angry. 'You old fool,' he cried, 'you'll keep on until you won't get a cent.'"[84]

A client once wounded Lincoln's feelings. Shortly after Stephen A. Douglas defeated him for the Senate, Lincoln received a complaint from Samuel C. Davis and Company, which thought the firm of Lincoln and Herndon had badly neglected its interests.[85] He wrote an exasperated reply suggesting that the whole matter, which involved the collection of judgments, be turned over to another attorney. Testily he declared, "My mind is made up. I will have no more to do with this class of business. I can do business in court, but I can not, and will not follow executions [of judgments on property] all over the world. . . . I would not go through the same labor and vexation again for five hundred [dollars]."[86] The outburst had something to do, in all probability, with his frustration not only with Samuel C. Davis and Company, but also with Stephen A. Douglas and Company. During the 1858 campaign, Douglas nettled Lincoln; at Charleston, site of the fourth debate, Lincoln told D. C. Donnohoe that if Douglas angered him further, he would state "that he (L) did not have to have his wife along to keep him sober."[87]

Another client, William Martin, exasperated Lincoln by insisting that important documents had been published in the press. "I have just seen a letter of yours," he wrote Martin on August 29, 1851, "to Mr. Hickox, in which you *reiterate* that the publications for the calls were all made in both the city papers at Springfield. May be they were; *but I tell you if they were, neither I, nor the editors or publisher's of the papers can find them.* . . . Surely you can not suppose I would be so pertenaceously urging you to send the publications, if I had them here already."[88]

Bullying in or out of court stirred Lincoln's ire. During the Black Hawk War of 1832, he intervened to stop his fellow militiamen from killing an old, hungry Indian bearing a safe-conduct pass. When this forlorn figure entered their camp, many soldiers, enraged by recent atrocities committed by the Indians, leveled their muskets at him. When Lincoln ordered the troops not to shoot, they reluctantly complied. His friend W. G. Greene recalled, "I never in all my life saw Lincoln so roused before."[89] In Springfield Lincoln angrily denounced the young son of a butcher who had loosed his bulldog on a gentle canine owned by a neighbor's child, who later recalled, "I shall never forget how big his fist looked as he shook it in the face of the butcher boy and denounced his accomplices."[90]

In 1856 Lincoln was evidently inflamed by the tactics of proslavery Missourians who terrorized Free Soil settlements in neighboring Kansas, and by South Carolina Representative Preston Brooks, who had bludgeoned Massachusetts Senator Charles Sumner into insensibility at the Capitol. Just days after the caning of Sumner, Lincoln delivered his celebrated "Lost Speech" in Bloomington, Illinois. Although the text has not survived, eyewitnesses recalled that he spoke with unwonted anger and passion. One student of the event concluded that "Lincoln stepped cleanly out of his character, and became . . . a different person— fiery, emotional, reckless, violent, hotblooded—everything which at other times he was not."[91] This feeling tone probably reflected his rage at proslavery bullies, a sentiment widespread in the North.[92]

With his highly developed sense of fair play, Lincoln grew incensed at cheating, especially in politics. On election day in 1840, when he heard that an Illinois railroad contractor had brought a construction gang to take over the polls, he told the contractor menacingly, "You will spoil & blow if you live much longer." That night Lincoln confided to his friend Joshua Speed, "I intended to knock him down & go aw[a]y and leave him a-kicking."[93]

In athletics as well as politics Lincoln scorned dirty tricks. Soon after arriving in New Salem in 1831, he was goaded into a wrestling match with Jack Armstrong, the champion scuffler of the area. As they struggled, an onlooker named Bill Clary, who had bet money on Armstrong, cried out, "Throw him any way, Jack." Armstrong then "grabbed Abe by the thigh and threw him in a second." According to one observer, "Abe got up pretty mad. He didn't say much, but he told somebody that if it ever came up right, he would give Bill Clary a good licking."[94]

Lincoln also grew angry when his good faith was impugned. In 1834, while serving as postmaster at New Salem, he received a request from a newspaper subscriber for a receipt for postage paid. Interpreting this as a reflection on his honor, Lincoln indignantly replied, "The law requires News paper postage to be paid in advance and now that I have waited a full year you choose to wound my feelings by insinuating that unless you get a receipt I will probably make you pay it again." Despite his irritation, he complied with the request.[95]

During his campaign for reelection to the state legislature two years later, Lincoln resorted to unusually strong language in denouncing a critic. One Robert Allen had claimed that he knew things that, if told, would ruin Lincoln at the polls but, as a favor to the candidate, he would not make his information public. Lincoln heatedly protested, "That I once had the confidence of the people of Sangamon is sufficiently evident, and if I have since done any thing, either by design or misadventure, which, if known, would subject me to a forfeiture of that confidence, he that knows of that thing, and conceals it, is a traitor to his country's interest."[96]

When accused in 1853 of misappropriating funds, he found it "difficult to suppress" his "indignation" at those who had filed a claim against him.[97] He used similar language when chastising George W. Rives, who, in 1849, had asked Congressman Lincoln to help him obtain a government job in the Wisconsin Territory. Because one of Lincoln's close friends had applied for a post in the same locale, he had reluctantly turned Rives down; later Lincoln was told that the disappointed office-seeker had openly abused him. When Rives once again asked for a letter of recommendation, Lincoln answered with some asperity that his "feelings were wounded" by the allegations that Rives had attacked him: "On receiving your last letter, the question occurred whether you were attempting to *use* me, at the same time you would *injure* me, or whether you might not have been misrepresented to me. If the former, I ought not to answer you; if the latter I ought, and so I have remained in suspense." Giving Rives the benefit of the doubt, Lincoln sent him an endorsement.[98]

That same year Lincoln took offense at charge that he had been willing to pay $1,000 to a Springfield clique dedicated to helping thwart his competitors, particularly Justin Butterfield of Chicago, for the commissionership of the General Land Office. Upon learning of this charge, he wrote a heated denial to the secretary of the interior: "This annoys me a little. I am unwilling for the Administration to believe or suspect such a thing." He assured the secretary that he knew of no such clique and insisted that he "opposed the appointment of Mr. B[utterfield] because I believed it would be a matter of discouragement to our active, working friends here [in Illinois]." Somewhat disingenuously he added, "I never did, in any true sense, want the office myself."[99]

When his friend William Butler, at whose Springfield home Lincoln took his meals from 1837 to 1842, protested that Lincoln had committed political treachery, he answered heatedly, "I only now say, that I am willing to pledge myself in black and white to cut my own throat from ear to ear, if, when I meet you, you shall *seriously* say, that you believe me capable of betraying my friends for any price."[100]

• • •

In the White House, Lincoln lost his temper more than once, despite what he may have told Governor Pierpont of Virginia. Although long-suffering, he found it difficult to tolerate insolence. In May 1861, the governor of Tennessee protested against the seizure of a ship at Cairo, Illinois. In response to such "cheekiness," to use John Hay's word, the president said, "He be d[amne]d."[101] Three days later another cheeky Southerner, state senator John M. Johnson of Kentucky, irritated the president with a letter indignantly denouncing the Union occupation of Cairo.[102] Lincoln had his secretary, John Hay, send the following response: "The President directs me to say that the views so ably stated by you shall have due consideration: and to assure you that he would certainly never have ordered the movement of troops complained of, had he known that Cairo was in your Senatorial district." Hay "wanted to add that the President respectfully requested that in future occasions he would spell 'solemnly' with an 'n'. But this hypercritical orthography the Chief disapproved."[103]

One day a low-ranking officer, after failing to get the president to rescind the order dismissing him from the service, finally exploded: "Well, Mr. President, I see you are determined not to do me justice!" Lincoln quietly set down the petitioner's papers, escorted him to the door, and said in parting, "Sir, I give you fair warning never to show yourself in this room again. I can bear censure, but not insult!" The officer protested that he must have his papers, to which Lincoln replied, "Begone, sir, your papers will be sent to you. I wish never to see your face again!"[104] He also threw out a profane caller, saying, "I thought Senator C. had sent me a gentleman. I was mistaken. There is the door, and I wish you good-night."[105] Once summoned from a cabinet meeting to hear a minor complaint, the president tried to humor his caller, who responded, "Mr. President, I think your course is decidedly insincere." Lincoln silently "wheeled the little man around, grabbed him by the collar and the seat of the pantaloons, threw him into the hall and returned to resume the other necessary work of the day."[106] He used force yet again to evict a gambler posing as a member of the clergy. A White House secretary recalled that as the gentleman left the president's office, he was hurried on his way by "a large foot just behind him, suggesting to any naval constructor the idea of a propeller."[107]

In 1863 General Daniel Sickles called at the White House and, after receiving warm praise from Lincoln, criticized the president for allowing his pro-Confederate sister-in-law to stay at the Executive Mansion. According to an eyewitness, "Lincoln instantly drew himself up and said in a quiet, dignified voice, 'Excuse me, General Sickles, my wife and I are in the habit of choosing our own guests. We do not need from our friends either advice or assistance in the matter.'"[108]

When Charles Gibson, a conservative Republican from Missouri, petulantly resigned his federal position in 1864, Lincoln, in the words of a member of his cabinet, was "incensed" and struck back "in blind impetuosity," showing "bad taste."[109] Lincoln's reply to Gibson, sent under the signature of John Hay, concluded, "He [the president] thanks Mr. Gibson for his acknowledgment that he has been treated with personal kindness and consideration; and he says he knows of but two small draw-backs upon Mr. Gibson's right to still receive such treatment, one of which is that he [the president] could never learn of his giving much attention to the duties of his office, and the other is this studied attempt of Mr. Gibson's to stab him."[110]

Sometimes Lincoln used his legendary storytelling skills to put down insolent callers. One day three gentlemen barged into the presidential office to demand that the government adopt their new weapon and thereby bring the war to a quick end. Their spokesman said impatiently, "We have been here to see you time and again; you have referred us to the Secretary of War, to the Chief of Ordnance, and the General of the Army, and they give us no satisfaction. We have been kept here waiting, till money and patience are exhausted, and we now come to demand of you a final reply to our application."

"You three gentlemen remind me of a story I once heard of a poor little boy out West," Lincoln responded. The youngster could not keep the names of Shadrach, Meschach, and Abednego straight, much to the annoyance of his religious instructor, who threatened to punish the boy.

After several unsuccessful attempts, the clergyman finally said, "'Now tell me the names of the men in the fiery furnace.'

"'Oh,' said the boy, 'here come those three infernal bores! I wish the devil had them!'" Thereupon the three petitioners left.[111]

He used humor in a similar fashion to express irritation at the governor-general of a Canadian coastal province that was used as a refuge by Confederate blockade-runners. The governor-general called at the White House during the election campaign of 1864 and "with a grain of sarcasm" asked if he could vote in November. Lincoln, who "had been very much annoyed by the [governor-general's] failure . . . to enforce, very strictly, the rules of neutrality," was reminded of a story about an Irishman who arrived from the old country one election day and was

> perhaps, as eager as Your Excellency, to vote, and to vote early and late and often. So, upon his landing at Castle Garden, he hastened to the nearest voting place, and, as he approached, the judge, who received the ballots, inquired, "who do you want to vote for? on which side are you?" Poor Pat was embarrassed, he did not know who were the candidates. He stopped, scratched his head, then, with the readiness of his countrymen, he said:
>
> "I am fornent the Government, anyhow. Tell me, if your Honor plases, which is the rebellion side, and I'll tell you how I want to vote. In Ould Ireland, I was always on the rebellion side, and, by Saint Patrick, I'll stick to that same in America."
>
> "Your Excellency," said Mr. Lincoln, "would, I should think, not be at all at a loss on which side to vote?"[112]

Lincoln also lost his temper at weapons inventors who, he thought, took advantage of his good nature. In January 1862, he "remarked witheringly" to a gentleman who proposed a new form of incendiary shell "that all the charlatans came to him with their worthless inventions because they knew he could be easily imposed upon." The victim of this verbal assault, Levi Short, later said, "Judge you, whether I winced under the lash."[113]

The inventor of a periscopelike device for rifles called at the White House to lobby the president, who suggested that he approach the War Department. When informed that the gentleman had already done so and been turned down, Lincoln, "evidently becoming somewhat impatient," said, "Well, do you want me to test it?"

"O, no," was the reply. "But I would like the privilege of allowing the soldiers to test it."

"Ah," responded the president, "what you want then is a license to go down to the Army and peddle your looking-glass machine among the soldiers, is it? Good day, sir."[114]

Reports on new weapons also could make the presidential gorge rise. When late in the war he received an exceptionally voluminous committee report on a cannon, he threw down the bulky document, exclaiming, "I should want a new lease of life to read this through! Why can't a committee of this kind occasionally exhibit a grain of common sense? If I send a man to buy a horse for me, I expect him to tell me his *'points'*—not how many *hairs* there are in his tail."[115] In December 1862, a noncommittal report on a new cartridge prompted Lincoln to respond: "In this, as in other cases, I am disgusted with the character of this report made by a supposed expert. An opinion whether the cartridge should be introduced into the service, and not how many pine boards it penetrated . . . is what is wanted."[116]

Bureaucratic obstructiveness as well as timidity could rouse Lincoln's ire. Delays in carrying out plans to equip the army with mortars in early 1862 caused him to circumvent normal channels. A caller noted in her diary that the president was *"mad about mortars"* and said "he believes he must take these army matters into his own hands." In order to rush essential mortar beds to General Grant, Lincoln had enlisted the aid of Abram S. Hewitt, who discovered that a Pennsylvania firm could produce the necessary wheels and rails for these beds. When the firm's owner expressed reluctance to fill the emergency order, Lincoln, at Hewitt's suggestion, dispatched an officer to seize the factory. The owner then agreed to produce the necessary items forthwith. The mortars helped Grant capture Fort Donelson in February.[117]

Lincoln would also protest against regulations that made little sense, like the army requirement that officers pass tests full of such irrelevant questions as "Why did the Roman Government declare war against Mithridates?" In 1863, for example, he ordered the War Department to appoint one Jacob R. Freese to a colonelcy in a black unit "regardless of whether he can tell the exact shade of Julius Caesar's hair."[118]

Lincoln also resented presidential dress requirements. One day as he was about to leave for the Capitol as a congressional session ended, his servant remarked, "Mr. President, you must change your clothes before going." A visitor recalled that Lincoln, "rather cross and impatient," asked what was wrong with the suit he was wearing. "Why you must wear your dress suit and coat for your appearance in the president's room of the capitol is official," replied the servant. Lincoln "protested and ridiculed the idea" but eventually agreed to change his garb.[119]

When an elderly gentleman in early 1863 tried to enlist Lincoln's help for a business deal, he listened patiently and mildly suggested that his caller launch the enterprise without presidential sanction and blessing. The would-be entrepreneur replied that the scheme would fare much better if Lincoln endorsed it. An observer recalled that Lincoln's eyes

> flashed with sudden indignation, and his whole aspect and manner underwent a portentous change. "No!" he broke forth, with startling vehemence, springing from his seat under the impulse of his emotion. "No! I'll have nothing to do with this business, nor with any man who comes to me with such degrading propositions. What! Do you take the President of the United States to be a commission broker? You have come to the wrong place, and for you and every one who comes for such purposes, there is the door!" The man's face blanched as he cowered and slunk away confounded, without uttering a word. The President's wrath subsided as speedily as it had risen.[120]

A Southerner who claimed to be loyal asked Lincoln to sign papers allowing him to recover substantial sums for property damaged in the war. The president heatedly observed that the claimant's documents did not prove that he deserved the money. "I know what you want," Lincoln snapped, "you are turning, or trying to turn me into a justice of the peace, to put your claims through. There are a hundred thousand men in the country, every one of them as good as you are, who have just such bills as you present; and you care nothing of what becomes of them, so you get your money."

The caller insisted that his claim was valid.

"Yes, but you know you can't prove what is in this paper by all the people in the United States, and you want me to prove it for you by writing my name on the back of it; yes, in plain words you wish me to lie for you that you may get your money. I shall not do it."[121]

Importunate office seekers occasionally felt the sting of Lincoln's anger. Congressman John B. Alley saw two of them accost the president as he walked from the White House to the War Department. When their persistence became unbearable, the "President, evidently worn out by care and anxiety, turned upon them, and such an angry and terrific tirade, against those two incorrigible bores, I never before heard from the lips of mortal man," Alley recalled.[122]

Another claimant rushed up to Lincoln on the street one day and pressed upon him a letter and requested a government post in Wisconsin. Alexander Milton Ross, who was with Lincoln, remembered that "the President was offended at the rudeness, for he passed the letter back without looking at it, saying, 'No, sir! I am not going to open shop here.'" As they continued their walk, Lincoln told Ross, "These office-seekers are a curse to this country. No sooner was my election certain, than I became the prey of hundreds of hungry, persistent applicants for office, whose highest ambition is to feed at the government crib."[123]

On the heels of Willie Lincoln's death in February 1862, a suppliant for a postmastership in Michigan loudly demanded to see the bereaved president. When Lincoln emerged from his office to learn the cause of the commotion, the office-seeker insisted on an interview. The request was honored. When Lincoln discovered his caller's business, he "got angry," as he later told Joshua Speed, and asked, "When you came to the door here, didn't you see crepe on it? Didn't you realize that meant somebody must be lying dead in this house?"

"Yes, Mr. Lincoln, I did. But what I wanted to see you about was important."

Heatedly the president replied, "That crepe is hanging there for my son; his dead body at this moment is lying unburied in this house, and you came here, push yourself in with such a request! Couldn't you at least have the decency to wait until after we had buried him?"[124]

"If this keeps on," Lincoln once lamented, "I shall be in the position of a man who is so busy renting rooms at one end of his house that he has no time to put out the fire that is consuming it at the other end."[125] Even some of his old friends became a burden. Four days after his first inauguration Lincoln complained to Henry C. Whitney about David Davis: "with expressions of extreme irritability, and with a countenance shrouded in densest gloom," the president "inveighed . . . in the bitterest terms against Judge Davis's greed and importunity for office, and summarized his disgust in these words: 'I know it is an awful thing for me to say, but I already wish I was back home, and some one else was here in my place.'"[126] Ward Hill Lamon recalled a similar outburst by Lincoln, who "greatly disturbed and much excited" called the presidency "a white elephant" and complained that "with a fire in my front and rear, having to contend with the jealousies of the military commanders and not receiving that cordial cooperation and support from Congress that could reasonably be expected with an active and formidable enemy in the field threatening the very life-blood of the Government, make my position anything but a bed of roses."[127]

Two years later Lamon and Davis irritated the president by lobbying on behalf of Colonel William Orme, who sought both a promotion and a leave of absence. "Lamon & I have been incessant in our endeavors," Davis reported in January 1863. On the twenty-second of that month, Lincoln "was much annoyed, saying that the whole thing was full of trouble—on account of the constant pressure . . .—that if leave was granted to Orme he w[oul]d have to grant leave to others." Davis noted that the "pressure upon Lincoln for offices & promotions is as great as ever—He sometimes gets very impatient—If ever a man sh[oul]d be sympathized with it is Lincoln—."[128]

Whitney too nettled the president by urging an appointment. When he asked that Sam Houston's brother William be given a government post, Lincoln, as Whitney recalled, "flew into a towering rage at once" and said "'don't bother me about Bill Houston. [H]e has been here sitting on his a[s]s all summer waiting for me to give him the best office I've got.'" When Whitney replied, "If he will select a small clerkship," Lincoln interrupted, roaring "with more impatience & disgust" than Whitney had ever heard him use, "I hain't got it." Whitney dropped the subject, and the president "at once became cheerful and jolly."[129] Cassius M. Clay aroused similar feelings. In December 1862 the president, "much annoyed," refused to see Clay, telling a confidant that the Kentuckian "had a great deal of conceit and very little sense, and that he did not know what to do with him, for he could not give him a command—he was not fit for it."[130]

As the war drew to a close, Lincoln reacted in somewhat the same manner when told that his vice president, Andrew Johnson, had with another politician come to visit him at City Point, Virginia. According to Admiral David D. Porter, the president became "greatly excited," "jumped up from the chair," and was "almost frantic" as he exclaimed, "Don't let those men come into my presence. I won't see either of them; send them away. . . . I won't see them now, and never want to lay eyes on them. I don't care what you do with them . . . but don't let them come near me!" The agitated chief executive then "sat down in his chair looking like a man it would be dangerous for anyone to anger."[131] During that same visit, Mary Lincoln, who claimed that her husband "hated" his new vice president, heard him exclaim, "For God's sake don't ask Johnson to dine with us."[132]

The president evidently believed that, as military governor of Tennessee, Johnson had been "too harsh" and "severe,"[133] and he was appalled by the vice president's conduct at the inauguration in March 1865. There Johnson had delivered a drunken speech before an embarrassed audience in the Senate chamber.[134] Humiliated, Lincoln listened to the "incoherent harangue" and "bowed his head with a look of unutterable despondency."[135] As the scandalized spectators filed out to hear Lincoln give his inaugural, the president said to officials in charge of arrangements, "Do not permit Johnson to speak a word during the exercises that are now to follow."[136] For the next six weeks, Lincoln shunned his vice president.[137]

Other high officials upset Lincoln. When he solved patronage problems, he naturally expected his wishes to be carried out; when they were not, he grew angry. The director of the Philadelphia mint once failed to obey instructions to employ one Elias Wampole. Lincoln sharply reproved him: "You must make a job of it, and provide a place for . . . Wampole. Make a job of it with the Collector, and have it done. You *can* do it for me, and you *must.*"[138]

When the naval officer in Baltimore refused to carry out the president's order to appoint one French S. Evans to a post in the Customs House, he received a stern letter from the White House: "I am quite sure you are not aware how much I am disobliged by the refusal to give . . . Evans a place. . . . I had no thought that the men to whom I had given the higher officers [offices] would be so ready to disoblige me."[139]

Three years later, he chastised David P. Holloway, the commissioner of patents, for failing to endorse the Republican party's congressional nominee in his home district. When that candidate, George W. Julian, appealed to Lincoln to have Holloway fired, the president said, "Your nomination is as binding on Republicans as mine, and you can rest assured that Mr. Holloway shall support you, openly and unconditionally, or lose his head." After a week or two without action from the commissioner, Lincoln summoned a messenger and "said to him in a very excited and emphatic way, 'Tell Mr. Holloway to come to me!' The messenger hesitated, looking somewhat surprised and bewildered, when Mr. Lincoln said in a tone still more emphatic, '*Tell Mr. Holloway to come to me!*'" A few days later, Holloway publicly backed Julian.[140]

Lincoln grew impatient one day when a pardon he had issued was questioned by the adjutant general, Joseph Holt, who dispatched a clerk to the White House. After the young man stated his business, the president "pointed to the paper containing the pardon and said: 'Is that my signature?' The clerk acknowledged that he recognized it. 'That's enough, then!'" Lincoln said, abruptly ending the interview.[141]

The Senate annoyed Lincoln one day when it rejected his nominees for high office. John W. Forney, secretary of the upper chamber, recalled him angrily saying, "Why did the Senate not confirm Mr.—— and Mr. ——? . . . My friends knew I wanted this done, and I wanted it done to-day." He then "used certain strong expressions" against the men whom the Senate did confirm for the posts. Forney protested that it was not his fault, to which the president replied, "Oh, no, I was not scolding you, my friend, but I fear I have been caught in a trap."[142]

In December 1862, Forney suggested to the president that a report on the recent Union defeat at Fredericksburg be published, "as the people were excited." Lincoln "answered warmly," saying "that he did not like to swear, but why will people be such damned fools?" As he was about to leave, Forney said "'that he hoped the President would not let Mr. Chase resign,' and added, 'nor Mr. Seward.' The President paused and reddened, then said suddenly, 'If one goes, the other must; they must hunt in couples.'"[143]

Cabinet members themselves sometimes angered Lincoln, notably Simon Cameron, his first secretary of war. He had been reluctant to appoint Cameron, whose "very name stinks in the nostrils of the people for his corruption," as he told a Pennsylvania politician.[144] In June 1861 the president, who "seemed in a temper" and "agitated," asked a journalist about dissatisfaction with War Department contracts.[145] Four months later Lincoln criticized his secretary of war to John G. Nicolay, whose memorandum of their conversation read: "Cameron utterly ignorant and regardless of the course of things and probable result. Selfish and openly discourteous to the president. Obnoxious to the country. Incapable either of organizing details or conceiving and executing general plans."[146] In December 1861, without consulting the president, Cameron indiscreetly recommended in his annual report that the slaves be liberated and recruited as Union troops. When Lincoln read that controversial passage, he exclaimed, "This will never do! Gen. Cameron must take no such responsibility. That is a question which belongs exclusively to me!"[147] On January 11, 1862, Lincoln sent Cameron a brusque dismissal that deeply wounded the Pennsylvania politico, who raged and wept.[148] Lincoln salved the wound with another note, more kind and generous.[149]

The president evidently grew exasperated with Secretary of the Navy Gideon Welles early in the war. According to one source (possibly Interior Secretary Caleb B. Smith), "The habit of Well[e]s in the Cabinet is to say nothing," to sit in meetings as "a sort of silent oracle." In June 1861 Lincoln asked him his opinion on a pressing matter. "Well," came the reply, "I d-o-n't exactly know." Lincoln, "turning sharply," asked "What the he-ll *do* you know?"[150]

A patronage squabble led to the resignation of another cabinet member, Treasury Secretary Salmon P. Chase, one of the few men who utterly exhausted Lincoln's patience.[151] The arrogant, self-righteous, sanctimonious, hyperambitious Chase had, by June 1864, so taxed the president's good humor that Lincoln avoided personal contact with him.[152] In accepting Chase's letter of resignation, Lincoln said, "You and I have reached a point of mutual embarrassment in our official relations which, it seems to me, cannot be overcome or longer sustained consistently with the public service."[153] When notified of this cabinet change, the astonished Senate Finance Committee called at the White House, where Lincoln explained why he had accepted Chase's resignation. A member of that body, John Conness, later described how the president rehearsed the history of his troubled relations with the treasury secretary, who had several times offered his resignation. Lincoln concluded that "I will not longer continue the association. I am ready and willing to resign the office of President, . . . but I will no longer endure the state I have been in."[154] Similarly, the president told John Hay that "I could not stand it any longer."[155]

Among the many problems that plagued relations between Lincoln and Chase was the secretary's autocratic demand for complete control his department's patronage. To harmonize the factions within the Republican party, the president had insisted that he and members of Congress be consulted about all government appointments.[156] In March 1863, Chase had arbitrarily replaced the chief federal officers in San Francisco without discussing the changes with the California congressional delegation or with the president. When Lincoln discovered this, he summoned Noah Brooks, a West Coast journalist who recalled that the president quizzed him about the story "with some asperity of manner." When Brooks confirmed the facts, Lincoln "angrily asked why I had not told him this before" and "expressed his astonishment that he had been kept in the dark about so grave a matter as the emptying and filling of the most important Federal offices on the Pacific Coast."[157]

Another West Coast officeholder, Victor Smith, further exacerbated the tension between Lincoln and Chase. A friend of Smith's called him "a queer man, [as] cranky as possible, imprudently partisan and zealous, always ready for a controversy" and "one of the fiercest of the devoted admirers of Chase."[158] The president, deluged with protests about Smith's corruption and ineptitude as collector of customs at Port Townsend, told Chase that he would have to be dismissed. The secretary balked. Finally, in May 1863, Lincoln removed Smith and explained to Chase that he was under intense pressure to do so but, to placate the secretary, would name Smith to some other post. Chase, a friend of Smith's, thereupon submitted his resignation, which the president rejected and then somehow managed to appease his temperamental secretary of the treasury.[159]

The final dispute between the two men arose when Lincoln refused to approve Chase's candidate for the assistant treasurer at New York, Maunsell B. Field, a sycophantic socialite with no business experience or political following. He had been a clerk in the New York Custom House, and to oblige Chase, Lincoln had promoted him to third assistant secretary but would go no further. The influential New York senator Edwin D. Morgan strenuously opposed Field, who was often inexplicably absent from his post.[160] Lincoln himself told the Senate Finance Committee that, "I could not appoint him. He had only recently at a social gathering, in [the] presence of ladies and gentlemen, while intoxicated, kicked his hat up against the ceiling, bringing discredit upon us all, and proving his unfitness."[161] Chase was obdurate and although Lincoln offered him a choice of three candidates acceptable to Senator Morgan, the secretary asked to see the president. But relations between the two men had deteriorated so badly that Lincoln said, "The difficulty does not, in the main part, lie within the range of a conversation between you and me."[162]

Chase then resigned, evidently hoping to force Lincoln to back down as he had done the previous year when the secretary won a contest over a patronage appointment in Connecticut by threatening to quit.[163] As Lincoln interpreted it, Chase's letter of resignation in effect said to the president, "You have been acting very badly. Unless you say you are sorry, & ask me to stay & agree that I shall be absolute and that you shall have nothing, no matter how you beg for it, I will go."[164] Lincoln was in no mood to trifle, and when Ohio governor John Brough tried to effect a reconciliation, Lincoln said, "This is the third time he has thrown this [resignation] at me, and I do not think I am called on to continue to beg him to take it back, especially when the country would not go to destruction in consequence." When the governor persisted, Lincoln finally cut him off: "I know you doctored the matter up once, but on the whole, Brough, I reckon you had better let it alone this time."[165]

Lincoln told the register of the treasury that Chase had developed an unfortunate belief that he was an indispensable man who should be president. Such convictions, said Lincoln, "seem to have spoiled him. They have made him irritable, uncomfortable, so that he is never perfectly happy unless he is thoroughly miserable, and able to make everybody else just as uncomfortable as he is himself." Lincoln concluded that Chase "is either determined to annoy me, or that I shall pat him on the shoulder and coax him to stay. . . . I will not do it."[166]

The most striking feature of this complicated story is not so much that Lincoln finally lost patience with Chase and would not even speak to him, but that he endured such an insufferable man in his cabinet for so long. Another president, Rutherford B. Hayes, described Chase as "cold, selfish, and unscrupulous" and concluded that "political intrigue, love of power, and a selfish and boundless ambition were the striking features of his life and character."[167] Similar judgments have been rendered by historians, including Don E. Fehrenbacher, who noted that Chase was "a treacherous associate" to Lincoln and had "a streak of egocentric opportunism, unrelieved by humor or any significant capacity for self-examination," "restless ambition," "vanity of the kind that shuts out self-criticism and indulges self-deception," and that his "behavior was at times outrageous."[168]

Lincoln had shown the utmost forbearance in dealing with Chase's presidential intrigues in 1863 and 1864, when the treasury secretary tried to wrest the Republican nomination away from him. On one occasion, however, the president did express some resentment. In his December 1863 annual message to Congress, he had proposed a reconstruction program that would begin when 10 percent of the voters of a Confederate state took a loyalty oath. Chase suggested that the language be changed from "voters" to "citizens," for the attorney general had recently declared that blacks were citizens. Another cabinet member, John P. Usher, told Lincoln that "Chase was very pertinacious about the word citizen instead of voters. 'Yes,' said Lincoln, 'Chase thinks that the negroes, as citizens, will vote to make him President.'" Usher recalled this as an "event showing Lincoln's temper."[169]

A few months after accepting Chase's resignation, Lincoln nominated his former treasury secretary to be chief justice of the Supreme Court, even though he feared that Chase's "head was so full of *Presidential maggots* he would never be able to get them out" and that his overweening ambition might interfere with the execution of his judicial duties.[170] Lincoln had used the same imagery a year earlier, according to Thurlow Weed, who told John Bigelow that "Mr. Chase's report is very able, and his huge banking machine will make him strong. But how pitiable it is to know that his eye is single—not to the welfare of his country, in an unselfish cause, but to the presidency! Mr. Lincoln says that he is 'trying to keep that maggot out of his head,' but he cannot."[171] The president named Chase to the high court despite his own personal feelings, for he would, to use his own language, "rather have swallowed his buckhorn chair" or "have eat[en] flat irons" than to have made that appointment.[172] This reaction lends credence to the claim of another cabinet member, Montgomery Blair, who said that Chase "was the only human being that I believe Lincoln actually hated."[173]

Underlying the tension between Chase and Lincoln was the secretary's voracious craving for deference, which the president apparently gave in insufficient measure. John Hay claimed that it was Lincoln's "intellectual arrogance and unconscious assumption of superiority" that Chase "could never forgive."[174] Hay clearly exaggerated, for Lincoln was hardly "intellectually arrogant."[175] But despite his courteous, self-abnegating manner and his self-deprecating humor, Lincoln had as president a deep-rooted sense of self that lent him dignity, strength, and self-confidence.[176] These qualities were perhaps interpreted as arrogance by Chase, who may have projected onto Lincoln some of his own extreme self-regard. In any event, when he accepted Chase's resignation, Lincoln did not act merely out of pique; Chase wanted to dominate the administration, and Lincoln would not let him.

Lincoln had problems with other Radicals, more because of their style than their ideology. Historians have amply demonstrated that Lincoln and the Radicals shared in common strong antislavery views and a desire to prosecute the war vigorously.[177] What Lincoln found exasperating was "the self-righteousness of the Abolitionists" and "the petulent and vicious fretfulness of many radicals," as he put it.[178] According to Eli Thayer, Lincoln spoke of abolitionists "in terms of contempt and derision."[179] That is true of at least one "well-known abolitionist and orator" whom he called "a thistle"; "I don't see why God lets him live!" he exclaimed.[180]

Lincoln grew angry when first told in the summer of 1864 about the Wade-Davis Manifesto, outlining Radical objections to his reconstruction policies. On the night of August 5, Seward apparently met the president and summarized for him the manifesto, which had appeared in that day's New York *Tribune*. According to J. K. Herbert, who called at the White House on August 5 but decided not to visit again on the following day because it was "no use to talk to L. when he is so angry," Lincoln replied to Seward, "I would like to know whether these men intend openly to oppose my election,—the document looks that way." The president thought it curious that Horace Greeley should publish the manifesto, because he supported the administration's reconstruction policy. By the next day, Lincoln had calmed down; he told painter Francis Carpenter, "It is not worth fretting about; it reminds me of an old acquaintance, who, having a son of a scientific turn, bought him a microscope. The boy went around, experimenting with his glass upon everything that came in his way. One day, at the dinner-table, his father took up a piece of cheese. 'Don't eat that, father,' said the boy; 'it is full of *wrigglers.*' 'My son,' replied the old gentleman, taking, at the same time, a huge bite, 'let 'em *wriggle;* I can stand it if they can.'" Two days later the president, according to Gideon Welles, "remarked that he had not, and probably should not read it. From what was said of it, he had no desire to, could himself take no part in such a controversy as they seemed to wish to provoke." When a leading Radical, personally close to both Wade and Davis, called at the White House shortly after the manifesto appeared, the president said, "Ashley, I am glad to see by the papers that you refused to sign the Wade and Davis manifesto." "Yes, Mr. President," the congressman replied, "I could not do that." The two men looked at each other "while tears stood in the eyes of both."[181]

The quarrels between radical and conservative factions in Missouri vexed Lincoln mightily; in early 1863 he told a radical from that state, "Either party would rather see the defeat of their adversary than that of Jefferson Davis. You ought to have your heads knocked together."[182] But later that year the president acknowledged to one of his secretaries that the Missouri radicals "are nearer to me than the other side, in thought and sentiment, though bitterly hostile personally. They are utterly lawless—the unhandiest devils in the world to deal with—but after all their faces are set Zionwards."[183]

Among the unhandier devils was Thaddeus Stevens, a leading Radical in the House of Representatives. The militant Pennsylvania congressman provoked Lincoln in August 1864 by insisting that the conservative Montgomery Blair be removed from the cabinet if the Radicals of Pennsylvania were to campaign vigorously for the president's reelection. Because Lincoln was, as Henry C. Whitney noted, "extremely jealous" of "power which was unmistakably his," he bristled at Stevens's demand.[184] "Am I to be the mere puppet of power?" he asked rhetorically. "To have my constitutional advisers selected beforehand, to be told I must do this or leave that undone? It would be degrading to my manhood to consent to any such bargain—I was about to say it is equally degrading to your manhood to ask it." Lincoln concluded emphatically, saying he would rather "refuse the office rather than to accept such disgraceful terms as really not to be President after I am elected."[185] When Shelby M. Cullom of Illinois also pressed for Blair's dismissal, the president grew "annoyed, even to the extent of petulance" and defended his postmaster general vigorously.[186] To a representative of a German meeting in St. Louis suggesting a change in the cabinet, Lincoln allowed that it "might be a misfortune for the nation that he was elected President," but in all events "he meant to be President, and to perform his duty according to his own views, and nobody should dictate to him a change in his Cabinet."[187]

Stevens's counterpart in the Senate, Charles Sumner, was, according to a White House observer, "the only man, so far as my knowledge goes, to obtain the President's bitter dislike." Once Lincoln's "intense antipathy" toward the Massachusetts senator prompted him to order the hall attendant, Elphonso Dunn, to deny him admission.[188] Early in the war Sumner pressed hard for emancipation. Sumner, who, like his friend Chase, could be overbearing, one day provoked the president to exclaim loudly: "Mr. Sumner, I will not issue a proclamation freeing the slaves now." Sumner then jumped up and rushed out of the room, slamming the door behind him. An observer of this colloquy said that he "had never seen . . . Lincoln anything like mad before." Later that day, Lincoln mollified Sumner and invited him to dinner.[189] Sumner held a low opinion of Lincoln's competence. He once told Henry Wilson that "there are twenty men in the Senate who are better qualified for the place."[190]

Sumner failed to understand Lincoln's humor or subtlety. One day at the time of the sailing of General Burnside's expedition to Roanoke Island, Congressman Hamilton Fish joined Sumner to call on the president. As Fish later described the event, the three men talked about several matters, including Burnside's operation. Sumner tried to get the president to reveal the destination of the Union forces. "Well," he replied, "I am no military man, and of course, I cannot [know] all about these matters—and indeed if I did know, the interest of the public service require that I should not divulge them." As Fish recalled, Lincoln rose and, "sweeping his long hand over a Map of the North Carolina coast which hung in a corner," and said, "Now see here. Here are a large number of inlets, and I should think a fleet might perhaps get in there somewhere. And if they were to get in here, don[']t you think our boys would be likely to cut some flip-flaps? I think they would."

After leaving the Executive Mansion, Sumner impatiently criticized Lincoln's secretiveness. Fish replied, "He told you where Burnside is going."

"Don't you think that was merely to put us off?" Sumner asked skeptically.

"The President was desirous of satisfying your curiosity so far as he could," Fish said, "but of course could not give you an official declaration on the subject. I think you ought to be well satisfied that he has been so frank. You will see by the result that he has correctly indicated the point of attack." Fish, who proved correct, later said, "The direct and angular nature of Sumner had been utterly blind to the president's subtle hint, and so far from giving him credit for his confidence was going away exasperated at what he outwardly mistook for an unobliging reserve."[191]

In June 1862, Sumner denounced to the president the newly appointed military governor of North Carolina, Edward Stanly, who had forbidden schools to be opened to blacks. Lincoln, "with an impatience which Mr. Sumner never encountered from him on any other occasion, exclaimed, 'Do you take me for a School-Committee-man?'" He quickly "changed his tone, and with perfect kindness proceeded to consider the case."[192] Despite their temperamental and ideological differences, the president and Sumner managed to get along, partly because, as Lincoln once said, "Sumner thinks he runs me."[193]

Sumner's friend and early biographer Edward L. Pierce irritated Lincoln in mid-February 1862. At the suggestion of Chase, Pierce called on the president to describe conditions among the freedmen at Port Royal, South Carolina. As Pierce later remembered the conversation, "He soon cut me short, saying that he ought not to be bothered with such details, that there seemed to be a great itching to get negroes within our lines." When Pierce tried to condense his report, Lincoln again interrupted. Indignant, Pierce rose to leave, but before he made his exit, Lincoln managed to placate him. Pierce speculated that the ill health of the president's son Willie, who died shortly after this conversation took place, doubtless affected his mood.[194]

When a Connecticut delegation, led by Governor William A. Buck-ingham, urged emancipation upon him, Lincoln "said abruptly, as if irritated by the subject: 'Governor, I suppose that what your people want is more nigger.'" Buckingham was "surprised" both at "an impatience unusual with him" and at the president's language. Lincoln quickly altered "his mode of address to one of intensest earnestness, saying in substance, that if anybody supposed he was not interested in this subject, deeply interested, intensely anxious about it, it was a great mistake."[195]

In August 1862 a delegation led by Radical senators James F. Har-lan of Iowa and Samuel Pomeroy of Kansas vainly lobbied the president to accept black troops. In response to their arguments he said, "Gentlemen, you have my decision. I have made my mind up deliberately and mean to adhere to it. It embodies my best judgment, and if the people are dissatisfied, I will resign and let Mr. Hamlin try it." One of the callers replied, "I hope in God's name, Mr. President, you will."[196]

When pressed by a Radical senator to emancipate the slaves, Lincoln asked, "will Kentucky stand that?" The senator replied, "Damn Kentucky!" to which the president, in an unwonted resort to profanity, exclaimed: "Then damn *you!*"[197] He once denounced a certain politician as a "d——d rascal," then quickly added, "God knows I do not know when I have sworn before."[198] In response to the threat of French intervention in the Civil War, he allegedly said he would "be d——d if he wouldn't get 1,000,000 men if France dares to interfere."[199] When informed of a plot to defraud Illinois, Lincoln, in "a towering rage" declared, "They shan't do it, d——n 'em!"[200]

Lincoln never used such language to religious delegations insisting that he liberate the bondsmen, although he lost patience with some of them. In June 1862 a Quaker group, while presenting him an antislavery memorial, implied that he had been "false and derelict" in carrying out his alleged campaign promises to eradicate human bondage. The president "sought to repel this covert imputation upon his integrity and veracity" by correcting their garbled version of his 1858 "House Divided" speech. A congressman who observed the exchange noted that Lincoln "replied with an asperity of manner of which I had not deemed him capable."[201]

Two months later a Chicago clergyman delivered to Lincoln the word of the Lord: "Open the doors of bondage that the slave may go free!" The president replied: "That may be, sir, . . . but if it is, as you say, a message from your Divine Master, is it not odd that the only channel he could send it by was that roundabout route by that awfully wicked city of Chicago?"[202]

Other clergy from the West visited Lincoln one day and harangued him at length. The president, with "unusual animation," replied,

> Gentlemen, suppose all the property you possess were in gold, and you had placed it in the hands of Blondin [a celebrated tightrope walker] to carry across the Niagara River on a rope. With slow, cautious, steady step he walks the rope, bearing your all. Would you shake the cable, and keep shouting to him, "Blondin! stand up a little straighter! Blondin! stoop a little more; go a little faster; lean more to the south! Now lean a little more to the north!"—would that be your behavior in such an emergency? No; you would hold your breath, every one of you, as well as your tongues. You would keep your hands off until he was safe on the other side. This government, gentlemen, is carrying an immense weight; untold treasures are in its hands. The persons managing the ship of state in this storm are doing the best they can. Don't worry them with needless warnings and complaints. Keep silence, be patient, and we will get you safe across. Good day, gentlemen. I have other duties pressing upon me that must be attended to.[203]

When in 1862 a minister gave the president his views on the conduct of the war, Lincoln replied, "Perhaps you had better try to run the machine a week."[204]

Another clergyman, Moncure D. Conway, called on the president with several abolitionist friends in early 1863 to voice dissatisfaction with the enforcement of the recent Emancipation Proclamation. Addressing the group, which included Wendell Phillips, Lincoln noted that most of the men present had been lifelong members of political minorities and had "got into a habit of being dissatisfied. At any rate it has been very rare that an opportunity of 'running' [down] this administration has been lost." When his callers urged the president to replace the North Carolina military governor, Lincoln said angrily, "Well, gentlemen, the people have entrusted the conduct of this matter to *me*, and I must do what *I* think best, and take the responsibility."[205]

Lincoln deeply resented intimidation tactics. As John Hay observed, he would "not be bullied—even by his friends."[206] The president took special interest in wartime reconstruction in Louisiana and helped create a civilian government that elected two representatives to Congress. The House had not yet decided whether to acknowledge them as legitimate members, and when Treasury Secretary Chase suggested that their credentials might be rejected, the president, "apparently irritated," said, "Then I am to be bullied by Congress am I? I'll be d——d if I will."[207] Soon thereafter, Congress seated the Louisiana representatives.

Much as Lincoln admired the Sanitary Commission's efforts to help sick and wounded Union troops, he snapped at a delegation from that forerunner of the Red Cross one day when they "were crowding him in a direction he did not fancy." He turned on them and "with some little asperity" said, "It looks to me as if you would like to run this machine."[208]

When choosing his cabinet, Lincoln as president-elect felt unduly pressured by Thurlow Weed, the intimate friend of William Henry Seward, to refuse a post to Gideon Welles of Connecticut. According to Welles, Seward resented him because at the 1860 Republican convention Welles had led the anti-Seward Connecticut delegation. When visiting Lincoln in Springfield, Weed urged the appointment of John P. Hale, Amos Tuck, Charles Francis Adams, John A. Andrew, or any New Englander other than Welles to the cabinet. "His intense opposition," Welles later wrote, "confirmed Mr. Lincoln in the opposite direction."[209]

Courts which encroached on the executive branch's domain also angered Lincoln, especially when they threatened to impede the draft. Attorney General Edward Bates noted in his diary on September 14, 1863 that the president "was greatly moved—more angry than I ever saw him" because state judges had been freeing civilians arrested by the military, as authorized by the president. Lincoln, according to Bates, "declared that it was a formed plan of the democratic copperheads, deliberately acted out to defeat the Govt., and aid the enemy" and that "no honest man did or could believe that the State Judges have any such power."[210] He even threatened to expel refractory state judges to the Confederacy.[211] Pounding the table, Lincoln "said with great emphasis: 'I'll not permit my officers to be arrested while in the discharge of their public duties.'"[212] Later in the day Lincoln penned a truculent opinion on the draft, castigating its critics for their "effrontery" and use of "false arguments," impugning their patriotism, and asking, "Are we degenerate? Has the manhood of our race run out?"[213] The following day, he suspended the privilege of the writ of habeas corpus and issued stern orders to provost marshals to reject any attempt by judges to counter the proclamation.[214] That day the president also replied testily to his Illinois friends Jesse K. Dubois and Ozias M. Hatch, who had recommended that Robert Allen be appointed quartermaster general: "What nation do you desire Gen. Allen to be made Quarter-Master-General of? This nation already has a Quarter-Master-General."[215]

Attacks on Secretary of State Seward roused Lincoln's ire. On September 10, 1862, when a delegation from the War Committee of New York called at the White House to complain about administration policies and about Seward, a "sharp encounter" developed between the president and John E. Williams. In response to James A. Hamilton's criticism of Seward's April 10, 1861, dispatch to Charles Francis Adams, Lincoln "in an excited manner" said, "Sir! you are subjecting some letter of Mr. Seward's to an undue criticism in an undue manner." Then, pointing to Williams and Hamilton, he continued, "You, gentlemen, to hang Mr. Seward, would destroy this Government." Hamilton retorted, "Sir, that is a very harsh remark."[216]

When congressional Radicals tried to force Seward's withdrawal from the cabinet in late 1862, Lincoln smoothly finessed their challenge to his leadership.[217] During that crisis, Senator Orville H. Browning told the president that "the attack in the Senate caucus upon Mr[.] Seward was by the partizans of Mr[.] Chase, and that I had reason to believe that he had set them on. That their game was to drive all the cabinet out— then force upon him the recall of Mr[.] Chase as Premier, and form a cabinet of ultra men around him." Lincoln replied "with a good deal of emphasis that he was master, and they should not do that."[218] He recounted to John A. Dahlgren how upset he was during that crisis: "'It was very well to talk of remodelling the Cabinet, but the caucus had thought more of *their* plans than of *his* benefit,' and he had told them so."[219] Soon afterward, when a pair of New Yorkers came to urge the dismissal of Seward, the president heatedly rebuked them. As he described the event to John Hay a year later, "For once in my life I rather gave my temper the rein and I talked to those men pretty damned plainly."[220]

· · ·

Military ineptitude stretched Lincoln's patience to the breaking point. As a telegraph operator who often saw the president noted, Lincoln "was sometimes critical and even sarcastic when [military] events moved slowly."[221] In October 1861, General Thomas W. Sherman asked that a regiment be diverted from George McClellan's command to join his expedition against the Sea Islands. John Hay noted that "the President was vexed at this and at Sherman's intimation that the fleet would not sail before Sunday." Lincoln told his secretary of state, "I think I will telegraph to Sherman that I will not break up McClellan's command and that I haven't much hope of his expedition anyway." Seward replied, "No, you won't say discouraging things to a man going off with his life in his hand. Send them some hopeful and cheering despatch." Taking only part this advice, Lincoln the next morning curtly telegraphed Sherman: "I will not break up McC's army without his consent. I do not think I will come to Annapolis." Hay found Lincoln's "petulance very unaccountable."[222]

Earlier that month the president got "his dander up a little" about a proposed amphibious operation to be headed by General Ambrose E. Burnside. During a conference about Sherman's expedition, the subject came up and Lincoln "with some warmth" denied "all knowledge of it" and asked that the matter "be sifted instanter." A War Department official soon arrived with a paper obtained from one of McClellan's staff, marked "expedition of 8,000 men, General McClellan to name the Commanding General and names General Burnside." No one in the group had seen that memo, including the president, who declared he had never been asked "or told a word on the subject" and talked "of going back to Illinois if his memory has become as treacherous as that."[223]

In May 1862, while visiting the Army of the Potomac, he took a hand in the operations around Norfolk. Upon learning that petty jealousy and squabbles over rank between two generals had prevented a coordinated movement against the retreating Confederates, the president "with vehement action threw his tall hat on the floor, and uttering strongly his disapproval and disappointment . . . said finally: 'Send me some one who can write.'" Lincoln then dispatched the troops himself.[224] Around that same time, when the president hoped to "bag" Stonewall Jackson's troops in the Shenandoah Valley, he grew angry at General John C. Frémont because he "had failed (he claimed) to throw himself in the way of Jackson's retreating forces." A White House visitor recalled that Lincoln "complained bitterly of the disobedience of orders by Fremont" and, when it was suggested that he criticize Frémont to the press, "he said rather bitterly that he had quite enough to do without writing for the papers."[225] The president had earlier been upset by Frémont's discourtesy.[226]

Later that year, delays in forwarding troops from Massachusetts exasperated the president. The state's governor had protested that he could not dispatch some regiments "because I can[']t get quick work out of the U.S. disbursing officer & the Paymaster." Lincoln replied, "Please say to these gentlemen that if they do not work quickly I will make quick work with them. In the name of all that is reasonable, how long does it take to pay a couple of Regts.?" Plaintively he closed, "We were never more in need of the arrival of Regts. than now—even to-day."[227]

Another paymaster taxed Lincoln's patience when he refused to authorize wages for a young woman who in disguise had joined an Indiana regiment and was severely wounded in battle. Regulations did not provide for the payment of women who passed themselves off as men. According to a member of the paymaster general's staff, the president, when informed of the circumstances, "blazed with anger" and ordered that she be paid forthwith.[228]

Few people tested Lincoln's patience more than General George B. McClellan, who commanded the Army of the Potomac for more than a year between 1861 and 1862. This arrogant, snobbish, insolent West Point graduate, deemed by one biographer to be "inarguably the worst" general to head the Army of the Potomac, often exasperated the president with his delays, petulant complaints, and lack of fighting nerve.[229] To his wife, McClellan described Lincoln as "an idiot," "the original gorilla," and "'an old stick'—& of pretty poor timber at that." He spoke of "the cowardice of the Presdt" and said that "I can never regard him with feelings other than those of thorough contempt—for his mind, heart, & morality."[230] To General Montgomery Meigs he complained that Lincoln was indiscreet: "If I tell him my plans they will be in the New York Herald tomorrow morning. He can't keep a secret, he will tell them to Tadd."[231]

On November 13, 1861, the general snubbed the president, an event Hay described in his diary:

> I wish here to record what I consider a dreadful portent of evil to come. The president, Governor Seward and I went over to McClellan's house tonight. The servant at the door said the General was at the wedding of Colonel Wheaton at General Buell's and would soon return. We went in, and after we had waited about an hour McClellan came in, and without paying any particular attention to the porter, who told him the president was waiting to see him, went up stairs, passing the door of the room where the president and Secretary of State were seated. They waited about half-an-hour, and sent once more a servant to tell the General they were there, and the answer coolly came that the General had gone to bed.[232]

Lincoln magnanimously endured such treatment, saying on a similar occasion, "I'll hold McClellan[']s horse if he'll only bring us success."[233]

But eventually he lost his monumental self-control. In January 1862, with McClellan sick and the Army of the Potomac idle, the despairing president summoned generals Irvin McDowell and William B. Franklin to the White House, where, according to McDowell's minutes, Lincoln

> said he was in great distress, and as he had been to General McClellan's house, and the general did not ask to see him; and as he must talk to somebody, he had sent for General Franklin and myself to obtain our opinion as to the possibility of soon commencing active operations with the Army of the Potomac.
>
> To use his own expression, "If something was not soon done, the bottom would be out of the whole affair; and if General McClellan did not want to use the army, he would like to *borrow* it, provided he could see how it could be made to do something."[234]

The following month, as McClellan's delays provoked vehement criticism, Lincoln stated that "there was probably but one man in the country more anxious for a battle than himself, and that man was McClellan." The president "repudiated in words of withering rebuke those who make the charge that he or Mr. Seward or General McClellan were tampering or delaying out of any consideration for rebels or rebel institutions, or that they indulged any thought of ending the war by any means other than by conquest on the battlefield."[235]

Later in February McClellan botched an advance into western Virginia by miscalculating the width of canals.[236] Upon learning the bad news, Lincoln, according to a journalist, "swore like a Philistine."[237] White House secretary William O. Stoddard "never knew Mr. Lincoln so really angry, so out of all patience, as when it was reported impossible to obey his celebrated order for a general advance of the army on the 22d of February, 1862."[238] Stoddard recalled the scene vividly: Lincoln "was alone in his room when an officer of McClellan's staff was announced by the doorkeeper and admitted. The president turned in his chair to hear and was informed, in respectful terms, that the advance movement [against Winchester] could not be made.

"'Why?' he curtly demanded.

"'The pontoon trains are not ready—'

"'Why in [hell] ain't they ready?'

"The officer could think of no satisfactory reply, but turned very hastily and left the room. Mr. Lincoln also turned to the table and resumed the work before him, but wrote at about double his ordinary speed."[239]

When the secretary of war confirmed the bad news, the president asked "What does this mean?"

"It means that it is a d[amne]d fizzle. It means that he doesn't intend to do anything," replied Stanton.

John Nicolay noted that Lincoln "was much cast down and dejected at the news of the failure of the enterprise. 'Why could he not have known whether his arrangements were practicable?'" The president then summoned McClellan's chief of staff, General Randolph B. Marcy, and had a "long, sharp talk with him":

> "Why in the Nation, General Marcy," said he excitedly, "couldn't the General have known whether a boat would go through that lock before spending a million dollars getting them there? I am no engineer, but it seems to me that if I wished to know whether a boat would go through a hole or a lock, common sense would teach me to go and measure it. I am almost despairing at these results. Everything seems to fail. The general impression is daily gaining ground that the General does not intend to do anything. By a failure like this we lose all the prestige we gained by the capture of Fort Donelson. I am grievously disappointed—almost in despair."

When Marcy attempted to defend McClellan, Lincoln abruptly dismissed him.[240] On March 1 he described to Charles Sumner the canal boat fiasco, which "excited him very much, so that he expressed himself angrily."[241]

After McClellan launched his campaign against Richmond in the spring of 1862, the president became "indignant" when he discovered that his general had violated his agreement to leave behind enough troops to safeguard Washington while the bulk of the Army of the Potomac sailed for the Virginia Peninsula.[242] After the failure of that campaign, Lincoln and Marcy had another sharp conversation. Hearing that Marcy had predicted that the Army of the Potomac might be forced to capitulate, Lincoln grew "excited" and summoned the general to the White House, where he "said to him sternly, 'Genl. I understand you have used the word "Capitulate"—that is a word not to be used in connection with our army.'" Marcy then "blundered out some kind of explanation, excuse or apology."[243]

According to Senator Zachariah Chandler, around that same time

Lincoln grew exasperated with McClellan's interminable delays: "His patience was now completely exhausted, and his passions carried him by storm." Chandler exulted to a fellow radical, "Old Abe is mad, and the war will now go on."[244]

In the late summer of 1862, Lincoln became incensed at McClellan's conduct during the Second Battle of Bull Run. On August 27, a journalist told his editor that in the White House there "is great mortification at the Manassas raid," with the president "blue, and cross."[245] Five days later it was reported that "the President was never so wrathful as last night against George [McClellan]."[246] After Lee had thrashed General John Pope, Lincoln explained to Gideon Welles "with much emphasis" that "there has been a design, a purpose in breaking down Pope, without regard of consequences to the country. It is shocking to see and know this. . . . We had the enemy in the hollow of our hands" and would have crushed them "if our generals, who are vexed with Pope, had done their duty. All of our present difficulties and reverses have been brought upon us by these quarrels of the generals." Despite his fury at McClellan, Lincoln hesitated to dismiss him because, as he told Welles, the Young Napoleon "has the army with him."[247]

On September 1, Lincoln and John Hay discussed the battle, which was still raging at Chantilly:

> The President was very outspoken in regard to McClellan's present conduct. He said it really seemed to him that McC[.] wanted Pope defeated. He mentioned to me a despatch of McC. in which he proposed, as one plan of action, to "leave Pope to get out of his own scrape, and devote ourselves to securing Washington." He spoke also of McC's dreadful cowardice in the matter of Chain Bridge, which he had ordered blown up the night before, but which order had been countermanded; and also of his incomprehensible interference with Franklin's corps which he recalled once and then when they had been sent ahead by Halleck's order, begged permission to recall them again & only desisted after Halleck[']s sharp injunction to push them ahead till they whipped something or got whipped themselves. The president seemed to think him a little crazy.

Four days later Lincoln said of McClellan, "Unquestionably he has acted badly toward Pope! He wanted him to fail. That is unpardonable. But he is too useful just now to sacrifice."[248]

The president displaced his anger at McClellan onto Major John J. Key, who had allegedly declared that the Army of the Potomac did not intend to crush Lee: "The object is that neither army shall get much advantage of the other; that both shall be kept in the field till they are exhausted, when we will make a compromise and save slavery."[249] When the president heard this, he "said he should have the matter examined and if any such language had been used, [Key's] head should go off."[250] Lincoln quizzed the major, who "said he thought slavery was a divine institution, and any issue in this conflict that did not save it would be disastrous." The president replied, "You may think about that as you please, but no man shall bear a commission of mine who is not in favor of gaining victories over the rebels at any and all times." Lincoln forthwith cashiered the major.[251] As he later explained to John Hay, "I dismissed Major Key for his silly treasonable talk because I feared it was staff talk & I wanted an example."[252]

He also felt wrathful at Fitz-John Porter, who was court martialed for his role at Second Bull Run. Robert Todd Lincoln recalled seeing his father plainly exhibit distress "when he learned of General Fitz-John Porter's conduct."[253] To Orville H. Browning the president said "that he knew no reason to suspect any one [involved in the Second Battle of Bull Run] of bad faith except Fitz John Porter, and that . . . at present he believed his disobedience of orders, and his failure to go to Pope[']s aid in the battle . . . had occasioned our defeat, and deprived us of a victory which would have terminated the war."[254] After signing the order to dismiss the general, Lincoln remarked that he should have been shot.[255]

Shortly after the battle of Antietam in September 1862, the president had hoped that McClellan would cut off General Lee's army before it retreated from Maryland. The general offered countless excuses for delay, including the weariness of his army's horses. Lincoln sarcastically wrote him: "I have just read your despatch about sore tongued and fatieuged horses. Will you pardon me for asking what the horses of your army have done since the battle of Antietam that fatigue anything?"[256] Two weeks later, the president sacked McClellan. As Lincoln explained to his secretary in 1864,

> After the Battle of Antietam, I went up to the field to try to get him to move and came back thinking he would move at once. But when I got home he began to argue why he ought not to move. I peremptorily ordered him to advance. It was 19 days before he put a man over the river. It was 9 days longer before he got his army across and then he stopped again, delaying on little pretexts of wanting this and that. I began to fear he was playing false—that he did not want to hurt the

enemy. I saw how he could intercept the enemy on the way to Richmond. I determined to make that the test. If he let them get away, I would remove him. He did so & I relieved him.[257]

To another White House secretary, Lincoln said, "For the organization of an army—to prepare it for the field—and for some other things, I will back General McClellan against any general of modern times—I don't know but of ancient times either—but I begin to believe that he will never get ready to fight."[258] At that same time the president was growing impatient with General William S. Rosecrans, who delayed his projected advance in the West.[259]

When telegrams to him from McClellan were routed first to Stanton, Lincoln grew "mad all the way through" and scolded the White House troops who had forwarded the communications to the war secretary. A boy working for the American Telegraph Company recalled how Lincoln, who "was very mad," exclaimed to a sentry at the gate, "Send up to the door for the officer in charge [of receipting telegrams] and tell him that when telegrams come here addressed to me they should and must be delivered to me. Tell him also that if he sends any more of my telegrams over to Mr. Stanton's house I'll drive him away from here. Mr. Stanton has enough telegrams of his own and should not have mine." To the messenger boy, he said, "Tell your folks that I must have my telegrams, and that if these soldiers about the door interfere any more I'll drive every one of them away. I don't want them and never did want them about the place."[260]

Lee's second invasion of the North in the spring of 1863 rekindled Lincoln's hopes for trapping the Army of Northern Virginia, especially after General George Gordon Meade fought a victorious defensive battle at Gettysburg. The president hoped Meade would deliver the coup de grace to Lee before he could escape across the Potomac River. Between July 3, when the fighting ended, and July 14, when Lee safely returned to Virginia, Lincoln's "anxiety seemed as great as it had been during the battle itself," according to an officer in the Washington telegraph office. The president, he recalled, "walked up an down the floor, his face grave and anxious, wringing his hands and showing every sign of deep solicitude. As the telegrams came in, he traced the positions of the two armies on the map, and several times called me up to point out their location, seeming to feel the need of talking to some one. Finally, a telegram came from Meade saying that under such and such circumstances he would engage the enemy at such and such a time. 'Yes,' said the president bitterly, 'he will be ready to fight a magnificent battle when there is no enemy there to fight!'"[261]

On July 13, Lincoln, according to his son Robert, "summoned Gen. [Herman] Haupt, in whom he had great Confidence as a bridge builder, and asked him how long in view of the materials which might be . . . available under Lee, would it take him to devise the means and get his army across the river." Haupt guessed the it would require no more than twenty-four hours. Lincoln "at once sent an order to Gen. Meade," either by telegraph or by special messenger, "directing him to attack Lee's army with all his force immediately, and that if he was successful in the attack he might destroy the order but if he was unsuccessful he might preserve it for his vindication."[262]

When word arrived the next day that the Army of Northern Virginia had crossed the Potomac, Lincoln's "grief and anger were something sorrowful to behold," according to the journalist who brought him the bad news.[263] That day John Hay recorded in his diary,

> This morning the Presdt seemed depressed by Meade's despatches of last night. They were so cautiously & almost timidly worded—talking about reconnoitering to find the enemy's weak place and other such. He said he feared he would do nothing.
>
> About noon came the despatch stating that our worst fears were true. The enemy had gotten away unhurt. The Presdt was deeply grieved. "We only had to stretch forth our hands & they were ours. And nothing I could say or do could make the Army move. . . ."
>
> Every day he has watched the progress of the Army with agonizing impatience, hopes struggling with fear. He has never been easy in his own mind about Gen[.] Meade since Meade's General Order in which he called on his troops to drive the invader from our soil. The Presdt says, "This is a dreadful reminiscence of McClellan. The same spirit that moved McC. to claim a great victory because Pa[.] & Md[.] were safe. The hearts of 10 million people sank within them when McClellan raised that shout last fall. Will our Generals never get that idea out of their heads? The whole country is our soil."

The following day, Robert Todd Lincoln reported that his father "is grieved silently but deeply about the escape of Lee. He said, 'If I had gone up there[,] I could have whipped them myself.'" Robert recalled seeing his father cry when word arrived that Meade would not attack.[264] Four days later the president lamented to Hay, "Our Army held the war in the hollow of their hand & they would not close it. . . . We had gone through all the labor of tilling & planting an enormous crop & when it was ripe we did not harvest it."[265]

Lincoln feared that the Army of the Potomac was determined to allow the enemy to escape. "There is bad faith somewhere," he told Gideon Welles. "Meade has been pressed and urged, but only one of his generals was for an immediate attack. . . . What does it mean, Mr. Welles? Great God! what does it mean?"[266]

The president wrote Meade an exceptionally harsh letter: "I do not believe you appreciate the magnitude of the misfortune involved in Lee's escape. He was within your easy grasp, and to have closed upon him would, in connection with our other late successes, have ended the war. As it is, the war will be prolonged indefinitely. . . . Your golden opportunity is gone, and I am distressed immeasureably because of it."[267] After penning these bitter lines, Lincoln filed them away with the endorsement, "never sent, or signed," although earlier that day General Halleck wired Meade that "the escape of Lee's army without another battle has created great dissatisfaction in the mind of the president, and it will require an active and energetic pursuit on your part to remove the impression that it has not been sufficiently active heretofore."[268] Soon thereafter Lincoln told Meade, "The fruit seemed so ripe, so ready for plucking, that it was very hard to lose it."[269]

On July 15 Lincoln wrote to Simon Cameron, "I would give much to be relieved of the impression that Meade, Couch, Smith and all, since the battle of Gettysburg, have striven only to get Lee over the river without another fight."[270] When, two months later, Gideon Welles asked what Meade was doing, Lincoln replied, "It is the same old story of this Army of the Potomac. Imbecility, inefficiency—don't want to *do*—is defending the Capital." The president then "groaned," saying, "Oh, it is terrible, terrible, this weakness, this indifference of our Potomac generals, with such armies of good and brave men."[271]

Lincoln told Hay on July 19, after expressing his anguish, "Still, I am very grateful to Meade for the great service he did at Gettysburg."[272] Two days afterward, the president wrote a corps commander in Meade's army, "I was deeply mortified by the escape of Lee across the Potomac. . . . A few days having passed, I am now profoundly grateful for what was done, without criticism for what was not done."[273] Later the president asked Meade, "Do you know, General, what your attitude towards Lee after the battle of Gettysburg reminded me of?"

"No, Mr. President—what is it?" replied the general.

"I'll be hanged if I could think of anything but an old woman trying to shoo her geese across the creek!"[274]

On at least three other occasions Lincoln wrote but did not send angry missives. In September 1863, General Ambrose E. Burnside was ordered to relieve the besieged army of William S. Rosecrans in Chattanooga. When the president received a telegram indicating that Burnside was moving away from Chattanooga and toward Jonesboro, he cried out, "Jonesboro? Jonesboro?? D[amn] Jonesboro!"[275] He composed but did not send a heated reply: "Yours of the 23rd. is just received, and it makes me doubt whether I am awake or dreaming."[276]

Later that fall, a Kentucky judge complained that Union troops had violated the rights of slaveholders. Lincoln dashed off "a hot tempered letter" but evidently kept it: "I believe you are acquainted with the American Classics, (if there be such) and probably remember a speech of Patrick Henry, in which he represented a certain character in the, revolutionary times, as totally disregarding all questions of country, and 'hoarsely bawling, beef! beef!! beef!!!' Do you not know that I may as well surrender this contest, directly, as to make any order, the obvious purpose of which would be to return fugitive slaves?"[277] The following year a crank denounced General George H. Thomas to Lincoln, who wrote a stinging reply but, after handing the document to a telegraph operator, thought better of it, saying, "I guess on the whole . . . you need not send that—I will pay no attention to the crazy fellow."[278] He urged Secretary of War Stanton to follow the same policy of composing but not sending angry letters.[279]

In 1864, when Jubal Early's Confederate army penetrated into the North, Lincoln once again hoped to see the Confederates trapped. Early escaped, however, and the president once again was "disgusted," according to John Hay.[280] The following day Lincoln told Orville H. Browning that "he was in the dumps" because "the rebels who had besieged us were all escaped."[281]

In the aftermath of the Union defeat at Fredericksburg, Lincoln angrily rebuked Henry W. Halleck for evading his responsibilities as the army's general-in-chief. He asked Halleck to visit Burnside, inspect his plan to cross the Rappahannock River, and either approve or disapprove it. "If in such a difficulty as this you do not help," the president said, "you fail me precisely in the point for which I sought your assistance. . . . Your military skill is useless to me, if you will not do this." The letter was withdrawn because Halleck, considering it too "harsh," had threatened to resign.[282] Three months earlier, Lincoln had evidently become angry at Halleck when he called on the general to discuss a projected campaign in the West. According to one source, Halleck "absolutely insulted the President," who then "resolved to [re]move" Halleck for this "act of personal indignity."[283]

To officers who pestered him unmercifully about promotion, reinforcements, injured dignity, and the like, Lincoln would sometimes react sharply. In September 1862 General Franz Sigel called on the president to protest that a junior officer had been put in command over him. Lincoln sent him to Halleck, whom Sigel accused of lying.[284] The general dispatched an aide to the White House to protest yet again the administration's mistreatment of Sigel and his men. In response, the president urged Sigel to do the best he could with his command and "not to keep up this constant complaining," which made it seem as if the general "were only anxious about himself." Lincoln stressed that he "was tired of this constant hacking," which "gave him more trouble than anything else."[285] When another caller raised Sigel's case a few weeks later, the president snapped, "Don't talk to me any longer about *that man!*"[286] In January, Lincoln mildly rebuked Sigel but promptly apologized, saying, "If I do get up a little temper I have no sufficient time to keep it up."[287]

Lesser military figures also felt Lincoln's wrath. When in October 1863 General Robert C. Schenck authorized the forcible recruitment of black troops in Maryland without War Department approval, he jeopardized the chances of Unionist candidates in the upcoming state election. Lincoln, who preferred only voluntary recruiting with compensation for loyal slaveowners, said, "The fact is, Schenck is wider across the head in the region of the ears, & loves fight for its own sake, better than I do."[288] So the president summoned the general and his chief of staff, Donn Piatt, to Washington, where they received a dressing down. Piatt later wrote, "I do not care to recall the words of Mr. Lincoln. . . . They were exceedingly severe, for the President was in a rage."[289]

More gently Lincoln chided Massachusetts Governor John A. Andrew about raising black troops. When Andrew sent a letter on the president's birthday in 1864 protesting that blacks wishing to migrate to his state had been forcibly detained, Lincoln sarcastically replied, "If I were to judge from the letter, without any external knowledge, I should suppose that all the colored people South of Washington were struggling to get to Massachusetts; that Massachusetts was anxious to receive and retain the whole of them as permanent citizens; and that the United States Government here was interposing and preventing this." The president explained, "You are engaged in trying to raise colored troops for the U.S. and wish to take troops from Virginia. . . ; and the loyal Governor of Virginia, also trying to raise troops for us, objects to your taking his material away; while we, having to care for all, and being responsible alike to all, have to do as much for him, as we would have to do for you, if he was, by our authority, taking men from Massachusetts to fill up Virginia regiments."[290]

One day the president asked Mrs. Andrew, "How do the Governor and [Benjamin F.] Butler get on?" She replied, "You probably know more about it than I do, Mr. L[incoln]." "Well," answered the president, "the more I hear of it [the quarrel between Butler and Andrew] the madder I get with both of them." When Mrs. Andrew endeavored to defend her husband, Lincoln said, "Oh, you know I never get fighting mad with anybody."[291]

When his cherished plans to colonize freedmen went awry, Lincoln did grow angry, however. The Rev. Dr. James Mitchell recalled the president's irritation when Secretary of War Stanton rejected Lincoln's scheme to have British agents help relocate American blacks overseas.[292] In 1863, Charles K. Tuckerman visited the White House to discuss a plan to colonize five hundred blacks in Haiti. Tuckerman later recalled,

> When keeping an appointment, and when my patience was nearly ex-
> hausted by waiting to be summoned to the president's room, the door
> of the adjoining apartment was opened by him with considerable ir-
> ritability of manner, and, in a loose dressing gown and carpet slip-
> pers, he exclaimed:
> "I thought you were to be here at nine o'clock. It is now ten." I
> stated that I had been there for more than an hour, but that the Sec-
> retary of the Interior, who also was to have been present, had not yet
> appeared, and that, naturally, I had supposed they were in consulta-
> tion together before calling me in. He instantly apologized, and trans-
> ferred his irritability to the absent Secretary.

On another occasion while consulting Lincoln about colonization, Tuckerman observed the president's "brusqueness." Tuckerman suggested "that all the preliminaries having been satisfactorily arranged, the easiest way to settle the matter would be for him to affix his signature to the document before him.

"'O, I know that,' he replied, 'and it would be "very easy" for me to open that window and shout down Pennsylvania Avenue, only I don't mean to do it—just now.'

"He was irritated, and justly irritated, by certain difficulties which had been thrown in his way . . . by opponents of the [colonization] scheme."

Tuckerman suggested that the president might want more time to consider the matter. "'No,' said Mr. Lincoln, 'you've had trouble enough about it, and so have I,' and he read over the document to himself with close attention. 'I guess it's all right,' he remarked, when he had done so, and, sending for the Secretary of the Interior, affixed his signature."293

Enlisted men as well as generals could stir presidential anger. A private complained in the summer of 1863 about a matter Lincoln thought best handled by the soldier's officer. The recruit persisted in his appeal, provoking Lincoln "in a peremptory tone" to say, "Now, my man, go away! I cannot attend to all these details. I could as easily bail out the Potomac with a spoon."294 In late March 1865, another soldier pestered Lincoln about his problems. When told that the fellow wanted to see him yet again, the president remarked, "Tell him I can't see him any more about that matter. I've seen him as many times as I can." To callers present at the time, he explained, "I wish that man would let me alone. I've seen him again and again. I've done everything for him that I can do, and he knows it just as well as I do; and I've told him over and over, and he ought to let me alone, but he won't stop following me up. He knows I can't do anything more for him. I declare, if he don't let me alone, I'll tell him what I did a fellow the other day, that I'll undo what I have done for him."295

· · ·

In addition to writing angry letters but not mailing them, Lincoln sometimes ignored criticism.296 If friends tried to tell him about attacks, he would steer the conversation to another topic or else simply say, "I guess we won't talk about that now."297

Seldom did he read hostile commentary in the press, because he was, as he told Francis Carpenter, too *"thin-skinned."*298 When an army officer volunteered to write a defense of the administration against attacks by the Committee on the Conduct of the War, Lincoln replied, "Oh, no, at least, not now. If I were to try to read, much less answer, all the attacks made on me, this shop might as well be closed for any other business. I do the very best I know how—the very best I can; and I mean to keep doing so until the end. If the end brings me out all right, what is said against me won't amount to anything. If the end brings me out wrong, ten angels swearing I was right would make no difference."[299] To Sidney Howard Gay, managing editor of the New York *Tribune*, he complained about the injustice of some minor criticism that the paper had made of the administration but added, "I don't care what they say of me. I want to straighten this thing out, and then I don't care what they do with me, [—] they may hang me."[300] Late in the war the president told General William T. Sherman that Grant and he were his favorite generals "because you never found fault with me."[301]

Mary Lincoln recalled that newspaper assaults gave her husband "great pain."[302] When she attempted to read aloud hostile commentary in the press, he would say, *"Don't do that,* for I have enough to bear."[303] One Sunday afternoon he perused a batch of Henry Ward Beecher's antiadministration editorials in the New York *Independent*. An observer later recalled that "as Mr. Lincoln finished reading them, his face flushed up with indignation. Dashing the package to the floor, he exclaimed, 'Is thy servant a *dog,* that he should do this thing?'"[304] On another occasion, Ward Hill Lamon heard the president cry out after learning of similar criticism, "I would rather be dead than, as president, thus abused in the house of my friends."[305] When early in his administration, Lincoln found a New York *Times* article "containing a savage attack on him," he made it clear that the editor of the paper, Henry J. Raymond, would receive no government post.[306]

Charles Sumner heard the president speak harshly of only two men, William H. Russell of the London *Times,* who had, in Lincoln's view, misrepresented both him and the Northern cause, and Lord John Russell, the British Minister for Foreign Affairs.[307] Lincoln grew irate at a Democratic editor who claimed that the president's salary was paid in gold while soldiers received greenbacks. "See to what depths of infamy a Northern Copperhead can descend," he said. "If the scoundrel who wrote that don't boil hereafter, it will be because the devil hasn't got iron enough to make gridirons."[308] On September 13, 1862, he bitterly complained to a delegation of clergy that *"I am very ungenerously attacked"* by the New York *Tribune* because Confederate forces were enslaving black prisoners. Lincoln related a specific instance of this misconduct and then asked plaintively, "What *could* I do?"[309] Such Confederate actions upset Lincoln as much as they did Horace Greeley. In the winter of 1863–64, the Jefferson Davis government "excit-

ed the rage and disgust of Mr. Lincoln" by forcing thousands of captured Union black troops to help fortify Mobile rather than exchang-
ing them for Confederate captives.[310] When Floridians complained in
the spring of 1861 that Captain Montgomery Meigs was using slaves
to help reinforce Fort Pickens, Lincoln gave them "a very caustic reprimand."[311]

In November 1862 the president angrily blamed the press, in part,
for Republican losses in the fall elections: "Our newspaper's, by vili-
fying and disparaging the administration, furnished them [the Demo-
crats] all the weapons" to defeat Republican candidates.[312] When Congressman John Covode at length told him about discontent in the army
and the way his policies were being criticized, the depressed Lincoln
suddenly interrupted, saying, "Covode, stop! Stop right there! Not
another word! I am full, brim full up to here," as he drew his hand
across his neck.[313]

Lincoln also would refuse to read hostile letters and pronounce-
ments.[314] In his last public address, he said, "As a general rule, I ab-
stain from reading the reports of attacks upon myself, wishing not to
be provoked by that to which I can not properly offer an answer."[315]
When a secretary brought him a "very cross" missive from the governor of Missouri, Lincoln wrote to that official, "As I am trying to preserve my own temper, by avoiding irritants, so far as practicable, I have
declined to read the cross letter." Alluding to the governor's grievance,
Lincoln explained that "I was totally unconscious of any malice, or
disrespect towards you, or of using any expression which should of-
fend you."[316]

On occasion Lincoln would send a sharp letter only after letting it
sit for weeks. When General David Hunter complained that Lincoln's
actions "mortified, humiliated, insulted and disgraced" him, the president replied, "It is difficult to answer so ugly a letter in good temper."
Yet he did manage to keep calm, reviewing Hunter's grievances and
concluding patiently, "I would say you are adopting the best possible
way to ruin yourself. 'Act well your part, there all the honor lies.' He
who does *something* at the head of one Regiment, will eclipse him who
does *nothing* at the head of a hundred." Lincoln kept this reply on his
desk for over a month, then dispatched it by special courier with instructions to deliver it when the general was in a good mood.[317]

Lincoln tried to remain aloof from patronage squabbles, which he
heartily detested.[318] In 1864 he told Kansas Senator Samuel C. Pomeroy that he would not see him regarding the appointment of an asses-

sor in his state, for which post Pomeroy and the other Kansas senator, James E. Lane, had proposed different candidates. The exasperated president told Pomeroy, "I wish you and Lane would make a sincere effort to get out of the mood you are in. I[t] does neither of you any good—it gives you the means of tormenting my life out of me, and nothing else."[319]

Lincoln also sought to preserve his equanimity by declining to see petitioners for whom he could do nothing. In August 1863 he reluctantly sent away eastern Tennessee loyalists who had come to implore help against their persecutors. Expressing the deepest sympathy for their plight, he wrote that "meeting you would do no good; because I have . . . done . . . the best for you I could. . . . I do as much for East Tennessee as I would, or could, if my own home, and family were in Knoxville." After explaining the difficulties of getting an army into that mountainous area, he concluded, "I know you are too much distressed to be argued with; and therefore I do not attempt it at length. You know I am not indifferent to your troubles."[320]

Although seldom ruffled by hostile press commentary, Lincoln now and then grew infuriated when newspapers leaked vital information. He became "exceedingly angry" when the New York *Evening Post* described a troop movement in the fall of 1863. The same paper made him "mad enough to cry" when in that same year it prematurely released his important campaign letter to James C. Conkling.[321]

In April 1865, at the suggestion of John A. Campbell, Lincoln ordered General Godfrey Weitzel to permit the Virginia legislature to reconvene in order to withdraw the state's troops from the war. Weitzel was also instructed to show the president's order to Judge Campbell, who then indiscreetly released to the press an account of his conversation with the president and the order to Weitzel. Lincoln was, according to a biographer, "very indignant. The breach of confidence on the part of Judge Campbell . . . quite exhausted his patience."[322] On the last day of his life, Lincoln complained to Schuyler Colfax about a letter from Campbell "suggesting & urging amnesty or armistice in favor of some leading Rebels as essential to assist in the work" of reconstruction. As Colfax later recalled, Lincoln read it aloud and commented on it "in indignant language as a violation of the explicit understanding between them, & as a breach of faith. This, with the Surrender of Lee . . . inclined him at once, he said, to revoke the authority for the reassembling of the Legislature, adding with emphasis that these Rebels did not appear to have either fairness or gratitude."[323] Two months earlier at the Hampton

Roads Conference, Judge Campbell had irritated Lincoln by saying that he never regarded his neck as in danger. Lincoln replied angrily that "there were a good many oak trees about the place where he [Campbell] lived, the limbs of which afforded many convenient points from which he might have dangled."[324]

Petitioners of suspect truthfulness roused Lincoln's anger. One day a restless man with "unsteady eyes" gave him a paper. After scanning it, he gazed long at the gentleman's face, then resumed reading. Abruptly the president set aside the document, pointed his finger at the caller, and asked, "What's the matter with you?"

"Nothing," came the stammered reply.

"Yes, there is. You can't look me in the face! You have not looked me in the face since you sat there! Even now you are looking out that window and cannot look me in the eye!"

"Flinging the paper in the man's lap, he cried, 'Take it back! There is something wrong about this! I will have nothing to do with it!'"[325]

Lincoln was similarly abrupt with General H. W. Benham, who called at the White House in August 1862 to appeal the revocation of his commission. The president indignantly charged that Benham was trying to "deceive" him by denying that Halleck had examined his case.[326]

When a man and a woman came seeking a pardon for a convicted spy, Lincoln heard their story "impatiently and with a darkening face." According to a woman who observed the conversation, Lincoln finally "burst in, abruptly and sternly" saying,

> There is not a word of this true! And you know it as well as I do. He *was* a spy, he has been a spy, he ought to have been hanged as a spy. From the fuss you folks are making about him, who are none too loyal, I am convinced he was more valuable to the cause of the enemy than we have yet suspected. You are the third set of persons that has been to me to get him pardoned. Now I'll tell you what—if any of you come bothering me any more about his being set at liberty, that will decide his fate. I will have him hanged, as he deserves to be. You ought to bless your stars that he got off with a whole neck; and if you don't want so see him hanged as high as Haman, don't you come to me again about him.[327]

When asked by a Presbyterian minister to pardon a deserter, Lincoln snapped, "Not a word more, Dr. Paxton. I can do nothing in the matter. I will not interfere. You should not come here trying to undermine the morale of my armies. Those increasing desertions must be stopped. If you had stopped to think, you would not have come on this foolish errand. So go back to Pittsburgh and try to be a more loyal citizen." Eventually, however, he relented and pardoned the soldier.[328]

Lincoln rarely took criticism personally, but he was incensed when good friends, such as Oregon Senator Edward D. Baker, were unfairly attacked. Baker and the president had been so close as young lawyers that Lincoln had named his second son after him. In March 1861 a California delegation, led by James William Simonton of the San Francisco *Bulletin,* called on Lincoln to complain about Baker's attempts to dictate patronage appointments for both his state and California. In Baker's presence, Simonton caustically denounced him and then presented a remonstrance with many signatures. The president listened quietly, took the document, and said in substance, "The protest deserves to be considered, but as to your speech, it is disrespectful to myself and Mr. Baker, and I can make no other disposition of it than this," as he tossed it into the fire. According to a congressman who spoke with one of the delegation, "The anger of Mr. Lincoln was kindled instantly, and blazed forth with such vehemence and intensity that everybody present quailed before it. His wrath was simply terrible, as he put his foot down and told the delegation that Senator Baker was his friend; that he would permit no man to assail him in his presence; and that it was not possible for them to accomplish their purpose by any such methods." The next day the president apologized to Simonton for acting hastily. Later he explained that "the paper was an unjust attack upon my dearest personal friend. . . . The delegation did not know what they were talking about when they made him responsible, almost abusively, for what I had done, or proposed to do. They told me that was my paper, to do with as I liked. I could not trust myself to reply in words: I was so angry."[329]

Lincoln had come to Baker's defense many years earlier during a heated political debate with Josiah Lamborn in Springfield. As one observer recalled, Baker "was a fiery fellow—and when his impulsiveness was let loose among the rough elements which constituted a large part of his audience, it was generally understood that there might be trouble at any time." Resting in his law office, Lincoln overheard from the courtroom below threats made against Baker. "Lincoln jumped off the bed, and in about three strides he went down the stairs and into the court room" where his friend confronted a menacing crowd.[330] Lincoln allegedly grabbed a stone pitcher and said, "I'll break it over the head of the first man who lays a hand on Baker!"[331]

Later he bristled when someone suggested that he might renege on his preliminary Emancipation Proclamation. "Why, it would be an astounding breach of faith! If I should do it, I ought to be damned in time and eternity," he exclaimed.[332]

Lincoln found it difficult to remain calm in the face of avarice. During the secession crisis, panicky businessmen urged him to avert war by compromising with the South on any terms. A New England manufacturer, Henry S. Sanford, alarmed by the decline in orders from the South, pleaded with Lincoln in November to "reassure the men honestly alarmed" in the cotton states. John G. Nicolay noticed that the caller's appeal "irritated Lincoln to a warmth of retort he seldom reached."

"'There are no such men,' bluntly replied Lincoln. 'This is the same old trick by which the South breaks down every Northern victory.'" The Yankee businessman persisted, submitting a compromise petition signed by eminent people. Asked whether he were familiar with those names, Lincoln replied, "I recognize them as a set of liars and knaves."[333] When in February 1861 William E. Dodge expressed fear that "the whole nation shall be plunged into bankruptcy" and that "grass shall grow in the streets of our commercial cities," and urged Lincoln to "yield to the just demands of the South," the president-elect replied with a "stern expression" that he would carry out his oath of office to defend the Constitution: "It must be so respected, obeyed, enforced, and defended, let the grass grow where it may."[334] On another occasion when pressed to compromise the differences between North and South, he reportedly told Illinois Governor Richard Yates that "he would rather be hanged by the neck till he was dead on the steps of the capitol than buy or beg a peaceful inauguration."[335]

Similarly, on November 10, 1860, Lincoln wrote to Truman Smith, saying, "I am not insensible to any commercial or financial depression that may exist; but nothing is to be gained by fawning around the *'respectable scoundrels'* who got it up. Let them go to work and repair the mischief of their own making; and then perhaps they will be less greedy to do the like again." In that same letter, he rejected an appeal to issue public statements about his future plans: "I could say nothing which I have not already said, and which is in print, and open for the inspection of all. To press a repetition of this upon those who *have* listened, is useless; to press it upon those who have *refused* to listen, and still refuse, would be wanting in self-respect, and would have an appearance of sycophancy and timidity, which would excite the contempt of good men, and encourage bad ones to clamor the more loudly."[336]

Also during the secession crisis, Lincoln erupted when his secretary announced that President James Buchanan had ordered Union soldiers in Charleston to surrender their fort if the South Carolinians attacked it. "With warmth," the president-elect exclaimed, "If that is true, they ought to hang him!"[337] When one of his favorite journalists wrote that the Lincoln administration would be "the reign of steel," Lincoln jokingly—and bitterly—asked, "Why not add that Buchanan's was the reign of *stealing?*"[338]

He grew impatient for his own inauguration. On New Year's Day, 1861, Lincoln, in a rather depressed mood, told Joseph Gillespie, "I would willingly take out of my life a period in years equal to the two months which intervene between now and my inauguration to take the oath of office to-morrow."

"Why?" queried Gillespie.

"Because every hour adds to the difficulties I am called upon to meet, and the present Administration does nothing to check the tendency toward dissolution. I, who have been called to meet this awful responsibility, am compelled to remain here, doing nothing to avert it or lessen its force when it comes to me."

Then, as Gillespie recalled, "with more bitterness than I ever heard him speak, before or after," Lincoln said, "It is not of myself I complain. . . . But every day adds to the difficulty of the situation, and makes the outlook for the country more gloomy. Secession is being fostered rather than repressed, and if the doctrine meets with a general acceptance in the border States, it will be a great blow to the Government. . . . Joe, I suppose you will never forget that trial down in Montgomery County where the lawyer associated with you gave away the whole case in his opening speech. I saw you signalling to him, but you couldn't stop him. Now that's just the way with me and Buchanan. He is giving away the case and I have nothing to say and can't stop him."

Lincoln was also upset at the Republicans in Congress, who during the secession winter voted to admit Colorado with no provision regarding slavery. While preparing to leave Springfield for Washington, he told Gillespie, "It seems to me that Douglas got the best of it at the election last fall. I am left to face an empty treasury and a great rebellion, while my own party indorses his popular sovereignty idea, and applies it in legislation."[339]

As the crisis reached its climax, Lincoln grew exasperated with his chief general, Winfield Scott. On March 29, he summoned the venerable Scott to the White House, where an observer noted, "The President said [Major Robert] *Anderson had played us false,* and he seemed to indicate a want of consistency in General Scott's own views concerning Fort Pickens. The president went so far as to say that his administration would be broken up unless a more dedicated policy was adopted, and if General Scott could not carry out his views, some other person might." Not surprisingly, this remark seemed "to have disturbed General Scott greatly."[340]

When war broke out, Lincoln could scarcely contain his anger at the Southern firebrands. In his April 15 proclamation, calling out troops to suppress the rebellion, he said the forces would be employed "to redress wrongs already long enough endured." Two months later he had Secretary of War Simon Cameron send a letter (probably composed by the president himself) denouncing secessionists as "a class of political adventurers" leading a "conspiracy against popular rights" that had been "matured for many years by secret organizations throughout the country, especially in the Slave states." He promised federal aid "to repel from Virginia the lawless invaders now perpetrating every species of outrage upon persons and property throughout a large portion of the State," and severely criticized state authorities for allowing Confederates to seize the important navy yard at Gosport.[341]

The president feared for the safety of the nation's capital, nestled as it was between two slave states, Virginia and Maryland. On April 19, 1861, a pro-Confederate mob attacked Union soldiers passing through Baltimore; three days later a group of Baltimoreans visited the White House and urged him to make peace with the South and reroute the troops away from their city. Lincoln replied testily:

You, gentlemen, come here to me and ask for peace on any terms, and yet have no word of condemnation for those who are making war on us. You express great horror of bloodshed, and yet would not lay a straw in the way of those who are organizing in Virginia and elsewhere to capture this city. The rebels attack Fort Sumter, and your citizens attack troops sent to the defense of the Government, and the lives and property in Washington, and yet you would have me break my oath and surrender the Government without a blow. There is no Washington in that—no Jackson in that—no manhood nor honor in that. I have no desire to invade the South; but I must have troops to defend this Capital. Geographically it lies surrounded by the soil of Maryland; and mathematically the necessity exists that they should come over her territory. Our men are not moles, and can't dig under the earth; they are not birds, and can't fly through the air. There is no way but to march across, and that they must do. But in doing this there is no need of collision. Keep your rowdies in Baltimore, and there will be no bloodshed. Go home and tell your people that if they will not attack us, we will not attack them; but if they do attack us, we will return it, and that severely.[342]

Lincoln had more sharp things to say about Baltimore's leaders in the summer of 1863, when a group urged him to pardon a young man named Compton, who had been condemned to death. After the appeals proved unavailing, one visitor asked, "Will you, Mr. President, receive a delegation of the most influential citizens of Baltimore, with the Hon. Reverdy Johnson at their head, if they will come in person and present a petition of behalf of Mr. Compton?" Lincoln, "with the fire of indignation," replied, "No! I will not receive a delegation from Baltimore for any purpose. I have received many delegations from Baltimore, since I came into office, composed of its most prominent citizens. They have always come to gain some advantage for themselves, or for their city. They have always had some end of their own to reach, without regard to the interests of the government. But no delegation has ever come to me to express sympathy or give me any aid in upholding the government and putting down the rebellion. No! I will receive no delegation from Baltimore."[343]

The following year Lincoln snapped at Baltimoreans who came to plead on behalf of a merchant accused of supplying blockade-runners. When told that his reelection campaign would be injured if the merchant were not pardoned, Lincoln replied, "No matter whether I am re-elected or not, I shall want the rebellion put down all the same."

One intercessor declared, "But your Excellency *can* do it."

Turning his head to the side and giving his caller a "peculiar look," Lincoln said, "Yes, I know I *can*. I can stop the war and let Jeff. Davis have his way; but . . . I'm not going to do it."

When his visitors persisted, Lincoln interrupted, saying, "See here, . . . if this man is innocent, as you say, why does he not patiently await his trial, and make his innocence appear? Why do his friends presume in taking up my time urging his release? If *I* was arrested for a crime, I should await my trial, look for justice, and ask no man for mercy."

One intercessor described how much money the accused merchant had contributed to the war effort. "If he gave a few hundred to the Union cause, as a cover to the thousands he has contributed to the rebellion, by furnishing supplies, it does not help the case," said the president.

"But he has not done this!" came the reply.

"Make it appear on his trial. I tell you what it is, my friend, we have big job on hand, putting down this rebellion. The War Department says to me plainly, we will not support your plank, if, every time we catch a rascal you release him!"

"But my friend, Mr. —— is not a rascal!"

"Beg your pardon, but I think he is."

"Our merchants have vouched for him, your Excellency. The Mayor of Baltimore has vouched for him. I vouched for him. He is a good Union man. We all voted for him [you]. We wish to vote for you again. . . . I have spent thousands in the Union cause, your Excellency. I once paid three hundred dollars for knocking a man down."

Lincoln, "with a look of mock alarm," said, "I hope you will not try that on me!"

"Even your enemys, your excellency, say you have a kind heart."

"Now not another word. I have no time for this, and I tell you, once [and] for [all."]

Lincoln did grant a permit to visit the accused, but when the recipient promised to call again, he said, "No. You must not come again. I have no time for this, and will not see you[.]"[344]

In 1862 Lincoln chastised a Louisianian who had protested against the conduct of the Union army in his state. He scorned timid Southern Unionists who "will do nothing for the government, nothing for themselves, except demanding that the government shall not strike its open enemies, lest they be struck by accident!" With unwonted sarcasm, he compared such men to reluctant crew members on a warship: "They are to touch neither a sail nor a pump, but to be merely passengers,—dead-heads at that—to be carried snug and dry, throughout the storm, and safely landed right side up. Nay, more; even a mutineer is to go untouched lest these sacred passengers receive an accidental wound." Impatiently he asked, "What would you do in my position? Would you drop the war where it is? Or, would you prosecute it in [the] future, with elder-stalk squirts, charged with rose water? Would you deal lighter blows rather than heavier ones? Would you give up the contest, leaving any available means unapplied."[345]

Gold speculators also angered the president. He asked the governor of Pennsylvania in May 1864, "What do you think of those fellows in Wall Street, who are gambling in gold at such a time as this?" When the governor replied, "They are a set of sharks," Lincoln banged his fist on a table and said, "For my part, I wish every one of them had his *devilish* head shot off!" Francis B. Carpenter called this "the strongest expression I ever heard fall from the lips of Mr. Lincoln."[346] As a young lawyer, Lincoln had denounced a similar class of men in Illinois, people commonly known as "land sharks." "I respect," he said, "the man who properly named those villains land-sharks. They are like the wretched ghouls of the sea that follow a ship and fatten on its offal."[347]

Lincoln despised corrupt exploiters of the war, like the retainers who swarmed around General John C. Frémont in Missouri. When a friend of the general's called to smooth over the troubled relations between the two men, Lincoln told him, "Sir, I believe General Fremont to be a thoroughly honest man, but he has unfortunately surrounded himself with some of the greatest scoundrels on this continent; you are one of them and the worst of them."[348] Lincoln also contemned war profiteers such as the New York railroad and canal operators who hiked prices when the rebel army cut off competing east-west routes further south. On November 25, 1862, he protested against the "grievous imposition" placed on the West by the high freight rates, adding "quite emphatically that adequate measures would be adopted to terminate this abuse."[349] Lincoln evidently wrote to Governor Horatio Seymour of New York, "urging him to drop attention to party interests and to concern himself somewhat for the interest of the nation; dwelling on the suffering of the West from the closing of the Mississippi river, and expressing the hope they will be able to alleviate that suffering somewhat, by preventing railroad monopolies and reducing the present enormous tariff on freight."[350]

He also had little patience with vigorous patriots who sought reductions in army enrollment quotas in their areas. When in 1864 a Chicago delegation appealed for such special treatment, Lincoln rejected them firmly, saying "in a voice full of bitterness," "Gentlemen, after Boston, Chicago has been the chief instrument in bringing this war on the country. . . . You called for war until we had it. You called for Emancipation, and I have given it to you. . . . Now you come here begging to be let off from the call for men which I have made to carry out the war you have demanded. You ought to be ashamed of yourselves." He went on to accuse a member of the delegation, Chicago *Tribune* editor Joseph Medill, of "acting like a coward."[351] Lincoln also snapped at John M. Palmer, who visited the White House on a similar errand. Interrupting his caller, the president said, "Palmer, I can get more men easily in Illinois than some other places. I directed the quota of Illinois myself, and I must have the men, and neither you nor 'Dick' [Yates] can make a fuss about it!" Seeing that "he meant what he said," Palmer quickly changed the subject.[352]

. . .

Although Lincoln urged a peace based on the principle of "charity for all and malice toward none," he could express pique at the effrontery of his opponents. In 1864 he rejected an appeal from Tennesseans protesting against the strict loyalty oath prescribed by their governor for the upcoming elections, including the presidential race between Lincoln and George B. McClellan. In reply Lincoln snapped, "May I inquire how long it took you and the New-York politicians to concoct that paper?"

The spokesman for the delegation, John Lellyett, protested that it was a spontaneous expression of the people of Tennessee. Scornfully, Lincoln retorted, "*I expect to let the friends of George B. McClellan manage their side of this contest in their own way; and I will manage my side of it in MY way.*"[353] This was, as Josiah G. Holland observed, "unquestionably an undignified and injudicious reply."[354] Lincoln's secretaries apologetically wrote that it "is not impossible that, in a moment of irritation at the presentation of a petition which was in itself an insinuation that he was making a selfish and corrupt use of his power, the president may have treated Mr. Lellyett with scant courtesy; but he took the protest, nevertheless, and told him he would answer it at his convenience."[355]

Holland ascribed Lincoln's intemperate response to "the condition of nervous and mental irritability, to which all the latter part of his life he was subject." In Holland's view, Lincoln during his last two years became "peevish," "querulous," "childish," and "petulant" more frequently than in earlier days because of "the protracted and irritable condition of his nervous system, resulting from excessive labor, mental suffering, and loss of sleep."[356] Noah Brooks also observed that as the war dragged on, Lincoln's "hearty, blithesome, genial, wiry" spirit changed: "The old, clear laugh never came back; the even temper was sometimes disturbed; and his natural charity for all was often turned into an unwonted suspicion of the motives of men."[357] William O. Stoddard noted a similar pattern: "Mr. Lincoln did not retain the external equanimity of his earlier days under the galling pressure of the burdens laid upon him in 1863." In the later stages of the war, Stoddard recalled, "he now and then gave way to short-lived fits of petulance."[358] Short-ly after the assassination, Mary Lincoln acknowledged that when "worn down," the president "spoke crabbedly to men, harshly so."[359]

He was most likely to lose control of his anger when bad news arrived from the front.[360] In July 1862, after the defeat of the Peninsular Campaign, "a prominent Senator with a very dejected bearing" called at the White House, where the president told him, "you have a very sad face to-day. It reminds me of a little incident."

The caller cut off his host and rebuked him, "Mr. President, this situation is too grave for the telling of anecdotes. I do not care to listen to one."

Lincoln, somewhat "aroused by this remark," said in reply, "Senator, do you think that this situation weighs more heavily upon you than it does upon me? If the cause goes against us, not only will the country be lost, but I shall be disgraced to all time. But what would happen if I appeared upon the streets of Washington to-day with such a countenance as yours? The news would be spread throughout the country that the President's very demeanor is an admission that defeat is inevitable. And I say to you, sir, that it would be better for you to infuse some cheerfulness into that countenance of yours as you go about upon the streets of Washington."[361]

Another act of lèse majesté provoked Lincoln shortly after a serious Union army defeat. At a public reception, one kind visitor said, "I hope, Mr. President, you are able to sleep, notwithstanding your heavy burdens." Then entered a general freshly arrived from the front, "a short stout man . . . with a blustering, pompous manner as if he thought the whole army was centered in himself." Overhearing the remark of the well-wisher, the general "added in a bold, confident tone, 'I presume, Mr. President, you sleep as much as the private soldiers on the Rappahannock.'"

The president "looked down upon him with a loftiness which was almost scorn, and said slowly and distinctly, and with indescribable pathos: *'For that matter, Sir, I would gladly change places with the poorest soldier in the ranks!'*"[362]

Early in the war, an army doctor bluntly criticized the president's rude attire, telling him that he resembled "a Virginia wood-chopper." A witness recalled that "this unexpected allusion to his appearance was a little too much for the President. A little red spot of hectic red burned for a moment on his cheeks." But instead of expressing his anger, Lincoln replied "pleasantly" and generously offered to expedite the physician's work.[363]

Lincoln also grew irritable when tired. One evening in the summer of 1862, Lt. Colonel Charles Scott asked presidential permission to go South to retrieve the body of his wife, who had drowned in a steamboat accident. Lincoln exclaimed, "Am I to have no rest? no privacy? Must I be dogged to my last fastnesses and worried to death by inches?"

When the officer replied that he had been turned down by Secretary of War Stanton, the president said, "Mr. Stanton has done just right. He knows what he is about. Your demands are unreasonable, sir."

"But, Mr. Lincoln, I thought *you* would feel for me."

"*Feel for you!* Good God! I have to feel for five hundred thousand more unfortunate than you. We are at war, sir: don't you know we are at war? Sorrow is the lot of all; bear your share like a man and a soldier."

The next morning Lincoln apologized to the colonel: "I treated you brutally last night. I ask your pardon. I was utterly tired out, badgered to death. I generally become about as savage as a wild cat by Saturday night, drained dry of the 'milk of human kindness.' I must have seemed to you the very gorilla the rebels paint me. I was sorry enough for it, when you were gone. . . . I thought I'd drive into town, in the cool of the morning, and make it all right. . . . I never should have forgiven myself, if I had let that ugly piece of work stand." The president arranged a leave for the officer and had a steamer dispatched to retrieve Mrs. Scott's body.[364]

On other occasions Lincoln expressed regret for angry outbursts. Early in the war, at the request of the Reverend Dr. Phineas D. Gurley, the president commuted a young soldier's death sentence. The boy's father, a congregant of the minister's church, then appealed to the president for his son's release, despite Gurley's advice to the contrary. Lincoln told the importunate gentleman,

> your son was convicted of the gravest possible crime, the just penalty of which is death. Had he succeeded in his scheme, the executive officers of this government would have been captured and perhaps the government itself destroyed. I have commuted his sentence from a death on the gallows to imprisonment, giving you every facility for ministering to his comfort. I have already done more for him than many will approve. At present, at least, I am sure I would not be justified in doing more. Your persistent applications have pained me and

annoyed me. If you do not cease, I may have cause to regret the clemency I have already shown.

A few days later Lincoln apologized to Gurley and handed him a pardon for the man's son. He explained, "Ever since he was here with you, the other day, about a pardon for his son I have felt grieved that I had to be so severe with him, and I fear I hurt his feelings so."[365]

During the Christmas season of 1864–65, the president was beseeched to pardon a condemned soldier whose mother wanted to plead on her son's behalf. Lincoln "cried out angrily, 'There is no use of her coming here crying about me. I can't do anything for her.'" At that point the chaplain who recorded those remarks stepped forward, explaining that he wanted to represent the interests of the accused man and some others as well, all of whom were quite young. "'Well,' said Lincoln, 'suppose they were old men, with families to support, would that make it any better?'" The chaplain pleaded earnestly, inducing Lincoln to relent.[366]

· · ·

The episodes of anger recounted here must be viewed in perspective. A secretary to the president, William O. Stoddard, asked rhetorically, "Does the good-natured, soft-hearted, easy-going . . . tenant of the White House ever really lose his temper? The country generally does not believe that he ever does or can, but the right answer to the question is that under exceedingly trying circumstances he *generally* succeeds in keeping down the storm which is continually stirred up within him by the treacheries, cowardices, villainies and stupidities, which, almost daily and hourly, he is compelled to see and understand and wrestle with and overcome."[367]

The remarkable thing about Lincoln's temper is not how often it erupted, but how seldom it did, considering how frequently he encountered the insolence of epaulets, the abuse of friends and opponents alike, and the egomaniacal selfishness of editors, senators, representatives, governors, cabinet members, generals, and flocks of others who pestered him unmercifully about their own petty concerns. It is no wonder that John Hay marveled in 1863, "While the rest are grinding their little private organs for their own glorification[,] the old man is working with the strength of a giant and the purity of an angel to do this great work."[368] Hay might well have added, "with the forbearance of a saint."

Late in the war, Lincoln told his old friend, "Speed, die when I may I want it said of me by those who know me best . . . that I always plucked a thistle and planted a flower when I thought a flower would grow." [369] The record indicates that Lincoln lived up to that credo, but that he did not believe that flowers would grow everywhere.

NOTES

1. Angle, *HL*, 96.
2. John G. Nicolay, "The Campaign of 1860," unpublished essay, Nicolay MSS, DLC.
3. Chicago *Herald*, 4 Dec. 1887.
4. William Crook, *Through Five Administrations: Reminiscences of Colonel William H. Crook, Body-Guard to President Lincoln*, ed. Margarita Spalding Gerry (New York: Harper and Brothers, 1910), 11.
5. Brandon to Herndon, Petersburg, Ill., 3 Aug. 1865, H-W MSS, DLC.
6. Charles A. Dana, *Lincoln and His Cabinet: A Lecture Delivered before the New Haven Colonial Historical Society* ([New York]: N.p., 1896), 31, 41.
7. Remarks at the meeting of the U.S. District and Circuit Courts, 17 June 1865, paraphrased in the Springfield *Daily State Journal*, 19 June 1865. Cf. William P. Schramm, "Why Lincoln Didn't Lose His Temper," *Catholic Young People's Friend*, Feb. 1936, 174–75.
8. St. Louis *Globe Democrat*, 13 Jan. 1887. Dowling, who married Dennis Hanks's daughter Sarah Jane, claimed the Lincoln stayed at his family's house when visiting Charleston.
9. Paul M. Angle, "Abe Lincoln Had a Temper," *Midwest: Magazine of the Chicago Sunday Times*, 12 Feb. 1956, 6.
10. Carl Sandburg, *Abraham Lincoln: The Prairie Years*, 2 vols. (New York: Harcourt, Brace, 1926), 1:392; Benjamin P. Thomas, *Abraham Lincoln: A Biography* (New York: Alfred A. Knopf, 1952), 84.
11. Herndon quoted in George Alfred Townsend's interview, Springfield correspondence, 25 Jan. 1867, New York *Tribune*, 15 Feb. 1867, 2.
12. John G. Nicolay's interview with Logan, Springfield, 6 July 1875, Hay MSS, reel 22, DLC.
13. Henry C. Whitney, *Lincoln the Citizen*, vol. 1 of *A Life of Lincoln*, ed. Marion Mills Miller, 2 vols. (New York: Baker and Taylor, 1908), 1:183.
14. Henry C. Whitney, "Abraham Lincoln: A Study from Life," *Arena* 19 (April 1898): 465.
15. Isaac N. Arnold, *The Life of Abraham Lincoln* (Chicago: Jansen, McClurg, 1885), 416.
16. Davis's address before the meeting of the U.S. District and Circuit courts, 17 June 1865, Springfield *Daily State Journal*, 19 June 1865, 3.
17. Henry B. Rankin, *Intimate Character Sketches of Abraham Lincoln* (Philadelphia: Lippincott, 1924), 137.
18. Ida M. Tarbell, *The Life of Abraham Lincoln*, 4 vols. (New York: Lincoln History Society, 1903), 1:43.

19. Charles H. Ambler, *Francis H. Pierpont: Union War Governor of Virginia and Father of West Virginia* (Chapel Hill: University of North Carolina Press, 1937), 259. This conversation probably took place sometime between April 11 and 13, 1865. Washington *Star,* summarized in the Albany *Evening Journal,* 12 April 1865.

20. Robert Bray, "'The Power to Hurt': Lincoln's Early Use of Satire and Invective," unpublished essay (1993). I am grateful to Robert Bray for providing me with a copy of this thoughtful work.

21. "Response to a Serenade," 10 Nov. 1864, in Basler, *CWL,* 8:101.

22. J. Edward Murr, "Lincoln in Indiana," *Indiana Magazine of History* 13 (Dec. 1917): 341, 344–45.

23. William H. Herndon, "Lincoln's Ways," manuscript, H-W MSS, DLC. Cf. James C. Conkling, *Recollections of the Bench and Bar of Central Illinois,* Fergus Historical Series no. 22 (Chicago: Fergus Printing Co., 1881), 54–55.

24. J. Edward Murr, "Lincoln in Indiana," *Indiana Magazine of History* 14 (March 1918): 58; Green B. Taylor's statement, 16 Sept. 1865, H-W MSS, DLC.

25. John W. Lamar, in the Indianapolis *News,* 12 April 1902, in J. T. Hobson, *Footprints of Abraham Lincoln* (Dayton: Otterbein Press, 1909), 24. Mrs. Lamar reported (21–22) that the Grigsbys had "let her lay too long." The Grigsbys denied the charge, arguing that Sarah was well cared for but that the only available doctor, who was reputedly competent when sober, had unfortunately been drunk when Sarah delivered her child. *The Monitor* [Grandview, Ind.], 13 Feb. 1930. Cf. reminiscences of James Gentry in the Rockport, Ind., correspondence, 25 Sept. 1902, Louisville *Courier-Journal,* 28 Sept. 1902; Sam E. Kercheval to Jesse W. Weik, Rockport, Ind., 2 Dec. 1887, and William Herndon to Weik, Chicago, 8 Jan. 1887, H-W MSS, DLC; Francis Marion Van Natter, *Lincoln's Boyhood: A Chronicle of His Indiana Years* (Washington: Public Affairs Press, 1963), 53; Louis A. Warren, *Lincoln's Youth: Indiana Years, Seven to Twenty-One, 1816–1830* (Indianapolis: Indiana Historical Society, 1959), 173–75.

26. Reminiscences of Eliza Tuley Hesson and Redmond D. Grigsby, Rockport, Ind., correspondence, 21 Dec. 1895, Chicago *Times-Herald,* 22 Dec. 1895; reminiscences of Redmond D. Grigsby, Elizabeth Crawford, and one of the brides, in Hobson, *Footprints of Lincoln,* 27–29; Albert J. Beveridge, *Abraham Lincoln, 1809–1858,* 2 vols. (Boston: Houghton, Mifflin, 1928), 1:92–94.

27. M. Grigsby to Herndon, Gentryville [Ind.], 25 Oct. 1866, H-W MSS, DLC; Beveridge, *Lincoln,* 1:93–94; Angle, *HL,* 48.

28. O. C. Terry to Jesse W. Weik, Mt. Vernon, Ind., July 1888, H-W MSS, DLC. Cf. Ward H. Lamon, *The Life of Abraham Lincoln; from His Birth to His Inauguration as President* (Boston: James R. Osgood, 1872), 51; Angle *HL,* 47; Elizabeth Crawford's statement, 16 Sept. 1865, in Hertz, *HL,* 365–66; Murr, "Lincoln in Indiana," *Indiana Magazine of History* 14 (March 1918): 45.

29. N. W. Brandon to Herndon, Petersburg, Ill., 3 Aug. 1865, H-W MSS, DLC. The gentleman in question may have been Samuel Hill, postmaster and storekeeper.

30. Letter signed by Samuel Hill but written by Lincoln, New Salem, 7 Sept. 1834, in the Beardstown *Chronicle and Illinois Military Bounty Land Advertiser,* 1 Nov. 1834, 1. I am indebted to Douglas L. Wilson of Knox College in Galesburg, Ill., who discovered this document and sent me a copy. One contemporary reader called it "a hard one" that "used the old man [Cartwright] very Ruff." So abusive was it that the editor of the *Sangamo Journal* refused print it; Lincoln therefore submitted it to the Beardstown *Chronicle,* which was not so finicky. Caleb Carman to Herndon, Petersburg, Ill., 30 Nov. 1866, and John McNamar to Herndon, Menard, Ill., 1 Dec. 1866, H-W MSS, DLC. McNamar identifies Lincoln as the author of the letter.

31. Joshua F. Speed, *Reminiscences of Abraham Lincoln and Notes of a Visit to California: Two Lectures* (Louisville: John P. Morton, 1884), 17–18.

32. Arnold, *Life of Lincoln,* 49.

33. J. McCan Davis to Ida Tarbell, Springfield, Ill., 11 March 1895, copy, JGR MSS, DLC. Davis here summarizes the views of several Springfield residents who knew Taylor.

34. Arnold, *Life of Lincoln,* 50. Cf. statement of James H. Matheny, [3 May 1866?], H-W MSS, DLC.

35. "To the People of Sangamon County," undated document, probably written on the eve of the 1836 election, in Basler, *CWL,* 8:429.

36. Paul M. Angle, *"Here I Have Lived": A History of Lincoln's Springfield, 1821–1865* (Springfield: Abraham Lincoln Association, 1935), 65.

37. Ibid., 66–69; Lincoln and Benjamin Talbott to James Adams, [Springfield], 6 Sept. 1837, and "Letter to the Public," 18 Oct. 1837, in Basler, *CWL,* 1:95–100, 101–6. Cf. Thomas F. Schwartz, "The Lincoln Handbill of 1837: A Rare Document's History," *Illinois Historical Journal* 79 (Winter 1988): 267–74, and Kent L. Walgren, "James Adams: Early Springfield Mormon and Freemason," *Journal of the Illinois State Historical Society* 65 (1982): 121–36.

38. *Sangamo Journal,* 14, 21, 26 June, 12, 20, 26 July, 6, 30 Sept. 1837. See also William L. Patton to Albert J. Beveridge, Springfield, Ill., 18, 23, 30 March 1925, and Beveridge to Patton, N.p., 5, 22 March 1925, copies in Beveridge MSS, DLC; Basler, *CWL,* 8:434. Beveridge attributes these "Sampson's Ghost" letters to Lincoln, although the editor of Lincoln's works thinks there is insufficient evidence to do so. Beveridge, *Lincoln,* 1:215–16. Earl Schenck Miers et al., in *Lincoln Day by Day: A Chronology, 1809–1865,* 3 vols. (Washington: Lincoln Sesquicentennial Commission, 1960), agree with Beveridge (1:73).

39. John J. Duff, *A. Lincoln: Prairie Lawyer* (New York: Holt, Rinehart and Winston, 1960), 49.

40. Usher F. Linder, *Reminiscences of the Early Bench and Bar of Illinois* (Chicago: Chicago Legal News Company, 1879), 62–64.

41. Lincoln to John T. Stuart, Vandalia, 14 Feb. 1839, in Basler, *CWL,* 1:143. This probably refers to an attempt to repeal the bill removing the state capital from Vandalia to Springfield. See also Paul Stroble, *High on the Okaw's Western Bank: Vandalia, Illinois, 1819–39* (Urbana: University of Illinois Press, 1992).

42. "Speech on the Sub-Treasury," [26] Dec. 1839, in Basler, *CWL*, 1:177; *Illinois State Register*, 23 Nov. 1839, in *Abraham Lincoln: A Press Portrait*, ed. Herbert Mitgang (Chicago: Quadrangle Books, 1971), 16. Lincoln had attacked Douglas two years earlier in a letter to the *Sangamo Journal* signed "The Conservative" (see the appendix in this volume).

43. John P. Frank, *Lincoln as a Lawyer* (Urbana: University of Illinois Press, 1961), 74. Frank refers to Lincoln's conduct in the case of *Todd v. Ware*.

44. David Davis, quoted in Willard L. King, *Lincoln's Manager: David Davis* (Cambridge: Harvard University Press, 1960), 38; Alfred Taylor Bledsoe in *The Southern Review*, April 1873, in *Lincoln among His Friends: A Sheaf of Intimate Memories*, ed. Rufus Rockwell Wilson (Caldwell: Caxton, 1942), 467; Whitney, *Lincoln*, 1:144–45; *Illinois State Register*, 24 July 1840, in "Lincoln—Author of the Letters by 'A Conservative,'" *Bulletin of the Abraham Lincoln Association*, no. 50 (Dec. 1937): 8–9. Cf. S. C. Parks to Herndon, Lincoln, Ill., 25 March 1866, H-W MSS, DLC.

45. Herndon's recollection of a story he heard Lincoln tell often, N.d., H-W MS, DLC. Cf. similar spoofing of Democrats in "Speech on the Sub-Treasury," [26] Dec. 1839, in Basler, *CWL*, 1:177–78.

46. J. A. Powell to the editor of *The Century*, copy; Powell to Nicolay, Homer, Ill., 11 Feb. 1889, both in Nicolay MSS, DLC.

47. Lincoln to William G. Anderson, Lawrenceville, [Ind.], 31 Oct. 1840, in Basler, *CWL*, 1:211.

48. "The 'Rebecca' Letter," 27 Aug. 1842, in Basler, *CWL*, 1:295.

49. Mark E. Neely, Jr., *The Abraham Lincoln Encyclopedia* (New York: McGraw Hill, 1982), 181.

50. Beveridge, *Lincoln*, 1:334–53. For a different version of the story from the one usually told, see Nicolay's interview with William Butler, Springfield, 18 June 1875, Hay MSS, RPB.

51. Beveridge, *Lincoln*, 1:353.

52. An unidentified Chicago newspaper, quoted in D. W. Bartlett, *The Life and Public Services of Hon. Abraham Lincoln* (New York: Derby and Jackson, 1860), 108.

53. Milton Hay to Thomas Venmun, Springfield, 26 Jan. 1892, Stuart-Hay MSS, IHi.

54. F. B. Carpenter, *Six Months at the White House with Abraham Lincoln: The Story of a Picture* (New York: Hurd and Houghton, 1867), 305.

55. Thomas J. Pickett's recollections in the Lincoln [Neb.] *Daily State Journal*, 12 April 1881, in *Intimate Memories of Lincoln*, ed. Wilson, 190–91. Cf. Miers et al., eds., *Lincoln Day by Day*, 1:237 [entry for 16 Oct. 1844].

56. Constable had differed with Lincoln about the Whig strategy for 1848. The previous year Lincoln had called a meeting of Illinois Whigs and urged that Zachary Taylor rather than Clay be the party's presidential candidate, and that steps be taken quickly to secure his assent lest the Democrats recruit the war hero. When this proposal was accepted, Constable left the meeting. This story was told by James W. Singleton, who joined Constable in walking out. See Petersburg [Ill.] *Semi-Weekly Axis*, 30 May 1860, copy, Harry E. Pratt Papers, University of Illinois, Urbana-Champaign.

57. Lincoln to John M. Clayton, Springfield, 13 May 1849, and to James A. Pearce, Springfield, 13 Jan. 1851, in Basler, *CWL,* 2:48, 97; Constable to David Davis, Mount Carmel, Ill., 2 July 1849, and David Davis to his wife, Paris, Ill., 27 Oct. 1851, David Davis MSS, IHi; J. G. Holland, *The Life of Abraham Lincoln* (Springfield, Mass.: Gurdon Bill, 1866), 97–98.

58. Unidentified newspaper article by Thornton, clipping collection, LMFW. Thornton said of Lincoln: "I never saw him angry but once. He became excited at some words of Judge Constable, an amiable gentleman. Strife was prevented by the interposition of mutual friends."

59. John Hay diary, 7 May 1861, Hay MSS, RPB.

60. "Speech in the U.S. House of Representatives on the Presidential Question," 27 July 1848, in Basler, *CWL,* 1:511, 510.

61. Rankin, *Intimate Sketches,* 136–37.

62. Henry C. Whitney, *Life on the Circuit with Lincoln* (Boston: Estes and Lauriat, 1892), 462, and "Lincoln: A Study from Life," 465; Duff, *Prairie Lawyer,* 63.

63. Thomas, *Lincoln,* 84.

64. Robert H. Wiebe, "Lincoln's Fraternal Democracy," in *Abraham Lincoln and the American Political Tradition,* ed. John L. Thomas (Amherst: University of Massachusetts Press, 1986), 24–25.

65. See the chapters elsewhere in the volume on Lincoln's depressions, women, and his hatred of slavery.

66. Herndon's interview with George Alfred Townsend, Springfield correspondence, 25 Jan. 1867, New York *Tribune,* 15 Feb. 1867, 2; William H. Herndon, "Analysis of the Character of Abraham Lincoln: A Lecture" [delivered in Springfield, 26 Dec. 1865], *Abraham Lincoln Quarterly* 1 (Dec. 1941): 429; Herndon to Jesse Weik, Springfield, 20 Nov. 1885, H-W MSS, DLC; Angle *HL,* 264–65. The case was *The State v. Peachy Quinn Harrison,* which is ably described and analyzed in Robert Bray's unpublished 1991 essay "When Lincoln Put Cartwright on the Stand: A New Look at the Harrison Trial." The trial record, discovered recently by staff members of the Lincoln Legal Papers Project, has little to say about Lincoln's outburst, although on page 60 of the document Stephen T. Logan is paraphrased thus: "As there was now a good deal of feeling excited on the subject at the moment, he would propose that the other evidence proceed, & this matter be postponed for further argument tomorrow morning." I am indebted to Cullom Davis, director of the Lincoln Legal Papers Project, for providing me with a photocopy of the relevant passages from the trial report. This document was unavailable to John Maxcy Zane, who expressed skepticism about Herndon's "wild statement about Lincoln, during the trial, flaying the judge [E. Y. Rice]." Zane, *Lincoln the Constitutional Lawyer* (Chicago: Caxton Club, 1932), 12n.

67. T. W. S. Kidd's lecture, "The Court Crier," excerpts in the Ida M. Tarbell MSS, Allegheny College.

68. Angle, *HL,* 274.

69. Herndon to Weik, Springfield, 12 Nov. 1885, H-W MSS, DLC; Angle, *HL,* 274–76.

70. Parks to Herndon, Lincoln, Ill., 25 March 1866, H-W MSS, DLC.

71. Lawrence Weldon in Rice, *RL*, 203.

72. Herndon, "Analysis of the Character of Lincoln," 432–33.

73. [John M. Scott], "Lincoln on the Stump and at the Bar," typescript, 14, Ida M. Tarbell MSS, Allegheny College.

74. Statement of Davis, 20 Sept. 1866, H-W MSS, DLC.

75. Davis to his wife, Urbana, 1 May 1851, David Davis MSS, ICHi.

76. Whitney, *Lincoln*, 1:179.

77. Thomas Wesley Shastid, paraphrased in Thomas Hall Shastid, *My Second Life: An Autobiography* (Ann Arbor: George Wahr, 1944), 62n.

78. Reminiscences of Henry Rickel, Cedar Rapids *Evening Gazette*, 6 Feb. 1909, enclosed in William J. Petersen to Harry E. Pratt, Iowa City, 25 Feb. 1941, Reminiscences File, folder 7, Lincoln Collection, IHi. Rickel's father, who was allegedly close to Lincoln in Springfield, told Rickel this story.

79. Newton M. Bateman, *Abraham Lincoln: An Address* (Galesburg: Cadmus Club, 1899), 11–13. The victim was probably Stephen T. Logan.

80. Henry C. Whitney to Herndon, Chicago, 27 Aug. 1887, H-W MSS, DLC.

81. Reminiscences of Adlai E. Stevenson, in Frederick Trevor Hill, *Lincoln the Lawyer* (New York: Century, 1906), 219–20. When an Iowa congressman during the Civil War recommended for office a man named H. Clay Caldwell, Lincoln replied that he would not appoint anyone who "parted his name in the middle." The congressman protested that Caldwell used only the initials H. C. when signing letters; the president then relented. *Pacific Commercial Advertiser*, N.d., reprinted in the New York *Sun*, 29 May 1908.

82. Recollections of Lawrence Weldon, in Hill, *Lincoln the Lawyer*, 212–15.

83. Henry McHenry to Herndon, Petersburg, Ill., 29 May 1865, H-W MSS, DLC.

84. Reminiscences of George M. Angell in an undated newspaper clipping marked "originally published in the Crickfield Bros. Papers," Reminiscences File, folder 7, Lincoln Collection, IHi.

85. Lincoln did a large volume of business for this firm, primarily collecting debts. Frank, *Lincoln as a Lawyer*, 7.

86. Lincoln to Samuel C. Davis and Company, Springfield, 17 Nov. 1858, in Basler, *CWL*, 2:338. See also Albert A. Woldman, *Lawyer Lincoln* (Boston: Houghton, Mifflin, 1936), 259.

87. D. C. Donnohue, interview with Jesse W. Weik, 13 Feb. 1887, Weik MSS, IHi.

88. Lincoln to Martin, Springfield, 29 Aug. 1859, in Basler, *CWL*, 2:110.

89. W. G. Greene to Herndon, Elm Wood, 30 May 1865, H-W MSS, DLC; Arnold, *Life of Lincoln*, 34–35. Cf. the statement of Roil A. Clary, N.d., H-W MSS, DLC.

90. Walter Graves to Ida Tarbell, Mound City, Mo., 15 Nov. 1929, Ida M. Tarbell MSS, Allegheny College; reminiscences of Colonel Hobart Graves, in "Across the Editor's Desk," *Better Homes and Gardens*, Feb. 1932.

91. Elwell Crissy, *Lincoln's Lost Speech: The Pivot of His Career* (New

York: Hawthorn Books, 1967), 152. Cf. Joseph Medill's description of the speech in a letter to Ida Tarbell, 15 May 1896, Ida M. Tarbell MSS, Allegheny College.

92. William E. Gienapp, *The Origins of the Republican Party, 1852–1856* (New York: Oxford University Press, 1987), 273–303, and "The Caning of Charles Sumner and the Rise of the Republican Party," *Civil War History* 25 (Sept. 1979): 218–45.

93. Statement of Joshua Speed, N.d., H-W MSS, DLC.

94. John Potter's reminiscences, in "Salem Traditions," Petersburg, Ill., correspondence, 18 Sept. [ca. 1887], St. Louis *Globe Democrat* [ca. 19 Sept. 1887], clipping, LMFW. Potter explained that "the hold Jack took was fair in a scuffle, but not in a wrestle, and they were wrestling."

95. Lincoln to George C. Spears, [1 July 1834], in Basler, *CWL*, 1:25.

96. Lincoln to Allen, New Salem, 21 June 1836, in Basler, *CWL*, 1:48–49.

97. Lincoln to George B. Kinkead, Danville, Ill., 27 May 1853, in Basler, *CWL*, 2:194. Cf. William H. Townsend, *Abraham Lincoln Defendant: Lincoln's Most Interesting Lawsuit* (Boston: Houghton, Mifflin, 1923).

98. Lincoln to Rives, Springfield, 7 May, 15 Dec. 1849, in Basler, *CWL*, 2:46, 69. According to Rives, Anson G. Henry, his rival for the post, had spread false rumors that Rives was disparaging Lincoln behind his back. When he learned of this calumny, Rives confronted Henry and demanded a retraction. Henry denied the charge but did go to Lincoln with Rives and exonerated him. Rives did not use Lincoln's letter of recommendation but eventually, with the help of Lincoln, won the appointment for his brother-in-law, John Stratton. Anonymous, "A Test of Friendship," *Memoirs of Abraham Lincoln in Edgar County* ([Paris: Edgar County Historical Society], 1925), 12–13. In the 1850s Rives became an enthusiastic supporter of Lincoln, whom he called "one of the best men God ever made." Rives to O. M. Hatch, Paris, Ill., 10 Nov. 1858, Hatch MSS, IHi.

99. Lincoln to Thomas Ewing, Springfield, 13 Oct. 1849, in *The Collected Works of Abraham Lincoln: Second Supplement, 1848–1865*, ed. Roy P. Basler and Christian O. Basler (New Brunswick: Rutgers University Press, 1990), 5–6. Cf. Thomas F. Schwartz, "'An Egregious Political Blunder': Justin Butterfield, Lincoln, and Illinois Whiggery," *Journal of the Abraham Lincoln Association* 8 (1986): 9–19.

100. Lincoln to Butler, Vandalia, 26 Jan. 1839, in Basler, *CWL*, 1:139. Cf. Edward D. Baker to Butler, Vandalia, 26 Jan. 1839, and Butler to Baker, Springfield, 29 Jan. 1839, 28 Feb. 1839, William Butler MSS, ICHi.

101. John Hay diary, 3 May 1861, Hay MSS, RPB.

102. Johnson to Lincoln, Paduca, 26 April 1861, Lincoln MSS, DLC.

103. John Hay diary, 6 May 1861, Hay MSS, RPB. Hay added, "It will take the quiet satire of the note about half an hour to get through the thick skull of this Kentucky Senator, and then he will think it a damned poor joke." Actually, Senator Johnson enjoyed the joke and told it to others. William F. G. Shanks, *Personal Recollections of Distinguished Generals* (New York: Harper and Brothers, 1866), 213–14.

104. Francis Fisher Browne, *The Every-Day Life of Abraham Lincoln*, 2d ed. (New York: G. P. Putnam's 1913), 477–78. This story was evidently told by Galusha Grow.

105. Noah Brooks, "Personal Reminiscences of Lincoln," *Scribner's Monthly* 15 (March 1878): 681.

106. John Hay is cited as the source of this story. "In the Interpreter's Chair: A Talk about Lincoln," *American Magazine*, Feb. 1909, 448.

107. William O. Stoddard, *Inside the White House in War Times* (New York: Webster, 1890), 56–58, 67.

108. Emilie Todd Helm's diary, in Katherine Helm, *The True Story of Mary, Wife of Lincoln* (New York: Harper and Brothers, 1928), 229–31.

109. Howard K. Beale, ed., *The Diary of Edward Bates, 1859–1866*, vol. 4 of the Annual Report of the American Historical Association for 1930 (Washington: Government Printing Office, 1933), 392–93 [entries for 30 July, 2 Aug. 1864].

110. Hay to James C. Welling (Gibson's assistant), Washington, 25 July 1864, in Basler, *CWL*, 7:462.

111. Titian J. Coffey, in Rice, *RL*, 237–38. For other versions of this story, see Adlai E. Stevenson, *Something of Men I Have Known* (Chicago: A. C. McClurg, 1909), 352–53, and Carpenter, *Six Months at the White House*, 256–57.

112. Isaac N. Arnold, *Abraham Lincoln: A Paper Read Before the Royal Historical Society, London, June 16, 1881* (Chicago: Fergus, 1881), 190.

113. Robert V. Bruce, *Lincoln and the Tools of War* (Indianapolis: Bobbs-Merrill, 1956), 179.

114. John J. McGilvra's 1896 reminiscences of a visit to the White House in November 1863, in Ivan Doig, ed., "The Genial White House Host and Raconteur," *Journal of the Illinois State Historical Society* 62 (1969): 310–11. This was, McGilvra said, "the only time I ever saw Lincoln exhibit any considerable amount of temper."

115. Bruce, *Lincoln and the Tools of War*, 280; Carpenter, *Six Months at the White House*, 253–54.

116. Bruce, *Lincoln and the Tools of War*, 222.

117. Ibid., 156–70; "Notes of an Interview with Abraham S. Hewitt, March 8, 1901," Ida M. Tarbell MSS, Allegheny College.

118. Lincoln to Stanton, Washington, 11 Nov. 1863, in Basler, *CWL*, 7:11. A West Point graduate, the deputy adjutant general of the New Jersey militia, and the editor of the Trenton *State Gazette*, Freese had applied to lead a regiment of black troops and was subjected to a nit-picking test. He wrote a pamphlet about his experience and sent a copy to the president. New York *Times*, 24 April 1886. He had early in the war volunteered to do anything he could to help subdue the rebellion. Freese to Ward Hill Lamon, Trenton, N.J., 4, 14 May 1861, and Charles Smith Olden to Lamon, Trenton, 18 May 1861, Lamon MSS, CSmH.

119. Leonard Swett, lecture on Lincoln, Chicago *Times*, 21 Feb. 1876.

120. C. Van Santwood, "A Reception by President Lincoln," *Century Magazine* 25 (Feb. 1883): 613.

121. Frazer Kirkland, ed., *Reminiscences of the Blue and Gray, '61–'65* (Chicago: Preston, 1895), 640–41.

122. Alley in Rice, *RL,* 589.

123. Alexander Milton Ross, *Recollections and Experiences of an Abolitionist; From 1855 to 1865* (Toronto: Rowsell and Hutchinson, 1875), 138–39.

124. Speed told this story to Judge Fontaine Talbott Fox. Francis B. Fox to Ida Tarbell, New York, 13 Nov. 1939, Ida M. Tarbell MSS, Allegheny College.

125. Noah Brooks, *Abraham Lincoln and the Downfall of American Slavery* (New York: G. P. Putnam's Sons, 1894), 425. Cf. A. K. McClure, *Abraham Lincoln and Men of War-Times: Some Personal Recollections of War and Politics during the Lincoln Administration* (Philadelphia: The Times, 1892), 64.

126. Whitney, "Lincoln: A Study from Life," 455–56. Cf. Whitney to Herndon, [Chicago], 23 June, 23 Aug. 1887, H-W MSS, DLC, and Whitney, *Lincoln,* 2:26–27. In March 1861 Davis lobbied for Simon Cameron and Caleb B. Smith for the cabinet; for Archibald Williams and William P. Kellogg for judgeships; for William P. Dole as head of the Indian Affairs Bureau; and Ward Hill Lamon as marshal of Washington. When Lamon tried to return the favor by recommending Davis as commissioner of patents, Lincoln was unreceptive. Davis to Lamon, Bloomington, Ill., 30 March 1861, Lamon MSS, CSmH; King, *Davis,* 350n1. The following month, Davis asked Lamon to urge Davis's claims to a judgeship. Davis to Lamon, Urbana, Ill., 14 April 1861, Lamon MSS, CSmH.

127. New York *Tribune,* 26 July 1885, 3.

128. Davis to Leonard Swett, Washington, 23 Jan. 1863, Davis MSS, IHi. Cf. Davis to Hanna, Washington, 8 Feb. 1863, Davis MSS, IHi: "The President . . . is not very patient now, when the subject of offices are mentioned to him." See also Lamon to Orme, Washington, 6 Jan. 1863, copy, Illinois Historical Survey, University of Illinois Library, Urbana-Champaign.

129. Conversation of 30 Sept. 1861, in Whitney, "Lincoln: A Study from Life," 465; undated statement by Whitney to Herndon, Lincoln Records, 2:430, Lamon MSS, CSmH.

130. Theodore C. Pease and James G. Randall, eds., *The Diary of Orville H. Browning,* 2 vols., vols. 20, 22, Collections of the Illinois State Historical Library (Springfield: Illinois State Historical Library, 1925), 1:595.

131. David W. Porter, *Incidents and Anecdotes of the Civil War* (New York: D. Appleton, 1885), 287. William Crook recalled a much milder reaction by the president: "Well, I guess he [Johnson] can get along without me." Crook, *Through Five Administrations,* 44. Cf. Hans L. Trefousse, *Andrew Johnson: A Biography* (New York: W. W. Norton, 1989), 192.

132. "Lincoln's Religion: Answer of William H. Herndon, Esq., to Mrs. Lincoln," Springfield, 12 Jan. 1874, *Illinois State Register* [Springfield], 14 Jan. 1874; Angle, *HL,* 413–14.

133. Daniel E. Sickles in the New York *Times,* 10 July 1891, 4.

134. Cf. LeRoy P. Graf et al., eds., *The Papers of Andrew Johnson,* 8 vols. to date (Knoxville: University of Tennessee Press, 1967–), 7:xxiv–xxvi.

135. William Pitt Kellogg to James R. B. Van Cleave, Washington, 8 Feb. 1909, copy, Lincoln File, Reminiscences, folder 4, IHi; John W. Forney, *Anecdotes of Public Men,* 2 vols. (New York: Harper and Brothers, 1874), 1:177. Kellogg claimed that he sat near Lincoln and observed his face closely.

136. Ervin S. Chapman, *Latest Light on Abraham Lincoln,* 2 vols. (New York: Fleming H. Revell, 1917), 2:294; Trefousse, *Johnson,* 190–91. Trefousse implausibly maintains that Lincoln was not disturbed by Johnson's conduct. Cf. Noah Brooks, *Washington, D.C. in Lincoln's Time,* ed. Herbert Mitgang (Chicago: Quadrangle Books, 1971), 211–12.

137. Graf et al., eds., *Johnson Papers,* 7:lxi–lxii. The president finally had a brief visit with Johnson on April 14.

138. Lincoln to James Pollock, Washington, 15 Aug. 1861, in Basler, *CWL,* 4:485.

139. Lincoln to Francis S. Corkran, Washington, 6 May 1861, in Basler, *CWL,* 4:357.

140. George W. Julian, *Political Recollections, 1840 to 1872* (Chicago: Jansen, McClurg, 1884), 244–45; Julian in Rice, *RL,* 52. Julian had opposed Holloway's appointment in 1861 (*Recollections,* 183).

141. Reminiscences by the clerk, J. C. Hesse, in "True Stories of Lincoln Never Published until Now," unidentified clipping, LMFW.

142. Forney, *Anecdotes of Public Men,* 1:176.

143. Journal of John A. Dahlgren, [entry for 22 Dec. 1862], in Madeleine Vinton Dahlgren, *Memoir of John A. Dahlgren, Rear-Admiral United States Navy* (Boston: James R. Osgood, 1882), 383.

144. J. K. Morehead, interview with John G. Nicolay, 12, 13 May [no year given], Nicolay MSS, DLC. This passage is in Nicolay's idiosyncratic shorthand. I am grateful to William Mohr for translating it for me.

145. On June 13, T. J. Barnett, who wrote for the New York *Journal of Commerce,* was asked by Lincoln if he "had heard any well founded rumors that *responsible* parties [in New York] were dissatisfied with the contracts of the War Dept." T. J. Barnett to S. L. M. Barlow, Washington, 14 June 1861, Barlow MSS, CSmH.

146. Nicolay memorandum, "Conversation with the President, October 2, 1861," Nicolay MSS, DLC.

147. Carpenter, *Six Months at the White House,* 136.

148. Lincoln to Cameron, Washington, 11 Jan. 1862, in Basler, *CWL,* 5:96; A. K. McClure, "Lincoln and Cameron," Philadelphia, 10 Dec. (no year given), St. Louis *Globe-Democrat,* clipping, LMFW; David Donald, ed., *Inside Lincoln's Cabinet: The Civil War Diaries of Salmon P. Chase* (New York: Longmans, Green, 1954), 60–62 [entry for 12 Jan. 1862]; Chase to Jeremiah Black, N.p., 4 July 1870, *The Green Bag,* July 1895.

149. Lincoln to Cameron, Washington, 11 Jan. 1862, in Basler, *CWL,* 5:96–97.

150. T. J. Barnett to S. L. M. Barlow, Washington, 14 June 1861, Barlow MSS, CSmH; Henry B. Stanton, *Random Recollections* (New York: Harper and Brothers, 1887), 232–33.

151. Burton J. Hendrick, *Lincoln's War Cabinet* (Boston: Little Brown, 1946), 517–29. Cf. McClure, *Lincoln and Men of War-Times*, 133–36.

152. Cf. John Niven, "Lincoln and Chase, a Reappraisal," *Journal of the Abraham Lincoln Association* 12 (1991): 1–15.

153. Lincoln to Chase, Washington, 30 June 1864, in Basler, *CWL*, 7:419. On Chase's disagreeable personality, see Frederick J. Blue, *Salmon P. Chase: A Life in Politics* (Kent: Kent State University Press, 1987), 5, 13, 72, 108, 117, 118, 320, 322; Howard K. Beale, ed., *Diary of Gideon Welles*, 3 vols. (New York: W. W. Norton, 1960), 2:121 [entry for 25 Aug. 1864]; and Hendrick, *Lincoln's War Cabinet*, 43–55.

154. Conness in Rice, *RL*, 561–64 [quote on 564].

155. John Hay diary, 30 June 1864, Hay MSS, RPB.

156. William Faxon to Mark Howard, Washington, 18 March 1861, Mark Howard MSS, Connecticut Historical Society, Hartford; Harry J. Carman and Reinhold H. Luthin, *Lincoln and the Patronage* (New York: Columbia University Press, 1943), 63–64, 111–12;

157. Brooks, *Washington in Lincoln's Time*, 112–13. At the time, Brooks reported that "when the President discovered what had occurred," he "was at once greatly exercised at what he considered to be an unfair and ungenerous treatment of the California Congressmen by the Secretary, and he directed that they be recalled to the Capital, if possible, informing them that their preference in the matter should be regarded. [Representative Frederick Ferdinand] Low and [Representative Aaron A.] Sargent returned to Washington a day or two since, [Representative Timothy Guy] Phelps having sailed for California in the meantime. The President expressed his regret at the hasty and somewhat arbitrary action which had deprived them of any opportunity of having a voice in the selection of the new appointees for the Federal positions to be made vacant by dismissal, and then asked them to submit names for Executive action." Washington correspondence, 21 March 1863, Sacramento *Daily Union*, 17 April 1863, 1.

158. Murat Halstead to Ida Tarbell, Cincinnati, 2 July 1900, Ida M. Tarbell MSS, Allegheny College.

159. A. G. Henry to his wife, [Washington, 12 April 1863], fragment, photostatic copy, JGR MSS, DLC; Brooks, *Washington in Lincoln's Time*, 114–17; Carman and Luthin, *Lincoln and the Patronage*, 230; Maunsell B. Field, *Memories of Many Men and Some Women* (New York: Harper and Brothers, 1874), 301–3; Lincoln to Chase, Washington, 8 May 1863, in Basler, *CWL*, 6:202. According to Noah Brooks, "The charges brought against Victor Smith, Collector of Port Angeles, Washington Territory, are very explicit, and his removal is asked for by all the Federal officers in the Territory, with but a single exception, and by a great number of loyal and influential citizens. It is charged that Smith removed the Collectorship from Townsend to Angeles for a private speculation; that he has misused the public moneys confided to his care, depositing a portion thereof for security for his private debts, and diverting cash to his own uses; that he has made false entries upon his books and has kept his business in a loose and disreputable manner. He has said that he was 'so linked into the fibers of the National Government that he could not be removed;' but

the appearances are the Father Abraham will try the experiment." Washington correspondence, 18 March 1863, Sacramento *Daily Union*, 14 April 1863, 1.

160. John Hay diary, 30 June 1864, Hay MSS, RPB; John P. Usher to Richard W. Thompson, Washington, 5 July 1864, photocopy, JGR MSS, DLC; L. E. Chittenden, *Recollections of President Lincoln and His Administration* (New York: Harper and Brothers, 1891), 371ff.

161. Conness in Rice, *RL*, 564. Cf. Brooks, *Washington in Lincoln's Time*, 118–21. According to a journalist, in 1865 Lincoln objected on similar grounds to another nominee for a federal post: "One of Mr. Lincoln's last acts was to decide upon the appointment of a gentleman in one of the Western States to an important office. He said to a friend of mine who called upon him: 'I am great[ly] embarrassed by the persistency of Mr. —— and Mr. —— in sticking to their candidate for the place.' My friend asked what was the objection to their man. The President quickly replied: 'He is a drunkard. I hear bad stories of his moral character, yet his backers are among the best Republicans in the State. I like the fellow's friends, but it goes against my conscience to give the place to a man who gambles and drinks.' The result was that Mr. Lincoln refused to give the appointment to the applicant, and gave it to another person who did not ask for it, but whose moral character was above suspicion." Washington correspondence, 27 April 1865, Boston *Daily Evening Traveller*, 29 April 1865, 2.

162. Lincoln to Chase, Washington, 28 June 1864, in Basler, *CWL*, 7:413. According to Noah Brooks, Chase was also upset over another matter: "The Ways and Means Committee of the House had declined to accede to Chase's request, just made, that Congress should provide, before the adjournment, for $100,000,000 additional to the estimate and appropriations already made, on account of a deficiency in the estimates of the Treasury Department." When the president "declined sending a special message to Congress asking for a supplemental tax bill to raise the additional $100,000,000 asked by Chase, preferring to postpone all such requests for this session," the secretary felt aggrieved. Washington correspondence, 1 July 1864, Sacramento *Daily Union*, 26 July 1864, 1.

163. John G. Nicolay and John Hay, *Abraham Lincoln: A History*, 10 vols. (New York: Century, 1890), 9:87–88. Thurlow Weed claimed that shortly before the crisis over Field, Chase had gotten Lincoln to withdraw his objections to another New York Customs House appointee. Albany *Evening Journal*, 16 July 1864.

164. John Hay diary, 30 June 1864, Hay MSS, RPB.

165. Brough told this story to William Henry Smith shortly after the conversation took place. Smith, "Private Memoranda—War Times," 12 July 1864, photostatic copy, JGR MSS, DLC. Cf. Field, *Memories*, 300–304.

166. Chittenden, *Recollections*, 378–79.

167. Hayes conceded that "Chase possessed noble gifts of intellect, great culture, and a commanding presence." Hayes's diary entry for 18 May 1873, in *Diary and Letters of Rutherford Birchard Hayes, Nineteenth President of the United States*, ed. Charles Richard Williams, 5 vols. (Columbus: Ohio State Archaeological and Historical Society, 1922–26), 3:243.

168. Don E. Fehrenbacher, "Comment" on John Niven, "Lincoln and Chase, a Reappraisal," *Journal of the Abraham Lincoln Association* 12 (1991): 18–19.

169. Recollections by John P. Usher, in *Humorous and Pathetic Stories of Abraham Lincoln*, 5th ed., 2d ser. (Fort Wayne: Lincoln Publishing Co., 1900?), 16.

170. Fragment of a letter from an unidentified Massachusetts political figure (probably John B. Alley), who spoke with Lincoln the night before Chase's appointment was announced, to Josiah G. Holland, Washington, 8 Aug. 1865, J. G. Holland Papers, New York Public Library; Chittenden, *Recollections*, 384; Nicolay and Hay, *Lincoln*, 9:394–95; Blue, *Chase*, 245; Carman and Luthin, *Lincoln and the Patronage*, 315–20. On the identity of the congressman who heard these remarks, see Crook, *Through Five Administrations*, 31ff. Senator Lafayette Foster told Lincoln on the day Chase was confirmed, "Mr. President you sent us up a Chief Justice today, whom we confirmed at once. There had been so many contradictory reports and rumors that we had begun to have some doubts and anxieties on the subject."
The president replied, "Mr. Chase will make a very excellent judge if he devotes himself exclusively to the duties of his office, and don[']t meddle with politics. But if he keeps on with the notion that he is destined to be President of the United States, and which in my judgment he will never be, he will never acquire that fame and usefulness as a Chief Justice which he would otherwise certainly attain[.]" John G. Nicolay's interview with Foster, 23 Oct. 1878, Nicolay MSS, DLC.

171. Weed to Bigelow, Albany, 13 Dec. 1863, in John Bigelow, *Retrospections of an Active Life*, 5 vols. (New York: Baker and Taylor, 1909–13), 2:110.

172. William E. Chandler, quoting Lincoln, in Beale, ed., *Welles Diary*, 2:196 [entry for 15 Dec. 1864]; Fox diary, Gist-Blair Papers, DLC, quoted in Miers et al., eds., *Lincoln Day by Day*, 3:301 [entry for 10 Dec. 1864].

173. Blair to Samuel J. Tilden, Washington, 5 June 1868, in *Letters and Literary Memorials of Samuel J. Tilden*, ed. John Bigelow, 2 vols. (New York: Harper and Brothers, 1908), 1:233.

174. Hay to Herndon, Paris, 5 Sept. 1866, H-W MSS, DLC.

175. See Norman A. Graebner, "Lincoln's Humility," in *Lincoln for the Ages*, ed. Ralph G. Newman (Garden City: Doubleday, 1960), 384–89.

176. See chapter 1 of this volume.

177. Hans L. Trefousse, *The Radical Republicans: Lincoln's Vanguard for Racial Justice* (New York: Alfred A. Knopf, 1969). Cf. Roger D. Launis, "Williams and the Radicals: An Historiographical Essay," *Louisiana History* 28, no. 2 (1987): 141–64, and LaWanda Cox, "From Emancipation to Segregation: National Policy and Southern Blacks," in *Interpreting Southern History: Historiographical Essays in Honor of Sanford W. Higginbotham*, ed. John B. Boles and Evelyn Thomas Nolen (Baton Rouge: Louisiana State University Press, 1987), 222–23 and citations listed on 233n43.

178. William D. Kelley to the editor of the New York *Tribune*, Philadelphia, 23 Sept. 1885, in William D. Kelley, *Lincoln and Stanton* (New York: G. P. Putnam's Sons, 1885), 86; John Hay diary, 1 July 1864, Hay MSS, RPB.

179. Undated memorandum by F. P. Rice, Eli Thayer MSS, folder 17, Box 6, RPB. James S. Wadsworth also complained about Lincoln's patronizing attitude toward radicals and blacks. Cf. Wadsworth's remarks, summarized in Adams Hill to Sydney Howard Gay, N.p., N.d., quoted in James Ford Rhodes, *History of the United States from the Compromise of 1850,* 7 vols. (New York: Macmillan, 1902–6), 4:64n.

180. John Eaton, *Grant, Lincoln and the Freedmen* (New York: Longmans, Green, 1907), 184.

181. J. K. Herbert to Benjamin Butler, Washington, 6 Aug. 1864, in *Private and Official Correspondence of Gen. Benjamin F. Butler during the Period of the Civil War,* ed. Jessie Ames Marshall, 5 vols. (Privately published, 1917), 5:8–9; Beale, ed., *Welles Diary,* 2:95, 98 [entries for 6, 8 Aug. 1864]; Carpenter, *Six Months at the White House,* 145; James M. Ashley, "Abraham Lincoln," *Magazine of Western History Illustrated* 14 (May 1891): 32. Cf. Herman Belz, *Reconstructing the Union: Theory and Practice during the Civil War* (Ithaca: Cornell University Press, 1969), 228–31.

182. Recollections of an unnamed Missouri radical, in Tarbell, *The Life of Abraham Lincoln,* 3:173.

183. John Hay diary, 28 Oct. 1863, Hay MSS, RPB.

184. Whitney, "Lincoln: A Study from Life," 471.

185. "The Interview between Thad Stevens & Mr. Lincoln as Related by Col. R. M. Hoe," Nicolay MSS, DLC. In a headnote, Nicolay states that "shortly before the election of 1864 Col. R. M. Hoe of N.Y. happened to be in company with Hon. S. Cameron and Hon. Thad. Stevens of Pa. when they went one evening to call on the President, and being there, by request of the parties remained present at what turned out to be a very noteworthy interview."

186. Shelby M. Cullom, *Fifty Years of Public Service: Personal Recollections of Shelby M. Cullom* (Chicago: A. C. McClurg, 1911), 96.

187. Unidentified clipping, ca. late Aug. 1863, LMFW.

188. William Henry Crook, "Lincoln as I Knew Him," ed. Margarita Spalding Gerry, *Harper's* 115 (June 1907): 45; Dunn, paraphrased in Crook, *Through Five Administrations,* 36–37. The order to Dunn was, Crook said, "a matter of my personal knowledge." Crook's description of the "intense antipathy" that Lincoln felt for Sumner is stronger in the *Harper's* article than it is in his memoirs. Despite Crook's claim, a modern biographer of Sumner argues that his subject and the president had a "generally amicable relationship." David Donald, *Charles Sumner and the Rights of Man* (New York: Alfred A. Knopf, 1970), 167.

189. John W. Forney, quoted by Hawkins Taylor, in *A Genealogy of the Descendants of John Walker of Wigton, Scotland,* in *Intimate Memories of Lincoln,* ed. Wilson, 12. In the summer of 1862, Lincoln, responding to Sumner's renewed pleas for emancipation, said, "I would do it if I were not afraid that half the officers would fling down their arms & three more States would rise." Sumner to John Bright, Boston, 5 Aug. 1862, in *The Selected Letters of Charles Sumner,* ed. Beverly Wilson Palmer, 2 vols. (Boston: Northeastern University Press, 1990), 2:122.

190. Wilson in an interview conducted in Washington by John G. Nico-

lay, 1 April 1874, Nicolay MSS, DLC. Cf. Sumner to John Bright, Boston, 27 Sept. 1864, in *Selected Letters of Charles Sumner,* ed. Palmer, 2:253.

191. John G. Nicolay's interview with Fish, 10 April 1874, Nicolay MSS, DLC.

192. Sumner's recollections of the event, in *The Works of Charles Sumner,* 15 vols. (Boston: Lee and Shepard, 1875–83), 7:112. Cf. Sumner to John Andrew, Washington, 5 June 1862, in *Selected Letters of Charles Sumner,* ed. Palmer, 2:118; Sumner to [?], Washington, 5 June 1862, typescript, Ida M. Tarbell MSS, Allegheny College. In the latter document, Sumner reassures his correspondent that the president "has no sympathy with Stanly in his absurd wickedness, closing the schools, nor again in his other act of turning our camp into a hunting ground for Slaves. He repudiates both—positively."

193. Tarbell, *The Life of Abraham Lincoln,* 3:73. For evidence to support Lincoln's assertion, see Edward Everett Hale's manuscript memo of a conversation with Sumner, 26 April 1862, Lincoln Collection, RPB .

194. Pierce to Herndon, Milton, Mass., 15 Sept. 1889, H-W MSS, DLC.

195. Samuel G. Buckingham, *The Life of William A. Buckingham, the War Governor of Connecticut* (Springfield: W. F. Adams, 1894), 262–63.

196. Washington correspondence, 5 Aug. 1862, Chicago *Tribune,* 6 Aug. 1862, 1; Chicago *Morning Post,* 7 Aug. 1862, copy, Allan Nevins MSS, Columbia University; Washington correspondence, 4, 5 Aug. 1862, Cincinnati *Gazette,* 5 Aug. 1862, 3, 6 Aug. 1862, 3. According to a letter by the *Gazette's* correspondent to the Washington *Republican* of 11 Aug., which appeared on 14 Aug. (3), the source was the senator who retorted so boldly. That was doubless Pomeroy, for Harlan did not include the insolent retort in his reminiscences. Undated reminiscences of James Harlan, and Harlan to Ida Tarbell, Mt. Pleasant, Iowa, 15 Dec. 1898, Ida M. Tarbell MSS, Allegheny College. In an anonymous newspaper dispatch, John Hay emphatically denied that such an insult had been uttered. Washington correspondence, 22 Sept. 1862, *Missouri Republican* [St. Louis], 26 Sept. 1862, 2. Cf. New York *Tribune,* 5 Aug. 1862, in Basler, *CWL,* 5:356–57.

197. Moncure Daniel Conway, "A Southern Abolitionist's Memories of Mr. Lincoln," *Fortnightly Review* [London], June 1865, in *Intimate Memories of Lincoln,* ed. Wilson, 182.

198. Samuel G. Suddarth to William Stewart and Dr. Walker (no first name indicated), Washington, 1 Nov. 1863, in *Concerning Mr. Lincoln: In Which Abraham Lincoln Is Pictured as He Appeared to Letter Writers of His Time,* ed. Harry E. Pratt (Springfield: Abraham Lincoln Association, 1944), 101.

199. Josephine Shaw Lowell, diary [entry for 20 May 1862], copy, Allan Nevins MSS, Columbia University.

200. An unidentified friend of Lincoln's, in Ichabod Codding, *A Republican Manual for the Campaign: Facts for the People* (Princeton, Ill.: The Republican, 1860), 10.

201. William D. Kelley to the editor of the New York *Tribune,* Philadelphia, 23 Sept. 1885, in Kelley, *Lincoln and Stanton,* 83–85; Kelley in Rice, *RL,* 281–83. Cf. "Remarks to a Delegation of Progressive Friends," 20 June 1862, in Basler, *CWL,* 5:278–79.

202. Schuyler Colfax, in Rice, *RL*, 334–35. Cf. Browne, *Every-Day Life of Lincoln*, 2d ed., 426–27.

203. Ward Hill Lamon, *Recollections of Abraham Lincoln, 1847–1865*, 2d ed., ed. Dorothy Lamon Teillard (Washington: Privately published, 1911), 92–93.

204. Albany *Evening Journal*, 30 June 1862.

205. [Moncure D. Conway], "President Lincoln, by an American Abolitionist," *Fraser's Magazine* (Jan. 1865), in *Conversations with Lincoln*, ed. Charles M. Segal (New York: Putnam's, 1961), 238–39.

206. Helen Nicolay, *Lincoln's Secretary: A Biography of John G. Nicolay* (New York: Longmans, Green, 1949), 83.

207. John G. Nicolay's interview with John P. Usher, Washington, 8 Oct. 1878, Nicolay MSS, DLC; Usher, in Rice, *RL*, 93. Cf. Peyton McCrary, *Abraham Lincoln and Reconstruction: The Louisiana Experiment* (Princeton: Princeton University Press, 1978).

208. Thomas M. Clark, *Reminiscences* (New York: Thomas Whittaker, 1895), 143.

209. Welles to Isaac N. Arnold, Hartford, 27 Nov. 1872, Isaac N. Arnold MSS, ICHi. Cf. Welles, "Recollections in regard to the Formation of Mr[.] Lincoln's Cabinet," and "Abraham Lincoln and His Cabinet," Manuscripts Department, Beinecke Library, Yale University, esp. 10. See also Nelson R. Burr, "Abraham Lincoln: Western Star over Connecticut, 1848–1865," typed manuscript, 1973, Connecticut State Library, Hartford, 119–27.

210. Beale, ed., *Bates Diary*, 306 [entry for 14 Sept. 1863].

211. Beale, ed., *Welles Diary*, 1:432 [entry for 14 Sept. 1863]. In fact, such judges, especially in Pennsylvania, seriously interfered with recruiting new troops and punishing deserters. See Mark E. Neely, Jr., *The Fate of Liberty: Abraham Lincoln and Civil Liberties* (New York: Oxford University Press, 1991), 69–74.

212. Statement by the son of Robert B. Carnahan, U.S. district attorney for the Western District of Pennsylvania, Pittsburgh, May 1896, Ida M. Tarbell MSS, Allegheny College.

213. "Opinion on the Draft," [September 14?] 1863, in Basler, *CWL*, 6:444–49. According to Neely, this document "seems . . . likely to have been provoked later, after the Pennsylvania Supreme Court declared the federal conscription law unconstitutional in Nov[ember]." Neely, *The Fate of Liberty*, 248n55.

214. Ibid., 69–74.

215. Lincoln to Hatch and Dubois, Washington, 15 Sept. 1863, in Basler, *CWL*, 6:450.

216. "Statement: Interviews with President Lincoln, September 10th and 11th, 1862," which Hamilton said were "noted down immediately after they were closed," in James A. Hamilton, *Reminiscences of James A. Hamilton; or, Men and Events, at Home and Abroad, during Three Quarters of a Century* (New York: Charles Scribner, 1869), 529–30. That night Hamilton described this interview to Salmon P. Chase, who recorded in his dairy: "The President became vexed, and said, in substance, 'It is plain enough what you want—you

want to get Seward out of the Cabinet. There is not one of you who would not see the country ruined, if you could turn out Seward.'" Donald, ed., *Chase Diary*, 130 [entry for 10 Sept. 1862].

217. Glyndon Van Deusen, *William Henry Seward* (New York: Oxford University Press, 1967), 345–47.

218. Pease and Randall, eds., *Browning Diary*, 1:604 [entry for 22 Dec. 1862].

219. Journal of John A. Dahlgren, entry for 22 Dec. 1862, in *Memoir of John A. Dahlgren*, ed. Dahlgren, 383–84.

220. John Hay diary, 30 Oct. 1863, Hay MSS, RPB. The two visitors were D. D. Field and George Opdyke.

221. David Homer Bates, *Lincoln Stories: Told by Him in the Military Office in the War Department during the Civil War* (New York: William Edwin Rudge, 1926), 24.

222. John Hay diary, 17 Oct. 1861, Hay MSS, RPB. In response to further pressure by Sherman and Isaac Stevens, the 79th Highlanders were transferred from McClellan to the Hilton Head expedition. Hazard Stevens to [Nicolay and Hay], Boston, 5 Jan. 1889, Nicolay-Hay Papers, IHi; William Todd, *The Seventy-ninth Highlanders: New York Volunteers in the War of the Rebellion, 1861–1865* (Albany: Brandow, Barton, 1886), 78.

223. Samuel F. DuPont to Henry Winter Davis, New York, 8 Oct. 1861, in *Samuel Francis DuPont: A Selection from His Civil War Letters*, ed. John D. Hayes, 3 vols. (Ithaca: Cornell University Press for the Eleutherian Mills Historical Library, 1969), 1:162–63. The meeting, which took place on October 1 at Seward's house, was called to go over the plans for Sherman's expedition.

224. Joseph B. Carr, "Operations of 1861 about Fort Monroe," in *Battles and Leaders of the Civil War*, ed. Robert Underwood Johnson and Clarence Clough Buel, 4 vols. (New York: Century, 1884–88), 2:152.

225. Oran Follett, "Account of an Interview with President Lincoln at Washington, [28] October 1862," evidently written in 1866, in Jake Zeitlin to Carl Sandburg, Los Angeles, 11 June 1940, in the Lincoln Collection, Reminiscences File, folder 2, IHi.

226. Henry D. Bacon to S. L. M. Barlow, N.p., 20 Jan. 1862, Barlow MSS, CSmH, copy, Allan Nevins MSS, Columbia University. Bacon reported that he and Lincoln "talked about Fremont. . . . He does not feel unkindly towards Fremont, but will never give him an independent command. Would have given him, probably the Mission to St. Petersburgh if he had treated him even civilly."

227. Lincoln to John A. Andrew, Washington, 12 Aug. 1862, in Basler, *CWL*, 5:367. Andrew's language is quoted in this response.

228. Reminiscences of a Captain Page of Philadelphia, "Lincoln in Anger," New York *Commercial*, N.d., clipping, LMFW.

229. Stephen W. Sears, *George B. McClellan: The Young Napoleon* (New York: Ticknor and Fields, 1988), xii; T. Harry Williams, *Lincoln and His Generals* (New York: Alfred A. Knopf, 1952), 15–178.

230. McClellan to his wife, Washington, 16 Aug. 1861, 31 Oct. 1861, 17 Nov. 1861, and Berkeley, Va., 17, 27 July 1862, in *The Civil War Papers*

of George B. McClellan: Selected Correspondence, 1860–1865, ed. Stephen Sears (New York: Ticknor and Fields, 1989), 85, 114, 135, 362, 374.

231. These remarks were made on January 13, 1862, at a council of war with the president, cabinet members, and military leaders. In response to McClellan's criticisms, Meigs said, "That is a pity, but he is the President,—the Commander-in-Chief; he has a right to know; it is not respectful to sit mute when he so clearly requires you to speak." Meigs later called McClellan's behavior a "spectacle to make gods and men ashamed!" Meigs, "The Relations of President Lincoln and Secretary Stanton to the Military Commanders in the Civil War," 1887 or 1888 article, *American Historical Review* 26 (Jan. 1921): 293, 295. Cf. Meigs's diary entry for 13 Jan. 1862, 303. At the meeting, either Salmon Chase or Montgomery Blair commented to William B. Franklin, "Well, if that is Mac's decision, he is a ruined man." W. B. Franklin, "The First Great Crime of the War," in *The Annals of the War Written by Leading Participants North and South, Originally Published in the Philadelphia Weekly Times,* ed. Alexander K. McClure (Philadelphia: Weekly Times, 1879), 78–79. Cf. "Memorandum of General McDowell," in Henry J. Raymond, *The Life and Public Services of Abraham Lincoln* (New York: Derby and Miller, 1865), 772–79.

232. Hay diary, 13 Nov. 1861, Hay Papers, RPB. This snub was not unprecedented. On October 9, 1861, William Howard Russell wrote in his diary: "Calling on the General the other night at his usual time of return, I was told by the orderly, who was closing the door, 'The General's gone to bed tired, and can see no one. He sent the same message to the President, who came inquiring after him ten minutes ago.'" Russell commented: "This poor President! He is to be pitied; surrounded by such scenes, and trying with all his might to understand strategy, naval warfare, big guns, the movements of troops, military maps, reconnaissances, occupations, interior and exterior lines, and all the technical details of the art of slaying. He runs from one house to another, armed with plans, papers, reports, recommendations, sometimes good humored, never angry, occasionally dejected, and always a little fussy." Russell, *My Diary North and South,* ed. Eugene H. Berwanger (New York: Alfred A. Knopf, 1988), 317. McClellan also kept Lincoln waiting when the president called at the general's house. Stoddard, *Inside the White House,* 114–15.

233. F. A. Mitchel to John Hay, E. Orange, N.J., 3 Jan. 1889, Nicolay-Hay MSS, IHi. Lincoln uttered these words (or words to the effect) to General Ormsby M. Mitchel and Governor William Dennison of Ohio after McClellan had failed to keep an appointment with them.

234. McDowell's manuscript minutes, 10 Jan. 1862, in William Swinton, *Campaigns of the Army of the Potomac,* rev. ed. (New York: C. Scribner's Sons, 1882), 80. In 1864 Lincoln told Swinton that this document accurately described what happened at the meeting. Cf. Franklin, "The First Great Crime of the War," 76–78.

235. Letter by New York Congressman A. S. Diven, quoted in the Columbia [Mo.] *Statesman,* 14 Feb. 1862, copy, Allan Nevins MSS, Columbia University.

236. Sears, *McClellan*, 156–58.

237. Horace White to Joseph Medill, Washington, 3 March 1862, Charles H. Ray MSS, CSmH. Cf. White to Ray, Washington, 3 March 1862, Allan Nevins MSS, Columbia University.

238. William O. Stoddard, "White House Sketches, No. VI," New York *Citizen*, 22 September 1866. He added: "I doubt if the impression then made upon his mind was ever afterward removed. It would not have surprised me to have heard of General McClellan's removal at any time thereafter, but I knew that the question of who should be his successor was even more perplexing than that of the propriety of a change. That question, like many another, finally settled itself to general satisfaction."

239. Dirk P. deYoung, "Lincoln's Secretary Talks of His Chief," *Dearborn Independent*, 7 Feb. 1925, 14.

240. Memorandum by Nicolay, 27 Feb. 1862, typed copy, Nicolay Papers, DLC. Helen Nicolay observed that "This is almost the only time in all my father's notes that he mentioned seeing the President shaken out of his usual calm." *Lincoln's Secretary*, 143.

241. The president said he had "made up his mind to talk plainly" to McClellan. Charles Sumner to John A. Andrew, Washington, 2 March 1862, in *Selected Letters of Charles Sumner*, ed. Palmer, 2:103.

242. Charles Sumner to John A. Andrew, Washington, 28 May 1862, in *Selected Letters of Charles Sumner*, ed. Palmer, 2:115. Lincoln's anger soon cooled and he wrote the general a gentle but firm letter explaining why he had withheld McDowell's corps. Williams, *Lincoln and His Generals*, 82–83; Lincoln to McClellan, Washington, 9 April 1862, in Basler, *CWL*, 5:184–85.

243. Pease and Randall, eds., *Browning Diary*, 1:559 [entry for 14 July 1862]. Cf. Lincoln to McClellan, Washington, 4 July 1862 and Marcy to McClellan, [Washington], 4 July 1862, in Basler, *CWL*, 5:305–6.

244. George W. Julian in Rice, *RL*, 52–53.

245. Unknown to Sidney Howard Gay, Tribune Rooms [Washington], 27 Aug. 1862, Gay Papers, Columbia University.

246. Adams Hill to Sidney Howard Gay, Washington, Sunday night [31 Aug. 1862], Gay Papers, Columbia University.

247. Beale, ed., *Welles Diary*, 1:113, 116 [entries for 7, 8 Sept. 1862].

248. Hay diary, 1, 5 Sept. 1862, Hay MSS, RPB.

249. Lincoln to Key, Washington, 26 Sept. 1862, in Basler, *CWL*, 5:442.

250. John Hay diary, 26 Sept. 1862, Hay MSS, RPB.

251. John Hay's anonymous Washington dispatch, 1 Oct. 1862, *Missouri Republican* [St. Louis], 6 Oct. 1862, 2; "Record of Dismissal of John J. Key," 26–27 Sept. 1862, in Basler, *CWL*, 5:442–43. Cf. Lincoln to Key, Washington, 24 Nov. 1862, in Basler, *CWL*, 5:508; Beale, ed., *Welles Diary*, 1:146 [entry for 24 Sept. 1862].

252. John Hay diary, 25 Sept. 1864, Hay MSS, RPB. Key's brother, Colonel Thomas Key of Cincinnati, reported that many of McClellan's staff officers wanted Lincoln to treat slavery conservatively. According to one journalist, some of those officers in mid-September planned to march on Washington to intimidate the administration. Nathaniel Paige, interviewed in the New York

Tribune, N.d., in the Washington *Capital,* 21 March 1880, copy, Allan Nevins MSS, Columbia University. The officers, according to the author of the *Capital* article, "had a contempt of Lincoln and a hatred of Stanton, with a fixed belief that the war was a folly and bound to be a failure." They referred to the president and his advisors as "old women."

253. Robert Todd Lincoln to Isaac Markens, Manchester, Vt., 13 July 1918, Robert Todd Lincoln Papers, ICHi. The only other time he saw his father so upset was when General George Gordon Meade failed to block Lee's escape across the Potomac after the battle of Gettysburg, an episode discussed at length later.

254. Pease and Randall, eds., *Browning Diary,* 1:589 [entry for 29 Nov. 1862].

255. Memorandum by Rush C. Hawkins, Hombourg-les-Bains, Prussia, 17 Aug. 1872, Hawkins MSS, RPB. This document was written immediately after a two-hour conversation between Hawkins and Robert Todd Lincoln. A note dated 21 Nov. 1919 and appended to a copy of Hawkins's memorandum, perhaps by a "Miss Stillwell," says: "The General [Rush C. Hawkins] once asked General Foster, a member of the Court Martial, 'Why didn't you give that —— traitor a stronger sentence?' (meaning death). And General Foster replied, 'We gave him as strong a sentence as we thought the President would approve.'" Cf. John G. Nicolay's interview with Joseph Holt, 29 Oct. 1875, Nicolay MSS, DLC. To William Dole and others, Lincoln said Porter should have been hanged. Memorandum by Ward Hill Lamon, copy, JGR MSS, DLC.

256. Lincoln to McClellan, Washington, 24 [actually 25] Oct. 1862, in Basler, *CWL,* 5:474. According to John Nicolay, when the Confederate cavalry rode around the entire Union army that fall, Lincoln "well-nigh lost his temper over it." Nicolay to Therena Bates, Washington, 13 Oct. 1862, Nicolay MSS, DLC.

257. John Hay diary, 25 Sept. 1864, Hay MSS, RPB. Cf. Pease and Randall, eds., *Browning Diary,* 1:589–90 [entry for 29 Nov. 1862]. Lincoln told a journalist a similar story: "I do not, as some do, regard McClellan either as a traitor or an officer without capacity. He sometimes has bad counsellors, but he is loyal, and he has some fine military qualities. I adhered to him after nearly all my constitutional advisers lost faith in him. But do you want to know when I gave him up? It was after the battle of Antietam. The Blue Ridge was then between our army and Lee's. We enjoyed the great advantage over them, which they usually had over us: we had the short line, and they had the long one, to the rebel capital. I directed McClellan peremptorily to move on Richmond, at once. It was eleven days after that before he crossed the last man. Thus, he was twenty-two days in passing the river at a much easier and more practicable ford than that where Lee crossed his entire army between dark one night and daylight the next morning. That was the last grain of sand which broke the camel's back. I relieved McClellan at once." Albert D. Richardson, *The Secret Service: The Field, the Dungeon, and the Escape* (Hartford: American, 1865), 323–24.

258. Stoddard, "White House Sketches, No. VI," New York *Citizen,* 22 Sept. 1866; William O. Stoddard, *Abraham Lincoln: The True Story of a Great Life* (New York: Fords, Howard and Hulbert, 1884), 274.

259. In late November, Illinois Senator Lyman Trumbull told the president that Grant would open the Mississippi River promptly "if let alone from Washington," to which Lincoln replied "that he would be let alone except to be urged forward, & such would be the case in regard to Rosecrans also. He even seemed a little impatient that Rosecrans should have delayed as long as he has at Nashville." Trumbull to [William Butler], Washington, 26 Nov. 1862, William Butler Papers, ICHi.

260. Reminiscences of Charles Frederick, Washington *Star*, 1899, clipping, Lincoln Scrapbooks, 4:65, Judd Stewart Collection, CSmH.

261. "Notes of an Interview with A. B. Chandler, September 16, 1898," Ida M. Tarbell MSS, Allegheny College.

262. Memorandum by Robert Todd Lincoln of a conversation he had with his father on July 14, 1863, dated 5 Jan. 1885, enclosed in R. T. Lincoln to John G. Nicolay, Washington, 5 Jan. 1885, photostatic copy, Robert Todd Lincoln MSS, DLC. Cf. Joseph Medill's statement to Newton Macmillan, Portland *Oregonian*, 28 April 1895; memorandum by Rush C. Hawkins, Hombourg-les-Bains, Prussia, 17 Aug. 1872, Hawkins Papers, RPB. In this document Hawkins reports, evidently based on what he had just heard, that "the day before [Lincoln received Meade's dispatch saying he would not attack], and that he (the President) would hold himself responsible for the result. The telegram, as I now understand it was, read as follows: 'To Major General Meade[e] Commanding the Army of the Potomac. You will follow up and attack Genl. Lee as soon as possible before he can cross the river. If you fail this dispatch will clear you from all responsibility and if you succeed you may destroy it.'"

A Lincoln collector in Seattle allegedly bought a copy of Lincoln's order to Meade, which read something like this: "This is your order to pursue the retreating army and annihilate them. If you succeed you may keep this order and take the credit. If you fail destroy this order I will take the blame." Roger L. Scaife to Albert J. Beveridge, Boston, 27 April 1925, enclosing an undated letter from "H.L." in Seattle to Scaife, Beveridge MSS, DLC. Robert Todd Lincoln told several others about this order.

In October 1863, Lincoln sent to Meade through Halleck a telegram stating, among other things, "If Gen. Meade can now attack him on a field no worse than equal for us, and will do so with all the skill and courage, which he, his officers and men possess, the honor will be his if he succeeds, and the blame may be mine if he fails." Basler, *CWL*, 6:518.

263. Brooks, *Washington in Lincoln's Time*, 94.

264. Memorandum by Rush C. Hawkins, Hombourg-les-Bains, Prussia, 17 Aug. 1872, Hawkins Papers, RPB. During his conversation with Hawkins, Robert Lincoln "stated . . . that he had never seen his father cry but once."

265. John Hay diary, 14, 15, 19 July 1863, Hay MSS, RPB. For an account of Meade's pursuit of Lee that support Lincoln's view, see Kenneth T. Williams, *Lincoln Finds a General: A Military Study of the Civil War*, 5 vols. (New York: Macmillan, 1949–59), 3:730–56. For a defense of Meade, see Edwin B. Coddington, *The Gettysburg Campaign: A Study in Command* (New York: Charles Scribner's Sons, 1968), 572.

266. Beale, ed., *Welles Diary*, 1:370–71 [entry for 14 July 1863]. The

president evidently confided similar forebodings to his son Robert. Herman Haupt, *Reminiscences of General Herman Haupt* (New York: John R. Anderson, 1901), 224. See also Lincoln to Simon Cameron, Washington, 15 July 1863, in Basler, *CWL*, 6:329–30.

267. Lincoln to Meade, Washington, 14 July 1863, in Basler, *CWL*, 6:328.

268. Halleck to Meade, 1 P.M., 14 July 1863, ibid.

269. William Swinton, *Campaigns of the Army of the Potomac* (New York: C. B. Richardson, 1866), 371n.

270. Lincoln to Cameron, Washington, 15 July 1863, in Basler, *CWL*, 6:329–30.

271. Beale, ed., *Welles Diary*, 1:439 [entry for 21 Sept. 1863].

272. Hay diary, 19 July 1863, Hay MSS, RPB.

273. Lincoln to Oliver O. Howard, Washington, 21 July, 1863, in Basler, *CWL*, 6:341. To Stanton, the president allegedly said, "Why should we censure a man who had done so much for his country because he did not do a little more." Stefan Lorant, "Two New Lincoln Finds," *Look*, 21 Oct. 1969, 118.

274. William A. Croffut, *An American Procession, 1855–1915: A Personal Chronicle of Famous Men* (Boston: Little, Brown, 1931), 102. The conversation, which Gideon Welles recounted to the journalist Homer Byington, who in turn related it to Croffut, took place when Meade came to Washington to report on Gettysburg.

275. Albert B. Chandler, "As Lincoln Appeared in the War Department," in *Abraham Lincoln: Tributes from His Associates: Reminiscences of Soldiers, Statesmen and Citizens,* ed. William Hayes Ward (New York: Thomas Y. Crowell, 1895), 222; Burnside to Lincoln, 23 Sept. 1863, in Basler, *CWL*, 6:470n. Cf. William Marvel, *Burnside* (Chapel Hill: University of North Carolina Press, 1991), 266–68.

276. Basler, *CWL*, 6:480–81.

277. Lincoln to George Robertson, Washington, 20 Nov. 1862, in Basler, *CWL*, 5:502. The characterization of this document appears in Roy P. Basler, "'Beef!, Beef, Beef!': Lincoln and Judge Robertson," *Abraham Lincoln Quarterly* 6 (Sept. 1951): 400. Cf. J. Winston Coleman, Jr., "Lincoln and 'Old Buster,'" *Lincoln Herald* 46 (Feb. 1944): 3–9.

278. Robert A. Maxwell to Lincoln, N.p., 23 Sept. 1863, Lincoln to Maxwell, Washington, 23 Sept. 1863, Charles A. Tinker to George H. Thomas, N.p., 27 May 1867, all in Basler, *CWL*, 6:475–76; Charles A. Tinker, "A Telegrapher's Reminiscence," in *Abraham Lincoln: Tributes*, ed. Ward, 163.

279. Crook, *Through Five Administrations*, 34.

280. Hay diary, 14 July 1864, Hay MSS, RPB.

281. Pease and Randall, eds., *Browning Diary*, 1:676 [entry for 15 July 1864].

282. Lincoln to Halleck, Washington, 1 Jan. 1863, in Basler, *CWL*, 6:31; Stephen E. Ambrose, *Halleck: Lincoln's Chief of Staff* (Baton Rouge: Louisiana State University Press, 1962), 80; T. Harry Williams, *Lincoln and His Generals* (New York: Alfred A. Knopf, 1962), 203–4.

283. T. J. Barnett to S. L. M. Barlow, Washington, D. C., 12, 27 Oct. 1862, Barlow MSS, CSmH.

284. Jacob Picard, "Life of Franz Sigel," copy of excerpt, Allan Nevins MSS, Columbia University.

285. Col. George C. Lyon to Sigel, Fairfax Courthouse, [Va.], 10 Oct. 1862, Sigel MSS, New York Historical Society.

286. Caspar Butz to Sigel, Chicago, 25 Dec. 1863, Sigel MSS, New York Historical Society.

287. Lincoln to Sigel, Washington, 26 Jan., 5 Feb. 1863, in Basler, *CWL,* 6:79–80, 93.

288. Hay diary, 22 Oct. 1863, Hay MSS, RPB.

289. Ibid. [entry for 23 Oct. 1863]; Donn Piatt, *Memories of the Men Who Saved the Union* (New York: Belford, Clarke, 1887), 44–45. Cf. Lincoln's "Reply to Maryland Slaveholders," 21 Oct. 1863, and Lincoln to Schenck, Washington, 21 Oct. 1863, in Basler, *CWL,* 6:529–30. Piatt argued that Lincoln's reputation as a sweet-tempered man "covered as firm a character as nature ever clad with human flesh, and I doubt whether Mr. Lincoln had at all a kind, forgiving Nature. Such traits are not common to Successful leaders." Richard N. Current, *The Lincoln Nobody Knows* (New York: Hill and Wang, 1958), 182.

290. Andrew to Lincoln, 12 Feb. 1864, and Lincoln to Andrew, 18 Feb. 1864, in Basler, *CWL,* 7:190, 191.

291. Mrs. Andrew told this story on the day the conversation took place to Sidney Howard Gay, who in turn related it to Josephine Shaw Lowell. J. S. Lowell diary [entry for 3 April 1862], copy, Allan Nevins MSS, Columbia University.

292. Interview with Dr. Mitchell, St. Louis *Globe-Democrat,* 26 Aug. 1894.

293. Charles K. Tuckerman, "Personal Recollections of Abraham Lincoln," *Magazine of American History,* May 1888, 412–13. Cf. Tuckerman, "President Lincoln and Colonization," *Rare Lincolniana,* no. 15 (*The Magazine of History,* extra no. 69 [1920]): 40–44.

294. John Hay, "Life in the White House in the Time of Lincoln," *Century Magazine* 41 (Nov. 1890): 33–34. Cf. James B. Fry, in Rice, *RL,* 392–93.

295. Recollections by H. P. H. Bromwell, in *Memoirs of Abraham Lincoln in Edgar County* ([Paris: Edgar County Historical Society], 1925), 27.

296. Cf. Don Phillips, "Abraham Lincoln—The Manager: Part II, Dealing with Severe and Unjust Criticism: How Lincoln Did It," *Lincoln Herald* 89 (Spring 1987): 25–31.

297. Noah Brooks, "Personal Recollections of Abraham Lincoln," *Harper's New Monthly Magazine* 31 (July 1865): 225.

298. Carpenter, *Six Months at the White House,* 230–31; Miers et al., eds., *Lincoln Day by Day,* 3:151; Stoddard, *Inside the White House,* 113–14.

299. Carpenter, *Six Months at the White House,* 258–59.

300. Josephine Shaw Lowell, diary [entry for 3 April 1862], copy, Allan Nevins MSS, Columbia University.

301. Rice, *RL,* xxviii.

302. Angle, ed., *Herndon's Lincoln,* 414.

303. William H. Herndon's statement, 12 Jan. 1874, Springfield [Ill.], *Register,* 14 Jan. 1874.

304. Carpenter, *Six Months at the White House,* 230–31.

305. Lamon, *Reminiscences of Lincoln,* 2d ed., 261.

306. Diary of John Bigelow, 3 July 1861, quoted in Carman and Luthin, *Lincoln and the Patronage,* 101.

307. Sumner to the Duchess of Argyll, Washington, 24 April 1865, to John Bright, Washington, 24 April 1865, and to Richard Cobden, Washington, 26 April 1863, 27 March 1865, in *Selected Letters of Charles Sumner,* ed. Palmer, 2:295–97, 160, 177. Lincoln told W. H. Russell that he objected not so much to the correspondent's dispatches as to the pro-Confederate stance of his newspaper. William Howard Russell to John T. Delane, Washington, 14 Oct. 1861, in *William Howard Russell's Civil War: Private Diaries and Letters, 1861–1862,* ed. Martin Crawford (Athens: University of Georgia Press, 1992), 150–51.

308. Don C. Seitz, *Lincoln the Politician: How the Rail-Splitter and Flatboatman Played the Great American Game* (New York: Coward McCann, 1931), 374.

309. "Reply to Chicago Emancipation Memorial, Washington D.C.," 13 Sept. 1862, in Basler, *CWL,* 5:421.

310. W. A. Croffut, ed., *Fifty Years in Camp and Field: Diary of Major-General Ethan Allen Hitchcock, U.S.A.* (New York: G. P. Putnam's Sons, 1909), 457–58.

311. Washington correspondence, 8 May 1861, Worcester *Spy,* 9 May 1861, 2.

312. Lincoln to Carl Schurz, Washington, 10 Nov. 1862, in Basler, *CWL,* 5:494.

313. Haupt, *Reminiscences,* 298.

314. See Lincoln to Salmon P. Chase, Washington, 29 Feb. 1864, in Basler, *CWL,* 7:212–13; endorsement concerning William Kellogg, [ca. 11 April 1863], 6:167; Beale, ed., *Welles Diary,* 2:98 [entry for 8 Aug. 1864].

315. Speech of 11 April 1865, in Basler, *CWL,* 8:401.

316. Lincoln to Hamilton R. Gamble, Washington, 23 July 1863, in Basler, *CWL,* 6:344.

317. Hunter to Lincoln, 23 Dec. 1861, and Lincoln to Hunter, Washington, 31 Dec. 1861, in Basler, *CWL,* 5:84–85.

318. See, for example, Lincoln to Mrs. L. H. Phipps, Washington, 9 March 1863, in Basler, *CWL,* 6:130.

319. Lincoln to Pomeroy, Washington, 12 May 1864, in Basler, *CWL,* 7:338.

320. Lincoln to John M. Fleming and Robert Morrow, Washington, 9 Aug. 1863, in Basler, *CWL,* 6:373.

321. Brooks, *Washington in Lincoln's Time,* 65–66; L. A. Gobright, *Recollections of Men and Things at Washington* (Philadelphia: Clayton, Remsen and Haffelfinger, 1869), 336–38. Cf. Lincoln to Conkling, Washington, 3 Sept. 1863, in Basler, *CWL,* 6:430.

322. Holland, *Lincoln,* 510–11.

323. Colfax to Isaac N. Arnold, South Bend, Ind., 1 May 1867, copy, Hay MSS, RPB.
324. Campbell told this to a Richmond colleague two days after the conference. Current, *Lincoln Nobody Knows,* 247.
325. T. B. Bancroft, "An Audience with Abraham Lincoln," *McClure's Magazine* 32 (Feb. 1909): 448.
326. Benham to Lincoln, Washington, 19 Aug. 1862, Joseph Holt MSS, DLC.
327. Mary A. Livermore, *My Story of the War* (Hartford: A. D. Worthington, 1889), 568.
328. J. D. Paxton, Lynchburg, Va., "Abraham Lincoln at Bay," JGR MSS, DLC. The author was the son of the minister who spoke with Lincoln.
329. Cincinnati *Daily Commercial,* 1 April 1861, quoted in John Denton Carter, "Abraham Lincoln and the California Patronage," *American Historical Review* 58 (April 1943): 502 [San Francisco *Bulletin,* 17 April 1861, 31 July 1865, quoted and paraphrased]; George W. Julian in Rice, *RL,* 50–51; Brooks, *Lincoln and the Downfall of Slavery,* 416–17. Cf. James M. Scovel in *Intimate Memories of Lincoln,* ed. Wilson, 522, and Miers et al., eds., *Lincoln Day by Day,* 3:31 [entry for 30 March 1861].
330. Milton Hay's interview with John G. Nicolay, 4 July 1875, Hay MSS, RPB.
331. Alonzo Rothschild, *Lincoln, Master of Men: A Study in Character* (Boston: Houghton Mifflin, 1906), 56.
332. Arnold, *Life of Lincoln,* 416.
333. Nicolay, personal memorandum, 5 Nov. 1860, Nicolay MSS, DLC.
334. Chittenden, *Recollections,* 74–75.
335. William Jayne to Lyman Trumbull, Springfield, 28 Jan. 1861, in Horace White, "Critical Period of Lincoln's Career," Chicago *Tribune,* 7 Feb. 1909. Lincoln said this after telling Yates to delay replying to the invitation to participate in the peace conference in Washington.
336. Lincoln to Smith, Springfield, 10 Nov. 1860, in Basler, *CWL,* 4:138.
337. Nicolay memorandum, Springfield, 22 Dec. 1860, Nicolay MSS, DLC.
338. Simon P. Hanscom, quoting Lincoln, in Ben: Perely Poore, "Reminiscences of the Great Northern Uprising," *Youth's Companion,* 26 July 1883, 301.
339. Gillespie's reminiscences, Springfield correspondence, 2 Feb. 1888, New York *Tribune,* 5 Feb. 1888, 9.
340. Journal of Erasmus Keyes, aide to General Scott, [entry for 29 March 1861], in Keyes, *Fifty Years' Observations of Men and Events* (New York: C. Scribner's Sons, 1884), 378.
341. Cameron to Peirpont, Washington, 25 June 1861, *Official Records of the Rebellion,* series 1, 2:723–24. Cameron's letter begins, "the President directs me to say" and may well, as Richard N. Current suggests, have been written by Lincoln. Current, review of Roy P. Basler and Christian O. Basler, eds., *The Collected Works of Abraham Lincoln, Second Supplement,* in *Illinois Historical Journal* 84 (Autumn 1991): 194; Richard N. Current, *Lincoln's*

Loyalists: Union Soldiers from the Confederacy (Boston: Northeastern University Press, 1992), 15–16.

342. "Reply to Baltimore Committee," 22 April 1861, in Basler, *CWL,* 4:341–42.

343. Robert Livingston Stanton, "Reminiscences of President Lincoln," manuscript written ca. 1883; cf. Robert Brewster Stanton, "Notes from My Notebook," manuscript memoirs written ca. 1916, both in Robert Brewster Livingston Stanton Papers, New York Public Library.

344. This interview took place on 29 Oct. 1864. Jane Grey Swisshelm, Washington correspondence, 31 Oct. 1864, in St. Cloud *Democrat,* 17 Nov. 1864, in *Crusader and Feminist: Letters of Jane Grey Swisshelm, 1858–1865,* ed. Arthur J. Larsen (St. Paul: Minnesota Historical Society, 1934), 280–82.

345. Lincoln to Cuthbert Bullitt, Washington, 28 July 1862, in Basler, *CWL,* 5:345–46. Cf. Lincoln to Reverdy Johnson, Washington, 26 July 1862, in Basler, *CWL,* 5:342–43, and Pease and Randall, eds., *Browning Diary,* 1:564 [entry for 26 July 1862].

346. Carpenter, *Six Months at the White House,* 84. Cf. Stoddard, *Inside the White House,* 69.

347. Browne, *Lincoln and the Men of His Time,* 1:259.

348. E. P. Whipple quoted in Thomas Wentworth Higginson to his mother, N.p., 1 Nov. 1861, in *Letters and Journals of Thomas Wentworth Higginson, 1846–1906,* ed. Mary Thatcher Higginson (Boston: Houghton, Mifflin, 1921), 160.

349. Samuel Ruggles to Edwin D. Morgan, N.p., 28 Nov. 1862, quoted in G. S. Boritt, *Lincoln and the Economics of the American Dream* (Memphis: Memphis State University Press, 1978), 224. Ruggles wanted to link the Mississippi River with the Great Lakes by enlarging canals. When Lincoln rebuffed him, the New York banker, lawyer, and politician grew "angry" and "threaten[e]d to arouse the legislature against the Prest." Beale, ed., *Bates Diary,* 267 [entry for 24 (and 25) Nov. 1862].

350. Washington correspondence, 10 Dec. 1862, Cincinnati *Gazette,* 11 Dec. 1862, 3.

351. Medill's statement to Ida M. Tarbell, Chicago, 25 June 1895, Ida M. Tarbell MSS, Allegheny College.

352. John M. Palmer, *Personal Recollections of John M. Palmer: The Story of an Earnest Life* (Cincinnati: R. Clarke, 1901), 223–24.

353. John Lellyett to the editor of the New York *World,* 15 Oct. 1864, in New York *World,* 18 Oct. 1864, in Basler, *CWL,* 8:58n.

354. Holland, *Lincoln,* 487.

355. Nicolay and Hay, *Lincoln,* 9:358. Cf. Stoddard, *Lincoln,* 438–39. The written reply of 22 Oct. is far milder than the president's oral reply of a week earlier. Basler, *CWL,* 8:58–72.

356. Holland, *Lincoln,* 487, 453.

357. Brooks, "Personal Recollections of Lincoln," 226. Brooks noted as early as December 1862 that Lincoln "has grievously altered from the happy-faced Springfield lawyer of 1856, whom I then met on the stump in Illinois for Fremont. His hair is grizzled, his gait more stooping, his countenance sal-

low, and there is a sunken, deathly look about the large, cavernous eyes, which is saddening to those who see there the marks of care and anxiety such as no President of the United States has ever before known." Washington correspondence, 4 Dec. 1862, Sacramento *Daily Union*, 30 Dec. 1862, 1.

358. Stoddard, *Lincoln*, 382.

359. Mary Todd Lincoln's statement to Herndon, 1866, quoted in "Lincoln's Religion: Answer of William Herndon to Mrs. Lincoln," Springfield, 12 Jan. 1874, Springfield [Ill.] *Register*, 14 Jan. 1874.

360. William D. Kelley, in Rice, *RL*, 281–83.

361. Theodore Burton, address given in 1909, in *Addresses Delivered at the Lincoln Dinner of the Republican Club of New York in Response to the Toast Abraham Lincoln, 1887–1909* (New York: Republican Club of New York, 1909), 307–8. According to Burton, "A man who was witness of this conversation is still living."

362. Edna Dean Proctor, "At a Lincoln Reception," *McClure's Magazine*, Feb. 1909, 519.

363. Reminiscences of Schuyler Hamilton, New York *Tribune*, 20 June 1889, 5.

364. *All the Year Round*, 7 Aug. 1869, 226–28. When this article appeared, Scott told a journalist "that the facts stated therein are in the main true. The interview with the President at his retreat [at the Soldier's Home], is perhaps a little overdrawn, though much of the conversation which occurred there, as well as the material facts stated in the story, are correctly reported." *Peterborough Transcript*, 4 Sept. 1869, quoted in Willard de Lue, "Tracking a New Hampshire Lincoln Legend," Boston *Globe*, 12 Feb. 1953, 15.

This episode probably occurred in late August, for on August 27, Captain John A. Cummings wrote from Alexandria, Va., to his mother, saying, "Col[.] Scott we have not seen. He has gone to recover the remains of his wife. He has succeeded in obtaining 20 days leave of absence." Ibid. Charles Dickens, editor of *All the Year Round*, at first did not credit this story, but after careful investigation, he found it confirmed by reliable sources. Headnote to an article by Charles Thomas White, "Lincoln's Humanity and Tenderness," *Christian Advocate*, 11 Feb. 1932, 3.

365. Alban Jasper Conant, "My Acquaintance with Abraham Lincoln," (N.p., N.d.), 180–81. Gurley told this to Conant in 1866. Cf. Rev. D. H. Mitchell, "An Anecdote of Lincoln," *The Independent*, 13 Dec. 1894.

366. E. S. Nadal, "Some Impressions of Lincoln," *Scribner's Magazine* 39 (March 1906): 370.

367. Stoddard, *Inside the White House*, 55, emphasis added.

368. Hay diary, 31 July 1863, Hay MSS, RPB.

369. Joshua Speed to Herndon, Louisville, 12 Jan. 1866, H-W MSS, DLC.

8

"The Most Ambitious Man in the World"

To think of Abraham Lincoln as an ambitious politician is, for some, as difficult as it was for respectable Victorians to think of their parents as sexual beings. Such prudery rankled William Herndon, who described his law partner as "inordinately ambitious," "a man totally swallowed up in his ambitions," and "the most ambitious man in the world." Herndon remarked on "his general greed for office" and "his burning and his consuming ambition," declared that his "ambition was never satisfied" and "was a consuming fire which smothered his finer feelings," and stated flatly that any "man who thinks Lincoln calmly sat down and gathered his robes about him, waiting for the people to call him, has a very erroneous knowledge of Lincoln. He was always calculating, and always planning ahead. His ambition was a little engine that knew no rest."[1]

Other friends and political allies in Illinois agreed. Horace White, secretary of the Republican State Committee in the 1850s, thought Lincoln "was extremely eager for political preferment" and "as ambitious of earthly honors as any man of his time."[2] Senator Lyman Trumbull said, "A more ardent seeker after office never existed. From the time when, at the age of twenty-three, he announced himself a candidate for the legislature . . . till his death, he was almost constantly either in office, or struggling to obtain one."[3] With less edge, Joseph Gillespie told Herndon that Lincoln "was unquestionably ambitious for official distinction."[4] Orville H. Browning concurred: "He was always a most ambitious man."[5] Lincoln's neighbor William Jayne called him "a man of exalted ambition," and David Davis acknowledged that Lincoln was "ambitious" but hastened to add that "office had no attractions for him, if attainable through a sacrifice of principle."[6] Paul Selby noted that Lincoln "had the reputation of being inspired by an almost unbounded ambition."[7] Ward Hill Lamon recalled that "ambition was one of the ruling characteristics of this great man from the cradle to the grave." When "riding over the prairies of Illinois with him long years ago, travelling from one county to another to attend the courts," Lamon "was told by him repeatedly that he did not recollect the time when he did not believe that he would at some day be President. It seemed to him manifest destiny. 'I will get there,' he would say, seemingly in the fullest confidence of realizing his prediction." One day during the Civil War, Lincoln told Lamon, "You know better than any man living that from my boyhood up my ambition was to be President."[8]

Indeed, from the beginning of his public career, Lincoln made little secret of his desire for "place and distinction as a politician," as he put it in an early campaign speech.[9] During his adolescence in Indiana, he had expressed a desire to escape the tedium of farm work. "I don't always intend to delve, grub, shuck corn, split rails and the like," he told Mrs. Elizabeth Crawford after several days spent pulling cornstalks.[10] Mrs. Crawford told Herndon that "Abe was ambitious, sought to outstrip and override others."[11] His cousin Sophie Hanks "said Abe always had a natural idea that he was going to be something" and that "he always talked like he would be something."[12]

Such evidence tends to confirm Orville Browning's assertion that "even in his early days he had a strong conviction that he was born for better things than then seemed likely or even possible." Browning speculated that "his ambition was to fit himself properly for what he considered some important predestined labor or work" and that it "had its origin in this sentiment, that he was destined for something nobler than he was for the time engaged in."[13]

Education appeared to Lincoln as the means to fit himself for his destiny. While working for Josiah Crawford in 1825, he allegedly said, "I'll study and get ready, and then the chance will come."[14] According to Joseph Richardson, five years later Lincoln inscribed the following verses in a friend's copybook: "Good boys who to their books apply / Will make great men by and by."[15] James Grigsby, with whom Lincoln pursued his studies, recalled that "Abe was just awful hungry to be somebody."[16] John W. Lamon thought "thar was one thing" about Lincoln "that any Body cud see and that is he was Determ[in]ed to make Something of him Self."[17]

Shortly after moving to New Salem in 1831, Lincoln discussed his ambition with Lynn McNulty Greene, who, as a student at Illinois College in Jacksonville, helped him puzzle out the meaning of Samuel Kirkham's *English Grammar in Familiar Lectures.* One day he said to Greene "that all his folks seemed to have good sense but none of them had become distinguished, and he believed it was for him to become so." Lincoln added that he "had talked with men who had the reputation of being great men, but [he] could not see that they differed from other men."[18] He also told the local school teacher, Mentor Graham, that he aspired to become a public man.[19] To an employer in New Salem he confided "his ambition . . . to be something more than a clerk in a country store."[20] In that village he lived with Mr. and Mrs. Bennett Abell. She was a "cultivated woman—very superior to the common run of women" on the frontier, according to William Butler, who thought it was from Mrs. Abell that Lincoln "first got his ideas of a higher plane of life—that it was she who gave him the notion that he might improve himself by reading &c."[21]

Lincoln's experience in the Black Hawk War encouraged his belief that he might be famous. When the Sauks and Foxes under Chief Black Hawk crossed the Mississippi River in April 1832, Lincoln joined the Illinois militia and was promptly chosen captain by his comrades in arms. Although he thought himself unqualified for the office, he delighted in the honor and accepted. He wrote in 1860, "He has not since had any success in life which gave him so much satisfaction."[22] In another autobiographical sketch, Lincoln called his election as captain of a militia company "a success which gave me more pleasure than any I have had since."[23]

Soon after the Black Hawk War, Lincoln lost his first race for public office, a seat in the Illinois legislature. At the start of the campaign, the twenty-three-year-old candidate introduced himself to the voters of Sangamon County with a frank avowal:

> Every man is said to have his peculiar ambition. Whether it be true or not, I can say for one that I have no other so great as that of being truly esteemed of my fellow men, by rendering myself worthy of their esteem. How far I shall succeed in gratifying this ambition, is yet to be developed. I am young and unknown to many of you. I was born and have ever remained in the most humble walks of life. I have no wealthy or popular relations to recommend me. My case is thrown exclusively upon the independent voters of this county, and if elected they will have conferred a favor upon me, for which I shall be unremitting in my labors to compensate. But if the good people in their wisdom shall see fit to keep me in the background, I have been too familiar with disappointments to be very much chagrined.[24]

He allegedly stated that, if defeated, he would run again five or six times before quitting politics.[25]

He did not have to run so often to achieve victory; in 1834 he captured the seat he had sought two years earlier. He was to hold it for four terms, commanding respect as the floorleader of the Whigs and twice standing as their nominee for speaker of the house. He aspired to become "the DeWitt Clinton of Illinois" by promoting a vast scheme of internal improvements.[26] While a member of the Illinois house, he laid plans to run for a seat in the state senate, but nothing came of it.[27] His experience in the legislature, as Paul Simon observed, "gave Lincoln confidence in himself." He had "dealt with issues that confronted the top men of the state and could not help observing that he handled these issues as well as any of them."[28]

With his confidence thus reinforced, Lincoln aspired to national office. Herndon recalled that "Mr. Lincoln told me that his ideas of [becoming] something burst on him in 1840. He was flattered in 1833–4, & 5 by Offutt and others in New Salem . . . & made to believe that he would be a great man & *he dreamed of* it then, as he told me—always delicately & indirectly."[29] A catalyst for this wider ambition may have been provided at the Whig convention in October 1839, where he was chosen a presidential elector in the upcoming campaign. In that canvass, Lincoln for the first time stumped throughout Illinois as one of the main Whig speakers.[30]

Even before stepping down from the legislature, Lincoln found his name mentioned as a gubernatorial candidate.[31] In July 1841, a western Illinois newspaper reported that "since his return from the circuit [in mid-June], Lincoln declines being considered as a candidate for Governor."[32] Five months later, the *Sangamo Journal* announced that "since Mr. Lincoln returned from the circuit, he has expressed his wishes not to be a candidate for Governor."[33] An item in that same paper the following year scotched the proposal formally: "We do not believe that he desires the nomination. He has already made great sacrifices in sustaining his party principles; and before his political friends ask him to make additional sacrifices, the subject should be well considered. The office of Governor, which would of necessity interfere with the practice of his profession, would poorly compensate him for the loss of four years of best portion of his life."[34] This refusal seems curious for an ambitious young man; he may have been preoccupied with his renewed courtship of Mary Todd and concerned about making sufficient money to support a wife, or he may have simply concluded that, in a Democratic state like Illinois, the Whig gubernatorial nomination was worthless. In 1844, another Whig attempt to elect Lincoln governor came to naught.[35]

His reason for not seeking reelection to the legislature in 1842 is also something of a mystery. Noting that Lincoln's attendance at legislative sessions fell off during his fourth term, Paul Simon concluded that he "was somewhat tired of life as a state representative" and that he "wanted a change of scenery."[36] Perhaps at Lincoln's own suggestion, a week after he quit the legislature the Whigs of Illinois asked Secretary of State Daniel Webster to appoint him chargé d'affaires at Bogata, Colombia.[37] Lincoln may have wished to give his new law partner, Stephen T. Logan, a chance to engage in politics; indeed, Logan did win election to the legislature in 1842.[38] Gabor Boritt believes that Lincoln's stubborn support of internal improvement schemes for Illinois grew unpopular during the depression of the late 1830s and early 1840s and "helped prompt his retirement from the General Assembly."[39] Douglas L. Wilson suggests that Lincoln's painful experiences of the heart in the winter of 1840–41 may have led him to quit the legislature.[40]

Others believe he quit the legislature "because he hoped to run for Congress in 1843."[41] That explanation seems borne out by Lincoln's actions, for in 1843 he did seek the Whig nomination for the seat in the House of Representatives that John T. Stuart was vacating. To one friend he wrote, "Now if you should hear any one say that Lincoln don't want to go to Congress, I wish you as a personal friend of mine, would tell him you have reason to believe he is mistaken. The truth is, I would like to go very much."[42] But his efforts proved vain, for his home district's delegation, of which he was a member, was instructed to vote for a rival, Edward D. Baker. Sorrowfully he remarked to Joshua Speed, "In getting Baker the nomination, I shall be 'fixed' a good deal like a fellow who is made groomsman to the man that has cut him out, and is marrying his own dear 'gal.'"[43]

More bitterly, Lincoln unburdened himself to a fellow delegate: "It is truly gratifying to me to learn that while the people of Sangamon [County] have cast me off, my old friends of Menard [County] who have known me the longest and best of any, still retain there confidence in me. It would astonish if not amuse, the older citizens of your County who twelve years ago knew me a strange, friendless, uneducated, penniless boy, working on a flat boat—at ten dollars per month [—] to learn that I have been put down here as the candidate of pride, wealth, and aristocratic family distinction."[44]

The depth of his anger and disappointment may have induced Lincoln to take an uncharacteristically vengeful step. In August 1843 he cast ballots only for candidates running for justice of the peace and constable; he refused to vote either for congressional or for county office nominees. Benjamin P. Thomas called this act "a mystery" and wondered whether Lincoln was "showing his displeasure at [John J.] Hardin [who had defeated Baker at the convention to become the Whig nominee for the House seat], or at the county organization that had thrown him over, or both?"[45] Donald Riddle concluded that "perhaps this was an implied protest against the Whig county or district organization, but more probably it was a reflection of personal antipathy to his rival."[46] The rare example of spiteful behavior shows how intense Lincoln's ambition was at this stage of his life.

In 1839 he had displayed similar antagonism toward another successful rival for political advancement, William L. D. Ewing, who had narrowly defeated him for speaker of the Illinois house. Shortly after that loss, Lincoln wrote with unwonted venom that Ewing was "not worth a damn."[47] Earlier, he and Ewing had nearly come to blows during a heated debate about the removal of the capital from Vandalia to Springfield.[48]

During the presidential campaign of 1844, Lincoln expanded his horizons beyond Illinois. As an elector for the Whig candidate Henry Clay, he stumped widely in Indiana as well as Illinois but to no avail; Clay, his "beau ideal of a statesman," lost to James K. Polk. Lincoln may well have been disappointed and discouraged at the result. One biographer asserted that "no personal defeat could have been more dispiriting to him than this failure before the people of his political idol," and "in the first gush of his disappointment," Lincoln "made a new resolution to let politics alone, and attend more devotedly to the duties of his profession."[49]

If he did make such a resolution, it was short-lived. In 1846 he renewed his bid for the seat in Congress and this time won, thanks partly to dogged effort. It was hard work; as he told an ally in the midst of the campaign, "I would rejoice to be spared the labour of a contest; but 'being in' I shall go it thoroughly, and to the bottom."[50] After a fierce struggle, Lincoln prevailed over Hardin for the nomination and then handily won the election in August.[51] Curiously, he found that his victory, as he told Joshua Speed two months later, "has not pleased me as much as I expected."[52] Even more curiously, he declined the opportunity to fill the unexpired term of E. D. Baker, who had resigned his seat in the House of Representatives to fight in the Mexican War. The Whigs had wanted to nominate Lincoln, thus allowing him to begin his congressional career in December 1846 instead of a full year later.[53]

In the House of Representatives, Lincoln hoped to distinguish himself, but in fact made little impression.[54] When he somewhat reluctantly stepped down after one term, in keeping with the rotation-in-office principle that the Whigs of central Illinois had adopted earlier, he sought high office from the newly installed administration of Zachary Taylor, for whom he had campaigned extensively. He met disappointment in his vigorous four-month struggle to become commissioner of the General Land Office.[55] As his chances dimmed, he complained bitterly to a Land Office official, "It will now mortify me deeply if Gen. Taylor's administration shall trample all my wishes in the dust."[56] When the post finally went to a rival from Chicago, Lincoln returned to his room and lay down in a deep depression for an hour or more.[57] Later, he stated that "I hardly ever felt so bad at any failure in my life."[58]

Although passed over for one high-ranking job, Lincoln was offered the secretaryship of the Oregon Territory, which, on the advice of his ambitious wife, he declined. When the administration then proffered him the governorship of that territory, he again said no.[59] His political ambitions thwarted, he returned disconsolate to Springfield in 1849 and essentially retired from politics for five years (chapter 1). According to Herndon, he "despaired of ever rising again in the political world."[60]

Although Lincoln's ambition slumbered, it did not die, and when the Kansas-Nebraska Act of 1854 stunned the North, he reentered political life with a remarkable sense of purpose and commitment to principle. Previously, his ambition had little ideological content; he was something of a party hack (chapter 1). But the repeal of the 1820 Missouri Compromise and the threatened spread of slavery into millions of acres previously set aside for freedom outraged Lincoln as well as thousands of others (chapter 2).

When political leaders in his district sounded him out regarding a bid for a congressional seat, he demurred. As one of them recalled, Lincoln "seemed gratified by the compliment" but refused to challenge the antislavery Whig incumbent, Richard Yates: "No," Lincoln said, "Yates has been a true and faithful Representative, and should be returned."[61] He campaigned eloquently on behalf of Yates and allowed his own name to be put on the ballot for state legislature. When the anti-Nebraska forces did surprisingly well at the polls, it seemed that they could dominate the legislature and choose the next U.S. senator from Illinois.

His ambition had been reawakened in the 1854 campaign. One

October day he read aloud to Henry C. Whitney passages from Byron's "Childe Harold," reciting the following canto "earnestly, if not, indeed, reverently":

> He who ascends to mountain tops, shall find
> Those loftiest peaks most wrapt in clouds and snow;
> He who surpasses or subdues mankind
> Must look down on the hate of those below;
> Though high above the sun of glory glow,
> And far beneath the Earth and Ocean spread,
> Round him are icy rocks, and loudly blow
> Contending tempests on his naked head,
> And thus reward the toils which to those summits lead.

Whitney concluded that Lincoln had a premonition that he would reach "the mountain tops of human achievement."[62] In political terms, that mountain top was a U.S. Senate seat.

Lincoln, as Herndon recalled, was "ambitious to reach the United States Senate, and, warmly encouraged in his aspirations by his wife," he campaigned for the post with "his characteristic activity and vigilance. During the anxious moments that intervened between the general election [in November] and the assembling of the Legislature [in January] he slept, like Napoleon, with one eye open."[63] He told political supporters that "I have really got it into my head to try to be United States Senator" and wrote them at length soliciting their votes and offering advice and suggestions.[64]

Thanks in part to his hard work over the years and to his eloquent denunciation of slavery expansion, Lincoln emerged as the first choice of the antislavery forces in the legislature. When that body convened in January 1855, he assiduously lobbied on his own behalf. According to one legislator, when Lincoln approached members, his "manner was agreeable and unassuming; he was not forward in pressing his case upon the attention of members." Yet before the conversation ended, the topic of the senatorship would arise, and Lincoln would say, in essence, "Gentlemen, this is rather a delicate subject for me to talk upon; but I must confess that I would be glad of your support for the office, if you shall conclude that I am the proper person for it."[65]

Although Lincoln was far stronger than the other antislavery candidate, Lyman Trumbull (who at first had only five votes), he magnanimously threw his support to Trumbull, sacrificing his own ambition in order to thwart a Democratic intrigue. Stoically he recounted this complex story to an ally and concluded, "I regret my defeat moderately, but I am not nervous about it." The successful scotching of the Democrats' scheme "now gives me more pleasure than my own [defeat] gives me pain. On the whole, it is perhaps as well for our general cause that Trumbull is elected." The opposition, he noted, "confess that they hate it worse than any thing that could have happened. It is a great consolation to see them worse whipped than I am."[66] To another friend he described the way that he yielded his forty-four votes to Trumbull: "It was rather hard for the 44 to have to surrender to the 5—and a less good humored man than I, perhaps would not have consented to it—and it would not have been done without my consent. I could not, however, let the whole political result go to ruin, on a point merely personal to myself."[67]

Despite the tone of these letters, Lincoln evidently felt quite downcast. As Herndon noted, Lincoln "thirsted for public notice and hungered—longed for approbation and when he did not get that notice or that approbation—was not thoroughly appreciated [—] he writhed under it."[68] Sam C. Parks, a pro-Lincoln legislator, believed that his candidate "was very much disappointed, for . . . it was the height of his ambition to get into the United States Senate."[69] When Parks consoled him by saying he would surely win the senatorship in 1858, Lincoln replied that "the taste for the senatorship would get out of his mouth" by then.[70] Joseph Gillespie, another legislator active on Lincoln's behalf, accompanied him home after the defeat and later recalled, "I never saw him so dejected. He said the fates seemed to be against him and he thought he would never strive for office again[.] He could bear defeat inflicted by his enemies with a pretty good grace; but it was hard to be wounded in the house of his friends."[71]

One of those friends was John M. Palmer, an antislavery Democrat who had refused Lincoln's request for his vote. Palmer explained that he had alienated his party by opposing the Kansas-Nebraska Act and could not vote for any candidate but a Democrat for the Senate. He later recalled that Lincoln "felt hurt and was a little angry."[72] However bitter he may have been, Lincoln, at a party in honor of the senator-elect, cheerfully responded to a query about his disappointment by saying he was "not *too* disappointed to congratulate my friend Trumbull."[73]

During the fall campaign, Lincoln had directed his new-found eloquence at Senator Stephen A. Douglas and his popular sovereignty doctrine. He followed Douglas around the state to rebut the Little Giant's speeches. Two years later he wrote a revealing memorandum contrasting his career and Douglas's: "Twenty-two years ago Judge Douglas and I first became acquainted. We were both young then; he a trifle younger than I. Even then, we were both ambitious; I, perhaps, quite as much so as he. With *me*, the race of ambition has been a failure—a flat failure; with *him* it has been one of splendid success. His name fills the nation; and is not unknown, even, in foreign lands. I affect no contempt for the high eminence he has reached."

Yet Lincoln deplored Douglas's lack of principle, especially his indifference to the "vast moral evil" of slavery. He envied Douglas's fame but wished to attain it without betraying the antislavery cause. Alluding to Douglas's renown, Lincoln thus closed that private fragment: "So reached, that the oppressed of my species, might have shared with me in the elevation, I would rather stand on that eminence, than wear the richest crown that ever pressed a monarch's brow."[74]

The brief document was an acknowledgment of the intensity of Lincoln's ambition, which during his twenties and thirties had not been rooted deeply in principle. After five years of semiretirement in his early forties, the nature of that ambition had changed (chapters 1 and 2). In 1858 he told his friend Joseph Gillespie that "he had but one complaint to make against Douglas in their discussions and that was Douglas arrogated a superiority over him on account of his national reputation." Lincoln protested, "If our positions were changed I would not do that."[75]

The very year when Lincoln wrote of his "flat failure" in life, the Illinois Republicans, as he put it, "probably would have given" him the nomination for governor, but he declined in order to allow a former Democrat, William H. Bissell, to head the state ticket and thereby lend it more strength than he, as a former Whig, could.[76] On similar grounds he discouraged attempts to nominate him for a seat in Congress.[77] He was also put forward at the Republican national convention as a candidate for the vice presidency and enjoyed a notable success with his address to the Republican state convention in May.

When Douglas sought reelection to the Senate two years later, Lincoln challenged him. During the campaign, he publicly and privately reiterated that he was ambitious for himself and also for the antislavery cause. Even if he failed to gain the Senate seat, he believed that he might at least win honor in the eyes of future generations. In preparing a speech, he jotted down thoughts on this subject, beginning with a candid avowal of his personal ambition: "I have never professed an indifference to the honors of official station; and were I to do so now,

I should only make myself ridiculous." But, he continued, "I have never failed—do not now fail—to remember that in the republican cause there is a higher aim than that of mere office." He then turned to the history of the long struggle in Great Britain to abolish the slave trade, a cause that "was agitated a hundred years before it was a final success." During that time, the defenders of the slave trade "got offices, and their adversaries got none." But ultimately, the supporters of the status quo were forgotten: "Though they blazed, like tallow-candles for a century, at last they flickered in the socket, died out, stank in the dark for a brief season, and were remembered no more, even by the smell." Meanwhile, their opponents achieved enduring fame and respect: "Schoolboys know that Wilbe[r]force, and Granville Sharpe, helped that cause forward; but who can now name a single man who labored to retard it?" This thought was a solace to Lincoln as he contemplated the risk of yet one more defeat: "Remembering these things I can not but regard it as possible that the higher object of this contest may not be completely attained within the term of my natural life. But I can not doubt either that it will come in due time. Even in this view, I am proud, in my passing speck of time, to contribute an humble mite to that glorious consummation, which my own poor eyes may not last to see."[78]

Lincoln did not confine these musings to his study. Just before the first of his debates with Douglas, he gave a speech in which he urged his audience to respect the basic tenets of the Declaration of Independence and to "do anything with me you choose, if you will but heed these sacred principles." With his peculiar habit of alluding to his own demise, he added, "You may not only defeat me for the Senate, but you may take me and put me to death." Candidly owning that he pretended "no indifference to earthly honors," he averred that "I *do claim* to be actuated in this contest by something higher than an anxiety for office." He charged the voters "to drop every paltry and insignificant thought for any man's success. It is nothing; I am nothing; Judge Douglas is nothing." In his final sentence, Lincoln appealed grandiloquently to his audience not to *"destroy that immortal emblem of Humanity— the Declaration of American Independence."*[79]

A few days later Lincoln drafted a speech in which he once again admitted that he was ambitious: "I claim no extraordinary exemption from personal ambition. That I like preferment as well as the average of men may be admitted."[80] In his final address of the campaign, he repeated this theme: "Ambition has been ascribed to me. God knows how sincerely I prayed from the first that this field of ambition might not be opened." But it did open, and Lincoln entered it. He wanted it understood, however, that he would cheerfully forgo the honor of office if the expansion of slavery could be halted: "I claim no insensibility to political honors; but today could the Missouri restriction [on slavery expansion] be restored, and the whole slavery question replaced on the old ground of 'toleration['] by *necessity* where it exists, with unyielding hostility to the spread of it, on principle, I would . . . gladly agree, that Judge Douglas should never be *out*, and I never *in*, an office, so long as we both or either, live."[81]

When the election returns in November gave the Democrats control of the Illinois legislature, and with it the power to name the next U.S. senator, Lincoln felt "fork end down and ready for another fight."[82] When told that the Democrats were boisterously celebrating their triumph, he replied, "Douglas has taken this trick, but the game is not played out."[83] Two weeks later he stoically told a friend that it did not much matter personally, for he had done work on behalf of the cause that would make a difference in the long run: "I am glad I made the late race. It gave me a hearing on the great and durable question of the age, which I could have had in no other way; and though I now sink out of view, and shall be forgotten, I believe I have made some marks which will tell for the cause of civil liberty long after I am gone."[84] In December he wrote in a similar vein, "While I desired the result of the late canvass to have been different, I still regard it as an exceeding small matter. I think we have fairly entered upon a durable struggle as to whether this nation is to ultimately become all slave or all free, and though I fall early in the contest, it is nothing if I shall have contributed, in the least degree, to the final rightful result."[85]

But when the legislature met and chose Douglas in early January 1859, Lincoln was dispirited.[86] Soon after the vote, he good-naturedly told a journalist, "I am in the predicament of a Kentucky boy I once heard of. Running up hill, he stumbled, and hurt his toe pretty badly. Some one coming up, asked him whether he was going to cry or laugh about it. 'Well,' said he, '*I am too big to cry about it, but it hurts too awful much to laugh.*'"[87] Somewhat ruefully he told a friend upon hearing the results, "Well, I shall now have to get down to the practice. It is an easy matter to adjust a harvester to tall or short grain by raising or lowering the sickle, but it is not so easy to change our feelings and modes of expression to suit the stump or the bar."[88] On the way back to the office, Lincoln, as he later recalled, found the path "had been worn hog-back & was slippery. My foot slipped from under me, knocking the other one out of the way, but I recovered myself & lit square, and I said to myself, 'It's a slip and not a fall.'"[89]

Yet he was not so stoic once he reached his office. There Henry C. Whitney found him "gloomy as midnight . . . brooding over his ill-fortune." Whitney "never saw a man so depressed." The inconsolable Lincoln "was simply steeped in gloom" and said "several times, with bitterness, 'I expect everybody to desert me.'"[90] He even considered retiring from politics. To Robert H. Browne he complained that party leaders regularly cast him in the role of sacrificial lamb: "I feel that, by some kind of happening, inscrutable to me, they are always putting me in the place where somebody has to be beaten and sacrificed for the welfare of the party or the common good; and you know there are few men who can be beaten very often whose party success is a possibility."[91]

During the 1858 campaign, Lincoln told a young journalist, Henry Villard, that, while clerking in New Salem stores, his ambition had been to enter the state legislature. "Since then, of course, I have grown some, but my friends got me into *this* business [the canvass]. I did not consider myself qualified for the United States Senate, and it took me a long time to persuade myself that I was. Now, to be sure, I am convinced that I am good enough for it; but, in spite of it all, I am saying to myself every day: 'It is too big a thing for you; you will never get it.'" He added that his spouse did not share this modest view: "Mary insists . . . that I am going to be Senator and President of the United States, too." He laughed heartily and then, "shaking all over with mirth at his wife's ambition," he exclaimed, "Just think of such a sucker as me as President!"[92]

Lincoln's presidential aspirations may have dawned as early as 1848. In a congressional speech that year, he humorously but perhaps significantly alluded to the possibility of his being nominated for the presidency. He ridiculed the war record of the Democratic standard-bearer, Lewis Cass, and said of the Democrats that "if . . . they shall take me up as their candidate for the Presidency, I protest they shall not make fun of me, as they have of Gen: Cass, by attempting to write me into a military hero."[93] Eight years later, after he had delivered an impassioned speech at the Illinois state Republican convention, Lincoln was told by a friend that people were saying that his address had "put him on the track for the presidency." He remained silent, assuming "a thoughtful, abstracted look."[94] Shortly thereafter, at the Republican national convention, Lincoln's name was put into nomination for the vice-presidency without his knowledge and received strong support.

James H. Matheny believed that this piece of news, which Lincoln modestly shrugged off, may have first inspired him to think of running for the White House.[95]

But during the months immediately after his defeat for the Senate in 1859, when talk of Lincoln as a presidential candidate began to circulate, he repeated to Illinois political figures what he had said to Villard: "I do not think myself fit for the Presidency."[96] To a newspaper editor who suggested organizing an effort for his candidacy, Lincoln replied, "I must, in candor, say I do not think myself fit for the Presidency. I certainly am flattered, and gratified, that some partial friends think of me in that connection; but I really think it best for our cause that no concerted effort, such as you suggest, should be made."[97] When the Aurora *Beacon* endorsed him for the presidency, he "was very much pleased" and showed the editorial to friends.[98]

His political ally Jesse W. Fell, whose travels in the East and Midwest had convinced him that Lincoln had a good chance to win the presidency, urged him to run. "Oh, Fell," he diffidently responded, "what's the use of talking of me for the presidency, whilst we have such men as Seward, Chase and others, who are so much better known to the people, and whose names are so intimately associated with the principles of the Republican party." He also thought justice demanded that the veterans of the movement be nominated. Fell pointed out that those veterans were not easily electable. Lincoln responded, "I admit the force of much that you say, and admit that I am ambitious, and would like to be President. I am not insensible to the compliment you pay me . . . *but there is no such good luck in store for me as the presidency.*"[99] In the spring of 1860, he told a law student in his office that "I haven't a chance in a hundred."[100] When Judge Thomas Drummond of Chicago informed Lincoln that people were discussing him as a presidential possibility, he replied, "I hope they will select some abler man than myself."[101] He considered Governor William Henry Seward of New York the best-qualified candidate; in early May 1860, Lincoln told Anson S. Miller of Rockford, "Judge, if I had the making of the President, I would make . . . Seward President."[102] If Seward were to be denied, Lincoln thought Edward Bates of Missouri might be the most available candidate.[103] Still, thoughts of the presidency may well have been stirring in Lincoln's mind.

After his defeat in January 1859, Lincoln began acting like a presidential candidate, thus belying his disclaimers. Early that year he evidently changed his mind about running for the presidency. According to David Davis, Lincoln put himself forward when Davis, Fell, Swett, and one or two others were discussing the strongest possible western candidate. As Davis recalled, "One name after another was mentioned and their strong and weak points considered. At last Lincoln spoke up and said: 'Why don't you run me? I can be nominated, I can be elected, and I can run the Government.' We all looked at him and saw that he was not joking. . . . The meeting adjourned without any action. But the more we thought of Lincoln's proposition to run himself the more we liked it."[104] During the summer and fall, he accepted invitations to speak in Illinois, Iowa, Indiana, Wisconsin, Kansas, and, most importantly, in Ohio, where he continued his oratorical duel with Douglas. Thus, without publicly avowing it, he was becoming a presidential candidate.

Possibly he did not really expect to win the presidency but merely hoped to improve his chances for a third bid for the Senate.[105] He did tell Norman B. Judd in December 1859 that "I would rather have a full term in the Senate than in the Presidency."[106] The following year he declared, "For personal considerations I would rather have a full term in the Senate—a place in which I would feel more consciously able to discharge the duties required, and where there was more chance to make a reputation and less chance of losing it—than four years in the presidency."[107] In late 1859 he allegedly told Dr. William Jayne that although he felt unqualified for the presidency, "I would like to be Attorney General of the United States."[108]

As the rift in the Democratic party widened in 1859 and 1860, Lincoln took heart. To Herndon and others he said, in substantially these words: "An explosion must come in the near future. Douglas is a great man in his way and has quite unlimited power over the great mass of his party, especially in the North. If he goes to the Charleston Convention, which he will do, he, in a kind of spirit of revenge, will split the Convention wide open and give it the devil; & right here is our future success or rather the glad hope of it." According to Herndon, Lincoln "prayed for this state of affairs," for "he saw in it his opportunity and wisely played his line."[109]

Another source claims that in early 1860, when Republican leaders, including Judd, asked permission to boost his presidential candidacy, Lincoln, after a day's reflection, authorized them to do so, adding that he was uninterested in the vice-presidency.[110] He told T. J. Henderson of the Illinois legislature, "My name has been mentioned rather too prominently for the first place on the ticket for me to think of accepting the second."[111] Doubtless he realized that the Seward forces sought to derail his candidacy by nominating him for the vice-presidency.[112]

On February 9, Lincoln urged Judd to help gain him the support of the Illinois delegation to the national convention.[113] Later that month he traveled to New York and, at Cooper Union, gave a masterful speech that spread his fame in the East, where few knew much of him. Several New Yorkers told him he had a good chance to become president.[114] Immediately thereafter, he delivered throughout New England a series of addresses, which also helped win him notice in the East. When he returned, he told an Ohio friend, "My name is new in the field; and I suppose I am not the *first* choice of a very great many. Our policy, then, is to give no offence to others—leave them in a mood to come to us, if they shall be compelled to give up their first love."[115]

A month later he acknowledged that "the taste *is* in my mouth a little."[116] This was doubtless an understatement. As Lincoln was to put it during the Civil War, "No man knows, when that Presidential grub gets to gnawing at him, just how deep in it will get until he has tried it."[117] By March 1860, that grub was gnawing very deeply.[118] Herndon wrote that Lincoln returned from the East believing "that the Presidential nomination was within his reach." Gradually he lost interest in the law and began "to trim his political sails at the same time." The accolades he won on his swing through the East "stimulated his self-confidence to unwonted proportions."

Herndon scorned the notion that "Lincoln sat still in his chair in Springfield, and that one of those unlooked-for tides in human affairs came along and cast the nomination into his lap." In fact, Herndon argued, "Lincoln was as vigilant as he was ambitious, and there is no denying the fact that he understood the situation perfectly."[119] Joseph Gillespie thought Lincoln's debates with Douglas in 1858 and his Cooper Union speech two years later "first inspired him with the idea that he was above the average of mankind."[120]

Early in May Lincoln privately told some delegates to the Illinois Republican convention, which had unanimously endorsed him for the presidency, that he was not sanguine about his chances: "I reckon I'll get about a hundred votes at Chicago, and I have a notion that will be the high mark for me."[121] A fortnight later his prognostication proved far too modest. He won the nomination thanks to the weaknesses of his opponents, his electability, his reputation as a forceful exponent of Republican principles, and the skillful management of his representatives in Chicago. Upon learning of his election in November, he acknowledged that he was "a very happy man." With "much feeling," Lincoln added, "Who could help being so under such circumstances?"[122]

The burdens of office soon tempered his enthusiasm. In April 1862 he told a Springfield visitor, "This getting the nomination for President, and being elected, is very gratifying to a man's ambition; but to be the President and to meet the responsibilities and discharge the duties of the office in times like these is anything but pleasant. I would gladly, if I could, take my neck from under the yoke, and go home with you to Springfield and live as I was accustomed to, in peace with my friends, than to endure this harassing kind of life."[123]

Despite these sentiments, Lincoln sought reelection. According to Leonard Swett, he "was much more eager" for a second term than he had been for his first.[124] One Pennsylvania politician believed that "anxiety for a renomination was the one thing ever uppermost in his mind during the third year of his administration."[125] A friend noted that although Lincoln "had no bad habits," he did have "one craving that he could not overcome: that was for a second term of the Presidency."[126] To a journalist he confided that although the burdens of office were oppressive, still "he would not deny that a re-election would also have its gratification to his feelings" and that "it would be a very sweet satisfaction to him to know that he had secured the approval of his fellow citizens and earned the highest testimonial of confidence they could bestow."[127]

In December 1863, he told Thurlow Weed and Leonard Swett, "Until very recently I expected to see the Union safe and the authority of the Government restored before my term of office expired. But as the war has been prolonged, I confess that I should like to see it out, in this chair. I suppose that everybody in my position finds *some* reason, good or bad, to gratify or excuse their ambition."[128] To Thaddeus Stevens, the president confided, "I confess that I desire to be re-elected. God knows I do not want the labor and responsibility of the office for another four years. But I have the common pride of humanity to wish my past four years Administration endorsed."[129] A relieved Lincoln told a friend after the election returns came in, "Being only mortal, after all, I should have been a little mortified if I had been beaten in this canvass."[130]

Lincoln probably would not have equated his desire for reelection with a bad habit. To be sure, he once called ambition an "infirmity," and he did tell Herndon during the war that "if ever American society and the United States government are demoralized and overthrown it

will come from the voracious desire of office—this struggle to live without toil—work and labor—from which I am not free myself."[131] Yet
he acknowledged his ambition candidly. In 1863 he wrote to General
Joseph Hooker: "You are ambitious, which, within reasonable bounds,
does good rather than harm."[132] Seldom in history has anyone's ambition produced as much good as Lincoln's.

The origins of Lincoln's ambition are obscure; contemporaries
despaired of understanding them. John W. Bunn, a political ally in
Springfield, wrote, "He no doubt had his personal ambitions but no
man then or now can say what they were or how they originated. He
never gave his confidence to any living person about what was strictly
private and personal to himself."[133]

In the absence of any direct evidence from Lincoln himself, scholars have been forced to speculate. Robert V. Bruce hypothesized that
his "uncommonly absorbing ambition" stemmed from a desire to
achieve "immortality through remembrance, eternal consciousness by
proxy in the mind of posterity."[134] Dwight G. Anderson has put forward a similar argument: "Lincoln's ambition was rooted in what can
only be described as an obsession about death. . . . Ambition provided the means by which immortality could be attained."[135] It is true that
Lincoln longed to have his name remembered after he died. As he told
Joshua Speed during a particularly debilitating bout of depression in
1841, "I am not afraid, and would be more than willing [to die]. But I
have an irrepressible desire to live till I can be assured that the world
is a little better for my having lived in it."[136]

Anderson detects something sinister in Lincoln's ambition, which
drove him to become a "tyrant," a "Robespierre" who presided over
the destruction of the Constitution.[137] To support his contention, Anderson, like Edmund Wilson and George Forgie before him, leans heavily
on "The Perpetuation of Our Political Institutions," an address the
twenty-eight-year-old Lincoln gave to the Young Men's Lyceum of
Springfield. In it he inveighed against the dangers of mob violence and
warned that "men of ambition and talents" might try to destroy the
government. Bombastically he spoke of men who belong *"to the family of the lion, or the tribe of the eagle"* and whose "towering
genius. . . . thirsts and burns for distinction; and, if possible, it will have
it, whether at the expense of emancipating slaves, or enslaving freemen." He asked whether it is "unreasonable then to expect, that some
man possessed of the loftiest genius, coupled with ambition sufficient
to push it to its utmost stretch, will, at some time, spring up among

us" and become a tyrant.[138] Anderson, Wilson, and others interpret this
as a projection onto a future Caesar of Lincoln's own ambition and an
accurate forecast of what he was to become.[139]

Such a reading of the Lyceum speech flies in the face of Lincoln's
history; his words and deeds lend no credence to the argument that he
became a power-mad dictator.[140] Rather than referring to himself, Lincoln's overheated rhetoric was a characteristic exercise in partisan ridicule aimed at Stephen A. Douglas, who was then campaigning against
Lincoln's law partner for a seat in Congress (see the Appendix of this
volume). He may also have been poking fun at the autocratic Andrew
Jackson and his successor Martin Van Buren. As a young politico, Lincoln delighted in sarcastic mockery of Democrats (chapter 7), and in
the Lyceum address he parroted some of Van Buren's language, especially that of his inaugural address.[141]

There is nothing unusual or alarming about wanting to be remembered after death. As Daniel J. Levinson, a psychologist, has observed,
the "desire for an immortalizing legacy is a powerful, 'normal' human
urge." It can "have destructive consequences if it grows, unchecked,
into overly elaborate, magical forms, as in the Faust legend."[142] Nothing in the Lincoln record suggests a parallel with Faust. Lincoln's ambition, as Don E. Fehrenbacher has aptly described it, was "notably
free of pettiness, malice, and overindulgence. It was, moreover, an
ambition leavened by moral conviction and a deep faith in the principles upon which the republic had been built."[143] In response to those
who suggest that Lincoln's ambition was rooted in his desire for immortality, Fehrenbacher observed sensibly that other ambitious men of
Lincoln's era, for example, Stephen A. Douglas and Salmon P. Chase,
had no death obsession.[144]

Although strong, Lincoln's ambition was not all-consuming and
probably would have not led him to aspire to the presidency had his
wife not goaded him on. Without her restless urging, he might well have
settled for a seat in the U.S. Senate;[145] he had said as much to Henry
Villard in 1858 and to Norman B. Judd the following year.

George Forgie's analysis of the effects of Lincoln's ambition is as
unpersuasive as Anderson's analysis of its origins. To be sure, Forgie
sensibly suggests that Lincoln's taste in literature cries out for explanation, especially his identification with three highly ambitious political figures in Shakespeare: Macbeth, Hamlet's uncle/stepfather Claudius, and Richard III. Forgie notes that "of all Shakespeare's creations,

Lincoln was drawn to the plays, characters, and indeed the very scenes that most vividly dramatize fratricidal ambition." Lincoln's favorite speeches evidently were Claudius' "O, my offense is rank"; Macbeth's "Better be with the dead"; and Richard III's "Now is the winter of our discontent." Because guilt about ambition tormented each of these characters, Forgie speculates that Lincoln may have felt guilty about his intense ambition that led to the defeat of Stephen A. Douglas, thus paving the way for fratricidal warfare.[146]

This interpretation is farfetched. Lincoln may well have suffered guilt pangs for a number of reasons. Perhaps, as the war dragged on and the casualties mounted, he wished that he had accepted compromise during the secession crisis. His conscience may have tormented him about signing the death warrants of 276 Union soldiers during the war. The large number of friends and relatives whose appeals for office he rejected when distributing the spoils may also have weighed on his mind.[147] But it seems highly unlikely that he would have felt guilty about defeating Douglas, a man opposed to his most deeply felt principles.

• • •

Intensely as he may have craved the admiration of future generations, Lincoln wanted even more the approbation of his contemporaries in order to salve the wounds that his self-esteem had suffered in his youth. Harold D. Lasswell has argued that political ambition is rooted in "an intense and ungratified craving for deference," and that for power seekers, "*power is expected to overcome low estimates of the self.*"[148] As Lincoln said in his first political campaign document, "I have no other [ambition] so great as that of being truly esteemed of my fellow men, by rendering myself worthy of their esteem."[149] That hunger for the admiration of others persisted throughout his life as he tried to heal his damaged self-esteem.

Lasswell argues that the compensatory psychological benefits of political power and fame have a special appeal to "the 'provincial' or the 'small-town boy' or the 'country boy'" who wants "to succeed against the stigma of rusticity."[150] Lincoln is a good case in point, for, as John L. Scripps said of a conversation with him in 1860, he "seemed to be painfully impressed with the extreme poverty of his early surroundings— the utter absence of all romantic and heroic elements." When Scripps asked him for biographical information, the future president replied, "Why, Scripps, it is a great piece of folly to attempt to make anything out of my early life. It can all be condensed into a single sentence . . . in Gray's Elegy: 'The short and simple annals of the poor.' That's my life, and that's all you or any one else can make of it."[151]

Lincoln nevertheless acceded to Scripps's request and wrote an autobiographical sketch. In that document, he seemed to apologize for his humble origins. He said that Thomas Lincoln, "by the early death of his father, and very narrow circumstances of his mother, even in childhood was a wandering laboring boy, and grew up litterally without education. He never did more in the way of writing than to bunglingly sign his own name." Speaking of himself, Lincoln ruefully alluded to his own lack of formal schooling: "He regrets his want of education, and does what he can to supply the want."[152] For the *Dictionary of Congress,* Lincoln in 1858 wrote a brief entry that contained the laconic observation, "education defective."[153]

In yet another autobiographical document prepared the following year Lincoln said, "My parents were both born in Virginia, of undistinguished families—second families, perhaps I should say." He again pointed out that his father "grew up, litterally without education." In childhood he had found "absolutely nothing to excite ambition for education."[154] When the people of Logan County, Illinois, proposed to name a town after him, Lincoln told them, "You better not do that, for I never knew anything named Lincoln that amounted to much."[155] The positive reception that he received in the East in early 1860 astonished him. To a Norwich, Connecticut, minister who lauded his address in that city, Lincoln replied, "Certainly I have had a most wonderful success for a man of my limited education." He was especially struck by the lavish praise of a professor of rhetoric at Yale.[156]

At the age of thirty-five, Lincoln visited the sites he had known as a boy in Indiana and wrote a poem about his impressions. Some of the verses suggest that much of Lincoln's childhood was spent among scenes "gross and vile."[157] On more than one occasion he told a Springfield neighbor that "I have seen a good deal of the back side of this world."[158] Scholars studying Lincoln's youth have divided into adherents of "the dunghill thesis," which stresses the poverty and squalor of his surroundings, and adherents of "the chin fly thesis," which paints a rosier, more bucolic picture of those environs. Modern Lincoln authorities tend to subscribe to the former school.[159] As he told voters during his first political campaign, he "was born and have ever remained in the most humble walks of life"; a decade later he referred to himself at twenty-two as "a strange, friendless, uneducated, penniless boy."[160] The psychologist

G. Stanley Hall speculated that Lincoln's ambition was rooted in his feelings about his appearance: "His height, long limbs, rough exterior, and frequent feeling of awkwardness must have very early made him realize that to succeed in life he must cultivate intrinsic mental and moral traits, which it is so hard for a handsome man or women to excel in. Hence he compensated by trying to develop intellectual distinction."[161]

Emotional as well as material and educational poverty seems to have plagued the young Lincoln, for evidently neither parent could meet his most basic psychological needs (chapters 2 and 6). Nancy Hanks Lincoln, about whom little is known, may have provided her young son with love and support during his first nine years, but it is likely that he viewed her death as a deliberate abandonment. In later life he seldom mentioned her; one of the few times he did so, it was in a patronizing fashion.[162]

His father, utterly different from Abraham, offered little nurturance (chapter 2). Perhaps the best thing Thomas Lincoln ever did for his son was to marry Sarah Bush Johnston, who cherished the lad.[163] But by the time she arrived on the scene, the boy's psyche had endured much. Lincoln thus seems to have suffered from emotional malnutrition. To compensate for the damage to his self-esteem, he sought in political life a surrogate form of the love and acceptance he had not found at home.

NOTES

1. William H. Herndon, "Analysis of the Character of Abraham Lincoln" [lecture of 26 Dec. 1865], *Abraham Lincoln Quarterly* 1 (Dec. 1941): 410–11; Herndon, "Lincoln's Ambition," H-W MSS, DLC; Herndon to an unidentified New York clergyman, Springfield, 24 Nov. 1882, New York *Tribune*, 21 Jan. 1883, 3; Angle, *HL*, 163, 304. Cf. Herndon to Jesse Weik, Springfield, 5 Jan. 1886, H-W MSS, DLC.

2. Horace White, *Abraham Lincoln in 1854: An Address Delivered Before the Illinois State Historical Society, at Its 9th Annual Meeting at Springfield, Illinois, Jan. 30, 1908* (Springfield: Illinois State Historical Society, 1908), 20; White's introduction to William H. Herndon and Jesse W. Weik, *Herndon's Lincoln: The True Story of a Great Life*, 2 vols. (New York: D. Appleton, 1892), 1:xxi.

3. Trumbull to his son, Walter, N.p., N.d., in Horace White, *The Life of Lyman Trumbull* (Boston: Houghton, Mifflin, 1913), 429.

4. Gillespie to Herndon, Edwardsville, 8 Dec. 1866, H-W MSS, DLC.

5. Nicolay's interview with O. H. Browning, Springfield, 17 June 1875, Hay MSS, RPB.

6. William Jayne, *Personal Reminiscences of the Martyred President, Abraham Lincoln, by His Neighbor and Intimate Friend* (Chicago: Grand

Army and Memorial Association, 1908), 15; Davis, speech of May 19, 1865, Indianapolis *Daily Sentinel,* 20 May 1865, reprinted in Sherman Day Wakefield, *How Lincoln Became President: The Part Played by Bloomington, Illinois, and Certain of Its Citizens in Preparing Him for the Presidency and Securing His Nomination and Election* (New York: Wilson-Erickson, 1936), 150.

7. Francis Fisher Browne, *The Every-Day Life of Abraham Lincoln,* 2d ed. (New York: G. P. Putnam's Sons, 1913), 159.

8. New York *Tribune,* 26 July 1885, 3.

9. Albert J. Beveridge, *Abraham Lincoln, 1809–1858,* 2 vols. (Boston: Houghton, Mifflin, 1928), 1:154.

10. Public statement by Mrs. Crawford at Lincoln City, 4 July 1881, Rockport [Ind.] *Journal,* 9 June 1916, quoted in Francis Van Natter, *Lincoln's Boyhood: A Chronicle of His Indiana Years* (Washington, D.C.: Public Affairs Press, 1963), 36.

11. Herndon's memo of a conversation with Elizabeth Crawford, Springfield, 16 Sept. 1865, in Hertz, *HL,* 367.

12. James LeGrande, recalling the words of his mother, undated memo, Arthur E. Morgan MSS, DLC.

13. Nicolay's interview with Browning, Springfield, 17 June 1875, Hay MSS, RPB.

14. Unpublished manuscript by "a Hoosier," quoted in Ida M. Tarbell with J. McCan Davis, *The Early Life of Abraham Lincoln* (New York: McClure, 1896), 62.

15. Joseph C. Richardson's undated statement, in Hertz, *HL,* 361.

16. Van Natter, *Lincoln's Boyhood,* 93.

17. Lamon to Herndon, Buffaloville, Ind., 18 May 1867, H-W MSS, DLC.

18. James Quay Howard's notes of a conversation with Greene, [May 1860], Lincoln MSS, DLC; William Dean Howells, *Life of Abraham Lincoln,* ed. Clyde C. Watson (Bloomington: Indiana University Press, 1960; reprint of a 1938 facsimile edition with Lincoln's emendations in the 1860 edition), 29–30. Lincoln read and corrected passages in Howells's 1860 campaign biography, based in part on Howard's notes. These observations by Howard, in Howells's paraphrase, evidently squared with Lincoln's recollections, for he penciled no comments on them. Cf. L. M. Greene to Herndon, Avon, Ill., 30 July 1865, H-W MSS, DLC.

19. Kunigunde Duncan and D. F. Nickols, *Mentor Graham: The Man Who Taught Lincoln* (Chicago: University of Chicago Press, 1944), 125.

20. Walter B. Stevens, *A Reporter's Lincoln* (St. Louis: Missouri Historical Society, 1916), 9.

21. John G. Nicolay's interview with William Butler, Springfield, 13 June 1875, Hay MSS, RPB.

22. "Autobiography Written for John L. Scripps" [ca. June 1860], in Basler, *CWL,* 4:64.

23. Autobiography enclosed in Lincoln to Jesse W. Fell, Springfield, 20 Dec. 1859, in Basler, *CWL,* 3:512.

24. "Communication to the People of Sangamo County," 9 March 1832, in Basler, *CWL,* 1:8–9.

25. J. R. Herndon to W. H. Herndon, Quincy, 28 May 1865, H-W MSS, DLC.

26. Joshua Speed, in Francis F. Browne, *The Every-Day Life of Abraham Lincoln* (Boston: Mason and Fowler, 1886), 142.

27. John Easton, a member of the legislature, recalled that "I received letters from Lincoln urging me to see to it that the members known to be in his favor for the State Senatorship should be held solidly together." St. Louis *Globe-Democrat*, 13 Jan. 1887. No such letters to Easton are known to have survived.

28. Paul Simon, *Lincoln's Preparation for Greatness: The Illinois Legislative Years* (Norman: University of Oklahoma Press, 1965), 290. Cf. William E. Baringer, *Lincoln's Vandalia: A Pioneer Portrait* (New Brunswick: Rutgers University Press, 1949), 4; Paul Stroble, *High on the Okaw's Western Bank: Vandalia, Illinois, 1819–39* (Urbana: University of Illinois Press, 1992).

29. Herndon to Ward Hill Lamon, Springfield, 25 Feb. 1870, Lamon MSS, CSmH.

30. Harry E. Pratt, "Lincoln—Campaign Manager and Orator in 1840," *Bulletin of the Abraham Lincoln Association*, no. 50 (Dec. 1937): 3–8.

31. *Sangamo Journal*, 8 Jan. 1841, 2.

32. Alton *Telegraph*, 20 July 1841, in *Lincoln Day by Day: A Chronology, 1809–1865*, ed. Earl Schenck Miers et al., 3 vols. (Washington, D.C.: Lincoln Sesquicentennial Commission, 1960), 1:164.

33. *Sangamo Journal*, 12 Nov. 1841, 2.

34. *Sangamo Journal*, 15 Oct. 1842, 2, replying to a piece in the Fulton *Telegraph*.

35. A newspaper editor discussed the upcoming gubernatorial election with Simeon Francis, who said he "had talked of Lincoln," but the editor "satisfied him it would not answer to have both the Congressman & Governor from Springfield, *as he knew* from the tone of the members of the late convention that there was a great deal of feeling against Springfield *asking everything.*" Francis then agreed to support John J. Hardin for governor. Less than two weeks later the editor reported that the "Springfield men have given up Lincoln" in favor of Hardin. George T. M. Davis to John J. Hardin, Springfield, 29 Jan., 10 Feb. 1844, John J. Hardin MSS, ICHi. The Whigs nominated Edward D. Baker of Springfield for Congress.

36. Simon, *Lincoln's Preparation for Greatness*, 272.

37. F. Lauriston Bullard, "When John T. Stuart Sought to Send Lincoln to South America," *Lincoln Herald* 47 (Oct.–Dec. 1945): 21, 29.

38. Donald W. Riddle, *Lincoln Runs for Congress* (New Brunswick: Rutgers University Press, 1948), 9–10.

39. Gabor S. Boritt, *Abraham Lincoln and the Economics of the American Dream* (Memphis: Memphis State University Press, 1978), 33.

40. Douglas L. Wilson, "Abraham Lincoln and 'that fatal first of January,'" *Civil War History* 38 (June 1992): 101–30.

41. Roy P. Basler and Lloyd A. Dunlap in their edition of John Locke Scripps, *Life of Abraham Lincoln* (New York: Greenwood Press, 1968), 77n.

42. Lincoln to Richard S. Thomas, Springfield, 14 Feb. 1843, in Basler, *CWL,* 1:307.

43. Lincoln to Speed, Springfield, 24 March 1843, in Basler, *CWL,* 1:319.

44. Lincoln to Martin S. Morris, Springfield, 26 March 1843, in Basler, *CWL,* 1:320.

45. Benjamin P. Thomas, *Abraham Lincoln: A Biography* (New York: Alfred A. Knopf, 1952), 104.

46. Riddle, *Lincoln Runs for Congress,* 20–21.

47. Lincoln to John T. Stuart, Vandalia, 14 Feb. 1839, in Basler, *CWL,* 1:143. Cf. Simon, *Lincoln's Preparation for Greatness,* 150, 159.

48. Usher F. Linder, *Reminiscences of the Early Bench and Bar of Illinois* (Chicago: Chicago Legal News Company, 1879), 62–64.

49. J. G. Holland, *The Life of Abraham Lincoln* (Springfield, Mass.: Gurdon Bill, 1866), 94. Cf. Noah Brooks, *Abraham Lincoln and the Downfall of American Slavery* (New York: G. P. Putnam's Sons, 1894), 100.

50. Lincoln to Benjamin F. James, Springfield, 14 Jan. 1846, in Basler, *CWL,* 1:354. Cf. the spate of letters he wrote in late 1845 and early 1846 on behalf of his own candidacy (1:349ff).

51. Riddle, *Lincoln Runs for Congress,* 76–185.

52. Lincoln to Speed, Springfield, 22 Oct. 1846, in Basler, *CWL,* 1:391.

53. Paul Findley, *A. Lincoln: The Crucible of Congress* (New York: Crown, 1979), 54–57. Findley calls this decision "one of the great mysteries of his life."

54. Lincoln to Herndon, Washington, 13 Dec. 1847, in Basler, *CWL,* 1:420.

55. Cf. Thomas F. Schwartz, "'An Egregious Political Blunder': Justin Butterfield, Lincoln and Illinois Whiggery," *Papers of the Abraham Lincoln Association* 8 (1986): 9–19. He told Herndon that he had no objection to being reelected, but that, having promised other aspirants that he would not run again, he did not want to go back on his word. If, however, "it should so happen that nobody else wishes to be elected, I could not refuse the people the right of sending me again." Lincoln to Herndon, Washington, 8 Jan. 1848, in Basler, *CWL,* 1:431.

56. Lincoln to Josiah M. Lucas, Springfield, 25 April 1849, in Basler, *CWL,* 2:43–44.

57. Thomas Ewing, "Lincoln and the General Land Office, 1849," *Journal of the Illinois State Historical Society* 25 (Oct. 1932): 152–53. Lincoln was defeated in part because some Illinois politicians thought he had become "a mere catspaw of [Edward D.] Baker" and that the Whigs in northern Illinois deserved patronage plums because the marshall and the district attorney posts had already gone to Whigs in the southern part of the state. E. B. Washburne to C. B. Smith, Galena, Ill., 21 May 1849, copy, Ewing Family Papers, DLC.

58. Browne, *Every-Day Life of Lincoln,* 2d ed., 107.

59. Undated statement of John T. Stuart, H-W MSS, DLC; John G. Nicolay's interview with Stuart, Springfield, 24 June 1875, Hay MSS, RPB; Angle, *HL,* 246–47; Emilie Todd Helm in Katherine Helm, *The True Story of Mary, Wife of Lincoln* (New York: Harper and Brothers, 1928), 107; Henry B.

Rankin, *Personal Recollections of Abraham Lincoln* (New York: G. P. Putnam's Sons, 1916), 181–82. Also see chapter 9 in this volume. Lincoln may have turned down the Oregon offer because he felt embarrassed to take such a post while friends whom he had recommended for office were rejected. See Lincoln to Thomas Ewing, Tremont, Ill., 23 Sept. 1849, in *The Collected Works of Abraham Lincoln: Second Supplement, 1848–1865,* ed. Roy P. Basler and Christian O. Basler (New Brunswick: Rutgers University Press, 1990), 5, and Anson G. Henry to Thomas Ewing, N.p., 24 Sept. 1849, in Paul I. Miller, "Lincoln and the Governorship of Oregon," *Mississippi Valley Historical Review* 23 (Dec. 1936): 392.

60. Herndon to Jesse Weik, Springfield, 28 Oct. 1885, in Hertz, *HL,* 6; Thomas, *Lincoln,* 128–29.

61. Recollections of Paul Selby, in Browne, *Every-Day Life of Lincoln,* 2d ed., 158–60.

62. Henry C. Whitney, *Life on the Circuit with Lincoln* (Boston: Estes and Lauriat, 1892), 141, and "Abraham Lincoln: A Study from Life," *Arena* 19 (April 1898): 479–80.

63. Angle, *HL,* 301–2.

64. Lincoln to Joseph Gillespie, Springfield, 1 Dec. 1854, in Basler, *CWL,* 2:290. Cf. 2:286–304, passim.

65. Reminiscences of Elijah M. Haines in Browne, *Every-Day Life of Lincoln,* 2d ed., 163.

66. Lincoln to Elihu B. Washburne, Springfield, 9 Feb. 1855, in Basler, *CWL,* 2:304. Cf. Lincoln to Jesse Olds Norton, Springfield, 16 Feb. 1855, in *Collected Works: Second Supplement,* ed. Basler and Basler, 9–11.

67. Lincoln to William H. Henderson, Springfield, 21 Feb. 1855, in Basler, *CWL,* 2:306–7.

68. Herndon, "Lincoln's Ambition," H-W MSS, DLC.

69. Parks's recollections, in White, *Trumbull,* 45.

70. LeRoy H. Fischer, ed., "Samuel C. Parks's Reminiscences of Abraham Lincoln," *Lincoln Herald* 68 (Spring 1966): 11.

71. Gillespie to General [?], Edwardsville, 22 April 1880, John J. Hardin Papers, ICHi. Gillespie told Herndon that Lincoln was "of course greatly disappointed and mortified at his own want of success." Gillespie to Herndon, 19 Sept. 1866, in Angle, *HL,* 307n. Beveridge stated, "When the struggle was over, young Whitney went to Lincoln's office and found his hero in the deepest depths of blackest melancholy. Never before or thereafter did Lincoln's associate on the Circuit see him so utterly dejected." Beveridge cited an undated letter from Whitney to Weik in the Weik Papers. Beveridge, *Lincoln,* 2:287. But elsewhere, Whitney says he saw Lincoln utterly dejected after his *second* defeat for the Senate four years later. Hertz, *HL,* 10.

72. Washington correspondence, 30 Sept. [1892?], Chicago *Evening Post,* N.d., clipping in the Lincoln Collection, Vertical File, "Reminiscences," folder 3, IHi.

73. White, *Trumbull,* 45. Cf. Lincoln to Trumbull, Springfield, 3 Feb. 1859, in Basler, *CWL,* 2:355–56. See also John W. Bunn, interview with John

G. Nicolay, Springfield, 21 Aug. 1879: "There was a party that night at Ninian Edwards: Lincoln was the lion of the evening—surrounded with condoling friends most of whom told him they would have preferred Matteson to Trumbull. But Lincoln reassured them and told them it was all right." Nicolay MSS, DLC.

74. "Fragment on Stephen A. Douglas," [Dec. 1856?], and Lincoln's speech of July 17, 1858, both in Basler, *CWL*, 2:382–83, 2:506. In 1852 Lincoln had made similar comments in a stump speech on behalf of the Whig presidential candidate, Winfield Scott: "He said that he had been told since he came to this town [Peoria], that Judge Douglass was coming here, & that he would skin me;—Well perhaps he would; Douglass had got to be a great man, & [be]strode the earth. Time was when I was in his way some; but he has outgrown me & [be]strides the world; & such small men as I, can hardly be considered as worthy of his notice; & I may have to dodge & get between his legs." No author given, memo of a speech by Lincoln at Peoria, 16 March 1852 [actually 17 Sept. 1852], Lincoln Collection, ICHi.

75. Gillespie to General [?], Edwardsville, 22 April 1880, John J. Hardin Papers, ICHi.

76. Lincoln's handwritten correction of a passage in Howells, *Life of Lincoln*, 73; Lincoln's response to a toast at a banquet, 22 Feb. 1856, quoted in Paul Selby, "The Formation of the Republican Party in Illinois," typescript, 22–23, Ida M. Tarbell MSS, Allegheny College. William J. Usrey, editor of the *Illinois State Chronicle* [Decatur], reported that Lincoln's name was put forward at this banquet for the U.S. Senate, and that Lincoln favored the proposal. *Illinois State Chronicle*, 28 Feb. 1856, in Otto R. Kyle, *Abraham Lincoln in Decatur* (New York: Vantage Press, 1957), 75.

77. Lincoln to Julian M. Sturdevant, Springfield, 27 Sept. 1856, in Basler, *CWL*, 2:378–79.

78. "Fragment on the Struggle against Slavery," [ca. July, 1858], in Basler, *CWL*, 2:482.

79. Speech at Lewiston, 17 Aug. 1858, in Basler, *CWL*, 2:547.

80. "Fragment: Notes of Speeches," [ca. 21 Aug. 1858], in Basler, *CWL*, 2:548.

81. "Fragment: Last Speech of the Campaign at Springfield," 30 Oct. 1858, in Basler, *CWL*, 3:334. In 1863 Lincoln said that his "proudest ambition . . . was to do something for the elevation of the condition of his fellow-man." "Reply to John Conness upon Presentation of a Cane," 13 Nov. 1863, 7:13.

82. Reminiscences of Bushrod E. Hoppin, typescript dated April 1921, Lincoln Collection, Watkinson Library, Trinity College, Hartford, Conn.

83. Charles S. Zane, "Lincoln as I Knew Him," *Sunset Magazine* 29 (Oct. 1912): 430–38, reprinted in the *Journal of the Illinois State Historical Society* 14 (1921–22): 74–84 [quote on 79–80].

84. Lincoln to Anson G. Henry, Springfield, 19 Nov. 1858, in Basler, *CWL*, 3:339.

85. Lincoln to H. D. Sharpe, Springfield, 8 Dec. 1858, in Basler, *CWL*, 3:344.

86. Reminiscences of E. M. Haines, member of the legislature, in Browne, *Every-Day Life of Lincoln*, 2d ed., 209–10.

87. Alton *Daily Courier*, 17 Jan. 1859, reprinting the Springfield correspondence of the Cincinnati *Commercial*, N.d., in the *Journal of the Illinois State Historical Society* 48 (1955): 329.

88. Zane, "Lincoln as I Knew Him," 76.

89. John Hay diary, 8 Nov. 1864, Hay MSS, RPB.

90. Whitney, *Life on the Circuit*, 467; Whitney to Herndon, N.p., N.d., in Hertz, *HL*, 10; Robert H. Browne, *Abraham Lincoln and the Men of His Time*, 2 vols. (New York: Eaton and Mains; Cincinnati: Jennings and Pye, 1901), 2:241.

91. Browne, *Lincoln and the Men of His Time*, 2:242, 251–52, 257.

92. Henry Villard, *Memoirs of Henry Villard, Journalist and Financier, 1835–1900*, 2 vols. (Boston: Houghton, Mifflin, 1904), 1:96.

93. "Speech in the U.S. House of Representatives on the Presidential Question," 27 July 1848, in Basler, *CWL*, 1:510.

94. Henry C. Whitney's remarks to Jesse W. Weik, in Weik, *RL*, 257.

95. Whitney, *Life on the Circuit*, 81.

96. Lincoln to Samuel Galloway, Springfield, 28 July 1859, in Basler, *CWL*, 3:395.

97. Lincoln to Thomas J. Pickett, Springfield, 16 April 1859, in Basler, *CWL*, 3:377.

98. J. Wainwright Ray to John G. Nicolay, Washington, 18 Oct. 1886, quoting Ward Hill Lamon, Nicolay MSS, DLC. Like several other editors, Ray claimed that his newspaper was the first to bring forth Lincoln's name as a presidential candidate. Ray told Nicolay, "When I met the Marshall, Lamon, here he said—'why you are the man who nominated Lin[coln]' & added, 'I was in court at Springfield when L. came in one morning & called Gen. Baker & me & showed [us] the *Beacon* & said "they have put me up for Prest." & was very much pleased.'" According to Joseph Medill, editor of the Chicago *Tribune*, the Illinois State Central Republican Committee arranged in 1859 for rural newspapers to champion Lincoln's candidacy. Reminiscences of Medill, galley proof dated 21 April 1895, Ida M. Tarbell MSS, Allegheny College.

99. Fell's recollections in *The Lincoln Memorial: Album-Immortelles*, ed. Osborn H. Oldroyd (New York: G. W. Carleton, 1883), 473–76. Cf. James A. Briggs's recollections, paraphrased in Ida M. Tarbell, *In the Footsteps of the Lincolns* (New York: Harper and Brothers, 1924), 381; Browne, *Lincoln and the Men of His Time*, 2:267–68.

100. John H. Littlefield, quoted in Joseph Fort Newton, *Lincoln and Herndon* (Cedar Rapids: Torch Press, 1910), 251.

101. Reminiscences of Drummond, in Browne, *Every-Day Life of Lincoln*, 2d ed., 144.

102. Moses Coit Tyler, "One of Mr. Lincoln's Old Friends," *Journal of the Illinois State Historical Society* 29 (Jan. 1936): 256 (reprinted from the New York *Independent*, 12, 19 March 1868).

103. Theodore Calvin Pease and James G. Randall, eds., *The Diary of Orville Hickman Browning*, 2 vols., Collections of the Illinois State Histori-

cal Library, vols. 20 and 22 (Springfield: Illinois State Historical Library, 1925–33), 1:395 [entry for 8 Feb. 1860].

104. Reminiscences given by David Davis to Ferdinand C. Iglehart, in an unidentified newspaper clipping, "With Lincoln," by Iglehart, Lincoln Collection, PRB.

105. William Baringer, *Lincoln's Rise to Power* (Boston: Little, Brown, 1937), 5–6, 69, 144, 147, 334.

106. Lincoln to Judd, Springfield, 9 Dec. 1859, in Basler, *CWL*, 2:505. Cf. Browne, *Lincoln and the Men of His Time*, 2:394–97.

107. Memo by John G. Nicolay, Springfield, 25 Oct. 1860, Nicolay MSS, DLC.

108. J. McCan Davis, "Lincoln and the Presidency," typescript, 2, Ida M. Tarbell MSS, Allegheny College.

109. Herndon to Horace White, Springfield, 28 April 1890, copy, JGR MSS, DLC.

110. Jackson Grimshaw's recollection, in Angle *HL*, 366–67. Joseph Medill claimed that he dissuaded Lincoln from thoughts of the vice-presidency. Reminiscences of Medill, galley proof dated 21 April 1895, Ida M. Tarbell MSS, Allegheny College.

111. Reminiscences of Thomas J. Henderson, Princeton, Ill., 28 Oct. 1895, 24, Ida M. Tarbell MSS, Allegheny College; cf. statement by E. M. Haines in Browne, *Every-Day Life of Lincoln*, 2d ed., 228–29.

112. John M. Palmer, undated interview with J. McCan Davis, Ida M. Tarbell MSS, Allegheny College.

113. Lincoln to Judd, Springfield, 9 Feb. 1860, in Basler, *CWL*, 3:517.

114. James A. Briggs's reminiscences, New York *Evening Post*, 16 Aug. 1867, in *An Authentic Account of Hon. Abraham Lincoln*, ed. Gilbert A. Tracy (Putnam, Conn.: Privately published, 1915), [4–5].

115. Lincoln to Samuel Galloway, Chicago, 24 March 1860, in Basler, *CWL*, 4:34.

116. Lincoln to Lyman Trumbull, Springfield, 29 April 1860, in Basler, *CWL*, 4:45.

117. Comments made to J. Russell Jones, in "Lincoln and Grant in 1863," statement of Jones to J. McCan Davis, 10 Dec. 1898, typescript, Ida M. Tarbell MSS, Allegheny College; cf. James Harrison Wilson, "Reminiscences of General Grant," *Century Magazine* 30 (Oct. 1885), 954; James B. Fry in Rice, *RL*, 390.

118. Horace White in the New York *Evening Post*, 12 Feb. 1909, in *Lincoln among His Friends: A Sheaf of Intimate Memories*, ed. Rufus Rockwell Wilson (Caldwell: Caxton, 1942), 174.

119. Angle, *HL*, 369–70.

120. Gillespie to General [?], Edwardsville, 22 April 1880, John J. Hardin Papers, ICHi.

121. Richard Price Morgan, in *Abraham Lincoln by Some Men Who Knew Him*, ed. Isaac N. Phillips (Bloomington, Ill.: Pantagraph Printing, 1910), 94.

122. Henry C. Bowen's recollections of a conversation during the week

of Lincoln's first inauguration, in *Abraham Lincoln: Tributes from Associates: Reminiscences of Soldiers, Statesmen and Citizens*, ed. William Hayes Ward (New York: Thomas Y. Crowell, 1895), 31.

123. Noyes W. Miner, "Personal Reminiscences of Abraham Lincoln," 10 July 1882, SC 1052, folder 2, 47, IHi. This account is based on "full notes" taken by Miner shortly after the conversation.

124. Swett to Herndon, Chicago, 17 Jan. 1866, in Angle, *HL*, 427.

125. A. K. McClure, *Lincoln and Men of War-Times: Some Personal Recollections of War and Politics During the Lincoln Administration* (Philadelphia: Times, 1892), 136.

126. James B. Fry, in Rice, *RL*, 390.

127. James M. Winchell, "Three Interviews with President Lincoln," *Galaxy* 16 (July 1873): 40. Cf. Brooks, "Personal Recollections of Abraham Lincoln," 226, and Brooks's Washington dispatch of 6 Oct. 1863, Sacramento *Daily Union*, 31 Oct. 1863, 1.

128. New York *Commercial Advertiser*, N.d. [ca. Nov. 1864], quoted in an unidentified clipping, JGR MSS, DLC. Cf. Weed to the editor, New York *Tribune*, 25 June 1878, New York *Tribune*, 5 July 1878, 5.

129. "The Interview between Thad. Stevens & Mr. Lincoln as Related by Col. R. M. Hoe," Nicolay MSS, DLC.

130. Holland, *Lincoln*, 489. Lincoln's desire to win reelection doubtless had roots not only in his psychological need for approval but also in his realistic belief that if his opponent triumphed, the Union cause would suffer.

131. Helen Nicolay, *Personal Traits of Abraham Lincoln* (New York: Century, 1912), 304–5; Herndon, "Analysis of the Character of Lincoln," 406–7.

132. Lincoln to Hooker, Washington, 26 Jan. 1863, in Basler, *CWL*, 6:78.

133. Bunn to Henry S. Pritchett, N.p., 12 Jan. 1905, SC 210 (copy), IHi. Bunn, twelve years Lincoln's junior, knew him in the 1850s and often ran political errands for him.

134. Robert V. Bruce, *Lincoln and the Riddle of Death* (Fort Wayne: Louis A. Warren Lincoln Library and Museum, 1981), 23. This thoughtful essay is the best description and analysis of Lincoln's attitude toward death.

135. Dwight G. Anderson, *Abraham Lincoln: The Quest for Immortality* (New York: Alfred A. Knopf, 1982), 79, 95.

136. Joshua Speed, *Reminiscences of Abraham Lincoln and Notes of a Visit to California: Two Lectures* (Louisville: John P. Morton, 1884), 39.

137. Anderson, *Lincoln*, 99, 61.

138. Basler, *CWL*, 1:113–14.

139. Anderson, *Lincoln*, 68–78 and passim; Edmund Wilson, *Patriotic Gore: Studies in the Literature of the American Civil War* (New York: Oxford University Press, 1962), 106–8; George B. Forgie, *Patricide in the House Divided: A Psychological Interpretation of Lincoln and His Age* (New York: W. W. Norton, 1979), 84–87 and passim. The most thoughtful commentary on this school of thought is Mark E. Neely, Jr., "Lincoln's Lyceum Speech and the Origins of a Modern Myth," *Lincoln Lore*, Feb. 1987, 1–4, March 1987, 1, in which Neely shows how historians have erred: "In the course of adopting Wilson's *approach* to Lincoln through psychoanalysis they also unconscious-

ly adopted part of the substance of Wilson's argument, that is, the view that Lincoln was a dictator" and thus have "perpetuated a Copperhead myth." Cf. Neely, *The Fate of Liberty: Abraham Lincoln and Civil Liberties* (New York: Oxford University Press, 1991), 224–35.

140. For a thoughtful discussion of Lincoln's purportedly dictatorial ways, see Herman Belz, *Lincoln and the Constitution: The Dictatorship Question Reconsidered* (Fort Wayne: Louis Warren Lincoln Library and Museum, 1984).

141. Fehrenbacher, *Lincoln in Text and Context,* 282; Major L. Wilson, "Lincoln and Van Buren in the Steps of the Fathers: Another Look at the Lyceum Address," *Civil War History* 29 (Sept. 1983): 203–4. The speech has also been viewed as an expression of the Whig party's traditional reverence for law and order. See George M. Fredrickson, "The Search for Order and Community," in *The Public and the Private Lincoln: Contemporary Perspectives,* ed. Cullom Davis et al. (Carbondale: Southern Illinois University Press, 1979), 92–94; Howe, *The Political Culture of the American Whigs,* 270–71. With some justice Neely has questioned this reading of the Lyceum address; see *The Fate of Liberty,* 215.

142. Daniel J. Levinson et al., *The Seasons of Man's Life* (New York: Alfred A. Knopf, 1978), 221.

143. Fehrenbacher, *Prelude to Greatness,* 161.

144. Fehrenbacher, "The Death of Lincoln," in *Lincoln in Text and Context,* 165–67.

145. William E. Baringer, *Lincoln's Rise to Power* (Boston: Little, Brown, 1937), 5–6, 48, 69, 144, 147, 334.

146. Forgie, *Patricide in the House Divided.*

147. Gabor S. Boritt suggested this hypothesis.

148. Harold D. Lasswell, *Power and Personality* (New York: Norton, 1948), 38, 39. In a study of highly ambitious entrepreneurs, Orvis F. Collins and his colleagues found that many of their subjects had in childhood either lost a parent or suffered from other forms of emotional abandonment. Collins et al., *The Enterprising Man* (East Lansing: Michigan State University Press, 1964), 54–56.

149. Basler, *CWL,* 1:8.

150. Lasswell, *Power and Personality,* 50.

151. Scripps to William Herndon, Chicago, 24 June 1865, in Scripps, *Life of Lincoln,* 13.

152. "Autobiography Written for John L. Scripps" [ca. June 1860], in Basler, *CWL,* 4:61, 62.

153. "Brief Autobiography," [15?] June 1858, in Basler, *CWL,* 2:459.

154. Enclosure in Lincoln to Jesse W. Fell, Springfield, 20 Dec. 1859, in Basler, *CWL,* 3:511. Cf. Lincoln to Solomon Lincoln, Washington, 6 March 1848, 1:456. It might be objected that in his autobiographical sketches for Scripps and Fell, Lincoln exaggerated the poverty of his origins for political effect. But that would not explain why he gave Scripps the impression that he "seemed to be painfully impressed with the extreme poverty of his early surroundings—the utter absence of all romantic and heroic elements." Nor would it explain his poetry, which described the bleakness of his early years.

155. Tarbell, *In the Footsteps of the Lincolns*, 312.

156. John P. Gulliver in the New York *Independent*, 1 Sept. 1864, quoted in Holland, *Lincoln*, 213–15. This may have been Professor Larned, who lectured his rhetoric class about the virtues of Lincoln's address in Norwich. Reminiscences of Horace Bumstead, who was a Yale freshman at the time, *Congregationalist and Christian World*, 30 Jan. 1913, 168.

157. "My Childhood Home I See Again," [25 Feb.?] 1846, in Basler, *CWL*, 1:367–70.

158. Miner, "Personal Reminiscences of Abraham Lincoln."

159. Mark E. Neely, Jr., "Lincoln's Peculiar Relationship with Indiana," *Inland: The Magazine of the Middle West*, no. 1 (1980): 4–7.

160. Basler, *CWL*, 1:8–9, 320.

161. Hall to William E. Barton, Worcester, Mass., 3 Oct. 1922, in scrapbook marked "The Life of Lincoln, Vol. 2," Barton MSS, University of Chicago.

162. Writing to Mrs. Orville Browning about how Mary Owens had changed between the first time he saw her in 1836 and her return to Illinois after two years, Lincoln said, "I could not for my life avoid thinking of my mother; and this, not from withered features, for her skin was too full of fat, to permit its contracting to wrinkles; but from her want of teeth, [and] weather-beaten appearance in general." Lincoln to Mrs. Browning, Springfield, 1 April 1838, in Basler, *CWL*, 1:118.

163. Angle, *HL*, 29–30.

9

The Lincolns' Marriage:
"A Fountain of Misery, of
a Quality Absolutely Infernal"

Abraham Lincoln seems to have been one of those men who regard "connubial bliss" as an oxymoron. In 1864 he pardoned a soldier who had deserted to go home and marry his sweetheart. As he signed the necessary documents, he told an intercessor on behalf of the condemned, "I want to punish the young man—probably in less than a year he will wish I had withheld the pardon."[1] Much evidence suggests that Lincoln regretted his marriage as much as he expected the soldier to rue his.

The Lincolns' marriage baffled some of their contemporaries. H. M. Powel, a Springfield neighbor, recalled that "Mr. and Mrs. Lincoln were not a congenial couple; their tastes were so different that when a boy I often wondered why they were married."[2] Later scholars have done little to answer Powel's question. Fawn Brodie optimistically predicted in 1974 that a "sensitive study of the Lincoln marriage will not always defy biographers," but it has.[3]

Two schools of thought have dominated writing on the subject. The first is that of William H. Herndon, who claimed that "Lincoln's married life was a domestic hell on earth," a "burning, scorching hell," "as terrible as death and as gloomy as the grave," and who deemed Mary Lincoln a "she wolf," "a tigress," and "the female wildcat of the age."[4] Adherents of this school share Carl Schurz's belief that the marriage was "the greatest tragedy of Mr. Lincoln's existence."[5] The second school is that of Ruth Painter Randall, whose sympathetic *Mary Lincoln: Biography of a Marriage* depicts "an appealing love story," cites a "flock of witnesses close to the Lincolns [who] have left testimony as to the happiness of their marriage," and concludes that "the nation can well be proud of this American romance."[6] Recently there has emerged what John Y. Simon calls the "legend of Lincoln's happy marriage."[7]

Two questions have been particularly troublesome for biographers, What did Mary Todd and Abraham Lincoln see in one another, and why were they, as Richard N. Current so delicately put it, "blessed with far less than their fair share of domestic happiness"?[8]

• • •

In 1818 Mary Todd was born, the third of seven children, to Eliza Parker Todd and Robert Smith Todd in Lexington, Kentucky, where she remained until the age of twenty.[9] She then moved to Springfield, Illinois, to live with her eldest sister. Soon after her arrival, she met the law partner of her cousin John Todd Stuart, a young attorney named Abraham Lincoln. They became engaged after a brief courtship. He broke the engagement, but they were eventually reconciled and became man and wife in 1842.[10]

It is hard to understand what drew two such different people together in the first place. As Albert J. Beveridge noted, "Few couples have been more unsuited in temperament, manners, taste, and everything else."[11] T. G. Onstot thought Mary Todd "entirely different from Abe in every particular,"[12] and Herndon concluded that she was "the exact reverse" of her husband in "figure and physical proportions, in education, bearing, temperament, history—in everything."[13] Henry B. Rankin of Springfield remembered that "physically, mentally, [and] emotionally" Mary Todd "was the extreme opposite of Mr. Lincoln."[14] Mary Lincoln herself referred to "our opposite natures" when discussing her marriage.[15] Ruth Painter Randall acknowledged that Mary Todd and Abraham Lincoln "had come into the world endowed with qualities of personality and temperament singularly opposite. In family background and environment up to the time of their meeting there was violent contrast."[16]

The contrasts were violent indeed. Nearly ten years after Abraham Lincoln was born to an uneducated and illegitimate mother and an obscure and scarcely literate father on the hardscrabble Kentucky frontier, Eliza Parker Todd, whose distinguished ancestors were friends of George Washington, and Robert S. Todd, son of the famous General Levi Todd, became parents of their third child—a girl named Mary. The Todd family was part of a very different Kentucky: the pinnacle of well-bred society in Lexington, then known as "the Athens of America." While young Abraham struggled to supplement his meager formal schooling (which amounted to less than one year all told) by reading whatever books he could lay his hands upon in whatever moments he could carve out of days filled with tedious, uncongenial farm labor, Mary Todd attended Lexington's finest private schools, including Madame Victorie Charlotte Leclere Mentelle's academy, where French was spoken and students mastered such social graces as conversation, dancing, and letter writing. Shortly after Lincoln's elder sister died bearing a child to a rough frontiersman in Indiana, one of Mary Todd's elder sisters wed the well-connected son of the governor of Illinois. At the time when Lincoln left his parents to start a life of his own in the tiny village of New Salem as "a strange, friendless, uneducated, penniless boy" (to use his own self-description),[17] Mary Todd visited the stately mansion of Ashland to show off her new white pony to Henry Clay, her father's close friend and political ally.

For all the glaring differences between their childhoods, however, Abraham Lincoln and Mary Todd shared a profoundly important common experience: the early death of their mothers. Mary was six when a postbirth bacterial infection killed Eliza Parker Todd; Lincoln was nine when Nancy Hanks Lincoln succumbed to the milk sick. Both children sustained wounds that crippled them emotionally and contributed mightily to the difficulties they would later experience as man and wife.

Mary Todd recalled her seemingly pampered childhood as "desolate"[18] for understandable reasons that have to do not only with the actual death of her mother but also with the metaphorical death of her father. Immediately after her mother's death, Mary evidently received little paternal attention. Robert S. Todd "probably spent more time sympathizing with his older children, Elizabeth and Frances (who both favored their mother in looks), and arranging a wet nurse for baby George." A few weeks later, business drew him from Lexington to Frankfort. There he courted Elizabeth "Betsey" Humphreys, whom he married fourteen months after his wife's death. The newlyweds promptly started a brood of half-siblings for Mary (nine in fifteen years), much to her dismay, it seems. She got along poorly with her stepmother and apparently felt betrayed, abandoned, and rejected by her father. One scholar has concluded that Robert Todd did not "provide the persevering affection that might have overcome" Betsey Todd's hostility to Mary and her siblings.[19]

To the traumatic shocks of her mother's death and her father's remarriage can be traced the "uncontrollable rages"[20] that were, more than anything else, to undermine her marriage. Those rages reflected her "very violent temper,"[21] which the wife of an Illinois politician described as "really a species of madness."[22] Her cousin, Martinette Hardin, recalled that in Springfield she and her friends "didn't like" Mary Todd "very well" because "she had such a bad temper."[23] Abundant evidence corroborates what James H. Matheny, the best man at Lincoln's wedding, told Herndon: "Mrs. Lincoln often gave L[incoln] Hell in general—. . . *Ferocity*—describes Mrs. L[incoln]'s conduct to L[incoln]."[24] Peter Van Bergen told a friend that "he has heard Mrs. L[incoln] yelling & screaming at L[incoln] as if in hysterics."[25]

Another of the Lincolns' neighbors in Springfield, James Gourley, now and then overheard domestic discord from next door. He recalled that they "got along tolerably well, unless Mrs. L[incoln] got the devil in her." Gourley noted that she "was gifted with an unusually high temper" that "invariably got the better of her." If "she became excited or troublesome, as she sometimes did when Mr. Lincoln was at home, . . . he would apparently pay no attention to her. Frequently he would laugh at her, which is a risky thing to do in the face of an infuriated wife; but generally, if her impatience continued, he would pick up one of the children and deliberately leave home as if to take a walk. After he had gone, the storm usually subsided, but sometimes it would break out again when he returned."[26]

Herndon also recalled that many times Lincoln, after a domestic row, would take Robert and come to the office very early, sitting silently and "full of sadness." Knowing "that Lincoln was driven from home, by a club—knife or tongue," Herndon would leave his partner for a while to allow him to recover his spirits.[27] One morning a carpenter working at a restaurant saw Lincoln and young Robert enter the establishment. After they finished breakfast, Lincoln said, "Well, Robby, this ain't so very bad after all, is it? If ma don't conclude to let us come back we will board here all summer."[28]

Domestic turmoil would often follow dinner parties, according to Herndon, who thought the "suppers were very fine indeed." Mary Lincoln would invite members of the local aristocracy, whereas Lincoln would "choose a few of his boon companions to make things lively." He would lead the men into a corner, where they would swap stories until the party ended. Once the guests left, Herndon related, the hostess "would be as mad as a disturbed hornet" and "lecture L[incoln] all night, till he got up out of bed in despair and went whistling through the streets & alleys till day &c. &c. It would take a ream of paper to write it all out just as it did often happen."[29]

Another neighbor, Joseph P. Kent, also recalled how Lincoln would retreat to his office when his spouse went on a rampage. According to Kent, it "was never difficult to locate" Mary Lincoln. "It mattered not who was present when she fell into a rage, for nothing would restrain her. . . . Her voice was shrill and at times so penetrating, especially when summoning the children or railing at some one whose actions had awakened her temper, she could easily be heard over the neighborhood." When she erupted, Kent said, it was "little wonder that Mr. Lincoln would suddenly think of an engagement he had downtown, grasp his hat, and start for his office."[30] Lincoln had a couch six and a half feet long placed in his office so that he could sleep there "on nights of domestic discord."[31]

At such times he might also seek refuge in other lawyers' offices. An attorney visiting a colleague in Springfield one morning noticed a tall gentleman enter and quietly proceed to the back room. After lunch, the host observed his visitor munching cheese and crackers and said, "Why, Mr. Lincoln, I had forgotten your coming in here. I did n't remember that you were in the back room, or I would have asked you to go home to dinner with me. Folks away?" Lincoln "looked very serious. 'No, folks are not away, I'm away.'" Later the attorney explained that "this has happened before. Sometimes Mr. Lincoln's home is not very agreeable, though he has never been known to speak of it, but I know that he takes it very much to heart and that it breaks him up when anything occurs. He has his own office near here with a partner and clerks, but he has come in to find a quiet place. I supposed when he went in that he had come to consult some law book that I had in the other room, but he has probably sat silently there all this time."[32]

One Sunday Herndon heard Mrs. Lincoln's loud voice as she berated her husband on the streets of Springfield. When attending worship services, she regularly left the children in his care, and once, emerging from church to discover Lincoln sitting on a curbstone chatting with a friend, she screamed at him and chased him home.[33] On another day, while deep in thought, he failed to notice that his child had fallen out of the wagon he was pulling along. By chance Mary Lincoln came up the street at just that moment, saw what had happened, and said some sharp things to her preoccupied spouse, who retreated home before she had finished scolding him.[34]

Such incidents also took place inside the Lincolns' house. One day Lincoln stayed home to supervise a carpenter while Mrs. Lincoln ran errands, leaving Tad in his charge. Just as the carpenter summoned Lincoln outdoors to ask his advice, Mary Lincoln returned home to discover her son howling. As the carpenter recalled, she "had rather a hasty temper and at once she sought her husband and berated him soundly for letting the child sit on the floor and cry." He replied, "Why, Mary, he's just been there a minute" and picked up the lad and snuggled with him in a rocking chair.[35]

A young woman who lived for a time in the house recalled that Mrs. Lincoln "had an ungovernable temper."[36] A servant girl recounted the following example of that temper at work: One day in 1857 Lincoln had allowed the fire in the sitting room to die down, prompting Mrs. Lincoln to leave the kitchen and ask him to put more wood on the fire. Evidently abstracted, as he often was, he failed to hear her. She asked him again, to no avail. Losing all patience, she returned yet again to the sitting room, grabbed a stick of stovewood, and said, "Mr. Lincoln, I have told you now three times to mend the fire and you have pretended that you did not hear me. I'll make you hear me this time." Thereupon she assaulted him with the stick of wood. The next day he came to work with a plaster covering his injured nose.[37]

Jesse K. Dubois witnessed a similar scene one day when he visited Lincoln's office and discovered him heading home with some breakfast meat. Dubois walked with him to the house, where Mary Lincoln was entertaining "some aristocratic company" from Kentucky. After unwrapping the meat, she "became enraged at the Kind L[incoln] had bought" and, as Dubois recalled, "abused L[incoln] outrageously and finally was so mad she struck him in the face." He then wiped the blood from his face and, with Dubois, returned to the office.[38]

On many occasions Mary Lincoln chided her husband for his uncouth manners and appearance. "Why don't you dress up and try to look like somebody?" she would ask.[39] Their different attitudes toward clothing and appearances were manifested one day in 1862 when a formal reception was to be held at the White House. Mary Lincoln began to dress for the event five hours early, fussily rejecting one garment after the next because of some perceived defect. Finally she and her attendants completed her toilet with half an hour to spare. A few minutes later Lincoln, weary from his administrative chores, began to don formal dress, including a pair of white kid gloves. Having trouble, he asked the children's nurse, "Won't you button this old rat skin?"[40]

When he read in his stocking feet, Mary Lincoln would order a White House servant to bring his slippers. Extremely conscious of dress and fashion, she would "criticize his cuffs for being a trifle more frayed than was becoming to his position"[41] and complained that he did not doff his hat "decently." She charged the courtly Ward Hill Lamon with instructing Lincoln how to do so, but Lamon reported that despite his best efforts and even with the assistance of William Henry Seward, the president could not master that fine art.[42]

In April 1862, a dinner guest at the White House noted a cat on a chair next to the president, who used Executive Mansion cutlery to feed the pet. "Don't you think it is shameful for Mr. Lincoln to feed tabby with a gold fork?" Mary Lincoln asked. The president replied, "If the gold fork was good enough for Buchanan I think it is good enough for Tabby" and continued to feed the cat throughout the meal.[43] In Springfield "she raised 'merry war' because he persisted in using his own knife in the butter, instead of the silver-handled one intended for that purpose" and complained "if he answered the door-bell himself instead of sending the servant to do so."[44]

When a friend observed one of her scoldings, she gently said, "Mary[,] if I had a husband with a mind like yours [has,] I wouldn['] care what he did." Pleased "very much" by this compliment to her spouse, Mary Lincoln replied, "It is very foolish. It is a small thing to complain of."[45] Yet one evening Lincoln, in his shirtsleeves, answered a knock at the door and told the two callers that he would "trot the women folks out." Witnessing the scene from an adjoining room, Mrs. Lincoln waxed indignant and roundly chastised him. He left the house, to return late at night by the rear door.[46]

Sometimes he did not come home at all, according to Anna Eastman Johnson, a neighbor during the 1850s. Mrs. Johnson recalled that one evening Lincoln, carrying "a prodigious carpet-bag," dropped by and appealed to her father, "Mary is having one of her spells, and I think I had better leave her for a few days. I didn't want to bother her, and I thought as you and I are about the same size, you might be kind enough to let me take one of your clean shirts! I have found that when Mrs. Lincoln gets one of these nervous spells, it is better for me to go away for a day or two."[47] The postmaster of Springfield, Abner Yates Ellis, recalled a similar episode: One evening Lincoln tarried at the post office, swapping stories until eleven. When he finally said, "Well I hate to go home," Ellis invited him to spend the night at his house; Lincoln accepted.[48]

Mary Lincoln had trouble keeping servant girls, for she treated them tyrannically and paid them poorly.[49] In Springfield, she was known to "put on plenty [of] style" but at the same time was "stingy

& short in dealing with people."[50] A relative who lived at the Lincoln home recalled that Mrs. Lincoln "was very *economical*[.] So much so that *by some she* might have been pronounced stingy."[51] Herndon noted that "Mrs. Lincoln was stingy & exclusive . . . cold & repulsive to visitors that did not suit her cold aristocratic blood." The Lincoln house reminded Herndon of "an ice cave" with "no soul—fire—cheer or fun in it."[52] A journalist who observed Washington affairs during the Civil War noted that Mary Lincoln "brought shame upon the President's House, by petty economies, which had never disgraced it before."[53] On one occasion in 1861, she "beat down a poor widow" by paying her fourteen cents instead of twenty for cloth, "after much chaffing."[54] On another occasion she wanted to sell milk produced by the White House cows and haggled unbecomingly over the price. She also canceled state dinners, which presidents had traditionally given and paid for themselves.[55] She further haggled over the salary of the tutor hired to teach Willie and Tad.[56] A servant who lived in the Lincolns' home in Springfield called Mrs. Lincoln "cranky."[57]

Shortly after the 1856 presidential campaign, during which her husband had labored mightily on behalf of the antislavery Republican candidate John C. Frémont, Mary Lincoln told her sister in Kentucky that she had preferred the nativist former president Millard Fillmore because he "feels the *necessity* of keeping foreigners, within bounds. If some of you Kentuckians, had to deal with the 'wild Irish,' as we housekeepers are sometimes called upon to do, the south would certainly elect Mr[.] Fillmore next time[.]"[58] In a similar vein, she told friends after a quarrel with a servant girl, "If Mr. Lincoln should happen to die, his spirit will never find me living outside the boundaries of a slave State."[59]

In order to keep one servant, Lincoln begged, "Stay with her, Maria; stay with her," and supplemented her wages.[60] According to Mary Lincoln's sister Elizabeth, the episode caused a family row:

> One day the girl threatened to leave unless she could get $1.50 per week. Mrs. L. could [—] rather would [—] not give the extra 25 cents; the girl said she would leave. Mrs. L. said leave. Mr. L. heard the conversation—didn't want the girl to leave—told his wife so—asked—begged her to pay the $1.50. Mrs. L. remained incorrigible. Mr. L. slipped around to the back door and said, ["]Don't leave. Tell Mrs. Lincoln you have concluded to stay at $1.25 and I'll pay the odd 25 cents to you.["] Mrs. Lincoln overheard the conversation and said to the girl and Mr. L.: ["]What are you doing? I heard some conversa-

tion—couldn't understand it—I'm not going to be deceived. Miss[,]
you can leave[,] and as for you, Mr. L.[,] I'd be ashamed of myself."[61]

Lincoln himself employed Margaret Ryan, agreed to give her a seven-
ty-five-cent bonus, and told her not "to fuss with Mrs. L."[62]

A like incident took place when a youngster asked Lincoln to contribute to a fire department's fund drive. According to the boy, Lincoln
replied, "Well, I'll go home to supper and ask Mrs. Lincoln what she
has to say. After supper she will be in good humor, and I will ask her if
we shall give fifty dollars. She will say, 'Abe, when will you learn some
sense? Twenty dollars is enough.' Come around in the morning and get
your money." The strategy worked.[63]

One hot day in July 1859, Lincoln intervened again to ameliorate
his wife's tightfisted ways. John F. Mendosa and his father had picked
blackberries from four in the morning until nearly noon, managing to
collect but three pints. When he offered them to Mrs. Lincoln for fifteen
cents a pint, she "started to run them down because they were so small"
and refused to pay more than ten cents. Lincoln then appeared and gave
the lad a quarter for a pint and told his wife to take them into the house.
She, according to Mendosa, "did not like that and scolded Mr. Lincoln
for taking them. Mr. Lincoln spoke up and told me to tell father that
it was cheap enough, that he had earned every cent of it, and more
too."[64]

In the White House, Mary Lincoln continued to have trouble keeping servants. According to a knowledgeable journalist, she inveigled a
maid in the service of the British ambassador, Lord Lyons, to join the
presidential staff. The young woman, who had evidently believed that
"she would have nothing to do but exhibit herself," quit shortly after
being hired because Mary Lincoln "wounded her feelings" by order-
ing her to make underwear for the president from "the linen sheets of
the establishment."[65]

Mary Lincoln felt degraded when she herself had to do chores,
which she evidently considered beneath her dignity. While washing
dishes one day in the mid-1840s, she was heard to sigh, "What would
my poor father say if he found me doing this kind of work."[66] Fanny
Grimsley, who lived near the Lincolns in Springfield for several years,
recalled that in dealing with her servants, "Mrs. Lincoln was hot tempered." She remembered that once she grew angry at a servant boy,
Philip Dingley, and "told him to get out, and threw his suit case out

the window after him." Another time she hired a servant woman to help the two she already had in service, "but fired them all the next day."⁶⁷

To be let go abruptly or unceremoniously was not the worst treatment that servants endured at the Lincoln house. According to a serving girl, she "often struck other girls,"⁶⁸ one of whom promptly quit and fled home in tears to her uncle, a miller named Jacob Taggart, who called on Mrs. Lincoln for an explanation. After she gave him a tongue-lashing and struck him in the face with a broom, he went to demand satisfaction of Lincoln, who was found "telling yarns" at Lavely's grocery store. With a mournful look, Lincoln calmly replied to Taggart, "*Friend,* . . . can't you endure this one wrong done to you. . . . without much complaint for old freindship's sake while I have had to bear it without complaint and without a murmur for lo these last fifteen years[?]"⁶⁹

Mary Lincoln also took the broom to her husband, according to Hillary Gobin, a neighbor of the Lincolns' in the 1850s. Mrs. Gobin recalled her mother saying that Mary and Abraham Lincoln "were very unhappy in their domestic life, and she was seen frequently to drive him from the house with a broomstick."⁷⁰ As a young girl, Lizzie DeCrastos visited the Lincoln home with her mother and observed Lincoln flee out the door as his angry wife attacked him with "very poorly pitched potatoes."⁷¹ A servant girl recalled that one day as Lincoln prepared to leave for Taylorville, "His wife ran him out [of the house] half dressed—as she followed him with [a] broom." Lincoln told the servant "not to get scared" but to go into the house and fetch him some clothes, which he donned and then "went up town through [the] woodhouse & alley."⁷² In a boardinghouse soon after the Lincolns' wedding, Mrs. Jacob M. Early helped clean Lincoln up after his bride, in a rage, had flung hot coffee in his face.⁷³ Jean Baker reports that Mary Lincoln sometimes threw books at her husband.⁷⁴ These episodes tend to confirm the judgment of Turner R. King, who deemed Mary Lincoln "a hellion—a she devil," who "vexed & harassed the soul out of that poor man" and "drove him from home . . . often and often."⁷⁵

Mary Lincoln treated merchants and tradesmen as she did servants. The family druggist, J. R. Diller, called her "very hard to deal with."⁷⁶ She would, for example, buy perfume, then return the bottles with the seals broken, explaining that the "contents were inferior or otherwise not as represented, and thus preventing their sale to others." In response, Diller refused to sell her more perfume.[77] Similarly, when she lost her temper at the iceman and accused him of cheating, that gentleman stopped calling at the Lincoln house.[78]

As the wife of the president, she continued to exasperate tradespeople. One day in New York, while sitting in her carriage, she imperiously summoned a clerk who was speaking with a friend at the front door of Genin's store. The clerk ignored her. When informed that Mrs. Lincoln was beckoning, he "replied somewhat indifferently, that he did not care." He explained, "I don't know any difference between Mrs. Lincoln and the wife of a mechanic. If she will come into the store, I will attend to her, but I am not employed to wait on people in the street."[79]

It is no wonder that, as David Davis put it in 1860, "The people of Springfield do not love Lincoln's wife, as they do him." Davis himself shared what he deemed the prevailing view: "I must say that Mrs. Lincoln is not to my liking. I don[']t think she would ever mesmerize anyone."[80] A minister corroborated Davis's view, telling a friend in late May 1860 that although Lincoln was admired in the Illinois capital as a "man of uncorrupted if not incorruptible integrity," he could not "speak as highly of his wife, as of Lincoln. On hearing of his nomination I gave my opinion that she ought to be sent to the cooper's and well secured against bursting by iron hoops. Her course since has not changed my mind."[81]

Usually Lincoln submitted to uxorial tirades stoically, believing that "it is better at times to let a woman have her way."[82] When friends teased him about his failure to stand up to his bossy wife, he replied, "If you knew how little harm it does me and how much good it does her, you wouldn't wonder that I am meek."[83] On election night in 1860, Mary Lincoln ordered the Republican presidential candidate to return home early or else she would lock him out. He simply took an extra key and let himself into the house. The next day, he revealed to callers that his wife had locked him out, prompting the first-lady-to-be to say, "Shut your mouth[,] never tell that again."[84] A woman who accompanied the Lincolns on a trip to Cincinnati recalled that at one point, Mary Lincoln "was almost hysterical about the baggage and fairly forced Mr. Lincoln to walk back three-quarters of a mile to Lafayette Junction to see that it was safe—which he did uncomplainingly."[85]

Not surprisingly people who knew the Lincolns in Springfield, like Herndon and Milton Hay, called the future president "woman whipt," "woman cowed," and *"hen pecked."*[86] Some compared the Lincoln marriage to that of Socrates and Xanthippe.[87] Hay, who noted that Mary Lincoln "had a very extreme temper and made things at home more or less disagreeable,"[88] pitied his neighbor: "Poor man! I think *some* woman ought to talk kindly to him, and I suppose he has got to go from home to hear it."[89] According to a servant, when Lincoln returned home at night from work, he first would enter the kitchen and ask whether Mrs. Lincoln was in a good mood before he entered the house through the front door.[90] Although he normally avoided or ignored his wife when she was in a rage, "sometimes he would rise and cut up the very devil for a while—make thing[s] more lively and 'get,'" as Herndon put it.[91] One Sunday morning, Lincoln, his enormous reservoir of patience evidently dry, wheeled on his wife and said, "You make the house intolerable, damn you, get out of it!"[92]

The Lincolns occasionally quarreled about his relatives. In 1851, Lincoln told his stepbrother John D. Johnston that Johnston's adolescent son Abraham was welcome to stay at his house in Springfield: "I understand he wants to live with me so that he can go to school, and get a fair start in the world, which I very much wish him to have." He promised that "when I reach home, if I can make it convenient to take him, I will take him."[93] At home, however, Mary Lincoln demurred. According to Abraham Johnston's brother, she "refused furiously" and "caused hard feelings." Thus what Lincoln "had proposed could not be filled on his part on account of domestic difficulty."[94] When in the mid-1840s Dennis Hanks's daughter Harriet lived with the Lincolns in Springfield, "Mrs. Lincoln tried to make a servant—a slave of her," and "this created a fight[,] a fuss[,] between Lincoln and his wife," Herndon recalled.[95]

A neighbor claimed that Mary Lincoln also "was quite disposed to make a servant girl of her husband." She allegedly compelled him "to get up and get the breakfast and then dress the children, after which she would join the family at the table, or lie abed an hour or two longer as she might choose." In either case, "it was a usual part of her husband's duties to wash the dishes before going to his office."[96] Another neighbor told an interviewer that Mary Lincoln made her husband "take care of the baby," whom "he rolled . . . up and down in [the] baby carriage."[97] Evidently, Lincoln sometimes resented the way she foisted child-rearing duties on him. One day when baby Robert was crying loudly, his father picked him up and walked him about the room of the boardinghouse where they were staying. Mary sat by, "silently weeping." The proprietress of the establishment assured the worried parents that the child merely had colic and was not about to die. "Does it do any good to pack him round this way?" he asked. When told, "None whatever," Lincoln, "glancing . . . at his wife . . . in a manner as though he expected her to protest," said, "If it don't do him any good, I'm damned if I don't put him down."[98] According to Thomas Dowling, Dennis Hanks's son-in-law, "Mrs. Lincoln loved the dance, and often left her husband to take care of the children while she enjoyed the pleasures of the ballroom."[99] Lincoln himself was "never given to dancing," and although he would accompany his wife to a ball, he would usually spend the evening in the cloakroom telling stories.[100]

Henry B. Rankin, who admired Mary Lincoln and maintained that she and her husband enjoyed a happy marriage, noted that she "could tolerate no delay without manifesting her displeasure and if possible enforcing her calls for him at meal-times." One day in the White House toward the end of the war, Rankin reported, the president was so deeply involved in pressing business with a high official of the Treasury Department that he ignored the butler's announcement that dinner was ready. He likewise paid no heed to subsequent entreaties from his son Tad. At last Mary Lincoln herself appeared "and in her emphatic tones of command, so characteristic of her when she was displeased" ordered Lincoln to join her. He rose, calmly went to his wife, gently but firmly guided her from the room, closed and locked the door, and resumed his business.[101] Charles A. Dana told a similar story about Lincoln's refusal to heed his wife's urgent summonses. Not long after the first inauguration, he sat conferring with a New York delegation when a messenger intruded to announce, "She wants you." Lincoln did not stir but simply said, "Yes, yes." Soon the message was repeated, to the president's evident annoyance, but he kept right on consulting with the New Yorkers.[102]

These stories lend credence to Donn Piatt's observation that Mrs. Lincoln "was treated by her husband with about the same good-natured indifference with which he regarded the troublesome boys." During the winter of 1860–61, Piatt recalled, Mary Lincoln acidly remarked, "The country will find how we regard that abolition sneak, Seward!" In response, her husband "put the remarks aside, very much as he did the hand of one of his boys when that hand invaded his capacious mouth."[103]

Most evidence about Mary Lincoln's nagging is secondhand, but a revealing story appears in Lincoln's 1857 correspondence. He had subscribed to a newly founded Republican newspaper, and when the first issue arrived at their home, she said, according to Lincoln, "Now are you going to take another worthless little paper?" Instead of defending his right to subscribe to any periodical he saw fit, he replied *"evasively"* (to use his own term), "I have not directed the paper to be left." She then canceled the subscription.[104]

Mary Lincoln did not mellow with age; she continued to berate her husband in the White House. On February 22, 1864, while attending a Patent Office fair to benefit the Christian Commission, Lincoln was caught off guard by the crowd's insistence that he make a speech. According to his friend Richard J. Oglesby, who had prevailed upon him to attend the meeting only by promising that he would not have to speak, Lincoln reluctantly acceded to the crowd's importunings and delivered a few remarks.[105] Afterward, while the Lincolns and Oglesby awaited their carriage, Mary Lincoln allegedly said to her husband, "That was the worst speech I ever listened to in my life. How any man could get up and deliver such remarks to an audience is more than I can understand. I wanted the earth to sink and let me go through." The president did not reply; in fact, during the ride home, no further words were spoken by Oglesby or the Lincolns.[106]

At times Mary Lincoln would, in effect, blackmail her husband by behaving like a spoiled child. One day in the White House, the painter Francis B. Carpenter, lying down in the guest quarters adjacent to the master bedroom, heard the following conversation:

"No, Mr. Lincoln, you *shan't* have them!"

"Now, Ma, you know I *must* have them!"

"Not at all, Mr. Lincoln! You *can't* have them: not until you promise me." Carpenter could not make out what she was demanding.

"But wife, you know right well that I need to. . . ."

"Need to be taught a lesson—yes, Sir! Promise me what I asked you, or I won't leave go of them."

Lincoln then said in "tired tones of a patient weariness: 'Ma,—come now! be reasonable. Look at the clock. I'm already late; let me have them—*please!'*"

"Never, Mr. Lincoln!—not till you promise me first. . . ." Again Carpenter could not discern her demand.

Finally, he pleaded, "Laws, Ma! How do you reckon I can go to a Cabinet meeting—without my pants!"[107]

She reportedly forced her husband to appoint William S. Wood to the post of commissioner of public buildings by locking herself in her room until he yielded.[108]

In February 1861, she threw a temper tantrum, insisting on the appointment of Isaac Henderson, publisher of the New York *Evening Post,* as naval agent in the New York Customs House. He was backed by William Cullen Bryant and Parke Godwin. An unsavory self-made man, Henderson evidently had sent Mary Lincoln diamonds as a bribe. Her hysterics delayed Lincoln, who was late for an appointment with Herman Kreismann. Curious about the president-elect's tardiness, Kreismann called at the hotel where the Lincolns were staying. There he found Mrs. Lincoln in the throes of a fit. Lincoln said, "Kreismann, she will not let me go until I promise her an office for one of her friends." As usual, he yielded to her and nominated Henderson as navy agent.[109]

Later that month, en route to Washington, she threw another tantrum in Harrisburg, Pennsylvania, where the president-elect learned that assassins might attempt his life in Baltimore. Hurried changes were made in Lincoln's route and schedule; lest spies discover this, the strictest secrecy was enjoined on all who knew about it. One of those who planned the revisions, Alexander K. McClure, later described how Mary Lincoln failed to cooperate:

> To our utter surprise Mrs. Lincoln became very unmanageable. She suspected that some movement was going on and insisted that if Mr. Lincoln's route was changed she must accompany him, and spoke publicly about it in disregard of the earnest appeals to her for silence. Prompt action was required in such an emergency, and several of us simply hustled her into her room with Colonel [E. V.] Sumner and Norman Judd, chairman of the Lincoln campaign in Illinois[,] and locked the door on the outside. The men with her explained what was to be done and forced her to silence as she could not get out of the door.

McClure "thought Mrs. Lincoln was simply a helpless fool and was so disgusted with her conduct that evening" that he "never spoke to her afterwards."[110]

Once in Washington, Mary Lincoln became something of an influence peddler, expediting the cases of importunate office-seekers and accepting such gifts as a black barouche and horses to draw it.[111] In 1867, Elizabeth Keckley "said that politicians used to besiege Mrs. Lincoln, and that presents would be sent to her from people whom she had never seen." The donors would attend White House receptions and declare, "*Mrs. President* Lincoln, I hope you admired that set of furs I sent you lately."

She would reply, "Oh, was it you sent them; really I am at a loss to thank you for your kindness."

"Not at all, madam, it was but a slight and worthless token of the deep esteem I have for the talents of one whose intrinsic merit would, irrespective of your present exalted station, make you an ornament in the highest circles of the most civilized society."

Pleased with such "fulsome flattery," Mary Lincoln found it "difficult to refuse" when the gentleman then asked a favor. After a few months of this, the president "shut down on it" (to use his own words) and "many scenes" occurred "when his wife was goaded on to ask for places by office-seekers."[112]

She scrutinized her gifts closely. When John A. Logan presented her with a ring he claimed "had cost him several hundred dollars," she sent it to a New York jeweler, who estimated its value at $18. She returned the bauble.[113]

In 1867, assuming "an attitude of threat very strongly savoring of extortion," Mary Lincoln publicly demanded that men appointed to high office by her husband aid her financially.[114] She agreed to write letters to be shown to political figures who had benefited from her husband's patronage. If those gentlemen did not then offer assistance, her brokers—S. C. Keyes and William Brady—would threaten to expose them by publishing the letters.[115] Evidently, one of her targets was Simeon Draper, who, according to David Davis, had given Mary Lincoln $20,000 to help him become the collector of the Port of New York.[116] One newspaper denounced her as "a termagant with arms akimbo, shaking her clenched fist at the country, and forgetful of her dead husband and all manner of propriety, demanding gold as the price of silence and pay that is her due because she was the wife of a President." The editor could not "imagine a more shocking exhibition, or one more calculated to put the country to the blush in her behalf."[117] Another paper found her acts consistent with earlier behavior: "Her conduct throughout the administration of her husband was mortifying to all who respected him. . . . The gaudy bad taste with which she dressed, and the constant effort to make a show of herself disgusted all observers. She was always trying to meddle in public affairs, and now she will have it known to the whole world that she accepted costly presents from corrupt contractors."[118]

She was outspoken regarding appointments at the highest level.[119] When Norman B. Judd was being considered for a cabinet post, she protested that "his business transactions, have not always borne inspection."[120] She opposed Jesse K. Dubois's aspirations for office because of her "contempt for his manners.[121] In early 1861, the president-elect asked George B. Lincoln his opinion of Edward Bates as a cabinet member. The guest replied positively and added that Seward should also be named to a cabinet post. At that point, Mrs. Lincoln interrupted: "Never! Never! Seward in the Cabinet! Never. If all things should go on all right—the credit would go to Seward—if they went wrong—the blame would fall upon my husband. Seward in the Cabinet! Never!"[122] When she later told her husband "Seward is worse than Chase," he replied, "Mother, you are mistaken; your prejudices are so violent that you do not stop to reason. Seward is an able man, and the country as well as myself can trust him." She shot back: "Father, you are too honest for this world! You should have been born a saint. You will generally find it a safe rule to distrust a disappointed, ambitious politician. It makes me mad to see you sit still and let that hypocrite, Seward, twine you around his finger as if you were a skein of thread." The discussion ended when the chief executive said bluntly, "It is useless to argue the question, mother. You cannot change my opinion."[123]

She declined to make an appearance when Seward, accompanied by his wife and children, called at the White House in September 1861. They waited some time before the usher announced that "Mrs. Lincoln begged to be excused, she was *very* much engaged." Seward's daughter Frances believed that this was "the only time on record that she ever refused to see company in the evening" and that Mrs. Lincoln lied about being engaged simply because "she did not want to see Mother."[124]

According to Senator Charles Sumner, Mary Lincoln meddled in nearly all patronage affairs early in her husband's administration.[125] Another learned Massachusetts politician, George Bancroft, heard that she "wished a rogue who had cheated the government made a lieutenant: the cabinet thrice put the subject aside. One morning in came Lincoln sad and sorrowful: 'Ah,' said he, 'to-day we must settle the case of Lieutenant ——. Mrs. Lincoln has for three nights slept in a separate apartment.'"[126] It was reported that she lobbied on behalf of Caleb Lyon, a candidate for a territorial governorship, because "he had published one or two fulsome puffs of Mrs. Lincoln in the newspapers."[127]

Jean Baker maintains that by fighting "to make herself her husband's chief adviser on patronage and appointments" she "meant to contribute to her husband's endeavors . . . the special intuition with which females—and none more than she—were endowed. . . . In her imaginative projection of their life together she had become his collaborator—a full-fledged, home-based counselor available for insightful judgments about the human motivations that were the core of politics."[128] She once boasted, "My husband placed great confidence in my knowledge of human nature. He had not much knowledge of men."[129]

There is little reason to believe that Lincoln seriously listened to her advice about important appointments. To be sure, he might have John Watt named a lieutenant, or William S. Wood commissioner of public buildings, or Isaac Henderson naval officer in the New York Custom House. As Herndon put it, he "had to do things which he knew were out of place in order to keep his wife's fingers out of his hair."[130] But her voice counted for little in significant cases. According to one of her best friends and closest confidantes, the modiste and former slave Elizabeth Keckley, Lincoln told her, "Mother, you are too suspicious. I give you credit for sagacity, but you are disposed to magnify trifles." On another occasion, he said, "If I listened to you, I should soon be without a Cabinet." When she criticized military leaders, Lincoln replied ironically, "Well, mother, supposing that we give you command of the army. No doubt you would do much better than any general that has been tried."[131] She recalled that her husband would, when she discussed "Chase and those others who did him evil," say, "Do good to those who hate you and turn their ill will to friendship."[132]

Like the president, Secretary of War Edwin Stanton also told Mary Lincoln to stop meddling in patronage matters. She lobbied to have a "half loafer, half gentleman" named a commissary, arguing that "I thought that as [the] wife of the President I was entitled to ask for so small a favor." Bluntly Stanton replied, "If I should make such appointments, I should strike at the very root of all confidence of the people in the government, in your husband, and you and me."[133]

She had been offering political advice well before 1861. When her husband was a member of Congress, his friend David Davis ran for a judgeship coveted by Benjamin S. Edwards, brother-in-law to her sister Elizabeth. In this contest, Lincoln remained neutral, evidently because of pressure from his wife. According to Davis's statement many years later, "Lincoln hadn't the manhood to come out for me in preference to Ben Edwards whom he despised. . . . because Ben was in the family."[134]

Just as she was protective of her husband's reputation, Mary Lincoln was "extremely jealous," according to Mrs. Keckley, whose memoirs note that "if a lady desired to court her displeasure, she could select no surer way to do it than to pay marked attention to the President. These little jealous freaks often were a source of perplexity to Mr. Lincoln."[135] Mrs. Keckley remembered that one evening, as the Lincolns were dressing for a reception, the president said, "Well, mother, who must I talk with to-night—shall it be Mrs. D.?"

"That deceitful woman! No, you shall not listen to her flattery."

"Well, then, what do you say to Miss C.? She is too young and handsome to practise deceit."

"Young and handsome, you call her! You should not judge beauty for me. No, she is in league with Mrs. D., and you shall not talk with her."

"Well, mother, I must talk with some one. Is there any one that you do not object to?"

"I don't know as it is necessary that you should talk to anybody in particular. You know well enough, Mr. Lincoln, that I do not approve of your flirtations with silly women, just as if you were a beardless boy, fresh from school."

"But, mother, I insist that I must talk with somebody. I can't stand around like a simpleton, and say nothing. If you will not tell me who I may talk with, please tell me who I may *not* talk with."

"There is Mrs. D. and Miss C. in particular. I detest them both. Mrs. B. also will come around you, but you need not listen to her flattery. These are the ones in particular."

"Very well, mother; now that we have settled the question to your satisfaction, we will go down-stairs."[136]

Miss C. was evidently the beautiful Kate Chase, of whom Mary Lincoln was especially jealous.[137] In January 1864, this belle, along with her father, Salmon P. Chase, and her husband, William Sprague, were excluded from the invitation list for a cabinet dinner at Mrs. Lincoln's insistence. When John G. Nicolay informed the president of this, he overruled his wife, and, as Nicolay reported, "There soon arose such a rampage as the House hasn't seen for a year." In response to Mary Lincoln's rage, White House secretary William O. Stoddard "fairly cowered at the volume of the storm," and Nicolay found himself buffeted by it; as he told his fiancée, "after having compelled Her S[atanic] Majesty to invite the Spragues I was taboo, and she made up her mind resolutely not to have me at the dinner."[138]

Mary Lincoln refused to attend Kate Chase's wedding and wanted her husband to boycott that occasion, the social event of the season. According to a woman who was in Washington at the time, the

Lincolns argued about the matter, "and the music of her voice penetrated the utmost end of the house." Lincoln broke away, donned formal attire, and then tried to calm his infuriated wife. In no mood for reconciliation, she "made a dash at his cravat, and captured a part of his whiskers." He then retreated from the White House. Upon his return, she locked him out of the bedroom.[139]

At White House receptions, traditionally the president would choose a woman to lead the promenade with him. "This custom is an absurd one," Mary Lincoln told Mrs. Keckley. "On such occasions our guests recognize the position of the President as first of all; consequently, he takes the lead in everything; well, now, if they recognize his position they should also recognize mine. I am his wife, and should lead with him. And yet he offers his arm to any other lady in the room, making her first with him and placing me second. The custom is an absurd one, and I mean to abolish it. The dignity I owe to my position, as Mrs. President, demands that I should not hesitate any longer to act."[140]

She expressed keen jealousy of generals' wives during visits that she and her husband made to the Army of the Potomac. In 1863, the president, while at the headquarters of the Third Corps, was besieged by many officers' spouses, including the beautiful Princess Salm-Salm, who wanted to kiss him. After clearing their proposal with General Daniel Sickles, the women carried out their friendly assault. The next day, when informed of this bit of levity, Mary Lincoln grew furious. "But, mother, hear me," Lincoln pleaded. "Don't mother me," was the indignant rejoinder, "and as for General Sickles, he will hear what I think of him and his lady guests. It was well for him that I was not there at the time." She treated Sickles frostily until Lincoln solved the matter with one of his more ingenious puns: "Sickles, I never knew you were such a pious man . . . they tell me you are more than a psalmist—they tell me you are a Salm-Salmist."[141]

Mary Lincoln flew into a rage at a female supplicant from Connecticut who lobbied the president late one night about a claim. The tall, attractive woman had fallen to her knees, grabbed Lincoln around his legs, and was pleading her case, when, as he told the story, Mrs. Lincoln entered and "jumped at conclusions. 'Out of the room, you baggage,' she cried, and going into the hall she shouted to Edward, one of the household servants, 'Put this woman out and never admit her again.'" The president conveyed a message to U.S. Representative Henry C. Deming of Hartford: "Send that long-legged woman back to Connecticut and keep her there."[142] Similarly, when he tried to help a poor Irish widow obtain a pension in July 1861, he reportedly told friends, "Mrs. Lincoln is getting a little jealous."[143]

Her intense jealousy and insistence that she alone escort the president led Mary Lincoln to humiliate her husband publicly less than three weeks before his death.[144] In the early spring of 1865, the Lincolns visited General Grant's headquarters at City Point, Virginia. On March 26, Mrs. Lincoln and Julia Dent Grant took an excursion to the front, along with Grant's aide Adam Badeau. That officer, to make conversation on the long carriage ride, speculated that a battle would soon occur, for officers' wives at the front had been ordered to the rear. The only exception in the Army of the Potomac had been Mrs. Charles Griffin, to whom the president had issued a special permit. Mrs. Lincoln bristled at the news: "What do you mean by that, sir? . . . Do you mean to say that she saw the President alone? Do you know that I never allow the President to see any woman alone?"

Mrs. Grant tried in vain to come to Badeau's assistance. Mary Lincoln asked Badeau to order the driver to stop the carriage, and when Badeau hesitated, she thrust her arms past him and seized the driver. Mrs. Grant finally convinced her to wait until they had reached their destination. There General George Gordon Meade, unaware of the trouble, relieved Badeau of his escort duty. When the ladies returned to the carriage, Mrs. Lincoln looked at Badeau "significantly" and said, "General Meade is a gentleman, sir. He says it was not the President who gave Mrs. Griffin the permit, but the Secretary of War."

The next day a similar scene occurred as the same party visited the command of General E. O. C. Ord, whose wife, like Mrs. Griffin, had been exempted from the requirement that all officers' wives leave the front. She was on horseback and rode beside the president for a while, thus going ahead of Mary Lincoln's carriage. Badeau recalled that as "soon as Mrs. Lincoln discovered this her rage was beyond all bounds. 'What does the woman mean,' she exclaimed, 'by riding by the side of the President? and ahead of me? Does she suppose that *he* wants *her* by the side of *him?*' She was in a frenzy of excitement, and language and action both became more extravagant every moment."

She grew angry when Mrs. Grant once again tried to calm her and said, "I suppose you think you'll get to the White House yourself, don't you?" Mrs. Grant replied evenly that she was quite content as she was, to which Mrs. Lincoln responded, "Oh! you had better take it if you can get it. 'Tis very nice."

At this sensitive moment an officer rode up and said, "The President's horse is very gallant, Mrs. Lincoln; he insists on riding by the side of Mrs. Ord."

"'What do you mean by that, sir?' she cried."

The embarrassed officer slunk off. When the carriage arrived at General Ord's headquarters, Mrs. Ord rode up. As Badeau remembered it, Mary Lincoln "positively insulted her, called her vile names in the presence of a crowd of officers, and asked what she meant by following up the President. The poor woman burst into tears and inquired what she had done, but Mrs. Lincoln refused to be appeased, and stormed till she was tired. Mrs. Grant still tried to stand by her friend, and everybody was shocked and horrified." That night at dinner the Lincolns entertained the Grants, and during the meal "Mrs. Lincoln berated General Ord to the President, and urged that he should be removed. He was unfit for his place, she said, to say nothing of his wife."

After dinner, at about eleven o'clock, she had the president summon John S. Barnes, a naval officer who had witnessed the day's fireworks. Barnes, who was already abed, got up, dressed hurriedly, and reported to the president, who, he recalled, "seemed weary and greatly distressed, with an expression of sadness that seemed the accentuation of the shadow of melancholy which at times so marked his features." Most of the talking was done by Mary Lincoln, "who had objected very strenuously to the presence of other ladies at the review that day, and had thought that Mrs. Ord had been too prominent in it, that the troops were led to think that she was the wife of the President, who had distinguished her with too much attention." The president "very gently suggested that he had hardly remarked the presence of the lady, but Mrs. Lincoln was hardly to be pacified and appealed to me to support her views." The embarrassed Barnes could not, of course, referee this dispute and did his best to stay neutral, merely stating what he had observed without drawing conclusions.[145]

According to Badeau, Mrs. Lincoln continued her vendetta throughout her week's stay at City Point. She "repeatedly attacked her husband in the presence of officers because of Mrs. Griffin and Mrs. Ord." Badeau later said, "I never suffered greater humiliation and pain . . . than when I saw the Head of State, the man who carried all the cares of the nation at such a crisis—subjected to this inexpressible public mortification." Lincoln, Badeau recalled, "bore it as Christ might have done; with an expression of pain and sadness that cut one to the heart, but with supreme calmness and dignity." With "old-time plainness" he called his wife "mother." He also "pleaded with eyes and tones, and endeavored to explain or palliate the offenses of others, till she turned on him like a tigress; and then he walked away, hiding that noble, ugly face that we might not catch the full expression of its misery."[146]

Thomas Stackpole, a White House steward, told Ward Hill Lamon that on the boat trip home from Richmond, Mrs. Lincoln struck her husband in the face, damned him, and cursed him.[147] At a dinner party on the boat, Elizabeth Keckley observed an unpleasant outburst. A young captain, "by way of pleasantry," said, "Mrs. Lincoln, you should have seen the President the other day, on his triumphal entry into Richmond. He was the cynosure of all eyes. The ladies kissed their hands to him, and greeted him with the waving of handkerchiefs. He is quite a hero when surrounded by pretty young ladies." As Mrs. Keckley recalled, the officer "suddenly paused with a look of embarrassment. Mrs. Lincoln turned to him with flashing eyes, with the remark that his familiarity was offensive to her. Quite a scene followed."[148] Mary Harlan, who was aboard the *River Queen,* similarly observed a young officer tell how, when the president passed through Richmond, all doors were closed to him save one, which "was opened furtively and a fair hand extended a bunch of flowers, which he took." Mrs. Lincoln "made manifest her dislike of the story, much to the narrator's chagrin."[149]

Back in Washington, Mary Lincoln continued seething with jealousy and resentment. On April 13, she asked General Grant to escort her to view the illuminated capital buildings.[150] At the urging of the president, he accepted, and as the two entered their coach, the huge crowd gathered at the White House lustily cried out "Grant" nine times, "whereupon Mrs. L[incoln] was disturbed, and directed the driver to let her out." But when the crowd then cheered for Lincoln, she gave orders to proceed. This "was repeated at different stages of the drive" whenever the crowd learned the identity of the coach's occupants. Evidently Mary Lincoln found it unsettling that Grant should be cheered first. The following day the general, when invited by the president to attend *Our American Cousin* at Ford's Theater, declined lest he endure Mary Lincoln's displeasure yet again.[151]

Little evidence suggests that Mary Lincoln had good reason for jealousy. To be sure, her husband did admire the beautiful young actresses and singers at Ford's Theatre. In the summer of 1864, while Mrs. Lincoln was out of town, John Hay and the president attended a concert at Ford's; to a friend, the young secretary confided that both he and his boss "carried on a hefty flirtation with the Monk girls in the flies."[152] Schuyler Colfax recalled that he and Lincoln "often went to Ford's opera house to regale ourselves of an evening, for we felt the strain on mind and body was often intolerable." They found "real relaxation" in watching "those southern girls with their well rounded forms, lustrous hair and sparkling voices. We thought it a veritable treat to see them dance and hear their song."[153]

It is not known how often Mary Lincoln fell into a rage and attacked her husband, but Mrs. Keckley stated that when "in one of her wayward impulsive moods, she was apt to say and do things that wounded him deeply," and she "often wounded him in unguarded moments."[154] She herself owned after her husband's death that, during their courtship, "I doubtless trespassed, many times & oft, upon his great tenderness & amiability of character."[155] These words, as Ruth Painter Randall observed, "could well be applied to the whole of their married life."[156]

The origins of Mary Lincoln's rage and volatility puzzled observers. A White House secretary found it difficult "to understand why a lady who could be one day so kindly, so considerate, so generous, so thoughtful and so hopeful, could, upon another day, appear so unreasonable, so irritable, so despondent, so even niggardly, and so prone to see the dark, the wrong side of men and women and events."[157]

Elizabeth L. Norris recalled that the young Mary Todd often indulged in sarcastic witticisms "that cut like a Damascus blade" and "was impulsive & made no attempt to conceal her feelings, indeed it would have been an impossibility had she desired to do so for her face was an index to every passing emotion." Norris described how Mary fought with a young, somewhat dictatorial tutor: "There was nothing but discord between them," although the other girls he taught managed to get along with him.[158]

Mary Lincoln's jealousy may have been rooted, at least partially, in her own flirtatiousness, which she unconsciously projected onto her husband.[159] In June 1861, the president received an anonymous letter about "the scandal of your wife and [William S.] Wood," the commissioner of public buildings, a New Yorker who spent time with Mrs. Lincoln, even taking trips with her to Manhattan. "If he continues as commissioner, he will stab you in your most vital part," the unknown correspondent warned.[160] The president evidently spoke sharply to his wife about the matter. Schuyler Colfax later recalled "the war she had with Mr. Lincoln" about her relations with Wood. According to Col-

fax, the Lincolns "scarcely spoke together for several days."[161] An Io-
wan, evidently referring to Wood, claimed that Mary Lincoln "used to
often go from the White House to the Astor House in New York to
pass the night with a man who held a high government office in Washington, given to him by her husband."[162] Wood had supervised arrangements for their train trip from Springfield to Washington in February
1861. The following month Wood presented her a gift of fine horses.[163]
One observer noted that his "attentions were devoted exclusively to
the whims and caprices of Mrs. Lincoln," who returned the favor by
insisting that he be named commissioner of public buildings.[164] David
Davis, who found the appointment "incomprehensible," was told by
the president that "it would be ruinous to appoint him—*ruinous to
him.*"[165] Wood later resigned under fire.

Other sources suggest that Mary Lincoln may have been unfaith-
ful. The White House gardener, John Watt, told a journalist in 1867
that "Mrs. Lincoln's relations with certain men were indecently improp-
er."[166] Edward McManus, doorkeeper at the White House, evidently
made a similar allegation.[167] Oswald Garrison Villard claimed that
Robert Todd Lincoln "systematically bought up any books that reflected [poorly] on Mrs. Lincoln," including one by "the Hungarian adventurer who very nearly succeeded in eloping with Mrs. Lincoln from the
White House."[168] In a letter to her confidant Abram Wakeman, Mary
Lincoln purportedly wrote, "I have taken your excellent advice and
decided not to leave my husband while he is in the White House."[169]
Sam Ward, a knowledgeable Washington insider known as "King of
the Lobby," suggested that there was something unsavory in the relations between Mary Lincoln and "Dennison," presumably either William Dennison, Lincoln's postmaster general in New York in 1864 and
1865, or George Dennison, naval officer in the New York Custom
House.[170]

The psychological mechanism of displacement, however, probably
explains more of Mary Todd Lincoln's rages than does the mechanism
of projection. She evidently harbored deep-seated anger at her "impet-
uous, high-strung, sensitive" father, Robert Todd.[171] No direct evidence
of her feelings toward him survives, but it would seem plausible that
his remarriage when she was seven made her feel abandoned, betrayed,
and rejected.[172] As Linda Schierse Leonard, a psychologist, has found,
"A woman's rage . . . is often rooted in feelings of abandonment, be-
trayal, and rejection which may go back to the relation with the father,
and which often come up over and over again in current relationships

[with men]." Such rage "is often mixed with feelings of jealousy and revenge that are strong enough to kill any relationship and the woman's capacity for loving herself as well." Thus "many women destroy their relationships . . . through continued hysterical outbursts."[173]

In addition, Mary Lincoln evidently shared the jealousy and resentment of her stepmother with her younger brother George, who "complained bitterly" about her "settled hostility" and charged that he had been forced to leave "his father's house in consequence of the malignant & continued attempts on the part of his stepmother to poison the mind of his father toward him." George added that his father was "mortified that his last child by his first wife should be obliged, like all his other first children, to abandon his house by the relentless persecution of a stepmother."[174]

George seems to have described a deep estrangement that the children of Robert Todd's first marriage, like many such children, felt toward their father and stepmother.[175] All four of the daughters left home when of age.[176] The eldest, Elizabeth, wed Ninian Edwards and settled in Springfield, where her three younger sisters moved, were introduced to society, and married. Robert Todd and his second wife did not attend their weddings and seldom visited these daughters, who in turn rarely went to Lexington. Compounding matters was the enmity of Mary Todd's maternal grandmother, the redoubtable Widow Parker, toward the remarriage of her son-in-law.[177]

There are hints that Mary Todd had some legitimate grievances against Betsey Humphreys Todd. She retained no fond memories of life in the house of her father and stepmother; as she confided to a close friend, "My early home was truly at a *boarding* school," referring to Madame Mentelle's Academy, which she entered at the age of fourteen.[178] Her niece recalled that she "was a bundle of nervous activity, wilful and original in planning mischief, and so the inevitable clashes with her very conventional young stepmother."[179] As a ten-year-old, Mary had a run-in with Betsey Todd over an attempt to dress up like an adult. With the aid of long willow branches, Mary had clumsily tried to convert her narrow muslin frock into a hoop skirt. When her stepmother saw this, she exclaimed, "What a fright you are" and ordered the child and her companion, Elizabeth L. Norris, to "take those things off, & then go to Sunday school." Norris later recalled that "we went to our room chagrined and angry. Mary burst into tears, and gave the first exhibition of temper I had ever seen or known her to make. She thought we were badly treated, and expressed herself freely on the subject."[180]

Another episode suggests that relations between the adult Mary and her stepmother were not entirely cordial. While Lincoln was serving his term in Congress in the late 1840s, his wife and two children stayed with the Todds in Lexington. One day Eddie Lincoln brought home a kitten and tenderly cared for it. As Mrs. Lincoln wrote to her husband, "In the midst of his happiness Ma [Betsey Todd] came in,[—] she[,] you must know[,] dislikes the whole cat race, [—] I thought in a very un-feeling manner, she ordered the servant near, to throw it out, which, of *course,* was done, Ed—screaming & protesting loudly against the proceeding, *she* never appeared to mind his screams, which were long & loud, I assure you." She added a significant commentary to the tale: "Tis unusual for her *now a days,* to do any thing quite so striking, she is very obliging & accommodating, but if she thought any of us, were on her hands again, I believe she would be *worse* than ever."[181] Mary Lincoln underlined *now a days,* suggesting that such heartless behavior toward children was not uncommon in earlier years. The callous indifference to Eddie's feelings may have rankled in part because it reminded her of similar treatment that she had once received at the hands of her stepmother. In any event, she could well have been as furious at her stepmother as was her brother George. She left Lexington in order "to avoid living under the same roof with her stepmother," according to Elizabeth Edwards.[182]

Mary Todd may also have resented Betsey Todd for producing nine children, rivals for paternal favor. During the Civil War, all but one sided with the Confederacy. Mrs. Lincoln astonished a friend in 1862 by saying that she hoped her brothers fighting in the Confederate army would be captured or killed. In response to the friend's amazed disbelief, she grimly said, "They would kill my husband if they could, and destroy our Government—the dearest of all things to us."[183] Upon the death of her half-brother Alexander, she made similar remarks to Elizabeth Keckley, "Lizzie, I have just heard that one of my brothers has been killed in the war."

"I also heard the same, Mrs. Lincoln, but hesitated to speak of it, for fear the subject would be a painful one to you."

"You need not hesitate. Of course, it is but natural that I should feel for one so nearly related to me, but not to the extent that you suppose. He made his choice long ago. He decided against my husband, and through him against me. He has been fighting against us; and since he chose to be our deadly enemy, I see no special reason why I should bitterly mourn his death."[184] Alexander and his siblings had already stolen Mary's father; now they were threatening to kill her husband, who, in effect, was her father surrogate.

It might be argued that Mary Lincoln had no good reason to mourn half-siblings, who meant little to her, but there is an almost inhuman coldness in these remarks. They resemble the harsh comment she made in 1867, when she told Mrs. Keckley that the Lord punishes her critics:

> The evening I left my house to come here, the young daughter of one of my neighbors in the same block, was in a house not a square off, and in a childish manner was regretting that I could not retain my house. The man in the house said: "Why waste your tears and regrets on Mrs. Lincoln?" An hour afterward the husband and wife went out to make a call, doubtless to gossip about me, [and] on their return they found their young boy had almost blinded himself with gunpowder. Who will say that the cry of the "widow and fatherless" is disregarded in *His* sight![185]

Such shards of evidence about Mrs. Lincoln's feelings toward her family are by no means conclusive, but they do suggest that she harbored rage that could not be openly expressed but needed an outlet. In Abraham Lincoln, Mary Todd seems to have found the ideal person upon whom to displace her feelings toward her father, both positive and negative.

In her psyche, Lincoln became a father surrogate; in fact, she probably married him because she needed someone to indulge, love, and protect her like a father. When Robert Todd remarried and began siring a new family, he left a void in Mary's life that Lincoln was well suited to fill. Not only was he more than a foot taller and almost a decade older than she, but he also radiated the quality of being old, even as a young man.[186] One observer during Lincoln's early years in Springfield said that the young attorney reminded him "of the pictures I formerly saw of old Father Jupiter, bending down from the clouds, to see what was going on below." At social occasions, Lincoln especially conveyed this impression as he talked with young women: Just "as an agreeable smile of satisfaction graced the countenance of the old heathen god, as he perceived the incense rising up—so the face of L[incoln] was occasionally distorted into a grin as he succeeded in eliciting applause from some of the fair votaries by whom he was surrounded."[187] One of those "fair votaries" was Mary Todd, who was particularly susceptible to the charms of a man who resembled old Father Jupiter.

Ruth Painter Randall speculated that Mary Todd, an "emotionally unstable girl," might "unconsciously have sensed" that Lincoln "was one who would pass her 'imperfections lightly by,' who would deal gently, understandingly, and paternally with her undisciplined and often headstrong spirit," and that she "needed a slow, balanced, deliberate person" like Lincoln "to look after her."[188] In their married life he treated her as a father would a child, in part because he recognized that she was psychologically troubled.[189] Herndon believed that Lincoln "held his wife partly insane for years."[190] At the first sign of a thunderstorm, he would hurry home from the office "to quiet her fears and comfort her until the storm was over."[191]

When Lincoln was absent for long periods on the circuit, he sometimes arranged for a neighbor to stay with his wife to calm her often baseless fears. She was given to hysterical outbursts, unreasonably suspecting that dogs or strangers would attack her.[192] One day she cried out to her Springfield neighbor, John B. Webber, "Keep this little dog from biting me." Webber recalled that the canine "was a little thing and was doing nothing" and that it was "too small and good natured to do anything."[193] Another Springfield neighbor, Elizabeth A. Capps, described a similar incident: "Mrs. Lincoln cried, 'Fire, Fire!' When the neighbors ran in they found just a little fat burning in a frying pan on the cook stove." Mrs. Capps also recollected an occasion when Mary Lincoln "screamed 'Murder!'" A neighbor came running "and found an old umbrella fixer sitting on the back porch, waiting for 'Mrs.' to come back, as he had seen her go thru the house to the front and supposed she would be right back." The neighbor "took the man by the arm and led him off the porch and told him how he had frightened the woman." The umbrella repairman left, muttering, "I wouldn't have such a fool for my wife!" Evidently, the "cause of her fright was the man's heavy beard, which was a rare sig[h]t in those days."[194]

A peddler once called at the Lincoln home and "knocked at Mrs. Lincoln's door, as at any door, and had stepped in when she answered the knock and had started to open his pack." By that point Mary Lincoln "had begun to scream and carry on, and had kept yelling for him 'to leave, to leave, to leave.'" The peddler later accosted Lincoln in the street and said, "If you have any influence over your wife[,] in God's world, go home and teach her some sense."[195] Her antagonistic behavior toward Springfield merchants and tradesmen also suggested mental imbalance.[196]

During the Civil War, Lincoln once warned his wife that he might be forced to institutionalize her. After the death of their beloved son Willie, Mary Lincoln was so overcome with grief that the president one day led her to a window of the White House, pointed to an insane asylum in the distance, and said, "Mother, do you see that large white building on the hill yonder? Try and control your grief, or it will drive you mad, and we may have to send you there."[197] To William P. Wood he confided, "The caprices of Mrs. Lincoln, I am satisfied, are the result of partial insanity."[198]

When the Reverend Dr. Phineas Gurley signed a petition urging clemency for a young man of dubious integrity, Lincoln asked him why the minister had done so against his better judgment. Gurley explained that the boy's father was fearful that his wife would lose her mind if her son remained in jail. "Ah, Doctor! these wives of ours have the inside track on us, don't they?" Lincoln responded.[199] After the assassination, Commissioner of Public Buildings Benjamin B. French remarked that Mary Lincoln had become "crazier than she used to be."[200] Gideon Welles thought that she should have been committed to a mental hospital long before 1875, when an Illinois court took that step.[201] A servant in the Lincoln home thought Mrs. Lincoln "was half crazy."[202] Mrs. Norman B. Judd considered her "slightly insane."[203]

In fact, Mary Lincoln evidently suffered from manic depression. Orville H. Browning, who considered her "demented," recalled that in her early twenties she "was a girl of much vivacity in conversation, but was subject to . . . spells of mental depression. . . . As we used familiarly to state it she was always 'either in the garret or cellar.'"[204] This labile quality was noted in childhood. Her friend Margaret Stuart said that as a youngster Mary was "very highly strung, nervous, impulsive, excitable, having an emotional temperament much like an April day, sunning all over with laughter one moment, the next crying as though her heart would break."[205] Manic depression is not the only possible diagnosis for what ailed Mary Lincoln; she had many of the symptoms associated with what is now termed "borderline personality disorder." Jean Baker believes that she suffered a related disorder, narcissism.[206]

At the White House, Lincoln told Browning "about his domestic troubles." On several occasions the president confided "that he was constantly under great apprehension lest his wife should do something which would bring him into disgrace."[207] In 1861 David Davis also worried that Mary Lincoln "will disgrace her husband."[208] Decades later Alexander McClure recalled that Mary Lincoln "was a consuming sorrow to Mr. Lincoln, yet he bore it all with unflagging patience.

She was sufficiently unbalanced to make any error possible and many probable, but not sufficiently so as to dethrone her as mistress of the White House."[209]

Lincoln's fears were justified. As McClure observed, "She was vain, passionately fond of dress and wore her dresses shorter at the top and longer at the train than even fashions demanded. She had great pride in her elegant neck and bust, and grieved the President greatly by her constant display of her person and her fine clothes."[210] Commenting on one such dress, Lincoln said to his wife, "Mother, it is my opinion, if some of that tail was nearer the head, it would be in better style."[211] Her sartorial taste offended others, including William Howard Russell, who thought her "the most preposterous looking female I never saw." At her gala ball in February 1862, she looked "like a damned old Irish . . . washerwoman dressed out for a Sunday," he said.[212] An Oregon senator also objected vehemently to the gown that Mrs. Lincoln wore at that event: "The weak minded Mrs Lincoln had her bosom on exhibition," he told his wife, "and a flower pot on her head, while there was a train of silk or satin drag[g]ing on the floor behind her of several yards in length." As he regarded her, the senator "could not help regretting that she had degenerated from the industrious and unpretending woman that she was in the days when she used to cook Old Abe[']s dinner, and milk the cows with her own hands." Now, he acidly remarked, "Her only ambition seems to be to exhibit her own milking apparatus to the public gaze." He regretted that "the wife of the President could not have brought something like republican simplicity to the White House."

This same legislator also objected to Mary Lincoln's extravagance in refurbishing the White House. He thought that the Executive Mansion "was sufficiently gorgeous for a prince" when the Lincolns moved in. Now, he said, Mrs. Lincoln had already spent the $25,000 that Congress appropriated for refurnishing the house "and contracted debts for six thousand more, for the payment of which Congress is now called upon to make an appropriation, and that too while our troops are suffering for the necessaries of life." Harshly he concluded that the "old Spanish proverb which says, 'put a beggar on horseback and he will ride to the D—l' was never better illustrated."[213]

When Mary Lincoln realized that a supplemental appropriation would be necessary to cover her redecorating expenses, she turned in desperation to Commissioner of Public Buildings French.[214] "I have sent for you to get me out of trouble," she pleaded on December 14, 1861, "if you will do it, I will never get into such a difficulty again." She explained that the contractor's bill exceeded the original congressional authorization by $6,700. "Mr. Lincoln will not approve it," she lamented. "I want you to see him and tell him that it is common to overrun appropriations—tell him how *much* it costs to refurnish, he does not know much about it, he says he will pay it out of his own pocket." She wept as she begged French's help: "Major, he cannot afford that, he ought not to do it. Major[,] you must get me out of this difficulty, it is the last,[.] I will always be governed by you,[;] henceforth, I will not spend a cent without consulting you,[.] now do go to Mr. Lincoln and try and persuade him to approve the bill. Do[,] Major[,] for my sake, but do not let him know that you have seen me." She gave him the bill with the annotation, dated December 13, "This bill is correct. Mr[.] Lincoln will please have it settled—this closes the house furnishing."[215]

French, whose position made him "almost a member of the President's household,"[216] explained to Lincoln that "a Mr. Carryl has presented a bill of some $7000 over the appropriation, for furnishing this house, and, before I can ask for an appropriation to pay it, it must have your approval." The president, "a little excited," exclaimed, "It never can have my approval—I'll pay it out my own pocket first—it would stink in the nostrils of the American people to have it said that the President of the United States had approved a bill overrunning an appropriation of $20,000 for *flub dubs* for this damned old house, when the soldiers cannot have blankets!! Who is this Carryl, and how came he to be employed[?]"

French replied, "I do not know sir—the first I ever heard of him he brought me a large bill for room paper."[217]

The president was particularly shocked by a "Rich, Elegant Carpet made to order" his wife had purchased: "I would like to know where a carpet worth $2,500 can be put."[218]

"In the East Room," French suggested.

Lincoln called it "a monstrous extravagance," adding, "Well I suppose Mrs. Lincoln *must* bear the blame, let her bear it, I swear I won't! . . . It was all wrong to spend one cent at such a time, and I never ought to have had a cent expended, the house was furnished well enough, better than any one we ever lived in, and if I had not been overwhelmed with other business I would not have had any of the appropriation expended, but what could I do? I could not attend to everything." He concluded "by swearing again that he *never* would approve that bill."[219]

At the funeral of Lincoln's close friend Edward Baker in 1861, Mrs. Lincoln shocked public taste by appearing in a "lilac silk dress, with bonnet and gloves to match." Some members of her circle, thinking she should be made aware of her breach of etiquette, dispatched one of her most intimate friends to bear the news to the White House. Upon arrival, the emissary was greeted by Mrs. Lincoln with the exclamation, "I am so glad you have come, I am just as mad as I can be. Mrs. Crittenden has just been here to remonstrate with me for wearing my lilac suit to Colonel Baker's funeral. I wonder if the women of Washington expect me to muffle myself up in mourning for every soldier killed in this great war?"

"But Mrs. Lincoln," came the reply, "do you not think black more suitable to wear at a funeral because there is a great war in the nation?"

"No, I don't. I want the women to mind their own business; I intend to wear what I please."[220]

Mary Lincoln also scandalized Washington in early February 1862 by giving a lavish White House party, which many thought "out of taste" at a time when war raged and when Willie Lincoln lay upstairs, gravely ill with the malady that killed him before the month was out. She reportedly believed that God took Willie away in order to punish her frivolity.[221]

In the winter of 1860–61, Mrs. Lincoln had offended women in Illinois when she traveled east to buy clothes. According to one Springfield matron, "Her friends here think [it] quite unnecessary in the present state of political affairs."[222] Throughout the war, similar criticisms filled the press. As one journalist summarized them, "While her sister-women scraped lint, sewed bandages, and put on nurses' caps, and gave their all to country and to death, the wife of its President spent her time in rolling to and fro between Washington and New York, intent on extravagant purchases for herself and the White House. Mrs. Lincoln seemed to have nothing to do but to 'shop.'" During the summer months, while her husband, "a lonely man, sorrowful at heart, and weighed down by mighty burdens, bearing the Nation's fate upon his shoulders, lived and toiled and suffered alone," Mary Lincoln relaxed "at the hotels of fashionable watering-places." While she "seemed chiefly intent upon pleasure, personal flattery and adulation; upon extravagant dress and ceaseless self-gratification," the nation was "goaded at last to exasperation."[223]

A leading Maryland Republican, Francis S. Corkran, one day "mentioned to Mr. Lincoln that Mrs. Lincoln was being criticized by the women of the U.S. [for] being in New York and leading a gay life while so many of the people were in mourning."[224]

Even more embarrassing than her tactlessness was Mary Lincoln's dishonesty. In the diary of Orville H. Browning are passages indicating that "Mrs. Lincoln was caught padding the expense accounts of the White House and that Lincoln was exceedingly indignant and angry when apprised of this situation," and that she offered Browning "money if he would obtain an appointment for a party in whom she was interested."[225] In the summer of 1861 she tried to charge the expenses of a state dinner for Prince Napoleon to the account of the White House gardener, John Watt, whose loyalty and basic integrity were suspect.[226] In September 1861, John F. Potter, chair of the House Select Committee on the Loyalty of Government Employees, informed Lincoln of damning testimony about Watt's pro-Confederate sympathies. Two independent witnesses confirmed that he had, shortly after the first battle of Bull Run, proclaimed that the South could not be defeated and that Union army consisted of human trash.[227] As White House gardener during the Buchanan administration, Watt had been chastised by the Commissioner of Public Buildings John B. Blake for submitting unreasonable bills and had also been accused by others of wrongdoing.[228]

Mary Lincoln apparently billed the Interior Department $900 for the August 3 banquet, but Interior Secretary Caleb B. Smith rejected it. Smith told Thurlow Weed that because he regarded the cost as exorbitant, he consulted with Secretary of State Seward, who "had also dined the Prince, having the same number of guests, and giving them a duplicate of the dinner at the White House. In fact," Weed recalled, "Mr. Seward ordered both dinners from the same restaurant, and, by his own bill, knew the cost of each. For what Mr. Seward paid $300, Mrs. Lincoln demanded $900." Thwarted by Smith's refusal, Mrs. Lincoln then "made her gardener make out a bill for plants, pots etc of the required amount, certified it herself and drew the money." This "occasioned scandal."[229]

The gardener's account used to disguise the money refunded to Mary Lincoln for the banquet was described by a White House gatekeeper, James H. Upperman, who complained to Interior Secretary Smith on October 21, 1861, about "sundry petit, but flagrant frauds on the public treasury," the products of "deliberate col[l]usion." According to Upperman, Watt had in mid-September authorized payments to Alexander McKerichar, a laborer on the White House grounds, for flowers that were not delivered ($700.75) and for 215 loads of manure ($107.50) as well as hire of a horse and cart for twenty-seven days in August to haul it to the Executive Mansion ($47.25). These bills were apparently for goods and services not provided. Another man, Charles F. Cone, was paid $33.75 for working at the White House for twenty-seven days in August and $47.25 for the hire of horse cart and driver, even though "this individual is no labourer and has rendered no such service as charged for[,] as can be proved by sundry persons, that he does not work at any kind of labour and was at the time refer[r]ed to, and can yet be found in a certain locality on P[ennsylvani]a Avenue anytime during working hours." As for Cone's delivery charges, Upperman contended that "it can be proved that no such horse cart or driver rendered any such service in said grounds." Moreover, Upperman claimed, William Johnson was paid $155 for 310 loads of manure that were never delivered. "I imagine his whereabouts to be doubtful as nobody knows him." Augustus Jullien, a French cook employed in the White House kitchen, received $67.50 for work done on the grounds in July and August, although he "has at no time rendered any such service." Similarly, Francis P. Burke, a presidential coachman, was paid $33.75 for labor on the grounds for August, as was White House butler Peter Vermeren.[230]

In late October 1861, Mary Lincoln, through Watt, begged Secretary Smith to see the president, evidently about these revelations. In response to a query from the commissioner of public buildings, Lincoln on October 26 said he would "determine in a few days what he would do." Watt insisted that "the arrangement of the accounts was made by [Commissioner of Public Buildings William S.] Wood & that he assured Mrs[.] L[incoln] that the transaction was right & legal and that she had no idea that any thing was done which was not authorized by law." Secretary Smith told his cabinet colleague Seward that he "would be glad to have her relieved from the anxiety under which she is suffering."[231]

Smith did so by covering up the scandal. After interviewing Watt, McKerichar, and B. B. French about the $700 flower bill, Smith concluded "that the voucher was correct, and that it had been rightfully paid by Mr. French" and therefore "pursued the matter no further."[232] He did not consult Upperman, Burke, Jullien, Johnson, Vermeren, Cone, or others knowledgeable about the matter. Upperman then protested to Solomon Foot, chair of the Senate Committee on Public Buildings and Grounds, citing as his sources Burke, Jullien, and Vermeren, as well as the former public gardener Thomas J. Sutter and George W. Dant, a messenger and clerk to the commissioner of public buildings.[233] According to Thurlow Weed, the Interior Department and Congress "measurably suppressed" the story out of "respect for Mr. Lincoln."[234] Congressman Benjamin Boyer of Pennsylvania confirmed Weed's story, adding that the president paid the bill himself and withdrew the government check.[235]

Later, when Watt threatened to blackmail Mrs. Lincoln, he evidently received some form of hush money. According to Isaac Newton of the Agriculture Division of the Interior Department, the gardener "entered into a conspiracy to extort [$]20,000 from the President by using three letters of Mrs. Lincoln."[236] In those documents she evidently asked Watt "to commit forgery and perjury for purpose of defrauding the Government."[237] Simeon Draper called on Watt and "with much bluster & great oaths" threatened to have him imprisoned. Watt then "fell on his literal marrow bones & begged, & gave up the letters & the conspiracy got demoralized & came down, down, to 1500 dollars which was paid, and the whole thing settled."[238]

In March 1862, Watt was named special agent for Newton's Agriculture Division and assigned to purchase seeds in Europe at an annual salary of $1,500 plus travel costs.[239] After failing to be paid for his services in Europe, in 1863 he billed the president $736 as compensation for Mary Lincoln's hotel bills, cash advances, and "Commissary stores." The vouchers for these payments and advances from Watt to Mrs. Lincoln were held by Simeon Draper.[240]

The Watt affair became the talk of the capital. David Davis told his wife in February 1862 that "I got a letter from Washington & the gossip is still about Mrs. Lincoln and the gardener Watt." Somewhat harshly, he added that the recent death of Willie Lincoln might cause Mary Lincoln to mend her ways: "Will not this calamity be a lesson to his wife? I am afraid not."[241] The press reported that Watt, at Mary Lincoln's instigation, bought two cows "and charged them to the manure fund—that is, a fund voted in one of the general appropriation bills to provide manure for the public lands." The bill was rejected, probably by Secretary Smith. When Watt facilitated the sale of a White House rug to a Washington photographer to pay an outstanding bill, the carpet was replaced at public expense.[242]

Smith also questioned other bills. According to the New York

World, when Mary Lincoln ordered $800 worth of china from E. V. Haughwout & Co., she evidently tried to hide other purchases, amounting to $1,400, by having the total bill ($2,200) applied to the china alone. When the skeptical secretary raised questions, the *World* alleged that the merchant acknowledged that the overcharge was made to disguise the unspecified items. Haughwout & Co. denied the allegations in a letter to Manton Marble, editor of the *World.* In turn, Marble defended the story and, rather than retract it, threatened to "expose what I know about Mrs. Lincoln's practices in her New York purchases—her silver service—the champagne[,] manure bills etc. etc. to say nothing of wall paper—seed commissions, shawls, contracts, etc. etc. etc."[243] John Watt claimed that "a bill of $6,000 contracted with Haughwout & Co. for silverware was paid for by a bill charged against gilding gas-fixtures."[244] It was rumored that Mary Lincoln also suggested to a New York merchant that he provide the White House with a $500 chandelier, charge $1,000 for it, and thus allow her to disguise $500 worth of jewelry purchases. The businessman refused to cooperate and apparently lost the sale of the chandelier.[245] John Hay angered Mrs. Lincoln by refusing to allow her to tap the White House stationery fund or to give her the salary once paid to Mrs. John Watt, who was fired from her post as stewardess in 1862.[246] It was widely rumored that Mary Lincoln "appropriated the manure piles which had always been the perquisites of the gardener" and used the proceeds from the sale of that commodity for her own purposes.[247]

Mary Lincoln's dishonesty became a national scandal in 1865, when she left the White House with scores of trunks and boxes containing, so it was said, "a great deal of Government silver, spoon[,] forks etc[.] and a large quantity of linen and stuffs."[248] Eight years later, Orville H. Browning, who knew Mrs. Lincoln well, told Supreme Court Justice David Davis that he "believed that all the charges against her of having pilfered from the White House were false." Davis "replied that the proofs were too many and too strong against her to admit doubt of her guilt; that she was a natural born thief; that stealing was a kind of insanity with her, and that she had carried away from the White House many things that were of no value to her, and she had carried them away only in obedience to her irresistable propensity to steal."[249]

In December 1861 Mary Lincoln, who had a reputation as "*one of the leaky vessels*—from whom contraband army news, gets afloat,"[250] further embarrassed the president by allowing her close friend and "social adviser," Henry Wikoff, to see a copy of Lincoln's forthcoming annual message to Congress. A charming, worldly rake convicted of abducting a woman, Wikoff was a secret correspondent for the New York *Herald*. He telegraphed portions of the document to his employer, which published excerpts before Congress received it.[251]

According to Alexander McClure, Mary Lincoln "was the easy prey of adventurers, of which the war developed an unusual crop, and many times they gained such influences over her as to compromise her very seriously."[252] Her friendship with Wikoff was a case in point; it scandalized proper society. In December 1861 David Davis told his wife, "Rumors are plenty—that Mrs. Lincoln is acting badly. . . . It is said that she has installed as Master of Ceremonies at the White House, the Chevalier Wikoff. 'My courtship & its consequences you read.' He is a terrible libertine, & no woman ought to tolerate his presence." Washington matrons were "in distress" at this news.[253] A journalist told his editor in November 1861 that "Mrs. Lincoln is making herself both a fool and a nuisance. *Chevalier Wikoff* is her gallant, and I have within the week seen two notes signed by him in her name sending compliments and invitations. . . . He is a beautiful specimen to occupy such a position."[254] In disbelief Joseph R. Hawley asked, "What does Mrs. Lincoln mean by . . . having anything to do with that world-renowned whoremonger and swindler Chevalier Wikoff? Is Lincoln an old saphead or is she a headstrong fool who thinks she can have a kitchen cabinet? It's a national disgrace."[255]

Echoing this sentiment, John Hay deemed Wikoff an "unclean bird," a "vile creature," a "marked and branded social Pariah, a monstrosity abhorred by men and women" and declared it "an enduring disgrace to American society that it suffers such a thing to be at large."[256] Henry Villard described him as "an accomplished man of the world, a fine linguist, with graceful presence, elegant manners, and a conscious, condescending way," who "showed the utmost assurance in his appeals to the vanity of the mistress of the White House." Villard overheard Wikoff pay Mary Lincoln compliments "upon her looks and dress in so fulsome a way that she ought to have blushed and banished the impertinent fellow from her presence." Instead, she made him a kind of "major domo in general and in special, as a guide in matters of social etiquette, domestic arrangements including her toilette, and as always welcome company for visitors in her salon and on her drives."[257]

Eventually, after Matthew Hale Smith, New York correspondent for the Boston *Journal,* warned the president of scandal, he intervened. In 1868, Smith revealed the full story: Wikoff, "with whom no reputable woman would willingly be seen on Broadway," had been "very officious in his attention to . . . Mrs. Lincoln." He "was an early and constant visitor" at all of Mrs. Lincoln's receptions. "No one went so early but this person could be seen cozily seated in a chair as if at home, talking to the ladies of the White House. None called so late but they found him still there." Wikoff was often "seen riding in the President's coach, with the ladies, through Pennsylvania Avenue" and "found lounging in the conservatory, or smoking in the grounds, very much at home, and not at all anxious to hide his presence." Wikoff's visits embarrassed the White House staff, and the press began to comment unfavorably.

Friends of the president, suspicious of Wikoff, investigated his background and discovered that he had been hired "by some parties in New York, who were using him as their tool." These men had "furnished him with money and instructions. He was to go to Washington, make himself agreeable to the ladies, insinuate himself into the White House, attend levees, show that he had power to come and go, and, if possible, open a correspondence with the ladies of the mansion." Once known as an insider, he would be able to wield influence that his backers might find useful in time.

Wikoff did his work well. Lincoln's friends "considered that the President should be made acquainted with this plot against his honor" and dispatched Smith to inform him. Evidently in early February 1862, Smith, accompanied by a U.S. senator, visited the White House. As he later recalled, Lincoln "took me by the hand, led me into the office of his private secretary, whom he drove out, and locked the door." When Smith showed him documents illuminating the purposes of Wikoff, who at that moment was downstairs, the president said, "Give me those papers and sit here till I return." He "started out of the room with strides that showed an energy of purpose," soon came back, shook Smith's hand, and had Wikoff "driven from the mansion that night."[258] According to another source, Lincoln "became jealous" of Wikoff and "taxed" his wife. The chevalier then "volunteered an explanation," telling "the wounded & incensed" president that "he was only teaching the madame a little European Court Etiquette."[259]

A further warning came from William P. Wood, superintendent of the Old Capitol Prison, who told Lincoln that Mrs. Lincoln was involved in a corrupt traffic in "trading permits, favors and Government secrets." In his reminiscences, Wood claimed that Thomas Stackpole, "a subtle[,] partisan, Yankee Democrat" who "had an eye to business and was anxious to make an extra dollar whenever occasion offered," managed to gain the confidence of Mary Lincoln. He then used her to gain trading permits, which he sold to his friend John Hammack, a Washington restaurateur and "a Virginia-bred Democrat and rabid secessionist." Hammack in turn peddled them to his customers. Wood recalled that as he described these shady practices during a long interview at the White House, the president "exhibited more feeling than I had believed he possessed" and ascribed his wife's behavior to mental derangement.[260] Mary Lincoln evidently had direct contact with Hammack, for in May 1865 she received $84 from him.[261]

On April 11, 1865, Lincoln was reportedly embarrassed by his wife as he delivered a speech from the White House to a joyful crowd celebrating Robert E. Lee's surrender. During his remarks, she and some female friends gathered at an adjacent window, chatting and laughing "with almost boisterous animation, until the noise quite drowned the voice of the speaker." At first the listeners below showed forbearance, but several eventually hushed the women emphatically. The president thought "that some word of his own had called forth the unwonted demonstration" but realized instantly that "no disrespect to him was intended." With "an expression of pain and mortification which came over his face as if such strokes were not new, he resumed his reading."[262]

. . .

Lincoln bore all these embarrassments stoically. According to Elizabeth Keckley, he "was a kind and an indulgent husband, and when he saw faults in his wife he excused them as he would excuse the impulsive acts of a child. In fact, Mrs. Lincoln was never more pleased than when the president called her his child-wife."[263] In turn, she addressed him, after they became parents, as "Father."[264] In widowhood, she said Lincoln had been "always—lover—husband—father & *all all to me*—Truly my all."[265] She deemed him "the kindest man and most loving husband and father in the world," who told her, whenever she asked for anything, "You know what you want, go and get it."[266]

After Lincoln's death, she turned to others for parental succor. According to her sister's niece, Mary sought to make Elizabeth Keckley a kind of surrogate mammy. Like many a widow or divorcée, she also looked to her sons as husband surrogates.[267] In 1869 she wrote that the teenaged Tad, who accompanied her as she wandered Europe, "is like some *old woman,* with regard to his care of me—and the two or three days since—when I was *so very* sick—his dark loving eyes—watching over me, reminded me so much of his dearly beloved father's—so filled with *his* deep love."[268]

Lincoln's eminent suitability as a father surrogate was not the only source of his appeal to Mary Todd; he also seemed to her destined for political fame. As Albert J. Beveridge suggested, the one thing they shared in common was "mutual ambition."[269] She had grown up in a highly political household; Robert Todd numbered among his close friends the leading public figures of Kentucky, including Henry Clay. One of Todd's pet projects had been to make Clay president. In such a heady atmosphere, it is not surprising that young Mary developed political interests and ambitions.[270] John T. Stuart and David Davis thought her "very ambitious,"[271] as did her sister Elizabeth and her cousin Martinette Hardin, both of whom called Mary "the most ambitious woman I ever saw."[272] Henry B. Rankin contended that Mary Lincoln "was more aggressively ambitious than her husband."[273] Another young man who worked in Lincoln's law office recalled that "Mrs. Lincoln had displayed more zeal in regard to the Presidential nomination than her husband had. In fact there is no doubt that she was constantly spurring him on for she was very ambitious."[274] A neighbor termed her "extremely ambitious."[275]

In that era women could not aspire to public office, but they could dream of becoming the president's wife. One of her sisters recalled that when Mary was little, her grandmother one day chided her for being noisy and asked, "What on earth do you suppose will become of you if you go on this way?" Mary allegedly replied, "Oh, I will be the wife of a President some day."[276] The response might seem implausibly prescient, but it gains some credibility from other sources, one of whom maintained that at age thirteen Mary told Henry Clay, "I wish I could go to Washington and live in the White House. I begged my father to be President but he only laughed and said he would rather see you there than to be President himself."[277] Later, after moving to Illinois, she repeated this determination "and said it in earnest." When friends in Springfield asked Mary Todd which of her beaux she would marry, she replied, "Him who has the best prospects of being President."

She told a friend who had married a rich, old man, "I would rather marry a good man—a man of mind—with a hope and bright prospects ahead for position—fame & power than to marry all the houses—gold & bones in the world."[278] She predicted to one of her servants in Springfield before Lincoln was nominated "that she would go to the White House yet."[279] In the late 1840s she predicted to Ward Hill Lamon that Lincoln "is to be President of the United States some day; if I had not thought so I never would have married him, for you can see he is not pretty."[280] One Springfield resident marveled at the "almost prophetic insight" that led Mary Todd to select "the most awkward & ungainly man in her train," one "almost totally lacking in polish."[281] When courted by Stephen A. Douglas, she allegedly remarked, "I cannot consent to be your wife. I shall become Mrs. President, or I am the victim of false prophets, but it will not be as Mrs. Douglas."[282] In the first year of her marriage, "anxious to go to Washington," she hoped to see her husband nominated for a seat in Congress. When John J. Hardin beat him at the Whig convention, "her anger got the better of her, and Lincoln had an unpleasant time in consequence," as she berated him for not exerting himself more to win. On the day that Hardin left for the capital, Mary Lincoln "shed buckets full of tears."[283] Three years later, Lincoln did win a seat in the U.S. House, and David Davis reported to his wife that Mary Lincoln, as she prepared to accompany her husband to Washington, "wishes to loom largely."[284]

In 1854 Mrs. Lincoln apparently forbade her husband to take a seat in the state legislature, an office she felt was beneath his dignity. When she read a newspaper article indicating that in his absence, he was being put forward for the state House of Representatives, she rushed to the paper's offices and ordered Lincoln's name stricken from the list of candidates. Later, when William Jayne called to ask permission once again to put Lincoln's name in nomination, he found the potential candidate "the saddest man I ever saw—the gloomiest." Lincoln, nearly in tears, paced the floor, resisting Jayne's blandishments by saying, "No—I can't—you don't know all. I say you don't begin to know one half and that's enough."[285] Henry Whitney explained that "it was Mrs. Lincoln's opposition which so much disturbed him. She insisted in her imperious way that he must now go to the United States Senate, and that it was a degradation to run him for the Legislature."[286] Lincoln may also have stepped down because he discovered that Illinois law forbade newly elected state legislators from running for the U.S. Senate.[287]

When Lyman Trumbull defeated Lincoln for the Senate seat in 1855, Mary Lincoln was so angry that she turned on Mrs. Trumbull (her old friend Julia Jayne), calling her "ungainly," "cold," "unsympathizing," and "unpopular." Shortly after the election, she snubbed Julia Jayne publicly, and in 1867 denounced Trumbull's "cold, selfish treachery" toward Lincoln.[288]

During the 1860 campaign, politicians eager to smooth relations between Lincoln and Trumbull recruited Mrs. Norman B. Judd to heal the breach. In Springfield Mrs. Judd found neither Mary Lincoln nor Julia Trumbull willing to take the first step; eventually, after much cajolery, Mrs. Trumbull consented. But as she prepared to call on her former friend, at whose wedding she had been a bridesmaid, Mrs. Trumbull balked when Mrs. Judd innocently observed, "You are doing a great service to the cause & the country by this act." Flinging down her bonnet, she declared that she would not be reconciled simply for political reasons. Undaunted, Mrs. Judd then turned to Mary Lincoln, who in time agreed to invite Julia Trumbull for a ride. At the Trumbull home, Mary Lincoln refused to accompany Mrs. Judd to the door.

"Why didn't Mrs. Lincoln come in?" asked a miffed Julia Trumbull. "I told her not to," replied Mrs. Judd. "I thought it was better."

Despite this inauspicious start, the two former enemies spoke as they passed by the court house, where Lincoln, Trumbull, Judd, and others observed them. Judd blanched as one of the men whispered, "How did she do it?"

The rapproachment was short-lived, for relatives and politicians soon persuaded Mary Lincoln that the peace overture had been part of a plot to make the former Democrats dominate erstwhile Whigs in the Republican coalition. When invited to a party at the Trumbulls', Mrs. Lincoln developed a convenient headache.

Early in the Lincoln administration at a presidential levée, Mrs. Trumbull paused in the receiving line to chat with Mrs. Lincoln, who instructed the usher, "Tell that woman to go on." "Will you allow me to be insulted in this way in your house?" Julia Trumbull asked the president.[289]

Mary Lincoln also feuded with family. For example, she refused to have anything to do with her half-sister Emilie Todd Helm, who had been her favorite sibling, after she wrote Lincoln a harsh letter in 1864.[290]

Mary Lincoln also vetoed her husband's plan in 1849 to accept the post of governor of the Oregon Territory.[291] Lincoln wanted to go, in part because was told he might well "come back from there a Senator when the State was admitted." When his wife objected, Lincoln tried to persuade Joshua Speed to move to Oregon, where he could have a government post. John T. Stuart recalled that "Lincoln evidently thought that if Speed, and Speed's wife were to go along, it would be an inducement for Mary to change her mind and consent to go." But this hope went glimmering when Speed turned down the office.[292] According to Noah Brooks, "Years afterward, when her husband had become President, she did not fail to remind him that her advice, when he was wavering, had restrained him from 'throwing himself away' on a distant territorial governorship." Brooks explained that Mary Lincoln "had had enough of frontier life."[293] An Oregonian suggested that she "was afraid of Indians."[294]

This was not the only time they disagreed about where to live. When late in the Civil War John T. Stuart asked the president whether he planned to retire to Springfield, Lincoln said, "Mary does not expect ever to go back there, and don[']t want to go—but I do—I expect to go back and make my home in Springfield for the rest of my life."[295] Mrs. Stuart recalled that Mary Lincoln expressed a desire to retire to Chicago, but her husband said, "No, we are going back to Springfield. That is our home, and there it will continue to be." She "was somewhat vexed at this, but nothing more was said."[296]

Mary Lincoln quashed the proposal, suggested early in 1860, that her husband become vice president. Lincoln told a friend that the Iowa delegation to the Republican convention would cast most of its votes for him as president and all of them for him as vice president. Thereupon "Mrs. Lincoln spoke up in a hard, bitter manner and said: 'If you can not have the first place, you shall not have the second.'"[297] Henry B. Rankin noted that some of her friends thought that Mary Lincoln was "officious" in her meddling and that they "said cruel, harsh things about her for it."[298]

In May 1860, as all of Springfield awaited the results of the Republican national convention, Mary Lincoln "said she thought she had more interest and concern in whom the Chicago convention nominated than her husband."[299] When word came that Lincoln had won, the candidate accepted congratulations from his friends at the *Illinois State Journal* office and then remarked, "I must go home: there is a little short woman there that is more interested in this matter than I am."[300] When Lincoln learned of his election in November, he hurried home and woke his wife, saying, "Mary! Mary! *we are elected!*"[301]

This frank expression might be interpreted as evidence of a marriage rooted, like the Macbeths', in "mutual ambition." If Lincoln thought of himself and his wife as a political pair, as this recollection suggests, it might help explain why he was so fond of Shakespeare's "Scottish play," which he lauded extravagantly. "I think nothing equals Macbeth," he told the actor James H. Hackett. "It is wonderful."[302]

Another Scottish literary figure inspired Mary Lincoln one day as she bolstered her husband's self-confidence. When she told him he was qualified for the presidency, he replied, "I admit that I am ambitious and would like to be President, but there is no such good luck in store for me as the Presidency." His wife dissented, "Oh, how you underrate yourself! But you are the only person in the world who does. You often quote Burns. 'Oh wad some power the giftie gie *you* to see yoursel' as ithers see you.'"

Lincoln objected: "I must in all candor say I do not think myself fit for the Presidency." Mary Lincoln then "laughed at him for thinking himself 'not fit.' 'You've got no equal in the United States,' she declared."[303]

Once she had achieved the status of First Lady, Mary Lincoln was eager to retain it. On election night in November 1864, the president scrutinized telegrams showing that he had won a second term by a larger majority than expected. He forwarded the good news to his wife, saying, "She is more anxious than I am."[304] She later told a friend that "I could have gone down on my knees to ask votes for him and again and again he said: 'Mary, I am afraid you will be punished for this overweening anxiety. If I am to be re-elected it will be all right; if not, you must bear the disappointment.'"[305]

Part of her anxiety stemmed from the fear that if Lincoln lost the presidency, creditors would demand payment of thousands of dollars of debt she had run up for her elaborate wardrobe.[306] According to Jesse K. Dubois, shortly after Lincoln's death the New York firm of Ball, Black & Company presented bills against his estate totaling $64,000 for jewelry that Mary Lincoln had purchased without his knowledge.[307] In March 1864, when told by a spiritualist that her husband would be defeated, she returned to the White House "crying *like a child!*"[308]

Mary Lincoln's desire for fame did not end with her husband's assassination. Fourteen years after that event, she described herself as "elated" at the prospect, then being discussed in the press, that Robert Lincoln might become president.[309]

The intense delight that she took "in prominence, excitement, and glory"[310] probably had its origins in her early psychological wounds. Harold Dwight Lasswell has argued that political aspirations often stem from "an intense and ungratified craving for deference" rooted in "low estimates of the self."[311] Lasswell's model fits Mary Lincoln's case, for the traumatic events of her childhood undermined her self-esteem and created within her a deeply embedded sense of "worthlessness." To be prominent, indeed, the most famous woman in the country, helped salve the old wounds and offset the feeling of being "unlovable and unloved."[312]

In addition, such fame might serve to vindicate her in the eyes of those members of her family, like Elizabeth and Ninian Edwards, who had disapproved of her decision to marry beneath her station.[313] Mary resented a family member's reference to Lincoln as a "plebeian." When on her wedding day Elizabeth Edwards told Mary that because time was so short they would have to send into town for gingerbread and beer instead of more suitable fare, Mary replied, "Well, that will be good enough for plebeians I suppose."[314] As one scholar has noted, Mary Todd "had taken a great risk in marrying Lincoln . . . and every contribution she made to her husband's career was a contribution to the justification of that risk."[315] If her husband were to become president, she could assuage the wound caused by the hateful word "plebeian."

• • •

Given Mary Todd's unconscious need for a father surrogate and her conscious need to be First Lady, it is not entirely surprising that she chose Abraham Lincoln. It is harder to understand why he married her. As even the defensive Ruth Painter Randall acknowledged, she could be willful, impulsive, imprudent, superficial, vain, childish, stingy, jealous, emotionally unstable, tactless, gossipy, malicious, materialistic, sharp-tongued, acquisitive, and indiscreet.[316] Another sympathetic biographer, W. A. Evans, listed the following characteristics as the major flaws in her personality: "too great seriousness and an inability to laugh at herself; capacity to ridicule others, but not herself; lack of humor. . . . inability to withstand restraint; a tendency to hysteria; and a disposition to disregard the point of view and feelings of others, to give offense, to resent criticism, to give way to anger, to remember hurts, to be revengeful."[317] Ida Tarbell deplored "her uncontrolled impulses and her inability ever to discipline herself properly," as well as "her indiscretions and her hysteria," and thought her "very foolish."[318]

These qualities are immediately obvious to even a casual reader of Mary Lincoln's letters. In one she refers to her younger sister Ann as a woman who "possesses such a miserable disposition & so false a tongue," one "whom no one respects, whose tongue for so many years, has been considered 'no slander'—and as a child & young girl, could not be outdone in falsehood. . . . I grieve for those, who have to come in contact with her malice, yet even *that*, is so well understood, [that] the object of *her wrath,* generally rises, with good people, in proportion to her *vindictiveness.*"[319] Anyone who peruses the more than six hundred extant letters by Mary Lincoln will probably agree with a Springfield resident who, upon reading this description of Ann, said, "Mary was writing about herself."[320] A person more unlike Lincoln is hard to imagine.

In trying to understand why Lincoln married such a woman, it must be recognized that his attitude toward women in general was puzzling, especially his passivity in his dealings with them. Nowhere is this more clearly illustrated than in his peculiar courtship of Mary Owens (chapter 6). A year after Mary Owens disappeared from Lincoln's life, he met Mary Todd. Lincoln was as passive with this new Mary as he had been with Miss Owens. Orville H. Browning, who observed the courtship and talked with Mary Todd about it, later said, "I always thought then and ever since that in her affair with Mr. Lincoln, Mary Todd did most of the courting." Browning added that "Miss Todd was thoroughly in earnest [in] her endeavors to get Mr. Lincoln" and stated flatly, "There is no doubt of her exceeding anxiety to marry him."[321] In pursuing her quarry, "she read much & committed much to memory to make herself agreeable," according to Mrs. Benjamin Edwards.[322] Mary's cousin, Martinette Hardin, shared Browning's view. On the day Lincoln broke the engagement, Hardin surmised, Mary "made up her mind that he should marry her at the cost of her pride to show us all that she was not defeated."[323]

More than her determination to wed him drew Lincoln to Mary Todd. She had, as Mrs. Benjamin Edwards recalled, "a naturally fine mind and cultivated tastes. She was a great reader and possessed of a remarkably retentive memory." Mary Todd's "brilliant conversation, often embellished with apt quotations" made her "much sought after by the young people of the town. She was quick at repartee and when the occasion seemed to require it was sarcastic and severe."[324] According to Elizabeth Edwards, Lincoln "was charmed with Mary's wit and fascinated with her quick sagacity—her will—her nature—and culture." Her sparkling conversation seemed to mesmerize Lincoln: "I have happened in the room where they were sitting often & often and Mary led the conversation. Lincoln would listen & gaze on her as if drawn by some superior power, irresistibly so: he listened [and] . . . scarcely said a word."[325]

Mary Todd's youthfulness may have been especially attractive to Lincoln. Just as she needed a father figure to indulge her, so it seems that Lincoln needed "someone of his very own to pet and humor."[326] Thus, in Ruth Painter Randall's words, Mary Todd "aroused the paternal instinct that was always so strong an element in his make-up."[327] A journalist who observed the Lincolns in Washington thought that the president found in his wife, "despite her foibles and sometimes her puerileness, just what he needed." Those foibles included "natural want of tact," "deficiency in the sense of the fitness of things," "blundering outspokenness," and "impolitic disregard of diplomatic considerations."[328]

This analysis may be only partly correct; rather than finding her attractive despite her puerileness, it was *because* of it that he was drawn to her. Lincoln had a deep paternal streak; some part of him needed to have children and child surrogates (chapter 4). Mary Todd was ideally suited for such a role. As Helen Nicolay observed, the president's "attitude toward his wife had something of the paternal in it, almost as though she were a child, under his protection."[329] Thus, when Lincoln proposed to Mary Todd in 1840,[330] when he was thirty-one and she twenty-one, he probably did so because he desired to have a "child-wife" and because he believed that she wanted him to do so.

He broke the engagement in late 1840 because he had fallen in love with another woman, the eighteen-year-old Matilda Edwards, a cousin of Ninian Edwards and "something of a coquette." According to Orville H. Browning, "Lincoln became very much attached to her" and "finally fell desperately in love with her, and proposed to her, but she rejected him." Lincoln then "told Miss Todd that he loved Matilda Edwards." Understandably, Mary "had very bitter feelings towards her rival."[331] After falling in love with Miss Edwards, Lincoln reportedly told John J. Hardin "that he thought he did not love her [Mary Todd] as he should and that he would do her a great wrong if he married her."[332] To Mrs. William Butler, he allegedly confided in early 1841, "it would just kill me to marry Mary Todd."[333]

In 1842, he resumed the courtship. According to Browning, "he undoubtedly felt that he had made [a mistake] in having engaged himself to Miss Todd. But having done so, he felt himself in honor bound to act in perfect good faith towards her—and that good faith compelled him to fulfill his engagement with her, if she persisted in claiming the fulfillment of his word." Browning "always doubted whether, had circumstances left him entirely free to act upon his own impulses, he would have voluntarily made proposals of marriage to Miss Todd."[334]

Lincoln harbored serious misgivings, which he discussed indirectly with his closest friend, Joshua Speed, in a series of letters concerning Speed's own courtship and anxiety about marriage. After his engagement to Fanny Henning, Speed endured "immense suffering" because he doubted that he really loved her.[335] Lincoln reassured him that his anxiety was groundless. In a document that tells as much about Lincoln's feelings toward Mary Todd as it does about Speed's toward Fanny Henning,[336] he asked:

> How came you to court her? Was it because you thought she desired it; and that you had given her reason to expect it? If it was for that, why did not the same reason make you court Ann Todd, and at least twenty others of whom you can think, & to whom it would apply with greater force than to *her?* Did you court her for her wealth? Why, you knew she had none. But you say you *reasoned* yourself *into* it. What do you mean by that? Was it not, that you found yourself unable to *reason* yourself *out* of it? Did you not think, and partly form the purpose, of courting her the first time you ever saw or heard of her? What had reason to do with it, at that early stage? There was nothing *at that time* for reason to work upon. Whether she was moral, amiable, sensible, or even of good character, you did not, nor could not then know; except perhaps you might infer the last from the company you found her in. All you then did or could know of her, was her *personal appearance and deportment;* and these, if they impress at all, impress the *heart* and not the head.
>
> Say candidly, were not those heavenly *black eyes,* the whole basis of all your early *reasoning* on the subject?[337]

From this it might well be inferred that Lincoln had several doubts about wedding Mary Todd; that he loved her because she wanted and expected him to do so; that he feared he was interested in her wealth; and that he had allowed his head to convince him of his love rather than his heart. He seemed to be telling himself in this letter that such doubts were ill-founded.

Having reassured Speed (and indirectly himself) that his love was genuine, Lincoln evidently felt confident enough to renew his courtship. But he required one more piece of evidence before he could actually marry. On October 5, 1842, he asked Speed, who had wed Fanny

Henning several months earlier, "Are you now, in *feeling* as well as *judgement,* glad you are married as you are?"[338] Apparently Speed replied in the affirmative, thus emboldening Lincoln to propose to Mary Todd once again. After a separation of a year and a half, they had begun seeing each other again in the summer of 1842. On November 4, they decided to wed that very day. Mary's sister hastily arranged a ceremony and reception, and in the evening Abraham Lincoln and Mary Todd were married.[339]

Lincoln's reasons for hesitating to marry probably went deeper than the correspondence with Speed indicates. Charles B. Strozier argues that he dreaded intimacy "because he had not fully consolidated the bases of his sexual or work identity."[340] This seems an insufficient explanation, for, as the psychologist Daniel J. Levinson has found, most men wed before they are "ready to make an enduring inner commitment to wife and family, and they are not capable of a highly loving, sexually free and emotionally intimate relationship." Levinson also concluded that most men require a long time to "form an occupation," or, in Strozier's parlance, "establish a work identity."[341]

Lincoln's uneasiness about women probably stemmed from the death of his mother in his tenth year. The bitter agony that Lincoln experienced as a youth in Indiana seems to have crippled his capacity for trusting and loving women lest they abandon him as his mother had done. He harbored irrational fears of abandonment throughout adulthood (chapter 6). Although he had sufficiently overcome his fear of intimacy and marriage to wed Mary Todd, he did so with foreboding. As he dressed for the ceremony, he was asked where he was going. "I guess I am going to hell," he replied.[342] His best man, James Matheny, thought "Lincoln looked and acted as if he were going to the slaughter" and "more like one going to his grave than one going to his wedding."[343] We have only an enigmatic statement from the groom himself about his true feelings. A week after the ceremony, he told a colleague, "Nothing new here, except my marrying, which to me, is [a] matter of profound wonder."[344] A wedding guest, Mrs. B. S. Edwards, detected little love between the newlyweds. "I have often doubted," she later wrote, "that it was really a love affair." Mrs. Edwards acknowledged that Lincoln had been "deeply in love with Matilda Edwards," but she believed that his marriage to Mary Todd was something different, a match "made up" by "mutual friends."[345]

If Lincoln did not marry for love, it is possible, but unlikely, that he did so to advance his political career by forming an alliance with the more aristocratic Whig element. But such a calculating approach to wedlock seems out of character for Lincoln, who, after all, fell in love with Ann Rutledge and later proposed to Sarah Rickard, neither of whom belonged to well-bred Illinois society. Moreover, as Ruth Painter Randall noted, in some ways "it was a political hazard . . . to ally himself with aristocracy."[346] A few months after wedding Mary Todd, he was defeated for the Whig congressional nomination partly because, as he told a friend, of his reputation "as the candidate of pride, wealth, and aristocratic family distinction."[347]

As a husband, Lincoln evidently provided his wife with little intimacy. A few months after his death, she stated frankly that, for all his "deep feeling," he was *"not, a demonstrative man, [—] when he felt most deeply, he expressed, the least."*[348] Elizabeth Edwards thought Lincoln "a cold man" who "had no affection."[349] The marriage, as Jean Baker describes it, was troubled by his "abstraction and forgetfulness" and "his infuriating self-containment," as well as "her histrionic claims on his attention by flirting with other men" and "her clamorous need for affection, probably physical, undoubtedly emotional."[350] In Illinois he spent much time away from home.

When Lincoln served in Congress in the late 1840s, his wife evidently got along poorly with some of the boarders at the roominghouse where they lived. He told her in April 1848, "All the house—or rather, all with whom you were on decided good terms—send their love to you. The others say nothing."[351] Absorbed with his duties as a freshman representative, Lincoln thought that his wife hindered him somewhat in attending to his business. Only four letters between the Lincoln exist for the year they were separated during his term in Congress in the late 1840s. Their tone indicates that he played the role of indulgent parent. When his wife asked whether she could return to be with him in the capital, he replied, "Will you be a *good girl* in all things, if I consent?"[352] During the Civil War, as Baker notes, "With Lincoln often depressed and preoccupied with the war news, she was lonely."[353] In need of a confidant, she turned to John Watt.[354]

Lincoln's incapacity for intimacy kept him from forming close bonds not only with his wife but also with men.[355] Herndon said that "Lincoln never had a confidant, and therefore never unbosomed himself to others."[356] David Davis recalled that "Lincoln had no spontaneity—no emotional nature—no strong emotional feelings for any person." Davis added that, contrary to the widespread belief that he "knew all about Lincoln's thoughts," in fact Lincoln "never confided . . . anything" to him.[357] Recalling that Lincoln was "secretive," Lyman Trumbull doubted "if any man ever had his entire confidence."[358] A conspicuous exception was Speed, but after Lincoln's marriage, the bonds between them weakened. During the Civil War he spoke candidly about personal matters with Orville H. Browning, but Browning never became the confidant that Speed had been.[359]

This emotional reserve would probably have antagonized any woman. In general, women sensed that something was missing in Lincoln. Mary Owens identified it as "the little links that make up the chain of a woman's happiness."[360] Herndon was probably right when he said that "Lincoln ought never to have married anyone. He had no quality for a husband. He was abstracted, [and] cool."[361] Other colleagues shared this view, including Henry Rankin, who called Lincoln a "perplexing husband" who was a "puzzle or sometimes a despair" to his wife.[362] Henry C. Whitney told Herndon that "so great & peculiar a man as Lincoln could not make any woman happy. I guess he was too much allied to his intellect to get down to the plane of the domestic relations."[363]

Lincoln's reserve doubtless infuriated his needy wife, who reacted with rages. In turn, he responded by withdrawing even more. His law practice required him to travel throughout central Illinois for long stretches of each spring and fall.[364] Ruth Painter Randall called these absences "one of the greatest hardships of the marriage."[365] Mary Lincoln, according to a Springfield neighbor, "always said that if her husband had staid at home as he ought to that she could love him better."[366] She told the wife of a businessman, "You are fortunate in having a husband who is not in politics. A politician is owned by everybody, and his wife has many lonely hours."[367]

Not content at home, Lincoln relished life on the circuit so much that he refused to accept the offer made to him by a Chicago firm because he preferred traveling about central Illinois, even if he earned smaller fees than he might in Chicago.[368] David Davis believed that "Mr. Lincoln was happy—as happy as *he* could be, when on this Circuit—and happy no other place."[369] Davis noted that generally "all the lawyers of a Saturday evening would go home and see their families and friends, [but] Lincoln would find some excuse and refuse to go."[370] This conduct at first puzzled Davis and the other circuit-riding attorneys, but, as Davis wrote later, they "soon learned to account for his strange disinclination to go home. Lincoln himself never had much to say about home, and we never felt free to comment on it. Most of us had pleas-

ant, inviting homes, and as we struck out for them I'm sure each one
of us down in our hearts had a mingled feeling of pity and sympathy
for him."[371] It seemed to Davis and the others that Lincoln "was not
domestically happy."[372]

Herndon claimed that "Lincoln took a wide circuit" because "his
home was *Hell*" and "absence from home was his *Heaven.*"[373] Henry
Whitney, who spent time on the circuit with Lincoln, recalled that
"nothing could be duller than remaining on the Sabbath in a country
inn of that time after adjournment of court. Good cheer has expended
its force during court week, and blank dullness succeeded; but Lincoln
would entertain the few lingering roustabouts of the barroom with as
great zest, apparently, as he had previously entertained the court and
bar, and then would hitch up his horse . . . and, solitary and alone, ride
off to the next term in course."[374]

Not only was Lincoln the sole lawyer on the circuit to stay away
from home on weekends, but he was also one of the few who attended every court on the circuit and remained on it until the end of the
term.[375] According to attorney John M. Scott, "After 1854 there was
no such thing in central Illinois as 'traveling the circuit' as was done in
earlier days. Mr. Lincoln was probably the last one to give it up in the
'old 8th Circuit.'"[376] Leonard Swett in 1860 claimed that "for perhaps
five years Lincoln and myself have been the only ones [lawyers] who
have habitually passed over the whole circuit."[377]

Unlike David Davis, who wrote home once or twice each week,
Lincoln evidently corresponded with his spouse rarely. Davis said in
1852 that Lincoln, while riding the circuit, had not heard from his wife
for six weeks.[378] Mrs. Norman B. Judd once inquired of Lincoln, who
was on the circuit at the time, how his wife was. When told that he
had not heard since he had started out three weeks earlier, Mrs. Judd
asked incredulously, "But Mr. Lincoln, aren't you married?" "No, no,"
he replied, "if there was anything the matter Mary would write." Mrs.
Judd, whose husband wrote to her daily when they were separated, was
nonplused.[379] Mary Lincoln and Robert Lincoln may have destroyed
some family correspondence, so it is hard to know exactly what to make
of the paucity of surviving letters between Lincoln and his wife.[380]

Lincoln began staying away from home early in the marriage. In
the first year, during the initial nine months of which Mary was preg-
nant, he was gone for nearly ten weeks. Although he was homesick
when away from Springfield during the early months of his marriage,[381]
as time passed he absented himself more and more until he was spend-

ing more than four months each year on the road.[382] David Davis told his wife in 1854 that "Mr. Lincoln is so much engaged here [on the circuit] that he will not find time to go home—so that before he gets home again he will have been absent six (6) weeks."[383] Mrs. Davis "was a little critical of Lincoln, whom she adored, for staying out on the circuit when Mary was expecting."[384] Even when in Springfield, Lincoln would frequently spend evenings away from home. Herndon recalled that he often left for work around seven or eight in the morning and would not return until midnight or later.[385]

To reduce conflict with his tempestuous wife, Lincoln not only avoided her but also gave her almost total control of their home.[386] He told a friend that "I myself manage all important matters. In little things I have got along through life by letting my wife run her end of the machine pretty much in her own way."[387] This pattern apparently began shortly after the Lincolns wed. According to Mrs. John A. Logan, Mary Lincoln one day "casually observed at the breakfast table that she was without a cook." Although she "did not ask him to procure her a cook," after finishing his meal, "he drove a distance of some thirty miles to attend court, and while in attendance at court he procured a competent help, hoping pleasantly to surprise his wife on his return home by the presentation of a cook." But his plan miscarried, for his wife, "having assumed to attend to her part of her husband's domestic affairs," refused "to accept the cook of her husband's selection, and thereby early in her married life established a precedent which to the lawyer-husband in subsequent life was a relief from any burdens about household affairs."[388]

When a gardener asked whether a certain tree should be cut down, Lincoln replied, "Have you seen Mrs. L[incoln]?" When told that his wife had approved the idea, he exclaimed, "Then in God's name cut it down clear to the roots!"[389]

Although a notoriously indulgent and kind father, Lincoln was also frequently absent, leaving Mary to raise the children more or less by herself (chapter 3). In addition to her spouse's long absences, Mary Lincoln also seemed to resent his failure to earn much money. To be sure, although Lincoln had a respectable law practice, it did not generate enough income for luxuries like travel abroad.[390] In 1857 Mrs. Lincoln complained to her half-sister that when she saw in New York harbor large passenger steamers ready to sail for Europe, "I felt in my heart, inclined to sigh, that poverty was my portion, how I long to go to Europe." She added significantly that "I often laugh & tell Mr.

L[incoln] that I am determined my next Husband *shall be rich.*"[391] J. G. McCoy of Springfield recalled that Mary Lincoln "was ambitious to shine in a social way, beyond Mr. Lincoln's inclination or financial ability to sustain, and was given to scolding and complaining of Mr. Lincoln in a manner and to a[n] extent exceedingly unpleasant to him."[392] Another neighbor in Springfield said Mary Lincoln "was very desirous of having a carriage to take herself and packages home, but was unable to persuade Mr. Lincoln to purchase one." She therefore, "with a view of shaming him," one day "mounted the steps of his office and announced that she had a conveyance at the door to take him home." Manifesting "no surprise," he "quietly started with her down the stairs." On the street "stood an old fashioned one-horse dray," to which Mrs. Lincoln pointed and said, "There is your carriage." Her spouse, "smiling in his quaint way, climbed on to the dray and invited his wife to join him; she failed to see the joke, and Mr. Lincoln then told Jake, the driver, to take him home."[393]

The Lincolns' sex life is undocumented. They had four children, the first arriving nine months after the wedding and the others at roughly three-year intervals.[394] Mary evidently suffered a gynecological injury delivering the last-born in 1853, and it is possible that sexual relations between the Lincolns ceased thereafter. In 1856 their house was enlarged to provide separate bedrooms for husband and wife, then aged forty-seven and thirty-seven.[395]

As David Davis and Herndon noted, Lincoln seldom talked about his home life, so it is difficult to determine how he felt about his wife.[396] Some indirect evidence is suggestive. Once when Lincoln was traveling the circuit with Mrs. Lincoln's cousin, John Todd Stuart, a landlady greeted them thus: "Stuart, how fine and peart you do look!, but Lincoln, whatever have you been a doing? you do look powerful weak."

"'Nothing out of common, Ma'am,' was his reply, 'but did you ever see Stuart's wife? or did you ever see mine? I just tell you whoever married into the 'Todd' family gets the worst of it.'"[397]

Lincoln relished jokes about henpecked husbands.[398] He underlined a passage from a poem entitled "Love of Fame" that chided shrewish wives:

> A dearth of words, a woman need not fear;
> But 'tis a task indeed to learn to *hear*.
> Doubly like Echo sound is her delight,

And the last word is her eternal right.
Is't not enough plagues, wars and famines rise
To lash our crimes, but must our wives be wise?[399]

It is possible that Lincoln knew what he was letting himself in for when he married, but some believe that Mary Todd changed dramatically after her wedding. According to Herndon, she was before marriage "rather pleasant—polite—civil . . . intelligent [and] witty." But "after she got married she became soured—got gross—became material—avaricious—insolent—mean—insulting—imperious; and a she wolf." Herndon thought that wolf "was in her when young and unmarried, but she unchained it . . . when she got married. Discretion when young kept the wolf back for a while, but when there was no more necessity for chaining it was unchained to growl—snap & bite at all."[400]

If Herndon was right, and the evidence seems to bear him out, Lincoln confronted a difficult situation early in his marriage. He believed in plowing around stumps not into them.[401] To make marriage with such a difficult woman bearable, he distanced himself physically and emotionally, let her run domestic matters, and invested most of his psychological capital in his career as a lawyer and a politician.

The Lincolns' marital difficulties did not stem solely from his incapacity for intimacy and her displacement onto him of rage against her father, however. The unconscious, as Carl Jung has argued, consists of both a personal and a transpersonal realm. The personal unconscious is shaped by specific life events, especially childhood traumas. The transpersonal unconscious is a given at birth. A major part of the latter is a dominant archetype that profoundly shapes a life, no matter what is experienced in early years.[402] Lincoln's archetype seems to have been the Old Man (chapter 4). In its negative phase, a person dominated by the Old Man archetype is nay-saying, rigid, cold, hard, bitter, joyless, and sapped of life; a positive Old Man is wise, supportive, paternal, generous, and kind.[403] Lincoln clearly fits the positive Old Man pattern.

The opposite archetype is the Eternal Youth.[404] Among other things, a positive Eternal Youth radiates vitality, enthusiasm, hope, wonder, zest, and charm. Many people dominated by this archetype have, as Marie Louise von Franz has put it, "the stirring quality of a drink of champagne."[405] In short, a positive Eternal Youth is childlike. The negative Eternal Youth is childish or puerile: irresponsible, dependent, naive, gullible, undisciplined, indecisive, demanding, and self-centered.

Mary Lincoln seems to have been a negative Eternal Youth. "In some ways she never grew up," Ruth Painter Randall noted; she "had a timidity and childlike dependence upon the strength and calmness of others," she "was a child" in the hands of unscrupulous men during the Civil War, and among the scheming women of Washington society she "was as defenseless as a trusting child."[406]

Julia Taft Bayne, who as an adolescent saw her often in the White House, recalled that it "was an outstanding characteristic of Mary Todd Lincoln that she wanted what she wanted when she wanted it and no substitute!"[407] W. A. Evans rightly called this tendency "an infantile quality."[408] Julia Bayne remembered how Mary Lincoln coveted a special ribbon she observed in her mother's bonnet and brazenly asked her to give it over. The astonished Mrs. Taft complied.[409] A similar incident occurred in Springfield in the late 1850s, when a merchant invited Mrs. Lincoln to take her pick from an order of fancy material that had just arrived. She chose some organdie patterns for dresses and was initially delighted that she had been allowed first choice. Her joy faded, however, when she discovered that the merchant's wife had selected a pattern even earlier. To calm his aggrieved spouse, Lincoln visited the merchant and explained the situation. Magnanimously the merchant's wife turned over her organdie to Mary Lincoln, whose husband later told the merchant, "Of course I don't understand. But you seem to have fixed it all right. I'm obliged. Queer, isn't it?"[410] In 1848, when one of Lincoln's grateful clients, noticing that he was clad in homespun, sent his wife a present of some broadcloth, she indignantly protested that she did not wear trousers or coats or vests.[411]

Mary Lincoln handled her adult responsibilities poorly. As a mother, she had conspicuous shortcomings.[412] In Springfield she mismanaged household funds, prompting Lincoln to rare outbursts of scolding.[413] Thus she seems to fit the description of a negative Eternal Youth. A positive Old Man and a negative Eternal Youth are, in archetypal terms, polar opposites and bound to get along only with great difficulty. The Lincolns were polar opposites in psychological typology as well. Lincoln was an introverted thinker, whereas Mary Todd was extroverted and feeling.[414] James C. Conkling observed her at parties in her youth and described her as "the very creature of excitement . . . [who] never enjoys herself more than when in society and surrounded by a company of merry friends."[415] Introverts and extroverts cannot easily understand and empathize with one another. William E. Barton had good reason to conclude that the Lincolns "were divinely constituted to make each other uncomfortable."[416]

The sad story of Lincoln's marriage is more than simply antiquarian gossip. The long years of dealing with his tempestuous wife helped prepare Lincoln for handling the difficult people he encountered as president. After examining the Lincoln marriage, Benjamin Thomas eloquently concluded that "over the slow fires of misery that he learned to keep banked and under heavy pressure deep within him, his innate qualities of patience, tolerance, forbearance, and forgiveness were tempered and refined."[417] Henry C. Whitney believed that "but for the domestic discipline which Mr. Lincoln underwent" living with his wife, he would not have succeeded as president.[418]

Lincoln might not ever have become president in the first place but for his wife's influence. Friends and neighbors like David Davis, Milton Hay, William Herndon, and James Matheny agreed that had he married a more amiable woman, in all probability "he would have been satisfied with the modest emoluments of a country lawyer's practice . . . and buried in the delights of an inviting and happy home."[419] J. G. McCoy, who knew Lincoln well in Springfield, ascribed his knowledge of history, constitutionalism, and "the laws of human government" to "an untoward domestic situation." Rather then spending evenings at his unhappy home, he became "a constant attendent" at the state library, where he read widely.[420]

Not simply as a shrew making home life unbearable did Mary Lincoln help pave her husband's way to the White House; she was also a useful goad to his wavering ambition. Eager as he was for distinction and fame, he might well have settled for a lesser office had she not spurred him to seek the presidency.[421] Her close friend, Judge James Bradwell, believed that "she made Mr. L. by constantly pushing him on in his ambition."[422] Henry Rankin thought that "without Mary Todd for his wife, Abraham Lincoln would never have been President. . . . Until 1858 he needed influences outside himself to push him to the political front and hold him there. She gave him this unstintingly."[423] According to Herndon, she was "like a toothache, keeping her husband awake to politics day and night."[424]

Lincoln once presented his wife a book entitled *The Elements of Character* by Mary G. Chandler. In it he had marked a passage suggesting that marriage could deteriorate from "the highest happiness that can exist on earth" to "a fountain of misery, of a quality absolutely infernal."[425] The Lincolns' marriage was such a fountain of misery, yet from it flowed incalculable good for the nation.

NOTES

1. David R. Locke, in Rice, *RL,* 449–50.
2. Reminiscences of H. M. Powel, Taylorville [Ill.] *Semi-Weekly Breeze,* 12 Feb. 1909. As a youth of twelve and thirteen, Powel was hired to spend the night at the Lincoln home while Lincoln was away on business. From the summer of 1851 to the fall of 1853, Powel often visited the Lincolns.
3. Fawn M. Brodie, *Thomas Jefferson: An Intimate History* (New York: W. W. Norton, 1974), 25.
4. Herndon to Jesse W. Weik, Springfield, 8, 15, 16 Jan. 1886, H-W MSS, DLC; to C. O. Poole, Springfield, 5 Jan. 1886, in Hertz, *HL,* 122; and to Truman H. Bartlett, Springfield, 22 Sept. 1887, Bartlett Scrapbook, Massachusetts Historical Society; Herndon's lecture, "Analysis of the Character of Abraham Lincoln" [delivered 26 Dec. 1865], in *Abraham Lincoln Quarterly* 1 (Dec. 1941), 419n. John Hay called Mary Lincoln "the Hellcat." Hay to John G. Nicolay, Washington, 5 April 1862, Hay MSS, RPB.
5. Carl Schurz, interview with Ida Tarbell, 6 Nov. 1897, Ida M. Tarbell MSS, Allegheny College.
6. Randall, *MTL,* 64, 112. Cf. Noah Brooks, *Abraham Lincoln and the Downfall of American Slavery* (New York: G. P. Putnam's Sons, 1894), 422. Douglas L. Wilson has termed Randall's studies of Mary Todd Lincoln "a highly partisan and self-conscious effort to rescue the character and reputation" of her subject. Wilson, "Abraham Lincoln, Joshua Speed, and 'that fatal first of January,'" chapter of a forthcoming book, 4. I am grateful to Douglas Wilson for providing me a copy of his manuscript.
Randall's work has in some ways been superseded by Baker, *MTL,* although Baker's study is in its way as defensive as Randall's. When describing how creditors dunned Mary Lincoln after her husband's death, Baker says, "Like cockroaches come out at dark, the merchants and jewelers who had so casually extended credit in the past now emerged, demanding payment for finery she had purchased on an income of $25,000" (258). Baker also denigrates contemporaries who said unflattering things about Mary Lincoln. She calls David Davis a "fat judge," William Herndon "cranky" and "alcoholic," and Isaac Arnold "steely-eyed" (264, 267, 255). For thoughtful analyses of Baker's strengths and weaknesses, and Baker's response to the analyses, see "Symposium I," in *The Psychohistory Review* 17 (Fall 1988): 5–48.
7. John Y. Simon, "Abraham Lincoln and Ann Rutledge," *Journal of the Abraham Lincoln Association* 11 (1990): 33. Cf. Turner and Turner, *MTL,* 413: "Whatever the public was led to believe, she knew the union had been, on balance, an extremely happy one."
8. Richard N. Current, *The Lincoln Nobody Knows* (New York: Hill and Wang, 1958), 50.

9. In some sources Mary Todd is considered the fourth child, but Baker concludes that she was the third-born; see *MTL,* 371n4.

10. Ibid., 3–98. A revealing sketch of young Mary Todd is contained in a long letter by Elizabeth L. Norris to Emilie Todd Helm, Garden City, Kan., 28 Sept. 1895, photostat, JGR MSS, DLC.

11. Albert J. Beveridge, *Abraham Lincoln, 1809–1858,* 2 vols. (Boston: Houghton, Mifflin, 1928), 1:312.

12. Beveridge, *Abraham Lincoln,* 1:312.

13. Angle, *HL,* 165.

14. Henry B. Rankin, *Personal Recollections of Abraham Lincoln* (New York: G. P. Putnam's Sons, 1916), 160.

15. Mary Lincoln to Abram Wakeman, Washington, 30 Jan. [1865], in Turner and Turner, *MTL,* 200.

16. Randall, *MTL,* 20. Baker observed that "clearly Mary Todd and Abraham Lincoln were an oddly matched couple." *MTL,* 83, see also 132.

17. Lincoln to Martin S. Morris, Springfield, 26 March 1843, in Basler, *CWL,* 1:320.

18. Mary Todd Lincoln to Eliza Stuart Steele, Chicago, May [23, 1871], in Turner and Turner, *MTL,* 588.

19. Baker, *MTL,* 24, 28–32, 330–32, 333. Baker suggests (28) that even before the death of her mother, Mary Todd had suffered dislocating shocks, including abrupt weaning at age one, when her mother delivered another baby; the loss of a brother when she was four; and the surrender of her middle name, Ann, when she was five.

20. Turner and Turner, *MTL,* 7.

21. John T. Stuart, interview with John G. Nicolay, 23 June 1875, Hay MSS, RPB.

22. Mrs. John A. Logan, *Thirty Years in Washington; or, Life and Scenes in Our National Capital* (Hartford: A. D. Worthington, 1901), 646.

23. Interview with Mrs. Alexander R. McKee (née Martinette Hardin), Marietta Holdstock Brown, "A Romance of Lincoln," clipping identified as "Indianapolis 1896," LMFW.

24. Statement by James H. Matheny, 3 May 1866, H-W MSS, DLC. Herndon's memo indicates that Matheny had heard stories about Mrs. Lincoln from the "Butler girls," presumably the daughters of William Butler, at whose Springfield home Lincoln had boarded for years before his wedding.

25. Notes of Jesse Weik's interview with Judge Anthony Thornton, Shelbyville, 18 June 1895, Weik MSS, IHi. Judge Thornton heard Van Bergen state this.

26. Undated statements by Gourley, H-W MSS, DLC, and Weik, *RL,* 121–22.

27. Herndon to Weik, Springfield, 16 Jan. 1886, H-W MSS, DLC.

28. Reminiscences of "Mr. Eaton" (probably Page Eaton), Belvedere [Ill.] *Standard,* 14 April 1868, 1. Eaton's life is summarized in Wayne C. Temple, *Builder of Lincoln's Home: Page Eaton* (Harrogate, Tenn.: Lincoln Memorial University Press, 1962), 1–3.

29. Herndon to Isaac N. Arnold, Springfield, 24 Oct. [18]83, Lincoln Collection, ICHi.

328   *The Inner World of Abraham Lincoln*

30. Statements of Joseph P. Kent, 21 Nov. 1916, H-W MSS, DLC and Weik, *RL,* 126.

31. Victor Kutchin to the editor of the New York *Times,* Green Lake, Wis., 21 Aug. 1934, New York *Times,* 26 Aug. 1934, sec. 4, 5, and 29 July 1934, sec. 4, 1. Kutchin was a close friend of Mason Brayman, to whom Lincoln entrusted the couch when he left Springfield in 1861. Brayman in turn gave it to Kutchin.

32. David Bigelow Parker, *A Chautauqua Boy in '61* (Boston: Small, Maynard, 1912), 47–48.

33. Herndon to Jesse Weik, Springfield, 19 Nov. 1885, H-W MSS, DLC.

34. Ibid.; Emilie Helm's reminiscences in Katherine Helm, *The True Story of Mary, Wife of Lincoln* (New York: Harper and Brothers, 1928), 113.

35. The carpenter's story reported by Mary Todd Melvin Dewing, a neighbor and close friend of the Lincoln family, *Christian Science Monitor,* 12 Feb. 1935.

36. Weik, *RL,* 94. The statement was made by Harriet Hanks Chapman.

37. Herndon to Jesse Weik, Springfield, 23 Jan. 1886, H-W MSS, DLC. Evidently alluding to this incident, Baker reports that Mary Lincoln once threw "a log at him"; see *MTL,* 134.

38. Dubois's undated interview with Jesse W. Weik, Weik MSS, IHi. I am indebted to Douglas L. Wilson for calling this to my attention. Herndon claimed that she sometimes drove "him out with a stick of stove wood in order to make him go to market for some beef for breakfast." Herndon to Isaac N. Arnold, Springfield, 24 Oct. [18]83, Lincoln Collection, ICHi.

39. Reminiscences of "Mr. Eaton," Belvedere [Ill.] *Standard,* 14 April 1868, 1. According to Eaton, she said this "often."

40. Reminiscence by Rebecca Pomroy, who spent several weeks in the White House in 1862, paraphrased in Galusha Anderson, *Hitherto Unknown* (New York: Cochrane, 1910), 156.

41. Julia Taft Bayne, *Tad Lincoln's Father* (Boston: Little, Brown, 1931), 33.

42. Henry W. Fis[c]her, *Mark Twain and Eugene Field: Tales They Told to a Fellow Correspondent* (New York: N. L. Brown, 1922), 118–19, quoted in *Mark Twain Laughing: Humorous Anecdotes by and about Samuel L. Clemens,* ed. Paul M. Zall (Knoxville: University of Tennessee Press, 1985), 129–30. Early in the Civil War, Robert Gould Shaw reported that while reviewing troops, Lincoln "took off his hat in the most awkward way, putting it on again with his hand on the back part of the rim, country fashion." Shaw to his mother, [Washington], 27 April 1861, in *Blue-Eyed Child of Fortune: The Civil War Letters of Colonel Robert Gould Shaw,* ed. Russell Duncan (Athens: University of Georgia Press, 1992), 82.

43. Reminiscences of Mary Miner Hill, daughter of the Rev. Dr. Noyes W. Miner, 1923, SC 1985, 11, IHi.

44. A "near relative of Mrs. Lincoln," quoted in Angle, *HL,* 345.

45. Norman F. Boas, "Unpublished Manuscripts: Recollections of Mary Todd Lincoln by Her Sister Emilie Todd Helm; An Invitation to a Lincoln Party," *Manuscripts* 43 (Winter 1991): 25. I am indebted to S. L. Carson for calling this to my attention.

46. Harriet Chapman's undated interview with Jesse W. Weik, Weik MSS, IHi; Angle, *HL*, 345.

47. A. Longfellow Fiske, "A Neighbor of Lincoln," *Commonweal*, 2 March 1932, 494. Lincoln's stepnephew John Hall alleged that Lincoln during the summer of 1846 or 1847 came to visit his family in Coles County, evidently to escape his wife. Eleanor Gridley, *The Story of Abraham Lincoln; or, The Journey from the Log Cabin to the White House* (Chicago: Monarch, 1902), 167.

48. Statement of Pascal P. Enos, N.d., H-W MSS, DLC.

49. Herndon to Jesse Weik, Springfield, 19 Nov. 1885, H-W MSS, DLC; Baker, *MTL*, 106–8.

50. Memo of an interview with Joseph P. Kent, 21 Nov. 1916, H-W MSS, DLC.

51. Harriet Hanks Chapman to Herndon, Charleston, Ill., 10 Dec. 1866, H-W MSS, DLC.

52. Herndon to Isaac N. Arnold, Springfield, 24 Oct. [18]83, Lincoln Collection, ICHi.

53. Mary Clemmer [Ames], *Ten Years in Washington; or, Inside Life and Scenes in Our National Capital as a Woman Sees Them* (Hartford: Hartford Publishing Co., 1882), 239.

54. Martin Crawford, ed., *William Howard Russell's Civil War: Private Diary and Letters, 1861–1862* (Athens: University of Georgia Press, 1992), [entry for 3 Nov. 1861].

55. Ames, *Ten Years in Washington*, 171–72, 239.

56. Interview with Alexander Williamson, New York *Press*, N.d., reprinted in an unidentified newspaper dated 30 June 1889, LMFW.

57. Margaret Ryan, interview with Jesse W. Weik, 27 Oct. 1886, Weik MSS, IHi. I am indebted to Douglas L. Wilson for calling this item to my attention.

58. Mary Lincoln to Emilie Todd Helm, Springfield, 23 Nov. 1856, in Turner and Turner, *MTL*, 46.

59. Statement of John S. Bradford in Weik, *RL*, 99.

60. Ibid., 100. Lincoln similarly augmented the wages of a young boy hired to drive Mrs. Lincoln about Springfield. Ibid., 123–24. The "Maria" referred to here was doubtless Mariah Vance, who from 1850 to 1860 served as a cook, laundress, and maid for the Lincolns but did not live in their house. Lloyd Ostendorf, "A Monument for One of the Lincoln Maids," *Lincoln Herald* 66 (Winter 1964): 184–86. Cf. Angle, *HL*, 346.

61. Statement of Mrs. N. W. Edwards, H-W MSS, DLC.

62. Margaret Ryan, interview with Jesse W. Weik, 27 Oct. 1886, Weik MSS, IHi.

63. Henry Haynie in "Success," N.d., *Youth's Companion*, 1 Sept. 1898.

64. John F. Mendosa to James R. B. Van Cleave, Springfield, 2 July 1908, Vertical File, "Reminiscences," folder 3, Lincoln Collection, IHi. Cf. Baker, *MTL*, 110.

65. New York correspondence by "Metropolitan," 9 Oct. 1867, Boston *Post*, 11 Oct. 1867, 1.

66. Interview with Harriet Hanks Chapman, 16 Oct. 1914, Weik MSS,

IHi. Harriet Chapman lived with the Lincolns for eighteen months in 1844 and 1845.

67. "Notes of Interview with Mrs. Fanny Grimsley, July 27, 1926," by Paul M. Angle, enclosed in Angle to W. E. Barton, Springfield, 10 Jan. 1927, William E. Barton MSS, University of Chicago.

68. Margaret Ryan, interview with Jesse W. Weik, 27 Oct. 1886, Weik MSS, IHi.

69. Jesse W. Weik, undated interview, either with Taggart or his daughter, Weik MSS, IHi.

70. Hillary A. Gobin to Albert J. Beveridge, South Bend, 17 May 1923, Beveridge MSS, DLC. In the mid and late 1850s, Mrs. Gobin's father was a minister in Springfield, living a few doors away from the Lincolns' house.

71. New York Times, 6 Feb. 1938, sec. 2:1.

72. Margaret Ryan, interview with Jesse W. Weik, 27 Oct. 1886, Weik MSS, IHi. For a similar story about Mary Lincoln in the White House, see an unidentified artist's account, unidentified clipping, Lincoln Scrapbooks, vol. 2, Judd Stewart Collection, CSmH.

73. Mrs. Early, née Catherine Miles, often told this story to her nephew Jimmy Miles, who in turn related it to Dale Carnegie. Carnegie, Lincoln the Unknown (New York: Perma Giants, 1932), 71–72. The episode took place before other boarders. Louis A. Warren, commenting on Mary Lincoln's reputation for having "a quick temper and a sharp tongue," wrote, "Possibly she threw coffee at Lincoln and drove him out of the house with a broom and probably he deserved it." Lincoln Lore, 15 Feb. 1937.

74. Baker, MTL, 134.

75. Statement of King to Herndon, N.d., H-W MSS, DLC; Beveridge, Lincoln, 1:508n.

76. Memo of a conversation between Jesse Weik and Diller, 21 Nov. 1916, H-W MSS, DLC.

77. Ibid.; Weik, RL, 93–94.

78. Memo of a conversation between Joseph P. Kent and Weik, 21 Nov. 1916, H-W MSS, DLC; Weik, RL, 123.

79. New York correspondence by "Metropolitan," 9 Oct. 1867, Boston Post, 11 Oct. 1867, 1. Mary Lincoln evidently complained to the management, but the clerk was not fired.

80. Davis to his wife, Urbana, 18 Oct. 1860, and Springfield, 15 Oct. 1860, David Davis MSS, ICHi. In 1847 he told his wife that "Mrs. Lincoln is not agreeable." Letter of 2 Aug. 1847 (misdated 1846), David Davis MSS, ICHi.

81. [Albert Hale] to [Theron Baldwin], Springfield, 31 May 1860, copy, Nicolay MSS, DLC.

82. John Jay Janney, "Talking with the President: Four Interviews with Abraham Lincoln," Civil War Times Illustrated 26 (Sept. 1987): 35.

83. Margarita Spalding Gerry, ed., Through Five Administrations: Reminiscences of Colonel William H. Crook, Body-Guard to President Lincoln (New York: Harper and Brothers, 1910), 16.

84. Judith A. Bradner to James R. B. Van Cleave, N.p., [27 June 1908], copy, Vertical Files, "Reminiscences," folder 3, Lincoln Collection, IHi. Cf. Mrs. Bradner's recollections in Walter B. Stevens, *A Reporter's Lincoln* (St. Louis: Missouri Historical Society, 1916), 60.

85. Reminiscences of Mary Scott Uda, recounting a story told by her mother, New York *Herald Tribune*, 7 Feb. 1916.

86. Herndon to Jesse Weik, Springfield, 8 Jan. 1886, H-W MSS, DLC; Milton Hay to his wife, Springfield, 6 April [1862], Stuart-Hay MSS, IHi.

87. Reminiscences of Mary Scott Uda, New York *Herald Tribune*, 7 Feb. 1916. Cf. the recollections of Dr. Gilbert Bailey, son of the Rev. Mr. Gilbert S. Bailey, a Springfield neighbor of Lincoln's, in Edith Ryan, "Memories of Abraham Lincoln," *Catholic World*, N.d., Lincoln files, RPB.

88. Weik, *RL,* 91.

89. Hay to his wife, Springfield, 9 April 1862, Stuart-Hay MSS, IHi.

90. Margaret Ryan, interview with Jesse W. Weik, 27 Oct. 1886, Weik MSS, IHi.

91. Herndon to Weik, Springfield, 8 Jan. 1886, H-W MSS, DLC.

92. Carl Sandburg and Paul M. Angle, *Mary Lincoln: Wife and Widow* (New York: Harcourt, Brace, 1932), 70–71. In Springfield in the mid-1850s, Mary Lincoln was observed chasing her husband through the yard with a knife. When Lincoln realized that passers-by were witnessing the scene, he abruptly turned about, seized his wife, and hustled her back into the house, telling her never to disgrace them again before the eyes of the world. Herndon's notes of a conversation in 1867 with Stephen Whitehurst, H-W MSS, DLC. Whitehurst had heard this story from a man named Barrett, who allegedly observed it in 1856 or 1857.

93. Lincoln to Johnston, Shelbyville, 9 Nov. 1851, in Basler, *CWL,* 2:112.

94. Statement of Thomas L. D. Johnston, [1865], H-W MSS, DLC. Cf. Charles H. Coleman, *Abraham Lincoln and Coles County, Illinois* (New Brunswick: Scarecrow Press, 1955), 70–71.

95. Herndon to Weik, Springfield, 1 Dec. 1885, H-W MSS, DLC; interview with Harriet Hanks Chapman, 16 Oct. 1914, Weik MSS, IHi.

96. "Anecdotes of Mrs. Lincoln," by "a neighbor of the family at the time of President Lincoln's funeral," quoted in *The News* [no city indicated], ca. 17 July 1882, unidentified clipping, LMFW.

97. Paraphrased remarks of a Mrs. Bradford to Ida Tarbell, memo in "Mary Todd Lincoln" folder, Ida M. Tarbell MSS, Allegheny College.

98. Reminiscences of a Mr. Beck, son of the proprietress, in Effie Sparks, "Stories of Abraham Lincoln" MS, 23–24, Ida M. Tarbell MSS, Allegheny College.

99. St. Louis *Globe-Democrat*, 13 Jan. 1887.

100. Recollections of Captain John Easton, St. Louis *Globe-Democrat,* 13 Jan. 1887.

101. Rankin, *Personal Recollections,* 176–79. For another example of Mary Lincoln's ire at her husband's late arrival for dinner one evening, see Helm, *Mary, Wife of Lincoln,* 112. She also had difficulty, at least early in their

marriage, getting him to come to bed. When first wed, they roomed at a boardinghouse. At bedtime, when he would go downstairs to fill a pitcher of water, he would often "sit down on the steps of the porch and tell stories to whoever happened to be near." His wife would cough to signal that she wanted him; sometimes he "kept her coughing until midnight or after." Reminiscences of a Mr. Beck, told in Sparks, "Stories of Abraham Lincoln," 20–21.

102. Charles A. Dana, "'The Rail Splitter,'" Cincinnati *Times Star,* 7 June 1885.

103. Piatt in Rice, *RL,* 481. Cf. "A Lincoln Incident," Piatt's description, told around 1884, of Lincoln shushing his wife when three Ohio visitors complained about Seward one Sunday afternoon during the first year of the war, submitted to George P. Hambrecht by William J. Anderson, 12 Nov. 1925, copy, William E. Barton MSS, University of Illinois Library, Urbana-Champaign.

104. Lincoln to John E. Rosette, Springfield, 20 Feb. 1857, in Basler, *CWL,* 2:389–90.

105. Ibid., 7:197–98.

106. Sandburg and Angle, *Mary Lincoln,* 110–12, citing "a responsible Illinois citizen" who had heard the story from Oglesby. Cf. Sydney Kramer, "Lincoln at the Fair," *Abraham Lincoln Quarterly* 3 (June 1945): 340–43.

107. Percy MacKaye, *Epoch: The Life of Steele MacKaye, Genius of the Theater,* 2 vols. (New York: Boni and Liveright, 1927), 1:105–6. MacKaye recorded this tale as told often by his mother, who heard it from Carpenter himself.

108. Crawford, ed., *William Russell's Civil War,* 162 [entry for 3 Nov. 1861).

109. Harry J. Carman and Reinhard H. Luthin, *Lincoln and the Patronage* (New York: Columbia University Press, 1943), 62–63; Henry Villard, *Lincoln on the Eve of '61: A Journalist's Story,* ed. Harold G. and Oswald Garrison Villard (New York: Alfred A. Knopf, 1941), 70–71; Horace White to Jesse Weik, [New York], 26 Jan. 1891, Herndon to Jesse Weik, Springfield, 5 Feb. 1891, both in H-W MSS, DLC; Carl Schurz, interview with Ida Tarbell, 6 Nov. 1897, Ida M. Tarbell MSS, Allegheny College. Herndon told White that this story "rings like one of Mrs. Lincoln[']s fits of rage. I have seen her often in just such spells of frenzy & I will venture all that I have that the story is correct. Unfortunate woman! Miserable man!" Herndon to Horace White, Springfield, 13 Feb. 1891, copy, JGR MSS, DLC. Cf. Henry Villard, *Memoirs of Henry Villard, Journalist and Financier, 1835–1900,* 2 vols. (Boston: Houghton, Mifflin, 1904), 1:147–48.

Henderson was appointed navy agent in April 1861 and dismissed when accused of misconduct three years later. Although eventually acquitted by a court in 1865, Henderson was believed guilty by Godwin and most other observers. Godwin to William Cullen Bryant, Roslyn, 31 July 1865, and Bryant to Gideon Welles, New York 25 June 1864, draft, both in the Bryant-Godwin MSS, New York Public Library; William E. Chandler to Welles, Washington, 2 June 1865, with enclosure, Welles MSS, New York Public Library; Basler, *CWL,* 4:334, 7:409–10; Howard K. Beale, ed., *Diary of Gide-*

on *Welles, Secretary of the Navy Under Lincoln and Johnson*, 3 vols. (New York: W. W. Norton, 1960), 2:54 [entry for 20 June 1864]. On Henderson, see Allan Nevins, *The Evening Post: A Century of Journalism* (New York: Boni and Liveright, 1922), 426–30.

110. A. K. McClure to an unidentified correspondent, N.p., 9 May 1907, in Emanuel Hertz, *Abraham Lincoln: A New Portrait*, 2 vols. (New York: Boni and Liveright, 1931), 1:248. McClure went on to observe (250–51): "The friends of Mr. Lincoln all knew the situation and her failings were overlooked, although few, if any, of Mr. Lincoln's close political friends entertained the respect for Mrs. Lincoln that should have been accorded the Mistress of the White House. Some were offensive in their criticisms. Bluff Ben Wade, then one of the leading Republican Senators, when asked by her to attend a reception at the White House that was to end in a dance, his answer was: 'Madam, I don't dance in a beleaguered capital.' Intimately as I knew Mr. Lincoln and frankly as he spoke to me of almost everything in which he was interested, I never heard him speak of Mrs. Lincoln."

111. The horses were presented to Mary Lincoln by William S. Wood on behalf of some New Yorkers; an "elegant carriage" was also given to her by New York citizens. Hartford *Courant*, 8 March 1861; Boston *Evening Transcript*, 1 March 1861; Baker, *MTL*, 200–202.

112. New York *World*, 16 Oct. 1867, 1.

113. This story allegedly appeared in a book written by Mary Lincoln in 1868 and submitted to an Illinois publisher, who related it to a journalist. "Mrs. Lincoln's Book," Albany *Argus*, 15 April 1868, in John A. Washington, *They Knew Lincoln* (New York: E. P. Dutton, 1942), 228–29. Such evidence casts doubt on Randall's conclusion that Mary Lincoln's "participation in politics, however injudicious, stemmed from her intense desire to watch out for and assist the mild and unself-seeking man she loved." Randall, *MTL*, 251. That judgment is true only in part; she sought practical rewards for her meddling. Moreover, as Baker maintains, "She expected to gain recognition, and thus her interest in public affairs displayed a quirky feminism located not in principle but in the psychological necessity to be somebody." Baker, *MTL*, 134.

114. "Deplorable—Exceedingly," editorial, New York *Citizen*, 5 Oct. 1867. Cf. New York *Herald*, 4 Oct. 1867, 7; New York *World*, 3 Oct. 1867, 4, 5.

115. As one pair of scholars put it, "The idea smacked more than slightly of blackmail." Turner and Turner, *MTL*, 431. Baker calls it a "shakedown." *MTL*, 274.

116. Orville H. Browning, diary, 3 July 1873, copy, uncatalogued addendum, William E. Barton MSS, University of Chicago. Draper's appointment is examined in Carman and Luthin, *Lincoln and the Patronage*, 279–81.

117. Albany *Express*, 7 Oct. 1867, reprinted in New York *World*, 16 Oct. 1867, 1.

118. Cincinnati *Commercial*, N.d., reprinted in New York *World*, 16 Oct. 1867, 1.

119. Villard, *Memoirs*, 1:156–57.

120. Mary Lincoln to David Davis, New York, 17 Jan. [1861], in Turn-

er and Turner, *MTL*, 71. Cf. Carman and Luthin, *Lincoln and the Patronage,* 29–30.

121. Statement by a Mrs. Forrest to Ida Tarbell, memo marked "Lincoln—Items," folder "Mary Todd Lincoln," Ida M. Tarbell MSS, Allegheny College.

122. George B. Lincoln to Gideon Welles, Riverdale, N.J., 25 April 1874, in "New Light on the Seward-Welles-Lincoln Controversy?" *Lincoln Lore* (April 1981): 2–3. On Mary Lincoln's hostility toward Seward, see Randall, *MTL*, 238–39, 251.

123. Elizabeth Keckley, *Behind the Scenes; or, Thirty Years a Slave and Four Years in the White House* (New York: G. W. Carleton, 1868), 131.

124. Frances Seward Diary, 9 Sept. 1861, Seward MSS, microfilm edition, reel 198, University of Rochester Library.

125. Sumner told this to Charles Francis Adams on March 10, 1861. Charles Francis Adams, Jr., *Charles Francis Adams, 1835–1915: An Autobiography* (Boston: Houghton, Mifflin, 1916), 103.

126. Bancroft to his wife, [Washington], 12 Dec. 1861, in M. A. De Wolfe Howe, *The Life and Letters of George Bancroft,* 2 vols. (New York: Charles Scribner's Sons, 1908), 2:144–45. The lieutenant in question was probably the notoriously corrupt John Watt, former White House gardener. Leech, *Reveille in Washington,* 299–300.

127. A. G. Henry to Isaac N. Newton, Olympia, Washington Territory, 21 April 1864, Lincoln MSS, DLC.

128. Baker, *MTL,* 134–36.

129. Herndon's statement, 12 Jan. 1874, Springfield *Register,* 14 Jan. 1874.

130. Herndon to Horace White, Springfield, 13 Feb. 1891, copy, JGR MSS, DLC.

131. Keckley, *Behind the Scenes,* 129, 131, 134. After Lincoln's death, his widow turned to Mrs. Keckley for solace. Her sister's niece recalled: "In her extremity and weakness she reverted to the impulse of her childhood, which had been to seek the love and help she had unfailingly found in her black mammy who had shielded her from many a deserved scolding. In the faithful, sympathetic . . . Elizabeth Keckley, formerly a slave in a good old Virginia family, Mary saw the only available substitute, and to her she turned blindly for sympathy and advice." Helm, *Mary, Wife of Lincoln,* 266. The slave alluded to was "Mammy Sally," who was, according to Baker, "the most constant adult presence in her early years." *MTL,* 65. I use Mrs. Keckley's memoirs extensively, for she was obviously quite close to Mary Lincoln and wrote her book (in cooperation with James Redpath, an unacknowledged ghost writer) shortly after the events she described. See Washington, *They Knew Lincoln,* 205–41.

132. Herndon's statement, 12 Jan. 1874, Springfield *Register,* 14 Jan. 1874.

133. "The Late Secretary Stanton," *Army and Navy Journal,* 1 Jan. 1870. Stanton told this story in the summer of 1869.

134. Davis's statement to Herndon, 19 Sept. 1866, in Willard L. King,

Lincoln's Manager: David Davis (Cambridge: Harvard University Press, 1960), 59–60.

135. Keckley, *Behind the Scenes*, 124.

136. Ibid., 124–26. According to Wendell Phillips, Mary Lincoln also disliked another strong-willed wife of a politician, Jesse Benton Frémont, who, she felt, had slighted her by "want of attention." [Samuel Wilkeson] to Sydney [Howard Gay], [Washington], N.d., Gay MSS, Columbia University.

137. Keckley, *Behind the Scenes*, 128.

138. Nicolay to Hay, Washington, 18, 29 Jan. 1864, Nicolay MSS, DLC. On the day of the event, Mary Lincoln changed her mind and allowed Nicolay to attend.

139. "Presidential Domestic Squabbles," Washington correspondence, N.d., Rochester *Union*, N.d., unidentified clipping, Lincoln Scrapbooks, 5:44, Judd Stewart Collection, CSmH (for a variation on this story, see 2:103).

140. Keckley, *Behind the Scenes*, 144–45.

141. Julia Lorrilard Butterfield, ed., *A Biographical Memorial of General Daniel Butterfield* (New York: Grafton Press, 1904), 160–62. Cf. Sickles's own version of the story, New York *Tribune*, 21 May 1899, in *Abe Lincoln Laughing: Humorous Anecdotes from Original Sources by and about Abraham Lincoln*, ed. Paul M. Zall (Berkeley: University of California Press, 1982), 117.

142. Congressman Augustus Brandegee in the New London *Day*, 8 Feb. 1894. I am indebted to Elizabeth Bohlen for calling this item to my attention. Cf. Brandegee's reminiscences of Lincoln, New York *Tribune*, 23 Jan. 1887, 1. Lincoln told the story to Deming, who related it to Brandegee. The woman was married to a colonel.

143. Reminiscences by Schuyler Hamilton, New York *Tribune*, 24 March 1889, 15.

144. In the account that follows, I rely heavily on Adam Badeau, *Grant in Peace: From Appomattox to Mount McGregor; A Personal Memoir* (Hartford: S. S. Scranton, 1887), 356–62. Confirmation of parts of the story can be found in *The Personal Memoirs of Julia Dent Grant*, ed. John Y. Simon (New York: G. P. Putnam's Sons, 1975), 146–47; Horace Porter, *Campaigning with Grant* (New York: Century, 1906), 413–14; William T. Sherman, *Memoirs of Gen. W. T. Sherman*, 4th ed., 2 vols. (New York: Charles L. Webster, 1891), 2:332; and John S. Barnes, "With Lincoln from Washington to Richmond in 1865," *Appleton's Magazine* 4 (May–June 1907): 515–24, 742–51. Cf. Donald C. Pflanz, *The Petersburg Campaign: Abraham Lincoln at City Point, March 20–April 9, 1865* (Lynchburg: H. E. Howard, 1989), 92–93.

145. Barnes, "With Lincoln from Washington to Richmond in 1865," 524.

146. Badeau, *Grant in Peace*, 356–60.

147. Undated manuscript in Herndon's hand, H-W MSS, DLC.

148. Keckley, *Behind the Scenes*, 166–67. Carl Schurz had, at Lincoln's request, accompanied Mary Lincoln back to Washington, presumably when she returned on April 2. Later Schurz "said he was alone with Mrs. Lincoln

for twenty-four hours and never passed such a time." Schurz interview with Ida M. Tarbell, 6 Nov. 1897, Ida M. Tarbell MSS, Allegheny College.

149. Evidently a summary of a letter by Mary Harlen Lincoln, in William H. Slade, "Abraham Lincoln's Shakespeare," typescript, JGR MSS, DLC.

150. Mary Lincoln to Grant, Washington, [13 April 1865], in Turner and Turner, *MTL*, 219.

151. Grant related this to his cabinet more than four years after the assassination. Hamilton Fish, diary, 12 Nov. 1869, Fish MSS, DLC. Mrs. Grant told Fish "that she objected strenuously to accompanying Mrs. Lincoln."

152. Hay to Nicolay, Washington, 20 June 1864, Hay MSS, DLC.

153. Colfax told this story to Franz Mueller, "Lincoln and Colfax," reminiscences by Mueller, enclosed in Mueller to Ida Tarbell, Spokane, 13 Feb. 1896, Ida M. Tarbell MSS, Allegheny College.

154. Keckley, *Behind the Scenes*, 146–47.

155. Mary Lincoln to Josiah G. Holland, Chicago, 4 Dec. 1865, and Mary Lincoln to Charles Sumner, Chicago, 10 April 1866, both in Turner and Turner, *MTL*, 293, 356.

156. Randall, *MTL*, 68.

157. William O. Stoddard, *Inside the White House in War Times* (New York: Charles L. Webster, 1890), 62.

158. E. L. Norris to Emilie Todd Helm, Garden City, Kan., 28 Sept. 1895, photostat copy, JGR MSS, DLC.

159. On Mary Lincoln's tendency to flirt, see Baker, *MTL*, 90, 109, 142–43, 231–32, 286.

160. "Union" to Lincoln, Washington, 26 June 1861, in Baker, *MTL*, 184.

161. Colfax to John G. Nicolay, South Bend, Ind., 17 July 1875, Nicolay MSS, DLC. Baker mistakenly identifies this as a letter from Nicolay to Colfax. *MTL*, 184. Cf. Randall, *MTL*, 308–9.

162. The source of this story was Lincoln King, who claimed that he knew Mrs. Lincoln's lover "intimately" in New York during the late nineteenth century. *The Sky Rocket* [Primghar, Iowa], 15 March 1929, 4; King to William E. Barton, Primghar, Iowa, 9 Aug. 1930, William E. Barton MSS, University of Chicago.

163. Hartford *Courant*, 8 March 1861, 2.

164. Reminiscences of William P. Wood, Washington *Sunday Gazette*, 23 Jan. 1887. She urged Ward Hill Lamon to help overcome her husband's reluctance to appoint Wood. Mary Lincoln to Lamon, Washington [11 April], 1861, in Turner and Turner, *MTL*, 83; Lamon to Mrs. Lincoln, Washington, 11 April 1861, Lamon MSS, CSmH. Later, when Wood accused the White House gardener, her accomplice in trying to defraud the government, of misconduct, Mary Lincoln denounced Wood as "a very bad man," a "most unprincipled man," who "is either deranged or drinking." Mary Lincoln to John F. Potter, Washington, 13 Sept. 1861 and to Caleb B. Smith, Washington, 8 Sept. 1861, Turner and Turner, *MTL*, 104, 102.

165. Davis to Ward Hill Lamon, Bloomington, Ill., 6 May 1861, and Clinton, Ill., 31 May 1861, Lamon MSS, CSmH.

166. George W. Adams to [David Goodman] Croly, Washington, 7 Oct. 1867, Manton Marble MSS, DLC.

167. McManus, fired by Mary Lincoln for obscure reasons in January 1865, apparently told Thurlow Weed that she was romantically linked with a man other than her husband. Mary Todd Lincoln to Abram Wakeman, Washington, 20 Feb. [1865], in Turner and Turner, *MTL*, 202.

168. Villard to Isaac Markens, New York, 26 March 1927, Lincoln Collection, RPB. The identity of this Hungarian adventurer is unknown. Villard may have been thinking of Wikoff, who was definitely an adventurer but not of Hungarian origin.

169. Letter to Wakeman seen by Wakeman's daughter, who described it to her daughter, Elizabeth M. Alexanderson of Englewood, N.J., *Newark Star*, 3 March 1951. No such document exists in Mary Lincoln's published letters.

170. Ward to S. L. M. Barlow, Washington, 21 Nov. [1864?], Barlow MSS, CSmH.

171. William H. Townsend, *Lincoln and His Wife's Home Town* (Indianapolis: Bobbs-Merrill, 1929), 46.

172. Baker, *MTL*, 28–32; Strozier, *Lincoln's Quest for Union*, 72–73. Curiously, Mary Lincoln's letters say almost nothing about her father, mother, or stepmother.

173. Linda Schierse Leonard, *The Wounded Woman: Healing the Father-Daughter Relationship* (Boston: Shambala, 1983), 127–28.

174. Deposition in the case of *George R. C. Todd v. Elizabeth L. Todd et al., regarding the estate of Robert S. Todd*, in Townsend, *Lincoln and His Wife's Home Town*, 229.

175. Irene Fast and Albert C. Cain, "The Step-Parent Role: Potential for Disturbances in Family Functioning," *American Journal of Orthopsychiatry* 36, no. 3 (1966): 485–91.

176. Baker, *MTL*, 74–75.

177. Townsend, *Lincoln and His Wife's Home Town*, 74; see also Helm, *Mary, Wife of Lincoln*, 17, and Baker, *MTL*, 29.

178. Mary Lincoln to Elizabeth Keckley, Chicago, 29 Oct. [1867], in Turner and Turner, *MTL*, 447; see also Baker, *MTL*, 40–45.

179. Helm, *Mary, Wife of Lincoln*, 17.

180. E[lizabeth] L. Norris to Emilie [Todd Helm], Garden City, Kan., 28 Sept. 1895, photostat, JGR MSS, DLC.

181. Mary Lincoln to her husband, Lexington, May 1848, in Turner and Turner, *MTL*, 37.

182. Elizabeth Edwards to Herndon, 3 Aug. 1887, in Baker, *MTL*, 75.

183. This conversation took place in April 1862, shortly after the battle of Shiloh. Noyes W. Miner, "Mrs. Abraham Lincoln: A Vindication," 2–3, manuscript, SC 1052, folder 1, IHi. This document, dated New York, 1 April 1888, appeared in the New York *Tribune*, 15 April 1888, 11.

184. Keckley, *Behind the Scenes*, 135–36.

185. Mary Lincoln to Elizabeth Keckley, N.p., [24 Oct. 1867], in Turner and Turner, *MTL*, 445–46.

186. See chapter 4.

187. James C. Conkling to Mercy Levering, [Springfield], 7 March 1841, in Sandburg and Angle, *Mary Lincoln*, 180–81.

188. Ruth Painter Randall, *The Courtship of Mr. Lincoln* (Boston: Little, Brown, 1957), 87, 41.

189. Randall, *MTL*, 316, 332.

190. Herndon to Weik, Springfield, 2 Jan. 1882, H-W MSS, DLC.

191. Helm, *Mary, Wife of Lincoln*, 120.

192. Reminiscences of H. M. Powel, Taylorville [Ill.] *Semi-Weekly Breeze*, 12 Feb. 1909; Baker, *MTL*, 109; Elizabeth Irons Folsom, "New Stories of Abraham Lincoln," *American Magazine* 96 (July 1923): 129–30. Cf. James Gourley's statement in Weik, *RL*, 121.

193. Statement of John B. Webber of Pawnee, Ill., N.d., H-W MSS, DLC.

194. Ibid.; Elizabeth A. Capps, "My Early Recollections of Abraham Lincoln," Vertical File, "Reminiscences," Lincoln Collection, IHi.

195. Reminiscences of Mrs. Cecelia McConnell, who in 1846, at the age of eighteen, went to Springfield to live with her aunt and uncle. Buffalo *Express*, 11 Aug. 1929. Her uncle had witnessed the peddler telling the story to Lincoln.

196. Weik, *RL*, 123; memos of Weik's interviews with J. R. Diller and Joseph P. Kent, 21 Nov. 1916, H-W MSS, DLC.

197. Keckley, *Behind the Scenes*, 104–5.

198. Washington *Sunday Gazette*, 16 Jan. 1887.

199. D. H. Mitchell, "An Anecdote of Lincoln," *The Independent*, 13 Dec. 1894. Baker denies that she was insane; see *MTL*, 330–31, cf. 277–78.

200. French to his sister-in-law Pamela French, Washington, 21 May 1865, French MSS, DLC.

201. Welles to [Robert Todd Lincoln], Hartford, 5 July 1875, enclosed in Robert Todd Lincoln to John G. Nicolay, Chicago, 11 Nov. 1876, Nicolay-Hay MSS, IHi. A decade after her husband's assassination, Mary Lincoln was judged insane and remanded briefly to a mental hospital. See Mark E. Neely, Jr., and R. Gerald McMurtry, *The Insanity File: The Case of Mary Todd Lincoln* (Carbondale: Southern Illinois University Press, 1986).

202. Margaret Ryan, interview with Jesse W. Weik, 27 Oct. 1886, Weik MSS, IHi.

203. Mrs. Judd's undated interview with Ida Tarbell, Ida M. Tarbell MSS, Allegheny College.

204. Nicolay's interview with Browning, Springfield, 17 June 1875, Hay MSS, RPB.

205. Helm, *Mary, Wife of Lincoln*, 32.

206. Baker, *MTL*, 330.

207. Nicolay's interview with Browning, Springfield, 17 June 1875, Hay MSS, RPB.

208. Davis to his wife, St. Louis, 15 Dec. 1861, David Davis MSS, ICHi.

209. McClure to an unidentified correspondent, N.p., 9 May 1907, in Hertz, *Abraham Lincoln: A New Portrait*, 1:248.

210. Ibid.

211. Keckley, *Behind the Scenes,* 101.

212. Crawford, ed., *William Russell's Civil War,* 185 [entry for 23 Nov. 1861] and 220 [letter to John T. Delano, Quebec, 11 Feb. 1862].

213. J. W. Nesmith to his wife, Washington, 5 Feb. 1862, photocopy, JGR MSS, DLC.

214. This story is told at length in Benjamin Brown French to Pamela French, Washington, 24 Dec. 1861, French MSS, DLC, and Benjamin Brown French, *Witness to the Young Republic: A Yankee's Journal, 1828–1870,* ed. Donald B. Cole and John J. McDonough (Hanover, N.H.: University Press of New England, 1989), 382 [entry for 16 Dec. 1861]. Cf. Harry E. Pratt and Ernest E. East, "Mrs. Lincoln Refurbishes the White House," *Lincoln Herald* 47 (Feb. 1945): 13–22. In August, Interior Secretary Smith had ordered painters to stop in the middle of work on the exterior of the White House, and the following month he warned Mrs. Lincoln that wallpaper imported from Paris could not be used because there was no money left in the budget for repairing the Executive Mansion. In October, Smith asked that French prepare a request to Congress for a supplemental appropriation. The following documents are all in Records of the Commissioner of Public Buildings, microfilm edition, Record Group 42, microcopy 371, National Archives: French to Mary Lincoln, Washington, 28 Sept. 1861, copy, Letters Sent, 14:18; French to Smith, Washington, 16 Oct. 1861, copy, 42–43; French to William P. Fessenden, Washington, 28 Jan. 1862, copy, 74–76; Smith to French, Washington, 22 Aug., 17 Oct. 1861, Letters Received, reel 26, vol. 36.

215. The bill from William H. Carryl & Bro., dated 31 July 1861, came to $6,858. First Auditor's Records, Miscellaneous Records, Treasury Department, Record Group 217, no. 143610, National Archives.

216. French to "Brother Reynolds," Washington, 20 April 1865, unidentified clipping, French MSS, DLC. In 1868 French recalled that during the war, "No week passed that I did not see him, and I was often with him many times a week. This, of course, with a man like him, led to numerous conversations between us, and enabled me, with no particular intention of doing so, to observe the peculiar characteristics of Mr. Lincoln." French, *Address Delivered at the Dedication of the Statue of Abraham Lincoln* (Washington: McGill and Witherow, 1868), 7.

217. French's predecessor, William S. Wood, had on June 19 authorized William H. Carryl & Bro. of Philadelphia to purchase wallpaper as Mary Lincoln directed. In Paris, Carryl bought what she wanted and presented French with a bill for $3,549. At the time, only $1,500 remained in the account for repairing the White House. In October, Mary Lincoln badgered French to pay the bill: "Mr[.] Carryl has bought the papering according to order,[.] he was particularly desired to select it for the rooms, of the richest style. His bill is correct." Later she wrote to the commissioner: "Major French, will please settle this, with Mr[.] Carryl as he promised to do. He paid for them himself in Paris."

Mary Lincoln's annotations on the back of Carryl's bill, dated 31 July 1861, First Auditor's Records, Miscellaneous Records, Treasury Department, Record Group 217, no. 143610, National Archives; French to Caleb B. Smith,

Washington, 16 Oct. 1861, Records of the Office of the Secretary of the Interior, Patents and Miscellaneous Division, General Records, Letters Received Concerning the Executive Mansion, 1853–69, Record Group 48, entry 113, box 1, National Archives; French to Mrs. Lincoln, Washington, 28 Sept. 1861; W. S. Wood to Mrs. Lincoln, Washington, 15 June 1861, and to William H. Carryl & Bro., of Philadelphia, Washington, 19 June 1861; French to William Pitt Fessenden, Washington, 20 Jan. 1862, and to Caleb B. Smith, Washington, 28 Jan. 1862, copies, Records of the Commissioner of Public Buildings, Letters Sent, Record Group 42, microcopy 371, reel 7, and Financial Records of the Office of Public Buildings and Grounds, Record Group 42, entry 19, box 13, National Archives.

218. The carpet cost $2,575 and was described in Carryl & Bro.'s bill, dated 31 July 1861.

219. French had warned Mrs. Lincoln three months earlier that funds were unavailable to pay for $3,500 worth of wallpaper purchased in Paris: "There is no money now appropriated to pay for this papering. The $6000 appropriated for unusual repairs &c. of the President's House is now nearly exhausted by the painters and other bills, and there is no other fund out of which the payment for papering can be made." French to Mrs. Lincoln, Washington, 28 Sept. 1861, copy, Records of the Commissioner of Public Buildings, Letters Sent, 14:18, Record Group 42, microcopy 371, reel 7, National Archives. Cf. French to Caleb B. Smith, Washington, 16 Oct. 1861, ibid., 42–43.

On top of everything else, the following month it was discovered that Mary Lincoln had incurred a cost overrun of $2,613 for silverware. Smith to William Pitt Fessenden, Washington, 28 Jan. 1862, ibid. On March 1, 1862, Congress passed a Civil Appropriation Act that included $4,500 "on account of papering and painting the President's House in the autumn of 1861." In addition to Carryl & Bro., which received $3,549, the firm of Parker & Spalding was paid $951 from this appropriation. Carryl & Bro. also received $6,858.80 from a separate appropriation in the March 1, 1862, act to pay a July 1861 bill for White House furniture. Financial Records of the Office of Public Buildings and Grounds, Record Group 42, entry 19, box 13, National Archives.

220. Clipping from the *Commercial Gazette* [New York], 9 Jan. 1887, copy, JGR MSS, DLC.

221. Comments of Mrs. Owen Lovejoy, paraphrased in the Reverend David Todd to the Reverend John Todd, Providence, Ill., 11 June 1862, copy, JGR MSS, DLC. Cf. Laura Catherine Redden Searing, writing under the pen name Howard Glyndon, "The Truth about Mrs. Lincoln," *The Independent* [New York], 10 Aug. 1882.

222. Mrs. James Conkling to Clinton Conkling, Springfield, 19 Jan. 1861, copy, JGR MSS, DLC.

223. Ames, *Ten Years in Washington*, 237–38.

224. Ruth C. Cockran to Ida M. Tarbell, Los Angeles, 1928, Ida M. Tarbell MSS, Allegheny College.

225. William H. Townsend, "Memorandum regarding an afternoon spent

with Senator Albert J. Beveridge and Dr. Wm. E. Barton enroute to Louisville, Ky[.]," 17 June 1924, typed copy, Lincoln Collection, ICHi. The passages dealing with Mary Lincoln are expurgated in the published version of the diary and unavailable to scholars in the original manuscript. Beveridge and Barton managed to read the document before such restrictions were applied.

226. In January 1861, the thirty-seven-year old Watt, a native of Scotland, had been living in Washington for more than a decade and became a major in the Washington, D.C., militia. On September 9, he was appointed first lieutenant in the Sixteenth U.S. Infantry, but the Senate revoked his commission on February 3, 1862, evidently because his loyalty seemed doubtful. He later told authorities that he "was commissioned by President Lincoln and detailed for special duty at [the] White House and never served with his Regiment," and that he "also acted as recruiting officer at Washington D.C." A congressional report stated that he served as "one of the commanders of the bodyguard of President Lincoln" and "one of his personal aids and attendants." In November 1861, a journalist recorded that Lieutenant Watt "is detached to W[hite] House to superintend ye cooking." He enlisted in the Thirteenth New York Artillery as a private on August 12, 1863, rose to the rank of corporal, and in 1865 accepted a commission as a second lieutenant in the Thirty-eighth U.S. Colored Troops, serving until 1867. He died in Washington in 1892, survived by his wife, Jane Masterson Watt. They had no children. U.S. Senate, 59th Cong., 2d sess., Report 69 (1903); Crawford, ed., *William Russell's Civil War,* 162 [entry for 3 Nov. 1861]; Watt, "Declaration for Invalid Pension," 25 Aug. 1890, and Jane M. Watt, "Dependent Widow's Declaration for Pension," 29 Jan. 1892, Pension Records, National Archives; Watt to General [name indecipherable], Washington, 16 Jan. 1861; Watt to Lorenzo Thomas, 10 Sept., 3 Dec. 1861, and Watt's service record, Records of the Adjutant General's Office, Letters Received, Main Series, Record Group 94, National Archives.

227. New York *Tribune,* 28 Jan. 1862, 3. Mary Lincoln told Potter that the charges evidently brought by William S. Wood were false. Turner and Turner, *MTL,* 103–4.

228. Blake, "astonished" at a seed bill, told Watt in 1859, "You must raise your own seed hereafter." Blake also protested against an "enormous" bill "for making and sharpening tools." Sternly the commissioner warned him not to "incur the smallest debt without first consulting the public gardener or myself." John B. Blake, commissioner, to John Watt, Washington, 10 June 1858, copy, enclosing "a copy of the decision of the Secretary of the Interior upon the charges preferred against you by Mr. John Saunders," and Blake to Watt, Washington, 5 July 1859, copy, Records of the Commissioner of Public Buildings, Letters Sent, vols. 13 and 14, Record Group 42, microcopy 371, reel 7, National Archives.

229. Bill from Watt to Abraham Lincoln, [1 Feb.] 1863, Lamon MSS, CSmH; New York *Commercial Advertiser,* 4 Oct. 1867, 2; Bayly Ellen Marks and Mark Norton Schatz, eds., *Between North and South: A Maryland Journalist Views the Civil War: The Narrative of William Wilkens Glenn, 1861–1869* (Rutherford: Farleigh Dickinson University Press, 1976), 175–76, 296

[entries for 16 March 1865, 4 Oct. 1867]; Randall, *MTL,* 254–58. Cf. Pratt and East, "Mrs. Lincoln Refurbishes the White House," 13–22. The garden-er, John Watt, denied the story, but according to a New York wine merchant, Secretary of the Interior Smith verified it. George W. Adams to [David Good-man] Croly, Washington, 7 Oct. 1867, and Frederic S. Cozzens to Manton Marble, New York, 12 Oct. 1867, Manton Marble MSS, DLC. Cozzens names Caleb B. Smith as his source. Donn Piatt claimed that Smith lost his cabinet post for refusing to approve the expenditure. *Mac-a-cheek Press,* N.d., quot-ed in New York *World,* 19 Oct. 1867, 2. Another source maintained that William S. Wood fell out of favor because he refused to hide the expense of the dinner in the White House manure account. See Crawford, ed., *William Russell's Civil War,* 162, 222 [entry for 3 Nov. 1861, letter to John T. Delane, Quebec, 11 Feb. 1862]. Some believed Mary Lincoln was "close" with mon-ey because she wanted to preserve her husband's salary "as much as possible to build them a house after [his] term at Washington expires." Comments of Mrs. Owen Lovejoy, paraphrased in the Reverend David Todd to the Rever-end John Todd, Providence, Ill., 11 June 1862, copy, JGR MSS, DLC.

230. Upperman to Caleb B. Smith, Washington, 21 Oct. 1861, copy, Records of the U.S. Senate, Committee on Public Buildings, 37th Cong., Record Group 46, National Archives. William H. Johnson was paid $50 for services as furnace-keeper at the White House for April, June, and August 1861; $43.75 for carting manure in June; and $37.75 for whitewashing the Executive Man-sion in July 1861. Alexander McKerichar received $50 as a laborer on public grounds for June 1861; $54 for hire of horse, driver, and covered wagon in July 1861; and $47.25 for cartage in August. Augustus Jullien and Charles F. Cone were paid for working in June as laborers under Watt on Lafayette Square. Burke received $31.25 as a laborer on the square south of White House for June 1861.

Upperman sent Smith copies of eight receipts. Financial Records of the Office of Public Buildings and Grounds, Record Group 42, entry 19, box 13, National Archives. The originals are located in the First Auditor's Records, Miscellaneous Records, Treasury Department, Record Group 217, National Archives. Thomas J. Sutter approved Watt's bills for monthly pay as superin-tendent of President's Square and for hire of his horse and cart in hauling ma-nure in June and July 1861. He also approved Watt's payroll for twenty-two laborers working under him. Records of the Commissioner of Public Build-ings, Letters Sent, vols. 13 and 14, Record Group 42, microcopy 371, reel 7, National Archives.

231. Caleb B. Smith to W. H. Seward, Washington, 27 Oct. 1861, Seward MSS, University of Rochester Library, microfilm edition, reel 66.

232. Memo by Smith, Washington, 11 Dec. 1861, Records of the Com-missioner of Public Buildings, Letters Received, Record Group 42, microcopy 371, reel 7, National Archives. Three days later French disallowed the pay-ments to Jullien, Burke, and Vermeren. French to Joseph Ingle, Washington, 14 Dec. 1861, First Auditor's Records, Miscellaneous Records, Treasury De-partment, Record Group 217, no. 143610, National Archives. Cf. penciled annotations on "Account No. 1, Annual Repairs of the President's House, 30

September 1861," enclosed in first auditor's certificate on the account of B. B. French, Record Group 217, no. 142505, National Archives. This "return" was evidently made on January 7, 1862. See annotation on the first auditor's certificate on the account of B. B. French, Record Group 217, nos. 142506, 142416, National Archives.

233. Upperman to Foot, Washington, 6 Dec. 1861, Records of the U.S. Senate, Committee on Public Buildings, 37th Cong., Record Group 46, National Archives. Cf. Washington correspondence by "Iowa," 4 Feb. 1862, Burlington [Iowa] *Hawk-Eye*, 8 Feb. 1862, 2.

234. New York *Commercial Advertiser,* 4 Oct. 1867, 2.

235. Boyer, a member of the House Committee on Ways and Means, told the story to a Maryland journalist. Marks and Schatz, eds., *Between North and South*, 175–76, 296 [entries for 16 March 1865, 4 Oct. 1867].

236. John Hay heard this in 1867 from Isaac Newton, who "launched off in his buzzing way about Mrs. Lincoln how imprudent she was—how he protected & watched over her & prevented dreadful disclosures." He added, "'that lady has set here on this here sofy & shed tears by the pint a begging me to pay her debts which was unbeknown to the President. There was one big bill for furs which give her a sight of trouble—she got it paid at last by some of her friends—I don't know who for certain—not Sim Draper for he promised to pay it afore Cuthbert but after Lincoln's death he wouldn't do it' & other horrors like that for half an hour." John Hay diary, 13 Feb. 1867, Hay MSS, RPB.

237. Washington correspondence, 16 Oct. 1867, New York *Tribune,* 17 Oct. 1867, 4.

238. John Hay diary, 13 Feb. 1867, Hay MSS, RPB.

239. D. P. Holloway to John Watt, Washington, 14 March 1862, copy, Lincoln MSS, DLC. When Watt asked for instructions, he was put off by the secretary of the interior. Caleb B. Smith to Watt, Washington, 29 March 1862, Lincoln MSS, DLC.

240. In the Ward Hill Lamon Papers at the Huntington Library is the following document, dated on its folder [Feb. 1] 1863:

"His Excellency
Abraham Lincoln
Due to John Watt
1863
To Commissary stores for the use of the President[']s House $361.00 the items and vouchers for this sum of money are in the hand [of] Genl Simm Draper
To Cash sent to Mrs Lincoln from this city [Washington?] to Mrs L by a draft at her request $350.00 the authority to send the same to Mrs Lincoln to New York is also in the hand of Mr Draper
To Cash paid Mrs Lincoln Hotel bill in Boston, receipt in Mrs Lincoln['s] hand 15.00
To Cash handed Mrs Lincoln NY   10[.00]
                                     $736.00

Mr Watts presents this account with reluctance & never intended to present it for payment and departs from his purpose originally intended as the wishes of the Hon Secretary Smith has not been carried out by Mr Newton the head of the Agriculture bureau in not compensation [compensating] him [*me* is crossed out] for his [*my* is crossed out] time and services in his [*my* is crossed out] visit to Europe for that Bureau, as that has not been done Mr Watts feels bound to present the above bill for payment as he cannot afford now to lose it. Mr Watts parted with the vouchers refer[ed]d to with the understanding that the account would be promptly paid."

Watt later told Simon Cameron, "You know very well what difficulties I had to contend with in regard to Mrs. Lincoln. . . . I paid about $700.00 for Mrs. Lincoln on one trip to Cambridge, Mass." Turner and Turner, *MTL*, 103n.

241. Davis to his wife, St. Louis, 23 Feb. 1862, same to same, St. Louis, 19 Feb. 1862, both in David Davis MSS, ICHi.

242. Washington correspondence by "Iowa," 4 Feb. 1862, in Burlington [Iowa] *Hawkeye*, 8 Feb. 1862, 2; Marks and Schatz, eds., *Between North and South*, 176 [entry of 4 Oct. 1867].

243. New York *World*, 26 Sept. 1864, 4; E. V. Haughwout & Co. to Marble, New York, 26, 27, 28 Sept. 1864, [Marble] to Col. Frank E. Howe, New York, 26 Sept. 1864, and Marble to [E. V. Haughwout & Co.], "Wednesday 2 AM," filed at the end of Sept. 1864, and [3 Oct. 1864], draft, all in Marble MSS, DLC. According to a Maryland journalist, Mary Lincoln "once bought a lot of china for $1500 in cash & sent in a bill for $3000. When Lincoln refused to put his signature to the Bill prior to sending it to the Department to be paid, on the ground that it was exorbitant [the merchant said,] 'You forget, sir, . . . that I gave Mrs[.] Lincoln $1500.[']'" Marks and Schatz, eds., *Between North and South*, 296 [entry for 4 Oct. 1867].

244. George W. Adams to [David Goodman] Croly, Washington, 7 Oct. 1867, Marble MSS, DLC. In 1862, Congress passed a supplemental appropriation of $2,613 to cover expenses involved in plating gas fittings at the White House. Elisha Whittlesey to George Harrington, Washington, 6 March 1862, Letters Received, vol. 27, Records of the Commissioner of Public Buildings, microfilm edition, Record Group 42, microcopy 371, National Archives. On July 30, 1862, Haughwout received $2,343 from the commissioner of public buildings for plating White House cutlery. Financial Records of the Commissioner of Public Buildings, entry 19, box 13, Record Group 42, National Archives.

245. New York correspondence by "Metropolitan," 9 Oct. 1867, Boston *Post*, 11 Oct. 1867, 1.

246. Hay to John G. Nicolay, [Washington], [ca. 15 Nov. 1861], 5 April 1862, Hay MSS, RPB. Mrs. Watt had served as White House stewardess from June 1861 to March 1862. See receipt of Jane Watt to Lincoln, 7 Feb. 1863, Lamon MSS, CSmH. Cf. Marks and Schatz, *Between North and South*, 176 [entry for 16 March 1865].

247. Ibid., 176 [entry for 16 March 1865].

248. Ibid., 296 [entry for 4 Oct. 1867]. Cf. Randall, *MTL*, 388–89.

249. Browning diary, Springfield, 3 July 1873, copy, William E. Barton MSS, University of Chicago.

250. A. H[omer] B[yington] to [Sydney Howard] Gay, Washington, 23 March [1864], Gay MSS, Columbia University.

251. Washington correspondence, 13 Feb. 1862, New York *Tribune*, 14 Feb. 1862, 5, and New York *Herald*, 14 Feb. 1862, 1; Randall, *MTL*, 303–6; Poore, *Reminiscences*, 2:143. Cf. Douglas Fermer, *James Gordon Bennett and the New York Herald: A Study of Editorial Opinion in the Civil War Era, 1854–1867* (New York: St. Martin's, 1986), 214–16; Villard, *Memoirs*, 1:156–67; Frank Malloy Anderson, *The Mystery of 'A Public Man': A Historical Detective Story* (Minneapolis: University of Minnesota Press, 1948), 126–29.

252. McClure to an unidentified correspondent, N.p., 9 May 1907, in Hertz, *Lincoln: A New Portrait*, 1:248.

253. Davis to his wife, St. Louis, 15 Dec. 1861, David Davis MSS, ICHi.

254. Henry Smith to Charles Henry Ray and Joseph Medill, [Washington], 4 Nov. 1861, Ray MSS, CSmH. Cf. Adam Gurowski to Horace Greeley, Washington, 1 Oct. 1861, Greeley MSS, New York Public Library.

255. Hawley to Charles Dudley Warner, N.p., N.d., in "Letters of Joseph R. Hawley," ed. Arthur L. Shipman, typescript, 387, dated 1929, Connecticut Historical Society, Hartford.

256. Hay's anonymous Washington dispatch, 21 Oct. 1861, [St. Louis] *Missouri Republican*, 25 Oct. 1861, 3.

257. Villard, *Memoirs*, 1:157.

258. Matthew Hale Smith, *Sunshine and Shadow in New York* (Hartford: J. B. Burr, 1868), 284–89. Another journalist confirmed that Lincoln had unceremoniously ejected Wikoff from the White House, presumably in early February. Washington correspondence, 11 Feb. 1862, New York *World*, 12 Feb. 1862, 1.

259. T. J. Barnett to S. L. M. Barlow, Washington, 27 Oct. 1862, Barlow MSS, CSmH.

260. Washington *Sunday Gazette*, 16 Jan. 1887.

261. Receipt on Executive Mansion stationery, 10 May 1865: "Received of John D. Hammack Eighty four dollars for Sundry &c in full payment[.] Mrs. Lincoln." Lamon MSS, CSmH.

262. Boston *Daily Advertiser*, 7 Oct. 1867, 2.

263. Keckley, *Behind the Scenes*, 235–36.

264. Randall, *MTL*, 75.

265. Mary Lincoln to Sally Orne, N.p., [12 Dec. 1869], in Turner and Turner, *MTL*, 534.

266. William H. Herndon's statement, Springfield, 12 Jan. 1874, Springfield *Register*, 14 Jan. 1874.

267. John Bowlby, *Attachment and Loss* (New York: Basic Books, 1980), 3:293.

268. Mary Lincoln to Sally Orne, Frankfort am Main, 29 Dec. 1869, in Turner and Turner, *MTL*, 538.

269. Beveridge, *Lincoln*, 1:312.

270. Helm, *Mary, Wife of Lincoln*, 3, 41; Baker, *MTL*, 60–61; Randall, *MTL*, 103.

271. James Quay Howard's notes of an interview with Stuart [May 1860], Lincoln MSS, DLC; Davis to his wife, Clinton, 12 Oct. 1860, David Davis MSS, ICHi.

272. Statement of Mrs. N. W. Edwards, 27 July 1887, H-W MSS, DLC; interview with Mrs. Alexander McKee, Marietta Holdstock Brown, "A Romance of Lincoln," clipping identified as "Indianapolis, 1896," LMFW.

273. Rankin, *Personal Recollections*, 122.

274. Interview with J. H. Littlefield, Brooklyn *Eagle*, 20 Jan. 1887.

275. Mrs. Olivia Leidig Whiteman, in the Vandalia, Ill., correspondence, 4 Feb. 1929, New York *Herald*, 10 Feb. 1929.

276. Keckley, *Behind the Scenes*, 228–29. Her sister Elizabeth recalled that, as a girl in Kentucky, Mary "often contended that she was destined to be the wife of some future President." Statement of Mrs. N. W. Edwards, 27 July 1887, H-W MSS, DLC.

277. Helm, *Mary, Wife of Lincoln*, 3.

278. Undated statement of Mrs. N. W. Edwards, H-W MSS, DLC. Cf. Helm, *Mary, Wife of Lincoln*, 5. Mrs. Edwards was also ambitious for her husband. See David Davis to Mrs. Davis, 23 March 1851, in King, *David Davis*, 74.

279. Margaret Ryan, interview with Jesse W. Weik, 27 Oct. 1886, Weik MSS, IHi.

280. Ward Hill Lamon, *Recollections of Abraham Lincoln, 1847–1865*, 2d ed., ed. Dorothy Lamon Teillard (Washington, D.C.: Privately published, 1911), 21.

281. Unidentified women, interviewed in 1895 by Ida Tarbell, Ida M. Tarbell MSS, Allegheny College.

282. Keckley, *Behind the Scenes*, 230.

283. Reminiscences of a Mrs. Beck, in Sparks, "Stories of Abraham Lincoln," 30–31.

284. Davis to his wife, Springfield, 8 Aug. 1847, David Davis MSS, ICHi.

285. Statement by Jayne, 15 Aug. 1866, H-W MSS, DLC.

286. Henry C. Whitney, *Lincoln the Citizen*, vol. 1 of *A Life of Lincoln*, ed. Marion Mills Miller, 2 vols. (New York: Baker and Taylor, 1908), 150. Cf. Rankin, *Personal Recollections*, 182–83.

287. Baker, *MTL*, 148.

288. Ibid., 150; Mary Lincoln to Leonard Swett, N.p., 12 Jan. [1867], in Turner and Turner, *MTL*, 406; Julia Jayne Trumbull to Lyman Trumbull, N.p., 14 April 1856 [1855?], in Mark M. Krug, *Lyman Trumbull: Conservative Radical* (New York: A. S. Barnes, 1965), 99–100; Anson G. Henry to his wife, [Washington], 18[?] Feb. 1863, in Strozier, *Lincoln's Quest for Union*, 76. Mary Lincoln, unlike her husband, bore grudges and treated those she disliked rudely. During the Civil War, friends from Illinois "on visiting Washington were *snubbed*" by her. Springfield correspondence, 22 Oct. 1867, New York *Commercial Advertiser*, 29 Oct. 1867, 2.

289. Mrs. Norman B. Judd, undated interview with Ida Tarbell, Ida M. Tarbell MSS, Allegheny College. A son of Mrs. Judd was known to make unfavorable remarks about Mrs. Lincoln based "on stories told him by his father." King Dykeman to W. E. Barton, Seattle, 11 Dec. 1923, William E. Barton MSS, University of Chicago.

290. In the last seventeen years of her life, Mary Lincoln refused to see Emilie Todd Helm or answer her letters. Statement of Mrs. Helm to William H. Townsend. Townsend, *Lincoln and the Bluegrass: Slavery and Civil War in Kentucky* ([Lexington]: University Press of Kentucky, 1955), 332–33.

291. Undated statement of John T. Stuart, H-W MSS, DLC; Nicolay's interview with Stuart, Springfield 24 June 1875, Hay MSS, RPB; Angle, *HL*, 246–47; Emilie Todd Helm in Helm, *Mary, Wife of Lincoln*, 107; Rankin, *Personal Recollections*, 181–82; New York *Tribune*, 17 July 1882, 5.

292. Speed told this story to John T. Stuart. Nicolay's interview with Stuart, Springfield, 24 June 1875, Hay MSS, RPB. One scholar thinks that Lincoln may have rejected the Oregon governorship because "Oregon, with its strongly Democratic population, would have been a poor field of action for an ambitious Whig." Don E. Fehrenbacher, *Prelude to Greatness: Lincoln in the 1850's* (Stanford: Stanford University Press, 1962), 20.

293. Brooks, *Lincoln and the Downfall of American Slavery*, 116. Cf. Baker, *MTL*, 144–45, and chapter 8 of this volume.

294. A Mr. Kelly, in "Capital Pageant Review," 12 Feb. 1936, paraphrased in an editorial, "Lincoln and Oregon," *Morning Oregonian*, 12 Feb. 1936.

295. Nicolay's interview with Stuart, Springfield, 24 June 1875, Hay MSS, RPB. On Lincoln's plan to return to Springfield, see the reminiscences of Russell H. Cornwell, Charlotte *Observer*, 9 Feb. 1936.

296. Unidentified clipping, LMFW.

297. Hawkins Taylor in *Intimate Memories of Lincoln*, ed. Wilson, 11. Cf. New York *Tribune*, 17 July 1882, 5.

298. Rankin, *Personal Recollections*, 184; see also chapter 8 of this volume.

299. Reminiscences of John H. Littlefield in "Abe Lincoln's Wisdom," unidentified clipping, LMFW.

300. Undated statement of C. S. Zane, H-W MSS, DLC. A contemporary newspaper account has him utter similar words: "Well boys, there is a little woman down at our house who is interested in this business." *Central Illinois Gazette* [Champaign], 23 May 1860, in *Journal of the Illinois State Historical Society* 48 (1955): 322. According to Mary's cousin, Martinette Hardin, Lincoln said, "Gentlemen, there's a little woman at my house who is more interested in this dispatch than I am." Hardin recalled that she and her friends "all thought when we heard it, Mary will be satisfied now." Interview with Mrs. Alexander R. McKee (née Martinette Hardin), Marietta Holdstock Brown, "A Romance of Lincoln," clipping identified as "Indianapolis 1896," LMFW.

301. Recollections of Henry C. Bowen in *Abraham Lincoln: Tributes from His Associates: Reminiscences of Soldiers, Statesmen and Citizens*, ed. William Hayes Ward (New York: Thomas Y. Crowell, 1895), 32.

302. Lincoln to Hackett, Washington, 17 Aug. 1863, in Basler, *CWL*, 6:392. I am indebted to Robert Bray for suggesting this interpretation.

303. Helm, *Mary, Wife of Lincoln*, 144. Lincoln told others that he thought himself unfit for the presidency. Cf. Lincoln to Samuel Galloway, Springfield, 28 July 1859, in Basler, *CWL*, 3:395. See also chapter 8 of this volume.

304. Helen Nicolay, *Lincoln's Secretary: A Biography of John G. Nicolay* (New York: Longmans, Green, 1949), 217.

305. *Some Incidents in the Life of Mrs. Benjamin S. Edwards* (edited by her daughter, "M[ary] E[dwards] R[aymond]," N.p., N.p., 1909), 16. Mary Lincoln told this to Mrs. Edwards a few months after the assassination.

306. Keckley, *Behind the Scenes*, 147–51. Cf. King, *David Davis*, 235. This is not to say, of course, that Mary Lincoln's interest in her husband's reelection was rooted solely in her fear of creditors.

307. Dubois's undated interview with Jesse W. Weik, Weik MSS, IHi. Dubois, an attorney, had helped to settle the estate; he visited New York to deal with Ball, Black & Co. I am indebted to Douglas L. Wilson for calling this to my attention.

308. A. H[omer] B[yington] to [Sydney Howard] Gay, Washington, 23 March [1864], Gay MSS, Columbia University. A New York *Tribune* correspondent, Byington assured his superior, "This is believed by everybody here— & *I* get it from such a source that I have no doubt of its truth." The seance allegedly took place the previous week.

309. Mary Lincoln to Edward Lewis Baker, Jr., Pau, France, 22 June 1879, in Turner and Turner, *MTL*, 683.

310. Randall, *MTL*, 103.

311. Harold D. Lasswell, *Power and Personality* (New York: W. W. Norton, 1948), 38–39.

312. Baker, *MTL*, 331, see also 28, 134, 180, 210–11.

313. Randall, *MTL*, 47–51

314. *Some Incidents in the Life of Mrs. Benjamin S. Edwards*, 14–15; letter by Mrs. B. S. Edwards, N.d., unidentified clipping, LMFW. Cf. T. G. Onstot, *Pioneers of Menard and Mason Counties* (Peoria: J. W. Franks and Sons, 1902), 36; Dorothy Meserve Kunhardt, "An Old Lady's Lincoln Memories," *Life*, 9 Feb. 1959, 57. Mary Lincoln's sister-in-law witnessed the scene and described it much later to Octavia Roberts. Roberts, "Our Townsman: Pictures of Lincoln as a Friend and Neighbor," *Collier's*, 12 Feb. 1909, 17, 24.

315. Kathryn Kish Sklar, "Victorian Women and Domestic Life: Mary Todd Lincoln, Elizabeth Cady Stanton, and Harriet Beecher Stowe," in *The Public and the Private Lincoln: Contemporary Perspectives*, ed. Cullom Davis et al. (Carbondale: Southern Illinois University Press, 1979), 34.

316. Randall, *MTL*, 22, 82, 153–54, 156, 163, 167, 192–93, 205, 218, 221, 255, 258–59, 266, 301.

317. W. A. Evans, *Mrs. Abraham Lincoln: A Study of Her Personality and Her Influence on Lincoln* (New York: Knopf, 1932), 302.

318. Tarbell to Mrs. Clifford Ireland, N.p., 3 Nov. 1927, copy; to T. A. Frank Jones, N.p., 12 Dec. 1922, copy; and to Charles Rollinson Lamb, N.p. 28 Feb. 1938, copy, all in Ida M. Tarbell MSS, Allegheny College.

319. Mary Lincoln to Elizabeth Todd Grimsley, Washington, 29 Sept. 1861, in Turner and Turner, *MTL*, 105.

320. Evans, *Mrs. Lincoln*, 47. The letters collected by Turner and Turner are full of such obvious examples of the common defense mechanism of projection.

321. Nicolay's interview with O. H. Browning Springfield, 17 June 1875, Hay MSS, RPB. In this document, Browning said, "In those times I was at Mr. Edwards' a great deal, and Miss Todd used to sit down with me, and talk to me sometimes till midnight, about this affair of hers with Mr. Lincoln."

322. Notes of a conversation with Mrs. Benjamin S. Edwards, 1895, "Lincoln Marriage" folder, Ida M. Tarbell MSS, Allegheny College.

323. Interview with Mrs. Alexander R. McKee (née Martinette Hardin), Marietta Holdstock Brown, "A Romance of Lincoln," clipping identified as "Indianapolis 1896," LMFW.

324. *Some Incidents in the Life of Mrs. Benjamin S. Edwards*, 11–12.

325. Mrs. Edwards's undated statement, H-W MSS, DLC. J. F. Newton speculated that "Lincoln had not met such a woman before, and he was captivated by her cleverness, vivacity, and beauty." Quoted in Evans, *Mrs. Lincoln*, 290.

326. Randall, *Courtship of Lincoln*, 88.

327. Ibid., 40; see also chapter 4 of this volume.

328. Searing [Glyndon], "The Truth about Mrs. Lincoln." Another journalist, Mary Clemmer Ames, also found her essentially childish. Sandburg and Angle, *Mary Lincoln*, 127–28.

329. Nicolay, *Personal Traits*, 205. Cf. Randall, *Courtship of Lincoln*, 193.

330. Lincoln evidently began to court Mary Todd through the mails in the summer of 1840, pursued her in person in the fall, and broke off the engagement in late November or early December. Douglas L. Wilson, "Abraham Lincoln and 'That Fatal First of January,'" *Civil War History* 38, no. 2 (1992): 101–30. Cf. John G. Nicolay's interview with O. H. Browning, Springfield, 17 June 1875, Hay MSS, RPB.

331. Two essays, both entitled "Abraham Lincoln and Matilda Edwards" by H. O. Knerr, enclosed in Knerr to Ida M. Tarbell, Allentown, 26 Oct. 1936, Ida M. Tarbell MSS, Allegheny College; Knerr's article in the *Allentown Morning Call*, 9 Feb. 1936; Wilson, "Abraham Lincoln and 'That Fatal First of January,'" 101–30; Nicolay's interview with Browning, Springfield, 17 June 1875, Hay MSS, RPB; Herndon to Ward Hill Lamon, Springfield, 25 Feb. 1870, Lamon MSS, CSmH. According to a young woman in Springfield at the time, Lincoln "had addressed Mary Todd and she accepted him and they had been engaged some time when a Miss Edwards of Alton came here, and he fell desperately in love with her and found he was not so much attached to Mary as he thought. He says if he had it in his power he would not have one feature of her face altered, he thinks she is so perfect (that is, Miss E.) He and Mr. Speed have spent the most of their time at [the home of Ninian and Elizabeth] Edwards this winter and Lincoln could never bear to leave Miss Edward's side in company. Some of his friends thought he was acting very wrong

and very imprudently and told him so." Jane D. Bell to Anne Bell, Springfield, 27 Jan. 1841, copy, JGR MSS, DLC.

A niece of one of Mary Todd's sisters said, "It was always known in our family . . . that Mr. Lincoln courted Matilda Edwards, a fact which for many reasons she divulged only to her nearest and dearest." Horace Green, "Mother's Appeal Granted," unidentified clipping, LMFW. Lincoln had earlier been smitten by beautiful girls. In August 1827, it is reported, "he was thoroughly captivated" by the "beautiful face and figure" of Julia Evans in Princeton, Indiana. Reminiscences of John M. Lockwood, in Jesse W. Weik, "When Lincoln Met the Wool-Carder's Beautiful Niece," typescript, Papers of the Southwest Indiana Historical Society, Evansville Central Library.

332. Interview with Mrs. Alexander R. McKee, "A Romance of Lincoln," clipping identified as "Indianapolis 1896," LMFW.

333. Sarah Rickard, sister of Mrs. Butler, interviewed by Nellie Crandall Sanford, Kansas City *Star*, 10 Feb. 1907. Elizabeth Grimsley thought Lincoln "doubted whether he was responding as fully as a manly generous nature" should to Mary Todd; his feeling for her "had not the overmastering depth of an early love." Mrs. Grimsley to Ida Tarbell, Springfield, 9 March 1895, copy, Ida M. Tarbell MSS, Allegheny College.

334. Nicolay's interview with Browning, Springfield, 17 June 1875, Hay MSS, RPB.

335. Lincoln to Speed, Springfield, 5 Oct. 1842, in Basler, *CWL*, 1:303.

336. "I fancy he [Lincoln] has described his own case in the advice to Speed." John G. Nicolay to John Hay, Washington, 24 Jan. 1879, Hay MSS, RPB.

337. Lincoln to Speed, N.p., [3 Jan.? 1842], in Basler, *CWL*, 1:266.

338. Lincoln to Speed, Springfield, 5 Oct. 1842, in Basler, *CWL*, 1:303.

339. Randall, *MTL*, 57–74.

340. Strozier, *Lincoln's Quest for Union*, 40.

341. Daniel J. Levinson et al., *The Seasons of a Man's Life* (New York: Alfred A. Knopf, 1978), 107, 101–6.

342. William J. Butler, grandson of William Butler, in the *Illinois State Journal*, 28 Feb. 1937, 11. Cf. Salome Butler, daughter of William Butler, in Octavia Roberts, "'We All Knew Abr'ham,'" *Abraham Lincoln Quarterly* 4 (March 1946): 28; statement by Speed Butler, William Butler's son, to Lincoln Dubois, in a questionnaire filled out by Dubois, 15 June 1924, enclosed in Lincoln Dubois to Albert J. Beveridge, 15 June 1924, Beveridge MSS, DLC.

343. Matheny's statement to Herndon, 3 May 1866, H-W MSS, DLC.

344. Lincoln to Samuel D. Marshall, Springfield, 11 Nov. 1842, in Basler, *CWL*, 1:305.

345. Mrs. B. S. Edwards to Ida Tarbell, Springfield, 8 Oct. 1895, Ida M. Tarbell MSS, Allegheny College.

346. Randall, *MTL*, 54.

347. Lincoln to Martin S. Morris, Springfield, 26 March 1843, in Basler, *CWL*, 1:320.

348. Mary Lincoln to Josiah G. Holland, Chicago, 4 Dec. 1865, in Turner and Turner, *MTL*, 293. Cf. Mary Lincoln to James Smith, [Marienbad, 8 June

1870]: "As you well know, notwithstanding Mr Lincoln's deep amiable nature, he was not a demonstrative man." Ibid., 566.

349. Interview with Herndon, [10 Jan. 1866?], H-W MSS, DLC.

350. Baker, *MTL*, 94.

351. Lincoln to his wife, Washington, 16 April 1848, in Basler, *CWL*, 1:465.

352. Lincoln to Mrs. Lincoln, Washington, 12 June 1848, in Basler, *CWL*, 1:477.

353. Baker, *MTL*, 205.

354. Ibid., 191.

355. Such a lack of intimate friends is not uncommon for males, at least in late-twentieth-century America. Levinson has suggested that "close friendship with a man or woman is rarely experienced by American men. . . . [M]ost men do not have an intimate male friend of the kind that they recall fondly from boyhood or youth." Levinson, *Seasons of a Man's Life*, 335.

356. Angle, *HL*, 348. Cf. Current, *The Lincoln Nobody Knows*, 12–13.

357. Davis's statement to Herndon, 19 Sept. 1866, quoted in King, *David Davis*, 231.

358. Trumbull to his son, Walter, N.p., N.d., in Horace White, *The Life of Lyman Trumbull* (Boston: Houghton, Mifflin, 1913), 427.

359. John G. Nicolay's interview with Browning, Springfield, 17 June 1875, Hay MSS, RPB; Browning to Isaac N. Arnold, Quincy, Ill., 25 Nov. 1872, Arnold MSS, ICHi. In 1864 Browning told his law partner that "I am personally attached to the President, and have faithfully tried to uphold him, and make him respectable, tho' I never have been able to persuade myself that he was big enough for his position. Still, I thought he might get through, as many a boy has got through College, without disgrace, and without knowledge, but I fear he is a failure." Browning to [Edgar] Cowan, Quincy, 6 Sept. 1864, photocopy, JGR MSS, DLC. Cf. Maurice G. Baxter, *Orville H. Browning: Lincoln's Friend and Critic* (Bloomington: Indiana University Press, 1957), 172–79.

360. Mary S. Vineyard to Herndon, Weston, Mo., 22 July 1866, in Angle, *HL*, 121.

361. Herndon to Henry C. Whitney, Springfield, 16 April 1887, in Hertz, *HL*, 183. Cf. Herndon to Jesse Weik, Springfield, 16 Jan. 1886, H-W MSS, DLC.

362. Rankin, *Personal Recollections*, 31.

363. Whitney to Herndon, Chicago, 4 July 1887, H-W MSS, DLC.

364. John J. Duff, *A. Lincoln: Prairie Lawyer* (New York: Holt, Rinehart and Winston, 1960), 168–220.

365. Randall, *MTL*, 79.

366. James Gourley's statement to Herndon, H-W MSS, DLC.

367. Gibson William Harris, "My Recollections of Abraham Lincoln," *Woman's Home Companion*, Feb. 1904, 11.

368. Angle, *HL*, 247.

369. Statement of Davis, 20 Sept. 1866, H-W MSS, DLC. Cf. "Personal Reminiscences of the Late Abraham Lincoln," by "a contributor to the Bulletin," San Francisco *Steamer Bulletin*, 22 April 1865, 4.

370. Davis in Angle, HL, 344.

371. Ibid., 249. A Springfield minister in 1860 told a colleague that Lincoln was frequently absent on the Sabbath because "for the last 3 or 4 years he has been away from home much of the time and engaged in very exhausting labors." The Rev. Mr. Albert Hale to the Rev. Mr. Theron Baldwin, Springfield, 31 May 1860, JGR MSS, DLC.

372. Statement of Davis, 20 Sept. 1866, H-W MSS, DLC. Cf. Weik, RL, 90.

373. Herndon to Isaac N. Arnold, Springfield, 24 Oct. [18]83, Lincoln Collection, ICHi.

374. Whitney, Lincoln, 1:189.

375. Herndon to Isaac N. Arnold, Springfield, 24 Oct. [18]83, Lincoln Collection, ICHi; reminiscences of Judge Lawrence Weldon, Springfield News, 12 Feb. 1902; John M. Palmer, Personal Recollections of John M. Palmer: The Story of an Earnest Life (Cincinnati: R. Clarke, 1901), 40; Henry C. Whitney, Life on the Circuit with Lincoln (Boston: Estes and Lauriat, 1892), 40; King, David Davis, 87. Leonard Swett said that in addition to Lincoln and himself, only Ward Hill Lamon and David Davis attended all sessions on the circuit. Swett, lecture on Lincoln, Chicago Times, 21 Feb. 1876.

376. [John M. Scott], "Lincoln on the Stump and at the Bar," typescript, 9, Ida M. Tarbell MSS, Allegheny College.

377. Swett to Josiah H. Drummond, Bloomington, Ill., 27 May 1860, copy, Ida M. Tarbell MSS, Allegheny College.

378. Davis to his wife, Shelbyville, 17, 20 May 1852, in King, David Davis, 84. In 1850 he noted that Lincoln had not heard from his wife since he left Springfield weeks earlier. Davis to his wife, Shelbyville, 20 May 1850, David Davis MSS, ICHi.

379. Mrs. Norman B. Judd, undated interview with Ida Tarbell, Ida M. Tarbell MSS, Allegheny College.

380. Carl Sandburg, The Lincoln Collector: The Story of Oliver R. Barrett's Great Private Collection (New York: Harcourt, Brace, 1950), 71–75; James T. Hickey, "Robert Todd Lincoln and the 'Purely Private' Letters of the Lincoln Family," Journal of the Illinois State Historical Society 74 (Spring 1981): 58–79; David C. Mearns, ed., The Lincoln Papers, 2 vols. (Garden City: Doubleday, 1948), 1:1–130; John S. Goff, Robert Todd Lincoln: A Man in His Own Right (Norman: University of Oklahoma Press, 1969), 256–57.

381. In the northern part of the Eighth Judicial Circuit, James C. Conkling found Lincoln "desperately homesick and turning his head frequently toward the south" during the spring of 1843. Conkling to his wife, Bloomington, 18 [and 19] April 1843, photostat copy, JGR MSS, DLC.

382. Strozier, Lincoln's Quest for Union, 116–20. Strozier contends that Lincoln stayed away longer and longer as time passed, especially after the early 1850s. But his source—Lincoln Day by Day: A Chronology, 1809–1865, 3 vols., ed. Earl Schenck Miers et al. (Washington, D.C.: Lincoln Sesquicentennial Commission, 1960)—does not support such a conclusion. The title of that estimable work is misleading, for the book does not indicate where Lincoln was every single day, yet it does suggest that he spent more time at home in

the mid and late 1850s than in the early years of that decade. Cf. Richard Friend Lufkin's series of articles, "Mr. Lincoln's Light from under a Bushel," *Lincoln Herald* 52 (Dec. 1950): 2–20; 53 (Winter 1951): 2–25; 54 (Winter 1952): 2–26; 55 (Winter 1953): 2–14; 56 (Winter 1954): 3–24.

Robert Todd Lincoln recalled that during his childhood and early youth, his father "was almost constantly away from home," but that "in 1859 . . . he was beginning to devote himself more to practice in his own neighborhood." Robert Todd Lincoln to J. G. Holland, Chicago, 6 June 1865, Robert Todd Lincoln MSS, DLC. In 1858, Lincoln somewhat inaccurately wrote that "I am [away] from home perhaps more than half my time." Lincoln to Samuel Caldwell, Springfield, 27 May 1858, in *The Collected Works of Abraham Lincoln: Second Supplement, 1848–1865*, ed. Roy P. Basler and Christian O. Basler (New Brunswick: Rutgers University Press, 1990), 14.

383. Davis to his wife, Pekin, 8 May 1854, in King, *David Davis*, 94.

384. Willard L. King to Ruth Painter Randall, Chicago, 21 Sept. 1953, JGR MSS, DLC.

385. Herndon to Weik, Springfield, 10 July 1888, in Hertz, *HL*, 214–15.

386. Baker, *MTL*, 132–33.

387. Henry B. Stanton, *Random Recollections* (New York: Harper and Brothers, 1887), 221.

388. New York *Evening Sun*, 12 Feb. 1912.

389. Statement of P. P. Enos, N.d., H-W MSS, DLC.

390. See Harry E. Pratt, *The Personal Finances of Abraham Lincoln* (Springfield: Abraham Lincoln Association, 1943), 25–57.

391. Mary Lincoln to Emilie Todd Helm, Springfield, 20 Sept. [1857], in Turner and Turner, *MTL*, 50.

392. Reminiscences of McCoy in an unidentified newspaper clipping, dated 12 Feb. 1901, Lincoln Scrapbooks, 3:40, Judd Stewart Collection, CSmH.

393. Preston H. Bailhache, "Abraham Lincoln as I Remember Him," copy, enclosed in David Wesson to James S. Lincoln, Montclair, N.J., 25 March 1930, Vertical File, "Reminiscences," folder 5, Lincoln Collection, IHi.

394. For a discussion of the unusual pattern of Mary Lincoln's childbearing, see Sklar, "Victorian Women and Domestic Life," 30–34.

395. Strozier, *Lincoln's Quest for Union*, 87–88; for a different conclusion, see Baker, *MTL*, 142, 227–28.

396. Angle, *HL*, 348.

397. Grimsley, "Six Months in the White House," 64–65.

398. Whitney, *Life on the Circuit*, 183; Chauncey Depew, in *Lincoln Talks: A Biography in Anecdote*, ed. Emmanuel Hertz (New York: Viking, 1939), 60–61; Isaac N. Arnold, *The History of Abraham Lincoln, and the Overthrow of Slavery* (Chicago: Clarke, 1866), 503. Cf. Harry E. Pratt, "Lincoln Liked 'Nothing to Wear,'" *Abraham Lincoln Quarterly* 2 (March 1942): 5–12.

399. From an anthology entitled *Elegant Extracts; or, Useful and Entertaining Passages from the Best English Authors and Translations*, quoted in Townsend, *Lincoln and His Wife's Home Town*, 158.

400. Herndon to Weik, N.p., 16 Jan. 1886, H-W MSS, DLC.

401. James B. Fry quoting Lincoln, in Rice, *RL,* 400.

402. For a lucid general introduction to Jung's thought, see M. Esther Harding, *The "I" and the "Not-I": A Study in the Development of Consciousness* (New York: Pantheon, 1965).

403. See James Hillman, "Senex and Puer: An Aspect of the Historical and Psychological Present," in Hillman et al., *Puer Papers* (Dallas: Spring, 1979), 3–53.

404. Marie-Louise von Franz, *Puer Aeternus,* 2d ed. (Santa Monica: Sigo Press, 1981).

405. von Franz, *Puer Aeternus,* 4.

406. Randall, *MTL,* 22, 119, 303, 217.

407. Bayne, *Tad Lincoln's Father,* 49.

408. Evans, *Mrs. Lincoln,* 70.

409. Bayne, *Tad Lincoln's Father,* 43–48.

410. Folsom, "New Stories of Lincoln," 47. C. M. Smith was the principal informant for this article.

411. Lincoln told this to Charles Hoyt in a letter that has been lost. Allen G. Hoyt to Ida Tarbell, Aurora, Ill., 13 June 1896, Ida M. Tarbell MSS, Allegheny College.

412. See chapter 3 of this volume.

413. James Gourley's statement, N.d., H-W MSS, DLC.

414. See chapter 1 of this volume. Lincoln was not a pure example of an introvert, but he was more introverted than extroverted.

415. Conkling to Mercy Levering, Springfield, 21 Sept. 1840, in Sandburg and Angle, *Mary Lincoln,* 172–73.

416. William E. Barton, "Mr. and Mrs. Lincoln," *Women's Home Companion,* Feb. 1930, 180.

417. Benjamin P. Thomas, *Abraham Lincoln: A Biography* (New York: Alfred A. Knopf, 1952), 91.

418. Whitney, *Life on the Circuit,* 99.

419. Weik, *RL,* 90. Cf. Angle, *HL,* 349–50; Herndon quoted by Hardin W. Masters, Portland [Maine] *Sunday Telegram,* 16 July 1922; Milton Hay interviewed by George Alfred Townsend, Cincinnati *Inquirer,* 26 Aug. 1883, in *Intimate Memories of Lincoln,* ed. Wilson, 47.

420. Reminiscences of McCoy in an unidentified newspaper clipping, dated 12 Feb. 1901, Lincoln Scrapbooks, 3:40, Judd Stewart Collection, CSmH.

421. See chapter 8 of this volume.

422. Bradwell's statement to Ida Tarbell, memo marked "Lincoln—Items," folder "Mary Todd Lincoln," Ida M. Tarbell MSS, Allegheny College.

423. Rankin, *Personal Recollections,* 181, 184. Baker properly notes that "Mary Lincoln's essential contribution to her husband's eventual success lay in her faith in his ability, a traditional spouse's donation. But in keeping with her need to make a mark, she transformed the usual wifely applause into an inspirational prophecy of his greatness, which cause she intended to advance." *MTL,* 144.

424. Herndon to Isaac N. Arnold, Springfield, 24 Oct. [18]83, Lincoln Collection, ICHi.

425. Mary G. Chandler, *The Elements of Character* (Boston: Otis Clapp, 1854), 222, quoted in Carl Sandburg, *Abraham Lincoln: The Prairie Years,* 2 vols. (New York: Harcourt, Brace, 1926), 2:275–76. Cf. Evans, *Mrs. Lincoln,* 294–97. Oliver Barrett owned Lincoln's marked copy of Chandler's book. Barrett to Ida Tarbell, Chicago, 9 Nov. 1927; Tarbell to Barrett, New York, 26 Oct. 1927 and 19 June 1928; Tarbell to M. L. Houser, New York, 2 Nov. 1929, copy; all in Ida M. Tarbell MSS, Allegheny College.

Epilogue

Some psychohistorians have misjudged Lincoln. Dwight Anderson deemed him "a Robespierre" and a "tyrant;"[1] George Forgie thought him guilt-ridden for having defeated a rival who countenanced the spread of an institution that Lincoln despised,[2] and Charles B. Strozier portrayed Lincoln as a man, who even in the 1850s, was more obsessed with preserving the Union than eradicating slavery.[3] I have tried to show why I disagree with some of their conclusions.

This book most closely resembles Strozier's, which persuasively argues that Lincoln's inner life profoundly affected his outer life, and which offers sensitive analyses of Lincoln's relations with his parents, with his wife, with his children, and with Joshua Speed. I have tried to build on those insights. For example, Strozier puts defensive accounts of Thomas Lincoln into perspective, maintaining that "revisionist research . . . has been fundamentally misplaced," and that Abraham "grew up with an abiding sense of disappointment and alienation from" his father.[4] I take Strozier's argument one step further and relate such "alienation" and "disappointment" to the core of Lincoln's political ideology.

I view that core as a deep hatred of slavery, whereas Strozier sees it as a strong love of the Union. He argues that "the confusion, contradictions, and specious distinctions built into Lincoln's thought about the interrelated issue of slavery and racial equality in the 1850s reflected the fact that his primary concern lay elsewhere—with the preservation of the Union."[5] But during the 1850s Lincoln spoke far more heatedly and often about the evils of slavery than about the sanctity of the Union, and did so without "confusions, contradictions, and specious distinctions." I agree with Herman Belz, who, in a commentary on Strozier's thesis, wondered, "Why, if Lincoln was so concerned with union, he assumed the leadership of an exclusively sectional party, the very existence of which threatened the national union."[6]

Had union been his principal concern, Lincoln during the secession crisis might well have accepted compromise proposals that could have saved the union while allowing slavery to expand. Belz asks, "Could we not say that the central issue for Lincoln and his generation was freedom rather than union?"[7] The answer to that question, I believe, is yes.

Strozier's central thesis seems to rest on the belief, which I endorse, that the Lincolns' marriage was unhappy. Although that thesis is at times "portentous and obscure,"[8] the gist of it seems to be that Lincoln's failure to create a sense of union between himself and Mary Todd between 1842 and 1854 impelled him to try preserving the union of the states: "After 1854 Lincoln turned outward and attempted, as Erik Erikson might say, to solve for all what he could not solve for himself alone."[9]

My assessment of the Lincolns' marital woes stresses the ways in which they taught Lincoln how to cope with difficult people, helped to fuel his ambition, and led him to invest much of his emotional capital in his political career. I focus more intensively than does Strozier on the reasons why Lincoln and Mary Todd were drawn to each other and on why their marriage was so troubled. My chapter on that subject is perhaps the most controversial one in this volume. In the past half-century, historians and biographers have performed scholarly contortions to defend Mary Todd Lincoln and to portray her marriage as happy. In some circles, unflattering comments about Mary Lincoln are deemed "subversive."[10]

In 1987, Jean Baker called the Lincolns' marriage "a success" and to prove her point relied heavily on a letter by Elizabeth Blair Lee ("Mary has her husband's deepest love. This is a matter upon which one woman cannot deceive another.") and a statement by Mary Lincoln's sister, Frances Todd Wallace ("They knew each other perfectly. They did not lead an unhappy life at all. She was devoted to him and his children and he was certainly all to her a husband could have been").[11] Thirty-four years earlier, Ruth Painter Randall averred that the letters between the Lincolns as well as the testimony of Henry B. Rankin, Henry C. Whitney, Joseph Kent, James Gourley, and Emilie Todd Helm constituted "evidence of a happy marriage that will hold in any court of law, or historical investigation, where theories based on hearsay and gossip will be stricken from the record."[12]

But surviving evidence from neighbors, relatives, friends, servants, colleagues, tradesmen, and other firsthand witnesses—evidence that cannot be dismissed as "hearsay and gossip"—indicates that Mary Todd Lincoln was an impossibly difficult woman who made Lincoln's home life miserable. One notable case in point is the Lincolns' neighbor in Springfield, James Gourley, who now and then overheard domestic discord from next door. As noted in the previous chapter, Gourley recalled that the Lincolns "got along tolerably well, unless Mrs. L[incoln] got the devil in her"; that her "unusually high temper" almost "invariably got the better of her." When "she became excited or troublesome," Lincoln would laugh at her or simply pick up the children and leave the house.[13] Ruth Randall cited this as an example showing the "congeniality" of the Lincoln marriage![14] Willing to accept reminiscences by Gourley and others if they indicate, even slightly, that the Lincoln marriage was "congenial," Randall was quick to brand contrary testimony "gossip and hearsay." Her husband, James G. Randall, used a similar approach in his treatment of the Ann Rutledge story.[15]

Joseph P. Kent, whom Ruth Randall quotes to prove that the Lincolns' marriage was happy, recalled how Lincoln would flee to his office when Mary Lincoln "fell into a rage" and denounced him in her "shrill, penetrating voice." Like Gourley, Kent said Lincoln would simply leave the house.[16] Henry B. Rankin, another witness summoned to the bar by Randall to demonstrate the happiness of the Lincolns' marriage, related how firmly Lincoln evicted his wife from his White House office when she, "in her emphatic tones of command, so characteristic of her when she was displeased," ordered him to the supper table. Rankin termed Lincoln a "perplexing husband" who was a "puzzle or sometimes a despair" to his wife.[17] Henry C. Whitney, also cited by Ruth Randall to prove how happily married the Lincolns were, agreed with Rankin. Lincoln "could not make any woman happy" because he was "too much allied to his intellect to get down to the plane of the domestic relations."[18]

Ruth Painter Randall to the contrary notwithstanding, the few surviving letters between the Lincolns do not suggest a deep love on either side. Although the correspondence contains some expressions of affection, they are rather perfunctory and not so striking as Mary Lincoln's complaint to her husband that "you are not *given* to letter writing."[19] In fact, the most remarkable feature of that correspondence is its sparseness.

Randall also twists evidence about Mary Lincoln's character as well as the nature of her marriage. She notes that Benjamin Brown French, the commissioner of public buildings during the Civil War, "recognized that the bedrock of her character was a fundamental goodness and kindness of heart." French, who saw her often, knew, "like all who

came in contact with Mrs. Lincoln," that "she was not the terrible
woman pictured in malicious gossip. He was indignant at the *'vile slander'* heaped upon her for political purposes. He noted at the White
House receptions how she 'bore herself well and bravely, and looked
queenly.' He spoke of her little acts of thoughtfulness for others, 'excellent lady that she is.'"[20]

Most of French's compliments were paid early in the war. On December 22, 1861, he noted in his journal, "I like Mrs. L. better and
better the more I see of her and think she is an admirable woman. She
bears herself, in every particular, like a lady and, say what they may
about her, I will defend her." By war's end, his views had changed. As
Mary Lincoln left the White House in May 1865, French wrote: "She
is a most singular woman, and it is well for the nation that she is no
longer in the White House. It is not proper that I should write down,
even here, all I know! May God have her in his keeping, and make her
a better woman." He compared her unfavorably with President Andrew Johnson's daughters Mary Stover and Martha Patterson, who
served as the White House hostesses during their father's term. In January 1866, French confided to his journal after a reception in the Executive Mansion: "I introduced hundreds to Mrs. Patterson and Mrs.
Stover. Oh how different it is to the introductions to Mrs. Lincoln! She
(Mrs. L.) sought to put on the airs of an Empress—these ladies are plain,
ladylike, republican ladies, their dress rich but modest and unassuming, their manners such as become an American woman."[21]

Another controversial argument made in this volume concerns the
difference between Lincoln's early career as a hack politician and his
later career as a statesman. Not all scholars accept such a view. Gabor
S. Boritt, in a trailblazing, insightful study of Lincoln's economic ideas,
maintains that he was consistent throughout his political career, with
"an intense and continually developing commitment to the ideal that
all men should receive a full, good, and ever increasing reward for their
labors so that they might have the opportunity to rise in life." He contends that "far from being a small opportunist turned statesman, Lincoln must be recognized as a man of consistent, high vision throughout his life."[22]

There is much truth in Boritt's thesis (I rely heavily on his work,
particularly his brilliant chapter "Watchman, What of the Night?" in
my discussion of Lincoln's opposition to slavery), but I believe that he
is mistaken in detecting no profound difference between the partisan
Lincoln of the 1830s and 1840s and the statesmanlike Lincoln of the

1850s and 1860s. Joel Silbey is more persuasive in arguing that Lincoln in the 1830s and 1840s "was a total political operator," a "party hack," "a virulent political point man," "a nineteenth century political partisan to his boots," possessed of "a very partisan outlook."[23]

Like Boritt, Daniel Walker Howe argues that Lincoln's political career displays no sharp break between his Whig principles in the 1830s and 1840s and his Republicanism in the 1850s and 1860s. Lincoln's course after 1854, Howe contends, "can best be understood as developing out of the internal logic of Whig values." But his argument loses some force when he notes that Lincoln's antislavery passion reflected "what was best in Jacksonian Democracy: the commitment to the rights of the common man," as well as a concern for Jeffersonian principles spelled out in the Declaration of Independence. Howe also claims that the Whigs placed "emphasis on controlling of others" as a fundamental value.[24] Yet in his forties and fifties, Lincoln devoted himself to *liberating* others.

I also disagree with some psychologists, most notably those who pronounce Lincoln "*clearly* psychotic,"[25] or "schizoid-manic,"[26] or a man with "a mother fixation of unusual intensity."[27] As the evidence adduced in these pages shows, Lincoln was emotionally crippled in certain ways, struggling as he did with depression and finding it difficult to relate to women. But as Mark Neely observed, "Lincoln's ability to cope with whatever melancholy afflicted him late in life was great." He was able to use "humor, fatalistic resignation, and, perhaps, some religious feelings" in order to become "his wife's principal prop in the losses of their children Eddie and Willie." Moreover, "no melancholy ever interfered with his ability to work in the White House."[28]

Lincoln's depressions and the problems Lincoln encountered in dealing with women pale into relative insignificance when we consider his psyche as a whole. In most areas, he was a model of psychological maturity, a fully individuated man who attained a level of consciousness unrivaled in the history of American public life. Most politicians, indeed most people, are dominated by their own petty egos. They take things personally, try to dominate one another, waste time and energy on feuds and vendettas, project their unacceptable qualities onto others, displace anger and rage, and put the needs of their own clamorous egos above all other considerations. A dramatic exception to this pattern, Lincoln achieved a kind of balance and wholeness that led one psychologist to remark that he had more "psychological honesty" than anyone since Christ.[29] If one considers Christ as a psychological paradigm,[30] the analogy is apt. In short, what stands out about Lincoln's inner life is not his psychological weakness but his remarkable strength.

NOTES

1. Dwight G. Anderson, *Abraham Lincoln: The Quest for Immortality* (New York: Alfred A. Knopf, 1982), 66, 91.

2. George Forgie, *Patricide in the House Divided: A Psychological Interpretation of Lincoln and His Age* (New York: W. W. Norton, 1978).

3. Charles B. Strozier, *Lincoln's Quest for Union: Public and Private Meanings* (New York: Basic Books, 1982).

4. Strozier, *Lincoln's Quest for Union*, 13.

5. Ibid., 176.

6. Herman Belz, "Commentary on 'Lincoln's Quest for Union,'" in *The Historian's Lincoln: Pseudohistory, Psychohistory, and History*, ed. Gabor S. Boritt and Norman O. Forness (Urbana: University of Illinois Press, 1988), 249.

7. Belz, "Commentary," 249.

8. Ibid., 248.

9. Strozier, *Lincoln's Quest for Union*, 123.

10. C. W. Hackensmith, "The Much Maligned Mary Todd Lincoln," *Filson Club History Journal* 44 (July 1970): 282: "One writer openly hints that she was capricious from her childhood. Another tells of moods of temper and instability in her youth. If there was a vestige of truth in these subversive remarks I feel sure there would have been something dropped about it by those who knew her intimately during that time."

11. Baker, *MTL*, 228, 132. Baker might also have included the following remark by David Davis: "Lincoln speaks very affectionately of his wife & children." Davis to his wife, Shelbyville, 3 Nov. 1851, David Davis MSS, ICHi. But Davis observed later, both in letters and reminiscences, that Lincoln was domestically unhappy and that his wife was a most disagreeable woman.

12. Randall, *MTL*, 109–13, 149, 155, 162–63 [quote from 113].

13. Undated statements by Gourley, H-W MSS, DLC; Weik, *RL*, 121–22.

14. Randall, *MTL*, 149, 545. On page 149 she paraphrases Gourley, removing much of his sting; on page 545, part of the index, she lists many sources illustrating "congeniality of marriage attested by intimates." In fairness to Randall, it is possible that she did not compile the index.

15. James G. Randall, *Lincoln the President: From Springfield to Gettysburg*, 2 vols. (New York: Dodd, Mead, 1945), 2:321–42; Douglas L. Wilson, "Abraham Lincoln, Ann Rutledge, and the Evidence of Herndon's Informants," *Civil War History* 36 (Dec. 1990): 301–23.

16. Memo of a conversation between Joseph P. Kent and Weik, 21 Nov. 1916, H-W MSS, DLC; Weik, *RL*, 123, 126. These statements tend to belie Kent's letter of 23 Jan. 1909 to J. R. B. Van Cleave: "Mr. Lincoln's home life was all happiness & content so far as I could ever know. He seemed to idolize

his wife and boys and they, one and all sincerely loved him." Randall, *MTL*, 155.

17. Rankin, *Personal Recollections*, 176–79, 31.

18. Whitney to Herndon, Chicago, 4 July 1887, H-W MSS, DLC.

19. Mary Lincoln to her husband, [New York], 2 Nov. [1862], in Turner and Turner, *MTL*, 139.

20. Randall, *MTL*, 266.

21. Donald B. Cole and John J. McDonough, eds., *Witness to the Young Republic: A Yankee's Journal, 1828–1870* (Hanover: University Press of New England, 1989), 383, 479, 497 [entries for 22 Dec. 1861, 24 May 1865, 12 Jan. 1866]. In fairness to Randall, it should be pointed out that French's journal, unlike his correspondence, was unavailable to scholars when she was conducting her research.

22. Gabor S. Boritt, *Lincoln and the Economics of the American Dream* (Memphis: Memphis State University Press, 1978), ix, x. Aryeh Maidenbaum argues that "Lincoln's political attitudes were . . . consistent throughout his career." Maidenbaum, "Sounds of Silence: An Aspect of Lincoln's Whig Years," *Illinois Historical Journal* 82 (Autumn 1989): 176.

23. Joel Silbey, "'Always a Whig in Politics': The Partisan Life of Abraham Lincoln," *Journal of the Abraham Lincoln Association* 8 (1986): 21–42.

24. Daniel Walker Howe, *The Political Culture of the American Whigs* (Chicago: University of Chicago Press, 1979), 275, 290, 300.

25. A psychotherapist identified only as "Karl," quoted in Martin B. Duberman, *Cures: A Gay Man's Odyssey* (New York: Dutton, 1991), 205.

26. A. A. Brill, "Lincoln as a Humorist," a paper given before a convention of the American Psychiatric Association in 1931, typesecript, Ida M. Tarbell MSS, Allegheny College. Brill said, "Judging by all the descriptions given of Lincoln's depressions, I feel that all one can say is that he was a schizoid manic personality, now and then harassed by schizoid manic moods. These moods never reached to that degree of profundity to justify the diagnosis of insanity." Brill argued that "two contrasting natures struggled within him, the inheritance from an untutored, roving and unstable father, who treated him brutally, and from a cheerful, fine, affectionate mother." Lincoln biographers Ida Tarbell, Emil Ludwig, and L. Pierce Clark all criticized Brill's paper. New York *Sun*, 6 June 1931. A thoughtful rejoinder can also be found in H. L. Koopman, "Lincoln's Divided Nature," typescript, Lincoln Collection, RPB.

27. Harold D. Laswell, paraphrased in "Professors Disagree on What Knowledge Is 'Most Important,'" Chicago *Daily News*, either 1 Aug. or 8 Jan. 1934.

28. Mark E. Neely, Jr., *The Abraham Lincoln Encyclopedia* (New York: McGraw Hill, 1982), 248.

29. Morton Prince to Albert J. Beveridge, Nahant, Mass., 13 Oct. 1925, Beveridge MSS, DLC.

30. Cf. Edward Edinger, *Ego and Archetype: Individuation and the Religious Function of the Psyche* (New York: G. P. Putnam's, 1972).

Appendix
Stephen A. Douglas as a Target of Lincoln's Lyceum Address

On January 27, 1838, Lincoln warned the Young Men's Lyceum of Springfield against a man "of ambition and talents" who would scruple at nothing to attain "distinction." The quest to identify the coming Caesar whom Lincoln described has spawned a cottage industry among historians. Following the suggestion of literary critic Edmund Wilson, some scholars have concluded that Lincoln was unconsciously alerting the public to his own overweening ambition. Others have speculated that he was harpooning Andrew Jackson or Martin Van Buren.[1]

The same day that Lincoln spoke to the Lyceum, the *Sangamo Journal* published a blistering, pseudonymous attack on Stephen A. Douglas under the byline "Conservative No. 2." Some Democrats at the time accused Lincoln of writing the "Conservative" letters, and at least one historian has endorsed that view.[2] But the editors of *The Collected Works of Abraham Lincoln* demurred, saying that such attribution rested on "insufficient evidence."[3]

The most thorough analyst of this question, Glenn H. Seymour, properly noted similarities between the style and construction of the Conservative No. 2 letter and the style and construction of some of Lincoln's contemporary writings.[4] But Seymour failed to draw attention to the striking parallels between the imagery used in Conservative No. 2 and the Lyceum address, parallels that not only help to clinch his argument but also suggest that Lincoln aimed his barbs about Caesarism at Stephen A. Douglas, who was running for Congress against Lincoln's law partner, friend, and mentor, John T. Stuart.[5] The twenty-four-year-old Douglas would be an obvious target for Lincoln's satiric pen, with which he recklessly skewered Democrats in his early adulthood (chapter 7).

Conservative described how Douglas was inveigled into running for Congress by a flatterer (probably John Calhoun) who coveted Douglas's post as register of the Springfield Land Office. This crafty would-be bureaucrat appealed to Douglas's vanity "by telling him that he regretted to see him confined to the dry and laborious occupation of writing answers to the endless and silly enquiries of every applicant about N. W. of S. E. of 23, T. 24 R. 3 W., etc., etc.; that for one whom nature designed for nothing else but to be

> 'Fixed to one certain spot,
> To draw nutrition, propagate, and rot.'[6]

such a plodding occupation was well enough; but that for one of his towering genius, it was absolutely intolerable."
Conservative had the flatterer say to Douglas:

> You may be President of these United States just as well as not. A seat in Congress is not worthy to be your abiding place, though you might with propriety serve one term in the capacity of Representative—not that it would at all become you; but merely in imitation of some king, who being called to the throne from obscurity, lodges for one night in a hovel as he journies to the palace. History gives no account of a man of your age occupying such high ground as you do now. At twenty-four Bonaparte was unheard of; and in fact so it has been with all great men in former times. Of the history of all of them, Mr. Van Buren alone approaches rivalship to yours. Indeed, the similarity is striking. The only difference, perhaps, is, that his own was but the miniature of what your's is the life size.

Conservative imagined Douglas replying: "But do you really think a seat in Congress within my reach?"
"Within your reach!" expostulated the flatterer. "What a question!—How strange it is, that while true genius can place a true estimate upon everything else, it never can upon its own powers. There is no doubt of a seat in Congress being within your reach. The only question is whether you will condescend to occupy it."[7]
In the Lyceum address entitled "The Perpetuation of Our Political Institutions," Lincoln used similar images as he limned the dangers presented by a man "of ambition and talents." Rhetorically he asked if such a man would be content following traditional paths to distinction: "Many great and good men sufficiently qualified for any task they should undertake, may ever be found, whose ambition would aspire

to nothing beyond a seat in Congress, a gubernatorial or a presidential chair; *but such belong not to the family of the lion, or the tribe of the eagle*[.]" In a passage that seems aimed at Douglas, whose ambition was notorious, he mockingly added: "What! think you these places would satisfy an Alexander, a Caesar, or a Napoleon? Never! Towering genius disdains a beaten path."[8]

The parallels between the Conservative No. 2 letter and the Lyceum address are notable. Sarcastically, Conservative called Douglas a man of "towering genius" (probably a belittling reference to Douglas's diminutive stature); sarcastically, Lincoln called the coming Caesar a man of "towering genius."[9] Conservative compared Douglas to Bonaparte; Lincoln warned against a man who, like Napoleon, belongs to the family of the lion and the tribe of the eagle. Conservative hinted that Douglas would not be content with a seat in Congress; Lincoln denounced a man whose ambition would be unsatisfied with such a post.

The context as well as the text of Lincoln's address to the Young Men's Lyceum must be considered. Although nonpartisan, the organization had members who cared about politics, and a hot electoral contest just then raged between Stuart and Douglas, a contest that Lyceum members doubtless followed closely.[10] Hours before Lincoln addressed them, they had probably read the letter by Conservative in the *Sangamo Journal.* As they listened to Lincoln, they could not forget what they had just read, nor could they forget his reputation as a fierce Whig partisan, celebrated for his belittling of Democrats. In all likelihood, they interpreted Lincoln's assault on the coming Caesar as a clever thrust at Douglas, yet another sortie in his ongoing war of words against Democratic office-seekers. Historians might well do the same.

NOTES

1. Mark E. Neely, Jr., "Lincoln's Lyceum Speech and the Origins of a Modern Myth," *Lincoln Lore,* Feb. 1987, 1–4, March 1987, 1; Edmund Wilson, *Patriotic Gore: Studies in the Literature of the American Civil War* (New York: Oxford University Press, 1962), 106–8.

2. Glenn H. Seymour, "'Conservative'—Another Lincoln Pseudonym?" *Journal of the Illinois State Historical Society* 29 (July 1936): 135–50, and "Lincoln—Author of the Letters by a Conservative," *Bulletin of the Abraham Lincoln Association,* no. 50 (Dec. 1937): 8–9.

3. Basler, *CWL,* 1:435.

4. Seymour, "'Conservative,'" passim.

5. On the 1838 campaign in the Third Congressional District of Illinois, see Robert W. Johannsen, *Stephen A. Douglas* (New York: Oxford University Press, 1973), 61–72.

6. These lines are from Pope, a poet known to Lincoln. See Edward Everett, diary, 1 Nov. 1861, Massachusetts Historical Society.

7. *Sangamo Journal,* 27 Jan. 1838. For Douglas's heated reply, see the enclosure in Douglas to George W. Weber, N.p., [30 Jan. 1838], in *The Letters of Stephen A. Douglas,* ed. Robert W. Johannsen (Urbana: University of Illinois Press, 1961), 51–55.

8. "Address Before the Young Men's Lyceum of Springfield, Illinois," 27 Jan. 1838, in Basler, *CWL,* 1:113–14.

9. I am grateful to Mark Steiner for suggesting this point. Steiner plausibly detects a parallel between this "sarcastic dig at Douglas's height" and Lincoln's reference in a letter about Douglas, written less than two months before the Lyceum Address: "We have adopted it as a part of our policy here, to never speak of Douglass at all. Is'nt that the best mode of treating so small a matter?" Lincoln to William A. Minshall, Springfield, 7 Dec. 1837, in Basler, *CWL,* 1:107.

10. Thomas F. Schwartz, "The Springfield Lyceum and Lincoln's 1838 Speech," *Illinois Historical Journal* 83 (Spring 1990): 45–49, argues that Lincoln gave a civics speech because the previous year his fierce partisanship in the Adams affair had aroused resentment: "He needed to select a nonpartisan topic that appealed to the interests of his audience, while allowing him an opportunity to demonstrate his knowledge and oratorical ability" (49). That may be true of most of the speech, but in the section on the coming Caesar, Lincoln indulged his fondness for political invective and satire.

Index

Throughout the index, the following abbreviations are used: *L*, Lincoln, *MTL*, Mary Todd Lincoln, and *RTL*, Robert Todd Lincoln.

Abandonment: L's fear of, 100, 317
Abell, Bennett, 238
Abell, Elizabeth (Mrs. Bennett), 125, 238; on Ann Rutledge death, 96; Mary Owens romance and, 133
Abolitionists, 173
Adams, James, 151
Allen, Robert, 160, 179–80
Alley, John B., 165
Alsopp (Ill. abolitionist), 25
Alton, Ill., 9, 25
American Baptist Home Mission Society, 32
Ames, Bishop Charles Gordon, 105
Anderson, Dwight G., 253, 254, 357
Anderson, William G., 152
Andrew, John A., 181–82, 191–92; Benjamin F. Butler and, 192
Andrew, Mrs. John A., 192
Angle, Paul M., 22, 147, 151
Archetypes: discussed, 5, 73, 74, 323
Armstrong, Hannah (Mrs. Jack), 125
Armstrong, Jack, 159
Arnold, Isaac N., 26, 76, 148, 150
Ashley, James M., 174
Aurora (Ill.) *Beacon,* 249

Badeau, Adam: MTL and, 288–90
Bailey v. Cromwell, 26–27
Baker, Edward D., 41, 98, 198, 240, 241; death of, 104; funeral of, 300; mentioned, 77
Baker, Jean, 69n26, 277, 284–85, 297, 318, 327n16, 333n113, 354n423, 358
Balch, George B., 40–41
Baltimore, Md., 33; delegations from to L, 131–32, 201–3
Bancroft, George, 284
Baptists, 22
Barnes, John S., 289

Barnett, T. J., 218n145
Barton Clara, 129
Barton, William E., 120n121, 325; mentioned, xix
Battles (Civil War): Antietam, 186; Bull Run (First), 104; Bull Run (Second), 185, 186; Chickamauga, 83; Chantilly, 185; Gettysburg, 187; Wilderness, 104
Bayne, Julia Taft, 60, 67, 324
Beecher, Henry Ward, 194; mentioned, 133
Belz, Herman, xiv, 14, 357, 358
Benham, Gen. H. W., 197
Bereavement in childhood: as cause of depression, 94
Beveridge, Albert J., xix, xxiv–v, 1, 3, 9, 10, 93, 126, 137, 153, 269, 308; mentioned, xi, xix, 107
Birch, Jonathan, 76–77, 93
Birney, James G., 50n85
Bissell, William, 27, 245
Bixby, Lydia, 78
Black Hawk War: L's service in, 159, 238; mentioned, 101
Black, John C., 80
Black, William P., 80
Black troops, 83, 195; mentioned, 191
Blacks, 83–84, 222n179. *See also* Douglass, Frederick
Blair, Francis P., Sr., 59
Blair, Frank P., 59
Blair, Montgomery, 173
Blanchard, John, 48n52
Bloomington, Ill., 92, 159
Boritt, Adam, 137
Boritt, Gabor S., xi, xviii–xix, 35, 137, 240, 266n147, 360
Boston *Journal,* 306
Boutwell, George S., 20
Bowen, Henry C., 251–52
Boyer, Benjamin, 303

Bradwell, James, 325
Brady, William, 283
Brandon, N. W., 124, 147
Breckinridge, John C., 127
Bright, John, 9
Brill, A. A., 363n26
Brodie, Fawn M., xi, 93, 268
Brooks, Noah, 79; on L and Joseph Hooker, 81; on John G. Nicolay, 88n48; on L and Chase, 170; on changes in L, 205; mentioned, 13
Brough, John, 171–72
Browne, Robert H., 25, 45n23, 58, 248
Brownell, Judge H. P. H., 23
Browning, Eliza Caldwell (Mrs. Orville H.), 133, 135, 143n70
Browning, Orville H., 99, 319, 236, 237, 351n359; cabinet crisis and, 180; on L's home life, 297–98; on MTL, 297, 314–16; on Matilda Edwards, 315; mentioned, 190
Bruce, Robert V., 96, 253
Buchanan, James, 200, 274
Buckingham, William, 177
Buell, Don Carlos, 182
Bunn, John W., 253
"The Burial of Sir John Moore," 6
Burnside, Ambrose E., 175–76, 190, 181
Butler, Benjamin F., 192
Butler, Evan, 145n88
Butler, William, 97, 144n78, 161, 238
Butler, Mrs. William, 135
Butterfield, Justin, 160–61, 242
Byron, Lord, 243

Cabinet crisis of 1862, 180
Caldwell, H. Clay, 214n81
Calhoun, John, 366
California, 170, 219n157
Cameron, Simon, 169, 201; mentioned, 189
Campaigns, political: *1834*, 150; *1836*, 150–51, 160; *1837*, 151; *1840*, 151–52, 159, 239; *1844*, 241; *1846*, 241; *1848*, 154; *1854*, 242; *1856*, 31, 154, 275; *1858*, 245–48; *1859*, 250
Campbell, John A., 196–97
Carpenter, Francis B., 64, 174, 204; mentioned, 193
Capps, Elizabeth A., 62, 296
Carroll, Anna E., 127–28
Carryl, William H. & Bro., 299

Cartwright, Peter, 150, 213n66
Cass, Lewis, 154, 248
Chambrun, Marquis de, 20
Chandler, Mary E., 325–26
Chandler, Zachariah, 184–85
Chapman, Augustus H., 94
Chapman, Ervin, 11–12
Chapman, Harriet Hanks, *see* Hanks, Harriet
Charleston, Ill., 33
Charleston, S.C., 83–84
Charnwood, Lord, 2, 9, 107
Chase, Salmon P., 50n85; relationship with L, 170–73, 220n162; MTL and, 284, 286; mentioned, 285
Chicago Convention (1860), 251
Chicago, Ill., 177–78, 178, 204, 319
Chittenden, Lucius, 172
Christian Commission, 281
"Chronicles of Reuben," 121n126; mentioned, 149
Cincinnati, Ohio, 30, 34, 98, 99; mentioned, 278
Circuit, Eighth Judicial (Illinois), 319, 320
City Point, Va., 288–90
Clary, Bill, 159
Clay, Cassius M., 28, 34, 49n63, 167
Clay, Henry, 30, 36, 241; MTL and, 270, 308
Clergy, 177–78
Close, George, 47n46
Coles County, Ill., 41
Colfax, Schuyler, xii, 196, 291, 291–92
Collins, Orvis F., 266n148
Colonization, 30, 192–93
Colonization Society of Illinois, 30
Committee on the Conduct of the War (Joint Congressional), 193
Cone, Charles F., 302
Congress, U.S.: relationship with L, 84, 200
Conkling, James C.: on L's moods, 93, 99; on MTL, 324; on L at Springfield parties, 338n187; mentioned, 196
Conness, John, 170
"Conservative," 365–66
Constable, Charles H., 153–54, 212n56
Conway, Moncure, 178
Corkran, Francis S., 301
Covington, Ky., 30
Covode, John, 195
Cowper, William, 109

Cox, LaWanda, 20, 43*n*6
Crawford, Elizabeth (Mrs. Josiah), 40, 237
Crawford, Josiah, 37–38, 149, 237
Crittenden, Mrs. John J., 300
Crook, William H., 84, 147
Cullom, Shelby M., 175
Current, Richard N., xiv, 38, 140*n*27, 269
Curtin, Andrew G., 105, 203–4

Dahlgren, John A., 106, 180
Dana, Charles A., 147, 280
Danville, Ill., 92
Davis, David: on L, 11, 93, 148, 154, 155–56, 236, 250, 292, 318–21; on MTL and her affairs, 278, 297, 303, 304, 305, 308, 325; anger toward L, 158; L's anger toward, 166; lobbying activities for others, 167, 217*n*126; judgeship and, 285; correspondence with wife, 320; mentioned, 22, 322
Davis, Jefferson, 82, 90*n*78
Davis, Samuel C. and Company, 158
Davis, Sarah Walker (Mrs. David), 321
DeCrastos, Lizzie, 277
Defrees, John, 104
Delany, Martin R., 50*n*85
Deming, Henry C., 84, 287–88
Democratic party, 250
Dennison, William, 226*n*233
Depression: L's problems with, xvii, 92–113; causes of, 98; types of, 106; origins of in L, 106–7; L's family and, 120*n*121
Dickey, John, 48*n*52
Dickey, T. Lyle, 154–55
Dickinson, Anna E., 126–27
Dickson, Mr. and Mrs. William Martin, 99
Diller, J. R., 277–78
Dingley, Philip, 276–77
Dix, Dorothea, 129
Dodge, William E., 199
Donnohoe, D. C., 158
Douglas, Stephen A., 31, 151, 158, 244–55, 250, 254, 255, 365–67, 309; mentioned, 31, 138, 200
Douglass, Frederick, 20, 36, 84
Dowling, Thomas, 147, 278
Drake, Dr. Charles D., 100
Draper, Simeon: MTL and, 283; extortion demands of, 303
Drummond, Thomas, 249
Dubois, Fred, 58

Dubois, Jesse K., 179–80; MTL and, 273, 284, 312; mentioned, 58
Duff, John J.: on L between 1849 and 1854, 2; on Herndon, 73

Early, Dr. Jacob M., 150
Early, Mrs. Jacob M., 277
Early, Gen. Jubal E., 190
Eastman, Zebina, 28, 49*n*63
Eaton, Page, 271
Edwards, Benjamin S., 285
Edwards, Mrs. Benjamin S.: on MTL, 314; on Lincolns' marriage, 317
Edwards, Elizabeth Todd (Mrs. Ninian): on fight between L and MTL, 275–76; marriage of, 293; on MTL, 294, 308; on Lincolns' courtship, marriage, 313–15; on L's personality, 318
Edwards, Frank, 63
Edwards, Matilda, 99, 315
Edwards, Ninian, 144*n*78; marriage of, 293; on Lincolns' marriage, 313
Elkin(s), Rev. David, 94
Ellis, Abner Y., 124, 274
Ellsworth, Elmer E., 79–80, 104
Emancipation, 175, 222*n*189
Emerson, Ralph, 45*n*32
Erickson, Erik, 358
Evans, French S., 168
Evans, Julia, 350*n*331
Evans, W. A., 313, 324
Ewing, Thomas, 160–61
Ewing, William L. D., 151, 241

Feeling function, 7
Fehrenbacher, Don E., xvii, xxi*n*15, xxv–vi, 2, 107, 172, 254
Feinstein, Howard M., 121*n*126
Fell, Jesse W., 249; mentioned, 250
Ficklin, Orlando B., 29
Field, Maunsell B., 171–72
Fifer, Joseph Wilson, 93
Fillmore, Millard, 154, 275
Finch, Gilbert, 73–74
Fish, Hamilton, 175–76
Foot, Solomon, 303
Forgie, George, 253, 254–55, 357
Forney, John W., 169
Forquer, George, 150
Fort Donelson, 184
Foster, Lafayette, 221*n*170
Fox, Benjamin, 25

Francis, Simeon, 259n35
Franklin, Gen. William B., 183, 226n231
Freeman, Douglas Southall, 13
Freese, Jacob, 164, 216n118
Free-Soilers, 28
Frémont, Jesse Benton (Mrs. John C.), 128–29; MTL on, 335n136
Frémont, John C., 128–29, 181, 204, 225n226; mentioned, 275
French, Benjamin Brown, 339n216; MTL and, 297–99, 359–60
Fry, James B., 252
Fugitive Slave Law (1850), 27, 28

Gamble, Hamilton, 195
Gay, Sidney Howard, 194
General Land Office, 34–35, 160–61, 242
Genin's store (New York City), 278
Gentry, E. Grant, 22
Gibson, Charles, 162
Giddings, Joshua, 26, 29
Gillespie, Joseph, 11, 29, 200, 244, 251, 256
Gobin, Hillary, 277
Gollaher, Austin, 107
Goodwin, Parke, 282
Gordon, Nathaniel, 23
Gourley, James, 271, 359; mentioned, 358
Graham, Christopher Columbus, 21
Graham, Mentor, 98, 238; on Ann Rutledge death, 96
Grant, Julia Dent (Mrs. U. S.), 288, 289, 336n151
Grant, U. S., 164, 290; mentioned, 194, 229n259
Greeley, Horace, 50n85, 194
Green, J. Parker, 157
Green, Mrs. M. J., 125
Greene, Bowling, 96, 102
Greene, Gilbert, 55n153
Greene, Lynn McNulty, 237–38
Greene, Nancy (Mrs. Bowling), 102, 125
Greene, William G., 39–41, 96, 124, 159
Greven, Phillip, 121n130
Grierson, Francis, 9
Griffin, Mrs. Charles, 288
Grigsby, Aaron, 96, 149
Grigsby, Charles, 149
Grigsby family, 96, 149
Grigsby, James, 38–39, 93, 237
Grigsby, Nathaniel, 40
Grigsby, Redmond, 95

Grigsby, Reuben, 149
Grimshaw, Jackson, 147
Grimsley, Elizabeth Todd, 62, 350n333
Grimsley, Fanny, 276
Grow, Galusha, 77
Guilt: L's sense of, 103, 255, 357
Gurley, Rev. Phineas D., 207–8, 297

Hackensmith, C. W., 362n10
Hackett, James, 312
Hall, John J., 115n35
Halleck, Henry, 190–91; mentioned, 185, 189, 197
Hamilton, Alexander, 77–78
Hamilton, James A., 180
Hamlet, 254–45
Hamlin, Hannibal, 28
Hammack, John, 307
Hampton Roads Conference, 196–97
Hanks, Dennis: on L's personality, 10; on violence of Thomas Lincoln, 38; 41; on L and women, 123
Hanks, Harriet: Lincoln family and, 42, 279; relationship with MTL, 279, 328n36
Hanks, John, 22; on L and farm work, 39; on L and women, 123; mentioned, 124
Hanks, Sophie: on Thomas Lincoln, 38; on L and women, 123; on ambition, 237; mentioned, 95
Hardin County, Ky., 21–22
Hardin, George, 98–99
Harlan, James F., 177
Hardin, John J., 241, 309, 315
Hardin, Martinette (Mrs. Alexander McKee): on L's personality, 99, 124; on MTL's personality, 271, 308, 314
Harlan, Mary (Mrs. Robert Todd Lincoln), 290
Harris, Gibson William, 74, 75
Harrisburg, Penn., 282
Harrison, P. Quinn, 155, 213n66
Harvey, Cordelia A. P. (Mrs. Lewis), 129–30
Hatch, Ozias M., 179–80
Haughwout, E. V. & Co., 304
Haupt, Gen. Herman, 188
Hawley, Joseph R., 305
Hay, John: on L's personality, 13, 173, 178, 180, 208; on L's love for Tad L, 67–68; relationship with L, 77–78, 336n152; on L's fondness for Shakespeare, 112; Ken-

tucky senator and, 161; Charles Gibson and, 162; Chase's resignation and, 170; relationship with MTL, 304; on MTL, 326*n*4; on Henry Wikoff, 305; mentioned, xix, 180, 182, 185, 186, 188, 189, 190
Hay, Milton, 112, 278; on MTL, 279, 325
Hayes, Rutherford B., 172
Head, Rev. Jesse, 21
Helm, Benjamin Hardin, 83, 104
Helm, Emilie Todd (Mrs. Benjamin Hardin), 83, 310; MTL and, 310; mentioned, 358
Helm, John B., 39
Henderson, Isaac: relationship with MTL, 282, 332*n*109
Henderson, T. J., 250–51
Henning, Fanny, 138, 316
Henry, Anson G., 151, 215*n*98
Herbert, J. K., 174
Herndon, William H.: on L's personality, xi–ii, 4, 5, 7, 8, 18*n*67, 36, 37, 75, 93, 106, 107, 125, 147, 148, 149, 155–56, 236, 242, 243, 244, 251, 318; on L's work habits, 320, 321; informants of, xxiii–v; career of, 6, 73, 74–75; on L and slavery, 22, 28; on L and suicide, 97; on L and Speed family, 101; on L at Harrison trial, 155; on L and politics, 250, 252–53; on Lincoln sons, 57, 63–64; on MTL, v–vi, 323, 332*n*109; on the Lincolns' marriage, 62, 268, 269, 271, 272, 279, 279, 285, 296, 319, 325, 328*n*38; L's discussions of family with, 42, 137, 138; mentioned, xix, 27, 322
Hewitt Abram S., 164
Highland, Ill., 11
Hill, Maj. Samuel, 149, 150, 211*n*30
Hillis, Lois, 136
Hillman, James, 7, 86*n*4
Hitt, Robert Roberts, 74
Hoe, Col. R. M., 222*n*185
Holland, Josiah G., 84; on L's anger and irritability, 205; mentioned, xix
Holloway, David P., 168
Holmes, Oliver Wendell, 6, 113
Holt, Joseph, 145*n*87, 168–69
Hooker, Joseph, 80–81, 105, 253
Hosmer, James H., 76
Hospitals, military, 129–30
House of Representatives, 242

Houston, William, 167
Howard, James Quay, 48*n*53
Howe, Daniel Walker, 361
Howells, William Dean, 100–101, 258*n*18
Humphreys, Elizabeth, 270, 293–94
Hunter, David, 195

Illinois State Colonization Society, 30
Indiana: antislavery and, 22; Lincoln family and, 94; politics and, 241, 250
Individuation, 2–3
Iowa, 250, 311

Jackson, Andrew, 254, 365
Jayne, Julia, *see* Trumbull, Julia Jayne
Jayne, William, 236, 250, 309
Johannsen, Robert W., xxi*n*18, 43*n*4, 46
"John Anderson's Lamentation," 112
Johnson, Andrew, 167–68; mentioned, 360
Johnson, Anna Eastman, 274
Johnson, John M., 161
Johnson, William, 302
Johnston, Abraham, 279
Johnston, John D., 39; mentioned, 279
Jones, John Albert, 59
Jonesboro, Tenn., 190
Judd, Adeline Rossiter (Mrs. Norman B.): MTL and, 297, 310; 320
Judd, Norman B.: on L and politics, 250, 251; MTL and, 282–84; mentioned, 310
Julian, George W., 168
Jullien, Augustus, 302
Jung, Carl: on the unconscious, xviii, 323; on individuation, 2–3; on uses of failure, 4–5; on psychological functions, 7; on archetypes, 73, 323

Kain, J. L., 58
Kansas, 250
Kansas-Nebraska Act, 30
Kaplan, Joan: on "family romance," 56*n*168
Keckley, Elizabeth: on L's grief at death of son, 103; on MTL, 282–83, 285–86, 290; on L's relationship to MTL, 291, 307; MTL's confidences and, 294, 295; relationship with MTL, 307, 334*n*131
Kelley, William D., 177, 141*n*36
Kelley, Zeno, 45*n*34
Kent, Joseph P.: on L and children, 57–58; on Lincolns' relationship, 271–72; on MTL, 359; mentioned, 358

Kentucky: slavery in Hardin County, 21–22; L and, 24, 94; constitutional convention (1849), 29; mentioned, 133
Kerr, Orpheus C. (Robert H. Newell), 106
Key, Maj. John J., 185–86
Keyes, S. C., 283
King Lear, 66
King, Turner R., 277
Kirkham's *English Grammar,* 237
Knox, William, 108–9, 136
Kreismann, Herman, 282

Lamar, John W., 237
Lamborn, Josiah, 198
Lamon, Ward Hill, 34, 64, 112, 131, 274, 309; on the presidency, 166–67, 263n98; David Davis and, 217n126; on L's ambition, 236–37; mentioned, xix, 200, 290
Land sharks, 204
Lane, James E., 195–6
Lanman, Laurinda Mason, 138
Lasswell, Harold D., xvii, 255, 312–13
"The Last Leaf," 6, 113
Lavely's grocery (Springfield), 277
Lawrenceville, Ind., 152
Lawyers, 10, 75–78
Lee, Elizabeth Blair, 358
Lee, Robert E., 82, 105; mentioned, 185–88
Leidig, Olivia, *see* Whiteman, Olivia Leidig
Lellyett, John, 205
Leonard, Linda Schierse, 292–93
Levinson, Daniel J., xiv, 5, 6, 8, 13, 15n9, 100–101, 254, 317, 351n355
Lightner, David, 20
Lincoln, Abraham
—ambition of: origins of, xvii, 257, 252–56; acknowledgment of, 237–38, 240, 245–47; intensity of, 244; for presidency, 248, 250, 251–52; for attorney generalship, 250; for Senate seat, 250; and trip East, 251; MTL and, 325
—ancestry of, 42, 137, 138
—anger of: at his children, 64–65; at female petitioners, 130–33; at wife-beater, 136–37; at White House caller, 147; as a child, 148; at political "abandoners," 155; in legal cases, 148, 155–58; expression of during presidency, 147, 161–208; at George W. Rives, 160; at Robert Allen, 160; at Justin Butterfield, 161–62; at governor of Tennessee, 161; at John

M. Johnson, 161; at Daniel Sickles, 162; at Charles Gibson, 162; at war contractors, 162–63; at Canadian official, 163; at Levi Short, 163; at weapons developers, 163–64; at presidential dress requirements, 164; at office-seekers, 165–67; at David Davis, 166–67; at Ward Hill Lamon, 167; at William Houston, 167; at Andrew Johnson, 167–68; at David P. Holloway, 168; at Joseph Holt, 168–69; at U.S. Senate, 169, 180; at John W. Forney, 169; at Simon Cameron, 169; at Gideon Welles, 169–70; at Salmon Chase, 170–73; at Radicals, 173–76; at Missourians, 174; at Thaddeus Stevens, 174; at Shelby Cullom, 175; at Charles Sumner, 175–77; at Edward L. Pierce, 176; at William A. Buckingham, 177; at James F. Harlan, 177; at France, 177; at Samuel C. Pomeroy, 177, 195–96; at clergy, 177–78; at Congress, 178–79; at Thurlow Weed, 179; at Pennsylvania courts, 179; at James A. Hamilton, 180; at John E. Williams, 180; at Thomas W. Sherman, 180–81; at John C. Frémont, 181; at Union paymasters, 181–82; at George B. McClellan, 182–87; at John J. Key, 185–86; at William S. Rosecrans, 187; at George G. Meade, 187–90; at Ambrose E. Burnside, 190; at escape of Jubal Early, 190; at Henry W. Halleck, 190–91; at delays in carrying out colonization, 192–93; at soldiers, 193; at press, 193–95; at William H. Russell, 194; at Lord John Russell, 194; at Henry J. Raymond, 194; at Confederate treatment of black Union POWs, 194–95; at James E. Lane, 195–96; at John A. Campbell, 196–97; at H. W. Benham, 197; at Dr. Paxton, 197–98; at James William Simonton, 198; at William E. Dodge, 199; at compromisers, 199; at James Buchanan, 200; at Winfield Scott, 200–201; at Robert Anderson, 200–201; at Simon Cameron, 201; at secessionists, 201; at Baltimoreans, 201–3; at southern Unionists, 203; at gold speculators, 203; at war profiteers, 204; at land sharks, 204; at John Lellyett, 205; at Charles Scott, 207; at MTL, 279, 291, 299–301, 324; at Henry Wikoff, 306

—antislavery views, 7, 20–37; summarized, 31.

—appearance of, 74, 164–65, 234*n*357, 273

—attacks on: Richard Taylor, 150–51; Peter Cartwright, 150; George Forquer, 150; Jacob M. Early, 150; William L. D. Ewing, 151, 241; Stephen A. Douglas, 151, 158, 365–67; Jesse B. Thomas, 152; James Shields, 152–53; W. L. May, 153; Lewis Cass, 154

—Black Hawk War and, 238

—blacks and, 27, 42

—depression and, xvii, 92–113; mother's death and, xvii, 94–95; future and, 4, 5, 97, 98; Ellsworth's death and, 80; origins of, 93–94, 114*n*11; sister Sarah's death and, 95–96; severe, 96, 99–100; Bowling Greene's death and, 102; sons' deaths and, 103; E. D. Baker and James S. Wadsworth deaths and, 104; military defeats and, 104–5; humor and, 106; on coping with, 106; sad songs and, 112; political defeats and, 242, 244, 248

—Douglas, Stephen A. and, 151, 158, 244–45, 248, 365–67

—economic views of, 35, 44*n*9, 204

—failure and 4, 245, 247–48

—as father, 57; relationship with RTL, 60–61, 64–65, 71*n*55; reaction to corporal punishment, 63; grief of at death of Eddie, 63; relationship with Willie, 65–67; relationship with Tad, 65, 67–68; child-drearing practices of, 68

—father: relationship with, 37–42; estrangement from, 102–3. *See also* Lincoln, Thomas

—fear of abandonment and, 100, 137, 138, 155

—guilt of, 103, 254–55, 357

—ideology of, 35, 357. *See also* antislavery views of, economic views of

—immortality and, 5, 6

—labor, views on, 35

—laziness of, 39

—legal career, 10; Herndon and, 73, 74–75; John Todd Stuart and, 100–101; life on circuit and, 319–20. *See also* as mentor; Logan, Stephen T.

—literary taste of, 108–13, 254–55

—loneliness of, 105, 107

—married life of, 268–326, 358–60; relationships with sons, xviii, 60–68; child-rearing practices, xvii–iii, 57, 279–80; as a husband, xvi, 318, 319; domestic arrangements, 42, 279, 321, 322, 324, 325; absences of from home, 60, 318, 319, 320–21; marital woes, 270, 274, 286, 288, 291, 295; effect of MTL's rages upon, 271–72, 274, 276–77, 278–79, 281, 289, 291, 307; effect of MTL's instability upon, 296, 297; MTL and patronage, 281, 283, 284, 285; MTL's ostentation and, 199–200, 298, 321–22; finances and, 301, 303; politics and, 311–12. *See also* Lincoln, Mary Todd; Lincoln, Robert Todd; Lincoln, William Wallace; Lincoln, Edward D.; Lincoln, Thomas ("Tad")

—as mentor, 6, 74–77

—pardons and, 136, 145*n*87. *See also* Gordon, Nathaniel and Kelley, Zeno

—pettiness of, 240–41

—political career of: state legislature campaigns (1832, 1834, 1836, 1838, 1840), 238–41; as presidential elector, 239; nomination to Congress (1843), 240, 318; campaigns for Clay, 241; congressional career, 26, 241, 294; commissionership of General Land Office and, 242; retirement from politics, 1–14, 309; Senate seat and, 243–44; Douglas and, 244–48; gubernatorial nomination and, 245; vice–presidential nomination and, 248; presidential campaign and, 249–51; re-election and, 252

—popularity of: in Illinois, 10–11; with young lawyers, 74–77; with children, 57–60; with Union troops, 82; with blacks, 83–84; sources of 8–14, 84–85

—on presidency, 252

—psychological makeup of, 8–13; Oedipal feelings of, xvii, 107, 121*n*126; as a "thinking type," 7, 324; feeling function and, 7; cruel streak in, 8, 149–57; sensitivity of, 8, 149; modesty of, 13, 85, 249, 312; self-reliance of, 36–37; paternal feelings of, 74, 85, 315; jealousy of, 100, 306; passivity of, 133, 314; equanimity of, 147; mother's death and, 317; as Old Man archetype, 323; nonconfrontational nature of, 323; psychological healthiness of, 324

—sex and, 136, 322

—speeches by: Temperance Address (1842), 26; Lyceum Speech (1838), 253–54, 365–67; first inaugural, 84
—suicide and, 96, 97, 105
—surrogate mothers of, 125
—uniqueness of, 8–13
—women and: in youth, 123–24; attitude toward, xvii, 123–26, 133, 137–39, 317; on sexual double standard, 136; on women's suffrage, 136; interest in showgirls, 290–91; female petitioners and, 130–33; Anna E. Carroll and, 127–28; Jesse B. Frémont and, 128–29; Cordelia Harvey and, 129–30; Lois Hillis and, 136; Mary Owens and, 314; Matilda Edwards and, 317
—writings of: letters, 78; poetry, 109–10, 256; anonymous letters, 151–53; autobiography, 256
—youth of: father and, 37–41; childhood, 37; desire to leave home, 19, 40; mother and, 107; girls and, 123–24; poverty of, 27, 255; schooling, 256; comments on, 256, 269–70
Lincoln-Douglas debates, 31, 251; mentioned, 245
Lincoln, Edward D.: birth of, 62; death of, xvii, 6, 63; 294; mentioned, 60, 65
Lincoln, George B., 284
Lincoln, James, 120n121
Lincoln, Mary Rowena, 120n121
Lincoln, Mary Todd
—alleged adultery of, 291–92
—ambition of, 254, 308–13
—childishness of, 324
—dishonesty of, 283, 301–7; bribes and, 283; blackmail and, 283; extortion and, 283, 333n115; financial dealings while in White House, 301–4; trading permits, favors, and state secrets, 306–7
—family of: early family life, 269–70; relationship with father, 292; relationship with stepmother, 293–94; brothers and, 294; feud with family, 310; relationship with sisters, 310, 313–14
—grief and, xv
—Hanks, Harriet and, 42, 279
—health of, 322
—indiscretions of, 282, 304, 307
—jealousy of, 285–91; toward Washington women, 286–88; social customs and, 287; generals' wives and, 287–90;

Grant's popularity and, 290; Matilda Edwards and, 315
—loneliness of, 318, 319
—mental instability of, 296–97, 304
—as a mother: ineptitude of, 62–63, 324; relationship with RTL, 61, 312; use of corporal punishment by, 62–63; sons as surrogate husbands, 307
—nativism of, 275
—Nicolay and, 286
—old clothes scandal and, 283
—patronage and: W. S. Wood, 281; Isaac Henderson, 282; influence peddling, 282–83; John A. Logan, 283; Stanton, 285; criticized, 311
—personality of, 269, 275; gullibility of, 282, 305, 324; volatility of, 291; inferiority feelings of, 313; character flaws of, 313, 315; puerileness of, 315–24; after marriage, 323; Eternal Youth archetype and, 323–24
—relationship with L: effects of on L's character and career, xvi–ii, 325; criticism toward L, 194, 272–73, 274, 280–81, 290, 321–22, 359; rages of, 270, 271, 272, 273, 274, 277, 278, 280, 282, 287, 290, 328n38, 332n109, 358–59; domestic life and, 279, 321; treatment by L, 280, 295, 307, 315; courtship and early married years, 313, 314–15; husband's career and, 309, 310–11, 312, 320; in White House, 288–90, 301; on L's emotional reserve, 318
—sarcasm of, 291
—servants, treatment of by, 274–77, 291
—Seward, William Henry and, 280
—Sickles, Dan and, 287
—slavery and, 275
—spending habits: penuriousness of, 274–76; creditors and, 312; household funds and, 324
—spiritualism and, 312
—taste of, 283, 298
—temper of, 270, 271, 273, 276, 277, 278, 279, 319
—tradesmen and, 277–78, 296
—unpopularity of, 271, 278, 288, 300–301, 318
—vindictiveness of, 295
—White House and, 298–300, 304, 339n217, 340n219
Lincoln, Mordecai, 42

Lincoln, Mordecai II, 120*n*121

Lincoln, Nancy Hanks, 21, 42, 107, 137–39, 257; death of, xvii, 93–94, 137–39, 270

Lincoln, Robert Todd: relationship with L, xviii, 60–61, 64–65, 279–80, 320, 353*n*382; relationship with MTL, 61–63, 67, 292; Thomas Lincoln and, 53*n*132; personality of, 64; mentioned, 41, 68, 186, 188, 271

Lincoln, Sarah, 40, 95–96, 149, 210*n*25

Lincoln, Sarah Bush Johnston, 39, 95, 137, 139*n*2

Lincoln, Thomas ("Tad"): relationship with L, xviii, 63, 65, 66, 67–68; learning disabilities of, 57; relationship with MTL, 63, 66, 272–73, 307–8; RTL and, 64; personality of, 57, 67; mentioned, 60, 275

Lincoln, Thomas, 21, 40–41, 95, 106, 257; relationship with L, xviii, 37, 38, 39, 40, 55*n*153, 68, 102–3, 107, 256, 357; death of, 6

Lincoln, William Wallace ("Willie"), xviii, 65–67; death of, xvii, 66, 103–4, 166, 300; mentioned, 60, 63, 275

Littlefield, John H., 263*n*100; on MTL's ambition, 346*n*274, 347*n*299

Little Mount Baptist Church (Ky.), 22

Locofocos, 152

Logan, John A., 283

Logan, Mrs. John A.: on MTL, xvi, 321

Logan, Stephen T., 29, 73, 98, 148, 213*n*66; mentioned, 240

"Lord Ullin's Daughter," 112

"Lost Speech" (1856), 159, 248

Lovejoy, Elijah, 25

Lowell, James Russell, 13

Lyon, Caleb, 284

Lyceum Address (1838), 25, 26, 253–54, 365–67

Maas, Grace Jeanettte Bullock, 40

Macbeth, 254–55, 312

Mackay, Charles, 110–11

Marble, Manton, 304

Marcy, Randolph B., 184

Martin, William, 158

"Mary's Dream," 112

Maryland, 127, 191

Matheny, James H., 45*n*23, 93, 99–100, 249, 271, 317, 325

Matson, Robert, 27

May, W. L., 153

McClellan, George B., 182–87, 226*nn*231–32, 228*n*257; mentioned, 181, 188, 205

McClure, Alexander K., 265*n*125, 282, 297, 298, 305

McCoy, J. G., 322, 325

McDowell, Irvin, 183

McGilvra, John J., 216*n*114

McHenry, Henry, 96

McIlvine, A. R., 48*n*52

McKee, Mrs. Alexander, *see* Hardin, Martinette

McKerichar, Alexander, 302

McKim, J. M., 127

McManus, Edward, 292

McWilliams, Amzi, 156

Meade, George G., 187–90, 229*n*262, 288

Medill, Joseph, 204, 263*n*978

Meigs, Montgomery, 226*n*231; mentioned, 182, 195

Mendosa, John F., 276

Mentelle, Victorie Charlotte Leclere, 270, 293

Mentor: Stuart to L, 100–101; L assuming role of, 6, 74–77

Metamora, Ill., 22

Midlife transition, 2–13

"Milk sick," 94

Miller, Anson S., 27, 249

Minnesota, 129

Mississippi, 13,

Missouri Compromise (1820), 242

Missouri Radicals, 174; mentioned, 8

Mob violence, 25

Morgan, E. D., 171

Morgan, John Hunt, 24

Morison, Samuel Eliot, xi

Morrill, Lot M., 132

"Mortality," 108–9, 136

Mudd, Benjamin, 120*n*121

Mudd, Elizabeth Lincoln, 120*n*121

Murr, J. Edward, 44*n*15

Napoleon, Prince, 301

Nashville, Tenn., 22

Neely, Mark E., Jr., 153, 265*n*139, 361; mentioned, xix

Nevins, Allan, xix

New Orleans, 22; mentioned, 27, 85

New Salem, Ill., 41, 57, 97, 124–25, 159, 160, 237, 248; mentioned, 133

New York *Evening Post,* 196
New York *Herald,* 305
New York *Independent,* 194
New York *Times,* 194
New York *Tribune,* 194
New York *World,* 11, 304
Nicolay, Helen, 67, 126, 315
Nicolay, John G., 4, 12, 77, 78–79, 103, 147, 286; mentioned, xix, 77, 184, 199
Norfolk, Va., 181
Norris, Elizabeth L., 291, 293
Northwest Ordinance (1787), 26
Norwich, Conn., 256.

Offutt, Denton, 239
Oglesby, Richard, 281
Ohio, 250
Old Man archetype, 5, 73, 74, 323
Onstot, T. G., 269
Ord, Mrs. E. O. C., 289
Oregon, 242, 310–11
Orme, Col. William, 167
Owens, Mary, 96–97, 133–35, 138, 314, 319

Palmer, John M., 204, 244
Parker, Widow, 293
Parks, Samuel C., 155–56, 244
Patent Office Fair, 281
Patronage, 195, 281–85
Paul, Mrs. Gabriel R., 130
Paxton, Dr. (Pittsburgh clergyman), 197–98
Pendel, Thomas F., 131
Peninsula campaign, 104, 184
Pennsylvania courts, 179
Peoria, Ill., 7, 24, 30–31, 153
Petersburg, Ill., 156; mentioned, 137
Piatt, Donn, 191, 231n289, 280
Pierce, Edward L., 176
Pierpont, Francis H., 148–49
Pigeon Creek, Ind., 94
Polk, James K., 241
Pollock, James, 48n52
Pomeroy, Samuel, 50n85, 177, 195–96
Pope, John, 105; mentioned, 185, 186
Popular sovereignty, 30–31
Porter, Fitz-John, 186, 228n255
Potter, John F., 301
Powel, H. M., 268
Press, 193–95
Puns, 200, 287

Quakers, 130, 177
Quarles, Benjamin, 83

Racial equality, 31
Radicals, 173–77
Randall, James G., xiii, xix, xxiii, 116n37, 144n79, 359
Randall, Ruth Painter, 64–66, 268, 269, 291, 296, 313, 315, 318, 319, 324, 333n113, 358–59; mentioned, xix
Rankin, Henry B., 12, 269, 280, 308, 319, 325, 359; mentioned, 358
Ray, Charles H., 28
Raymond, Henry J., 194
Reconstruction policy, 127
Reid, Susan, 124
Rhodes, James Ford, xiii
Rice, Judge E. Y., 155
Richard III, 254–55
Richardson, Joseph C., 123, 237
Rickard, Sarah, 135, 144n78, 318
Rives, George W., 160, 215n98
Robertson, George, 49n67
Roby, Anna C., 123
Roll, John E., 36
Rosecrans, William S., 187, 229n259; mentioned, 190
Rosewater, Edward, 105
Ross, Alexander Milton, 166
Ross, Dr. Frederick A., 32–33
Ruggles, Samuel, 234n349
Russell, Lord John, 194
Russell, William Howard, xvi, 194, 226n232, 232n307
Rutledge, Ann, xxiii, 96, 135–36; mentioned, 318
Ryan, Margaret, 63, 275, 276, 277

St. Louis, 25
Salm-Salm, Mrs. Felix, 287
San Francisco *Bulletin,* 198
Schenck, Robert C., 104, 191
Schmink, Rosanna, 134
Schurz, Carl, 82, 335n148
Schwartz, Thomas F., 368n10
Scott, Lt. Col. Charles, 207
Scott, John M., 77, 320
Scott, Winfield, 200–201
Scripps, John L., 255–56
Secession crisis, 199
Second Bull Run, 104–5
Seward, Frances, 284

Seward, William H., 29, 174, 180, 249, 274, 284, 301; mentioned, 181, 182, 183
Seymour, Glenn, 365–66
Seymour, Horatio, 204
Shakespeare, 111–12, 254–55; *King John*, 103–4; *King Lear*, 66; *Macbeth*, 254–55, 312; *Hamlet*, 254–55
Sharpe, Granville, 246
Shelbyville, Ill., 29
Sherman, Gen. Thomas W., 180–81
Sherman, William T., 194
Shields, James, 152
Short, Levi, 163
Sickles, Daniel, 162, 187
Sigel, Franz, 191
Silbey, Joel, 2, 361
Simon, John Y., 39, 53*n*132, 268; mentioned, xix
Simon, Paul, 239, 240
Simonton, James William, 198
Singleton, James W., 154
Slavery: in New Orleans, 22; L's views of, 30–34
Slave traders, 22, 23–24
Smith, Caleb B., 301, 303–4, 339*n*214
Smith, Matthew Hale, 305–6
Smith, Mrs. Stephen, 59
Smith, Truman, 199
Smith, Victor, 170–71, 219*n*159
"The Soldier's Dream," 112
Soldiers (Union), 82, 193
Somers, William H., 76
Sparrow, Betsy, 94
Sparrow, Thomas, 94
Spears, J. Q., 124
Speed, Joshua, 10, 24, 26, 27, 61, 97–98, 99, 100, 101, 106, 138, 159, 166, 241, 253, 311, 319; mentioned, 209
Speed, Mrs. Lucy G., 101–2
Sprague, William, 186
Stackpole, Thomas, 290, 301
Stanly, Edward, 176, 223*n*192
Stanton, Edwin M., 98, 105, MTL and, 285; mentioned, 184, 187, 190
Steiner, Mark, 368*n*9
Stevens, Thaddeus, 174–75, 252
Stimmel, Smith, 59
Stoddard, William O.: on John G. Nicolay, 78–79; on L and women, 126; on L's anger, 205–6, 208; MTL and, 286; mentioned, 77, 183
Stone, Dan, 46*n*40

Stowe, Harriet Beecher, 50*n*85, 84
Strozier, Charles B., xvii, 21, 65, 93, 107, 317, 352*n*382, 357–58
Stuart, John T., 29, 92, 93, 100–101, 311; partnership with L, 73, 100; career of, 240, 322, 365; on MTL, 308; mentioned, 26, 269
Stuart, Mrs. John T., 311
Sumner, Charles, 23, 159, 175–76, 222*n*188; on MTL, 284; mentioned, 184, 194
Sumner, E. V., 282
Sutter, Thomas J., 342*n*230
Swett, Leonard, 27, 93, 252, 320; mentioned, 250
Swisshelm, Jane Grey, 12, 129

Taft, Horatio Nelson, 59–60
Taft, Julia, *see* Julia Taft Bayne
Taggart, Jacob, 277
Tarbell, Ida M., 64, 313; mentioned, xix
Taylor, Col. Richard, 150–51
Taylor, Zachary, 242
Taylorville, Ill., 277
Temperance address (1842), 26
Tennessee, 161, 196, 205; mentioned, 32
Thayer, Eli, 173
Thomas, Benjamin P., 1, 96, 155, 241, 325
Thomas, Jesse B., 152
Thompson, Mrs. Mary Virginia Pinkerton, 63
Thompson, William B., 58
Thornton, Anthony: on L's anger, 154, 213*n*58
Todd, Alexander, 294
Todd, Ann, 313–14; mentioned, 316
Todd, Elizabeth "Betsey," 293
Todd, Eliza Parker, 269; death of, 270
Todd, George, 293
Todd, Robert S., 269, 270, 293, 295, 308
Treat, Samuel H., 93
Trumbull, Julia Jayne: MTL and, 309–10
Trumbull, Lyman, 50*n*85, 236, 243, 309, 310, 319
Truth, Sojourner, 126
Tuckerman, Charles K., 192–93
Tuley, Elizabeth, 124
Turnham, David, 123
"Twenty Years Ago," 112

Underground Railroad, 27
Union troops, 82
Upperman, James H., 301–3

Urbana, Ill., 125
Usher, John P., 172

Van Bergen, Peter, 97, 271
Van Buren, Martin, 254, 365
Vance, Mariah, 329n60
Vandalia, Ill., 97
Verduin, Paul H., xix, 146n102
Vermeren, Peter, 302
Viele, Egbert L., 37
Villard, Henry, 148, 305
Villard, Oswald Garrison, 292
von Franz, Marie Louise, 323–24

Wade, Benjamin F., 50n85, 333n110
Wade-Davis Manifesto, 173–74
Wadsworth, James S., 104, 222n179
Wakeman, Abram, 292
Walker, William, 77
Wallace, Frances Todd, 358
Wallace, William, 41
Ward, Sam, 292
Washburne, E. B., 74, 76
Washington, D.C., 29
Waters, Lewis H., 58–59, 76
Watt, John: MTL and, 292, 301, 304, 318, 334n126, 343n240; corruption and, 302, 303; on financial irregularities at White House, 304; W. S. Wood and, 336n164; described, 341n226
Watt, Mrs. John (Jane), 304
Webber, John B., 296
Weed, Thurlow, xvi, 173, 179, 252; on MTL's financial problems, 301, 303

Weik, Jesse W., 92–93; mentioned, xix
Weldon, Lawrence, 93
Welles, Gideon, 169–70, 174, 297; mentioned, 185, 189
White, Horace, 12, 236
White, Martha Todd, 131
Whitney, Henry C., 10, 36, 76, 77, 79, 92, 96, 106, 113, 125, 174–75, 243, 248, 320; on L's anger, 148, 154–56, 166, 167; on L's marriage, 319, 325, 359; mentioned, 358
Wikoff, Henry, 305–6
Wilkinson, Morton S., 82
Williams, John E., 180
Willis, Nathaniel P., 66
Wilmot Proviso, 28–29
Wilson, Douglas L., xxiii–iv, 240; mentioned, xix
Wilson, Edmund, 253–54, 365
Wilson, Henry, 50n85
Wilson, Robert, 97
Winchell, James B., 252
Wisconsin, 9, 129, 250
Wood, William, 40, 41
Wood, William P., 297, 306–7
Wood, William S., 281, MTL and, 291–92, 336n164; White House bills and, 302, 339n217; John Watt and, 336n164, 341n227
Women's suffrage, 136
Wright, Erastus, 49n63, 155

Yates, Richard, 242; mentioned, 199
Young, John Russell, 12, 77–78

MICHAEL BURLINGAME is a professor of history at Connecticut College in New London. He received his Ph.D. in history from Johns Hopkins University. Among other Lincoln-related projects, he is currently editing a new edition of the diary of John Hay and writing a book on Lincoln scholarship.

More Books about Abraham Lincoln

The Historian's Lincoln: Pseudo-History, Psychohistory, and History
Edited by Gabor S. Boritt

Lincoln and the Tools of War
Robert V. Bruce

Lincoln, Land, and Labor, 1809–60
Olivier Frayssé; translated by Sylvia Neely

The Lincoln Murder Conspiracies
William Hanchett

Out of the Wilderness: The Life of Abraham Lincoln
William Hanchett

Lincoln the President: Last Full Measure
J. G. Randall and Richard N. Current

Lincoln's Preparation for Greatness: The Illinois Legislative Years
Paul Simon

Lincoln's Quest for Union: Public and Private Meanings
Charles B. Strozier

The Shadows Rise: Abraham Lincoln and the Ann Rutledge Legend
John Evangelist Walsh

The University of Illinois Press also publishes semiannually
The Journal of the Abraham Lincoln Association.

University of Illinois Press
1325 South Oak Street
Champaign, Illinois 61820-6903
www.press.uillinois.edu